Reviews of the first edition

"This book will afford enjoyment and enlightenment to layman and specialist alike. Duffy sweeps the reader along . . . by his lively and absorbing detail, his piercing insights, patient analysis, and his vigour in debate."—Peter Heath, *Times Literary Supplement*

"Deeply imaginative, movingly written, and splendidly illustrated. . . . Duffy's analysis, in his richly detailed book, of what happened at the Reformation to the religion of the laity of England . . . carries conviction."—Maurice Keen, *New York Review of Books*

"Revisionist history at its most imaginative and exciting. . . . [An] astonishing and magnificent piece of work."—Edward T. Oakes, *Commonweal*

"Duffy wants to show the vitality and appeal of late medieval Catholicism and to prove that it exerted a diverse and vigorous hold over the imagination and loyalty of the people up to the very moment of Reformation. He succeeds triumphantly."—Susan Brigden, *London Review of Books*

"A landmark book in the history of the Reformation."—Ann Eljenholm Nichols, *Sixteenth Century Journal*

"Sensitively written and beautifully produced, this book represents a major contribution to the Reformation debate."—Norman Tanner, *The Times*

"With the publication of this book, a kind of map or illustrated atlas of late medieval English Christianity, English Reformation studies will never be the same again."—Patrick Collinson, *Times Higher Education Supplement*

"Duffy offers an unrivaled picture of late medieval parochial religion, with all its ritual symbolism and visual imagery."—Keith Thomas, *The Observer*

"This is a quite remarkable, indeed brilliant, study, which puts flesh on the bones of the so-called 'revisionist' interpretation of the English Reformation. . . . This is essential reading for all those who wish to understand late medieval religion and the means by which it was undermined against the wishes of the vast majority of its practitioners."—Christopher Harper-Bill, *Theology*

"This magnificently produced volume must rank as one of the most important landmarks in the study of late medieval English religion to have hitherto appeared, and it is unlikely to be superseded for quite some time. . . . The sheer scale of Duffy's achievement, the enormous value of the information he provides and the vigour and elegance with which he presents it, make his book, in every sense, a must."—Robert Peters, *History Review*

"This is a monumental work. . . Duffy writes elegantly, handling complex and controversial subject matter in a way at once sober and factual. . . . It should be read by every historian of the medieval and early modern periods, by every Catholic, indeed by every Christian with a serious interest in the history of Christendom."—Evelyn Birge Vitz, *Theological Studies*

"A valuable source of information supported with excellent illustrations and bibliography."—*Choice*

"A very illuminating and satisfying book, which takes a major step towards better understanding of the English reformation."—Margaret Aston, *English Historical Review*

"This is a work of exceptional importance, demonstrating massive erudition, great sympathy, and eloquence of style. It presents a marvelously detailed new picture of traditional religious belief and practice in England during the century prior to the Reformation and it shows exactly when and how the customs of faith and ceremony were stripped away in the sixteenth century. Our interpretation of the Reformation and our understanding of Tudor religion will never be the same."—Stanford Lehmberg, *Sixteenth Century Journal*

"Scholarly, compulsively readable and revolutionary in thesis. . . Scholars of the period will enjoy the controversy and the general reader will . . . be carried back empathetically to the days when religion was not as we know it now."—Gillian Mottram, *Faith and Freedom*

"[This book] at last gives the culture of the late Middle Ages in England its due, and helps us to see the period as it was and not as Protestant reformers and their intellectual descendants imagined it to be. . . . A monumental and deeply felt work."—Gabriel Josipovici, *Times Literary Supplement*

"An outstanding history of the English Reformation."—*Commonweal*

THE STRIPPING OF THE ALTARS

THE STRUCTURE OF EVOLUTIONARY

THE STRIPPING
OF THE ALTARS

Traditional Religion in England

c.1400–c.1580

EAMON DUFFY

YALE UNIVERSITY PRESS

NEW HAVEN AND LONDON

Designed by John Nicoll

Set in Linotron Bembo by Best-set Typesetters Ltd, Hong Kong
Printed in China through Worldprint

ISBN 0-300-10828-1 (pbk)

Library of Congress Catalog Number 92-50579

Deus, qui nos patrem et matrem honorare praecepisti,
miserere clementer animabus patris et matris meae, eorumque
peccata dimitte, meque cum illis in aeternae claritatis gaudio fac vivere.
Per Christum Dominum Nostrum. Amen.

From the Mass for the Dead,
Missale ad Usum Insignis et Praeclarae Ecclesiae Sarum,
ed. F. H. Dickinson, 1861–83, col. 873★.

CONTENTS

ACKNOWLEDGEMENTS

In the course of more than seven years' work on this book, I have accumulated many debts. Much of that indebtedness has grown from the writings, conversations and arguments of workers in the same or related fields: Margaret Aston, John Bossy, Susan Brigden, Pat Collinson, Christopher Haigh, Dorothy Owen, Miri Rubin, Jack Scarisbrick, Bob Scribner, and Margaret Spufford have all helped to stimulate my thoughts and provoke me to question, though they will not always approve of the answers. Ann Nichols and Dick Pfaff not only shared their learning in late medieval liturgy, iconography, and sacramental theology, but drove with me through rural East Anglia in search of its material traces.

One of the many benfits of working in Cambridge is the unflagging and unostentatious expertise of the staff of the University Library. The endless patience and helpfulness which I have found in the Rare Books and Manuscripts Rooms there have smoothed many a rugged mile in my research.

Getting hold of the pictures in this book would have been a nightmare without the help of many institutions and individuals. Particular thanks must go to the staff at the Conway Library and the Cambridge University Library for their patient assistance, to David Hoyle and Jan Rhodes for lending photographs, and especially to Melissa Garnett, who acted as unpaid research assistant in the Bodleian Library. I am greatly indebted to the Morshead–Salter fund of my college for financial help with the cost of illustrations.

My greatest debt is to the many friends and colleagues who have patiently (for the most part) read through all or part of the book, in its many drafts, and have helped reduce its tally of errors and idiocies. Colin Armstrong, John Bossy, Nicholas Boyle, Pat Collinson, Peter Cunich, David Hoyle, Jane Hughes, John Morrill, Geoffrey Nuttall, Michael O'Boy, Bob Ombres, Richard Rex, John Stevens, and Helen Weinstein have all at one time or another shouldered this burden. In addition, Jan Rhodes put her unrivalled knowledge of Tudor devotional literature and her apparent gift of total recall at my disposal. Sandra Raphael was the firmest but kindest of copy-editors. With superhuman generosity, Christopher Brooke and Ruth Daniel read every word of the proofs. The sympathetic but critical vigilance of all these friends has materially improved both the style and the content of the book: the remaining lapses of fact, taste, and judgement are all my own work.

My wife and children have not only suffered, and suffered from, my growing preoccupation with the religion of fifteenth- and sixteenth-century English parishioners, but have supported me through it. If the dedication of this book had not already been made, it would go by rights to them.

E.D.

College of St Mary Madgalene, Cambridge
Lent, 1992

PREFACE TO THE SECOND EDITION

I

One of my schoolmasters liked to tell of a visit in his own schooldays to Gloucester Cathedral, during which he had overheard two tourists, one of them a Roman Catholic priest, holding forth on the iniquities of the Reformation, and deploring the sad fact that the great church was now in Protestant hands. "Just think", declared the priest, "all this was *ours* once upon a time".This was too much for a Cathedral verger, who had also been listening with visibly mounting indignation to this tirade. Unable to contain himself any longer, he bustled forward: "if you don't mind me saying so sir," he declared, "it would *still* be yours, if only you'd behaved yourselves"!

The verger's unbeatable repartee captured precisely an account of the Reformation which was widely accepted in England, by scholars as well as the man in the pew, till fairly recently. Even entirely secular people took it as axiomatic that Protestantism was, if not necessarily true, then at least not obviously and ludicrously false, like Roman Catholicism. Believers and unbelievers were agreed that whatever the true claims of Christianity, the Reformation was a vital stage along the road to modernity, the cleansing of the English psyche from priestcraft, ignorance and superstition.

The basic assumptions of this historiography were hilariously fictionalized in Kingsley Amis's novel *The Alteration,* set in a hypothetical 1960s, in which the English Reformation had never happened. Martin Luther himself had not rebelled, but had become Pope Germanicus I, and Prince Arthur of England had not died, so his younger brother Henry had not become King Henry VIII. Instead, Henry had led a rebellion of Protestant malcontents, and his followers had all been banished to New England.The whole course of Western history had thus been utterly altered, and Europe in the 1960s was therefore locked into a suffocating Catholic Habsburg tyranny, where papal talent scouts roamed the continent to identify boys with lovely voices, who were then castrated and taken back to Rome to grace the Sistine Chapel choir. Electricity, free thought and modern civilization had become the monopoly of Protestant New England, and the book turns on the attempts of a group of misfits and anticlericals to rescue a choirboy from Coverley Cathedral from a fate worse than death.

The Stripping of the Altars, first published in 1992, was, among other things, an attempt to contribute a shovelful of history to the burial of the venerable historiographical consensus which underlay both the verger's riposte and Amis's brilliant satire. The book was informed by a conviction that the Reformation as actually experienced by ordinary people was not an uncomplicated imaginative liberation, the restoration of true Christianity after a period of degeneration and corruption, but, for good or ill, a great cultural hiatus, which had dug a ditch, deep and dividing, between the English people and their past. Over the course of three generations a millennium of splendour – the worlds of Gregory and Bede and Anselm and Francis and Dominic and Bernard and Dante, all that had constituted and nourished the mind and heart of Christendom for a thousand years – became alien territory, the dark ages of "popery". Sixteenth-century Protestantism was built on a series of noble affirmations – the sovereignty of the grace of God in salvation, the free availability of that grace to all who sought it, the self-revelation of God in his holy word. But it quickly clenched itself round a series of negations and rejections. As its proponents smashed the statues, whitewashed the churches and denounced the Pope and the Mass, Protestantism came to be constituted in large part by its NO to medieval religion.

The Stripping of the Altars, then, was at one level an elegy for a world we had lost, a world of great beauty and power which it seemed to me the reformers – and many historians ever since – had misunderstood, traduced and destroyed. It was only after the book had been published, and began to be debated, that I came to realize that the energy and engagement which had helped to produce it, and which gave it some of its rhetorical force, did not belong entirely in the fifteenth and sixteenth centuries. Till my early teens I had been brought up in the Ireland of the 1950s, and the religion of my childhood had a good deal in common with the symbolic world of the late Middle Ages. My later teens had exactly coincided with the Second Vatican Council, of which I was an eager observer. That Council had triggered the dismantling of much of what had seemed immemorial and permanent in my own inner imaginative landscape, as the externals of the ritual life of the Catholic Church were drastically altered and simplified. My account of the English Reformation presented it less as an institutional and doctrinal transformation than a ritual one, "the stripping of the altars": in retrospect, I see that the intensity of focus I brought to my task as an historian was nourished by my own experience of another such ritual transformation. In Seamus Heaney's poem Station Island, the nineteenth-century writer William Carleton declares that

> We are earthworms of the earth, and all that
> Has gone through us is what will be our trace.[1]

True of poets, that is also supremely true of historians, for there is, of course, no such thing as a presupposition-less observer. All historians who aspire to be more than chroniclers derive their imaginative insight and energy from somewhere, and if reading and research provide the core materials, our own experience provides us with the sensitivities – and no doubt the blind-spots – which make what we do with that material distinctive. The book, as rigorously and exhaustively based as I was capable of making it on a mass of historical, literary and material evidence, was also shaped and informed by the imaginative and symbolic revolution through which I myself had lived in the 1960s and 1970s.

II

As an intellectual project, then, *The Stripping of the Altars* was conceived as a contribution to an adequate understanding of both medieval English Catholicism, and of the Reformation which swept that Catholicism away. But it should be read neither as a *Summa* of late medieval religion nor, in any straightforward sense, as a history of the English Reformation. An exhaustive exploration of late medieval English religion would have to have included extended discussion of the role of the religious orders, especially the Friars, whose influence on urban religion in particular was profound throughout the later Middle Ages, and remained so to the very eve of the Dissolution. *The Stripping of the Altars*, however, is focused primarily on the religion of the lay parishioner, and has almost nothing to say about the religious orders (or, for that matter, about the clergy in general). By the same token, the second part of the book, which deals with the processes and impact of the Reformation on the traditional religion of the parishes and parishioners of mid-Tudor England, has little to say about the positive attractions of the Protestant Gospel, or about those who willingly embraced it. As a result, some readers and reviewers have scratched – or shaken – their heads over what to make of a history of the Reformation which appeared to call in question the very existence of convinced Protestants.

Any such puzzlements will be resolved, I hope, by attention to the book's defining subtitle – "*Traditional* Religion in England c. 1400–1580". It is the religion of the conservative majority which this book sets out to explore, and it ends at the point at which I believe majority adherence to the forms and belief-system of late medieval Catholicism

---

[1]   Seamus Heaney, *Opened Ground, Poems 1966–1996*, London, 1998, p. 247.

was tipping or had tipped over into widespread acceptance of a contrasting and inimical Reformation world-view.

The book was thus intended as a contribution towards a reassessment of the popularity and durability of late medieval religious attitudes and perceptions, which had already begun, but which in 1992, the year of the book's first appearance, was still far from generally accepted. Three years earlier, the doyen of English Reformation studies, A. G. Dickens, had reissued and updated his classic study *The English Reformation*, which had deservedly dominated English Reformation studies for a generation. Dickens was a learned and generous-minded scholar, but in the last edition of his book, as in its first, the component elements of medieval religiosity were presented less as integrated elements in a coherent religious symbol-system than as exhibits in a freak-show. Like Erasmus, one of his intellectual heroes, Dickens looked at the framework of medieval Catholicism and saw no coherence or design, only a monstrous heap of littleness.

The first chapter of *The English Reformation* began with the words "There was once a certain knight", and went on to tell at length an elaborate and improbable medieval miracle-story of the rescue of a knight from a demon by the Virgin Mary, culled from the commonplace book of a late medieval Yorkshire cleric, Thomas Ashby. Dickens continued by itemising the rest of the contents of Ashby's book – prayer-texts to the Virgin Mary and St John of Bridlington, a commentary on the Hail Mary, assorted miracle stories, an account of the value of the opening words of St John's Gospel in Latin as a charm, an exposition of the penitential Psalm 50, a treatise on the privileges and rites of various festivals, a scholastic disputation about whether the resurrected will be naked or clothed on Judgement Day, an English rhyme teaching Transubstantiation, and so on. Dickens commented wonderingly that this material was written "not round the year 1200 but by a man who mentions Pope Julius II as still alive". In Ashby, therefore, "a twelfth-century world lingered on while Machiavelli was writing *The Prince*, while the sophisticated talkers at Urbino were giving Castiglione the materials for his *Book of the Courtier*". [2] This world of fable, relic, miracle and indulgence, he thought, was manifestly religiously inferior, for it allowed "the personality and teaching of Jesus to recede from the focus of the picture", and it could be demonstrated "with mathematical precision" that its connection with the Christianity of the Gospel was "rather tenuous". Medieval lay people, he thought, must have been alienated by such stuff, not least by the unscriptural horrors of purgatory, which cut them off from the mercy and love of Christ: "faced with quite terrifying

---

[2]   A. G. Dickens, *The English Reformation*, London, Fontana edn, 1974, pp. 13–16.

views of punishment in the life to come… it was small wonder that they felt more comfortable with the saints than with God."[3]

As these passages suggest, Dickens's book begged many questions about the nature of late medieval piety. It never seems to have occurred to him that those who flocked and jostled to "see their Maker" at the elevation in the Mass could hardly be said to be remote from or uncomfortable with their God, or that the clergy who led prayers to the saints or commended pilgrimage, promoted also a religion focussed on their daily celebration of the Eucharist, and thus on a resolutely Christocentric action. Dickens also operated with a sharply polarized and essentially anachronistic understanding of the difference between the medieval and humanist world views: the world of Machiavelli, Castiglione, and Erasmus, on the one hand; and the wonder-world of the *Golden Legend*, indulgences, and what he more than once called the "crazed enthusiasm for pilgrimage" on the other. This distinction, singularly inapplicable to the careers and convictions of those two greatest of early Tudor English humanists, John Fisher and Thomas More, was clear and stark in Dickens's mind. Humanism, he believed, looked forward to a rational religious world in which belief was firmly based on solid biblical evidence, not on unwritten verities and ecclesiastical tradition: it stood in marked contrast to the world of "scholastic religion", petering out in "disharmony, irrelevance and discredit".[4]

Dickens's work therefore revealed the fundamentally negative assumptions which underlay much contemporary understanding of the pre-history of the English Reformation, as well as the course of that great revolution itself. Ground-breaking work by other historians, notably Jack Scarisbrick,[5] Christopher Harper-Bill[6] and (especially) Christopher Haigh,[7] had already by 1992 challenged this "Dickensian" account of the Reformation, not merely on its own terms, but as representative of a widely shared historiography which was culturally if not confessionally Protestant in its terms of reference. Both Haigh and Scarisbrick, however, had focused on the sixteenth century, and the immediate context of the Tudor religious revolution. The first and larger part of *The Stripping of the Altars* was an attempt to place the debate

---

[3] Ibid. p. 20.

[4] Ibid. p. 444.

[5] J. J. Scarisbrick, *The Reformation and the English People*, Oxford, 1984.

[6] C. Harper-Bill, "Dean Colet's Convocation Sermon and the pre-Reformation Church in England", *History* 73, 1988, pp. 191–210.

[7] C. Haigh (ed), *The English Reformation Revised*, Cambridge 1987; other "revisionist" works on the late medieval church offering (sometimes reluctantly) a more positive account of the early Tudor church included Peter Heath's pioneering study of the late medieval clergy: *English Parish Clergy on the Eve of the Reformation*, London, 1969, and Robert Whiting's regional study of the South-west of England: *The Blind Devotion of the People: Popular Religion and the English Reformation*, Cambridge, 1989.

about the Reformation in a longer perspective, to grapple with the evident inability of many Reformation historians to take medieval religion seriously, and to help modern readers recover a sense of the power, integrity and internal logic of that distinctive religious culture. In particular it seemed important to contest the widely shared perception that by 1500 this was a failing religion that had already alienated or lost the commitment of the more intelligent and forward-looking of its lay English audience. I sought to show that, on the contrary, medieval English Catholicism was, up to the very moment of its dissolution, a highly successful enterprise, the achievement by the official church of a quite remarkable degree of lay involvement and investment, and of a corresponding degree of doctrinal orthodoxy. To explicate that convergence of lay practice and official teaching was therefore one of my main objectives, and the focus on religion before and around 1500 was probably the book's most distinctive contribution to the wider revision of historical opinion about the period, which others had already initiated, and which in its broad outlines has since gained widespread acceptance.

III

The Stripping of the Altars was received remarkably favourably by the general public: despite its bulk and its academic target audience, it escaped the confines of the academy, became a best seller (by the modest standards which pertain in such matters) and has since been through ten printings. I can still recall my own somewhat startled pleasure on glancing down a crowded London tube-carriage during the rush hour in the spring of 1993, and noticing that no fewer than four of my harassed fellow-passengers were clutching copies of the book. Perhaps more surprisingly, given its attempts to straddle two periods more commonly studied separately, it was also well received (for the most part) by both medieval and Reformation historians.[8]

In so far as there was consistent criticism in the book's reception, it was a sense among some reviewers that in seeking to demonstrate the internal coherence of late medieval religion, I was in danger of imposing an idealized harmony on the period, smoothing out dissent, conflict, and, in general, difference. So some commentators, while welcoming the book's detailed exposition of the practice of medieval religion, detected in it a dehistoricizing tendency, in which fifteenth-century English Christianity appeared as a calm, timeless equilibrium which minimized

---

[8] See the reviews by Peter Heath in the *Times Literary Supplement*, 15 January 1993, p. 4, Susan Brigden in *The London Review of Books*, 27 May 1993, p. 15, Maurice Keen in the *New York Review of Books*, 15 September 1993, pp. 50–1, and Ronald Hutton in the *Journal of Theological Studies*, vol. 44, October 1993, pp. 762–4.

conflict and tension, and marginalized the importance of dissent. This criticism I believe arose particularly from the absence in the book of any extended treatment of Lollardy.[9]

That omission, like the corresponding absence of any sustained discussion of witchcraft, was in fact a considered one, explicitly addressed in the introduction to the original edition. *The Stripping of the Altars* offered, first and foremost, an overview of the complex web of symbol, action and belief which constituted mainstream Christianity at the end of the Middle Ages. Much modern writing about the period, it seemed to me, had unwittingly distorted our perception of the place of Christianity in late medieval and early modern society by focusing disproportionately on the *outré*, the dissident and the dysfunctional. Thus studies of magic, witchcraft or of Lollardy abounded, but studies of orthodox – that is, mainstream – fifteenth-century religious practice were rarely undertaken. *The Stripping of the Altars*, nevertheless, did not argue for the *insignificance* of magic, or witchcraft, or of Lollardy. Quite simply, they were not its subject matter, and in omitting them I assumed that my book would be read alongside, not instead of, the many works which did treat of those things.

In attempting to offer a corrective to conventional assessments of medieval religion, I opted for a thematic, analytic treatment of a vast and intractable mass of source material. That decision about procedure exacted a price, similarly acknowledged in the introduction, in terms of the elimination of narrative, and the consequent muting of a sense of change and development within the thematic sections of the first and longer part of the book. I had indeed gone so far as to use the phrase "the social *homogeneity*" of late medieval religion.[10] By that phrase, however, I certainly did not mean to suggest that all was well in an harmonious pre-Reformation Merry England, a consensual garden of Eden only spoiled by the arrival of the serpent of reform. I recognized, as any historian with even a nodding acquaintance with the records of the medieval parish or the church courts must do, that late medieval England was a divided society, full of conflicting and diverging interests, above all the fundamental divide which runs through all human societies between the haves and have-nots, between rich and poor. And in the articulation and construction of the multiple identities which constituted that divided society, religion unquestionably had an intimate, even a dominant role – or rather, range of roles. Thus Lollard doubts and anti-sacramental polemic featured prominently in the book's central discussion of Eucharistic belief, just as class and economic distinctions were

---

[9] A conspectus of criticisms of the *Stripping of the Altars* by medievalists can be gained from the contributions to the New Chaucer Society symposium published in *Assays: Critical Approaches to Medieval and Renaissance Texts*, vol. IX, 1996, pp. 1–56.
[10] Below, p. 265.

explored in discussing the social functions of the liturgy. Part I of the book thus contained a number of extended discussions of the role of late medieval religious forms and institutions in establishing or supporting the social and political pecking-order.[11] In speaking of the "social homogeneity" of late medieval religion, my contention was not that there were no tensions within it, but that those tensions would not be found to run directly along the lines often laid down by those seeking conventional explanations of the Reformation. The divisions of late medieval religion were subtler and more various than had commonly been suggested, and did not, for example, seem to me to run along such obvious fault-lines and divides as the distinctions between *élite* and *popular, clerical* and *lay*. My concern in 1992 was to contest the claim, implicit in the work of Keith Thomas,[12] A. G. Dickens,[13] Jean Delumeau[14] and others, that the essential differences in late medieval religion were those between the educated and ill-educated, the clerically orthodox and the superstitious populace at large. Hence, I argued, even the most apparently heterodox or bizarre magical practices might employ ritual and symbolic strategies derived directly and, all things considered, remarkably faithfully, from the liturgical paradigms of blessing and exorcism: they thus represented not magic or superstition, but lay Christianity. Hence also, people at opposite ends of the social scale, like the young Henry VIII and the Norfolk church-reeve Robert Reynes, might both own and use, in roughly the same way, charms on the names of God or the nails of the Crucifixion.[15]

IV

The Stripping of the Altars, therefore, does not exclude or ignore difference, dissent, or doubt. But the book was written in the conviction that it was a mistake to set such dissidence and doubt at the centre of an overarching discussion of the content and character of traditional religion. I was clear, in particular, that I did not wish to devote separate treatment to the phenomenon of Lollardy, the distinctive English heresy propagated in the parishes of early Lancastrian England by the clerical disciples of the Oxford philosopher and theologian John Wycliffe.

It is, I think, worth spelling out here the rationale behind that decision

---

[11] For example, see below pp. 12–14 (social functions of the liturgy), pp. 102–7 (miracle stories and the demonization of dissent, pp. 114–16, 126–9 (power and conflict in lay experience of the Mass, and the proprietary control of the liturgy by individuals, families or social groups): pp. 164–5 (the political management of the cult of the saints).

[12] Keith Thomas, *Religion and the Decline of Magic*, Harmondsworth, 1973.

[13] In his *English Reformation*.

[14] Jean Delumeau, *Catholicism between Luther and Voltaire*, London, 1977.

[15] Below, pp. 71–4, 295–8, plates 110, 112.

about procedure. Wycliffe has often been accorded the pious and honorific title "morning star of the Reformation", and historians have conventionally credited much of the early success of the Reformation to expectations and attitudes planted by a continuing tradition of Lollardy in early Tudor England.[16] By contrast, I believe that the impact of Lollardy on fifteenth- and early sixteenth-century religious awareness has been grossly exaggerated. The mainstream of fifteenth-century piety was indeed conventionally censorious of heresy, but not in my view greatly affected, much less shaped, by reaction to it, while the over-whelming majority of early Protestant activists were converts from devout Catholicism, not from Lollardy.[17]

When I devised a title for *The Stripping of the Altars* I adopted, for convenience sake, a starting date of "c. 1400". In fact, the real focus of the medieval section of the book falls, as more than one reviewer com-mented, predominantly on the second half of the fifteenth century. Unfortunately, the date 1400, even with its softening "circa", led some readers to expect that I would deal with the crisis of Lollardy from the enactment of the notorious act authorising the burning of heretics, *De heretico Comburendo*, in 1401, through Arundel's *Constitutions* of 1409, to the fiasco of Oldcastle's riot (it scarcely merits the name rebellion) in 1414. Professor David Aers, in what was certainly the most ferocious response to the book, insisted that I had occluded the complexity and contested nature of fifteenth-century Christianity in England by writing Lollardy out of the picture.[18] Professor Aers pointed to the structural contrast between the thematic arrangement of the first part of the book, and the narrative arrangement of the first four chapters of the second part. That Reformation narrative, he argued, offered an account of the violent impact of royal power on Tudor religion as the novel intrusion of a usurping secular force into the timeless tranquilities of late medieval religion. On the contrary, he claimed, there was nothing new about such violence. The long history of the suppression of Lollardy by the alliance of the Church and Crown meant that royal enforcement was central to the character and history of late medieval as well as Reformation religion. By the time of Henry VIII, he argued "nothing could have seemed more 'traditional' than the role of the sovereign or secular authorities in the determination of what forms of Christianity should be enforced and what forms criminalised."[19]

---

[16] For a recent example, alleging the fusion of Norfolk Lollardy with the new Evangelical movement to create "a vigorous popular Protestantism" see A. Fletcher and Diarmaid MacCulloch, *Tudor Rebellions*, fifth edn, London, 2004, p. 87.

[17] A point robustly made in Richard Rex, *The Lollards*, London, 2002, ch. 5.

[18] David Aers, "Altars of Power: Reflections on Eamon Duffy's The Stripping of the Altars: Traditional Religion in England 1400–1580," *Literature and History* 3, 1994, 90–105.

[19] Ibid. p. 97.

This insistence on the equivalence of the role of the Crown in fifteenth- and in sixteenth-century England, however, seems to me misconceived, because based on an implicit counter-narrative to that offered in *The Stripping of the Altars*. In this counter-narrative Lollardy is presented as a major rival to orthodox Catholicism, needing sustained persecution and counter-propaganda to contain it, and hence functioning as a major determinant of official religious policy. In such an account, the character of fifteenth-century Catholicism had to be maintained by brute force, in a way directly comparable to the force exercised in pursuit of revolutionary religious change by successive Tudor regimes. Aers saw in the book's portrayal of late medieval religion as consensual and essentially unchallenged a deliberate and collusive act of injustice, writing out of the history of late medieval religion the victims of church and state brutality, the "ruthless exclusion of the already excluded 'others'."

The counter-narrative undergirding Professor Aers's criticism, and the over-estimation implicit in it of the role of Lollardy and of anti-Lollard state violence as determinants of the shape of late medieval English Christianity, however, seem to me simply mistaken. In imposing Protestantism the Tudor monarchy was manifestly working *against* the grain of popular religious sentiment and culture, in a way which the early Lancastrian monarchy manifestly was not. The bulldozing away of the externals of medieval Catholicism in Edward's reign in particular destroyed or defaced generations of lay donation to the parish churches, and finally and decisively halted lay investment in a form of religious conspicuous consumption which had been booming into the 1530s.[20] The Lancastrian campaign against heresy, by contrast, sought dynastic legitimacy by aligning itself with an orthodoxy which the regime knew had in fact overwhelming popular support – that, indeed, was the whole point of the alignment. There is thus no equivalence or symmetry between Crown intervention in the two cases.

In assessing the character of English religion in the century after Chaucer it is, in any case, highly misleading to place too much weight on Lollardy as a cultural determinant. Lollards of course continued to surface in ecclesiastical court proceedings after 1430, and there were to remain significant concentrations of them in Wealden Kent, Berkshire (above all in the Chiltern Hills round Amersham), and in a handful of urban enclaves such as Coventry.[21] Yet if we are to believe the surviving

---

[20] A sense of the scale and lavishness of this investment in Early Tudor England can be gained from Richard Marks and Paul Williamson (eds), *Gothic Art for England 1400–1547*, London, Victoria and Albert Museum, 2003.

[21] J. A. F. Thompson, *The Later Lollards, 1414–1525*, Oxford, 1965.

vide Wilson, Derek: 'The Peoples Bible',
for contrary view of the power of Lollardy.

PREFACE TO THE SECOND EDITION　　　xxiii

visitation and court records, fifteenth-century Lollardy seems to have
been less of an irritant to most diocesan authorities than local cunning-
men or womanising priests, and there is no convincing evidence that it
served as *the* shaping factor in any of the major developments of late
medieval English piety. Even in its acknowledged strongholds, it is hard
to be certain of the real extent of its popular base, and the leading
authority on the religion of fifteenth-century Bristol has recently
argued that the city's reputation as a hot-bed of heresy in the late
Middle Ages is the product of skewed documentation, largely an
illusion.[22] Certainly even at the height of the struggle against Lollardy,
in the decades on either side of 1400, it is possible to exaggerate its
cultural and political impact. Paul Strohm's delvings into the language
and mindset of Ricardian and Lancastrian England have alerted us to
the political and dynastic resonances of the anti-Lollard campaign.[23] The
new Lancastrian dynasty did indeed ostentatiously embrace and enforce
religious orthodoxy as a means of legitimating its dubious dynastic
claims, and of cementing the allegiances of powerful churchmen. All the
same, it is worth noting that under Henry IV more Franciscan friars
were executed for preaching against Lancastrian dynastic usurpation
than Lollards were burned for heresy.[24]

　　The character of the popular appeal of early Lollardy – but perhaps
also its evanescence – is vividly suggested by the hold it established in
Leicester in the 1380s. The movement there was centred on the disused
leper hospital of St John the Baptist, just outside the city, converted into
a hermitage by a local layman, William Smith, who was joined by a
chantry-chaplain named Richard Waytestaythe, and by the hermit-priest
William Swinderby, a protégé of Philip Repingdon's.[25] These men must
have looked familiar to the citizenry of Leicester, standing in a tradition
of devotional reform that went back to Richard Rolle and beyond.
Rolle's first entry into the life of a hermit is worth recalling here.
Dressed in a bizarre costume improvised from two of his sister's kirtles
and an old rainhood of his father's, he appeared unannounced in the
Dalton family chapel in the parish church of Pickering one summer day
in 1318. John Dalton was bailiff of Pickering, keeper of the forest and
constable of the castle, a considerable man. Rolle's father had probably
been in his service, and Rolle himself had known Dalton's sons at
Oxford. Though Rolle was a layman, the parish priest permitted him to
preach an English sermon, and the Daltons were sufficiently impressed

---

[22] Clive Burgess, "A Hotbed of heresy? Fifteenth-century Bristol and Lollardy reconsidered," in
Linda Clerk (ed), *The Fifteenth Century III: Authority and Subversion*, Woodbridge, 2003, pp 43–62.
[23] Paul Strohm, *England's Empty Throne: Usurpation and the Language of Legitimation 1399–1422*, New
Haven and London, 1998.
[24] An observation I owe to my colleague Dr Richard Rex.
[25] Anne Hudson, *The Premature Reformation*, Oxford, 1988, p. 74 ff.

to take him into their house, and to clothe him formally as a hermit.[26] The whole incident suggests a religious culture hospitable to the extraordinary, and not by any means slavishly subordinated to clerical control: Rolle does not seem to have had or indeed to have sought official approval for his adoption of the eremitical life. Lollardy undoubtedly brought a new and dangerous edge to this sort of charismatic religious culture, but the welcome it received must in many cases have built on this non-heretical tradition of lay devotional independence.

Swinderby, who famously preached to large crowds from a pulpit improvised round mill-stones displayed for sale outside the Leper Chapel, did eventually preach unmistakeably Wycliffite teachings, such as the rejection of Transubstantiation, but that was after he had left Leicester. To judge by the propositions he was forced to repudiate by Bishop Buckingham, his Leicester preaching seems to have consisted of issues which would have resonated with many non-Wycliffite critics – which means *members* – of the contemporary church, in particular the injustices of tithe and the defectiveness of the ministrations of unworthy priests. Waytestaythe and Smith anticipated what was to become the familiar Lollard polemic and polemical style against the cult of images, denouncing the shrine images of the Virgin of Walsingham and of the mother church of the diocese at Lincoln as "witches", and giving a practical demonstration of the powerlessness of holy images by cooking a cabbage over the broken fragments of a statue of St Catherine. Anne Hudson considers that this polemic against images was particularly popular with the laity of Leicester, though it should be noted that the chronicler Knighton, our principle source, seems to imply exactly the opposite, noting that "so, banishing shame they did not bother to conceal the deed, but boasted about it in jest. But they did not go unpunished, for many heard of it, and not long afterwards they were expelled from the chapel".[27] Nevertheless, this cocktail of anti-clerical, anti-sacramental, and anti-symbolic teaching does seem to have attracted support in the town, including that of the mayor and some of the town council. Ten years on, there would be a similar body of support among the urban *élite* of Northampton, where the principal Lollard leader was another hermit, this time a woman, the piquantly named Anna Palmer [i.e. pilgrim], ancress of St Peter's Church.[28]

Just how extensive long-term lay support for Lollardy was, how wide its social spread, and how enduring its appeal in communities where it

[26] Jonathan Hughes, "Rolle, Richard (1305–1349)," in *Oxford Dictionary of National Biography*, ed. H. C. G. Matthew and Brian Harrison, Oxford, 2004; Jonathan Hughes, *Pastors and Visionaries: Religion and Secular Life in late Medieval Yorkshire*, Woodbridge, 1988, pp. 82–126.

[27] Hudson, *op. cit.*, p. 76; G. H. Martin (ed.), *Knighton's Chronicle 1337–1396*, Oxford, 1995, pp. 296–7.

[28] Hudson, *op. cit.*, p. 79.

had once taken root would be hard to say. By the time Margery Kempe arrived in Leicester in 1414, overt support for religious deviance among the ruling elite had evidently evaporated, and she was denounced by the Mayor as a "fals strumpet, a fals Loller and a fals deceyver of the pepyl".[29] Indeed the meaning of the term "Lollard" itself was at this early stage far from fixed. For Chaucer it was something joylessly akin to the later term "Puritan", for Langland something more complicated, and recognisably related to the sort of phenomenon we have seen at Leicester – "such manere hermytes/ Lollen ayen the byleyve and maner of holy chyrche".[30] Lollardy must often have seemed to some of its early supporters not much more than the left wing of a generally "reformist" piety, which emphasised the value of vernacular religious texts, the dangers of a sterile or hypocritical ritualism, and the evils of a worldly clergy. Devotional compendia like the *Pore Caitiff* of c. 1400 notoriously shared much of the same reformist platform as Lollard writings and preaching, and drew on similar materials, yet remained nevertheless entirely orthodox. The characteristics of the "Lollard Wills" identified by K. B. MacFarlane as the unifying mark of Wycliffite gentry – a loathing of the physical body and an insistence of simple burial characterised by alms to the poor in place of funeral pomp – are, as is well known, replicated in the wills of testators of impeccable orthodoxy, not least those of Archbishop Arundel and of the renegade ex-Lollard Philip Repingdon, Bishop of Lincoln. Repingdon, indeed, in common with several of the other "lost leaders" among the apostles of early Wycliffism, was to prove himself a determined opponent of his former associates.[31] Denied the oxygen of educated clergy leadership and of gentry protection, Lollardy declined inexorably into negativity, a form of rejection of the dominant sacramental and symbolic expressions of contemporary Christianity. From about 1430 in most places it was almost certainly in recession, and no new texts were produced to nourish it.

V

The positive religious attraction of Lollardy is in any case elusive. It must certainly have centred on its Biblicism, the draw of the vernacular scriptures, an attraction which certainly extended far beyond the bounds of the heretical movement itself. The domestic reading or recitation of biblical material emerges from all our sources as the single most constant and sustaining feature of Lollard communities. The favoured

---

[29] Barry Windeatt (ed), *The Book of Margery Kempe*, London, 2000, p. 229.
[30] On Langland and Lollardy, Hudson, *op. cit.*, pp. 398–408.
[31] J. A. F. Thompson, "Knightly Piety and the Margins of Lollardy," in Margaret Aston and Colin Richmond, *Lollardy and the Gentry in the Later Middle Ages*, Stroud, 1997, pp. 95–111.

material was often didactic (the Ten Commandments, the Sermon on the Mount, the Epistle of St James) or apocalyptic (The Book of Revelation), helping to nourish a sense of a lay religion based round moral action independent of clerical ceremonial, or to fuel an urgent and angry sense that the official church had gone disastrously astray. But the appeal of vernacular scripture was clearly a powerful one in an increasingly literate lay population. The ban imposed in 1409 was therefore pregnant with consequence for the future, leaving unsatisfied a need attested by the fact that many and perhaps most fifteenth-century owners and readers of Wycliffite bibles were impeccably orthodox Catholics, like the Suffolk wool magnate John Clopton of Long Melford. Clopton built himself a tomb in the chancel of the parish church which doubled as the Easter Sepulchre for the adoration of the reserved Sacrament at Easter, so he was clearly no Lollard: yet his will made careful arrangements for the bestowal of his English bible, just as it did for his collection of relics and his gold pectoral cross.[32]

In addition, Lollardy shared with the Franciscan movement it so much detested a powerful critique of the extravagant excess of much contemporary ritual provision, and the consequent neglect of the poor. Many sensitive late medieval Christians may have suspected that gold lavished on statues would be better spent feeding and clothing the hungry and naked, that the real image of Christ was not so much the carved crucifix as the flesh of suffering humanity. Hence Lollard insistence that "it wer better to give a poor bitynel or lame man a peny than to bestow their mony in pilgre goyng and worshipping the immagys of sentys, for man is the very ymage of godde which ought only to be wurshipd and no stokkys ne stonys",[33] went unerringly to one of the nerve-centres of medieval Christianity. More positively expressed, that perception is the main substance of many of the stories in the Franciscan *Fioretti*, and something like it seems implicit in the eloquent gesture of the Norfolk Lollard Margery Baxter, when she rebuked her neighbour Joan Clifland for lavishing attention on images made by "lewed wrightes of stokkes", and instead stretched out her arms cross-wise , saying "Look, here is the true cross of Christ, which you can and you should venerate every day in your own home".[34] In some cases at least that insight appears to have been translated into practice. Derek Plumb has demonstrated the relatively wide social distribution of Lollardy in the Chilterns, and has discerned in the wills of the Lollards and ex-Lollards there a greater concern for the relief of the poor than is apparent in the

[32] J. Jackson Howard (ed), *The Visitation of Suffolk*, Lowestoft and London, 1866, I, p. 38; Peter Marshall, *Reformation England 1480–1642*, London, 2003, p. 17.
[33] Isabel Dorte of East Hendred in Berkshire, 1491, quoted in Diana Webb, *Pilgrimage in Medieval England*, London, 2000, p. 233.
[34] Norman Tanner (ed), *Norwich Heresy Trials*, London, 1977, p. 44.

wills of their orthodox neighbours.[35] Lollardy appealed also to a desire for simplicity which must often have been felt amidst the lavishness of late medieval Catholicism. Many laymen would have approved the Lollard sentiment that "a simple Pater noster of a ploughman that is in charity is better than a thousand masses of covetous prelates and vain religious full of covetousness and pride and false flattering and nourishing of sin": the same sentiments would not have been out of place in the *sermone volgare* of Bernardino of Siena.[36]

But in Lollardy that perception characteristically seems to have articulated itself less in the formulation of a positive religious code than in the disparagement of the sins of others, and you cannot build a healthy religious life on the disparagement of your neighbours, even your clerical neighbours. For all its biblicism, Lollardy presented itself primarily as a critique of religion rather than an alternative religion, and after 1414 it seems to have displayed an unstoppable tendency to slide into the ideology of the village know-all. The hostile court records which are our principal sources admittedly bristle with obvious difficulties as an accurate or adequate picture of a clandestine religious tradition. Yet what they reveal to us seems essentially a family tradition with little apparent evangelical appeal or motivation. This may have been because the popular movement had little constructive religious content, drawing its vigour apparently from its deconstruction of alternative forms of religiosity, its character (often memorably) preserved in ale-house belly-laughs at the expense of "Our Lady of Foulpit" or "Our Lady of Falsingham", rather than in any more positive folk wisdom.

But the same seems to me true of Wycliffism even at its most sophisticated. The Wycliffite Sermon Cycle is the largest and most systematic body of Lollard teaching, a stupendous and learned labour providing 294 sermons for the whole year, produced in Oxford or in some aristocratic Lollard household in the last years of the fourteenth century.[37] It is a chilling and depressing body of material, all too obviously infected by the spiritual dyspepsia of the movement's founder, monotonous in its moralism and its relentless polemic against the religious orders and the "folly of prelates", entirely lacking in the affective warmth and devotion to the suffering humanity of Christ which is the distinctive mark of late medieval popular Christianity. It is hard to imagine this sour diet satisfying anyone's religious hunger for long.

I am suggesting that there was something religiously – by which I suppose I mean imaginatively – sterile about Lollardy. To put the matter

---

[35] Derek Plumb, "The social and economic spread of rural Lollardy," in W. J. Sheils and D. Wood (eds), *Voluntary Religion: Studies in Church History*, vol. 23, Oxford, 1986, pp. 111–29; see also his even more emphatic essays in M. Spufford (ed), *The World of the Rural Dissenters 1520–1725*, Cambridge, 1995, chs 2 and 3.

[36] Hudson, *op. cit.*, p. 196.

in less value-laden terms, there was in Lollardy at the very least a literal-istic hostility to symbol and metaphor which put it at odds with some of the most characteristic energies of late medieval Christianity, and which, for all their overlaps of interest and emphasis, contrasts with Langland, who shared many of the concerns of Wycliffe and his disci-ples, yet whose poem is in the end so very un-Lollard a document. Like the Lollard preachers, Langland had no interest in and no sympathy for the affective tradition of meditation on the Passion which was the dom-inant devotional mode of the late Middle Ages. But Peter Dronke and others have commented on the extraordinary fluidity and fusion of Langland's use of symbol and metaphor, the symbolic complexity and creative instability of his poetic method, the roots of which Dronke found in the mystical tradition.[38] By contrast, Kantik Ghosh has demonstrated Wycliffe's extreme unease with the ambiguities of symbol, metaphor and even parable, his "obsessive interest in justifying the domain of figurative language by pointing to 'real' and not merely 'perceived' correspondence between vehicle and tenor", and his "extraordinary reluctance to admit that spiritual truths can be commu-nicated by means of 'fictions'." [39] As in the Master, so in the disciples, and the same suspicion of fiction is evident in Lollard polemic against "Myracles Playing". It was the Wycliffite refusal or incomprehension of this polysemic resourcefulness of late medieval religion, as much as royal or episcopal persecution, which made it marginal to the course of main-stream religion in England in the later fifteenth century.

VI

The Stripping of the Altars is, as some commentators quite rightly saw, essentially a book about religion in the century from about 1450 onwards,[40] the "c. 1400" of the subtitle being adopted to acknowledge the fact that I had drawn on some earlier texts – principally the *Book of Margery Kempe*. It may be, as Miri Rubin has suggested,[41] that the harmonies of traditional religion as I portray them can be understood as the strenuous mid-century outcome of a prolonged earlier struggle with, and process of enforcement of orthodoxy upon, the Lollards. I should myself, however, be reluctant to concede even this much. It has been argued by Professor Nicholas Watson that the condemnation of Lollardy by Archbishop Arundel's *Constitutions* in 1409 effectively

---

[37] Anne Hudson and Pamela Gradon (eds), *English Wycliffite Sermons*, 5 vols, Oxford 1983–96.
[38] Peter Dronke, "Arbor Caritas," in P. L. Heyworth (ed), *Medieval Studies for J. A. W. Bennett*, Oxford, 1981, pp. 207–43.
[39] Kantik Ghosh, *The Wycliffite Heresy*, Cambridge, 2001, pp. 32, 34.
[40] For example, Miri Rubin, in *Assays ix* (note 8 above), p. 19.
[41] Ibid.

sterilised English vernacular religious writing for the rest of the century. After the intellectual daring of Ricardian writing – Langland, Chaucer, Julian of Norwich, and lesser writers, Watson argued – we get the dumbed-down flatness of Lydgate and Gower, and the unquestioning devotionalism of Nicholas Love. After 1409, he considers, no-one dared *think* about religion in English, and the use of the vernacular for religious purposes in itself became suspect and problematic. In this general argument, the mid-century trial and condemnation for heresy of Bishop Reginald Pecock, whose many controversial works against the Lollards are written in English, has been seen as a key piece of evidence, it being contended – or at times assumed – that Pecock fell foul of the general ban on the vernacular which flowed from Arundel's *Constitutions*.[42]

But there just isn't enough evidence to claim so much. It has been recently demonstrated that Pecock's use of the vernacular was never central to the case against him. He was condemned not for writing in English, but for an exaltation of human reason which threatened the authority of scripture in matters of faith. Pecock had certainly crossed the boundaries of fifteenth-century orthodoxy, but because of what he said, not because of the language in which he said it. Moreover, his fall was almost certainly orchestrated by political enemies, and should not be understood as the inevitable outcome of some supposed general hyper-vigilant orthodoxy, fuelled by panic about Lollardy.[43] I myself doubt that Lollardy had a sufficiently deep or wide hold over the laity as a whole to justify a rereading of the remarkable catechetical and devotional achievement of the fifteenth-century church, simply or primarily in terms of its response to heresy.

There certainly were fifteenth-century devotional texts, like Nicholas Love's *Mirror of the Life of Jesu,* with its anti-Lollard appendix on the Blessed Sacrament,[44] which register for us the alarmed orthodox response to vernacular heresy. The life-work of Bishop Pecock was itself based on a continuing preoccupation with the Lollard threat and the need for a response in kind. But Pecock's writings were themselves evidence of considerable theological experiment, and the impact of Arundel's *Constitutions*, which have been described as initiating "a regulatory frenzy [which] changed the whole texture of religious culture in England"[45] should not be exaggerated. Fifteenth-

---

[42] Nicholas Watson, "Censorship and Cultural Change in Late Medieval Vernacular Theology," *Speculum* 70, 1995, pp. 822–64.

[43] In the unpublished 2003 Cambridge PhD dissertation by Sarah James, "Debating Heresy: 15th-century Vernacular Theology and Arundel's Constitutions".

[44] Nicholas Love, *The Mirror of the Blessed Life of Jesus Christ, a Reading Text*, ed. Michael G. Sargent, Exeter, 2004, pp. 223–39, esp. pp. 235–7.

[45] By Steven Justice in D. Wallace (ed), *The Cambridge History of Medieval English Literature*, Cambridge, 1999, p. 676.

century England simply did not possess the resources or infrastructure needed for a theocratic police-state, and the *Constitutions* were never consistently or systematically enforced. Orthodox attitudes to vernacular religious writing after 1409 were far from uniformly hostile. Even the gargantuan Latin anti-Lollard treatise of the Carmelite theologian Thomas Netter, the *Doctrinale Fidei Catholicae*, was probably already essentially otiose by the time of its early circulation in the 1420s, for Wycliffism by that date was in retreat in its Oxford stronghold. Netter's book was probably compiled at least as much with an eye to re-establishing the orthodox credentials of the English church with the papacy and Continental churchmen alienated by Wycliffe's reputation as an heresiarch during the anti-heretical proceedings of the Council of Constance, as to any English audience.[46] The fight against Lollardy would continue to provide a motive for the foundation of colleges and the provision of preachers, but the vernacular teaching of the faith in the remainder of the fifteenth century seems relatively and curiously untouched by anti-Lollard themes. Even at the height of the Lollard crisis, a London-based poet like the author of the alliterative verse narrative *St Erkenwald* was able to treat sacramental themes in terms which harked back to the theological preoccupations of the early fourteenth century, without any hint of overt engagement with or embarrassment by the teachings of Wycliffe.[47] And by the mid-fifteenth century, so apparently promising a platform for anti-Lollard polemic as the *Croxton Play of the Sacrament*, probably written in Suffolk, contains no obvious connections or allusions to contemporary heresy.[48] The anti-sacramentalists of the play are Jews, not Lollards, and there is not even the most oblique reference in the play to any continuing tradition of East Anglian heresy. If Lollardy provided an extra spur to the late medieval church's catechetical activity, it did not fundamentally alter the nature of the exercise. Indeed, the Lollard tradition itself seems to have been confined to a cluster of dynastically dominated and perpetuated Lollard communities. Despite the continuing insistence by some historians on the deep-rooted persistence of Lollardy as a feature of fifteenth-century religion, and even when all due allowance is made for the accidents of the survival of documentation, there is surprisingly little hard evidence of *widespread* popular appeal. Though there were periodic revivals of Episcopal concern about the Lollard threat, like that at Coventry in the 1480s, pastoral preoccupation in the fifteenth cen-

---

[46] For Netter and his work, Hudson, *op. cit.*, pp. 50–5.
[47] E. Duffy, "St Erkenwald: London's Cathedral Saint," in J. Backhouse (ed), *The Medieval English Cathedral, Papers in Honour of Pamela Tudor-Craig*, Donington, 2003, pp. 150–67.
[48] N. Davis (ed), *Non-Cycle Plays and Fragments*, Oxford, 1970, pp. 58–89.

tury seems by and large very much more concerned with ignorance than with heresy.[49]

This difficulty in attributing a decisive role to Lollardy in the formation of later fifteenth-century orthodoxy was highlighted by the publication in 1994 of Professor Ann Nichols's superb study of the carved Seven-Sacrament fonts of East Anglia, *Seeable Signs*.[50] Professor Nichols's book demonstrated that these extraordinary ritual objects, (forty-two survive) unlike many comparable continental depictions of the sacraments, precisely and remarkably embodied the best fifteenth-century academic teaching about the form and matter of the seven sacraments of the Catholic Church. She went on to suggest that this iconographical precision had perhaps been elicited by the Lollard threat. She pointed out that the fonts were to be found in the same region – and sometimes in the same places – as earlier manifestations of Lollardy, and that they should perhaps therefore be read as direct responses to Lollardy.

Tempting as such an interpretation might be, however, the problem is that the geographical overlap on which it rests was in fact only very approximate. Moreover, in the West Country, where Lollardy made little or no impact, equally striking and orthodox Seven-Sacrament artifacts – in this case stained-glass windows depicting the sacraments – had also proliferated in the fifteenth century. Above all, there is in every case at least a two-generation gap between the last recorded incidence of Lollardy, and the commissioning of the East Anglian fonts. The classic instance here is perhaps Martham, the hometown of the notorious Lollard Margery Baxter, and a parish which possesses a fine Seven-Sacrament font dating from the 1470s. Margery Baxter had made a special point of denouncing infant baptism,[51] so it is tempting to see the Martham font as a rebuttal, maybe by the wealthy of the parish, of her lower-class heresies. But fifty years is a long time to ponder such a rebuttal, and there is no independent evidence of continuing heterodoxy in the Martham region to explain the timing of such a gesture in the 1470s. Concern over Lollardy probably did form part of the prehistory of such artifacts, just as heresy in general was one contributory cause among others of the heightened concern for theological correctness which is so striking a feature of late medieval religious culture (notably in France and the Low Countries). Such concern, however, hardly constitutes evidence of a continuing panic about heresy, but rather the

[49] Coventry Lollardy has now been magnificently documented in Shannon McSheffrey and Norman Tanner, *Lollards of Coventry, 1486–1522*, Camden Society, 5th Series, vol. 23, Cambridge, 2003.

[50] Ann Nichols, *Seeable Signs, the Iconography of the Seven Sacraments 1350–1544*, Woodbridge, 1994.

[51] Norman P. Tanner (ed), *Heresy Trials in the Diocese of Norwich 1428–31*, Camden Society, 4th Series, vol. 20, Cambridge, 1977.

pearly precipitation of heightened orthodoxy round an ancient piece of heretical grit, which in most places had long since ceased to irritate directly. And to concede even so much for fifteenth-century England may be to falsify, for a preoccupation with catechetical precision is a feature of fifteenth-century religion in Western Europe as a whole, as the growing popularity of decorative schemes involving the iconography of those symbols of the teaching authority of the hierarchy, the Four Latin Doctors, suggests.[52]

VII

The interpretation of the English Reformation offered in this book looks less contentious now than it did in 1992.[53] Even the least enthusiastic reviewers then agreed that the book had "amply proved" that the late medieval church was "a flourishing and popular institution", and that the shift to Protestantism "was at first the work of a small minority".[54] In an England rapidly shedding, and indeed sometimes sadly embarrassed by, its own patriotic Protestant foundation–myth, the book's main contentions have since been quietly absorbed into public perception. It has become an historical commonplace that in the course of the three generations from 1530 to the end of Elizabeth's reign "one of the most Catholic of European countries" became "one of the most anti–Catholic".[55] I doubt myself whether England's Catholicism was in fact all that strikingly different in intensity from that of its northern–European neighbours, but however that may be, this acceptance of the book's main contentions is perhaps clearest in recent thinking about the visual arts and material culture in medieval and Tudor England, and more widely in Europe. *The Stripping of the Altars* was thus one of the shaping influences behind the National Gallery's hugely successful millennium exhibition, *Seeing Salvation*,[56]

[52] F. E. Hutchinson, *Medieval Glass at All Souls College,* London, 1949, pp. 38, 43, 49 and plates xxviii and xxix; Hilary Wayment, *King's College Chapel Cambridge: the Side-Chapel Glass*, Cambridge, 1988, pp. 194–5, illustrated p. 196: G. McN. Rushforth, *Medieval Christian Imagery as illustrated by the painted windows of Great Malvern Priory Church*, Oxford, 1936, pp. 253–4, 316–20: Emile Mâle, *Religious Art in France: the Late Middle Ages*, Princeton, 1986, pp. 212–13 and plates 122–3: Henk Van Os, *The Art of Devotion in the late Middle Ages in Europe 1300–1500,* Amsterdam, 1994, pp. 118–22; J. Leclerq, in F. Cabrol and H. Leclerq (eds), *Dictionnaire d'Archéologie Chrettienne et de Liturgie*, Paris, 1920, iv (i) cols 1260–1 ("Docteurs de l'Eglise"); Eugene F. Rice, *Saint Jerome in the Renaissance*, Baltimore, 1988, pp. 89–90.

[53] Two outstanding recent surveys of the English Reformation provide an overview of the current state of research: Felicity Heal's *Reformation in Britain and Ireland*, Oxford, 2003, as its title suggests, offers a unique "three kingdoms" perspective, while Peter Marshall's briefer *Reformation England 1480–1642*, London, 2003, is specially strong in its judicious appraisal of the historiography.

[54] Professor Lawrence Stone, in *The Guardian*, Tuesday 26 January 1993.

[55] Patrick Collinson, *The Reformation*, London, 2003, p. 107.

[56] Catalogued in Gabriele Finaldi (ed), *The Image of Christ*, London, National Gallery, 2000.

and the Victoria and Albert Museum's 2003 exhibition *Gothic, Art for England*.[57]

In historical writing, however, we are now in a self-consciously "post-revisionist" era. Recent treatments of the Reformation, while taking the main contentions of this book, and similar positions in the work of Haigh, Scarisbrick, and others as essentially proven, group them together under the blanket term "revisionism", and seek ways, some more successful than others, of moving beyond the terms of the debate about the English Reformation laid down in those works. As one such self-consciously "post-revisionist" historian has written, "few historians today would deny that in a simple contest between A. G. Dickens's interpretation on the one hand, and Haigh's or Duffy's interpretation on the other, Haigh and Duffy win hands down" – before proceeding, nevertheless, to argue for the radical unsatisfactoriness of "the revisionist model" of the history of the Reformation.[58]

In fact, this "revisionist model" is largely a critical construct, for the differences between "revisionists" are at least as significant as their agreements. It is, for example, a fundamental contention of *The Stripping of the Altars* that the Reformation represented a deep and traumatic cultural hiatus; it is a fundamental contention of Christopher Haigh's masterly and mischievous *English Reformations*, published in 1993, by contrast, that when the dust had settled on all the Crown-imposed religious upheavals, nothing very much had in fact happened.[59] But at least almost everyone now agrees that "although there were some English people excited about Protestantism in Henry VIII's reign, there was not much popular support for a change", despite which "over the course of three generations the way the English worshipped...and related to their place in the universe underwent a sea change".[60]

Historical enquiry into the English Reformation has therefore shifted now from consideration of the reluctances and resistances to reformation which "revisionism" highlighted, to the *processes* by which in the course of those three generations the assimilation of Protestant practice and belief took place. In that sense, my own study, published in 2001, of the conservative Devon village of Morebath, and its priest Sir Christopher Trychay, from the 1520s to the 1570s, is a "post-revisionist" work.[61] It is "post-revisionist" also in its correction of some of the

---

[57] Richard Marks and Paul Williamson, *Gothic: Art for England 1400–1547,* London, Victoria and Albert Museum, 2003.

[58] Ethan Shagan, *Popular Politics and the English Reformation*, Cambridge, 2003, p. 5.

[59] For a generalising discussion which tends to conflate several varieties of "revisionism" as a unitary phenomenon, see the Introduction to N. Tyack (ed), *England's Long Reformation 1500–1800*, London, 1998.

[60] Norman Jones, *The English Reformation: Religion and Cultural Adaptation*, London 2002, p. 2.

[61] E. Duffy, *The Voices of Morebath: Reformation and Rebellion in an English Village*, New Haven and London, 2001.

emphases of *The Stripping of the Altars*. Writing about Morebath in 1992, I had fully grasped neither the fact nor the implications of the remarkable promptitude and punctiliousness of Morebath's conformity with successive phases of the Henrician and early Edwardine Reformations (Morebath acquired an English bible, for example, before many of the urban parishes of Exeter), nor the extent of their conservative loathing of reform.[62] In 1549, it is now apparent, the formerly docilely acquiescent Morebath, bankrupted by the crippling financial demands of the Reformation, and demoralized by the collapse of vital social institutions structured round the cult of the saints, had armed and financed five unmarried men, and sent them to off join the traditionalist rebels besieging Exeter in protest against the Reformation and the Book of Common Prayer. Both Morebath's conformity and its eventual rebellion throw light on what has been called "the compliance conundrum",[63] which "revisionist" accounts of the Reformation like *The Stripping of the Altars* posed in a specially acute form. If early and mid-Tudor England was so Catholic, why and how was the Reformation accepted? But on that complex question, the jury is still out.

If the treatment of Morebath in this book needs some fine-tuning, by and large the Reformation section of *The Stripping of the Altars* seems to me to have worn surprisingly well, provided it is borne in mind that what is offered here is not a general history of the coming of Protestantism, but an account of its impact on the conservative majority. In retrospect, the chapter on Mary seems the most original in the second part of the book. Negative perceptions of the church under "Bloody Mary" have rather unsurprisingly proved the most resilient aspect of the traditional Protestant understanding of the Reformation. The section on the Marian church in a recent widely used survey of the Reformation is headed, characteristically, "Mary: Reaction and Persecution".[64] Persecution is certainly a major part of the story of Marian Catholicism,[65] but recognition of its horrors, and (rather less certainly) its counter-productivity, should not blind us to the more positive religious achievements of the Marian regime. Historians still regularly comment on the "limited intellectual horizons" of Marian

---

[62] For the evolution of my own understanding of the significance of Morebath's experience of Reformation, compare the book cited in the previous note with E. Duffy, "Morebath 1520–1570: a Rural Parish in the Reformation," in J. Devlin and R. Fanning (eds), *Religion and Rebellion*, Dublin, 1997, pp. 17–39.

[63] The phrase is Christopher Marsh's, in *Popular Religion in Sixteenth-Century England*, London, 1998, pp. 197 ff.

[64] Helen Parish in A. Pettegree (ed), *The Reformation World*, London, 2000, p. 229.

[65] For a survey of the Marian persecution of Protestants , see my "The repression of heresy in England," in Agostino Borromeo (ed), *L'Inquisizione, Atti del Simposio internazionale, Citta del Vaticano, 29–31 Octobre 1998*, Vatican 2003, pp. 445–68.

Catholicism.[66] By contrast, I would want now to emphasize and extend my insistence in this book on the Counter-Reformation character of Marian Catholicism. In particular, I would now argue even more strongly than I did in 1992 for the Marian regime's alertness to the power of popular religious culture, and its ability to harness and direct it.

One instance must suffice here: the creation by Cardinal Pole's Legatine Synod in 1555 of an annual commemoration on St Andrew's Day (30 November) of the restoration of papal obedience, at which a sermon was to be preached on papal primacy in every parish in the land, and before which there was to be a parish procession with banners. Pole thereby initiated a propagandist device, the public anniversary religious celebration, which is normally thought of as a characteristically *Protestant* institution, and which would indeed be exploited as a key element in the later formation of a Protestant popular culture, most notably in commemorations of Queen Elizabeth's Accession day on 17 November, and, in the seventeenth century, of Gunpowder, Treason and Plot on 5 November.[67]

VIII

Because my concern in chapters eleven to fifteen of the book was with the impact of Protestantism on the religion of the majority, the Reformation features here as an essentially destructive force, a movement for which, as I claimed in a consciously hyperbolic phrase, "iconoclasm was the central sacrament".[68] So, finally, it is worth stressing here that I do of course recognize that Tudor Protestantism was far more than the mere refusal of Catholicism, and that, in contrast to Lollardy, the Reformation had a positive and powerful message, which might and did inspire large numbers of devout men and women. Unlike Lollardy, Protestantism was both an expansive and a potent evangelizing movement. Indeed the very act of iconoclasm might make the force and nature of that positive vision clear. In the people's portion of the shared parish and monastic church of Binham priory in North Norfolk there survive the remains of an early Tudor rood-screen, the lower part or dado of which was painted in the usual manner with rows of holy

---

[66]   A. Pettegree, "A. G. Dickens, his critics, and the English Reformation," *Historical Research*, vol. 77, February 2004, p. 58.

[67]   David Cressy, *Bonfires and Bells. National Memory and the protestant calendar in Elizabethan and Stuart England*, Berkeley, 1989. I have dealt with this aspect of the Marian regime's religious policy more fully in "Cardinal Pole preaching: St Andrew's day 1557," in Eamon Duffy and David Loades (eds), *The Church of Mary Tudor*, Aldershot, 2005.

[68]   Below, p. 480.

figures, Christ and his saints and angels. In Edward's reign the screen was purged of the carved crucifix which surmounted it, and the lower panels, with their rows of painted saints, were whitewashed over. On the blank surface thus secured, handsome black letter passages were copied from the First Epistle of St Peter and the Epistles of St Paul. The text used was that of Cranmer's Great Bible, the 'Bible of the largest volume' commanded to be set up in churches by the 1538 Injunctions. The passages selected replaced the screen's former representation of the saints as intercessors, healers and protectors, with a scriptural message of inner sanctity, in which the reader is urged to unity, charity, and holiness of life. So, one of the panels reads , in the words of Colossians chapter 3 verses 12–15.

> [Wherefore as electe of God,] Holy and beloved, put on tender mercye, kyndnes, humblenes of mynde, mekenes, longe suffringe, forbearynge one another, yf any man have a quarrell agaynst another: as Christ forgave you, even so do ye. Above all these thinges put on love, which is the bonde of perfectnes. And the peace of God rule in your heartes: to the which peace ye are called in one body.

69   The Binham inscriptions in full are as follows:
From north to south
       Panel 1: I Peter chapter 1 verses 13–17:
[Wherefore gyrde up the loynes of your mynde,] Be sober and trust perfectly on the grace that is brought unto you by the declaryng of Iesus Chryst as obedient chyldren, that ye geve not your selves over unto youre old lustes by whych ye were led, when as yet ye were ignorauaant of Chryst, but as he which called you is holy, even so be ye holy also in all maner of conversacyon, because it is written: Be holy, for I am holy, [saith the Lord].
       Panel 2: Colossians chapter 3 verses 12–15.
[Wherefore as electe of God,] Holy and beloved, put on tender mercye, kyndnes, humblenes of mynde, mekenes, longe suffringe, forbearynge one another, yf any man have a quarrell agaynst another: as Christ forgave you, even so do ye. Above all these thinges put on love, which is the bonde of perfectnes. And the peace of God rule in your heartes: to the which peace ye are called in one body.
       Panel 3: I Peter chapter 3 verses 15b–17
Be ready allwayes to geve an answere to every man that asketh you a reason of the hope that is in you, and that with meaknes and feare: havynge a good conscience that where as they backbyte you as evyll doers, they may be ashamed, that falsely accuse your good conversacion in Chryst. For it is better yf the wyll of God be so that ye suffre for well doynge then for evyll doinge.
       Panel 4: I Timothy chapter 6 verses 6–9
Godlynes is great ryches if a man be content with what he hath. For we brought nothing into the worlde, nether maye we cary any thynge out. But when we have fode and rayment we must therwith be content. They that wylbe ryche fall into temptacyon and snares, and into many folysshe and noysome lustes, whiche droune men into perdicyon and destruccyon.
       Framed and glass-covered panel with the risen Christ continues the passage from I Timothy on panel 4, with verses 10–12.
For covetousnes of money is the roote of all evyll: which whyll some lusted after, they erred from the fayth, and tanglyd them selves with many sorrowes. But thou man of God, flye soch thynges. Folowe ryghtewsnes, godlynes, fayth, love, patience, meaknes. Fyght the good fyght of fayth. Laye hande on eternall lyfe, wher unto thou art also called, and hast professed a good professyon before many witnesses.

Nearby in the modern church is a small single-framed and glass-covered panel, a fragment from another section of the screen, now lost. It represents the risen Christ carrying a resurrection flag, hand raised in blessing. The fragment of text covering it is what remains of a longer extract from I Timothy chapter 6, verses 10–12.

> For covetousnes of money is the roote of all evyll: which whyll some lusted after, they erred from the fayth, and tanglyd them selves with many sorrowes. But thou man of God, flye soch thynges. Folowe ryghtewsnes, godlynes, fayth, love, patience, meaknes. Fyght the good fyght of fayth. Laye hande on eternall lyfe, wher unto thou art also called, and hast professed a good professyon before many witnesses.[69]

The reformers at Edwardine Binham, whether the parishioners themselves or, more likely, the diocesan or royal official enforcing drastic change, were doing more than obliterating the Catholic past. Their choice of texts suggests that they sought to replace what they believed to be an alienated and false holiness, embodied in the idolatrous figures of external heavenly mediators and helpers, with an internalized Gospel of personal responsibility and gracious renewal. The whitewash and black-letter text are flaking now, to reveal the gilded and painted remnants of the older piety beneath. In their combination of resonant biblical exhortation superimposed over the cult figures of late medieval Catholicism, the Binham panels are among the most poignant survivals of that violent age, in which the lives of ordinary men and women were caught up in the collision of contrasting understandings of the Christian Gospel.

E.D.
College of St Mary Madgalene, Cambridge
Feast of the Epiphany, 2005

INTRODUCTION

I

This book attempts two tasks usually carried out separately, and by at least two different sets of practitioners. In the first part I have sought to explore the character and range of late medieval English Catholicism, indicating something of the richness and complexity of the religious system by which men and women structured their experience of the world, and their hopes and aspirations within and beyond it. In the second part I have tried to tell the story of the dismantling and destruction of that symbolic world, from Henry VIII's break with the Papacy in the early 1530s to the Elizabethan "Settlement" of religion, which I take to have been more or less secure, or at least in the ascendant, by about 1580. There have, of course, been studies of aspects of English religion which have covered much the same period, notably Keith Thomas's *Religion and the Decline of Magic*, and many of those who have written about one or other of my two periods have reached out before or after to establish context or to suggest connections: Colin Richmond's sensitive explorations of the religion of the gentry in late medieval Norfolk and Suffolk, Clive Burgess's pioneering work on the parishioners of late medieval Bristol, or Robert Whiting's study of the Reformation in South-west England, provide cases in point.

But a good deal of writing about late medieval religion has been dogged by disciplinary or chronological divisions of labour. Late medieval devotion has been studied largely from within faculties of literature, with a consequent tendency to emphasize the culture of social élites and a stress on individuals or groups, such as the fourteenth-century mystics Rolle, Hilton, the "Cloud" writer, and Julian of Norwich, out of all proportion to their actual impact on the religion of ordinary men and women. Historians who *have* addressed themselves to the religion of the majority, as Keith Thomas did in his book, have been sceptical about or uninterested in the interconnections between "élite" or clerical culture and that of the people at large, and they have therefore presented a picture of the religion of the people which is seriously incomplete and one-sided. It is an extraordinary feature of Thomas's work, for example, that there is in it virtually no sustained discussion of the liturgy and its effect on the religious world-view of ordinary men and women. Yet, as I shall argue, the liturgy was in fact the principal reservoir from which the religious paradigms and beliefs of the people were drawn.

Again, much writing about late medieval and early modern religion has taken it as axiomatic that there was a wide gulf between "popular" and "élite" religion, that the orthodox teaching of the clergy was poorly understood and only partially practised, that paganism and superstition were rife. That conviction, crudely expressed in tens of thousands of undergraduate and sixth-form essays, has been absorbed from and is certainly amply reflected even in the work of sophisticated historians, for whom heresy, witchcraft, and magic have seemed more interesting, and, presumably, more important, than religious orthodoxy or orthopraxis. Ironically, even the growing number of excellent studies of the religion of the gentry and aristocracy of the period, by Malcolm Vale, Jeremy Catto, Colin Richmond, Christine Carpenter, and others, while adding greatly to our grip of the main features of late medieval piety, have also perhaps contributed to a sense that orthodoxy was the peculiar preserve of the well-educated and well-to-do. To judge by the amount of interest that has been shown in them, the English religious landscape of the late Middle Ages was peopled largely by Lollards, witches, and leisured, aristocratic ladies.[1]

It is my conviction, and a central plank of the argument of the first part of this book, that no substantial gulf existed between the religion of the clergy and the educated élite on the one hand and that of the people at large on the other. I do not believe that it is helpful or accurate to talk of the religion of the average fifteenth-century parishioner as magical, superstitious, or semi-pagan. Nor does it seem to me that the most interesting aspect of late medieval religion lay in the views and activities of those who, like the relatively small number of Lollards, rejected its central tenets and preoccupations. The fifteenth and early sixteenth centuries in England witnessed a period of massive catechetical enterprise on the part not only of the bishops and parochial clergy, whose responsibility it mainly was, but also on the part of members of

[1] An excellent bibliographical survey of recent work on the late medieval church is to be found in Peter Heath's "Between Reform and Reformation: the English Church in the Fourteenth and Fifteenth centuries", *Journal of Ecclesiastical History*, XLI, 1990, pp. 647–78.

religious orders and private individuals, like the printers Caxton, Wynkyn de Worde, and Richard Pynson. The teachings of late medieval Christianity were graphically represented within the liturgy, endlessly reiterated in sermons, rhymed in verse treatises and saints' lives, enacted in the Corpus Christi and Miracle plays which absorbed so much lay energy and expenditure, and carved and painted on the walls, screens, bench-ends, and windows of the parish churches. It is true that the wealthy and literate had increasing access to and interest in types of spirituality previously confined to the monastery. Yet within the diversity of medieval religious options there was a remarkable degree of religious and imaginative homogeneity across the social spectrum, a shared repertoire of symbols, prayers, and beliefs which crossed and bridge even the gulf between the literate and the illiterate.

For that reason, in talking of the religious beliefs and practices of the late medieval parishioner, I have avoided all but the occasional use of the notion of "popular religion", a term laden with questionable assumptions about the nature of *non-popular* religion and the gap between the two. Instead I have used the phrase "traditional religion", which does more justice to the shared and inherited character of the religious beliefs and practices of the people, and begs fewer questions about the social geography of pre-Reformation religion. Alas, in history every generalizing term begs some question: How traditional is "traditional"? Not every religious custom in the fifteenth century, however apparently well-established, was immemorial. The greatest feast of the late medieval church, Corpus Christi, was of comparatively recent institution, and the Corpus Christi play cycles, which absorbed the energies of a large proportion of the citizens of towns like York for months on end every year, were new in the fourteenth century. New feasts emerged as optional pious practices, and were eventually imposed as universal observances. New saints were venerated and the old, if not forgotten, at least gracefully retired. New devotional fads were enthusiastically explored by a laity eager for religious variety, increasingly literate, and keenly if conventionally devout. My use of the term "traditional", therefore, is not meant to imply stasis or impassibility, but to indicate the general character of a religious culture which was rooted in a repertoire of inherited and shared beliefs and symbols, while remaining capable of enormous flexibility and variety.

In attempting to delineate the character of that traditional religion I have drawn on a wide variety of sources, from liturgical books to painted images, from saints' lives and devotional treatises to play-texts, and from churchwardens' accounts and ecclesiastical court records to personal commonplace books and wills. I have also drawn on a good deal of local and parochial material, especially on the riches of the churches of East Anglia, for my non-documentary evidence, but, somewhat unfashionably, this is not a regional study. I am well aware of the importance of regional variation in many of the institutions and practices I have attempted to describe, from parish structures to the cult of the saints, but it was an overview I was seeking. In attempting to provide it I hope I have not imposed a distorting unity on the variety and complexity of the evidence.

It is the contention of the first part of the book that late medieval Catholicism exerted an enormously strong, diverse, and vigorous hold over the imagination and the loyalty of the people up to the very moment of Reformation. Traditional religion had about it no particular marks of exhaustion or decay, and indeed in a whole host of ways, from the multiplication of vernacular religious books to adaptations within the national and regional cult of the saints, was showing itself well able to meet new needs and new conditions. Nor does it seem to me that tendencies towards the "privatizing" of religion, or growing lay religious sophistication and literacy, or growing lay activism and power in gild and parish, had in them that drive towards Protestantism which some historians have discerned. That there was much in late medieval religion which was later developed within a reformed setting is obvious, but there was virtually nothing in the character of religion in late medieval England which could *only* or even *best* have been developed within Protestantism. The religion of Elizabethan England was of course full of continuities with and developments of what had gone before. Even after the iconoclastic hammers and scraping-tools of conviction Protestantism had done their worst, enough of the old imagery and old resonances remained in the churches in which the new religion was preached to complicate, even, in the eyes of some, to compromise, the new teachings. The preservation within the prayer-book pattern of the old rites of passage and some of the old forms of reverence made a totally fresh beginning an impossibility, doubtless to the relief of most of the population. The voracious lay appetite for religious literature which had already been in evidence in the fifteenth century, and which the advent of printing stoked furiously, continued to be catered for in books and broadsides which, for a time at least, freely employed the old types of religious imagery or passable imitations of it. Yet when all is said and done, the Reformation was a violent disruption, not the natural fulfilment, of most of what was vigorous in late medieval piety and religious practice.

That contention, if true, obviously raises a series of major problems for the historian of the Reformation. If medieval religion was decadent, unpopular, or exhausted, the success of the Reformation hardly requires explanation. If, on the contrary, it was vigorous, adaptable, widely understood, and popular, then we have much yet to discover about the processes and the pace of reform. In the second part of the book, therefore, I have tried to address some of the problems raised by the argument of the first part. I have provided a narrative of the religious changes which took place in England in the fifty years after the break with Rome, focusing in particular on the impact of those changes in the parishes, as traditional belief and practice came under ever fiercer pressure from Protestant regimes. In the process I have offered a reassessment of some of the central issues in current Reformation historiography. In particular, I have tried to penetrate the documentary evidence for the apparently ready implementation of the reform measures imposed on the localities from the centre, and to suggest that compliance should not be taken to imply agreement with the Protestant theology underlying the changes. Moreover, I suggest here that the evidence of the spread of Protestantism discerned by many historians in changing will preambles from the late 1530s onwards is largely an optical illusion. Historians have failed to note the pre-Reformation Catholic precedents for types of will formulae taken to be distinctively "Protestant", and have ignored or discounted the prudential factors which led Catholic testators to omit or change Catholic formulae and bequests. Finally, I have tried to explore the implications for our understanding and perception of the Marian religious regime of my central claim about the vitality and popularity of traditional religion. If it is the case that liturgy, ritual, and traditional religious forms and imagery remained central to lay religion into the 1540s and beyond, the preoccupation of the Marian regime with such matters, usually cited as evidence of blinkered reaction and disastrously mistaken priorities, takes on a radically different complexion. The Marian episcopate grasped, just as the reformers themselves did, the continuing vitality and importance of the ritual structures, both material and conceptual, of traditional religion. Bonner, Pole, and their fellow bishops therefore devised and launched a campaign for the restoration of those structures, and for the re-education of the laity in their significance and use, which was both far-seeing and practical, and which was in fact displaying unmistakable signs of success, till the death of Queen Mary wrecked the entire enterprise. In my final chapter I have tried to demonstrate the anxiety of the Elizabethan episcopate about the persistence and vitality of the forms of traditional religion, an anxiety reflected in the determination with which they set themselves to achieve the destruction of them.

My object in this book is to map the range and vigour of late medieval and early modern English Catholicism, and in the process to exorcize certain types of writing about the English Reformation. But this is not a history of the late medieval English Church, nor of the Reformation in its other aspects. In the interests of keeping an already lengthy work within manageable bounds, I have largely confined my exploration of traditional religion to the parish setting, saying almost nothing about the important and widespread influence of the religious orders. The reader will also search in vain in these pages for any extended discussion of Lollardy, or of the earliest English Protestants. This is not because I doubt the existence or significance of either group, though I do think that Reformation historians have by and large overestimated their numbers and their significance. Because, until comparatively recently, English medieval historians have tended to concentrate on earlier periods, the late medieval English Church has largely been studied by Reformation historians, and hence through the eyes of its critics, Lollard or Protestant, and in the light of its demise at the hands of the Crown – the fifteenth century diminished to the status of a set on which the real drama of Reformation was to take place. The assumptions underlying such an approach to late medieval religion have already been vigorously questioned by sixteenth-century historians like Jack Scarisbrick and Christopher Haigh. If this book with its broader time-span does anything to persuade its readers of the intrinsic interest and vitality of fifteenth- and early sixteenth-century English Catholicism, and to set a question mark against some common assumptions about the character and progress of the Reformation up to the middle years of Elizabeth's reign, it will have served its purpose.

II

The narrative framework of the second part of this book is, I hope, self-explanatory and self-justifying. Something, however, needs to be said here about the structure of the first part. Late medieval religion was both enormously varied and extremely tightly knit: any thread pulled from the multicoloured pattern will lead us eventually to its centre. To select a starting-point and set out themes is therefore to some extent an arbitrary exercise. I have elected to present my material in four clusters, which I hope will help to steer the reader through the sometimes daunting riches of late medieval English religion.

In the first section, "Liturgy, Learning, and the Laity", which consists of two chapters, I explore two ways in which lay folk appropriated for themselves traditional religion, as a system of worship and as an inherited belief system. Since it was in Latin, the late medieval liturgy is often thought of as the preserve of the clergy, a complex and imperfectly intelligible spectacle in which lay folk were passive onlookers. In the first chapter, "Seasons and Signs", I attempt to show that this is in fact a misleading perception, and to examine some of the ways in which the laity were able to appropriate, develop, and use the repertoire of inherited ritual to articulate their experience of community and their own role and status within it, their personal hopes and aspirations, and their sense of the larger order and meaning of the world in which they lived and out of which they would one day die. In the second chapter, "How the Plowman Learned his Paternoster", I explore the formal and informal means by which the official teaching programme of the Church, articulated in synodal and episcopal acts and countless pastoral handbooks, was transmitted to and appropriated by the ordinary parishioner. I argue that this process was one in which lay and clerical initiative had as important a role as hierarchical directives. The evidence of surviving church iconography in painting, carving, and glass, and of the contents of the religious commonplace collections produced by growing lay literacy, suggests that the late medieval Church was a highly successful educator. The fundamentals of Christianity as then conceived had been absorbed, internalized and improvised on by lay people, a process which the advent of printing did not challenge, but endorsed.

The second section of part I, "Encountering the Holy", examines what I take to be three of the central, focal points of the late medieval Catholic sense of the sacred: the Mass, the holy communities of parish and gild, and the saints. Widely different as they are, all three of these focal points have in common a shared preoccupation with the communal, and a sense of the intimate interweaving of this world and the next; all three are concerned with the visible and tangible embodiment of absolute value, of the sacred within the human community.

Prayer is the fundamental religious activity, and in section three, 'Prayers and Spells", I consider the ways in which late medieval lay people prayed. The late Middle Ages saw an astonishing proliferation of texts aimed to help lay people to pray, a development in which the advent of printing played a crucial part. On the eve of the Reformation there were probably over 50,000 Books of Hours or Primers in circulation among the English laity. No other book commanded anything like such a readership, and they offer an unrivalled insight into the religious preoccupations of the people who used them, yet the Primers have been virtually ignored by religious historians. Taking these Primers as a basic source, in these chapters I analyse the modes, methods, and matter of lay prayer, and the beliefs which underlay it. The range of material used by lay people in these books was enormous, from the liturgical prayers of the Little Hours of the Virgin or the Office of the Dead, to bizarre and apparently magical incantations based on the names of God. They therefore pose in an acute form the question of the relation between orthodox Christianity and magic in the religion of the late medieval laity. It is my contention that this "magical" dimension of late medieval religion can best be understood in the context of the official liturgy, from which it borrowed most of its rhetoric and ritual strategies: in this perspective it represents not superstition, a largely meaningless pejorative term, but lay Christianity.

The fourth and final section of part I, "Now, and at the Hour of our Death", deals with late medieval belief about death and the world beyond death. There is a case for saying that *the* defining doctrine of late medieval Catholicism was Purgatory. These two chapters seek to set that belief in context, to explore late medieval thinking about death and judgement, to examine the deathbed ministry of the Church, to analyse the imagery and institutions in which the doctrine of Purgatory was articulated. But I also suggest that the cult of the dead, so central in the pieties of every late medieval Catholic, was also in an important and often overlooked sense a cult of the living, a way of articulating convictions about the extent and ordering of the human community, and hence of what it was to be human. In this perspective, the Reformation attack on the cult of the dead was more than a polemic against a "false" metaphysical belief: it was an attempt to redefine the boundaries of human community, and, in an act of exorcism, to limit the claims of the past, and the people of the past, on the people of the present.

PART I

THE STRUCTURES OF
TRADITIONAL RELIGION

A: Liturgy, Learning,
and the Laity

CHAPTER 1

SEASONS AND SIGNS: THE LITURGICAL YEAR

Any study of late medieval religion must begin with the liturgy, for within that great seasonal cycle of fast and festival, of ritual observance and symbolic gesture, lay Christians found the paradigms and the stories which shaped their perception of the world and their place in it. Within the liturgy birth, copulation, and death, journeying and homecoming, guilt and forgiveness, the blessing of homely things and the call to pass beyond them were all located, tested, and sanctioned. In the liturgy and in the sacramental celebrations which were its central moments, medieval people found the key to the meaning and purpose of their lives.

For the late medieval laity, the liturgy functioned at a variety of levels, offering spectacle, instruction, and a communal context for the affective piety which sought even in the formalized action of the Mass and its attendant ceremonies a stimulus to individual devotion. Ecclesiastical law and the vigilance of bishop, archdeacon, and parson sought to ensure as a minimum regular and sober attendance at matins, Mass, and evensong on Sundays and feasts, and annual confession and communion at Easter. But the laity expected and gave far more in the way of involvement with the action and symbolism of the liturgy than those minimum requirements suggest.

It is widely recognized, for example, that the liturgy's ritual structures provided a means of ordering and perhaps also of negotiating social relations. The etiquette of liturgical precedence in the late Middle Ages reflected deep-seated anxieties about order and influence within the "secular" reality of the community. Mervyn James has written eloquently of the way in which the Corpus Christi procession in late medieval communities "became the point of reference in relation to which the structure of precedence and authority in the town is made visually present". This was the "social miracle", the sacramental embodiment of social reality. But it was often, perhaps always, a precarious and difficult process, an attempt to tame and contain disorder, or to impose the hegemony of particular groups, rather than the straightforward expression of the inner harmonies of a community at peace with itself. Bloody riots broke out during the Chester Corpus Christi procession in 1399, and an ordinance, made at Newcastle in 1536 but referring to earlier events, spoke of regulating the procession "in avoideing of dissencion and discord that hath been among the Crafts of the . . . Towne as of man slaughter and murder and other mischiefs . . . and to induce love charity peace and right".[1]

What was true of the social complexities of the great towns was true also for individuals and for villages, where the passion for one's own proper "worship" was just as highly developed. The Wife of Bath's determination that

> In al the parisshe wif ne was ther noon
> That to the offrynge bifore hire sholde goon

is well-known and, as we shall see, far from singular.[2] Mere participation in ceremony, therefore, was no infallible indicator of either individual piety or social harmony. As the village or urban community's most usual gathering-place, the church and the ceremonies conducted there certainly had many functions not envisaged by the rubrics. Young men went to church to survey the young women, and a neighbour attempted the seduction of Margery Kempe as they both went in to evensong on the patronal festival of their parish church. Margery's is our only account of such an encounter by a participant, but the situation was evidently sufficiently common to provide the material for a number of ribald carols:

> As I went on Yol Day in our procession,
> Knew I joly Jankin by his mery ton.
>   *Kyrieleison.*
> Jankin at the Sanctus craked a merie note,
> And yet me thinketh it dos me good, – I payed for his coat.
>   *Kyrieleison.*
> Jankin at the *Agnus* bered the pax-brede;
> He twinkled, but said nout, and on min fot he trede
>   *Kyrieleison*
> *Benedicamus Domino,* Crist fro schame me shilde.

---

[1] Mervyn James, "Ritual, Drama and the Social Body", *Past and Present*, XCVIII, 1983, p. 5: John Bossy, *Christianity in the West 1400–1700*, 1985, pp. 57–72, and "The Mass as a Social Institution", *Past and Present*, C, 1983, pp. 29–61; Alan Nelson, *The Medieval English Stage*, 1974, p. 13; M. Rubin, *Corpus Christi*, 1991, pp. 266–70.

[2] Prologue to the *Canterbury Tales*, lines 449–50; see below, chapter 3, "The Mass" pp. 126–9.

Deo Gracias, therto – alas, I go with childe!
Kyrieleison.[3]

Some days, like St Agnes's Eve, were less noted for their religious observances than for the rituals by which young women sought to discover the identity of their future sweethearts.[4] And there were in the parish calendar days which hardly seem religious at all. The hock ceremonies, held on the Monday and Tuesday of the second week of Easter, when bands of men and women held travellers of the opposite sex to ransom for fines, are a case in point, but they received some sort of sanction by being used to augment church funds. The plough ceremonies, held on the first working day after Christmas, were fertility rites, when the young men of the village harnessed themselves to a plough which they dragged round the parish, ploughing up the ground before the door of any household which refused to pay a token. Once again, these patently pagan observances were absorbed into the religious calendar: many churches had a "plough-light", perhaps burning before the Sacrament or the Rood. At Cawston in Norfolk the magnificently carved beam of the plough gallery survives, with its fertility prayer and its final pun on the fund-raising plough ales or festivals:

God spede the plow
And send us all corne enow
our purpose for to mak
at crow of cok of the plowlete of Sygate
Be mery and glade
Wat Goodale this work mad.[5]

There were, too, a number of feast-days which had a clear, Christian, religious rationale, but which had absorbed round them ludic and parodying observances which were always problematic for the sternly orthodox. The boy-bishop celebrations associated with St Nicholas's day on 6 December, and similar celebrations in which children carried out episcopal or priestly functions and exercised rule over their seniors, associated with the feasts of St Katherine, St Clement, and the Holy Innocents, are a case in point. A perfectly good Christian justification could be offered for these popular observances, however close to the bone their elements of parody and misrule brought them: Christ's utterances about children

[3] Margery Kempe, *The Book of Margery Kempe*, ed. S. B. Meech and H. E. Allen, EETS, 1940, p. 14; M. S. Luria and R. L. Hoffman, *Middle English Lyrics*, 1974, no. 86, and see also nos 85, 87.

[4] J. Brand, *Popular Antiquities of Great Britain*, ed. H. Carew Hazlitt, 1870, I pp. 19–20, 103–7.

[5] N. Pevsner, *Buildings of England: North-East Norfolk and Norwich*, 1962, p. 112.

and the Kingdom of Heaven, Isaiah's prophecy that a little child shall lead them, and the theme of inversion and the world turned upside-down found in texts like the "Magnificat" could all be invoked in their defence. Equally clearly, more explosive, more complex, and less pious social tensions were at work here, in a society in which age and authority could bear heavily on the young.[6]

The relation of the Christian calendar to turning-points of the seasons – Christmas and the winter solstice, Easter and spring – meant also that many observances associated with the religious feast served to articulate instincts and energies which were not exclusively Christian, however readily they could be accommodated within a Christian framework. The dances and games with balls and eggs and flowers played in many communities at Easter, sometimes in the church itself, are a case in point, for they are clearly related to the spring theme of fertility, but perhaps the clearest examples are the battles, staged all over Europe, between the flesh and the spirit, Christmas and Lent, on Shrove Tuesday.[7] One such battle was enacted in Norwich in January 1443, when John Gladman (aptly named) disguised himself as King of Christmas, and rode crowned round the city on a horse decked out in tinfoil, preceded by a pageant of the months "disguysed as the seson requiryd" and with Lent (March) clad in "whyte and red heryngs skinns and his hors trappyd with oystershells after him, in token that sadnesse shuld folowe and an holy tyme". This masking was perhaps not as innocent as it was subsequently made out to be: for one thing, it came a month too early, and riots ensued, in which deep-seated and long-standing resentments against the authority over the city of the bishop and priory of Norwich found vent. The church authorities were convinced that the masking was no laughing matter, and that Gladman was the leader of an insurrection. The details need not concern us, for, whatever his motives, Gladman was clearly able to call on a vocabulary derived from the ritual calendar, in which secular and sacred themes, the polarities of fast and feast and downright misrule, were difficult to disentangle.[8]

[6] On the boy-bishop celebrations see Brand, *Antiquities*, I pp. 232–40; R. L. de Molen, "Pueri Christi Imitatio: the Festival of the Boy Bishop in Tudor England", *Moreana*, X1, 1975, pp. 17–29; S. E. Rigold, "The St Nicholas Tokens or 'Boy Bishop' tokens", *Proceedings of the Suffolk Institute of Archaeology*, XXXIV/2, 1978, pp. 87–101.

[7] Brand, *Antiquities*, I pp. 28–57; E. O. James, *Seasonal Feasts and Festivals*, 1961, pp. 225–7, 232–4, 237–8.

[8] Brand, *Antiquities*, I pp. 38–9; N. Tanner, *The Church in Late Medieval Norwich*, 1984, pp. 146–52; more generally, P. Burke, *Popular Culture in Early Modern Europe*, 1978, pp. 178–243.

Yet while acknowledging the secular functions, respectable or otherwise, of liturgy and liturgical time in late medieval England, it is impossible not to be struck also, and more forcibly, by the abundant evidence of the internalization of its specifically religious themes and patterns and their devotional elaboration in lay piety. This aspect of late medieval devotion is perhaps most familiar to the twentieth century in connection with Christmas, particularly in the enormous richness of the late medieval carol tradition, designed for convivial use yet pervasively indebted to liturgical hymnody: the constant allusive use in carols of Latin tags and whole lines from the hymns and proses of the Offices and Masses of Advent and the Christmas season argues a widespread lay familiarity with those parts of the liturgy. Less obviously, the same familiarity is presupposed in the highly compressed liturgical framework of reference which underlies apparently simple vernacular nativity poems like "I sing of a maiden" and "Adam lay abounden".[9] But the centrality of the liturgy in lay religious consciousness was not confined to Christmas, and even more dramatic if less familiar evidence may be found in a connection with other festivals. Miri Rubin has explored one such, the feast of Corpus Christi.[10] I shall consider here two rather different feasts, Candlemas and Holy Week.

Candlemas, the feast of the Purification of the Blessed Virgin Mary or, alternatively, of the Presentation of the Infant Jesus in the Temple, was celebrated forty days after Christmas, on 2 February, and constituted the last great festival of the Christmas cycle. The texts prescribed for the feast in breviary and missal emphasize the Christmas paradoxes of the strength of the eternal God displayed in the fragility of the new-born child, of the appearance of the divine light in the darkness of human sin, of renewal and rebirth in the dead time of the year, and of the new life of Heaven manifested to Simeon's, and the world's, old age.[11] Celebrated as a "Greater Double" – that is, of lesser solemnity only than the supreme feasts such as Christmas, Easter, and Pentecost, but of equal status to Trinity Sunday, Corpus Christi, and All Saints – its importance in the popular mind is reflected in the fact that it was one of the days on which, according to the legend of St Brendan, Judas was allowed

[9] *The Early English Carol*, ed. R. L. Greene, 2nd ed. 1977, pp. lxxxi–cix; for "I sing of a maiden" see the essays in Luria and Hoffman, *Middle English Lyrics*, pp. 325–49.
[10] Rubin, *Corpus Christi*, passim.
[11] *Missale ad Usum Insignis et Praeclarae Ecclesiae Sarum*, ed. F. H. Dickinson, 1861–83, cols 696–706; *Breviarium ad Usum Insignis Ecclesiae Sarum*, ed. F. Proctor and C. Wordsworth, 1882–6, III cols 131–48.

out of Hell to ease his torment in the sea.[12] The Purification was marked by one of the most elaborate processions of the liturgical year, when every parishioner was obliged to join in, carrying a blessed candle, which was offered, together with a penny, to the priest at Mass. The candles so offered were part of the laity's parochial dues, and were probably often burned before the principal image of the Virgin in the church.[13] An account survives from fourteenth-century Friesthorpe in Lincolnshire of a row between the rector and his parish because on the day after Candlemas "maliciously and against the will of the parishioners" he took down and carried off all the candles which the previous day had been set before the Image of the Blessed Virgin, "for devotion and penance".[14] The blessing of candles and procession took place immediately before the parish Mass, and, in addition to the candles offered to the priest, many others were blessed, including the great Paschal candle used in the ceremonies for the blessing of the baptismal water at Easter and Pentecost. The people then processed round the church carrying lighted candles, and the "Nunc Dimittis" was sung. Mass began immediately afterwards with the singing of verses from Psalm 47, "We have received your mercy, O God, in the midst of your temple."[15]

The imaginative power of all this for the laity is readily understood, for the texts of the ceremony are eloquent evocations of the universal symbolism of light, life, and renewal, themes which were carefully expounded in Candlemas sermons.[16] But there was more to the appeal of Candlemas than mere symbolism, however eloquent. The first of the five prayers of blessing in the ritual for Candlemas unequivocally attributes apotropaic power to the blessed wax, asking that "wherever it shall be lit or set up, the devil may flee away in fear and trembling with all his ministers, out of those dwellings, and never presume again to disquiet your servants".[17] Here, undoubtedly, lay one of the principal keys to the imaginative power of Candlemas over lay minds. The people took blessed candles away from the ceremony, to be lit during thunderstorms or

---

[12] *Mirk's Festial: a Collection of Homilies by Johannes Mirkus*, ed. T. Erbe, EETS, 1905, p. 80.

[13] Though not always: the Candlemas wax offering at Spelsbury in Oxfordshire was burned before the Trinity. See J. Cox, *Churchwardens' Accounts*, 1913, p. 164.

[14] D. M. Owen, *Church and Society in Medieval Lincolnshire*, Lincoln Record Society, 1971, p. 111. This seems also to be the reason for the third *exemplum* given by Mirk in his Candlemas sermon, a conventional story of a wicked woman saved from Hell by the fact that, despite her evil ways, she had maintained a candle before the image of the Virgin in a church; there is no other link with the Candlemas feast.

[15] *Missale*, cols 696–703.

[16] *Speculum Sacerdotale*, ed. E. H. Weatherly, EETS, 1935, pp. 24–9.

[17] *Missale*, col. 697.

in times of sickness, and to be placed in the hands of the dying.

> Whose candelle burneth cleere and bright, a wondrous force
>   and might.
> Doth in these candelles lie, which, if at any time they light,
> They sure believe that neither storm nor tempest dare abide,
> Nor thunder in the skie be heard, nor any divil spide,
> Nor fearfull sprites that walk by night, nor hurt by frost and
>   haile.[18]

The Tudor jest-book, *A Hundred Merry Tales*, tells the story of John Adoyne, a Suffolk man who unwittingly terrifies his neighbours by wandering around the town in his demon's costume after a local religious play. The squire, on being told that the devil is at his door, "marvelously abashed called up his chaplain and made the holy candle to be lighted and gat holy water" to conjure him away.[19] The beliefs suggested in the jest were no laughing matter. The *Golden Legend* has a story of a devout woman who, unable to attend the Candlemas celebrations at her local church, was granted a dream vision of a heavenly celebration of the Candlemas liturgy, in which Christ was the priest, assisted by the deacon saints Laurence and Vincent, while a company of virgins sang the Candlemas antiphons. The Blessed Virgin herself led the procession and offered a candle. Angels gave the dreamer a candle to offer in her turn to the priest, according to custom, but she refused to part with so great a relic: the angel tried to wrest it from her grip, and she awoke to find the broken stump in her hand (Pl. 1). This piece of holy candle was henceforth reverenced as a "a grete jewel, tresoure and a relyck", so that "alle the seke whomever it touchid afterward were there-through hole delyvered". This story, almost invariably included in Candlemas sermons and vividly illustrated at Eton and in the Winchester Cathedral Lady Chapel series of frescos of the miracles of the Virgin, was clearly designed to impress on congregations the solemnity and importance of the Candlemas observances, and the rewards of devotion to the Virgin. But the celestial candle-stump must also have provided a paradigm for lay perception of the holiness and power of the candles, the "highly prized sacramental" which they took away from the ceremony.[20] Not surprisingly, the distribution of these holy candles, and the

---

[18] Barnabe Googe, quoted in R. T. Hampson, *Medii Aevi Kalendarium*, I n.d., p. 156.

[19] *A Hundred Merry Tales*, ed. P. M. Zall, 1963, p. 69.

[20] *The Golden Legend or Lives of the Saints as Englished by William Caxton*, ed. F. S. Ellis, 1900, III pp. 25–6; *Festial* 60–1: *Speculum Sacerdotale*, pp. 28–9; L. Eisenhofer, *The Liturgy of the Roman Rite*, 1961, p. 228; M. R. James and E. W. Tristram, "The Wall-Paintings in Eton Chapel and the Lady chapel of Winchester Cathedral", *Walpole Society*, XVII, 1929, pp. 1–44.

empowerment of lay people against hostile and evil forces which they represented, tended to override every other aspect of the feast in popular consciousness, so much so that the clergy might make a point of distinguishing between popular usage and the official character of the feast – "this day is callyd of many men Candylmasse. But that is of non auctorite, but of custom of folke."[21] This clerical suspicion of "custom of folk" is understandable, since according to the author of *Dives and Pauper* the laity were capable of diverting such sacramentals to nefarious ends: witches were known to drop wax from the holy candle into the footprints of those they hated, causing their feet to rot off.[22]

Of course none of the scriptural passages associated with the Feast of the Purification makes any mention of candles. The imagery of light in the ceremonies was derived from Simeon's song, in which the child Jesus is hailed as "a light to lighten the Gentiles". The *Golden Legend* made it clear that the processional candles on the feast were carried to represent Jesus, and underlined the point with an elaborate exposition of the significance of wax, wick, and flame as representing Jesus' body, soul, and godhead, an exposition invariably taken over into Candlemas sermons.[23] In lay consciousness, however, the annual procession with candles, far from remaining a secondary symbolic feature, invaded and transformed the scriptural scene. In late medieval paintings of the Purification like the Weston Diptych, in the Order of St John Museum, St John's Gate, London, the setting is clearly a parish church and the scriptural figures, including the child Jesus Himself, carry candles, like good fifteenth-century parishioners, as they do in the Purification scene in the window at East Harling (Pl. 2). Similarly, in the Chester Purification play Mary offers the scriptural doves, but Joseph declares to Simeon

> A signe I offer here allsoe
> of virgin waxe, as other moo,
> in tokeninge shee has lived oo
> in full devotion.[24]

Mary and Joseph and Anne made a "worshipful processioun" to the Temple with the Child, according to the Candlemas sermon in the *Speculum Sacerdotale*, a phrase which reveals the extent to which popular liturgical observances had come to shape perceptions of the scriptural event which they commemorated.[25]

---

[21] *Speculum Sacerdotale*, p. 25.
[22] *Dives and Pauper*, ed. P. H. Barnum, EETS, 1976, I pp. 162–3.
[23] *Golden Legend*, III p. 23; *Festial*, p. 60; *Speculum Sacerdotale*, p. 28.
[24] *The Chester Mystery Cycle*, ed. R. M. Lumiansku and D. Mills, EETS, 1972, I p. 209.
[25] *Speculum Sacerdotale*, p. 28.

The Candlemas ceremonies help to emphasize a distinctive feature of late medieval liturgy, one which brings it close to the practice of private meditation. This tradition, embodied in such works as the *Meditationes Vitae Christi*, stressed the spiritual value of vivid mental imagining of the events of the life of Christ, especially his Passion, to "make hym-selfe present in his thoghte as if he sawe fully with his bodyly eghe all the thyngys that be-fell abowte the crosse and the glorious passione of our Lorde Ihesu".[26] This search for spiritual communion with God through vivid picturing of the events of Christ's life and death was, of course, evolved as part of an individual and intensely inner spirituality. But it came to be applied to the liturgy itself, and to be seen as the ideal way of participating in the Church's worship. The pious lay person at Mass was urged to internalize by such meditation the external actions of the priest and ministers. The early sixteenth-century treatise *Meditatyons for goostely exercyse, In the tyme of the masse* interprets the gestures and movements of the priest in terms of the events of Maundy Thursday and Good Friday, and urges the layman to "Call to your remembrance and Imprinte Inwardly In your hart by holy meditation, the holl processe of the passyon, frome the Mandy unto the poynt of crysts deeth."[27] The effect of this sort of guidance was to encourage the development of representational elements in the liturgy and to set the laity looking for these elements. The Candlemas procession and ceremonies, enacting the journey up to Jerusalem and Mary's offering in the Temple there, were ideally suited to such an understanding of the working of liturgy, and this was certainly an element in their popularity with lay people. Margery Kempe tells how at Candlemas

> whan the sayd creatur be-held the pepil wyth her candelys in cherch, hir mende was raveschyd in-to beholdyng of owr Lady offeryng hyr blisful Sone owre Savyowr to the preyst Simeon in the Tempyl, as verily to hir gostly undirstondyng as [if] sche had be ther in hir bodily presens.

This inner contemplation was so intense that, beholding it and

> the hevynly songys that hir thowt sche hard whan owr blisful Lord was offeryd up to Symeon that sche myth ful evyl beryn up hir owyn candel to the preyst, as other folke dedyn at the

[26] C. Horstmann (ed.), *Yorkshire Writers*, 1895, I. p. 198.
[27] *Tracts on the Mass*, ed. J. Wickham Legg, Henry Bradshaw Society, XXVII, 1904, pp. 25–6, and see below pp. 118–23.

tyme of the offeryng, but went waveryng on eche syde as it had
ben a drunkyn woman.[28]

Margery's response was characteristically extreme, but in essence
her expectation of the liturgy was very much that of her neighbours, and there is no reason to think that the "hevynly songys"
were anything other than the liturgical chants for the day, sung
with all the splendour and resources which a great urban church
like St Margaret's, Lynn, could command. The Candlemas ceremonies were designed to summon up the scenes they commemorated, and the quest for the visionary vividness which made Margery
unsteady on her feet lay behind the tendency in late medieval
England to elaborate and make more explicit the representational
and dramatic dimension of the liturgy.

There were limits to how far this process could be carried
within the formal structure of the liturgy itself, so the Candlemas
ceremonies generated para-liturgical and dramatic elaborations. The
gild of the Blessed Virgin Mary at Beverley, founded in the 1350s,
moved from liturgical re-enactment to dramatic impersonation.
Each year on the morning of Candlemas the gild assembled at some
place distant from the church. One of their number, "qui ad hoc
aptior invenietur", nobly and decently dressed and adorned as the
Queen of Heaven, carried a doll in her arms to represent the Christ
child. Two other gild members dressed as Joseph and Simeon, and
yet another two dressed as angels carried a candelabrum or hearse
of twenty-four thick wax lights. Surrounded by other great lights,
and to the accompaniment of "music and rejoicing", they processed
to the church, the sisters of the gild immediately after the Blessed
Virgin, followed by the brethren, two by two, each carrying a
candle of half a pound weight. At the church, the Virgin was
to offer her Son to Simeon at the high altar, and then the gild
members, one by one, offered their candles and a penny apiece.

There is no explicit mention in the gild certificate of a Mass, but
it is very unlikely that this would have taken place without one.
The Beverley gild of St Helen, which mounted a similar costumed
procession and tableau of the finding of the Holy Cross once a
year, and whose gild certificate very closely resembles that of the
Candlemas gild, made their offerings at a Mass: the presumption
must be that the Candlemas tableau was part of a procession and
Mass.[29] But at any rate, what we have here is clearly an elaboration

---

[28] *Book of Margery Kempe*, p. 198.
[29] Candlemas gild certificates are printed in Karl Young, *The Drama of the Medieval
Church*, 1933, II pp. 252–3; summarized, with that of St Helen's gild, in L. Toulmin-Smith,
English Gilds, EETS, 1870, pp. 148–50.

and extension of the parochial Candlemas celebrations, encouraging an even deeper or more immediate sense of imaginative partici-pation in the biblical event by gild members than that offered by the prescribed liturgy. And the observances of other Candlemas gilds, even where they lacked the mimetic elements of the Beverley ceremony, must have served similarly to heighten and internalize the themes of the parochial liturgy. Margery Kempe's intense imagining of the scriptural scene may well be connected with the activities of the Candlemas gild which we know functioned in her parish church.[30]

Nevertheless, it is the liturgical celebration which shaped and defined such gild observances, and the same centrality of the pattern of the liturgy is evident in a number of the surviving Corpus Christi plays of the Purification. In the East Anglian *Ludus Coventriae* play of the Purification, for example, Simeon receives the child Jesus with a speech which is simply a literal verse rendering of the opening psalm of the Mass of the feast. While he holds the child in his arms, a choir sings "Nunc Dimittis", almost certainly to the Candlemas processional music. Joseph distributes candles to Mary, Simeon, and Anna, and takes one himself. Having thus formed, in the words of the *Speculum*, a "worshipful processioun", they go together to the altar, where Mary lays the child, and Joseph offers the temple priest five pence. For the audience, the whole play would have been inescapably redolent of the familiar Candlemas liturgy, and in essence an extension of it.[31]

Deliberate evocation of the Candlemas liturgy is even more obvious in the Digby play of Candlemas, where, after Simeon has received the Child and expounded the "Nunc Dimittis", Anna the prophetess calls together a band of girls, and forms them up:

> Ye pure Virgynes in that ye may or can,
> with tapers of wax loke ye come forth here
> and worship this child very god and man
> Offrid in this temple be his moder dere.

Simeon, as priest, takes charge

---

[30] V. B. Redstone (ed.) "Chapels, Chantries and Gilds in Suffolk", *Proceedings of the Suffolk Institute of Archaeology*, XII, 1906, p. 25: this is a reference to the Candlemas gild at Bury St Edmunds, which processed to the Lady altar in St James's church on Candlemas. For the Lynn Candlemas gilds see H. F. Westlake, *The Parish Gilds of Medieval England*, 1919, nos 243–5, 280. For other Candlemas gilds see also nos 9 (Great St Mary's, Cambridge), 93 (Castor, Lincs.), 147 (in the church of St Benedict, Lincoln), 168, 169 (Spalding, Lincs.), 310 (Outwell, Norfolk), 337 (Upwell, Norfolk), 461 (unnamed, but in Yorkshire).
[31] *Ludus Coventriae or the Plaie Called Corpus Christi*, ed. K. S. Block, EETS, 1922, pp. 167–9.

Now, Mary, I shull tell you how I am purposed:
to worshipe this lord / I will go procession;
ffor I se anna,. with virgynes disposed,
mekly as nowe, to your sonys laudacion.[32]

Mary and Joseph agree and they all process in order "abought
the tempill", the virgins singing "Nunc Dimittis", again almost
certainly to the liturgical setting for the Candlemas liturgy. At the
end of the procession Simeon preaches a little sermon, comparing
the candle, wax, wick, and flame, to Christ's body, soul, and
divinity. This is a homiletic commonplace, found in the *Golden
Legend* and from there in Mirk's Candlemas sermon, and so a staple
in Candlemas homilies in parish churches up and down the
country. Anna then urges the maidens to follow her

    . . . and shewe ye summe plesur as ye can,
    In the worshipe of Iesu, our lady, and seynt Anne.[33]

She then leads the company in a dance. This and the final dance of
virgins to the accompaniment of minstrels, with which the play
concludes, takes it beyond the scope of liturgy, but not perhaps
worlds away from para-liturgical observances like those of the
Beverley Candlemas Gild, which, the gild certificate states, were
to conclude "cum gaudio". What is beyond argument, however,
is that the spectrum of Candlemas observances evident in these
sources testifies to a profound and widespread lay assimilation and
deployment of the imagery, actions, and significance of the liturgy
of the feast. And the introduction of a "folk" element into the
Digby play, in the form of dances "in the worshipe of Iesu, our
lady, and seynt Anne", serves to warn us against underestimating
the links between liturgical observance and the "secular" celebratory
and ludic dimensions of lay culture at the end of the Middle Ages.[34]

The Ceremonies of Holy Week

Holy Week, the period from Palm Sunday to Easter Day, constituted the heart of the late medieval Church's year, just as the
Passion of Christ, solemnly commemorated then, lay at the heart
of late medieval Christianity. The ceremonies of Holy Week were
extremely elaborate, especially from the Wednesday onwards, when

---

[32] *The Digby Plays with an Incomplete Morality*, ed. F. J. Furnivall, EETS, 1896, pp. 18–23.
[33] *Golden Legend*, III p. 23; *Festial*, p. 60.
[34] The "Anna" of the play is not Anna Propheta, but the Lord's grandmother, with whom
she was sometimes identified. The Digby play was performed on 26 July 1512, the feast of
St Anne.

each day had its distinctive ritual observances. But much of the ceremonial prescribed in the Sarum rite had by the fifteenth century long since lost its imaginative power for lay people. The Easter Vigil, for example, with its elaborate ceremony of light, even now one of the most striking and moving parts of Catholic liturgy, was not held in darkness but on the morning of Holy Saturday, in broad daylight, and appears to have attracted no lay interest whatever. Lay people did attend the Tenebrae services on Wednesday, Thursday, and Friday. These were celebrations of the divine Office during which candles were snuffed out one by one to symbolize the abandonment of Jesus by his disciples: the standard sermon collections include explanations of this striking ceremony.[35] But to judge by lay sources of the fifteenth and sixteenth centuries, the aspects of Holy Week which consistently seemed to matter to parishioners were the Palm Sunday procession, the veneration or "creeping to the cross" on Good Friday, the observances associated with the Easter sepulchre, and of course the annual reception of communion – "taking one's rights" – on Easter Sunday, an action which was necessarily preceded by going to confession. Confession and communion will be dealt with elsewhere, but an exploration of the other components of Holy Week observance will do much to flesh out our sense of the ways in which the laity appropriated and used the liturgy.

The Palm Sunday procession was by the end of the Middle Ages the most elaborate and eloquent of the processions of the Sarum rite, with the possible exception of the special case of Corpus Christi. The parish Mass began as usual with the blessing and sprinkling of holy water. Immediately that had been done the story of Christ's entry into Jerusalem and greeting by the crowds with palms was read from St John's Gospel. The priest then blessed flowers and green branches, which were called palms but were usually yew, box, or willow.[36] The palms were distributed and clergy and people processed out of the church, led by a painted wooden cross without a figure. The procession moved to a large cross erected in the churchyard, normally on the north side of the building at its east end, the choir singing a series of anthems recapitulating the biblical story of Palm Sunday (Pl. 3).

While the palms were being distributed a special shrine supported on two poles was prepared, into which the church's principal relics

---

[35] *Festial*, pp. 117–18; *Speculum Sacerdotale*, pp. 101–2.

[36] *Missale*, cols 253–7. The palms were intended, of course, for use in the procession, but were certainly taken back to people's homes and put to apotropaic use; one of the benedictions prayed for the banishment of "adverse powers" wherever the palms were brought and blessings for the inhabitants of any such home.

were placed, along with the Blessed Sacrament to represent Christ. According to the rubrics, this shrine, carried by two clerks and sheltered by a silken canopy, was now brought in procession to join the parishioners and clergy at the churchyard Palm cross. By the end of the Middle Ages this aspect of the rite had been simplified in many places, the Host being carried instead in a monstrance by a single priest. In the meantime the story of Christ's triumphal entry into Jerusalem from Matthew's Gospel was read to the parishioners in the churchyard. The procession with the Blessed Sacrament now approached the parochial procession gathered at the Cross, and, according to the ritual, three clerks wearing surplices and plain choir copes sang an anthem, "Behold, O Sion, thy king cometh", after which clergy and choir venerated the Sacrament by kneeling and kissing the ground before it. In popular English practice this part of the ritual was elaborated, the singers of the anthem being costumed as Old Testament prophets with flowing wigs and false beards: payments "for hyering of the heres for the p[ro]fetys uppon Palme Sundaye" are a regular item of expense in many surviving sets of churchwardens' accounts.[37] At Long Melford in Suffolk the part of the prophet was played by "a boy with a thing in his hand", a wand or staff of some sort or possibly a scroll, who stood on the turret over the Rood-loft stairs, on the outside of the Clopton aisle on the north side of Melford church, and pointed to the Sacrament while the "Ecce Rex Tuus" was sung.[38] The two processions then merged, and a series of invocations to the Host were sung:

Hail, thou whom the people of the Hebrews bear witness to as
    Jesus . . .
Hail, light of the world, king of kings, glory of heaven
Hail, our salvation, our true peace, our redemption, our
    strength . . .

During the singing the procession moved round the east end of the church to the south side, where a high scaffold had been erected (Pl. 4). Seven boys stood on this scaffold and greeted the Host with the hymn "Gloria, Laus et honor" ("All glory, laud and honour to Thee, Redeemer King"). In a further elaboration of the prescribed ritual, flowers and unconsecrated Mass-wafers ("obols" or "singing-cakes") were usually strewn before the Sacrament from this

---

[37] H. J. Feasey, *Ancient English Holy Week Ceremonial*, 1893, pp. 75–6; J. C. Cox, *Churchwardens' Accounts*, 1913, pp. 254–5.

[38] Sir W. Parker, *The History of Long Melford*, 1873, p. 72: for the reduction of the rite by the replacement of shrine by a monstrance (probably in the interests of visibility, and in parishes where there was only one priest) see R. Pecock, *The Repressor of Over Much Blaming of the Clergy*, ed. C. Babington, 1860, I. p. 203.

scaffolding, to be scrambled for by the children. At Long Melford they were "cast over among the boys". There is no doubting the attraction of this picturesque feature of the Palm Sunday ceremonies to lay people, or its dramatic potential, and the singing of the hymn "Gloria, Laus" and scattering of flowers before the procession were adopted wholesale in the "N-Town" play of the Entry into Jerusalem.[39]

The procession then moved to the west door, where the clerks carrying the Sacrament in its shrine stood on either side of the door and raised the poles above their heads. In many parishes the priest elaborated the prescribed ceremony at this point by taking the processional cross and striking the door with its foot, symbolically demanding entry for Christ, a gesture interpreted as representing Christ's harrowing of Hell, after bursting the gates of death. For some reason this gesture was expressly forbidden by the rubricists, but it was clearly widespread and evidently spoke to many parishioners: Margery Kempe comments specifically on its devotional effect on her.[40] The clergy and people entered the church, passing under the shrine with the Sacrament, and then the whole procession moved to its culminating point before the Rood-screen. All through Lent a great painted veil had been suspended in front of the Crucifix (Pl. 5) on the Rood-screen. This veil was now drawn up on pulleys, the whole parish knelt, and the anthem "Ave Rex Noster" was sung, while the clergy venerated the cross by kissing the ground:

Hail, our King, Son of David, Redeemer of the World, whom the prophets proclaimed the saviour of the house of Israel who is to come. You indeed are the saving victim whom the Father has sent into the world, for whom the saints have waited from the beginning of the world. Blessed is he who comes in the name of the Lord, Hosanna in the highest.[41]

Mass then began, but at the Gospel there was a final, striking deviation from the normal Sunday liturgy. The whole of the Passion story from St Matthew's Gospel was sung, by three clerks in churches which had the resources, the words of Jesus in a bass

---

[39] Cox, *Churchwardens' Accounts*, loc. cit.; *Ludus Coventriae*, p. 241.

[40] For official disapproval see Clement Maydeston, "Crede Michi" in *Tracts of Clement Maydeston with the Remains of Caxton's Ordinale*, ed. C. Wordsworth, Henry Bradshaw Society, VII, 1894, pp. 50–1; for the actual practice see *The Book of Margery Kempe*, pp. 186–7, and J. Strype, *Ecclesiastical Memorials*, 1822, III part 2, p. 392; for similar observances in Germany, but associated there with Easter Sunday, see R. W. Scribner, *Popular Culture and Popular Movements in Reformation Germany*, 1987, p. 27.

[41] *Missale*, col. 260.

register, the narrator in a tenor one, and the words of the crowd in an alto. It was widely believed that crosses made during this reading of the Passion narrative had apotropaic powers, and many people brought sticks and string to church on Palm Sunday to be made up into crosses, a dimension of popular participation in the ritual which became a particular target of reformed criticism. Less controversially, in many parishes the reading of the Gospel was elaborated in the interests of dramatic effect and it was often sung by clerks standing in the Rood-loft itself, at the foot of the Crucifix which the whole parish had just venerated. With regional variations, this highly dramatic ritual was enacted all over late medieval Europe, but the English versions had a number of distinctive features, of which the most important was the use of the Blessed Sacrament to represent Christ. In many parts of Europe the presence of Christ was symbolized by a cross or a Gospel book, in Germany usually by a life-sized wooden carving of Christ on a donkey, which ran on wheels, the *Palmesel*.[42]

The *Palmesel* was an obvious manifestation of a feature of late medieval worship we have already noticed in connection with the Candlemas rituals, the tendency to turn liturgy into "sacred performance". The use of the Sacrament in English Palm Sunday ceremonies was at once more and less dramatic than the representational realism evident in the *Palmesel*, which looked like Jesus and directly represented the ride into Jerusalem. The Blessed Sacrament did not look like Jesus, but, far more vividly, *was* Jesus, body, blood, soul, and divinity, taking part in the communal re-enactment of his entry into the city not by a wooden proxy, but with all the overwhelming reality which late medieval believers attributed to the Host.

The Host was rarely carried in procession outside the church: the other festival on which this was done, Corpus Christi, was conceived and presented in late medieval communities as a celebration of the corporate life of the body social, created and ordered by the presence of the Body of Christ among them. The Palm Sunday procession, from which much of the Corpus Christi ritual was derived, was also a celebration of the redeeming presence of the divine within the community, made visible and concrete as the Host was carried around the churchyard, surrounded by the entire parish. The York play of the entry into Jerusalem catches this dimension of the Palm Sunday celebrations particularly clearly,

[42] Scribner, *Popular Culture*, pp. 25–6; L. Eisenhofer, *The Liturgy of the Roman Rite*, 1961, pp. 186–7; Terence Bailey, *The Processions of the Sarum Rite and the Western Church*, 1971, pp. 116–17.

when eight citizens of Jerusalem greet Christ in a series of invocations which are highly reminiscent of, and probably modelled on,
the "Ave" invocations of the Palm Sunday procession

> Hayll conqueror, hayll most of myght,
> Hayle rawnsoner of synfull all,
> Hayll pytefull, hayll lovely light,
> Hayll to us welcome be schall,
> Hayll kyng of Jues.
> Hayll comely corse that we the call
>   With mirthe that newes.
> Hayll domysman dredful, that all schall deme,
> Hayll that all quyk and dede schall lowte,
> Hayll whom our worscippe most will seme
> Hayll whom all thyng schall drede and dowte.
> We welcome the,
> Hayll and welcome of all abowte
>   To owre cete.[43]

The similarity of these invocations to the prayers used by the laity
at the elevation at Mass is very striking. The dramatic Christ of the
play has been subsumed into the Eucharistic Christ. The play's
"Burghers of Jerusalem" are patently citizens of York, welcoming
the presence of Christ among them, like the four yeomen who
carried the canopy over the Sacrament on Palm Sunday at Long
Melford, instead of the solitary clerk stipulated in the rubrics. It
was precisely this entry into "owre cete" of Christ, ransomer and
doomsman, in the form of the "comely corse" (Pl. 6), Corpus
Christi, surrounded by "al the pepil", that the parish liturgy of
Palm Sunday celebrated. As the *Ludus Coventriae* play of the entry
has it, "Neyborys gret joye in our herte we may make that this
hefly kyng wole vycyte this cyte."[44]

Palm Sunday was emphatically a celebration of the saving work
of Christ: the cross and the miracle of the Mass which perpetuated
the effects of the cross within the community lay at its centre. But
the last days of Holy Week, from Maundy Thursday to Easter Day,
formed a distinctive unit by themselves. They were packed with
striking ceremonial and charged with intense religious emotion,

[43] R. Beadle (ed.) *The York Plays*, 1982, p. 219.
[44] Cf. *Chester Mystery Cycle*, p. 258; *Ludus Coventriae*, p. 240; Parker, *History of Long Melford*, p. 72. It is notable that Roger Martin's account of the liturgical year at Long Melford focuses on processions and other communal forms of celebration, and moves straight from Palm Sunday to Corpus Christi. In *The Book of Margery Kempe*, p. 187, the communal language and emphasis on "the pepil" in Margery's account of the Holy Week liturgy is also striking.

for the ceremonies and texts of these days gathered up and gave eloquent expression to all the major themes of late medieval piety. There can be no question of the importance of these ceremonies for lay people, an importance reflected in the extended Holy Week meditation which forms chapters 78–81 of *The Book of Margery Kempe*.[45] It is not perhaps surprising to find an aspirant to sanctity like Margery interested in these solemn ceremonies, but their wider appeal was grudgingly acknowledged by John Mirk, in his *Festial*. In addition to the model sermons for each of the major days of Holy Week, Mirk provided a compendium of ritual notes for unlearned clergy unable to make "a graythe answer" to the eager questions put to them by parishioners anxious to make sense of the unusually rich ceremonial of the season. Mirk, writing at a time of anxiety about the spread of Lollardy, chose to interpret such questioning as springing from a desire to expose the ignorance of the clergy, but there was no denying the phenomenon. "Lewde men," he complained, "wheche buthe of many wordys and proude in hor wit" will insist on asking priests questions "of thynges that towchen to servyce of holy chyrche, and namly of thys tyme".[46]

The Easter Triduum began with Maundy Thursday, when Mass was celebrated with extra solemnity, the priest consecrating three Hosts, one for his communion at the Mass, one for his communion at the Good Friday liturgy, and the third to be used in the sepulchre ceremonies. After Mass the altars of the church were ritually stripped of all their coverings and ornaments, while a series of responsories from the Passion narratives and the prophets were sung. As each altar was stripped the priest intoned a collect of the saint to whom it was dedicated. Each of the altars then had water and wine poured on it and was washed, using a broom of sharp twigs.[47] Every detail of this vivid ceremony was allegorized in popular preaching – the stripping of the altars was the stripping of Jesus for death, the water and wine were the water and blood from his side, the broom of twigs the scourges or the crown of thorns.[48] In cathedrals, religious houses, and great churches this ceremony was followed immediately by the Maundy, or solemn washing of feet, in imitation of Christ in the account of the last supper in St John's Gospel. To judge by the silence on this subject of surviving Holy Week parish sermons explaining the ritual, this foot-washing was omitted in many parish churches. In Mirk's compendium of information on the ceremonies of Holy Week the scriptural foot-

[45] *Book of Margery Kempe*, pp. 184–97.
[46] *Festial*, pp. 124–9.
[47] *Missale*, cols 308–11.
[48] *Festial*, pp. 125–7.

washing is mentioned, but he is more directly concerned to explain a feature of the ceremonies of the day which would have impinged directly on lay liturgy, the absence of the pax from the Maundy Mass, "for Iudas betrayd Crist thys nyght wyth a cosse".[49]

Good Friday in the late Middle Ages was a day of deepest mourning. No Mass was celebrated, and the main liturgical celebration of the day was a solemn and penitential commemoration of the Passion. The whole of the narrative from St John's Gospel was read, with a small dramatic embellishment: at the words "They parted my garments among them" the clerks parted and removed two linen cloths which had been specially placed for the purpose on the otherwise bare altar. After the Gospel there was a series of solemn prayers for the world and the Church. A veiled Crucifix was then brought into the church, while the "Improperia" or "Reproaches" were sung, a series of scriptural verses contrasting the goodness of God and the ingratitude of his people. The cross was then unveiled in three stages, the priest singing, each time on a higher tone, "Behold the wood of the cross, on which hung the saviour of the world. Come, let us worship."

Clergy and people then crept barefoot and on their knees to kiss the foot of the cross, held by two ministers. After the adoration of the cross, a Host consecrated at the previous day's Mass was brought, and the priest, having recited the Lord's Prayer, communicated as if at Mass. The service concluded with the recitation of vespers without any music.[50]

Creeping to the cross was one of the most frequent targets of Protestant reformers from the 1530s onwards, and there can be no doubt of the place it held in lay piety: well into the Elizabethan period Bishop Grindal would complain that on Good Friday "some certeyn persons go barefooted and barelegged to the churche, to creepe to the crosse."[51] But the most imaginatively compelling of the Good Friday ceremonies, though associated with the cross, came after the solemn liturgy had ended. This was the custom of the "burial" of Christ in the Easter sepulchre, an observance which left a deep mark not only in the minds of medieval English men and women but in the very structure of many parish churches. At the end of the liturgy of Good Friday, the priest put off his Mass vestments and, barefoot and wearing his surplice, brought the third Host consecrated the day before, in a pyx. The pyx and the Cross which had been kissed by the people during the liturgy were

[49] *Festial*, p. 126.
[50] *Missale*, cols 316–33.
[51] Brand, *Antiquities*, I. p. 86.

wrapped in linen cloths and taken to the north side of the chancel, where a sepulchre had been prepared for them. This was normally a timber frame, probably the shape and size of the "hearse" which, covered with a pall, formed the focus of the normal obituary ceremonies at funerals and month's minds. Like those hearses, the sepulchre was covered with a rich cloth, often stained or embroidered with scenes from the Passion and a picture of the Resurrection, and candles burned before it. The Host and Crucifix were laid within it while the priest intoned the Psalm verse "I am counted as one of them that go down to the pit," and the sepulchre was censed. A watch was then kept before it continually till Easter. Since large numbers of candles needed tending during this period, and since the pyx in which the Sacrament was "buried" was usually extremely valuable, payments to parishioners or parochial officers like the sexton or clerk for maintaining this watch, and for "brede, ale and fyre" to see them through the chilly night hours are common in pre-Reformation churchwardens' accounts. Early on Easter Morning, before Mass was rung, the clergy assembled, all the lights in the church were lit, and a procession formed to the sepulchre, which was censed. The Host was removed without ceremonial to its normal position in the hanging pyx above the high altar. The Crucifix was then solemnly "raised" from the sepulchre and carried triumphantly round the church while all the bells were rung and the choir sang the anthem "Christus Resurgens".

> Christ, rising again from the dead, dieth now no more. Death shall no more have dominion over him. For in that he liveth, he liveth unto God. Now let the Jews declare how the soldiers who guarded the sepulchre lost the king when the stone was placed, wherefore they kept not the rock of righteousness. Let them either produce him buried, or adore him rising, saying with us, Alleluia, Alleluia.

The cross was placed on an altar on the north side of the church, and was once more venerated by people creeping towards it. In many places, especially cathedrals and the great town churches, growing devotion to the Host led to ritual development: the image used in this ceremony was often not a simple Crucifix, but an image of Christ which had a hollow space in the breast covered with a crystal in order to form a monstrance for the Host. The ceremony of creeping to the cross thereby became an act of solemn eucharistic worship. Matins and Mass were then sung, with a more than usually elaborate procession. Throughout the week the empty sepulchre remained a focus of devotion – candles burned before it during service time and it was solemnly censed at vespers each evening, before being finally removed before Mass on the Friday in Easter week.[52]

The Easter sepulchre and its accompanying ceremonial constitute something of an interpretative crux for any proper understanding of late medieval English religion. The sepulchre was emphatically a central part of the official liturgy of Holy Week, designed to inculcate and give dramatic expression to orthodox teaching, not merely on the saving power of Christ's cross and Passion but on the doctrine of the Eucharist. With its abundance of lights and night watches it constituted an especially solemn form of public worship of the Host, in many communities far more elaborate even than the Corpus Christi procession. At the same time it had become by the fifteenth century an intense and genuinely popular focus for lay piety and devotional initiative. The complexity of the cluster of ideas and observances which gathered around the sepulchre in popular understanding and practice also suggests that we should not too hastily accept the widely held view of the theological imbalance of late medieval Christianity, where it sometimes seems that "piety is becoming fevered, and that Christ's *humanitas* has become synonymous with his passibility".[53] Expressing to the full as it did the late medieval sense of the pathos of the Passion, the sepulchre and its ceremonies were also the principal vehicle for the Easter proclamation of Resurrection.

It is not difficult to establish the ubiquity of lay awareness of and interest in the Easter sepulchre. Since every church was obliged to provide one for the Holy Week and Easter ceremonies, expenses for the making, maintenance, lighting, and watching of the sepulchre feature in most surviving churchwardens' accounts.[54] In most places it was a movable wooden frame, which was adorned with drapery and carved or painted panels. Such structures could be immensely elaborate. In the 1470s St Mary Redcliffe in Bristol acquired "a new sepulcre well gilt with golde", which had an image of the risen Christ, a model of Hell complete with thirteen devils, four sleeping soldiers armed with spears and axes, four painted angels with detachable timber wings, as well as representations of

---

[52] Feasey, *Holy Week*, pp. 168–9; E. K. Chambers, *The Medieval Stage*, 1903, II pp. 19–24; A. Heales, "Easter Spulchres: their Object, Nature and History", *Archaeologia*, XLI, 1869, pp. 263–308; V. Sekules, "The Tomb of Christ at Lincoln and the Development of the Sacrament Shrine: Easter Sepulchres Reconsidered" in *British Archaeological Association Conference Transactions*, VIII, 1982, pp. 118–31; P. Sheingorn, "The Sepulchrum Domini, a Study in art and Liturgy", *Studies in Iconography*, IV, 1978, pp. 37–61. Sekules considers that some of these sepulchres were used as Sacrament shrines for reservation all the year through.

[53] J. A. W. Bennett, *The Poetry of the Passion*, 1982, p. 59; Bennett was characterizing a view he did not himself hold.

[54] Cox, *Churchwardens' Accounts*, pp. 259–60; Feasey, *Holy Week*, pp. 158–63.

God the Father and the Holy Ghost "coming out of Heaven into the Sepulchre".[55] But in many churches it was a permanent architectural and sculptured feature. This might take the form of a canopied niche set in the north wall of the chancel or a table-tomb on the north side of the high altar with its east end against the east wall of the chancel. Either way, lay financial resources were lavished on the elaboration of the sepulchre. There was an established iconography – the sleeping soldiers, Christ rising or risen, the three Maries or St Mary Magdalene, adoring angels. Magnificent and elaborately carved examples survive in Lincoln Cathedral, at Heckington in Lincolnshire (Pl. 7), at Northwold in Norfolk, and at Hawton, Arnold, and Sibthorpe in Nottinghamshire.[56]

Sepulchres of this sort represented major pieces of patronage, but the desire to associate oneself with the parish's annual worship of Christ in the Easter mysteries extended right across the social spectrum and took many forms. For the very wealthy there was the opportunity to build a tomb for oneself which was also the tomb of Christ, and to adorn it with Resurrection imagery which spoke of personal hopes as well as beliefs about Christ. Scores of such burials survive, like John Hopton's tomb at Blythburgh or the Clopton tomb in Long Melford (Pl. 8), with the donor's family painted round the arch of the sepulchre and the risen Christ in its vaulting. A fascinating and distinctive group of Easter sepulchre monuments, all of them probably dating from after the break with Rome, survives in the Chichester area. The sepulchre erected by William Ernley at West Wittering, possibly as late as 1540, has a sculpted Christ vigorously striding out of his box-tomb while the soldiers slump around it. On Agatha George's proprietorial sepulchre at Selsey the donor and her husband kneel, flanked by St Agatha and St George, the patrons who encode her name. Paradoxically, the central figure of the risen Christ has been chiselled away by iconoclasts. On the Sackville monument at Westhampnett (Pl. 9) the donors kneel on either side of a Corpus Christi image of the dead Christ, supported by the other members of the Trinity.[57]

These lavish tombs were designed to replace the temporary framework which formed the sepulchre in most churches, and thereby to create a permanent association between the memory of the donor and the parish's most solemn act of worship. Sometimes donors did not aspire to incorporate their dust quite so inescapably within the liturgy: mere proximity to the sepulchre might be

[55] A. Heales, "Easter Sepulchres", p. 301; for an equally elaborate sepulchre at St Stephen's, Coleman St., in London see Feasey, Holy Week, pp. 166–7.

[56] J. C. Cox and A. Harvey, English Church Furniture, 2nd ed. 1908, pp. 74–8.

[57] N. Pevsner, The Buildings of England: Sussex, 1965, pp. 320, 373, 377.

enough. Richard Clerke of Lincoln requested in 1528 to be buried "in the quere nere to the place where the sepulchre usyth to stande, yf so conveniently soo may". Thomas Mering of Newark in 1500 sought burial "by twix the two pillars next the altar, as at the tyme of Esturr itt is used to sett the sepulcur of Jhesu Criste". And somewhere between these two types of patronage, the donor might request burial in a tomb which formed a base for the sepulchre frame, like John Pympe of Nettlestead in Kent who asked in 1496 for burial "in the place where as the sepulture of oure lorde is wounte to stonde at the Fest of Ester and to be leyde there in a tomb of stone, made under such fourme as the blessid sacremente and the holy crosse may be leide vpon the stone of the saide tombe in the maner of sepulture at the Feast abovesaide".[58]

The association of one's own burial with that of the Host at Easter was a compelling, eloquent, and above all a permanent gesture. But for the merely moderately prosperous with less purchasing power there were other possibilities. Thomas Hunt of Cransley in Northamptonshire left ten ewes for making a sepulchre in 1516, and this could only have procured a much more modest structure than any so far discussed – presumably a movable wooden frame, the normal form taken by the sepulchre. Or one might seek an even humbler, though still apt association of one's own long sleep in death with the Lord's resting-place, by leaving embroidered bed-hangings to drape the sepulchre frame, like Cecily Leppington of Beverley, who left "my best oversee bed called the Baptest as an ornament to the sepulchre of oure Saviour Criste Jhesu at the fest of Ester", or Henry Williams of Stanford on Avon who bequethed "my coverled to the use of the sepulcre".[59]

All these were the benefactions of the rich, for in religion as in everything else the rich dominated the communities in which they lived. But the sepulchre was the possession of the parish, and the middling and the poor too sought to associate themselves with this aspect of the Easter liturgy. The sepulchre and its ornaments formed a complex collection of devotional paraphernalia, any one of which might be the object of individual or cooperative endowment. The specification of the sepulchre at St Mary Redcliffe or the

---

[58] *Lincoln Wills*, ed. C. W. Foster, 1914–30, II p. 89; L. L. Duncan, "The Parish Churches of West Kent, Their Dedications, Altars, Images and Lights", *Transactions of the St Paul's Ecclesiological Society*, III, 1895, p. 248; Feasey, *Holy Week*, pp. 139–40.

[59] Cox and Hervey, *English Church Furniture*, pp. 74–8; G. H. Cook, *The English Medieval Parish Church*, 1970, pp. 170–3; *Testamenta Eboracensia*, ed. J. Raine and J. W. Clay, Surtees Society, 1836–1902, IV p. 179, V pp. 224–5; R. M. Serjeantson and H. Isham Longden (eds) "The Parish churches and Religious Houses of Northamptonshire: their Dedications, Altars, Images and Lights", *Journal of the British Archaeological Association*, LXX, 1913 (hereafter = *Northants Wills* II) p. 407.

one at St Stephen's, Coleman Street, London illustrate the range of objects associated with its veneration:

> Item one sepulchre over gilded with a frame to be set on with 4 posts and crests thereto.
> Item four great angels to be set on the sepulchre with divers small angels.
> Item 2 stained clothes with the Apostles and Prophets beaten with gold with the Creed.
> Item 8 bears beaten with gold to be set about the sepulchre with divers small pennons.[60]

Just as individuals and gilds contributed single panels or sections of larger structures like Rood-screens, so individuals and gilds associated themselves with the provision, maintenance, and adornment of the sepulchre, like the gild at Chesterton, which provided a new frame for use in the liturgy at the cost of £11.[61] Though wealthy lay people frequently left bequests of hangings to adorn these frames, the commonest form of individual benefaction to the sepulchre for rich and poor alike was the endowment of one or more lights to burn around it during the watch period from Friday to Sunday morning. There was ample scope here: at St Edmund's, Salisbury, over a hundred candles blazed on prickets before the sepulchre, and all over England bequests of wax to the sepulchre lights are among the commonest of all mortuary provisions.[62] And for those whose resources did not extend even so far, there was the possibility of joining a Resurrection gild, whose central function was the maintenance of the sepulchre, or a Corpus Christi gild, many of whom maintained sepulchres as well as elevation or Corpus Christi lights.[63] Membership of such a gild offered the middling and the respectable poor some of the symbolic benefits the rich could secure by building tombs which were also Easter sepulchres, for Resurrection gilds often burned the great sepulchre lights they maintained at the funerals of their dead brethren. There can be little doubt that the "thirteen square wax lights in stands", and the "four angels and four banners of the passion" which stood round the hearses of deceased members of the Lincoln Resurrection

---

[60] Feasey, *Holy Week*, pp. 166–7: Heales, "Easter Sepulchres" *passim*.

[61] Westlake, *Parish Gilds*, p. 141.

[62] From thousands of possible examples, see the following at random – *Lincoln Wills*, I pp. 70–3, II pp. 148–9, 183: *Northants Wills*, II pp. 282, 345, 348, 405: *Somerset Medieval Wills*, ed. F. W. Weaver, Somerset Record Society, I pp. 209–10: *Transcripts of Sussex Wills*, ed. R. Garraway Rice and W. H. Godfrey, Sussex Record Society, 1935–41, III p. 52: Feasey, *Holy Week*, pp. 158–63.

[63] Westlake, *Parish Gilds*, nos 13, 67, 92, 135, 136, 139.

gild were part of the ornaments of the Easter sepulchre which the gild existed to maintain.[64]

These sorts of devotional gesture imply a great deal about lay religious sophistication. Such symbolic equations of one's own death and hopes of resurrection with those of Christ argue a widespread comprehension and internalization of the central message of the Easter liturgy. And the imaginative force of the ceremonial and imagery surrounding the sepulchre at the end of the Middle Ages is testified to by a poem preserved in the commonplace book of a devout London tradesman, Richard Hill, the so-called "Corpus Christi Carol". The meaning of this mysterious and moving poem has been much discussed and debated: though often associated with the Grail legend, in its present form it cannot long predate the Henrician Reformation and it is even possible that, like the West Sussex sepulchres I have already discussed, it is a product of the 1530s. It has been argued that it might even be a conservative Catholic lament for the divorce of Catherine of Aragon and Henry's marriage to Anne Boleyn, whose heraldic emblem was a falcon. However that may be, there can be no question whatever that one of the major sources of the poem's haunting power lies in the strange cluster of images which derive directly from the cult of the Easter sepulchre, with its Crucifix, Host, and embroidered hangings, and the watchers kneeling around it day and night.

> Lully, lelley, lully, lulley,
> The fawcon hath born my mak away.
> He bare him up, he bare him down,
> He bare him into an orchard brown.
> In that orchard ther was an hall,
> That was hanged with purpill and pall.
> And in that hall there was a bed:
> It was hangid with gold so red.
> And in that bed ther lythe a knight,
> His woundes bleding day and night.
> By that bedes side ther kneleth a may,
> And she wepeth both night and day.
> And by that bedes side ther stondeth a ston,
> "Corpus Christi" wreten theron.[65]

There was in late medieval England an established iconography of the Corpus Christi, the Eucharistic body of Christ portrayed as

[64] Toulmin-Smith, *English Gilds*, pp. 175–7.
[65] R. Davies, *Medieval English Lyrics*, 1963, p. 272 cf. pp. 363–4; R. L. Greene, "The Meaning of the Corpus Christi Carol", *Medium Aevum*, XXIX, 1960, pp. 10–21.

the dead Jesus, held in the arms of the Father and hovered over by the Spirit, displaying "His woundes bleding day and night" (Pl. 10). A number of painted windows in York associated with the Corpus Christi gild there contain this striking image (Pl. 11), and the Sackville monument at Westhampnett links it directly with the Holy Week veneration of the Corpus Christi in the sepulchre.[66] This image of Corpus Christi resembles that of Our Lady of Pity (Pl. 12), in which Mary rather than the Father displays the wounds of her Son. The images, despite their points of similarity, differ in intent. In those in which the Father appears the point is Trinitarian: the sufferings of Christ are revealed not to evoke pity or compunction for sins but as a theological statement, the sacrament of the love of the Trinity for humanity, a pledge, perpetuated daily in the Eucharist, of God's will to redeem and renew. In the image of Our Lady of Pity, in which Mary supports the dead Christ, the message is affective not theological, an appeal for repentance and compassion with the suffering of Christ – "Who cannot weep, come learn of me." The image of Our Lady of Pity is emphatically a Good Friday one, just as the "Corpus Christi Carol" is certainly a Good Friday poem: the Christ portrayed here is bleeding, and the watcher by the Host is a weeping maiden who inevitably recalls Mary. It is part of the theological complexity of the sepulchre that it stood at one and the same time for the affectivity of such piety and for a wider and profounder theological affirmation. The sepulchre was the place of lamentation for the havoc sin had wrought: the parishioners kneeling around it on Good Friday evening were encouraged by preachers to lament their sins, to experience the desolation of the burial of injured Innocence.

Yonder it lyes, yonder is hys bodye, in yonder tombe, in yonder sepulchre. Lett us goo thidre, lett us wepe with these Maryes, lett us turne and wynde thys bodye of Christe, lett us turne it thys wayes and that wayes, to and froo, and pytussely beholde hit. And what shall we fynde. We shall fynde a bloody bodye, a body full of plages and woundes. Not that hit nowe is full of woundes and plages, or nowe deede: but y[e]t thowe oughtest nowe as the tyme of the yere falleth, with the churche to remembere this body. Howe it was for the broken, howe it was for the rente and torn, howe bloody it was, howe full of plages, and howe it was wounded. And in recollection and remembrance thereof, wepe and lament, for it was doon for the.[67]

[66] J. A. Knowles, *Essays in the History of the York School of Glass-Painting*, 1936, pp. 169–77.

[67] John Longland, *A Sermond made be fore the kynge 1535*, RSTC 16795.5, sig. R4.

Longland's phrase "pytussely beholde" is significant, for it is the technical term for meditation on the Passion used in the indulgence rubrics which accompanied the devotional woodcuts of the wounded Christ surrounded by the Arms of the Passion which were in wide circulation as devotional aids in late medieval England: the liturgy is being used here as a trigger for penitential meditation. But the liturgy of the sepulchre moved the devotee on from the desolation and pathos of Good Friday to the affirmations of Easter. The sacramental presence hidden in the tomb till then became the housel received in a solemn act of communal reconciliation and solidarity, while the Easter morning creeping to the cross which immediately followed the raising of the image and the Host from the sepulchre was an act not of penitence, but of celebration of the healing and redeeming power of the cross triumphant. Langland caught this dimension of the sepulchre liturgy of Easter morning perfectly.

> Men rongen to the resurexion – and right with that I wakede
> And called Kytte my wife and Calote my daughter
> Ariseth and reverenceth Goddes resurexion
> And crepeth to the cros on knees, and kisseth it for a jewel
> For Goddes blissede body it bar for our boote
> And it fereth the fend – for swich is the myghte
> May no grisly goost glide there it shadweth.[68]

Sacred Place, Sacred Time

Sometime during the reign of Elizabeth the Suffolk recusant, Roger Martin, decided to write down what he could remember of the furnishings and pre-Reformation religious observances of his parish church of Holy Trinity, Long Melford. Martin, who was born in the early 1520s, had been a churchwarden under Mary. At the reintroduction of Protestantism he had rescued and hidden those Catholic ornaments of the church in which his family had proprietary rights. His detailed account of the parish before the iconoclastic storms of Edward's reign does, as one might expect, allude in passing to the anxious years of the Marian reaction and the work of restoration which had gone on in the church then, but its main aim was to evoke the richness and beauty of the immemorial observances of late medieval piety before the deluge of reform and iconoclasm, in one of the most prosperous and, if externals are anything to go by, one of the most pious of the Suffolk wool villages.[69]

[68] William Langland, *The Vision of Piers Plowman*, B text, ed. C. Schmidt, 1978, Passus XVIII lines 428–34 (p. 234).
[69] Parker, *History of Long Melford*, pp. 70–3.

Martin's account of Long Melford seems at first sight to fall into two quite distinct parts. In the first he is concerned with the images and furnishings of the church, especially the chancel and the south aisle, the Jesus aisle, where his own family had their burial place. He describes the Rood-screen with its images, its organs, and its paintings of the Apostles, the sepulchre frame set up each year within John Clopton's great Easter sepulchre-cum-tomb on the north side of the chancel. Behind the high altar was the enormous retable of Calvary, "made of one great Tree" and "carved very artificially with the story of Christ's passion", crowded, in typically late medieval style, with incident and minor characters. On either side of the high altar were elaborate carved tabernacles, that on the north side having the church's patronal image of the Trinity, that on the south (though he does not tell us so) with the image of the Virgin. In "my Ile called 'Jesus Ile'", the Martin family burial chapel, was another altar retable of the Crucifixion. Here too there were flanking tabernacles containing, to the north, the image of Jesus as Salvator Mundi "holdinge a round bawle in his hand, signifying I think that he containeth the whole round world", and to the south an image of Our Lady, "having the afflicted body of her dear Son, as he was taken down off the Cross lying along on her lap, the tears as it were running down pitifully upon her beautiful cheeks, as it seemed bedewing the sweet body of her Son, and therefore named the *Image of Our Lady of Pity*".[70]

In the second part of his account Martin turns from furnishings and iconography, and a piety which seems rooted in stillness and looking, to ritual activity and a piety which seems geared to move-ment and elaborate communal celebration. In the process the account itself moves from the inside of the church and the privacies of chancel, chantry, vestry, and proprietary aisle to the public processional ways round the churchyard and out into the parish at large. As it does so, it also begins to take account of time. He describes in some detail the Palm Sunday liturgy with the Host carried under "a fair canopy borne by 4 yeomen", a description already used in our treatment of the Holy Week ceremonies. Martin also describes the other major processions of the year: Corpus Christi when "they went likewise with the blessed Sacrament in procession about the Church green in Copes"; St Mark's day and the Rogation days, when the litanies were sung and the parish processed with handbells and banners "about the bounds of the

---

[70] *History of Long Melford*, loc. cit. Martin's account, with a good deal of relevant additional documentation, has been re-edited by D. Dymond and C. Paine, *The Spoil of Melford Church: the Reformation in a Suffolk Parish*, 1989.

town", each day's march culminating in communal drinking. In addition to these processions Martin includes four bonfires in his picture of the ritual year at Long Melford, one associated with the chapel of St James near his house and held on St James's day (25 July) after an elaborate sung Mass. The other bonfires took place on Midsummer eve, on the eve of St Peter's and Paul's day four days later (28/29 June), and then one week further on, on the eve of the summer festival of St Thomas of Canterbury (6/7 July). These three bonfires and feasts, at which the poor were entertained at the expense of Martin's grandfather, were evidently all assimilated to the "St John's fires", since on these occasions watch-candles were maintained throughout the night before an image of St John the Baptist. They were by no means peculiar to Melford or to eastern England, and similar communal religious fires and feasts occurred on these days all over England.[71]

It is tempting to see in the two parts of Martin's account two distinct aspects of late medieval religion, the inner and the outer. His nostalgic evocation of the imagery of the church, the various carvings of the Passion, Jesus altar, and statue of Our Lady of Pity, seems a clear manifestation of the inward-looking, meditative, and affective dimension of the piety of the period, with its emphasis on sweetness, on the pathos of the cross, on Mary's tears and the response of the individual heart to those tears. Neither season nor distance seem relevant within this type of religious world. By contrast his picture of the year's liturgical round is full of the clangour of handbells and the leather-lunged chanting of the litany, the rattle of processional paraphernalia, censer and holy-water bucket and cross, of yeomen sweating under the burden of the Eucharistic canopy, children scrambling for cakes and flowers, and the poor jostling for the beer and mutton and peascod pies laid out on boards on the green before Martin's grandfather's door at the other end of the village from the church, or at the parsonage on procession or bonfire days.

In fact any such distinction would be artificial: what is striking about Martin's account is the convergence between inner and outer, private and public, the timeless and meditative on one hand, the seasonal and external on the other. The carvings behind the altars or in the tabernacles were there to move piety, to signify to the observer the creating and saving power of Jesus or the pathos of his Passion, and Martin's comments on them, with his use of words like "afflicted" or his evocation of Mary's tears "as it were running

---

[71] C. Phythian-Adams, "Ceremony and the Citizen", in P. Clark (ed.) *The Early Modern Town*, 1976, pp. 112–13.

down pitifully upon her beautiful cheeks", indicates his own affective response to them. But this iconography was also geared to the liturgy and the public cycle of celebration and penance which made up the Christian year. The Rood-screen was not merely the chief image in the church of the Crucifixion of Jesus and of the intercessory power of Mary, John, and the other saints depicted on it: it was also a ritual prop which served as the culminating focus of the Palm Sunday liturgy which Martin so lovingly described. The less prominent carving of Calvary behind the high altar was similarly integrated into the seasonal variations of the church's year, for it was fitted with painted doors which were normally kept shut, concealing the carving, but which "were opened upon high and solemn Feast Days, which then was a very beautiful show".

Even so apparently private and individualistic a thing as a chantry chapel, dedicated to a ceaseless round of intercession on behalf of one man and decorated, as the Clopton chantry at Melford was, with devotional verses by Lydgate, could be drawn into this pattern of public seasonal observance. The Clopton chapel was built for the benefit of John Clopton and his family, but it served also as part of the stage for the liturgical drama of Holy Week: as the processions skirted it on Palm Sunday its turret roof was the platform from which was sung the antiphon "Behold, your king comes". Clopton himself directed that his tomb, set in the wall between the chantry and the north side of the chancel, should serve as an Easter sepulchre, and he left rich hangings, probably from his own bed and chamber, to dress it worthily for the parish's solemn public veneration of the Sacrament, and of Christ's cross, in Holy Week.[72]

This integration of personal devotional gestures into the seasonal pattern of the liturgy was a universal feature of late medieval religion. Gifts of ornaments in wills often specified their use "at every pryncipill feste".[73] Such bequests, designed to evoke prayers for the donor at the high points of the parish's devotional intensity, also contributed to the fostering of that intensity by ensuring a seasonal and festal variety in the ornaments of worship, alerting fellow-parishioners to the passage of sacred time, just as the provision of extra music on special days or the ringing of curfews and other bells "in pryncipall fests and oder dobull festes" might do.[74] Even the bequest to the parish of so personal an object as one's own rosary might be geared to the liturgical year in this way. Beatrice Kirkemer in 1509 left beads to be hung on the images in

---

[72] For Clopton's will see *Visitation of Suffolk*, I pp. 34–40; and see Gail McMurray Gibson, *The Theater of Devotion*, 1989, pp. 84–96.
[73] Louth CWA, p. 94; Leverton CWA, p. 355.
[74] Louth CWA, p. 13; St Michael Cornhill CWA, p. 1.

her parish church "on good dayes", and Alice Carre in 1523 left her small beads to adorn the image of St Anne in the north aisle through the year, but her best coral beads to hang on the image on the feast of St Anne itself.[75]

It is not difficult to understand the importance of the liturgical calendar for late medieval people. There was, in the first place, no alternative, secular reckoning of time: legal deeds, anniversaries, birthdays were reckoned by the religious festivals on which they occurred, rents and leases fell in at Lady Day, Lammas, or Michaelmas. The seasonal observances of the liturgical calendar affected everyone. No one could marry during the four weeks of Advent or the six weeks of Lent. Everyone must fast during the forty days of Lent, abstaining not merely from meat but from other animal products, "whitemeats" such as eggs and cheese. In addition to Lent, fasting was obligatory on the ember days, that is, the Wednesdays, Fridays, and Saturdays after the feast of St Lucy (13 December), Ash Wednesday, Whit Sunday, and Holy Cross Day (14 September). There was also an obligation to fast on the vigils of the feasts of the twelve Apostles (excepting those of Sts Philip and James and St John), the vigils of Christmas Day, Whit Sunday, the Assumption of Our Lady (15 August), the Nativity of St John the Baptist (24 June), the feast of St Laurence (10 August), and the feast of All Saints (1 November). Though not obligatory everywhere, it was also customary to fast on some at least of the days of Rogationtide.

There were therefore almost seventy days in the year when adults were obliged to fast, the bulk of them in spring for the great fast of Lent, but the rest spread more or less evenly through the rest of the year. The Embertide fasts in particular, originally occurring three times in the year, were made up to four groups of three days, one in each of the four seasons. Their seasonal occurrence was emphasized in commentaries and sermons, related to the four humours, the cardinal virtues, and the seasons of human life.[76] In addition, late medieval devotional custom made penitential fasting on bread and water a conventional and common way of honouring saints to whom one had a particular devotion (Pl. 13).[77] A custom like the Lady fast, in which the devotee noted which day of the week Lady Day in Lent (the feast of the Annunciation, 25 March) fell on, and observed that day throughout the year as a fast in honour of the Virgin, was established by 1410, much to the disgust

---

[75] F. Blomefield and C. Parkin, *An Essay towards a Topographical History of the County of Norfolk*, 1805–10, IV pp. 153–4.

[76] *Golden Legend*, I p. 66; *Festial*, pp. 253–4.

[77] *Festial*, p. 199.

of the author of *Dives and Pauper*, since "the mede of fastynge ne the vertu of fastynge is nought assyngnyd ne lymyt be the letterys of the kalender ne folwyn nout the cours of the kalender ne changyn nout from o day to another day."[78] The laity quite clearly thought otherwise, and the Lady fast was elaborated even further. In the parish church at Yaxley there survives a "sexton's wheel", a bizarre roulette-like device with six spokes, each assigned to one of the major feasts of the Virgin. Coloured strings were attached to each spoke and the wheel was spun: the devotee seized a string and observed the weekday on which the relevant feast fell as a fast in honour of the Virgin throughout the ensuing year (Pl. 14).[79]

As important as fast days were feast days, in particular the *festa ferianda*, on which total or partial abstention from servile work was required and the laity were expected to observe the Sunday pattern of attendance at matins, Mass, and evensong, fasting on the preceding eve. There were between forty and fifty such days, with variations in the precise list from region to region. The number of *festa ferianda*, as well as the degree of rigour in their observance, was in a continuous state of evolution throughout the fifteenth century, both because of the widespread divergence in local customs and observance and as a result of the introduction in the southern and northern provinces of *nova festa* such as the Transfiguration or the Holy Name in the 1480s and 1490s. The observance and the status of holy days were much contested issues, since holy days were also holidays. Workers sought to secure days free from secular toil, landowners and employers sought to extract the maximum work from their tenants or employees, and a particular bone of contention was the question of whether servants or lords should bear the expense of the loss of a day's work involved in each feast. Hence considerable variation was the rule in the degree of solemnity of particular days, some requiring the cessation of all work (except activities such as milking cows, feeding livestock, or the saving of crops in harvest), other days requiring only women to abstain from work. Both secular and ecclesiastical authorities throughout the Middle Ages showed considerable sensitivity to these sorts of questions, and a tendency to seek to limit the number of holidays. This trend achieved its starkest and most drastic expression after the break with Rome, when in 1536 the Crown abolished most of the local and national *festa ferianda* occurring in the Westminster law terms and in the busy summer months, on the grounds that the excessive numbers of holidays were impoverishing

[78] *Dives and Pauper*, I pp. 173–4.
[79] W. H. Sewell, "The Sexton's Wheel and the Lady Fast", *Norfolk Archaeology*, IX, 1884, pp. 201–14; Gibson, *Theater of Devotion*, p. 152.

the people by hindering agriculture. Widespread resentment of this action was a contributory factor in the Pilgrimage of Grace, and subsequent anti-reform feeling.[80]

Naturally, degrees of awareness of the niceties of the liturgical calendar varied. Ignorance was not necessarily the monopoly of the laity. The early Tudor jest-book, *A Hundred Merry Tales*, has a story of a country curate "which was not very learned" who sent to a neighbouring cleric on Easter eve to know what Mass to celebrate. His boy is told the Mass of the Resurrection, but forgets the word on his way home, and can recall only that it begins with R. "By God" quoth the priest, "I trow thou sayest truth, for now I remember well it must be 'requiem eternam', for God almighty died as on yesterday, and now we must say mass for his soul."[81] But this was a story for the well-informed laity to laugh at, and it depends in part for its point on the assumption that the correct performance of the appropriate liturgy was a matter of some general concern. Indeed, as the custom of devotional fasting suggests, the late medieval laity were intensely conscious of the liturgical calendar, and often displayed a startlingly detailed knowledge of it. Undoubtedly the most distinctive and striking manifestation of this lay liturgical awareness is the Pope Trental and related observances, in which lay people specified as part of their mortuary provision the singing of specific Masses, "Diriges", and fasts in a pattern closely geared to the major feasts of the liturgical year. The provisions of such testators often reveal a detailed knowledge of the prayers of the missal and breviary, and an awareness of the complexities of the calendar which must certainly reflect clerical instruction, but equally clearly a conviction on the part of the laity that such things mattered greatly.[82]

Despite the desire of those in authority, for economic and other reasons, to limit the number of festivals, in practice the calendar continued to grow during the late Middle Ages right up to the break with Rome. The most spectacular addition was Corpus Christi, kept on the Thursday after Trinity Sunday. Observed in England from 1318 and seized on by the authorities as an occasion for the promotion of both charity and Christian catechesis, the feast

[80] On *Festa Ferianda* see Barbara Harvey, "Work and Festa Ferianda in the Middle Ages", *Journal of Ecclesiastical History*, XXIII, 1972, pp. 289–308; C. R. Cheney "Rules for the observance of feast days in Medieval England", *Bulletin of the Institute of Historical Research*, XXXIV, 1961, pp. 117ff: E. C. Rodgers, *Discussion of Holidays in the Later Middle Ages*, 1940; on the 1536 abolition see below, chapter 11, "The Attack on Traditional Religion I" pp. 394–8.

[81] *A Hundred Merry Tales and Other English Jest Books of the Fifteenth and Sixteenth centuries*, ed. P. M. Zall, 1963, p. 135.

[82] See below, pp. 370–5.

rapidly won popular allegiance. Its progress in lay affections can be traced in the fourteenth and fifteenth centuries by the foundation and spread of Corpus Christi gilds to honour the Host as it was carried in procession, and the emergence of the Corpus Christi processions as major civic events. Craft gilds and urban corporations saw in the ritual order of the great processions associated with the feast an opportunity for civic and social iconography, the display of piety an opportunity for the display of the worship and the social clout of those involved. In Tudor York it was required that "for the honour of god and worship of this Citie" the citizens whose houses lay along the route of the procession with the Host should "hang before ther doores and forefrontes beddes and coverynges of beddes of the best that thay can gytt and strewe before ther doores resshes and other such flowres . . . for the honour of god and worschip of this Citie". In the same way, at Hull in the late fifteenth century testators left sumptuous bed-hangings to drape their hearses on their anniversary obsequies: all these hangings were displayed together in Holy Trinity Church on St George's day to add splendour to the town's celebration of the feast, "emong other worshipfull beddes", thereby presenting an opportunity for a con-certed display of conspicuous consumption persisting even in the tomb.[83] Particularly in urban parishes Corpus Christi became a focus of elaborate ceremonial and lavish expenditure on banners, garlands, lights: the gilds, not the clerks, took over the manage-ment of the processions. These celebrations also became the prin-cipal occasions for the performance of cycles of devotional and didactic plays on the theme of salvation history, which in some places involved virtually the whole community.[84]

But Corpus Christi was merely the best example of a much wider phenomenon. There were many other new feasts. The cult of St Anne led after 1383 to the widespread keeping of her day and a number of existing feasts were raised in status by being made binding throughout England in the course of the period: St George, St David, St Chad, and St Winifred, for example, in 1415. Feasts already observed, such as the nativity of the Virgin, were raised in solemnity by having a vigil (involving fasting) attached to them. In some cases the new feasts were the result of a new or revived cult – the canonization of St Osmund of Salisbury in 1456 is a case in

[83] A. H. Nelson, *The Medieval English Stage: Corpus Christi Pageants and Plays*, 1974, pp. 46–7; cf. the will of Thomas Wood of Hull, draper, in 1490, stipulating that his best bed, "of Arreys werk" should cover his grave each year at his "Dirige" and requiem in Holy Trinity, Hull, and should be hung up in that church each year on the feast of St George, "emong other worshipfull beddes". *Testamenta Eboracensia*, IV, p. 60.

[84] Rubin, *Corpus Christi, passim*, esp. pp. 213–87.

point. Others emerged after a lengthy history as private devotions. The liturgy was in flux, responsive to pressure from below, a mirror of the devotional changes and even fashions of the age. The multiplication within the Sarum rite of hymns and sequences in the metre of the "Stabat Mater" and "Dies Irae", reflecting late medieval devotional trends, lent a distinctive emotional colouring to many Masses. The mortuary benefactions of individuals and gilds, often specifying the celebration of particular votive Masses and prayers, could and did shape the daily pattern of the liturgy in parish churches and chapels alike. The emergence of new votive Masses on themes such as the Crown of Thorns or the Five Wounds was another sign of the power of popular piety to shape the liturgy itself, and was strikingly demonstrated in the raising of the characteristically English affective devotion to the Holy Name of Jesus to the status of a feast, with its own compulsory Mass and Office, in the late 1480s. The 1480s and 1490s in fact saw a good deal of innovation within the calendar, with the arrival of the feasts not only of the Holy Name but of the Visitation of the Virgin and the Transfiguration.[85] The arrival of these national observances within specific localities can often be traced by churchwardens' expenditure for the addition of the Mass and Office of the feast to the church's liturgical books. Some Kent parishes in 1511 had not got around to providing for the celebration of these new feasts twenty years after their introduction.[86] Occasionally one encounters more vivid evidence of the imaginative arrival of a new feast in a community. In the early sixteenth century the wealthier parishioners of Westhall in Suffolk clubbed together to provide a painted Rood-screen with sixteen panels. Most of these panels were filled in the traditional way with helper saints, one to a panel, but three panels on the north screen were set aside to depict the Transfiguration, with Jesus, Moses, and Elijah (Pl. 15). The choice of this subject, unique on English screens, suggests the existence of a devotion directly inspired by the liturgy. On the other side of England, and with a far greater degree of sophistication, the Chudleigh family had their chapel at Ashton in Devon painted with texts from the Office of the Transfiguration, as well as texts and images bearing on another of the new feasts, the Visitation, an example of the role of educated patronage "with access to skills and imaginative

---

[85] These changes are tabulated in C. Wordsworth and H. Littlehales, *The Old Service Books of the English Church*, 1904, pp. 190–3. The definitive work on the new feasts is R. W. Pfaff, *New Liturgical Feasts in Late Medieval England*, 1970.

[86] *Kentish Visitation of Archbishop Warham and his Deputies, 1511*, ed. K. L. Wood Legh, *Kentish Archaeological Society: Kent Records*, XXIV, 1984, p. 110.

theological understanding of a high order" in raising the liturgical awareness of a remote rural parish.[87]

"Sacred" and "Secular" Time?

Medieval liturgical books were divided into two distinct sections, reflecting two types of sacred time. On the one hand was the proper of seasons – Advent, Christmastide, Lent, Easter, and Whit, and, attached to the Whitsun season, the feasts of the Trinity and Corpus Christi. Of these only Christmas fell on a fixed date, running from 24 December to 6 January (or, if Candlemas was taken as the last festival of Christmas, 2 February). The other liturgical seasons were linked to the lunar calendar, and there were consequently huge variations in the dates on which these feasts fell – Easter Sunday, for example, could occur on any date between 22 March and 25 April. The other type of sacred time was that attached to fixed dates – the anniversaries of the saints and the new feasts we have just discussed, the Visitation (2 July), the Transfiguration (6 August), the Holy Name of Jesus (7 August).[88]

Some historians of late medieval religion have sought to draw a very sharp distinction between these two types of sacred time. The latest day on which Corpus Christi could fall was 24 June, Midsummer, which was also the major feast of the birth of John the Baptist, and the Corpus Christi observances brought to an end the great cycle of celebrations of the Incarnation and Redemption which ran effectively from Christmas to Pentecost. From the end of June until the end of November only the feasts of the saints served to break the unspectacular procession of Sundays after Trinity, until the season of Advent came again, and the cycle of Christmas, Lent, and Paschal tide, with its elaborate ceremonial and processions, began once more. Many commentators have noted this cramming of "all the major observances connected with the birth, life, death and resurrection of Christ" into the six-month period from 24 December to 24 June, from the winter solstice at the birth of Jesus to the summer solstice at the birth of John the Baptist. In a highly influential study of late medieval Coventry one historian has even suggested that the pre-Reformation year broke into two clearly

---

[87] The Westhall screen once had traces of an inscription naming the donors, from which its approximate date, *c.*1500, can be established; they are given in H. M. Cautley, *Suffolk Churches and their Treasures*, revised ed., 1982, p. 364; for Ashton see Marion Glascoe, "Late Medieval Paintings in Ashton Church", *Journal of the British Archaeological Society*, CXL, 1987, pp. 182–90; for a mention of a donor of the "image of the Transfiguration" at Bristol see C. Burgess, "For the Increase of Divine Service", *Journal of Ecclesiastical History*, XXXVI, 1985, pp. 63–4.

[88] Conventionally, the two types of celebration were arranged before and after the text of the ordinary of the Mass in missals, and before and after the psalter in breviaries.

marked divisions, a "ritualistic" half and a "secular" half.[89]

There is obviously something in this, but we need to beware of oversimplification. Though there is abundant evidence of the fascination which the liturgical calendar exercised over late medieval English men and women, there is very little evidence that they were aware of the sharp dichotomy and certainly not the "absolute contrast" perceived by modern social historians. To fifteenth- and early sixteenth-century sensibilities the liturgical year was spread over twelve months, not six, and none of it was secular.

This is readily grasped by considering some of the celebrations which fell outside the so-called ritual half of the year which ran from December to June. A major feast of England's most important saint, Thomas Becket, the translation of his relics, fell on 7 July, and with it was associated the general feast of relics, kept on the following Sunday and an occasion for pilgrimage and the granting of indulgences in many churches with notable relics. In the same month there were also the feasts of St Mary Magdalene, St Margaret, St James the Apostle, and St Anne. Not all of these days were obligatory feasts or *festa ferianda*, requiring attendance at matins, Mass, and evensong, as well as abstention from work, but all were immensely popular and very widely kept; Mirk supplied sermons for all of these days in his *Festial*. And all of the so-called secular months had feasts of this sort, some of great solemnity. August had the new feasts of the Transfiguration and the Holy Name of Jesus, and the feast of the Beheading of John Baptist, as well as the most important feast of Our Lady, the Assumption, or "Our Lady in Harvest". September had Mary's Nativity, Holy Cross Day, the feast of the Apostle Matthew, and, most important of all, the feast of the Archangel Michael, Michaelmas, the great autumnal celebration of the triumph of celestial powers over those of the underworld.[90] October, in addition to the *festa ferianda* of St Luke and Sts Simon and Jude, was rich in major local saints not venerated equally throughout England, but whose feasts were of primary importance within their own regions: Wilfrid, Thomas Cantilupe, Etheldreda, the translation of Hugh of Lincoln. November began with the major feast of All Saints, and was immediately followed by All Souls' Day, the focus of the late medieval cult of the dead. It had also many major saints' days with both universal and local importance: St Katherine, one of the most popular of all saints in the period, as well as Edmund, king and martyr, St Hugh, St Winifred, and St John of Bridlington.

---

[89] Charles Phythian-Adams, "Ceremony and the Citizen", pp. 106–28, and his *Local History and Folklore: a New Framework*, 1975.
[90] James, *Seasonal Fasts and Festivals*, pp. 226–7.

Given the number and importance of these celebrations, it makes very little sense to talk of a secular half of the year, over against the ritual half from Easter to Corpus Christi. In some communities, such as Coventry, it is true that there was a particular matching of sacred and secular, because most of the major secular celebrations, such as the election and installation of civic officials, fell within and derived a special resonance from the ritual half. In a number of English towns the Corpus Christi play cycles brought this period to a fitting close by an enactment of the whole of salvation history involving the community at large. Still, in many places this sort of inclusive celebration happened outside the ritual half: at Lincoln the greatest convergence of civic and sacred ceremonial came on Saint Anne's day, at the end of July, when the city gilds organized an elaborate series of pageants.[91] Even at York, where the most famous Corpus Christi cycle in England was normally played on the feast day itself, the Creed play and the Paternoster plays which sometimes replaced the Corpus Christi plays were performed in Lammastide, in the heat of August. And of course the ritual focus of communities with their own shrines and patrons varied according to the feast and translation days of the patron saint. So at Ely the great moments fell in late June and mid-October (the feast and translation of St Etheldreda), at Bury in November and April, at Hereford in early October, at Durham in March and September, at Chichester and the Thames valley in early April and mid-June.

Nor was this sort of variation confined to the great shrines. Every substantial parish had a cluster of gilds within the church, each one with its own patron, and with gild celebrations geared to their feast days. Norfolk had an elaborate cult of St Anne, and her gilds met for Masses, processions, and feasts at the end of July; during such feasts rhymed versions of St Anne's legend might be read.[92] A Norfolk town like Swaffham, with gilds dedicated to St Peter, St Helen, St John the Baptist, St Thomas Becket, the Trinity, the Ascension, and St Nicholas, would have had ceremonial and commensal events ranging from gild Masses and feastings to boy bishop rituals, all involving a large proportion of the population, in June, July, August, and early December.[93]

This blurring of the distinction between a ritual and a secular half of the calendar was further promoted by the production of Books

---

[91] I. Lancashire, *Dramatic Texts and Records of Britain*, 1984, no. 866; Nelson, *The Medieval English Stage*, pp. 104ff.

[92] *The Common-Place Book of Robert Reynes of Acle*, ed. L. Cameron, 1980 (hereafter = *Reynes Commonplace*) pp. 191–228, 406–49; P. Meredith, *The Mary Play from the N Town Manuscript*, 1977, pp. 9–12.

[93] F. Blomfield and C. Parkin, *An Essay towards a Topographical History of the County of Norfolk*, 1805–10, VI pp. 202–3.

of Hours – primers – for a wider public, and the inclusion in all
these books of calendars and related material. Late medieval people
were fascinated by the passage of time and the significance of its
divisions, and this for a variety of reasons, both practical and
occult. Seed-time and harvest, when to gather acorns or to kill
the pigs, the right time to let blood or take a laxative: all these
were determined by the calendar. Many of the Christian festivals,
whether by design or by serendipity, roughly coincided with pagan
festivals or fell at key moments in the turning of the year – the
summer and winter solstices, Our Lady's feast in harvest, the
autumn festivals of the angels at Michaelmas, All Saints and All
Souls at the change from autumn to winter, and so on. Men and
women who were not particularly devout, and who could not read,
sought to remember the saints' days and other festivals by which
the year was mapped out, and resorted to mnemonic devices to
imprint the pattern of the year in their minds. The most common
of these devices was the "Cisio-Janus", a series of nonsensical
rhymes, at first in Latin but later in English, which listed the major
feasts of each month. Prognostications based on the dominical
letter, or on the day on which festivals like Christmas or the feast
of St Paul fell, were extremely common, as were observances
connected with auspicious and inauspicious days. The ecclesiastical
authorities might fulminate against "they the whiche vowen never
to kembe them on the fryday or not to spynne on the satyrdaye / or
other semblable superstucyon" but the laity continued to observe
days and seasons, and for the most part the church tolerated while
trying to control such beliefs. Even astrology, within certain limits,
was permitted and endorsed.[94]

The outcome of all this was the close interweaving of the
Church's calendar with divisions and uses of time which in essence
had little to do with the Christian year. Astrological patterns and
the theme of the ages of man or the labours of the month became
woven into religious calendars (Pl. 16) or the sevenfold division
of the Hours of the breviary, and constantly recur in religious
contexts, on church doors and arches, even on baptismal fonts. In
manuscript Books of Hours the custom grew of illustrating the
calendar for each month not only with emblems of the principal
saints whose feasts occurred then, but with a picture of the secular
activities appropriate to that month – pig-sticking in December,
sitting by the fire in January, and so on. Later this seasonal theme
was applied to the life of a man, divided into six-year units, one

---

[94] *Ordynarye of crystyanyte or of crysten men*, W. de Worde 1502, RSTC 5198, sig. x iv (v)
and see *Dives and Pauper*, I pp. 182–5.

for each month. Once printed primers began to proliferate, this calendrical material could be elaborated, expanded, and made available across a wide social spectrum: printed primers for the English market incorporate what is effectively a mini-almanac, with a zodiacal man as a guide to phlebotomy, material on the humours (also for medical purposes and linked to the four seasons), and moralistic and calendrical material like the labours, the ages of man, and the anglicized "Cisio-Janus" rhymes for each month. In the cheap primers of the 1520s and 1530s, additional didactic material of the same sort is added, such as the set of pious rhymes, "The days of the week moralised".[95]

These trends were summed up in one of the runaway best-selling books of the sixteenth century, the *Kalender of Shepherdes*. First published in French in 1493, it was first translated into English (apparently by a Frenchman who knew only Scots English) in 1503. Richard Pynson issued a fresh translation in 1506, Wynkyn de Worde produced another in 1508, and there were further editions in 1518, 1528, and again in both Mary's and Elizabeth's reigns.[96] The *Kalender of Shepherdes* is a delightful, well-illustrated, but bizarre book. It is two-thirds astrological almanac, one-third religious vade-mecum, containing the essentials of Christian belief and practice for lay people as they had been worked out by catechists over the preceding three centuries. We shall have occasion to explore this dimension of the book in a later chapter. The aspect of the book which concerns us here is its shameless combination of religious divisions of time with astrological divisions. It advertised itself as containing "a Kalendar with the Fygures of euery Saynt that is halowed in the yere / in the whiche is the signes / the houres / the monethes / the momentes & the newe Mones", and much of the book was devoted to astrological characterizations and predictions. It moralized not only the days of the week but the months of the year, in a remarkable combination of sacred and profane:

> Amonge all the monthes I am lusty Apryll
> Fresshe and holsom unto each creature

---

[95] J. A. Burrow, *The Ages of Man*, 1986, esp. pp. 1–54, 75, 79ff; Mary Dove, *The Perfect Ages of Man's Life*, 1986, chapters 8 and 10; James Fowler, "On Medieval representations of the Months and Seasons", *Archaeologia*, XLIV, 1873, pp. 137–224; E. Clive Rouse and Andrew Baker "The Wall-Paintings of Longthorpe Tower near Peterborough", *Archaeologia*, XCVI, 1955, pp. 1–58; Russell Hope Robbins "English Almanacs of the Fifteenth Century", *Philological Quarterly*, XVIII, 1939, pp. 321–31; Willard Famham "The Dayes of the Mone", *Studies in Philology*, XX, 1923, pp. 70–82; D. Pearsall and E. Salter, *Landscapes and Seasons of the Medieval World*, 1973, pp. 129–34, 137–40, 142–6.

[96] Modern reprint with introduction by H. Oscar Sommer, *The Kalender of Shepherdes*, 1892.

And in my tyme the dulcet droppes dystyll
Called crystall as poetes put in scripture
Causyng all floures the longer to endure
In my tyme was the resurrecyon
Of god and man / by dyvyne elleccyon . . .

Among the other October I hyght
Frende unto vynteners naturally
And in my tyme Bachus is redy dyght
All maner wyne to presse and claryfy
Of which is sacred as we se dayly
The blyssed body of Cryst in flesshe and blode
Whiche is our hope / refeccyon / and fode.[97]

To lay sensibilities nourished by such material, the notion of a
contrast between a ritual and a secular half of the year cannot have
had much imaginative force. The sacred, while having climactic
moments in the great festivals, was an aspect of the whole year, and
those festivals themselves seem more likely to have been perceived
as falling into a symmetrical summer–winter disposition than seen
as crammed into a single half-year. It might be tempting to see in
this trend to moralize the weeks and months of the year, as opposed
to dramatizing a few focused, ritual, high points, a "bourgeoisifi-
cation" of time, part of the smoothing and regulating process
which would ultimately seek to abolish the festival calendar
altogether in favour of the regular weekly observance of the
sabbath. There might be something in this: certainly the emergence
of the morality plays in the later fifteenth and early sixteenth
centuries points to the growth of a type of religious sensibility
orientated to moral and religious generalities, rather than to the
narrative and festive sweep of the Corpus Christi cycles. The
morality play *Mundus et Infans*, published by Wynkyn de Worde in
1522, is little more than a dramatization of the moralizing of the
stages of man's life and the ills which beset him, long familiar from
the calendrical material and the illustrations in the primers and such
related works as the *Kalender of Shepherdes*.[98] But there are few
signs of these different approaches to sacred time pulling apart
before the Reformation. The regulated and regular piety of the
middling sort, geared to the daily and weekly observances of the
parish churches and the steady patterns of urban living, could
accommodate both the seasonal cycles of Advent and Easter and the

---

[97] *Kalender of Shepherdes*, pp. 17–19.
[98] Modern edition ed. G. A. Lester, *Three Late Medieval Morality Plays*, 1981, pp. 107–57.

sober pursuit of virtue, day in and day out, urged in the devotional material which printers like Caxton, Pynson, and Wynkyn de Worde poured out. For townsmen and countrymen alike, the rhythms of the liturgy on the eve of the Reformation remained the rhythms of life itself.

1.   The dreaming woman and the miraculous Candlemas procession: from the Miracles of the Virgin sequence in the Lady chapel of Winchester Cathedral.

2.   In the Purification scene at East Harling, the scriptural characters carry blessed candles.

3. The "Palm Cross", damaged by Protestant iconoclasts, stands in its original place at Hillesden in Buckinghamshire. It formed the first "station" in the Palm Sunday procession.

4. Late fourteenth-century rebuilding extended the church of Walpole St Peter to the edge of the consecrated churchyard. A Palm Sunday processional way was preserved by raising the chancel and building an arcaded tunnel.

5. The dramatic position of the great Crucifix unveiled and venerated on Palm Sunday at Cawston in Norfolk, revealed by the markings above the arch.

Ju eleuatïõe co2pis rþi.   fo.lrrrbï.

SACRAMENTV ALTARIt

A Ue verû co2pus natû de maria bgie
  Uere paffum inmolatû iu cruce p
hoïe. Cuius latus perfo2atumbnda flurit
fanguine. Æ fto nobis þguftatû mo2t3 i era
mine. O dulcis. O pie. O iefu fili marie.

6. "The Comely Corse": laymen carry the canopy over the Blessed Sacrament, as at Melford.

7.   The Easter sepulchre at Heckington, Lincolnshire.

8. John Clopton's tomb and Easter sepulchre, Long Melford.

9. The Sackville monument and Easter sepulchre, Westhampnett, Sussex.

10. The "Corpus Christi" image on the sepulchre at Westhampnett.

11 (below left). The "Corpus Christi" window (top centre), Holy Trinity, Goodramgate, York.

12 (below right). Our Lady of Pity, Long Melford.

The xij fridayes to fast Seynt Barnardis fast

The first fryday is the fryday in the first woke of Clene lent
The fryday next before our lady day in marche
The good fryday before Ester day
The fryday next before the Ascencion day
The fryday next before Wightsonday
The fryday in the Whitsonwoke
The fryday next before Seynt John Baptist
The fryday next before the first day of August
The fryday next before the Assumption of our lady
The fryday next before the Nativite of our lady
The fryday next before the Conception of our lady
The fryday next before Cristmas day

To knowe the stacions of our lord conteyneth xxxij pater nostres & xxxij aues & a crede

To honour the stacions of our lady conteyneth vij pater nostres lxxij aues & a crede

Cuj venit ad veniam qui negat ante viam

13. Devotional fasting: directions for "the xii fridays to fast Seynt Bernards fast", copied into a manuscript Book of Hours.

14. Devotional fasting: the sexton's wheel, Yaxley, Suffolk.

15. The arrival of a new feast: the north screen at Westhall, with the Transfiguration panels.

16. This primer calendar encodes four types of time – astrological time in the zodiac signs (top right panels), the occupations of the months (top left panels), the seasons of human life, here courting and marriage (bottom), and the liturgical year represented by th emblems of the chief saints of the months (side panels).

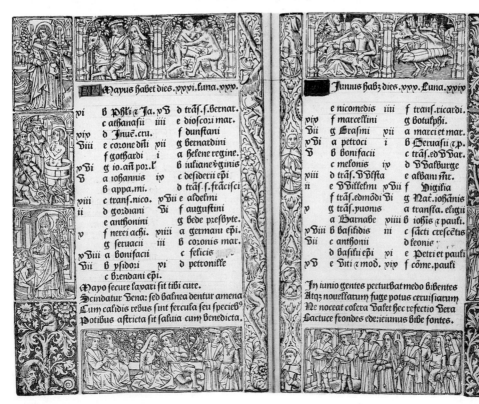

17. Fifteenth-century pulpit, with the
Four Latin Doctors, Castle Acre, Norfolk.

18. Fifteenth-century pulpit, Burlingham
St Edmund, Norfolk.

19. Holy Week confession in a town church: the parish priest is being assisted by a friar and another priest
(right and left); he holds his confession textbook in his left hand.

20. Parochial confession during Lent at Walsoken, Norfolk. On this font, completed in the last years of Henry VIII's reign, waiting parishioners jostle the kneeling penitent.

21. Relieving prisoners, from the Works of Mercy window, All Saints, North Street, York.

22. Feeding the hungry, from a Works of Mercy window at Combs, Suffolk.

23. Giving drink to the thirsty, from Combs, Suffolk.

24. Visiting the sick (often wrongly called Sloth), Blythburgh, Suffolk.

25. Relieving prisoners, Blythburgh, Suffolk.

26. Lust, Wigginhall St Germans, Norfolk. Below the sinners, Hell's mouth yawns.

27. Avarice, Wigginhall St Germans, Norfolk.

28. Hypocrisy (Pride), Blythburgh, Suffolk.

29. The Apostles with the Creed, Weston Longville, Norfolk.

31. St James the Great and St John, Mattishall –
"Who was conceived by the Holy Ghost, Born of
the Virgin Mary".

30. Apostle from a Creed window, Bale,
Norfolk.

32 (facing page, above). The spandrel carvings to the St James and St John panel at Mattishall portray the
moment of Christ's conception, the Annunciation.

33 (facing page, below). The Four Latin Doctors at Cawston: note that Pope Gregory's papal tiara (left) has
been scraped out, probably in Henry VIII's reign.

34. Seven-Sacrament fonts: Baptism, Westhall, Suffolk.

35 (below left). Seven-Sacrament fonts: Matrimony, Little Walsingham, Norfolk.

36 (below right). Seven-Sacrament fonts: Eucharist, Little Walsingham, Norfolk.

CHAPTER 2

HOW THE PLOWMAN LEARNED HIS PATERNOSTER

Priests, People, and Catechesis

Round the fourteenth-century font in the parish church of Bradley, Lincolnshire, is carved an English inscription, which runs

> Pater Noster, Ave Maria, Criede,
> Leren the childe yt is nede.

That injunction was directed to the godparents and was a formal part of the rite of baptism in late medieval England. Just before the blessing of the font at baptisms the priest was required to admonish the godparents to see that the child's parents kept it from fire, water, and other perils, and themselves to "lerne or se yt be lerned the Pater noster, Aue Maria and Credo after the law of all holy churche".[1] The Lord's Prayer, Hail Mary, and Apostles' Creed were in fact the irreducible core of a more elaborate catechetical programme for the laity which had been decisively formulated for the English Church at Archbishop Pecham's provincial Council of Lambeth in 1281. The Council drew up a schema of instruction for the laity, *De informacione simplicium*, better known by its opening words *Ignorantia Sacerdotum*, which was to be expounded in the vernacular to parishioners four times in the year. This scheme was structured round the Creed, the Ten Commandments and Christ's summary of these in the dual precept to love God and neighbour, the seven works of mercy, the seven virtues, the seven vices, and the seven sacraments, and was intended to provide a comprehensive guide to Christian belief and practice.

The *Ignorantia Sacerdotum* was to prove an immensely influential and long-lived schema. Adapted and translated into verse for the Northern Province at the command of Archbishop Thoresby in

---

[1] F. Bond, *Fonts and Font Covers*, 1908, p. 113; *Manuale ad Usum Percelebris Ecclesie Sarisburiensis*, ed. A. Jefferies Collins, Henry Bradshaw Society, XCI, 1960 (hereafter = *Manuale*) p. 32.

1357 as the so-called *Lay Folk's Catechism*, with an indulgence of
forty days attached to it for all who learned it or taught it to others,
it was imitated or directly used in dioceses all over England up to
the Reformation. John Stafford, Bishop of Bath and Wells from
1425, had it translated into English and placed in every church in
his diocese, instructing his archdeacons to provide copies to all the
clergy at a cost of not more than six pence. It was reissued by
Archbishop Neville in the Northern Province after 1465, and again
by Cardinal Wolsey in 1518.[2]

The educational priorities promoted by English bishops from the
late thirteenth century onwards were intimately linked to a new
religious obligation imposed on lay people by the Fourth Lateran
Council in 1215, that of annual confession to their parish priests.
In principle, this ruling put into the hands of the parish clergy an
immensely valuable pastoral and educational tool, for the priest
in confession could explore not only the moral condition of his
parishioners, but also their knowledge of Catholic faith and practice.
Confessors were to examine each penitent in the articles of the
Creed and on their ability to recite the Lord's Prayer. But the
obligation of annual confession placed enormous demands on both
confessor and penitent. The penitent needed to know how, what,
and when to confess, the priest needed to be able to distinguish
between what was serious and what trivial, to impose the appropriate penances, and to apply the best remedies for his parishioners'
spiritual ailments. Theologians and bishops alike were realistic
about the extent to which the average priest could be expected to
rise to this challenge,[3] but a whole literature emerged to help equip
curates to discharge their responsibilities, of which the best-known
was probably William of Pagula's *Oculus Sacerdotis*, produced in
the early fourteenth century.[4] The *Oculus* was divided into three
sections. The first was a manual for confessors, teaching the priest
how to hear confessions, in particular how to interrogate a penitent
using the seven deadly sins as a framework. It had a series of
particular interrogations for different states of life and types of

---

[2] W. A. Pantin, *The English Church in the Fourteenth Century*, 1955, reprinted 1980,
pp. 189–95, 211–12; Roy M. Haines, *Ecclesia Anglicana: Studies in the English Church of the
Later Middle Ages*, 1989, pp. 129–37; P. Hodgson, "Ignorantia Sacerdotum: a Fifteenth-
century Discourse on the Lambeth Constitutions", *Review of English Studies*, XXIV, 1948,
pp. 1–11.

[3] Leonard Boyle, *Pastoral Care, Clerical Education and Canon Law*, 1981, pp. 19–32.

[4] On the literature see Pantin, op. cit.; T. F. Tentler, *Sin and Confession on the Eve of the
Reformation*, 1977; R. M. Ball, "The Education of the English parish Clergy in the Later
Middle Ages with Particular reference to the Manuals of Instruction", Cambridge PhD thesis
1976; H. G. Pfander, "Some Medieval Manuals of Religious Instruction in England and
Observations on Chaucer's Parson's Tale", *Journal of English and Germanic Philology*, XXXV,
1936, pp. 243–58.

person, such as drunkards or those who are wrathful. This section also provided the priest with canonical information about sins whose absolution was reserved to bishop or pope, and about the different ways in which excommunication might be incurred. The second part of the *Oculus* provided a programme of instruction for lay people in essential religious knowledge, such as how to baptize babies in case of emergency, the age at which children should be confirmed, and questions of sexual and social morality, as well as doctrinal knowledge. As in the *Ignorantia Sacerdotum*, the doctrinal section followed the pattern of the Creed, the seven sacraments, seven works of mercy, seven virtues, Ten Commandments of the law and two of the Gospel, and the seven sins, these latter elaborately treated. All this the priest was to explain regularly to his people in English. This section concluded with material on remedies against sins, how to deal with temptations, and a final devotional passage, taken from James of Milan's *Stimulus Amoris*, on Christ and his wounds as the refuge of sinners, which moved the whole exercise away from the merely canonical towards a devotional context. The third and final part of the *Oculus* provided the priest with theological, canonical, and practical material on the sacraments and their administration.[5]

A large number of works of this sort, some derived from the *Oculus*, others independently composed, were in circulation in the fourteenth and fifteenth centuries. John Mirk's *Instructions for Parish Priests*, for example, was a short treatise in English verse derived from the *Oculus* and designed to help simple and unlearned priests to carry out their duties in pulpit, confessional, and at the deathbed.[6] It has been suggested that in the early fifteenth century there was a slackening in commitment to the improvement of the pastoral activities of the rank and file clergy, and that clerical manuals were acquired and used mostly by better educated urban clergy, more interested in the liturgical dimension of priestly work than in the confessional or the pulpit.[7] The evidence for this suggestion is equivocal and inconclusive, being largely dependent on surviving notes of provenance and the character of the annotations in some surviving manuscripts, and the astonishing abundance of catechetical and penitential material for the laity produced and used in fifteenth- and early sixteenth-century England suggests that this area of pastoral activity remained a high priority. Certainly the advent of printing at the end of the fifteenth century saw the publication

[5] L. Boyle, "The *Oculus Sacerdotis* and some other works of William of Pagula", *Transactions of the Royal Historical Society*, 5th series V, 1955, pp. 81–110.

[6] *Instructions for Parish Priests by John Myrc*, ed. E. Peacock, EETS, 1868.

[7] Ball, "Education", p. 363.

of a whole range of manuals designed to assist parish clergy in their pastoral work, notably the eminently practical and simple fourteenth-century manual, the *Manipulus Curatorum*, with its emphasis on the practical skills of the priest and its insistence, like that of Mirk, that the priest should know the scriptures. The *Manipulus* was first printed in England in 1498, and went through at least nine editions before the Edwardine Reformation made it obsolete.[8]

The *Manipulus* was in Latin, but there was also a series of vernacular treatises in print at the end of the fifteenth century, in addition to Mirk's perennially popular work. Caxton translated a French pastoral manual, the *Doctrinal of Sapyence*, in 1489, for "symple prestes that understande not the scriptures" to "lerne and teche to theyre paryshens", which had an indulgence of twenty days attached to it for anyone who read a portion of it to another. Caxton clearly envisaged that lay people might also read the *Doctrinal* and produced two editions, one containing and one omitting material on the mishaps that can occur during the celebration of Mass, "by cause it is not conyenyent ne aparteynyng that every layman sholde knowe it".[9] There were a number of vernacular pastoral manuals printed at about this time, mostly translated from French originals and principally designed for confessors, catechists, and preachers, but also aimed at a literate lay audience, for example, the *Ordynarye of Crysten Men* (1502) and the *Floure of the Commandements* (1510). Production of specifically clerical treatises, following the same basic pattern and designed to help priests hear confessions and expound the duties of the faith and the doctrine of the sacraments, went on right up to the break with Rome. In 1531 Wynkyn de Worde published an edition of the *Stella Clericorum*, first produced in France in the 1490s and devoted to the dignity and obligations of priesthood. In 1534 Thomas Godfray reissued an English version of the *Exonoratorium Curatorum*, a practical work modelled on Pecham's *Ignorantia Sacerdotum*. As late as 1542 Thomas Petyt produced an edition of the *Cura Clericalis*, which had had its first printing in England as recently as 1532, but whose instructions about pilgrimages and indulgences were by 1542 effectively illegal.[10]

---

[8] *Manipulus Curatorum*, R. Pynson 1508, RSTC 12474.

[9] *The Doctrinal of Sapyence*, W. Caxton 1489, RSTC 21431; George D. Painter, *William Caxton*, 1976, p. 170.

[10] *Here foloweth a notable treatyse . . . named the Ordynarye of crystyanyte or of crysten men*, Wynkyn de Worde 1502, RSTC 5198; *The floure of the commaundementes of god with many examples and authorytees . . . the whiche is moche utyle and prouffytable unto all people*, W. de Worde 1510, RSTC 23876; *Stella Clericorum*, W. de Worde 1531, RSTC 23244 – first published in England in 1497 and again 1503 by Pynson; *Exonoratorium Curatorum*, T. Godfray 1534 (?) RSTC 10634 – the first English edition is thought to have been in 1516; *Cura Clericalis*, Thomas Petyt 1542, RSTC 6128.

The *Cura Clericalis*, reflecting the received wisdom on the subject, defined four roles for the priest. He was to be a celebrant of Masses, and so needed to understand the basic texts and be able to pronounce the Latin grammatically and clearly. He must be a minister of the other sacraments and so needed to know what and how many they were, to grasp the essential matter of the sacrament and be able to distinguish it from the peripheral features, and to know the proper mode of administration. He was to be a confessor, and so must be able above all to distinguish venial from deadly sin – "inter lepram et non lepram". Finally he was to be "plebis doctor", the teacher of his people, able to instruct them in the articles of the faith and the other precepts of God.[11]

It will be noticed that preaching is not given a high priority in this list, or rather it is assimilated to catechesis, instructing the people in the precepts of God. Fifteenth- and early sixteenth-century lay people were enthusiastic sermon-goers, where preaching was to be had, and Margery Kempe records "how fast the pepyl cam rennyng to heryn the sermown" when a notable preacher came to King's Lynn, but this very fact suggests that it was something of an event. Preachers themselves could be sceptical of the motivation of those who flocked to hear them, and dubious about the value of the growth in choice of preachers:

> These days mochyl folk wyl nowt lowyn hem to syttyn doun at the sermoun, ne welyn heryn it with meek herte, but thei welyn stondun that they moun redely gon awey yif the prechour plese hem nout. Summe comuyn obstinat in here synne . . . Summe comyn only to heryn coyouste and newe thyngis . . . Summe comyn only to be seyn. Some comyn only for the maner and for non devocion ne for no profyght of here soule and swyche fallyn sone on slepe.[12]

Mirk expected that parish priests would expound the essentials of the faith and the meaning of the major feasts on Sundays, and his *Festial* was designed to provide simple priests with material for these short Sunday homilies. It is difficult to be sure just how widespread Sunday preaching was: over two hundred pre-Reformation pulpits survive in England, most of them from the fifteenth century, a remarkable number which does suggest a growth in the perceived importance of preaching as part of parochial life. It is true that pulpits had a variety of uses, and parish priests almost certainly used them more regularly for "bidding the bedes" at the parish Mass than for preaching, but inscriptions and paintings on

---

[11] *Cura Clericalis*, sig. a ii.
[12] *Book of Margery Kempe*, p. 149; Anne Hudson, "The Sermons of MS Longleat 4", *Medium Aevum*, LIII, 1984, p. 223.

some pulpits do suggest that pulpits in general were seen primarily as platforms for teaching, not for prayer. The practice of painting or carving the Four Latin Doctors on the panels or posts of the pulpit, as at Castle Acre (Pl. 17) or Burnham Norton in Norfolk, or the reference to John the Baptist, the archetypal preacher, on the pulpit at South Burlingham (Pl. 18) – "Inter natos mulierum non surrexit major Johanne Baptista" – certainly suggest this.[13]

At any rate, everyone agreed that the average parish priest was by and large ill-equipped for preaching, hence the production of Mirk's *Festial*. Most treatises for priests concentrated on the final two functions listed in the *Cura Clericalis*, the priest as confessor and as "plebis doctor", since these were held to be intimately related. It was assumed that the priest would have to help the majority of his parishioners to make a full and coherent confession, since most would be unlettered folk. So the priest, especially when dealing with the young "or other symple persones and rude", was instructed to work through the Ten Commandments, the seven sins, the corporal works of mercy, the five bodily senses, asking the parishioner whether they had fulfilled the commandments, committed the sins, carried out the works, and so on. This served simultaneously to elicit confession of the penitent's particular sins and to instruct them in the practice of the faith, but the *Ordynarye of Crysten men* warned the priest to be careful here, since simple people, overawed by the occasion, tended to answer "yes syre unto that / that a man them demandeth be it trouth or lesynge."[14]

Manuals, printed or manuscript, produced by experts for the instruction of parish clergy, tell us the theory of the confessional. A remarkable fifteenth-century manuscript at St John's College, Cambridge, allows us to see something of the actuality in practice. This manuscript is a compilation, assembled by at least two different priests and with a considerable amount of consequent overlapping, of practical material to assist them in the shriving pew (Pl. 19). Carvings of confession on several of the East Anglian Seven-Sacrament fonts, like those at Gresham and Alderford in Norfolk, show priests' handbooks of this sort actually in use.[15] The St John's collection includes exhortations to penitents to encourage them to a full and true confession, different formulae of absolution

---

[13] G. R. Owst, *Preaching in Medieval England*, 1926; T. Harjunpaa, *Preaching in England During the Later Middle Ages*, Acta Academiae Aboensis, Ser. A, XXIX no. 4, 1965; J. C. Cox and A. Harvey, *English Church Furniture*, 1908, pp. 148–50; M. D. Anderson, *The Imagery of British Churches*, 1955, pp. 42–3.

[14] *Ordynarye*, sig. S iii (v): on the didactic roll of the confessor see V. Gillespie, "Doctrina et predicatio: the Design and Function of Some Pastoral Manuals", *Leeds Studies in English*, ns XI, 1980, pp. 36–50.

[15] St John's College, Cambridge, MS S 35.

and reassurance, prayers for repentance and forgiveness, verses from the Psalms, theological notes on contrition, confession, and satisfaction, procedure to be followed in absolving the dying, including forms of absolution for use with those who possess bulls of indulgence, and prescribed remedies against the sins. The main body of the collection, however, consists of a systematic set of inquisitions for use by the priest in confession, structured round the seven deadly sins, the Ten Commandments, and the five bodily wits. After the inquisitions comes a section of instruction on the cardinal and theological virtues, with an exposition of 1 Corinthians 13 as a practical treatise on charity, the beatitudes, the seven gifts of the Holy Ghost, and a series of queries about the sins of people in particular states of life – merchants, artificers, magistrates, house-wives, and so on. In the section of inquiries about the deadly sins which forms the principal part of the compilation, the main text on each sin has a line drawn under it, below which the first compiler has jotted down a series of one-word headings which serve as a summary of the longer text and an *aide-mémoire* to himself in the course of hearing a confession. It is unmistakably a working book designed to help the owners to carry out their duties thoroughly and sympathetically.

The tone of the collection, and something of the social realities to which it was addressed, can be gathered from the enquiries about the sin of envy:

> Have ye hadde anie envie to your neighbores or to your even cristen and be glad of here harmes and of here evel fare and loth of here good, or of the adversite or desese that hath falle to hem and be sorie or hevie of here prosperite or welfare . . . and of here good name and good fame. Have ye backbited and dispreised your even cristen or tolde evill tales of hem to a pewn [?] here good name or wolde not heere noo good spoke of hem bi your wille but lette it or stopped it as much as ye might. Also sterid or procured other to hate hem . . . Also when ye have mette hem that ye hatith or hadde [anger] to: have ye made hem good chere and feire face withoute forthe and hatid hem with yn forth. And saide worse bi hinde him thene ye wolde avowe afore him for hatrade and envie that ye hadde to him.[16]

This is entirely standard material, closely resembling, for example, the equivalent section of Mirk's *Instructions for Parish Priests*. So, as in Mirk, or even in the confession of the deadly sins in Langland's *Piers Plowman*, the sin of sloth is treated largely in terms of failure to fulfil religious duties: "Have ye be slowe to lerne your be leve

[16] St John's MS S 35.

and the comanndmentes and the lawe of God and to teche it to them that beth under your governaunce . . . to come to chirche to here dyvine service and prechinge of the worde of god and to worship your lorde god of heven."[17] The significance of the St John's manuscript is not in any originality it contains, but in the evidence it provides of the actual employment of the theories and advice of the textbooks by working priests in their day-to-day practice.

Confession following the pattern prescribed in the textbooks or even the St John's compilation could have been a lengthy and harrowing business. In practice it must usually have been much abbreviated, for confessors were sensibly advised to save their close enquiries for the sins particular people were likely to have committed – "as unto the people of the chirche of symonye . . . unto yonge people of temptacyons carnalles".[18] Most people in most parishes confessed once a year, in Lent, and as often as not delayed coming till Holy Week. In any community with more than a hundred or so "houselling folk" a systematic confession of the sort envisaged by the manuals would have occupied the priest and his people for most of Lent. Pious and leisured lay people with spiritual guides were by the later fifteenth century confessing more regularly, using the confessional as a form of spiritual direction. There was a growing literature of penitence and compunction designed to help lay people to use confession in this way. But we should not take the devout introspection of a Lady Margaret or the scrupulous anxieties of a Luther as our model of what a late medieval confession entailed. For the majority of parishioners it remained a less subjective exercise, a time for practical reassessment, reconciliation with neighbours, and settling of spiritual accounts. It was, moreover, an exercise carried out with queues of waiting fellow-parishioners looming close behind, the mutter of their rosaries or their chatter plainly audible (Pl. 20). Pastoral realism therefore demanded that the confession be kept within manageable dimensions; in a time-honoured formula the penitent was to be brief, be brutal, be gone.[19]

---

[17] Cf. Mirk's *Instructions for Parish Priests*, pp. 37–8: *Piers Plowman* B Text, Passus 5 lines 392–461.

[18] *Ordynarye*, sig. S iii (v).

[19] Professor Ann Nichols, whose forthcoming book, *Seeable Signs*, explores the iconography, theology, and history of the Seven-Sacrament fonts, tells me that waiting penitents queue up in one-third (thirteen) of the confession panels on the fonts. Given the space available to the sculptor on the panel, the queue is usually made up of one or two people, but there are four at Nettlecombe. For discussion of the conditions in which late medieval confession was heard see L. G. Duggan, "Fear and Confession on the Eve of the Reformation", *Archiv für Reformationsgeschichte*, LXXV, 1984, pp. 153–75; A. E. Nicholls, "The Etiquette of Pre-Reformation Confession in East Anglia", *Sixteenth Century Journal*, XVII, 1986, pp. 145–63.

And quite apart from pastoral realism, many clergy were slap-dash or negligent. The jest-book *A Hundred Merry Tales* has a joke about a priest hearing confessions on Ash Wednesday with a massive hangover as a result of Shrove Tuesday junketing. He falls asleep in the midst of one woman's confession that she had stolen a pot, and in disgust she gets up and goes away. The next woman in the queue kneels down and begins with the conventional opening request for blessing. "Benedicite", at which the priest wakes confused and exclaims, "What, art thou now at 'benedicite' again! Tell me what didst thou when thou hadst stolen the pot."[20]

Nevertheless, it is clear that the framework of sins, commandments, works of mercy, and bodily wits did form the basis not only of clerical enquiry in the majority of confessions but of lay examination of conscience in preparation for confession. The brief English "Form of Confession" provided in some of the most popular primers of the 1520s and 1530s follows this form, taking the penitent through a check-list of the seven deadly sins, the Ten Commandments, the five wits, the seven works of mercy both corporal and spiritual, the seven gifts of the Holy Ghost, the seven sacraments and the eight beatitudes.[21] When in February 1536 John Stanton, a Protestant *agent provocateur*, denounced his confessor to Cromwell for papalist views revealed in the course of confession, his report revealed the traditional framework in operation:

First the said John Stanton said Benedicite, and the priest said Dominus. And then the said John said Confiteor, and afterwards rehearsed the seven deadly sins particularly, and then the misspending of his five wits. And then the priest said, Have you not sinned in not doing the five [*sic*] works of mercy? The said John said, Yea, forsooth, for the which and all other I cry God mercy and beseech you, my ghostly father, of forgiveness, and give me penance of my sins.[22]

Confessional practice and the catechetical and preaching programme of the English Church in the fifteenth century were closely linked: expositions of the Lord's Prayer by the parish clergy, for example, normally presented the seven petitions of the prayer as remedies against the deadly sins, and related them to the three theological and four cardinal virtues.[23] To assist and supplement the efforts of the parish clergy there evolved a massive and growing literature

[20] *A Hundred Merry Tales*, p. 139.
[21] E. Hoskins, *Horae Beatae Mariae Virginis, or, Sarum and York primers with Kindred Books and Primers of the Reformed Roman Use*, 1901 (hereafter = Hoskins) p. 133.
[22] G. Elton, *Policy and Police: The Enforcement of the Reformation in the Age of Thomas Cromwell*, 1972, p. 28.
[23] *Festial*, pp. 282–8; *Middle English Sermons edited from British Museum MS Royal 18 B xxiii*, ed. W. O. Ross, EETS, 1940, pp. 46–59.

in English designed to instruct and edify the laity and to provide
the simple clergy with material for their preaching and teaching.
Some of this material, such as the publications of John Mirk, was
by working parish priests. Some was directly commissioned or
inspired by the bishops, like Nicholas Love's immensely popular
translation of the *Meditationes Vitae Christi* usually attributed to
Bonaventura, the *Mirrour of the Blessed Lyfe of Jesu*. But much was
the product of private initiative or the activities of religious orders
such as the Brigittines of Syon or the Carthusians of Sheen or
Mount Grace, not directly involved in pastoral work. Though
almost entirely the work of clerics, the growth of an English
theological literature in this period "was largely unofficial, informal,
and supererogatory"[24] both promoting and responding to a
growing lay demand for religious instruction and edification. This
vernacular literature was also enormously varied. Compilations like
the *Poor Caitiff*, a series of didactic and devotional treatises aimed at
the growing number of devout literate lay folk, or *Dives and Pauper*,
a systematic exposition of the Commandments probably intended
to assist clergy in preaching and confession, relate very closely
to the catechetical aims of the clergy, though the *Poor Caitiff*
incorporates much devotional material and is heavily influenced by
Richard Rolle and his school.[25]

As all this suggests, the original modest aims of the thirteenth-
century Church, to equip the laity with basic prayers, the means of
examining their consciences, and the bare essentials of belief, had
expanded by the fifteenth century. Meditation on the Passion or the
life of Christ, affective devotion to his sufferings, to the Sacrament,
or to the saints, the recognition of a desire for a more structured
and elaborate prayer-life, had all been accepted by the early fifteenth
century as legitimate for lay people as well as for religious, and a
literature emerged to cater for it. The career of Margery Kempe
reveals the extraordinary accessibility of the devotional classics of
the period to a bourgeois laywoman, and the range of clerical and
religious guidance she could draw on, from parochial or monastic

[24] A. I. Doyle, "A Survey of the Origins and Circulation of Theological Writings in
English in the 14th, 15th and early 16th centuries", Cambridge PhD thesis, 1953, p. 283;
M. G. Sargent, "The Transmission by the English Carthusians of some Late Medieval
Spiritual Writings", *Journal of Ecclesiastical History*, XXVII, 1976, pp. 225–40; J. Hogg,
"Mount Grace Charterhouse and Late Medieval English Spirituality", *Analecta Cartusiana*,
LXXXII/2, 1983, pp. 1–43.
[25] M. Aston, "Devotional Literacy" in *Lollards and Reformers*, 1984, pp. 101–33; H. G.
Pfander, "Some Medieval Manuals of Religious Instruction", *Journal of English and Germanic
Philology*, XXXV, 1936, pp. 243–58; G. H. Russell, "Vernacular Instruction of the Laity in
the Late Middle Ages in England", *Journal of Religious History*, II, 1962, pp. 98–119; M. T.
Brady, "*The Poor Caitiff*: an Introductory study", *Traditio*, X, 1954, pp. 529–48; for a survey
and listing of surviving catechetical manuscripts see P. S. Joliffe, *A Check-List of Middle
English Prose Writings of Spiritual Guidance*, 1974.

clergy willing to read and expound the works of Rolle, Hilton, or Nicholas Love, or the lives and writings of modern saints like Christina of Markyate or Bridget of Sweden to serve as role models and exemplars, to expert spiritual guides like the parish priest Richard of Caister or the anchorite Julian of Norwich, willing and able to advise her on her own spiritual development.[26] Margery was a formidably determined woman with some means, living in what was possibly the most religiously privileged part of early fifteenth-century England, for the towns of East Anglia had far more in the way of religious resources than the scattered communities of Derbyshire, Cumberland, or Wales. The religious horizons of villagers in remote areas probably remained fairly constricted even late into the century, but in Yorkshire, the East Midlands, East Anglia, the South-east, and many parts of the West Country, a common and extremely rich religious culture for the laity and secular clergy had emerged by the fifteenth century, which far exceeded the modest expectations of Pecham and the thirteenth-century bishops who devised the catechetical strategies of the medieval English Church.[27]

The Impact of Catechesis: Imagery and Dramatic Evidence

The ubiquity of the catechetical preoccupations of the late medieval Church in the imaginative world of the laity is testified to in a range of types of evidence. From the late fourteenth century onwards wall-paintings illustrating the moral framework of the teaching of the confessional manuals abound. A particularly well-preserved one at Trotton in Sussex shows Christ in judgement, enthroned on the rainbow. Below him stands Moses, holding the tables of the Commandments. To Christ's left stands the figure of a man surrounded by circular medallions in which are portrayed the seven corporal works of mercy. On Christ's right is a gigantic naked figure, from whose body dragons emerge: in their gaping jaws small human figures enact the seven deadly sins. The painting would have provided the fifteenth-century parishioners of Trotton with a pictorial rendering of a standard examination of conscience.[28] Paintings of this sort were extremely common in the late fourteenth and early fifteenth centuries. As windows became larger and wall-space smaller, such representations were shifted into the

---

[26] C. M. Atkinson, *Mystic and Pilgrim: the Book and the World of Margery Kempe*, 1983.

[27] For a good account of its development in northern England, which probably over-emphasizes its regional distinctiveness, see Jonathan Hughes, *Pastors and Visionaries*, 1988, esp. pp. 127–73.

[28] M. D. Anderson, *History and Imagery in British Churches*, 1971, pp. 145–6 and plate 46.

painted glass. The works of mercy in particular were increasingly represented in the painted windows paid for by prosperous merchants or yeomen in the hundred years before the Reformation (Pl. 21). At Lamas in Norfolk the north window had a picture of the Doom, with Christ uttering the words of the Matthean parable: "Venite Benedicti", "Ite Maledicti". In the other panels of the window the works of mercy were represented, with the cry of the poor answered by the charity of the donor: "For hunger gredy – Thee to fede, lo me nogh reedy, Hostel I crave – Come wery in and you shal have." Parts of a similar window survive at Combs in Suffolk (Pl. 22–3).[29]

At Blythburgh visiting the sick is carved on a bench-end, the bedridden man turning hands of supplication upwards, while on the bench behind him a prisoner in the stocks implores help with the same gesture (Pl 24–5). The vices were also carved: at Wigginhall St German Lust is represented by a man and woman embracing, Avarice clutches his money-bags, while Gluttony pours wine from a bottle into a cup (Pl. 26–7). At Thornham Sloth dozes over his rosary. At Blythburgh Gluttony hugs a distended paunch, while Pride is a hypocritical devotee (Pl. 28), pretending to pray while actually peering over devoutly poised hands to see who is taking notice, a direct borrowing from the standard treatments of Pride in the confessional textbooks: "Have ye synned in ypocrisie and schewid you holier and better owte warde than ye were inwarde. And desired to be holde holie or good . . . have ye doo your almes or maide your prioures . . . or do the other goode dedis openlie that thei schulde be knowen."[30]

Other aspects of the catechetical programme were also presented visually. The twelve articles of the Apostles' Creed were conventionally attributed to the twelve Apostles, Peter having composed the first article "Credo in Deum, Patrem Omnipotentem", Andrew the second, "et in Iesum Christum", and so on. Portrayals of the twelve Apostles, each carrying a banner or a scroll on which the relevant article of the Creed is inscribed, became extremely common in windows and on the dados of Rood-screens in fifteenth-century England. They were also portrayed in alabaster altar-pieces and they can be found on the west front of Wells Cathedral. A complete Creed window survives at Drayton Beauchamp in Buckinghamshire,

[29] Blomefield, *Norfolk*, VI, pp. 291–2. There is discussion of this and related windows in C. Woodforde, *The Norwich School of Glass-Painting*, 1950, pp. 192–6. The best surviving examples are at All Saints, North Street, York (which contains only the six works mentioned in Matthew 25, omitting the burial of the dead, which was derived from the Book of Tobit). The remains of another fine set are at Combs in Suffolk.

[30] St John's College, Cambridge, MS S 35.

and Rood-screens with the Creed survive at Gooderstone, Ringland, Mattishall, Thetford, and Weston Longville, all in Norfolk (Pl. 29–30). At Mattishall the didactic purpose of the paintings with their texts was elaborated by the carver who framed the paintings within the screen. The clause of the Creed associated with the Apostle James the Great is "who was conceived by the Holy Ghost, born of the Virgin Mary" (Pl. 31). In the spandrels above the painting of St James with this text the carver has set the biblical scene of the Annunciation by Gabriel to Mary, thereby providing the parishioners with a portrayal of the moment at which the conception took place (Pl. 32).[31] In general, the emergence of the common arrangement on East Anglian Rood-screens in which the dado was occupied by the Apostles, with or without their clauses of the Creed, and the doors or pulpit by the Four Latin Doctors, Ambrose, Augustine, Gregory, and Jerome, symbols of the Church's teaching, suggests a heightened awareness of the importance of preaching and catechesis in parishes in the second half of the century (Pl. 33).[32]

One of the most remarkable manifestations of the impact of the Church's catechetical concerns on the laity is the collection of forty or so octagonal baptismal fonts, the majority of them in Norfolk and Suffolk, which portray the Seven Sacraments around the bowl. These fonts date from the three generations before the Reformation. One of the earliest is at East Dereham, acquired in 1468, and the last, at Walsoken, was made ten years after the break with Rome, in 1544. Many, perhaps most, of these fonts are the result of lay benefactions to the parish church, and in some cases the donors are known, as at Blythburgh, where John Mason and his wife are commemorated on the top step of the font pedestal. The choice of subject-matter on the fonts must at the very least have met with the approval of the donors and the rest of the parish.

The fonts are common in areas where Lollardy had been particularly strong in the generation prior to their appearance, as at Martham in Norfolk, the home of the redoubtable Margery Baxter, and it has been plausibly suggested by Professor Ann Nichols, the leading authority on the subject, that they represent a considered response to the Lollard attack on the sacramental teaching of the Church, and mark the understanding and acceptance of that

---

[31] There is an account and listing of the Apostles with their clauses in M. R. James, *Suffolk and Norfolk*, 1930 reprinted 1987, pp. 215–19.

[32] F. Cheetham, *English Medieval Alabasters*, 1984, p. 69. The Apostles and Doctors are found together at Salle and Cawston, Gooderstone and Castle Acre (where the doctors are on the pulpit, as at Burnham Norton). It is likely that they occupied the doors (now mostly vanished) in many other Apostle screens.

teaching by the most influential laity of East Anglia.[33] Certainly the iconography of the sacraments on the fonts is extraordinarily precise and "correct". In many continental and some English representations of the sacraments in other media they are represented by some peripheral part of the ritual, such as the anointings in baptism, or the handing over of the chalice in ordination, the tying of the chrisom-cloth in confirmation, or the blessing of the ring in marriage. On these fonts, by contrast, the scene depicted is almost always that of the action held by the theologians to be constitutive of the sacrament – the sacring at Mass (Pl. 36, 40, 42), the actual immersion of the child in baptism (Pl. 34), the laying on of hands in ordination, the hand-fastening of bride and groom in the presence of witnesses in token of the vow which constitutes the sacrament of matrimony (Pl. 35). Often the priest or bishop in these panels has a book open before him, on which the key words of the ritual might be painted. The carvings therefore represent an extremely precise and full form of catechetical teaching, perhaps designed to counteract heresy. At any rate the very large number commissioned in the later fifteenth century bear witness to lay interest in and enthusiasm for the teachings they enshrine. After the Reformation, Protestant activists recognized in the iconography of these fonts a rallying point for Catholic belief and a means of propagating it, and attacked them accordingly.[34]

The Seven-Sacrament fonts represent an appropriation by the laity of the catechetical concerns of the clergy. A similar and even more emphatic appropriation is evident in another medium, drama. The Corpus Christi gild and the Pater Noster gild at York regularly mounted plays designed to teach the citizens the elements of the faith. The Pater Noster gild had been founded to present a play "setting forth the goodness of the Lord's Prayer . . . In which play all manner of vices were held up to scorn, and the virtues held up to praise".[35] The Creed play was designed to impart "instruction and information of the Christian faith" to the glory of God "and especially to the instruction of the people" and to teach the Creed "to the ignorant". It was in twelve pageants, each with a banner

[33] Till Professor Nichols's book appears, the essential works are A. C. Fryer, "On Fonts with representations of the Seven Sacraments", *Archaeological Journal*, LIX, 1902, pp. 17–66, LXXXVII, 1930, pp. 24–59, Supplement XC 1933, pp. 98–105; G. McN. Rushforth, "Seven Sacrament Compositions in English Art", *Antiquaries Journal*, IX, 1929, pp. 83–100; John Foxe, *The Acts and Monuments of John Foxe*, ed. G. Townsend and S. R. Cattley, 1837–41, iii pp. 594–6; there is a selection of images of the Sacraments in H. S. Kingsford, *Illustrations of the Occasional Offices of the Church in the Middle Ages*, Alcuin Club, XXIV, 1921.

[34] See below, chapter 17, "Elizabeth" pp. 582–3.

[35] Toulmin-Smith, *English Gilds*, p. 137; Meg Twycross, "Books for the Unlearned", *Themes in Drama*, V, 1983, pp. 65–110; Alexandra F. Johnston, "The Plays of the Religious Guilds of York: the Creed Play and the Pater Noster Play", *Speculum* L, 1975, pp. 55–90.

on which the relevant clause of the Creed was painted, and it frequently replaced the longer Corpus Christi cycle, which was also the Corpus Christi gild's responsibility. The articles of the Creed were probably illustrated with the relevant plays from the Corpus Christi cycle, the article on the forgiveness of sins, for example, by the play of the woman taken in adultery. The Pater Noster play was clearly linked, as it generally was in contemporary preaching, to the seven sins and the seven virtues, though petitions like "give us this day our daily bread," which will certainly have had a play illustrating Sloth, might also have borrowed the Last Supper play from the Corpus Christi cycle to represent the Eucharistic dimension of the petition often discussed in sermons and expositions of the prayer.[36]

Whatever their precise content, these plays clearly involved a massive corporate effort by the laity of York to foster knowledge of the elements of the faith. The Pater Noster play had originally been a private initiative, and the gild certificate described how the first performance had such an effect "that many said, 'Would that this play could be put on a permanent basis in this city for the good of souls and for the consolation of citizens and neighbours.'" The formation of the Pater Noster gild had been the result, but in the course of the fifteenth century the city itself took over responsibility for both of these cycles of plays, and the catechetical and devotional enterprise they represented became the responsibility of the citizens as a whole.[37]

Few communities could match this sort of commitment to the task of instruction and consolation, but religious plays everywhere were a fundamental means of transmitting religious instruction and stirring devotion. William Revetour, chaplain of St William's Ousebridge, York, who left the text of the Creed play to the Corpus Christi gild, along with other play-texts and properties, in 1446, also left a small library. This contained a number of pastoral and liturgical treatises, and a handful of works which reveal his catechetical preoccupations – a treatise on the Lord's Prayer and an illustrated table setting out its petitions and the related vices and virtues, a copy of the *Prick of Conscience*, a book of the Gospels, some saints' lives in English, and a book of sermons for Lent.[38] He was clearly actively engaged in teaching, and it is probably significant that he left his English books to lay friends, his Latin books to clerics. His involvement with the York plays was an entirely consistent extension of this activity.

[36] Johnston, "Plays of the Religious Guilds", pp. 70–80.
[37] Ibid. pp. 80, 87.
[38] Twycross, "Books for the Unlearned", pp. 65–6.

What was true of Revetour at York was also true more generally. The Tudor reader was meant to smile but not to sneer at the Warwickshire curate in *A Hundred Merry Tales* who, though "no great clerk nor graduate of the university", was wont to expound the Creed to his parish on a Sunday, and told them that "if you believe not me then for a more sure and sufficient authority, go your way to Coventry and there ye shall see them all played in Corpus Christi play."[39] Relatively few communities mounted an entire cycle of plays, of course, but the many miracle and saints' plays performed by gilds and other groups in the villages and towns of England into the 1560s served much the same function. The Croxton miracle play of the sacrament vividly combined orthodox sacramental instruction, a devotional set piece derived from the cult of the Image of Pity, and farcical elements borrowed from mumming plays into a highly effective piece of religious drama, possibly designed to consolidate orthodox lay repudiation of Lollardy.[40] The story of the old man quizzed in James I's reign about his knowledge of Jesus Christ who replied that he had certainly heard of him, for he had attended in his youth the Corpus Christi play at Kendal, where there was a man on a tree and the blood flowed down, is usually told to illustrate the religious ignorance of the peasantry in the early modern period. What it actually attests is the enormous didactic and imaginative effectiveness of the religious plays of the late Middle Ages: once seen, never forgotten. The old man's ignorance of other aspects of the faith is a tacit testimony to the disastrous effect of the suppression of the plays by the Protestant authorities from the mid-1560s onwards.[41]

The Impact of Literacy: Lay Didactic and Devotional Collections

But the crucial factor in the growth of a well-instructed laity in fifteenth-century England was the spread of literacy down the social scale, even to many women. We have already considered the impact of this development in connection with the multiplication of primers, but many other types of religious texts also circulated – didactic treatises on the virtues or vices, saints' lives, rhymed moral fables, accounts of visions or visits from or to the afterlife, and collections of prayers and devotions. Much of this material was originally intended for reading aloud to the laity by clerics, as was

[39] *A Hundred Merry Tales*, pp. 115–16.

[40] See below, chapter 3, "The Mass," pp. 106–8.

[41] Charles Jackson (ed.), "The Life of Master John Shaw" in *Yorkshire Diaries and Autobiographies in the Seventeenth and Eighteenth Centuries*, Surtees Society, LXV, 1877, pp. 138–9, quoted in I. Lancashire, *Dramatic Texts and Records of Great Britain*, 1984, p. 160.

the case with the long fourteenth-century didactic poem *Speculum Vitae*, designed to be read piecemeal to gatherings of unlettered lay people:

> And that for lewd men namely
> That can no maner of clergy
> to teche hem were most nede
> For clerkis can both se and rede
> In diverse bokis of holy writte
> How thei schuld liven if thei loke it . . .

Such pious reading brought religious instruction out of the church, into the household and the gildhall, and thereby into direct competition with secular entertainment, something the author of the *Speculum* felt bound to warn his listeners about.

> I warne yow first at the begynnyng
> I wil make no vayn spekyng
> Of dedis of armes ne of amours
> As done mynstrels and gestours
> that makyn spekyng in many place
> Of Octavyan and Isambrace
> and of many other gestis
> and namely when thei come to festis
> Ne of the life of Bevis of Hamtoun
> That was a knyght of grete renoun
> Ne of Gy of warwick . . . [42]

In fact many didactic poems, like Mannyng's *Handlyng Synne*, did mix entertainment with edification, by providing vivid and often amusing exempla as illustrations of their serious points. Moreover, as the number of laymen able to read grew in many communities and even in many households, so too did demand for reading-matter, and well-to-do households and larger bodies like gilds acquired collections of material which might include both entertainment and uplift, romances of Sir Isumbras or Bevis of Hampton alongside saints' lives and sermons. One such collection from the later fifteenth century has been preserved in the Cambridge University Library and was recently published in facsimile. Its editors consider that it provides "a good index to the religious and literary tastes and preoccupations of the bourgeoisie in the late fifteenth century", with religious and devotional material alongside items

---

[42] Quoted in Doyle, "A Survey". p. 78; there is no printed edition of the *Speculum* but its opening lines, including those quoted above, were edited by J. Ullmann in *Englische Studien*, VII, 1884, pp. 468–72.

stressing the "domestic virtues and practical wisdom", and "popular romances which are pious, lively and full of incidents and marvels". The collection is highly stereotyped, for many of the same items, in more or less the same order, are found in other devotional and didactic collections of the period. This was the conventional religion of the day, and its contents admirably illustrate the way in which the programme outlined by the Council of Lambeth in 1281 had been absorbed into lay religious consciousness.[43]

The collection opens with a series of texts in verse, most of which are paraphrases of the parts of scripture familiar to the laity from their inclusion in the primers – the nine lessons from Job included in the "Dirige"and the penitential Psalms, together with some long devotions addressed to God and the Virgin. There follow a series of much simpler and more accessible texts probably aimed at children and young people, and directly geared to catechizing: rhymed versions of the Ten Commandments, the corporal and spiritual works of mercy, the five bodily and five spiritual wits, the seven deadly sins and their contrary virtues, a prose exposition of the Creed from the *Merure de Seinte Eglise* of St Edmund Rich, and an account of the seven sacraments from the same source. Then comes a series of saints' lives, some in prose, taken from Mirk's *Festial*, a poem on the Assumption of Mary, and a verse life of St Katherine. After these comes a verse devotion to Christ's Wounds known as the "charter of Christ", a poem about the end of the world called "The xv tokenys before the day of dome", a popular subject much illustrated in woodcuts and windows and forming part of the material covered in the Chester play of Antichrist. After this comes a series of cautionary tales illustrating the benefits of being moral and the disadvantages of wickedness, whose titles tell all one needs to know about them: "how the goode man taght hys sone", "the Adulterous Falmouth Squire", "how a merchande dyd hys wyfe betray", "a gode mater of the marchand and hys sone". This part of the collection is interspersed with some affective poems on the sorrows of the Virgin, and a miraculous tale of a woman whose wavering faith in the Blessed Sacrament was miraculously confirmed. The collection concludes with a series of verse romances, several of which combine entertainment with edification – the Earl of Toulouse, Syr Eglamour, Syr Tryamoure, Octavian, Bevis, the Seven Sages of Rome, Guy of Warwick, Le Bone Florence of Rome, Robert of Sicely, and Sir Degare.

[43] F. McSparran and P. R. Robinson (eds), *Cambridge University Library MS Ff.2.38*, 1979. An analytical table of contents is on pp. xxi–xxv.

The preoccupations and concerns evident in this collection extended beyond the urban bourgeois for whom it was compiled. The title of one of its treatises, "How the goode man taght hys sone", was symptomatic of a general desire among the pious laity to further within one's own household or sphere of interest godliness and good learning. The Oxfordshire landowner and minor courtier, Peter Idley, who died in 1473, devoted a good deal of his leisure to the compilation of a series of verse "Instructions to his Son" which similarly encapsulate these concerns. The instructions are in two books, the first based on moral and homiletic material by Albertanus of Brescia, and dealing in general terms with the meaning of life, the values his son should have, the evils of poverty and the need for faith – much the same mixture of devotion with "domestic virtues and worldly wisdom" evident in the Cambridge manuscript. The second book is derived from Robert Manning of Brunne's *Handlyng Synne*. Idley left it unfinished, but like Manning's work it was intended to treat the Commandments, the sins, and the sacraments, diversified and enlivened by vivid and entertaining exempla.[44]

At the other end of the social scale, the commonplace book of the rural artisan and church-reeve, Robert Reynes of Acle, active in the last third of the fifteenth century, reveals many of the same concerns and convictions, but also something of the limitations and difficulties of the catechetical impulse at the time. Reynes, a reeve's son, was agent and man of business for the ecclesiastical lord of the manor of Acle, and was a man of some consequence in his own community, but he was clearly far less sophisticated and far less well educated than either Idley or the compilers of the Cambridge manuscript. He is as near as one is likely to get to the typical representative of the class of men who became churchwardens in the parishes of late fifteenth-century England, and his commonplace book is an invaluable indicator of their religious concerns.[45] It is much more varied than either of the other collections we have been considering. This is in part because it contains a good deal of secular material, reflecting Reynes's own daily activities – notes on the assize of bread, on fires in Norwich and Acle, family dates, notes on manorial court procedures, Latin proverbs of a generally pessimistic and moralizing kind, a coded instruction about the location of a silver cup, lists of major events in world history, the principal battles in the Wars of the Roses, memoranda on taxes, markets, and assorted contracts and legal formularies. The religious

[44] Charlotte D'Evelyn (ed.), *Peter Idley's Instructions to his Son*, 1935.
[45] Robert Reynes, *The Commonplace Book of Robert Reynes of Acle*, ed. C. Louis, 1980.

items, which form the largest part of the book, are similarly varied, and elements representing the central didactic aims of the fifteenth-century Church jostle charms and other items which the upper clergy and the catechists might well have disapproved of.

Much in the book reflects Reynes's activities as parishioner and churchwarden: notes of church repairs, the purchase of vestments, details of the Peter's Pence tax in Acle and obituaries of rectors of the parish, a rhyme to be attached to a rosary placed in the parish church for the use of those who had forgotten to bring their own, encouraging them to gain the indulgences attached to recitation of the rosary against the day of doom, parts of the scripts or epilogues to pageants and plays organized for church funds. There are lists of fasting days and saints' days, and a "Cisio-Janus", designed to help Reynes memorize the major feasts in the calendar. The longest set of items consists of material connected with the cult of St Anne, including a verse life of Anne for reading at the patronal feast of a local gild, of which Reynes was probably an officer.[46]

The devotional fashions of the late fifteenth century have also left their trace in Reynes's book – a rhymed devotion on the number of the drops of Christ's blood, an account of the shrine images at Walsingham, which Reynes must certainly have visited, a moralistic poem on the transience of life and the evils of the world, the need for virtue in the three estates, and an appeal for mercy to Christ. There are a number of other poems of a pessimistic character on the brevity of life and the need to prepare for death by receiving the sacraments. Reynes included a long version of the legend of the "woman solitary and recluse" often prefaced to the "Fifteen Oes", the Passion prayers attributed to St Bridget, but he does not give the prayers themselves, though doubtless he had a respectable copy of the prayers in his primer or elsewhere, lacking the legend with its colourful tale of the defeat of demons and the efficacy of the "Oes" in freeing souls from Purgatory. He also had an incomplete version of the popular poem on the fifteen tokens of the day of doom: he copied the final sections, which treat of the appearance of Christ in judgement, where the major emphasis in Christ's speech is on those who have done no merciful deeds and those who have wounded him by swearing. This was a frequent theme of preaching in the period, often illustrated in wall-paintings and glass, in which Christ's bleeding and dismembered body is surrounded by the figures of people who have sworn by the afflicted part. This moralistic material reflects the preaching and catechetical concerns of the period, and so it is not surprising to find alongside it a series

---

[46] P. Meredith (ed.), *The Mary Play*, pp. 9–12.

of mnemonic texts designed to inculcate the fundamentals as set
out in Pecham's schema – brief summaries, in both English and
Latin, of the Ten Commandments, the seven sins, the works of
mercy, the virtues, the sacraments, including notes on which of
the sacraments were repeatable and which could be received only
once.[47]

Reynes, then, was certainly affected by the Church's official
programme of catechesis. But there is some indication that the
process may have been fairly elementary in his case. Standard
treatments of the Commandments in the confessional manuals and
catechetical textbooks consistently warned against the use of charms
and against divination, but Reynes's commonplace book is rich in
evidence of his use of both. Most of the charms would probably
have passed muster with the parish clergy – a prayer charm to
St Apollonia against the toothache, an invocation of Christ, the
Apostles, prophets, angels and saints against fever, a narrative charm
in the form of a conversation between Christ and St Peter against
malaria. But he also collected zodiacal material and prognostications
which were certainly widely disapproved of by the clergy, and one
of the odder items in the book is an elaborate formula for conjuring
angels, for purposes of divination, into a child's thumbnail. This
was evidently a widespread practice, but it is explicitly condemned
by Idley, in his *Instructions to his Son*

> Allso if in ony swerde or in a basen
> Or in a thombe or in a cristall
> Thow made ony childe to loke therein –
> Wichcraft men cleped this all.
> Beware of this, it woll have a fall.[48]

Reynes knew the Ten Commandments, but had evidently not
internalized the standard comments on the First Commandment,
which prohibited quasi-magical practices of this sort.

It is tempting to attribute the cruder and less inward piety of
Reynes's book to the social and educational gulf between his
world and that which produced the more sophisticated and securely
orthodox piety revealed in Idley's book or the Cambridge manuscript. But as we shall see in the context of the primer devotions
such assumptions about élite and popular religion can be misleading. The contents of a commonplace book from the Norfolk–
Suffolk border near Scole, contemporary with Reynes's book but

---

[47] On the images of Christ see Anderson, *Imagery of British Churches*, p. 172, and
Woodforde, *Norwich School*, pp. 183–92.
[48] *Peter Idley's Instructions to his Son*, p. 113.

from a gentry household, is sufficiently similar to Reynes's collection to suggest that the contrast may in fact be less to do with high and low, élite and popular, than with town (or, in Idley's case, court) and country.

The so-called Brome commonplace (from its place of discovery) contains many fewer items than either the Cambridge manuscript or Reynes's book, and most of these are extended poems rather than the sort of short pieces which Reynes collected, but there is a striking similarity of interest and ethos in the two rural East Anglian collections.[49] The catechetical and moralistic material in Reynes's book is matched in the Brome book by a handful of moralizing rules in verse, including one which also occurs, in a somewhat different version, in Reynes's collection.

> Fyrst arise erly
> Serve thy God deuly,
> And the warld besylly . . .

The main catechetical item in the Brome book, however, is an extraordinary poem, attributed to St John the Evangelist (!) "The Catechism of Adrian and Epotys", in which the child Jesus instructs the emperor Adrian in the story of Creation and Fall, the seven sins of Adam, the virtues, the methods of avoiding Hell, and the thirteen reasons for the Friday fast. This catechetical material is rounded off with a poem on the cardinal virtues by Lydgate. The fragments of religious plays in Reynes's collection are matched in the Brome book by a play of Abraham and Isaac, his hagiographic material on St Anne is matched in Brome by a verse life of St Katherine, his long account of the power of the "Oes" over demons and the souls in Purgatory by a metrical version of the story of St Patrick's Purgatory, "The Knight Sir Owen". Reynes's astrological and divinatory material is matched in Brome by a set of instructions in verse on divination by the casting of dice. And a later hand has completed the correspondences with Reynes by adding an incomplete charm prescribing an elaborate series of devotions, including the recitation of fifteen Paternosters and Aves daily in honour of a series of obscure saints, and a set of instructions of the performance of St Gregory's Trental. The religious section of the manuscript ends with a type of item not found in Reynes, a carol of the Annunciation.[50]

---

[49] L. Toulmin Smith (ed.), *A Common-Place Book of the Fifteenth Century*, 1886. List of contents on pp. "B" and 7–8.

[50] The Brome book was used by two separate owners, the second of whom, Robert Melton, a wealthy yeoman farmer and probably steward to the Cornwallis family at Sturston in Suffolk *c*.1506, added little religious material, and used the book largely for business entries.

Reynes was a poor man, the compiler of the Brome book was a gentleman. Both books display, however, a remarkably similar religion. It was a religion in which there was little evidence of the deep religious introspection and interiority encouraged by monastic and mystical devotional writers, concentrating rather on the objective things of religion, the observance of feast and fast, the changing pattern of the annual liturgy. It was somewhat credulous, avid for colour and spectacular incident, preferring religious instruction to come in the form of entertainment, rhymed saints' lives, or religious plays. It was interested in the afterlife and especially in the avoidance of Purgatory, about which both compilers were entirely orthodox. Both valued the Church's sacraments, both believed in the power of the Mass to save and heal, both placed a high value on the virtues of the rosary and devotion to the Virgin. Both feared the Devil, were much concerned with judgement, thought the end of the world might be near, and believed that the surest way to avert God's wrath was by being merciful to the poor and avoiding swearing. Both accepted and sought to remember the doctrinal outlines offered them by the contemporary Church, but neither was greatly interested in the intricacies of doctrine. Somewhere near the heart of their religion was a sober and conformist morality, encouraged no doubt by the clergy's concentration of their catechetical endeavours on the confessional, and the location of instruction on the Creed within a more elaborate scheme which put as much or more emphasis on the Commandments, the virtues, the sins. And both collections provide evidence of an entrenched area of lay religious belief and practice resistant to attempts at reform, and likely to be frowned on by the more austere medieval clerical catechists and devotional writers, just as it would be by humanists and reformers, the world of charms and divination.

One other commonplace book will help to complete this survey of lay assimilation of the catechetical programme of the late medieval church. Richard Hill was a London grocer, active in the 1520s and 1530s, for much of which time he seems to have lived in the parish of St Andrew Undershaft. His commonplace book, now at Balliol College, Oxford, is one of the most remarkable collections of the period, containing a wealth of devotional verse and carols, including the unique text of the Corpus Christi carol.[51]

[51] R. Dyboski (ed.), *Songs, Carols and other Miscellaneous Poems from the Balliol Ms 354, Richard Hill's Commonplace Book*, EETS, 1908. (hereafter = Dyboski, *Songs*). As the title suggests, this includes only the verse items from the Balliol MS 354, but there is an analytical table of the complete contents of the MS on pages xxxiv–lix of Dyboski's edition. The manuscript is now in a very fragile state, and in quoting items not included in Dyboski's selection I have used the typed transcript by D. C. Browning, kept at Balliol.

Like Reynes's collection, it mixes secular matter with religious, and in addition to the devotional material and notes of family baptisms, confirmations, and deaths, has recipes for brewing beer, making gunpowder, and dosing sick horses, notes on weights and measures, the sale of cheese, the assize of bread, and legal formulae. Like the Cambridge manuscript, it contains metrical romances and gestes – the Seven Sages, the Siege of Rome, the story of the Basin, the Friar, and the Boy. It has an enormous collection of devotional verses, some of them modelled on prayers found in the primers, some of them general reflections on the transience of worldly things. It has a version of the poem on St Gregory's Trental, and it has a series of Latin prose texts directly bearing on the catechetical programme we have been considering in this chapter. Hill was clearly a traditional Catholic, untouched by the reforming currents already evident in the city in the 1520s, as the presence of texts like the "Pope Trental" or the "Merits of the Mass" indicate. As might be expected, therefore, his collections include a significant number of catechetical texts. The most striking of these are in Latin, notably a "Tabila [sic] Christiane religionis valde utilis et necessaria" which looks as if it has been derived fairly directly from one of the shorter clerical manuals like the *Manipulus Curatorum*, and which gives a schematic but exhaustive analysis of the faith on the familiar Pecham model of Creed (complete with allocation of each article to an Apostle), Lord's Prayer, Commandments of law and Gospel, the laws of the Church, the sacraments, the sins, the virtues, the works of mercy. Each item is subdivided and minutely defined, giving the skeleton framework for an exhaustive treatment of its subject.[52] This tract also includes material on reserved sins, the ways of incurring excommunication, laws of fasting, days of obligation, and all the other rules and regulations governing orthodox Catholic practice. A briefer Latin tract expounds the Ten Commandments and the ways of breaking them.[53] A third Latin piece, longer than either of these, comprises a complete treatise on confession, obviously designed for use by a priest, and providing the sort of pattern of inquisition into the penitent's sins which we have already encountered in the St John's manuscript or the primer form of confession, as well as a good deal of supplementary material on the theology and practical conduct of confession.[54]

This rather dry and schematic material is supplemented by English and Latin verses designed to help the layman memorize and

[52] Balliol MS 254 transcript pp. 249–57.
[53] Ibid. pp. 257–9.
[54] Ibid. pp. 361–6.

flesh it out, such as a set of quatrains characterizing each of the deadly sins, poems on the Eucharist and other sacraments, metrical lists of the sins, virtues, sacraments and the rest, and moralizing rules and aphorisms like the "Aryse early, serve God devoutly" poem we have already encountered in Reynes and the Brome book, or the equally common riddling verses on the Commandments, sins and five bodily wits:

> Kepe well X and flee from sevyn
> Spend well V and cum to hevyn.[55]

Hill's religion was much richer in content and wider in range than that of Reynes. In particular, the extensive collection of carols and prayers addressed to Christ and Mary in his book, including items like the haunting Corpus Christi carol, add a depth and resonance largely lacking in the other collections. But much of that material is in turn indebted to the primers, which would have supplied the owners and compilers of books like Reynes's or the Brome collection with the affective warmth and interiority we miss in their commonplace books. What is perhaps more striking is the extent to which Hill, like them, has absorbed, assumed, and built on the catechetical framework and priorities mapped out for clergy and laity alike three centuries before.

The Coming of Print

In a famous passage of *Actes and Monumentes*, John Foxe asserted the incompatibility of popery and printing: "How many presses there be in the world, so many block houses there be against the high castle of St Angelo, so that either the pope must abolish knowledge and printing, or printing must at length root him out."[56] Had Foxe attended to the history of printing in and for England until the early 1530s, he would not have made this claim. The advent of printing in the 1470s and the enormous surge in numbers of publications after 1505 did not flood the reading public with reforming tracts or refutations of the real presence. Instead, alongside the grammar-books, almanacs, conduct-books, statutes, and law reports which formed so much of the stock-in-trade of printers, there flooded out liturgical books to serve the parish churches, letters of indulgence for hospitals, gilds, and other charities, a vast range of devotional and didactic tracts, designed to promote traditional piety and a better knowledge of the faith and practice of Catholicism, and

---

[55] Dyboski, *Songs*, p. 140.
[56] *Acts and Monuments*, III, p. 720.

above all tens of thousands of Latin primers, vying with each other to advertise the indulgenced prayers and pictures with which they were furnished. Caxton, Wynkyn de Worde, and Richard Pynson, who between them dominated the English printing trade until the break with Rome, were all religiously conservative, as well as being shrewd businessmen determined to tap and cater for the expanding lay market for traditional religious material.[57]

Much of this printed matter was reissuing classics which had long since circulated in manuscript. Nicholas Love's *Mirror of the Blessed Life of Jesu*, Mirk's *Festial*, assorted works by Richard Rolle, and several versions of the *Ars Moriendi* all went through multiple editions. We have already noted the stream of clerical manuals produced in both English and Latin, most of them established classics going back to the fourteenth century or earlier. Caxton produced a new version of the *Somme le Roi*, the thirteenth-century Carmelite classic on the Ten Commandments, the deadly sins, and the virtues which had been translated into English as the *Ayenbite of Inwyt*. It had circulated in at least nine other English versions before the advent of printing.[58] Caxton also translated a similar work, the *Book of Good Manners*, from an early fifteenth-century French original. His account of his reasons for undertaking this translation throws a fascinating light on the drive behind the steady flow of such material which was to come from the presses right up to the break with Rome. Caxton recorded how his friend William Pratt, a devout city mercer who died in 1486, leaving instructions for an austerely religious funeral without pomp, had brought him the French original not long before his death, declaring that he wanted it translated and published "to the end that it might be had and used among the people for the amendment of their manners". The impetus here is not from the clergy, certainly not the result of official *fiat*, but the suggestion of a devout layman, anxious to improve the moral and religious tone of the community at large.[59]

The overwhelmingly traditional and orthodox character of the religious literature printed in England before 1530 did not mean that it was all of one sort. Variety was the essence of fast sales, and Wynkyn de Worde and Pynson provided it. There were pamphlets advocating the merits of the rosary, treatises on a good death or providing comfort and reassurance for troubled consciences, visions

[57] H. S. Bennett, *English Books and Readers 1475–1557*, 1970, pp. 65–7, 69–71, 182–93. There is a checklist of Wynkyn de Worde's publications on pp. 239–76. On Pynson's output see S. H. Johnston's unpublished PhD dissertation for the University of Western Ontario, 1977, "A Study of the Career and Literary Publications of Richard Pynson".
[58] N. F. Blake, *Caxton and His World*, 1969, pp. 96–7.
[59] G. D. Painter, *William Caxton*, 1976, pp. 155–6.

and revelations about Purgatory such as the *Gast of Gy* and the *Monk of Eynsham*, the fourth book of the *Imitation of Christ* (on the Blessed Sacrament), a series of individual saints' lives, some of them, like the life of St Werburge, St Thomas, or Joseph of Arimathea, designed to promote pilgrimage to particular shrines.[60] Pynson published similar pamphlets to promote pilgrimage to the Holy Blood of Hailes and to Walsingham.[61] There were also hagiographical collections, some on a grand scale, as in Caxton's translation of the *Golden Legend*, expanded in successive editions to include newly popular saints and summaries of Old Testament stories, or, more modestly, Pynson's abbreviated translation of Capgrave's *Nova Legenda Angliae* of 1516, probably issued for the religious of Syon, but intended more generally to promote pride in and devotion to English saints among the married laity.[62] And among the runaway best-sellers of the first quarter of the century were the sermons of John Fisher on the seven penitential Psalms, a searching and sombrely magnificent verse-by-verse exposition by the greatest preacher of the period. The sermons not only appealed to growing lay interest in scripture, but explored and expounded with great pastoral sensitivity the theology of repentance and forgiveness, and the doctrine of the sacraments.[63]

Though some of this material was in Latin, most was in English, and printing gave an enormous impetus to the movement for vernacular religious instruction. This development brought its own tensions. Fear of Lollardy had made most Church leaders nervous of translations of scripture, even of such basics as the Lord's Prayer, the Hail Mary, and the "De Profundis" Psalm recited for the dead. The problems this created for religious instruction in the face of growing literacy had been met in a variety of ways. The ban on English versions of the New Testament had to a large extent been ameliorated by the production of Nicholas Love's translation of the *Meditationes Vitae Christi*, for that work was essentially an expanded Gospel harmony, and went a long way towards satisfying lay eagerness for knowledge of the Gospels.[64] Other portions of

[60] Johnston, "Pynson", pp. 30, 32, 35, 160–1.

[61] J. C. T. Oates, "Richard Pynson and the Holy Blood of Hayles" *The Library*, 5th Series, XIII, 1958, pp. 269–77; J. C. Dickinson, *The Shrine of Our Lady of Walsingham*, 1956, appendix on "The Pynson Ballad."

[62] There is a good discussion of Caxton's treatment of the *Golden Legend*, and his distinctive additions, including a catechetical exposition of the Ten Commandments in the life of Moses, in Blake, *Caxton and His World*, pp. 117–23; *Here Begynneth the kalendre of the new Legende of England*, Pynson 1516, RSTC 4602.

[63] On the sermons see Richard Rex, *The Theology of John Fisher*, 1991, pp. 30–50.

[64] M. Deanesly, "Vernacular Books in England in the Fourteenth and Fifteenth Centuries", *Modern Language Review*, XV, 1920, pp. 354–5.

scripture circulated in loose verse translations and paraphrases. We have already encountered "Pety Job", the verse rendering of the readings from the "Dirige", and countless Psalm paraphrases also circulated. Nevertheless, the fear of Bible translations was a major weakness in the educational and devotional programme of late medieval English Catholicism, and a principal reason why serious interest in religious education in the vernacular could tip over into, or be confused with, Lollardy. That educational programme sought to deepen and extend the religious knowledge and fervour of the common people, but the restriction of English Bible-reading to those who secured an episcopal licence effectively confined licit Bible ownership and readership to wealthy devotees like John Clopton of Long Melford.[65] Foxe was therefore right, to the extent that printing fed the aspirations of a swelling English readership eager for devotional material and increasingly used to the deployment of biblical stories and imagery in plays, paintings, and glass. It seems likely that even had the Reformation not reached England, and given the emphasis laid on the centrality of scripture by Erasmus, More, and Fisher, this particular ban would have had to go, sooner or later. Without the goad of Reformation, of course, the advent of an English version of the New Testament might well have been absorbed into the devotional mood which dominated English religious reading, without the doctrinal uncertainty and conflict which in fact ensued.[66]

However that may be, the pressure for the extension of the vernacular to all religious fundamentals, including the use of English versions of the Our Father, Hail Mary, and Creed, had been achieved long before the Reformation reached England. More than a century before Mirk had urged parish clergy to encourage their parishioners to say their prayers in English, for "hit ys moch more spedfull and meritabull to you to say your Pater Noster yn Englysche then yn suche Lateyn, as ye doth. For when ye speketh yn Englysche, then ye knowen and understondyn wele what ye sayn."[67] Though the basic texts of the primers remained in Latin till after the break with Rome, the demand for vernacular material was evident in the evolution of the early sixteenth-century primers, as more and more English material was added. A range of primers from a variety of publishers before 1530 were adding didactic and devotional matter in English, such as the "three verities', a brief

---

[65] For a good discussion of lay Bible readership before the Reformation see Dr Richard Rex's (forthcoming) *Henry VIII and the English Reformation* (London 1993), for the ultra-orthodox John Clopton's English Bible, see his will, *Visitation of Suffolke*, I p. 38.

[66] Rex, *Fisher*, pp. 158–60.

[67] *Festial*, p. 282.

instruction on Faith, Hope, and Charity attributed to Gerson, the "Form of Confession", and the "Maner to live well".[68]

That emphasis was even more evident in the history of printed instruction and devotion outside the primer. In 1500 the Syon monk Thomas Betson produced a catechetical treatise aimed at promoting religious knowledge and devotion among the simpler members of the community. This *Ryght Profytable Treatyse* advertised the inclusion of English versions of the Paternoster, Ave, and Credo, "medefull to religyous people as to the laye people". Within a few years the circulation of catechetical treatises teaching English prayers was commonplace.[69] In 1505 Wynkyn de Worde published *The Arte or Crafte to Lyue well*,[70] a comprehensive catechetical and devotional treatise adapted from the French and profusely illustrated. The pictures included a woodcut of Jesus teaching the Apostles how to pray, with the words of the Lord's Prayer in English above their heads (Pl. 37): another English version of the prayer was given in the text. A similar woodcut of Moses and Aaron gave the words of the Ten Commandments, a device repeated on the title-page of another catechetical treatise, *The Floure of the Commaundementes*.[71] *The Arte or Crafte* was a remarkable collection of materials, expounding Lord's Prayer, Hail Mary, Creed, Commandments (including the commandments of the Church about such things as fasting and payment of tithes), the virtues, the gifts of the Holy Ghost, the works of mercy, and the sacraments. The long and very comprehensive section on the sacraments was illustrated with vivid woodcuts, displaying the sacrament itself with, above it, a smaller picture of its Old Testament type. Over the picture of the Mass was a vignette of Melchizedek offering bread and wine, above the picture of marriage Adam and Eve were joined together by God in the garden (Pl. 38).[72] Each article of the Creed similarly had its own illustration, complete with Old Testament type, the type being explained both in a quatrain at the foot of the picture and in the main body of the text. The seven deadly sins were treated separately in a treatise dealing with the apocryphal vision of Lazarus, each sin being illustrated with a lurid woodcut of the appropriate punishment. The collection also included a crudely illustrated prose version of the

[68] Mary C. Erler, "*The Maner to Lyve Well* and the Coming of English in François Regnault's Primers of the 1520s and 1530s", *The Library*, 6th Series, VI, 1984, pp. 229–43.

[69] Thomas Beston, *A ryght profytable treatyse*, STC 1978. See Jan Rhodes's forthcoming article in the *Journal of Ecclesiastical History*, "Religious Instruction at Syon in the Early Sixteenth Century".

[70] *The Arte or Crafte to Lyve well*, STC 792.

[71] *The Floure of the Commaundementes of God*, W. de Worde 1505, RSTC 23875.1. Wynkyn de Worde produced further editions in 1510 and 1512.

[72] *Art or Crafte*, fols xxxvi (r) ff.

fifteen tokens of the day of doom, and the history of Antichrist. The book was a commercial speculation, with no indication of clerical involvement in its English production, yet it certainly provided a full and lively coverage of the traditional catechetical programme, in a form likely to appeal to the widest possible lay audience.[73]

It was outclassed in this regard, however, by one of the most remarkable books of the century, once again translated from a French original. *The Kalender of Shepherdes*, which first appeared in a barbarous Scots version in 1503, was retranslated for Pynson in 1506, and again for Wynkyn de Worde, with smaller and inferior woodcuts, in 1508. It had a fourth edition in 1518, a fifth in 1528, and was reissued in both Mary's and Elizabeth's reigns.[74]

The *Kalender* is both a beautiful and an unmistakably lay book. It is an extraordinary mixture of calendrical, astrological, and medical lore, together with orthodox religious instruction imaginatively presented. Less comprehensive than the *Arte or Crafte to Lyue well*, it nevertheless offered a basic course of religious instruction and exhortation in a form which was to prove popular and accessible thoughout the century. A major attraction of the book was the fine woodcuts, illustrating both the religious and the secular parts. The whole book sustains the conceit that it is written for and by simple men, symbolized by the shepherd "whiche was no clerke ne understode no manere of scrypture nor wrytynge but only by his naturall wyt". The shepherd knows the stars and therefore can give guidance on astrology, and he is natural man face to face with the mysteries of life and death. The religious sections of the book, apart from a calendar "with the Fygures of every Saynt that is halowed in the yere" (a gross exaggeration), include a lengthy and elaborate treatment of the seven deadly sins depicted as trees with all their branches, and a shortened version of the vision of Lazarus, with its unforgettable woodcuts of the torments that await each of the deadly sins. In the text the visionary and macabre elements in the original have been edited out, and instead each section is a short and generalized meditation on the evils of each of the deadly sins, well adapted to catechesis or pious reading. After the analysis and punishment of the sins, the *Kalender* moves on to treat the Paternoster, giving first a brief exposition of the seven petitions, relating it to one of the gifts of the Holy Ghost, then providing a slightly expanded devotional paraphrase, a large woodcut of Christ teaching the Apostles, with a literal English translation of the

---

[73] On the Lazarus vision and the deadly sins see below chapter 10, "The Pains of Purgatory", pp. 340–1.

[74] Modern reprint ed. H. Oskar Sommer, *The Kalender of Shepherdes*, 1892.

Lord's Prayer, followed by a brief exposition of the excellences of the prayer. The Hail Mary (Pl. 39), Creed, and Commandments are similarly treated. This whole section is extremely effective, approaching the prayers it expounds in a variety of ways well calculated to bring out its meaning for simple readers or listeners and using the illustrations to drive home the text. The same resourcefulness is shown in the handling of the other religious items in the book. There are a good many vigorous woodcuts – a man in a storm-tossed boat illustrates an extended reflection on the mutability of life, Death with his dart accompanies a stirring poem on judgement and the need to repent. The text is equally resourceful, for the treatment of the Commandments is varied by the inclusion of "The X commaundementes of the deuyll":

> Be dronkyn upon thy holy daye
> And cause other to synne and thou may.
> Thy fader nor thy moder loke thou love nor drede.
> And helpe them never thou they have nede.
> Hate thy neyghboure and hure hym by enuy
> Murder and shede mannys blode hardely.[75]

Throughout the book short sections of basic religious instruction are inserted on such matters as the best way to help souls in Purgatory, the nature of contrition, the love of God, and the dignity of the human soul. All this is set in the context of elaborate and finely illustrated astrological and calendrical material of the sort found in almanacs. The whole book reads as if it was compiled to cater for the tastes, but also to improve the theology, of Robert Reynes of Acle.

Pynson, in commissioning his new translation, clearly saw himself as contributing to the basic task of catechesis. The book, he claimed, was "very profytable bothe for clerkes and laye people to cause them to have greate understondyng and in espessyal in that we be bounde to lerne and knowe on peyne of averlastinge deth". It was not enough to know the Paternoster, as everyone did. We must also know the laws of God and of the Church, and the remedies against the deadly sins. There were many men and women, Pynson thought, who "thynkes them selfe wyse and knowes and lernes many thyngis but that that they be bounde to lerne . . . as perfectly as there pater noster". The book was therefore, in his view, principally a contribution to teaching people the Commandments. Complaints about the ignorance of the people were of course a commonplace of all catechetical literature, as was Pynson's contrast

[75] Sommer, *Kalender*, pp. 89–90.

between the worldly wisdom of men and women and their religious ignorance. The *Ordynary* had made much the same point when it insisted that "Many faders and moders be moche desyrous to nourysshe / to clothe/ and to make purchases / and to gader goodes for the bodyes of theyr children. But ryght fewe there be the whiche thynke on the soule in techyng them and makynge them to kepe the doctryne and the lyffe of holy crystyente."[76] There is no need to doubt Pynson's sincerity in declaring his desire to rectify the situation; few Tudor tradesmen saw any conflict between serving God and making money.

The *Kalender of Shepherdes* is of particular importance because it establishes the assimilation into popular culture, by commercial publishers for a mass audience, of the official educational programme of the Church. It was once again a commercial speculation, emphatically a lay book. The success of that assimilation is of course a moot point: many clergy would have been disturbed by the placing of theology cheek by jowl with popular astrology and prognostication. Yet the *Kalender* certainly found a readership which would have considered unpalatable many more sober didactic treatises, for it was a commonplace of the time, despite the efforts of the clergy and the torrents of paper discharged from the presses, that the people were often resistant to catechesis. In 1510 Wynkyn de Worde published an amusing pamphlet in lively doggerel, illustrating this truism, "a lytell geste how the plowman lerned his pater noster".

The poem derives in fact from a story used by St Bernardino to illustrate the duty of a parish priest to teach his people, and appears to have been translated from a French version into English, an interesting reflection of the openness of English religious culture in the late Middle Ages to a common European set of concerns and resources. But the whole pace of St Bernardino's story has been tightened up and the humour adapted to English conditions.[77] It tells of a wealthy plowman, his house and barn stocked with the abundance his farming skills have brought him, who comes in Lent to his curate to be confessed. The curate begins to test his religious knowledge, first asking him to recite his belief:

> The plowman sayd unto the preste
> Syr I beleue in Jhesu Cryste
> Which suffred deth and harrowed hell
> As I have herde myne olders tell.

[76] Ibid. p. 7.

[77] *Here beynneth a lytell geste how the plowman lerned his pater noster*, Wynkyn de Worde 1510, RSTC 23004. I am grateful to Richard Rex for drawing my attention to the link with St Bernardino, for whose version of the story see A. G. F Howell, *St Bernardino of Siena*, 1913, p. 286.

The Paternoster, however, defeats him: asked to recite it by the curate, he is stumped, and the priest, warning him of the peril of his soul, refuses to shrive him. The plowman is in no mind to take to his primer with the children:

> I wolde threshe sayd the plowman yeres ten
> Rather than I it wolde leren.
> I praye the syr persone my counsyll kepe
> Ten wethers wyll I gyve the or my best shepe . . .
> So ye me shewe how I may heven reache.
> Well says the preest, I shall the teche.

The method he adopts is unorthodox, for he recognizes that the way to the plowman's soul is through his wallet. He reminds him of the famine which is killing poor men all over the country, while the plowman has plenty, and promises to send him forty hungry men. Each will have a Latin name which forms part of the Paternoster: to each the plowman must give what corn he asks, and he must remember their names, and the order in which they come. If he does so, the priest promises, he will repay double and give him absolution as well. The plowman agrees, and the priest rounds up every pauper in the district and sends them to the plowman. The poem relates gleefully how the ragamuffins come, first "pater noster" then "qui es in coelis", and strip the plowman of his hoarded riches, only to blow it on a spree at the alehouse.

> They had ten bushelles withouten fayle
> And layde fyve to pledge for a kylderkyn of ale.

After a fevered night trying to memorize their names, the plowman successfully recites his Paternoster, but when he demands his corn the priest tells him his reward is a hundredfold in Heaven. Outraged, the plowman cites the priest before the Church courts, where the case is dismissed and the parson commended.

> Thus for his corne that he gave there
> His pater noster he dyde lere.

The tale of the plowman is a jest: the enjoyment of the Tudor audience lay in the virtuous slyness of the priest and the discomfiture of a greedy farmer who was expert in everything to do with heaping up wealth but did not know the most basic of all prayers. We certainly should not take it as an indicator of the general educational level of wealthy plowmen, but its effect does depend on the audience's sense of the general plausibility of the situation, as well as the enormity of the plowman's ignorance. Clergy and laity alike in early Tudor England perceived the centuries old catechetical enterprise as still very much a priority.

That enterprise was being pursued with inventiveness up to the very moment of Reformation and the break with Rome. Richard Whytford's *A Werke for Householders*, published in 1530, is one of the last pre-Reformation products of the catechetical programme which had underlain the English Church's teaching activity since the thirteenth century, and it is one of the most distinctive.[78] Whitford, a Cambridge graduate and a friend of More, Fisher, and Erasmus, was a monk of Syon, the Brigittine house on the Thames which was responsible for much of the devotional material in circulation in late medieval and early Tudor England. Much of that material was specifically intended for religious, and aimed to cultivate the inwardness and ascetic spirit which underlay their conception of the religious life. But the visionary writings of St Bridget, herself a married woman and a courtier, had exercised a profound influence over the spirituality of men and women engaged in secular affairs. Some of the tensions in Margery Kempe's quest for sanctity sprang from her efforts to emulate Bridget without withdrawing into religious life or entering a hermitage. The English Brigittines had an extensive lay clientele, and the remarkable group of Brigittine writers who contributed so much to the devotional output of early Tudor England never wrote exclusively for a monastic readership, as the very act of printing their books indicates.[79] We have already encountered Thomas Betson's treatise on the English Paternoster, and many of the Brigittine writings of the period have this dual audience in mind. Something of the extent of their impact is reflected in the painted screen at Horsham St Faith's in Norfolk, dating from 1528 and funded by wealthy parishioners. Two of the panels most unusually depict mystics whose writings were propagated from Syon, St Catherine of Siena and St Bridget herself. Their presence is difficult to account for except through the contact of the donors with Syon or at least the literature emanating from there. This conjecture is strongly borne out by the fact that the painting of St Bridget is directly copied from a woodcut used in a number of Brigittine tracts, including one published by Wynkynde Worde in 1520, the *Dyetary of Ghostly Helthe*, which also included the image of St Catherine holding her burning heart, as she appears on the Horsham screen.[80]

[78] *A Werke for Householders* went through seven editions 1530-7, RSTC 25421.8 – 25425.5. I have used the modern edition by J. Hogg, Salzburg Studies in English Literature no. 89, Salzburg 1979. The *Werke* is discussed by Helen C. White, *The Tudor Books of Private Devotion*, 1951, pp. 167–71.

[79] Rhodes, "Religious Instruction at Syon".

[80] *The Dyetary of Ghostly Helthe*, W. de Worde 1520, RSTC 6883. There were some parochial gifts to the "new perke" at Horsham from the 1490s, but the main donor was a William Wulcy and his wives Joan and Alice. See S. Cotton, "Medieval Roodscreens in Norfolk – their construction and painting dates", *Norfolk Archaeology*, XL, 1987, p. 49, and see below, chapter 5, "The Saints", pp. 167–8, and Pl. 62–3.

In this dissemination of devotional and instructional literature from Syon, Whitford was an active figure, concerned with both monastic formation and the education and edification of a wider lay audience. *A Werke for Householders* is directed exclusively to the latter, and demonstrates considerable sensitivity to the need to adapt the traditional catechetical programme to the circumstances of lay people. The treatise is, yet again, an exposition of the Lord's Prayer, Hail Mary, Creed, Ten Commandments, and the seven deadly sins, the last set out in the traditional form of an examination of conscience for confession. To this traditional list of contents Whitford adds a basic form of morning prayer and a brief meditation on the main events of Christ's life, Passion, and Resurrection, designed for daily use. It is the tone and practicality of Whitford's treatment of all this which is new. He allows his reader to argue with him, protesting that devotions in the morning are all very well for monks in their cells, "but we be done lye ii or iii somtyme togyder and yet in one chambre dyvers beddes and so many in comany / yf we shulde use these thynges in presence of our felowes / some wold laugh us to scorne and mocke us." Whitford's exposition of the elements of the faith is racy, earthy, and practical. Nothing in it is particularly original, but his fondness for proverbs and cracker-barrel wisdom, and his use of vivid and personalized exempla which anticipate some of the more gruesome efforts of later writers like Thomas Beard give the book an immediacy and appeal which brings it closer in spirit to commercial enterprises like the *Kalender of Shepherdes* than to many of the fifteenth-century catechetical texts produced by clerics. Above all, his emphasis encapsulated in the title on the responsibility of householders and parents for basic Christian teaching, his sense of the necessary difference between lay religion and monastic or clerical religion, anticipates much that would be developed more fully by reformed writers like Thomas Becon. On the eve of its dissolution, the old catechetical formula was showing its ability to adapt effectively to changing circumstances.

B: Encountering the Holy

CHAPTER 3

THE MASS

The liturgy lay at the heart of medieval religion, and the Mass lay at the heart of the liturgy. In the Mass the redemption of the world, wrought on Good Friday once and for all, was renewed and made fruitful for all who believed. Christ himself, immolated on the altar of the cross, became present on the altar of the parish church, body, soul, and divinity, and his blood flowed once again, to nourish and renew Church and world. As kneeling congregations raised their eyes to see the Host held high above the priest's head at the sacring, they were transported to Calvary itself, and gathered not only into the passion and resurrection of Christ, but into the full sweep of salvation history as a whole (Pl. 40).

> Then shal thou do reverence
> to ihesu crist awen presence,
> That may lese alle baleful bandes;
> knelande holde up bothe thi handes,
> And so tho leuacioun thou behalde,
> for that is he that iudas salde,
> and sithen was scourged & don on rode,
> And for mankynde there shad his blode,
> And dyed & ros & went to heuen,
> And yit shal come to deme vs euen,
> Ilk mon aftur he has done,
> That same es he thou lokes opone.[1]

The body of Christ, greeted as "journey-money for our pilgrimage, solace of all our longing",[2] was the focus of all the hopes and aspirations of late medieval religion. The sacrifice of the Mass was the act by which the world was renewed and the Church was constituted, the Body on the corporas the emblem and the instrument of all truly human embodiment, whether it was understood as

---

[1] *The Lay Folk's Mass Book*, ed. T. F. Simmons, EETS, 1871 (hereafter = *LFMB*) p. 38.

[2] "viaticum nostre peregrinationis . . . solatium nostre expectationis", phrases from the indulgenced prayer "Salve lux mundi", prescribed for use at the elevation at Mass in many primers. See Hoskins, p. 127.

individual wholeness or as rightly ordered human community.[3]

Accounts of late medieval spirituality often emphasize the growth of individualism, not least in the intense devotion to the Blessed Sacrament evident in works like the *Imitatio Christi*. Yet the unitive and corporative dimension of the Blessed Sacrament is in fact repeatedly insisted on in late medieval sources. That theme is set out at length in the prologue to the ordinances of the York Corpus Christi gild, established in 1408, which may be taken as representative here. The Body of Christ, "beaten and crucified by the Jews", is the true "medium congruentissimum", the instrument of harmony. That Body is made present daily in the Mass, so that "as Christ unites the members to the Head by means of his precious Passion, so we shall be united in faith, hope and charity by the daily celebration of this sacrament of remembrance." The Mass is the sign of unity, the bond of love: whoever desires to live, must be "incorporated" by this food and drink. Thus the unity and fellow-ship of the Corpus Christi gild is just one aspect of the "mystical body of Christ", a unity rooted in charity and expressed in the works of mercy. Only in that unity can anyone be a member of Christ, and all the natural bonds of human fellowship, such as the loyalty and affection of one gild member for another, or the care of rich for poor, or of the whole for the sick, is an expression of this fundamental community in Christ through the Sacrament.[4]

Such an insistence on the communal dimension of the Sacrament is readily grasped in the context of Corpus Christi gilds. Its centrality in the ordering and control of the late medieval town, through the Corpus Christi processions and plays, has been explored by Mervyn James and Charles Phythian-Adams. The coercive and hegemonic exploitation of this unitive theme by late medieval power-brokers in both church and secular community has recently been emphasized by Miri Rubin.[5] But it is important to grasp that the Eucharist could only be used to endorse existing community power structures because the language of Eucharistic belief and devotion was saturated with communitarian and corporate imagery. The unitive theme was not simply a device in the process of the establishment of community or the validation of power structures. It was a deeply felt element in the Eucharistic piety of the indi-vidual Christian too. The sense that the Host was the source simultaneously of individual and of corporate renewal and unity is

---

[3] Though the quizzical remarks of Miri Rubin, *Corpus Christi*, 1991, pp. 265–7 need to be weighed.

[4] Edited by Paula Lozar, "The Prologue to the Ordinances of the York Corpus Christi Guild", *Allegorica*, I, 1976, pp. 94–113.

[5] Rubin, *Corpus Christi*, esp. chapter 4.

perfectly caught in the striking prayer regularly printed in early sixteenth-century primers for use before receiving communion, the "Salve salutaris hostia".

In this prayer the communicant greets Christ in the Sacrament as the "saving victim" offered for them and for all humanity on the altar of the cross, and prays that the blood flowing from the side of the Crucified may wash away all their sins, so that they may be worthy to consume His body and blood. Pleading that Christ's sufferings for humanity may be to them the means of mercy and protection and not of condemnation, the communicant asks for a renewal in heart and mind, so that the old Adam may die and the new life begin. And at the climax of the prayer this new life is seen as essentially communal, not individualistic. The communicant prays that

> I may be worthy to be incorporated into Your body, which is the Church. May I be one of Your members, and may You be my head, that I may remain in You, and You in me, so that in the resurrection my lowly body may be conformed to Your glorious body, according to the promise of [St Paul] the Apostle, and so that I may rejoice in You and your glory eternally.[6]

The Host, then, was far more than the object of individual devotion, a means of forgiveness and sanctification: it was the source of human community. The ways in which it was experienced in communion underpinned and endorsed this. It is true that frequent reception of communion probably did encourage religious individualism, as it certainly often sprang from it. Margery Kempe's weekly reception, representing a claim to particular holiness of life, marked her off from her neighbours, and was almost certainly resented by them.[7] But frequent communion was the prerogative of the few. Lady Margaret Beaufort received only monthly, and even so was considered something of a prodigy. For most people receiving communion was an annual event, and it was emphatically a communal rather than an individualistic action. In most parishes everyone went to confession in Holy Week and received communion before or after high Mass on Easter Day, an act usually accompanied by a statutory offering to the priest. Only after the completion of all this was one entitled to break one's Lenten fast and resume the eating of meat.[8] In large communities extra

---

[6] Hoskins, p. 127: *Horae Eboracenses: the Prymer or Hours of the Blessed Virgin Mary, According to the Use of the Illustrious Church of York*, ed. C. Wordsworth, Surtees Society, CXXXII, 1919 (hereafter = *Hor Ebor*) p. 73.

[7] See *The Book of Margery Kempe*, p. 11, for an example of her neighbours' irritation with her ostentatious piety.

[8] Cf. Foxe, *Acts and Monuments*, III p. 593.

clergy were drafted in to help deal with the numbers involved, as row after row of communicants lined up before the chancel screen, holding the long houseling towel which prevented any fragments of the Host falling to the ground. The priest addressing his people at the Easter Day Mass, therefore, was expected to emphasize the bonds of community which were so visibly being celebrated. The sins which specially damaged community – wrath, envy, backbiting – were to be particularly eschewed, and those at odds were to be reconciled:

> Thys day ych cristen man, in reverence of God, schulde forgeve that have gylt to hom, and ben in full love and charyte to Godis pepull passyng all other dayes of the yere; for all that is mysdon all the yere befor, schall be helyd thys day wyth the salve of charyte . . . wherfor, good men and woymen, I charch you heyly in Godys byhalve that non of you today com to Godys bord, but he be in full charyte to all Godis pepull.[9]

Receiving communion at Easter (Pl. 41) was called "taking one's rights", a revealing phrase, indicating that to take communion was to claim one's place in the adult community. Exclusion was a mark of social ostracism. At All Saints, Bristol, the right to take Easter communion was linked to payment of parish dues, in particular one's contribution to the parish clerk's wages; defaulters were denied their Easter housel. Shame and outrage at exclusion from the honesty of the parish, rather than simple piety, seem to be at work in an incident at Little Plumstead in Norfolk on Easter Day 1530. Nicholas Tyting had quarrelled with his rector, who therefore refused him communion. He went weeping into the churchyard after Mass, other parishioners gathering round, and one of them went to the rector on his behalf, saying "How is it, Mr Parson, that Titing and you can not agree, it is pitie that he should goo his way without his rightes."[10]

The importance of parochial unity, endlessly reiterated in Easter homilies and exhortations, has rightly been stressed by John Bossy and others. It was of course an ideal which was probably rarely attained, as late medieval people themselves were well aware, and as the clergy often pointed out. The parishioners were required to come to communion "arayde in Godys lyvere, clothyd in love and charyte", not "the fendys lyvere, clothyd in envy and dedly

---

[9] *Festial*, pp. 130–1; for a very similar from of exhortation to be used by curates see W. Maskell, *Monumenta Ritualia Ecclesiae Anglicanae*, 1846–7, III pp. 348–9.

[10] *The Clerk's Book of 1549*, ed. J. Wickham Legg, Henry Bradshaw Society, XXV, 1903, p. 64; E. D. Stone and B. Cozens-Hardy (eds), *Norwich Consistory Court Depositions*, Norfolk Record Society, X, 1938, no. 428.

wrathe", but one of the standard exempla for Easter sermons told of a bishop or priest at the Easter communion granted a vision of the true state of the communicants' souls "when the pepull com to Godys bord". Many came "wyth hor face red as blod, and blod droppyng out of hor mouthys". These, an angel explained, were "envyous men and woymen, and full of dedly wrathe, and woll not amend hom". One much repeated exemplum told of a rich woman with a grudge against a poor neighbour, forced to reconciliation at Easter by the parson, who threatened that unless she "forgeve the pore woman here trespasse" he would "with-drawe fro hure here ryghtes that day": the wealthy woman dissembles forgiveness, and is choked by the Host.[11] The ideal of parochial harmony and charity was often just that, an ideal. It was, however, a potent one, carrying enormous emotive and ethical weight. In 1529 Joanna Carpenter, of the parish of St Mary Queenhithe, sought to exploit that weight by seizing the arm of her neighbour Margaret Chamber, with whom she was at odds, as Mistress Chamber knelt waiting her turn to receive Easter communion. "I pray you let me speke a worde with you," she said, "for you have need to axe me forgyvenes, before you rescyve your rights." This disruption of the annual parochial houseling landed Carpenter in the church courts, but the incident is eloquent testimony to the force of the theme of reconciliation and charity in lay perception of the Eucharist.[12]

Seeing the Host

But the reception of communion was not the primary mode of lay encounter with the Host. Everyone received at Easter, and one's final communion, the viaticum or "journey money" given on the deathbed, was crucially important to medieval people. As we shall see, many people recalled that final communion at every Mass.[13] But for most people, most of the time the Host was something to be seen, not to be consumed. Since the end of the twelfth century it had been customary for the consecrating priest to elevate the Host high above his head immediately after the sacring (the repetition of the words of institution, "Hoc est enim Corpus Meum" which brought about the miracle of transubstantiation) for adoration by the people. The origin of the custom is debated, but it was probably designed as a protest against the view that the consecration of both elements was incomplete till the words of institution were

---

[11] *Festial*, pp. 131–2; *Middle English Sermons*, pp. 62–3, 347.
[12] W. Hale (ed.), *A Series of Precedents and Proceedings in Criminal Causes, Extending from the Year 1475–1640*, 1847, p. 108; Rubin, *Corpus Christi*, pp. 149–50.
[13] See below, pp. 120, 311.

pronounced over the chalice as well as the Host. Although a matching elevation of the chalice was subsequently added, it was never so important in the lay imagination: seeing the Host became the high point of lay experience of the Mass.[14] When artists sought to portray the sacrament of the Eucharist, as in the many Seven-Sacrament fonts surviving in East Anglian churches, or the related Seven-Sacrament windows in churches such as Doddiscombsleigh in Devon, it was the moment of the elevation of the Host which they almost invariably depicted (Pl. 42). In churches with elaborately carved or coloured altar-pieces the custom emerged of drawing a plain dark curtain across the reredos at the sacring, to throw the Host into starker prominence. In some places this provision was improved: at St Peter Cheap in London the cloth displayed at the elevation had a Crucifixion scene on it. In 1502 a Hull alderman left money for the construction of a mechanical device above the high altar which caused images of angels to descend on the altar at the sacring, and ascend again at the conclusion of the Paternoster – he had seen such a device in King's Lynn.[15]

The provision of good wax lights, and especially of torches, flaring lights made with thick plaited wicks and a mixture of resin and wax, which burned from the elevation to the "Agnus Dei" or the priest's communion, became one of the most common of all activities of the gilds. It was also very common for individual testators to specify that the torches burned around their corpses at their funerals should be given to the parish church, to burn around the altar at the sacring time.[16] The provision of such lights was often indulgenced, and they may in addition have had the utilitarian function of lighting up the chancel to make the Host more visible, but they were also conceived of as forming a sort of proxy for the adoring presence of the donor close by the Sacrament at the moment of elevation. This was probably particularly true of funeral torches used as elevation lights, just as testators often left kerchiefs or bedlinen to make altar-cloths and corporases, a gesture clearly designed to bring their domestic intimacies into direct contact with the Host.[17] The notion of the torch as a proxy for the worshipping donor is certainly uppermost in the explanation offered by the group of shepherds and herdsmen of their motives in

[14] H. Thurston, "The Elevation" in *Catholic Encyclopedia*, V pp. 380–1.

[15] Rubin, *Corpus Christi*, p. 62.

[16] See e.g. *Bedfordshire Wills Proved in the Prerogative Court of Canterbury 1383–1548*, ed. M. McGregor, *Publications of the Bedfordshire Historical Records Society*, LVIII, 1979 (hereafter = *Beds Wills* III) pp. 19–21; for gilds providing elevation torches see Westlake, *Parish Gilds*, nos 13, 21, 23, 25, 34, 36, 40, 57, 58, 60, 67, 104, 108, 119, 121, 135, 165, 223, 224, 225, 226, 313, 330, 331, 333.

[17] See below, pp. 128–9, 330–4.

founding a gild of the Blessed Virgin at Holbeach. The gild, they explained, maintained torches at the elevation, because its members were often unable by reason of their work to be at Mass themselves.[18] Such torches were normally held by the clerk or the altar-boys in the sanctuary, and they often appear thus in carvings and pictures of the elevation (Pl. 43). But where gilds provided large numbers of torches for Sundays and festivals – sometimes up to a dozen or more – the gild members themselves would have gathered round the altar at the moment of elevation. In fifteenth-century Eye on All Saints' Day, and probably other festivals as well, "at the time of the elevation of high mass . . . many of the parishioners . . . lighted many torches, and carried them up to the high altar, kneeling down there in reverence and honour of the sacrament", in all probability in accordance with the ordinances of the parish gild.[19]

Just before the sacring in every mass a bell was rung to warn worshippers absorbed in their own prayers to look up, because the moment of consecration and elevation was near, and here different aspects of cult came into conflict. If the Mass was being celebrated at the high altar, those kneeling near the Rood-screen might have their view of the Host blocked by the dado. It was difficult to do anything about this in churches with panel-paintings of the saints on the dado: but where the screen was ornamented only with floral or geometric designs, or the names of the donors, the dado might be pierced with rows of "elevation squints" placed at eye-level for kneeling adults, as they are at Burlingham St Edmund (Pl. 44) and South Walsham in Norfolk, or Lavenham in Suffolk. At Roxton in Bedfordshire, where there were saints in the panels, squints were nevertheless drilled above their heads, those on the north screen, where a nave altar prevented the devotee getting close, being made much larger than those on the south (Pl. 45).[20] In great churches where many Masses were celebrated simultaneously, those at side altars were timed so that their sacrings were staggered, none preceding that at the main Mass at the high altar. Side altars were sometimes provided with squints which enabled the celebrating chantry or gild priest to see when his senior colleague at the high altar had reached the sacring. An especially elaborate arrangement of this sort survives at Long Melford, where the priest celebrating

[18] Westlake, *Parish Gilds*, no. 120.

[19] Westlake, *Parish Gilds*, nos 23, 67, 165; Foxe, *Acts and Monuments* III, p. 599.

[20] I deduce the presence of the altar from the abrupt line below which the wood is unpainted under the figures, and the fact that the figures on the north side are much shorter than those on the south. But if so the screen must have been placed higher up the wall, or the nave floor, as is likely, lower.

at the altar at the east end of the north aisle was provided with a double squint enabling him to see across the rear angle of the Clopton chantry and through the north wall of the chancel to the exact centre of the high altar. The same arrangement survives at St Matthews, Ipswich (Pl. 46).[21]

This staggered arrangement of Masses allowed the laity to see the Host at several sacrings within a short space of time. The warning bell might summon devotees at prayer in another part of the church, or even hearing a sermon, to view the Host. At Exeter the bishop legislated to prevent sacring bells being rung while the choir Offices were being recited, in case the clergy and choir should be deflected from the task in hand.[22] The early fifteenth-century Lollard priest William Thorpe was enraged when preaching to a crowd of lay people in the church of St Chad in Shrewsbury, "bisiinge me to teche the heestis of God", when "oon knyllide a sacringe belle, and herfor myche peple turned awei fersli, and with greet noyse runnen frowardis me" to see the Host at an altar elsewhere in the church.[23] A century and a half later Cranmer testified to the same eagerness on the part of the laity when he asked bitterly:

> What made the people to run from their seats to the altar, and from altar to altar, and from sacring (as they called it) to sacring, peeping, tooting and gazing at that thing which the priest held up in his hands, if they thought not to honour the thing which they saw? What moved the priests to lift up the sacrament so high over their heads? Or the people to say to the priest "Hold up! Hold up!"; or one man to say to another "Stoop down before"; or to say "This day have I seen my Maker"; and "I cannot be quiet except I see my maker once a day"? What was the cause of all these, and that as well the priest and the people so devoutly did knock and kneel at every sight of the sacrament, but that they worshipped that visible thing which they saw with their eyes and took it for very God?[24]

It is a commonplace of the literary and religious history of the period that royalty. aristocracy, and the gentry habitually heard several Masses each day. The glimpse Margaret Paston affords us of

---

[21] One of the reasons for this "staggering" was to make sure that parishioners did not shirk their duty of attending the (usually longer) main parish Mass on Sundays, by attending one of the chantry Masses in the same church; see K. L. Wood-Legh, *Perpetual Chantries in Britain*, 1965, p. 294.

[22] Rubin, *Corpus Christi*, pp. 59–60.

[23] Foxe, *Acts and Monuments*, III p. 263; Douglas Grey (ed.), *The Oxford Book of Fifteenth Century Verse and Prose*, 1985, p. 15.

[24] Thomas Cranmer, *Miscellaneous Writings and Letters of Thomas Cranmer*, ed. J. E. Cox, 1846 (hereafter = *Remains*), p. 442.

the devotional habits of her neighbour, Sir John Hevingham, who went to church one morning and heard three Masses, "and came home again never the merrier, and said to his wife that he would go say a little devotion in his garden and then he would dine", could in its essentials be matched for hundreds of the well-to-do in the period. The desire for ready access to daily Masses, rather than any more fundamental detachment from the parish, is no doubt one of the principal reasons why the fifteenth- and early sixteenth-century gentry increasingly sought licences to keep altars, and therefore priests, in their households.[25] But Cranmer clearly implies here that many "lewd" lay people also sought to see the Host at least once a day, and the records of gilds and parishes all over England testify to the anxiety of communities and individual testators to provide for "the increase of Divine Service" by securing several daily celebrations in their parish churches, including the dawn or "morrow Mass" for servants, labourers, and travellers. Doncaster parish church, in addition to daily sung matins, Mass, and evensong, had six "low" Masses, provided by the various chantry chaplains, hourly from five in the morning each day, "as well for th'inhabitants of the sayde towne as other strangers passing through the same". At Pontefract there were two chantry Masses daily, in addition to the "morrow Mass" said at dawn and the daily parish Mass at the high altar.[26] Archbishop Warham's Kent visitation of 1511 provides abundant evidence of parishes seeking to maintain a routine of daily Masses, with the help of chantry and gild priests as well as the parochial incumbent, and makes clear too the sense of grievance and deprivation which ensued in places where "many times in the yere they have no mass in the said church not in a hole weke togidre."[27] Jean Quentin's "Maner to lyve well", printed in many of the best-selling primers produced in the 1520s and 1530s and intended as spiritual advice for persons of "mean estate", stipulated that each day after saying matins from his primer the layman should "go to the chyrche or ye do ony worldly werkes yf ye haue no nedefull besynesse, & abyde in the chyrche the space of a lowe masse."[28] Clearly, daily Mass attendance was commonplace, and in

[25] N. Davis (ed.), *Paston Letters and Papers of the Fifteenth Century*, 1971, I pp. 39, 250, and see below chapter 4, "Corporate Christians", pp. 132, 139–40.

[26] C. Wordsworth, *Notes on Medieval Services*, 1898, pp. 83–8; Wood-Legh, *Perpetual Chantries*, pp. 291–5.

[27] *Kentish Visitation of Archbishop Willaim Warham and his Deputies 1511*, ed. K. L. Wood-Legh, *Kent Archaeological Society: Kent Records*, XXIV, 1984 (hereafter = *Kentish Visitation*), pp. 56, 62, 67, 112, 132, 140 etc.

[28] *This prymer of Salysbury use* 1531, Hoskins 98, RSTC 15973, see p. 15v: Hoskins, pp. 147–8 for modernized text (from another edition). On the "Maner to lyve well" see Mary C Erler "The Maner to Lyve Well and the Coming of English", *The Library*, 6th series, VI, 1984, pp. 229–43.

communities divided by heresy, which consequently put a high value on sacramental orthodoxy, to "come not to church oftener on the work day" might even be taken as a sufficient indication of Lollardy.[29]

Behind all was the sense that those cut off from the opportunity of hearing Mass devoutly and seeing the Host were being deprived of precious benefits for body and soul. Mothers in labour could secure safe delivery, travellers safe arrival, eaters and drinkers good digestion, by gazing on the Host at Mass.

> Thy fote that day shall not the fayll;
> Thyn eyen from ther syght shall not blynd;
> Thi light spekyng, eyther in fabill or tale,
> That veniall synnes do up wynd,
> Shall be forgeven, & pardon fynd . . .
> Thy grevouse othes that be forgett,
> In heryng of messe are don a-way;
> An angel also thi steppis doth mete,
> & presentith the in hevyn that same day . . .
> Thyn age at messe shall not encrease;
> Nor sodeyn deth that day shall not the spill;
> And without hostill [housel] yf thou hap to dissease,
> It shall stond therfore; & beleve thou this skyll,
> Than to here messe thou maste have will,
> Thes prophitable benefitts to the be lent,
> Wher God, in fowrm of bred, his body doth present.[30]

It was this sense of the blessings which flowed from seeing the Host which lay behind the increasing elaboration of all movement of the Blessed Sacrament, especially the founding of gilds or private endowments to provide a light to go before it in the street as it was carried to the sick, thereby alerting all who passed by to a further opportunity to kneel (whatever the weather and the state of the street) and reverently see the Host.

> For glad may that mon be
> That ones in the day may hym se.[31]

Margery Kempe, in a passage on her attendance at deathbeds, records the special veneration accorded to the Sacrament in fifteenth-

---

[29] Foxe, *Acts and Monuments*, IV p. 227.

[30] Dyboski, *Songs*, p. 70. The list is standard – Cf. LFMB, pp. 131–2, 366–73; *Festial*, pp. 169–70; *The Doctrinal of Sapyence*, fol. 63r.

[31] Westlake, *Parish Gilds*, nos 38, 135, 279, 367; Mirk, *Instructions for Parish Priests*, pp. 312–13: in this context of seeing the viaticum go by, he goes on to outline the benefits of seeing the Host.

century Kings, Lynn, as it was borne to the dying "abowte the town wyth lyte and reverens, the pepill knelyng on her kneys". This reverence was probably due to the work of the Corpus Christi gild which had functioned in Margery's parish church since 1349. In that year pestilence had swept through the town, and the sight of the sacrament being hurried through the streets to the dying, "with only a single candle of poor wax burning in front of it, whereas two torches of the best beeswax are hardly sufficient" scandalized some of the parishioners. In the heightened devotional atmosphere brought by the imminence of death three men resolved to fund more lights to be carried before the viaticum: they were quickly joined by others, and a gild devoted to Corpus Christi was the outcome.[32]

To see the Host, however fleetingly, was a privilege bringing blessing. Those robbed of this privilege by misfortunes such as poor eyesight might be rescued by heavenly intervention.[33] Conversely, the sacrilegious might be deprived of the ability to see the Host which they profaned. A mid-fifteenth-century chronicler recorded a spate of robberies in London churches, in which the pyxes hung over the altars to reserve the Host had been the only targets. It was widely believed that the thefts were motivated by heresy, and indeed the organizer was a Lollard who boasted at a supper that he had eaten "ix goddys at my sopyr that were in the boxys". But his accomplices were not heretics, and "it was done of very nede that they robbyd." One of the thieves, a lockyer and coppersmith, was in fact shocked to the core by the gang-leader's blasphemy, and went to Mass, and "prayde God of marcy". But Heaven was deaf, for

> whenn the pryste was at the levacyon of the masse, he myght not
> see that blessed sacrament of the auter. Thenn he was sory, and
> abode tylle anothyr pryste went to masse and helpyd the same
> pryste to masse, and say howe the oste lay apon the auter and
> alle the tokyns and sygnys that the preste made; but whenn
> the pryste hylde uppe that holy sacrament at the tyme of
> levacyon he myght se nothynge of that blessyd body of Cryste
> at noo tyme of the masse, not so moche at Agnus Dei.

A stiff drink at the local alehouse and attendance at three more Masses with the same result convinced him that his selective blind-

[32] *The Book of Margery Kempe*, p. 172: it is just possible that Margery is talking here about the Corpus Christi procession, but the context makes it more likely that the parish priest's journey with the viaticum is intended; Westlake, *Parish Gilds*, no. 279. For the growth of devotion to the Host as it was carried to the sick, see more generally, Rubin, *Corpus Christi*, pp. 77–82.
[33] See below, pp. 189–90.

ness was not "febyllnes of hys brayne", but that "bothe he and hys felescyppe lackyd grace." Only after a sincere confession to a priest was he enabled to "see that blessyd sacrament well inowe" and so make a good end.[34]

Seeing and Believing

That story was recorded to refute the impieties of the Lollards, and there is an evident preoccupation with the refutation of attacks on the sacramental teaching of the Church in much fifteenth- and early sixteenth-century writing about the power and pre-eminent sanctity of the Eucharist. In part this sprang from the audacity and strangeness of the Church's Eucharistic faith, and the discrepancy it seemed to posit between perception and reality. Grace came by gazing on the Host: to see it was to be blessed. But what one saw was misleading, and Lollardy was only possible because the appearance of bread in the Host cloaked the divine reality which was the true source of blessing. The Host did not look like the thing it was.

> Hyt semes quite [white], and is red
> Hyt is quike, and seemes dede:
> Hyt is flesche and seemes brede
> Hyt is on and semes too;
> Hyt is God body and no more.[35]

Late medieval Eucharistic piety was underscored by the problem of doubt, inevitably understood by the orthodox as the work of the Devil: as one preacher insisted, "If there cum any wickyd temptacion to thee of the fende by the whiche thou semyst be thy foly that it scholde nat be the very body of criste then it commyth from the devyll."[36]

Many of the stories routinely used to expound the meaning and power of the Host addressed themselves to this problem of seeing and not seeing. And as in the story of the blinded coppersmith, the true nature of the Host is almost always approached and endorsed in the standard exempla by means of a story about a doubter. A representative example is included by Robert Mannyng in his *Handlyng Synne*, and tells of a learned monk who doubts the Real Presence. At the prayers of two older monks to whom he confided his doubts, he and they were granted a vision during Mass. As the

---

[34] Gray, *Oxford Book*, pp. 11–12.
[35] R. H. Robbins, "Popular Prayers in Middle English Verse", *Modern Philology*, XXXVI, 1939, p. 344.
[36] R. L. Homan, "Two Exempla: Analogues to the Play of the Sacrament and Dux Moraud", *Comparative Drama*, XVIII, 1984, p. 248.

priest broke the Host after the consecration, they saw in his hands a child being stabbed by an angel, so that the child's blood ran into the chalice. At the communion the doubting monk was offered the sacrament, and was horrified to see in the priest's hands bleeding morsels of flesh. On acknowledging his error and crying for mercy, the sacrament returned to its normal appearance, and the monk is duly houselled.[37] Mirk tells a very similar story of "St Ode that was bishop of Canterbury", who convinced doubting clergy in his entourage by showing them the blood oozing over his fingers from the broken Host and dripping into the chalice: after their confession of error "the sacrament turnet into his forme of bred as hit was beforn."[38] The story has endless variants, but in its most common form Pope Gregory the Great convinced a woman who, having made the bread for the Mass, laughed aloud at the communion because she could not accept that her handiwork had become the very body of God. Once again the doubter was convinced and terrified by the sight of "raw flessch bledyng", and the Host only returned to its normal appearance after the Pope and all the people prayed that it should.[39]

There is here a striking fusion of devotional and polemical concerns. A preoccupation with inculcating the shared belief about the Eucharist which forms the community is expressed in the form of stories attacking the unbelief which breaks the bonds of community. Maybe this reflected actual experience of heresy: Lollards frequently seem to have set out to shock and antagonize their neighbours by ridiculing not merely their beliefs, but the forms in which these beliefs found expression. At the elevation at high Mass at Eye in Suffolk on Corpus Christi Day 1431, "when all the parishioners and other strangers kneeled down, holding up their hands and doing reverence unto the sacrament" Nicholas Canon went behind a pillar, turned his back on the altar, and "mocked them that did reverence unto the sacrament", an outrage on communal convictions and communal proprieties which he was to repeat on other festivals.[40] Holding up of the hands and the more or less audible recitation of elevation prayers at the sacring was a gesture expected of everyone: refusal or omission was a frequent cause of the detection of Lollards. And the refusal of such gestures might be held to exclude one from the human community, since they excluded one from the church, as when Thomas Halfaker denounced a group of his Buckinghamshire neighbours because

---

[37] C. Horstmann (ed.), *Minor Poems of the Vernon Mss*, EETS, 1892, 1901, I pp. 201–2.
[38] *Festial*, pp. 170–1.
[39] L. G. Powell (ed.), *The Mirrour of the Blessed Lyf of Jesu*, 1908, pp. 308–9: *Festial*, p. 173.
[40] Foxe, *Acts and Monuments*, III p. 599.

"coming to church, and especially at the elevation time, [they] would say no prayers, but did sit mum (as he termed it) like beasts."[41] Indeed, the very beasts might offer heretics an edifying example of how community should be structured by faith in the sacrament. A common Corpus Christi exemplum concerns a parson of Axbridge, in the Mendips. Rushing to bring the viaticum to a dying parishioner, he let fall a host from the pyx, and unbeknown to him it trundled away into the grass of a meadow. On discovering his loss he went to the meadow, to find all the beasts of the field gathered in adoration round the lost Host. Caesarius of Heisterbach has a similar story about a hive of bees who create a chapel for a stolen Host placed in the hive in order to promote honey production, and gather round to worship, thereby confounding the sacrilegious hive-owner.[42]

In many of these Eucharistic miracle stories the doubter is portrayed as a culpable deviant, an outsider, who is restored to the company of believers, made an insider, by a shocking revelation of the fleshly reality of the Sacrament. The bleeding child, the morsels of flesh, are ghastly, and have to be hidden once again under sacramental forms before they can be consumed. The overwhelming physical realism of these stories is an inescapable element of late medieval Eucharistic piety, but it is important to grasp that, for the late medieval believer, the horrifying vision of bleeding flesh was not intended as the only or even the normative image of the saving reality of the sacrament. It could not be, for such stories offered an image of Christ's blood which, like Abel's, cried out for vengeance. Its presentation to the eye of the unbeliever was meant to be frightening, designed to convict of sin and shock into faith. For this reason, in the early sixteenth-century legend of the Blood of Hailes, when a Lollard priest attempts to say mass

> The holy sacrament of cristes owne blod there
> Reboyled anone up: unto the chalyce brynke.[43]

The angry boiling blood was not designed to provide a model of how the sacrament should be understood by the believer. Christ in the sacrament was not a wounded child, nor was the Host mangled flesh. In one sense such images did indeed convey "the form and truth of the Blessed Sacrament"[44] and calming and beautiful versions

[41] Foxe, *Acts and Monuments*, IV p. 225.

[42] *Festial*, pp. 173–4; Rubin, "Mastering the Mystery": I am greatly indebted to Dr Rubin for allowing me to see this unpublished paper.

[43] J. C. T. Oates, "Richard Pynson and the Holy Blood of Hayles", *The Library*, 5th series, XIII, 1958, pp. 260–77.

[44] Love, *Mirror*, p. 310.

of them might be told, like the tender revelation of the Christ-child in the hands of the priest granted to Edward the Confessor.[45] But in the versions of such stories current in fifteenth- and early sixteenth-century England, the visionary images more frequently emphasize an aspect of the Eucharistic reality which was only presented to sin and unbelief, to those outside the household of faith. To those within, by contrast, the Host was manna, food, the bond of unity, the forgiveness of sins.

The classic medieval representative of culpable unbelief, the ultimate outsider, is of course the Jew, and unbelieving Jews regularly feature in Eucharistic miracle stories. In one example a Jew following a Christian friend into a church witnesses what he thinks is a revolting act of cannibalism, when he sees the priest and every member of the congregation devour a beautiful child.[46] His friend explains that this vision is in fact a sign of God's wrath against the Jews who crucified his Son; had he been a faithful Christian, he would have seen only the Host.

> This is the skille, quath the Cristene man,
> That god nout soffreth the than
> The sacrament that ben so sleye,
> That his Flesh mihte ben so hud
> To us cristene with-inne the bred.
> And thy kun made hym dye,
> Therfore al blodi thou hym seye.

What is torn and bleeding flesh to the Jew, in other words, is the bread of Heaven to believers, and is intended by God to be experienced in the reassuring form of bread. This is enough for the Jew, who immediately seeks baptism, so that he may never again be harrowed by such a vision:

> Help that I were a Cristene mon;
> For leuere ichaue cristned ben
> Then euere seo such a siht ayen.[47]

The late medieval audience for such stories would have recognized in the behaviour attributed to the Jew not a personal squeamishness, but a much more generally applicable reference to the Last Judgement. That was the moment when the sinner or unbeliever would

---

[45] Rubin, *Corpus Christi*, pp. 117–19.
[46] Rubin, *Corpus Christi*, pp. 123–4, 130–1. Interestingly, although the Jew sees all eat, only the priest has actually received communion. As the congregation views the Host a replica child flies to each of them and is eaten, a revealing manifestation of belief in "spiritual communion".
[47] Horstmann, *Minor Poems from the Vernon MS*, I p. 177.

see once more the gruesome images of the Eucharistic miracle stories, the terrifying sight of Christ with bloody wounds: "they shall look on him whom they have pierced."[48] Mirk has a macabre story in the Lenten section of the *Festial* which illustrates that dimension of the image of the wounded Christ. It tells of a Norfolk chapman who, though gravely ill, refuses to go to confession: Christ appears to him in a dream "bodyly with blody wondys" to plead with him. When the chapman remains obdurate, Christ casts a handful of his blood in the chapman's face and warns him that it will be a witness against him on Judgement Day. The chapman dies and is damned.[49]

This is the conception at work in these Eucharistic miracle stories, and the most sustained late medieval English treatment of the miracles of the Host embodies just this theme of the appearance of the bloody Christ in the Sacrament as a warning of the need to repent. The *Croxton Play of the Sacrament* was written in East Anglia in the later fifteenth century.[50] It tells the story of a miracle which took place in Aragon and was reputedly authenticated at Rome in 1461. A group of Jews, led by one Jonathas, bribe a Christian businessman to steal and sell them a consecrated Host. Determined to prove for themselves the falsehood of Christian belief, Jonathas and his friends subject the Host to a series of indignities which re-enact the torments of the Passion. They pierce it with five wounds, from which of course it bleeds profusely. They then "crucify" it by nailing it to a post with three large nails. In a scene of pure farce, Jonathas's hand ludicrously comes away from his arm and cleaves to the Host he has abused, and there follows a comic interlude based on traditional mumming plays, complete with a drunken quack doctor and his smart-alec assistant. The Host and the hand are cast into boiling oil, but the cauldron, like the Lollard priest's chalice, fills with blood and spills over. Finally the Host is "buried" with the hand in an oven. Like the tomb on Easter Day the oven is riven open, and Christ appears standing in the ruins as the Image of Pity, displaying his wounds and reproaching the Jews for once more crucifying him. Jonathas and his friends repent and believe, Jonathas is healed, and all seek baptism from the bishop. In a phrase reminiscent of other Eucharistic miracles they tell the Bishop that Christ has shewed himself to them as "A chyld apperyng with wondys blody". As in the story of Gregory and the unbelieving woman, the bishop cries to Christ for mercy and

---

[48] See below, pp. 247–8.
[49] *Festial*, pp. 91–2.
[50] Edited by Norman Davis, *Non-Cycle Plays and Fragments*, EETS, 1970.

forgiveness, and the terrifying and reproachful image of Christ displaying his bleeding wounds is changed again into the comforting of the sacramental bread. Thus "dread" is changed to "grett swettnesse". The bishop takes up the Host, and the Jews, the merchant, and his chaplain form a Corpus Christi procession. The bishop preaches a sermon on the importance of the sacrament of penance, the merchant confesses his sins, the Jews are baptised, and the play ends with a "Te Deum" in honour of the Holy Name of Jesus.[51]

The Croxton play is an extraordinary amalgam of a whole series of late medieval devotional *topoi*. It should perhaps be called the Croxton play of the sacraments, for it is almost as directly concerned with the sacrament of penance as with that of the Eucharist. The play also dramatises the conventional devotional call to repentance which was part of the cult of the Image of Pity. It is true that the sin of the Jews in the play in recrucifying the Sacramental Christ is specifically that of unbelief: to an East Anglian audience they would perhaps have recalled those other unbelieving outsiders, the Lollards. But their repentance is also presented in terms which assimilate it to the repentance required not only of heretics, but of all sinners, and hence of the audience itself.[52]

"Dredd" into "Sweetness"

When Christ appears in the Croxton play the stage direction stipulates that "Here the owyn must ryve asunder and blede owt at the crannys, and an image appere owt with woundys bledyng." When Jesus first speaks the direction runs "Here shall the image speke to the Juys." Despite the use of the word "image", we are not dealing here, of course, with a puppet or a ventriloquist's dummy, but with an actor painted with wounds and scourge marks, naked to the waist, representing the "Imago pietatis", The Image of Pity or "Man of Sorrows" (Pl. 47). The reproaches spoken by the Croxton Jesus are modelled on the appeals which usually accompanied the prints and drawings of the Image which circulated so widely in the period, such as Hawes's "See me, be kind".[53] In the Croxton play, as in so many of the Host stories, the

---

[51] *Non-Cycle Plays*, pp. 83, 89.

[52] C. Cutts, "The Croxton Play: an Anti-Lollard Piece", *Modern Language Quarterly*, V, 1944, pp. 45–60; the thesis is tellingly criticized in A. E. Nichols, "The Croxton Play of the Sacrament: a Re-Reading", *Comparative Drama*, XXII, 1988–9, pp. 117–37. Cutts's approach to the Croxton play is extended to the Towneley cycle in L. Lepow, *Enacting the Sacrament: Counter-Lollardy in the Towneley Cycle*, 1990.

[53] *Non-Cycle Plays*, p. 80; see below, pp. 244–8.

bleeding Christ behind the Host is intended to be seen as a figure of Judgement, as one of the Jews declares:

> They that be ded shall come agayn to Judgement,
> And owr dredfull Judge shalbe thys same brede.

But the bleeding Christ displaying his wounds was not only an image of justice and of judgement. The devotional ubiquity of the Image of Pity in late medieval England testifies to its ability to console as well as to frighten or disturb. If Christ's wounds reproached, the believer might respond, as the characters in the Croxton play did, by repentance and compassion. In that response to the blood of Christ, grace flowed.

All the sacraments, it was believed, took their meaning and power from the blood of Christ. As John Fisher explained:

> This moost holy and dere blode of Ihesu cryste shedde for our redemcyon, bought and gave so grete and plenteous vertue to the sacramentes, that as ofte as any creature shall use and receyve ony of them, so ofte it is to be byleved they are sprencled with the droppes of the same moost holy blode.[54]

This perception was no theological abstraction, the possession of clerical or lay élites, for it was given vivid iconographic expression in the popular art of the period. All over England, though perhaps especially in the West Country and the West Midlands, late fifteenth- and early sixteenth-century donors paid for the installation of Seven-Sacrament windows in their parish churches. These windows all contained a centrally placed figure of Christ, displaying his wounds. From the wounds rays or bands of red glass, representing the precious blood, flowed to the other panels of the window, in each of which one of the seven sacraments was portrayed (Pl. 48).[55]

But of all the sacraments, the Mass was supremely the sacrament of Christ's blood, and it had its own distinctive iconographical representation of that special link. The "Mass of Pope Gregory", modelled on one of the many Host miracles associated with the saint, shows the Pope celebrating Mass (Pl. 49). As he bends to consecrate the elements, kneels to worship them, or stands to elevate them, the figure of Christ emerging from his tomb, displaying his wounds and surrounded by the implements of the Passion, appears above the altar. This was a highly compressed

---

[54] Fisher, *English Works*, p. 109.
[55] For a list of surviving Seven-Sacrament windows and fragments see Painton Cowen, *A Guide to Stained Glass in Britain*, 1985, p. 252; for a discussion of their iconography see G. McN. Rushforth "Seven Sacrament Compositions", *passim*.

theological image, teaching the real presence and the unity of
Christ's suffering with the daily sacrifice in every church in
Christendom. Though it certainly evolved out of a fusion of
the story of the doubting woman who had baked the Eucharistic
bread[56] with the devotional Image of Pity, because both were
associated with the name of Gregory, it was emphatically an image
of forgiveness and grace, not of judgement. Its consolatory power
for English men and women is attested by the fact that both in its
full-blown form and in the simpler version of the Image of Pity,
without the figure of the Pope, it found its way into primers and
other prayer-books, devotional paintings, and prints circulating
with or without text, into stained glass, and even on to tomb
brasses and carvings. In the tiny Norfolk parish church of
Wellingham in the 1530s the parishioners erected an altar which
dominated the south side of their new Rood-screen. Over the altar
the painter set as reredos a naively painted version of the Image of
Pity (Pl. 50). Rather more lavishly, Alice Chester in the 1470s gave
to the Jesus altar in her church of All Saints Bristol an altar-piece
with the same image, "our Lord rising out of the sepulchre, sometimes called our Lord's Pity".[57] Every Mass at these altars thus
became a re enactment of the Mass of Pope Gregory, and the
presence of the crucified Lord in the Host was impressed on everyone who raised their eyes at the sacring. And because it did portray
"Our Lord rising out of the Sepulchre", it had a particular appropriateness to the Easter observances associated with the Host. It was
in a three-dimensional image of this sort, "an ymage of silver of
our Saviour with yhs woundes bledyng" and with "a little pixe for
the saccrament upon the breste" that the parishioners of St Peter
Mancroft, Norwich, buried the Host each year in their Easter
sepulchre, clinching the image's Eucharistic resonances.[58]

Spectators or Participants? Lay Religion and the Mass

The power to consecrate the Host was priestly power. Christ had
left to his Apostles "yee and to al othyr prestes, power and dignite
forto make his body of bred and wyne yn the auter, so that eche
prest hath of Cristis geft power forto make this sacrament, be he
bettyr, be he wors."[59] Margery Kempe, grilled by the Abbot of
Leicester about her belief concerning the Sacrament, knew what
was expected of her, and replied that

[56] See above, pp. 102–3.
[57] Bristol All Saints CWA (b) pp. 258–9.
[58] Norwich, St Peter Mancroft CWA, p. 209.
[59] Festial, p. 169.

Serys, I beleue in the Sacrament of the awter in this wyse, that what man hath takyn the ordyr of presthode, be he neuyr so vicyows a man in hys levyng, yef he say dewly tho wordys over the bred that owr Lord Ihesu Criste seyde whan he mad hys Mawnde among his disciplys ther he sat at soper, I be-leve that it is hys very flesch & hys blood & no material bred ne never may be unseyd be it onys seyd.[60]

The prestige of the Sacrament as the centre and source of the whole symbolic system of late medieval Catholicism implied an enormously high doctrine of priesthood. The priest had access to mysteries forbidden to others: only he might utter the words which transformed bread and wine into the flesh and blood of God incarnate, those "fyue wordes. withouten drede / that no mon but a prest schulde rede".[61] No layman or woman might even touch the sacred vessels with their bare hands. When the laity drank the draught of unconsecrated wine which they were given after communion to wash down the Host and ensure they had swallowed it, they had to cover their hands with the houseling-cloth, for the virtue of the Host and blood affected even the dead metal of the chalice. Power "leaked" from the Host and the blood: whooping cough could be cured by getting a priest to give one a threefold draught of water or wine from his chalice after Mass.[62]

The mystery that surrounded the central sanctities of the Mass were reflected in the language in which, like the rest of the liturgy, it was celebrated. The combination of the decent obscurity of a learned language on one hand, and clerical monopoly – or at least primacy – in the control and ordering of the liturgy on the other, has led to the view that the worship of late medieval England was non-participatory. The fact that in most churches the high altar was divided from the nave by a Rood-screen has lent support to this notion. Bernard Manning, in what remains one of the most suggestive and sympathetic accounts of late medieval religion, nevertheless wrote of a tendency "to leave the service more and more to the clerks alone", and a more modern commentator has even talked of a "lay society separated by rood screens and philo-

[60] *The Book of Margery Kempe*, p. 115.

[61] LFMB, p. 147. The *Golden Legend*, in making this point, tells a theologically rather confused story of some shepherds who recited the words of institution, turned bread into flesh, and were promptly roasted by a thunderbolt, "and therefore the holy fathers stablished these words to be said low, also that none should say them without he were a priest." *Golden Legend*, VII p. 239.

[62] *Letters and Papers, Foreign and Domestic, of the Reign of Henry VIII*, ed. J. S. Brewer, J. Gairdner, and R. H. Brodie, 1862–1910 (hereafter = L&P) XVIII/2 p. 309; *A Hundred Merry Tales*, pp. 100–1.

sophical abstractions from the 'alienated liturgy' of the altar".[63]
Enough has been said in the first chapter about lay assimilation of
liturgical themes to make any such notion of general lay alienation
from the liturgy untenable. But what of the specific case of the
Mass: to what extent was lay involvement with this most sacred
and central of the rites of Christendom passive or alienating?

Any attempt to tackle this question must start from the recognition that lay people experienced the Mass in a variety of ways and
in a range of settings. The parish Mass was indeed celebrated at the
high altar, and that altar was often physically distanced even from
the nearest members of the congregation, and partially obscured by
the screen. In some of the great parish churches, like St Margaret's,
Lynn, or Walpole St Peter, parishioners would have been well out
of earshot of anything said, as opposed to sung, at the altar. During
Lent, moreover, a huge veil was suspended within the sanctuary
area, to within a foot or so of the ground, on weekdays completely
blocking the laity's view of the celebrant and the sacring.[64] However, we need to grasp that both screen and veil were manifestations
of a complex and dynamic understanding of the role of both
distance and proximity, concealment and exposure within the
experience of the liturgy. Both screen and veil were barriers,
marking boundaries between the people's part of the church and the
holy of holies, the sacred space within which the miracle of transubstantiation was effected, or, in the case of the veil, between
different types of time, festive and penitential. The veil was there
precisely to function as a temporary ritual deprivation of the sight
of the sacring. Its symbolic effectiveness derived from the fact that
it obscured for a time something which was normally accessible; in
the process it heightened the value of the spectacle it temporarily
concealed.

[63] B. L. Manning, *The People's Faith in the Time of Wyclif*, 1919, p. 11; G. McMurray
Gibson, *The Theater of Devotion*, 1989, p. 41 – she is paraphrasing, apparently with approval,
a paper by Clifford Flanigan.

[64] W. H. Frere, *The Use of Sarum*, 1898–1901, I pp. 139–40; Rock, *Church of Our Fathers*,
IV pp. 257–62; Ludlow CWA, p. 3 records payments for the cords to draw up the cloth
"that hangyth in the mydes of the heygh chancelle in the Lent". It should not be confused
with the cloth which hung "afore the roode on Palme Sunday". Similar payments for the
"velum templi" are recorded at Leverton in Lincolnshire – Leverton CWA, p. 347. The phrase
"velum templi" was no idle one, since the veil was dramatically lowered at the mention of
the rending of the veil of the Jerusalem temple, during the reading of the Matthean Passion
narrative in Holy Week. The veil was not used during the canon of the Mass on the solemn
days of Lent and was raised for the reading of the Gospel at masses on the ferial days. On
these days it was lowered again at the "Orate Fratres", just before the canon of the Mass, in
order to conceal the elevation, though it appears that pressure from the laity to see the Host
was eroding this custom at the end of the Middle Ages (*Use of Sarum*, I p. 140). Brackets and
attachments for the Lent veil can still be seen in the chancels at Horsham St Faith and
Haddiscoe in Norfolk, and at Monk's Soham, Troston, and Norton in Suffolk.

The screen itself was both a barrier and no barrier. It was not a wall but rather a set of windows, a frame for the liturgical drama, solid only to waist-height, pierced by a door wide enough for ministers and choir to pass through and which the laity themselves might penetrate on certain occasions, for example, when, as at Eye on festivals, they gathered with torches to honour the sacrament, and in processions like the Candlemas one and the ceremonies and watching associated with the Easter sepulchre. Even the screen's most solid section, the dado, might itself be pierced with elevation squints, to allow the laity to pass visually into the sanctuary at the sacring.[65] This penetration was a two-way process: if the laity sometimes passed through the screen to the mystery, the mystery sometimes moved out to meet them. Each Mass was framed within a series of ritual moments at which the ministers, often carrying sacred objects, such as the Host itself at Easter, or, on ordinary Sundays, Gospel texts, the paxbred, or sacramentals like holy water or holy bread, passed out of the sanctuary into the body of the church. We shall explore some of these moments shortly.

But in any case, it is vital to remember that the parish Mass, important as it was for lay experience of the liturgy, was by no means the only or perhaps even the most common lay experience of the Mass. Many lay people, perhaps even most of them, attended Mass on some weekdays. These weekday masses were not usually the elaborate ritual affairs, with a procession, the blessing of holy water and holy bread, and some singing, which most parishes could have mustered on Sundays. The daily Masses to which the laity resorted to "see my Maker" were "low" Masses, short ceremonies celebrated at altars which, far from being concealed behind screens and out of earshot of the worshippers, were often within arm's reach. In his version of the *Doctrinal of Sapyence*, a treatise aimed at instructing "symple prestes . . . and symple peple", Caxton complained that far from standing well back in awe and reverence at Mass,

> moche peple . . . go nyghe and about the aulter and stond so nyghe the aulter that they trouble oftimes the preest for the dissolucions that they doo in spekyng in lawhing and many other maners and not only the laye men and women but also the

---

[65] Regional variation was a factor here; the heavily carved screens of Devon, stretching across the whole width of the church and having massive lofts, or like the one at Flamborough in Yorkshire, similarly massive, may have had a different ritual "feel" to the more slender and open screens of eastern England. For general discussion of these differences see Aylmer Vallance, *English Church Screens*, 1936, and F. Bond and B. Camm, *Roodscreens and Roodlofts*, 1909.

clerkes by whom the other ought to be governed and taken ensample of.[66]

The surviving evidence of the ritual arrangements of countless English churches confirms this picture of the accessibility of the daily celebration to the laity. Great churches, of course, had many altars, in side chapels, in chantries divided from the body of the church by parclosing or wainscot, or against pillars. But even small churches had their quota of altars for the celebration of gild and chantry Masses, all crammed into the nave. Often these altars made use of the Rood-screen, not as a barrier against contact with the Mass, but as the backdrop for it. At Ranworth in Norfolk these altar arrangements survive intact, with two altars flanking the central portion of the screen, using the paintings on its extreme northern and southern sections as reredos. An identical arrange-ment operated at Bramfield in Suffolk (Pl. 51), where the elaborate piscina to the south of the screen reveals the presence of an altar of some importance.[67] Even the tiny church of Wellingham, only sixteen feet wide, had an altar pushed up against the south screen, while at South Burlingham the mark of an even more substantial altar against the north screen is still visible. The altars at Wellingham and South Burlingham must have crowded the east end of the nave, and awkwardly interrupted the decorative schemes of the screens against which they were placed. But many of these nave altars were much more carefully integrated into the planning of the screen, as at Ranworth, Bramfield, and, even more spectacularly, at Attleburgh.[68] They were clearly among the most important focuses of ritual activity in the building. This prominence given to nave altars was no merely regional phenomenon. Jesus altars in many parishes attracted multiple benefactions for the maintenance of the worship of the Holy Name, and the Jesus altars in cathedrals like Durham, in great town churches like St Lawrence, Reading, and smaller buildings like All Saints, Bristol, were prominently placed in the people's part of the church, and had elaborate sung services endowed at them. The Jesus Mass at All Saints, Bristol, was celebrated several times a week, had a choir of its own and a set of organs; in addition to the Mass the priest and singers performed the "Salve" anthem at night.[69]

[66] *Doctrinal of Sapyence*, fol. 63v.
[67] H. Munro Cautley, *Suffolk Churches and their Treasures*, 5th ed. 1982, p. 228 and plate 119.
[68] Illustrated in N. Pevsner, *Buildings of England: North-West and South Norfolk*, 1962, plate 31(a).
[69] Bristol All Saints CWA (b) pp. 237–8.

The laity controlled, often indeed owned these altars. They provided the draperies in which they were covered, the images and ornaments and lights which encoded the dedication and functions of the altar and its worship. They specified the times and seasons at which the appearance and worship of the altar was to be varied. Their wills show an intense awareness of varying season and occasion – particular frontals or curtains for "good days", sombre array for requiems and year's minds, velvet or silk coats and bonnets and silver shoes to dress the altar images on festivals, and so on. The liturgy celebrated at these altars reflected the greater degree of lay involvement possible at them. The parish liturgy was fixed, following the order specified in calendar, missal, breviary, or processional. But most of the Masses said at the nave altars were votive or requiem ones, or Masses in honour of Our Lady or some favourite saint. As a consequence, the laity who paid for these celebrations could have a direct control over the prayers and readings used at them. It was standard practice for testators, whether founding a long-term chantry or less elaborately laying out a fiver on endowing an "annualer", to specify the use of particular collects, secrets, and post-communion prayers, or the celebration of a specific Mass or sequence of Masses on particular days of the week, or to stipulate the use of variant or even additional Gospels within the structure of a particular Mass. These extra Gospels were inserted at the end of Mass, just before the reading of the first chapter of St John's Gospel, with which every Mass concluded.[70] And since this was a culture in which specific prayers or Gospel passages were believed to be especially powerful, to bring particular blessings or protection from certain evils, even the unlettered laity noticed, and valued, such variations. In many cases, perhaps in most, these variant liturgical prescriptions would have been arrived at in consultation with clerical advisers, "my ghostly father". But the fact remained that it was lay men and women who hired, and who could often fire, the clergy who carried out their instructions. It makes no sense to talk here about an 'alienated liturgy of the altar". This was Eucharistic worship in which lay people called the shots.

The proprietary control of individuals, families, or larger groups like gilds over the liturgy of the nave altars raises another difference between the Masses said there and at the parish altar. Among the furnishings of these nave altars were their own "paxes", with their attendant peace rituals. Consequently, they represented a different ordering of community from that expressed or imposed by the Sunday Mass. Some of the implications of this can be teased out by

[70] Wood Legh, *Perpetual Chantries*, pp. 295–6.

considering the arrangements made in many places for the provision of a Jesus Mass at a nave altar.

The Mass in honour of the Holy Name of Jesus was, throughout
the fifteenth century, one of the most popular of all votive Masses.
From the 1470s onwards, Jesus brotherhoods proliferated throughout England, dedicated to the maintenance of a regular celebration
of the Mass of the Holy Name, often on a Friday, at an altar over
which there might be its own Jesus image, distinct from the
Crucifix.[71] These Masses often began as the specific devotion of
a small group, or as an individual benefaction, but invariably
generated other donations and bequests, large and small, "to the
sustentation of the Mass of Jesus". Wherever it occurs, the Jesus
Mass has all the hallmarks of a genuinely popular devotion.[72] Yet
the Mass of Jesus was also emphatically an observance seized on by
élites in every community as a convenient expression, and perhaps
an instrument, of their social dominance. From its beginnings in
England the cult of the Holy Name had aristocratic backing, and it
achieved status as a feast in the 1480s under the patronage of Lady
Margaret Beaufort, whose domestic clergy composed the Office.[73]
In many towns, the well-to-do and powerful emulated the court's
patronage of the cult. At Reading, the Jesus Mass at the church of
St Lawrence began on the initiative of one of the town's wealthiest
clothiers, Henry Kelsall, "fyrst mynder, sustayner and mayntayner
of the devocyon of the Masse of Jhu". The Jesus altar dominated
the nave at St Lawrence's, and the Mass itself was funded and
controlled by an exclusive gild of ten wealthy men and their wives.
The gild acquired considerable land in the area, and was responsible
for paying the sexton's wages, in return for his care of the gear
of the altar and gild. The importance of this group in the life of
the parish can be gauged from a town ordinance of 1547, which
stipulated that the wives of former members of the Jesus gild "shall
from henseforth sitt & have the highest scats or pewes next unto the
Mayors wifs seate towardes the pulpitt".[74]

The Jesus Mass at the town church of All Saints, Bristol, was
similarly sustained by the benefactions of the wealthy, and celebrated at the former Lady altar (increasingly in the late fifteenth

---

[71] As at Long Melford, but the precise nature of "Jesus" images in late medieval England
is a subject yet to be researched.
[72] The evidence from Kent is conveniently accessible in *Testamenta Cantiana: East Kent*, ed.
A. Hussey, 1907, pp. 14, 19, 30, 48, 53, 55, 57, 61, 90, 101, 107, 113, 126, 163, 202, 234,
235, 260, 285, 336, 355, 360, 367. A wide range of material on Jesus Masses, anthems,
and fraternities was brought together by E. G. C. Atchley, "Jesus Mass and Anthems",
Transactions of the St Paul's Ecclesiological Society, V, 1905, pp. 163–9.
[73] Pfaff, *New Feasts*, chapter 4.
[74] Reading, St Lawrence CWA, pp. 28–32.

and early sixteenth century called the Jesus altar) in what was effectively the private chantry chapel of Thomas Halleway, a former mayor of Bristol, who had installed fixed pews with doors for himself and his family directly in front of the Jesus altar.[75] On the other side of England, the Jesus Mass at Long Melford was celebrated at an altar in "my aisle, called Jesus aisle", as Roger Martin wrote. The aisle was the burial chapel of the Martin family, and when iconoclasm reached Long Melford in Edward's reign Martin took the reredos of the Jesus altar to his home, as much a manifestation of proprietary rights as of his undoubted traditionalist piety. As elsewhere, the wealthy of Long Melford were conspicuous in their bequests to the ornaments and maintenance of the Jesus Mass.[76]

That the parishioners of St Lawrence, Reading, All Saints, Bristol, or Holy Trinity, Long Melford, came in numbers to the Jesus Masses is not to be doubted, and the existence of bequests to these masses and to hundreds like them up and down the country leaves no doubt that they felt that, whoever had begun it, the Mass was now the possession of the community at large. But the altars, vestments, vessels, and clergy belonged not to the community at large, but to Henry Kelsall and his gild brethren, to Thomas Halleway, to the Martin family. The pax kissed at those masses was not the property of the parish, but the possession of the gilds, families or individuals who had established the devotion. The Mass belonged more to some than to others (Pl. 52–3).

This is not to suggest that the liturgy at these altars was in any simple sense an instrument of social hegemony or, worse, social control. The founders and donors of such Masses saw themselves, and were seen by others, as benefactors bestowing a spiritual amenity on their parish, and such benefactions earned one an honoured place in the parish bede-roll.[77] But the implications for the perception of the religious dimensions of community in towns and villages at such Masses were clearly more narrowly defined and more problematic than that at the parish altar on Sundays. We shall explore further dimensions of the complexities of the notion of communality in a late medieval religious community in a later chapter. Here it is sufficient to notice that in this respect, as in others, it is impossible to talk of a single type of experience of the Mass.

[75] Bristol All Saints CWA (b), pp. 236–7.
[76] Parker, *History of Long Melford*, pp. 73, 221.
[77] See below, pp. 139–41, 327–337.

37. The Our Father, from the *Arte or Crafte to Lyve Well.*

38. Matrimony, from the *Arte or Crafte to Lyve Well.*

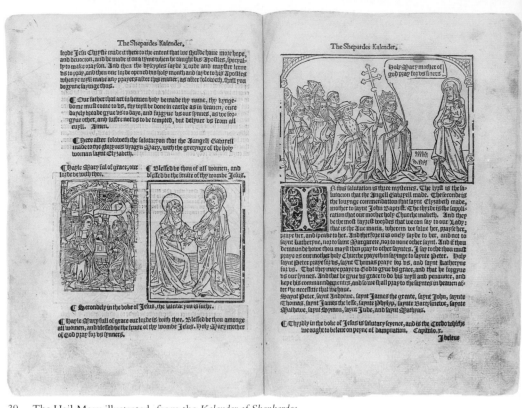

39. The Hail Mary illustrated, from the *Kalender of Shepherdes*.

40. The Mass, from the font at Westhall, Suffolk. Note the hands of the kneeling worshippers raised in the conventional gesture of adoration.

41. Easter communion, from the font at Gayton Thorpe, Norfolk. The houseling towel hangs over the communicants' hands, and the parish clerk follows the priest with a chalice of unconsecrated wine, to facilitate swallowing the Host.

42.   The elevation at the sacring, from the font at Badingham, Suffolk. Note the sacring bell in the parish clerk's left hand, and the parishioners peering across the parclosing (top left and right) to see the Host.

⁋ The vertue of ỹ masse.

43.   Parishioners gather round the priest at Mass; the clerk holds an elevation torch.

46 (above left). This piscina and squint allowed the priest celebrating at the altar of St Erasmus in St Matthew's Ipswich to see his colleague at the high altar.

47 (above right). The Image of Pity, Wigginhall St Germans.

44 (facing page, above). Elevation squints in the screen at Burlingham St Edmund. Note the unpainted marks of a nave altar.

45 (facing page, below). Elevation squints above the heads of St Sebastian and St Dorothy, Roxton, Bedfordshire.

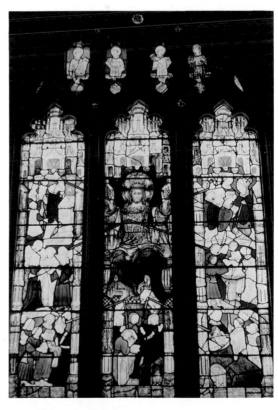

48. The Seven-Sacrament window, Doddiscombsleigh, Devon. The central figure of Christ is Victorian, replacing the medieval image smashed by iconoclasts.

49. The Mass of Pope Gregory, from a Sarum primer of 1497.

50. The south screen, Wellingham, Norfolk. The blank space beneath the Image of Pity marks the former nave altar site.

51. The south screen at Bramfield; the two blank bays at the end next to the elaborate piscina indicate a nave altar.

52. Private liturgy? The Spring chantry chapel at Lavenham, 1523.

53. Private liturgy breached: elevation squints at the west end of the Spring chantry enabled those kneeling outside to see the sacring.

54. The restored Rood-screen at Eye, Suffolk.

55. The Doom tympanum at Wenhaston, Suffolk. Bare patches mark the position of the carved Rood, Mary, and John. The Bible texts at the bottom, enjoining obedience to the monarch, are the remains of the Reformation overpainting of the Crucifixion and Doom scene.

56. The Apostles from the north screen at Ranworth, Norfolk.

57. The Apostles Sts Simon and Jude from the screen at Carleton Rode, Norfolk.

58.   The north screen at Burlingham St Andrew, donated by the Benet family.

59.   St John the Baptist and St Cecilia from the south screen, Burlingham St Andrew, given by John and Cecily Blake.

60.   St Apollonia and St Zita, Barton Turf, Norfolk.

61. St Bridget receiving her
revelations, from the *Dyetary of
Ghostly Helth*, 1520.

62. St Bridget of Sweden
receiving her revelations, from the
screen at Horsham St Faith,
Norfolk.

63. St James as a pilgrim, Martham, Norfolk.

64. Great miracles: St Martin raises a dead man, from the east window, St Martin's, York.

65. St Erasmus disembowelled.

67.   St Katherine and St Margaret, Ufford, Suffolk.

68. St Barbara, St Cecilia, St Dorothy, North Elmham, Norfolk.

69. St Agatha, Wigginhall St Mary, Norfolk.

70. Scene from the legend of St Margaret, Combs, Suffolk.

71. Helper saints: the presence of plague saints like St Roche (right) on this late screen at North Tuddenham, Norfolk, reveals anxieties about the growth of epidemic disease.

72. Helper saints: Master John Schorne, portrayed (right) at Gateley in Norfolk, was invoked against the ague.

Praying the Mass: the Individual's Experience

According to Lyndwood, the canon of the Mass was recited by the priest in silence "ne impediatur populus orare", so that the people might not be hindered from praying.[78] As that explanation reveals, it was not thought essential or even particularly desirable that the prayer of the laity should be the same as that of the priest at the altar. According to John Mirk, the parish priest should teach his people that

> whenne they doth to chyrche fare,
> Thenne bydde hem leve here mony wordes,
> Here ydel speche, and nyce bordes,
> And put a-way alle vanyte,
> And say here pater noster & here ave.

While at Mass they were neither to stand nor to slouch against pillars or walls, but to kneel and pray meekly and quietly on the floor. There were certain moments in the Mass when they might rise:

> whenne the gospelle i-red be schalle
> Teche hem thenne to stonde up alle,
> And blesse feyre as they conne,
> Whenne gloria tibi is begonne.[79]

These were the fundamental requirements for the laity at Mass: to kneel quietly without idle chatter, saying Paters and Aves, to respond to certain key gestures or phrases by changing posture, above all at the sacring to kneel with both hands raised in adoration, to gaze on the Host, and to greet their Lord with an elevation prayer. Mirk supplies a sample:

> Ihesu Lord, welcome thow be,
> In forme of bred as I the se;
> Ihesu! for thy holy name,
> Schelde me to day fro synne & schame.
> Schryfte & howsele, Lord, thou graunte me bo,
> Er that I schale hennes go,
> And verre contrycyone of my synne,
> That I lord never dye there-Inne;
> And as thow were of a may I-bore,
> Sofere me never to be for-lore,

[78] LFMB, p. xx.
[79] *Instructions for Parish Priests*, 9, lines 265–81.

But whenne that I schale hennes wende,
Grawnte me the blysse wyth–owten ende. Amen.[80]

A century on, Richard Whytford gave the devout Tudor householder almost identical advice, telling him to instruct his children
that the church was "a place of prayer / not of claterynge and
talkynge . . . charge them also to kepe theyr syght in the chirche
cloce upon theyr bokes or bedes. And whyle they ben yonge / let
them use ever to knele / stande or syt / and never to walke in the
chirche." They were to hear the mass "quyetly and deuoutly /
moche parte knelynge. But at the gospell / at the preface / and at
the Pater Noster, teche them to stande / and to make curtsy at this
worde Jesus as the preest dothe."[81] This was indeed a modest
requirement. It demanded from the laity no more than decency in
church and the recitation of the rosary while the priest got on with
the sacrifice at the altar. His liturgy and theirs converged only at the
climactic moment when Earth and Heaven met in the fragile disc of
bread he held above his head, and everyone found some heightened
form of words to greet and to petition the sacramental Christ for
salvation, health, and blessing. The parishioners of Woodchurch in
Kent, complaining about their neighbour Roger Harlakinden in
1511 that "he janglith and talkithe in the chirche when he is there
and lettithe others to say their divociones" give us a glimpse of that
modest ideal actually in practice.[82]

In fact this minimum requirement was frequently felt to be
inadequate both by the church authorities and by the laity themselves. Texts to assist the devout laity to a fuller participation in the
Mass were produced thoughout the later Middle Ages, of which the
best known is the rhyming *Lay Folk's Mass Book*, perhaps originally
produced in Norman French, and Englished in the fourteenth
century. Lydgate produced a somewhat more elaborate but essentially similar work for the Countess of Suffolk in the mid fifteenth
century, and Caxton published a lengthy prose guide, "the Noble
History of the Exposition of the Mass" at the end of his version of
the *Golden Legend*.[83] None of these works is a translation of the
Mass itself, though they all contain paraphrases of some of the
prayers in the outer sections of the mass, such as the "Gloria
in Excelsis" or the Lord's Prayer. All adopt essentially the same
method, offering moralized or allegorized meditations on the stages

---

[80] Ibid, lines 290–301.
[81] *Werke for Householders*, p. 34.
[82] *Kentish Visitation*, p. 160.
[83] LFMB, *passim*; *Minor Poems of John Lydgate: Part I*, ed. H. N. MacCraken, EETS, 1911,
pp. 84–117; *Golden Legend*, VII pp. 225–62; Rubin, *Corpus Christi*, pp. 98–108, 155–63.

of the Mass, in which the more distinctive actions of the priest, such as ascending or descending the altar steps, changing position at the altar, extending his arms, or turning towards the congregation, are related to the incidents of Christ's life and Passion, or to generalized aspects of Christian doctrine. So at the offertory the *Lay Folk's Mass Book* provides a prayer which recalls the gifts of the Magi, while Lydgate moralizes the priest's departure at the end of Mass as recalling Moses' leading of Israel through the Red Sea.[84] In some later medieval Mass devotions, such as those associated with the Brigittine house of Syon, the correspondences with the Passion are very closely worked out, on the premise that "the processe of the masse representyd the verey processe of the Passyon off Cryst." Thus as the priest places the fanon or maniple on his arm the devotee is to recall the rope with which Christ was led "fro Tyrant to Tyrant", while the chasuble was to recall the purple vestment in which Christ was mocked.[85]

Devotion at Mass on this method became a matter of inner meditation on the Passion, using the stages of the liturgy as triggers or points of departure, and Margery Kempe's visionary practice shows how far it could be carried. But all fifteenth- and early sixteenth-century methods of hearing Mass, however reflective or comparatively learned, were essentially elaborations of the basic method outlined by Mirk: intense prayer at the elevation, preceded and followed by private prayers keyed to a few significant moments in the ceremony – the confession of sins, the Gloria and Sanctus, the offertory, the commemorations of the living and of the dead before and after the sacring, the receiving of the pax. And these few moments did, in fact, encompass the essentials of Christian prayer – praise and self-surrender to God, confession of sins, intercession for one's own needs and those of one's "even-christians", and for the building of community in charity. All these were focused on the event which made all of them possible and meaningful, the consecration which renewed and gave access to the salvation of mankind on Calvary.

The overwhelming majority of prayers provided for the laity at Mass were, therefore, elevation prayers. The primers invariably included a range of such prayers in Latin, many of them with indulgences; some sixteenth-century printed primers supplied dozens. Though often repetitious and litany-like in form, these prayers offered a remarkably balanced and comprehensive Eucharistic theology. Linked firmly to the death of Christ on the altar of the

[84] LFMB, pp. 22–3.
[85] *Tracts on the Mass*, pp. 19–21.

cross, they nevertheless emphasized the glorious and risen character
of the body on which the devotee gazed. The prayers invoked
Christ not only by his death but by his resurrection, by the descent
of the Spirit, by his coming again in glory. His flesh was seen as
life-giving "salus, victoria et resurrectio nostra", and the Host was
seen as the pledge of delivery from every type of evil afflicting
humanity, spiritual or physical.[86] The primer prayers were generally
in Latin, but vernacular prayers proliferated, often in verse for easy
memorization: they follow fairly closely the pattern found in Mirk's
Instructions. Lay people attending Mass regularly collected such
vernacular devotions for their own use. A manuscript Sarum
primer compiled in London about 1500, whose owner was a
member of the Jesus gild at St Paul's, has an English prayer of
adoration of the sacrament for every day of the week copied into
blank spaces on the back of the illuminations which precede the
Hours. The prayers typify the tone of this Eucharistic piety, and the
cult of spiritual communion by gazing on which it was built:

> O thu swettest manna aungyll mete o thu most likyng gostly
> drynke brynge in to myn inwarde mowthe that honyful tast of
> thin helthful presence and also thin charite. Quenche in me alle
> maner of vices, send in to me the plente of vertues, encrese in
> me giftis of graces and geve to me hele of body and sowle to thi
> plesyng.[87]

One preoccupation in particular is especially notable in vernacular
elevation devotions, though it is also found in many of the Latin
prayers. This was prayer for delivery from sudden and unprepared
death, without the benefit of communion. Late medieval believers,
gazing on the Host, were often moved to reflect on the last moment
when they would gaze on it, the hour of death. Petitions for
"schrift, housil and good ending" are one of the most frequently
encountered elements in such prayers, and it was believed that for
those who did die suddenly, the mere sight of the Host that day
would be accounted to them as housel.[88] It may be significant that
the sight of the Host was thus linked instinctively with the solitary
communion of the deathbed, and the lonely journey into the other
world for which it was preparation. But there was here no necessary contradiction with the communal character of most Eucharistic
experience. Communal and individual experience could be held
together without tension as the rhythm of the Mass, from pro-

[86] *Hor. Ebor.* pp. 70–4.
[87] E. S. Dewick, "On a manuscript Sarum Prymer" *Transactions of the St Paul's
Ecclesiological Society*, V, 1905, pp. 170–5.
[88] See below, chapter 9, "Last Things", pp. 311–3.

cession to prayer to rapt gaze and outwards once again to the bustle of offertory or pax. And as we shall see, the solitary character of the medieval experience of the deathbed may itself be questioned. The hour of death was one not of isolation, but itself an experience of community.

Praying the Mass: Privatization?

Nevertheless, the private and privatizing dimensions of lay Eucharistic experience have tended to catch the attention of some historians of late medieval religion, not without apparent justification. Richard Whitford, as we have already seen, thought that devout lay people at Mass should "kepe theyr syght in the chirche cloce upon theyr bokes or bedes", except at the sacring and other key moments. Colin Richmond has argued that the religion of the gentry was developing away from the religion of the rest of the parish in this period, precisely because they, more than others, had their sights "cloce upon theyr bokes". They sat in their private pews, even sometimes in their own family chapels screened off from the rest of the church, and read.

> Whether they followed the Mass in the liturgical books or in a paraphrase and devotional commentary, or they read something unconnected with the service, they were, so to speak, getting their heads down, turning their eyes from the distractions posed by their fellow worshippers, but at the same time taking them off the priest and his movements and gestures. Such folk, in becoming isolated from their neighbours, were also insulating themselves against communal religion.[89]

Pamela Graves has taken this argument further, arguing that the primers and similar texts encouraged lay people "to muster their own thoughts, rather than construct a communal memory of the passion through the action of the Mass", and has suggested that literate people at Mass "already isolated in their pews and chapels" may even have "experience[ed] religion in probably quite different ways from their illiterate neighbours".[90]

There are several causes for unease with any such arguments. In the first place, too much is being assumed here about the difference between literate and illiterate experience of religion.[91] In the

[89] C. Richmond, "Religion and the Fifteenth century Gentleman", in B. Dobson (ed.), *The Church, Politics and Patronage*, 195, p. 199.
[90] Pamela Graves, "Social Space in the English Medieval Parish Church", *Economy and Society*, XVIII, 1989, pp. 297–322.
[91] See below, pp. 295–8.

second, the evidence on the relationship of the literate and the gentle to parochial or communal religion in the late fifteenth and early sixteenth century seems to this observer at least to run overwhelmingly in the opposite direction. It was often the gentry who paid for the vestments, vessels, processional crosses, monstrances, sepulchres which beautified the parish's Eucharistic worship, for these simultaneously established within the community the "worship" and importance of the Host and of the donors. The Cloptons, Martins, Halleways, Chesters did indeed have their private pews and even chapels, but those chapels were the location for observances valued by the whole community, and many gentry loaned vestments, vessels, and books from their private chapels to beautify the parish worship on feast days. Our most valuable single commentator on early sixteenth-century parochial religion in East Anglia is Roger Martin. His grandfather seems to have managed Long Melford's summer processional round, and the family's estate chapel was one of the focuses of that round. Roger Martin himself played a leading role in the reconstruction of parochial religion under Mary. Yet the Martin family owned and sat in one such proprietary chantry chapel in their parish church, and Martin's writing about the figure of Christ and his Mother reveal a sensibility saturated in the devotional commonplaces which filled the literature being read by the pious. There seems little tension here between the communal and the private. Martin is not unrepresentative. In most communities the gentry and the urban élites chose not to withdraw from communal worship, but to dominate it. To call this process privatization seems unhelpful.[92]

But did the gentry and other literate people experience the Mass in a qualitatively different way from those who could not read? Everyone at Mass was expected to participate in two quite different modes – private prayer, focusing on the relation between the Host and the Passion of Christ, and ritual action, geared to the community. The gentry may be assumed to have valued ritual participation, since they so often provided its props. Clearly, the scope of their private devotion was enormously broadened and deepened by literacy. There was a qualitative difference between those who could greet the Host only with a Pater or an Ave, and those who were able after the sacring to read the Eucharistic and Passion prayers of the primers, most of them in Latin and many of them with a long tradition of learned and patristic imagery behind them.

[92] See C. Carpenter, "The Religion of the Gentry in Fifteenth-Century England", in D. Williams (ed.), *England in the Fifteenth Century*, 1987, pp. 53–74.

But here above all we need to beware of attractively stark polarities. *The Book of Margery Kempe* is a formidable warning against any assumption that the religion of ritual, relic, and miracle is somehow at odds with the religion of meditation, reading, and the quasi-monastic devotion of the mystics and spiritual guides, as filtered into the devotional handbooks of the later Middle Ages. For Margery as for many of her contemporaries, the liturgy and above all the Mass was the natural focus of her private religion. She, of course, was no gentlewoman, but it is a mistake to see the access to primers and related books as the preserve of the gentry, especially once printing dramatically reduced the cost of a Book of Hours. As we shall see, such books were used by a very wide range of lay people, especially in the towns.[93] To read during Mass a religious book which no one else has access to might indeed cut one off from communal religion. To read a book which in its essentials might be read by a duchess or by a brewer's wife, and which was jammed with highly conventional phrases, metaphors, and images which were part of the stock repertoire of devotional *topoi*, derived from or echoed in the liturgy itself, and in the paintings, screens, carvings, and windows of the church, was hardly to retreat into élitist privacies. The illiterate gazing during Mass on a cheap indulgenced woodcut of the Image of Pity was not necessarily worlds away from the gentleman reading learned Latin prayers to the wounds of Jesus, and both of them would have responded in much the same way when summoned to put aside book or block-print to gaze at the Host. We shall return to this issue in the next chapter, and also when we come to consider the prayers of the primers themselves.

Praying the Mass: the Parochial Experience

None of the devotional guides to the Mass produced for lay people in the later Middle Ages can really be said to have had the main parish Mass on Sundays in mind, for none of them refer to the ceremonies which differentiated the parish Mass from low Masses said at other altars. The Mass fell into four main sections. In the first the priest vested himself, on weekdays often at the altar, recited the "Confiteor" and an opening prayer or collect, read the scripture lessons of Epistle and Gospel, and if it were a solemn day recited the Creed. The second section of the Mass was called the offertory, when the priest received the Mass pennies, if any were to be offered, and prepared the bread and wine for consecration. He

[93] See below, chapter 6, "Lewed and Lerned", pp. 212–3.

ritually washed his hands, and at this point in requiem and chantry Masses would turn to the congregation and invite them, in English, to pray for the deceased in whose memory the Mass was being said. The third section, the canon, was the most solemn, the long prayer of consecration at the centre of which the priest recited Christ's words at the Last Supper, and during which he elevated the Host and chalice for adoration by the people. In the final section, starting with the Lord's Prayer, he received communion and then dismissed the people with a blessing. As he left the altar, or while still standing at it, he recited the last Gospel, the first fourteen verses of St John's Gospel, "In principio". Indulgences were attached to hearing this Gospel read, perhaps in order to encourage the laity to remain to the end of Mass, even after the climactic moment of elevation: to gain the indulgence one had to kiss a text, an image, or even one's own thumbnail, at the words "The Word became flesh."[94]

To this basic weekday pattern a number of crucially important ceremonies were added at the high Mass on Sundays. Mass began with an elaborate procession round the church, at the commencement of which salt and water were solemnly exorcised, blessed, and mixed. In the course of the procession the altars of the church, and the congregation, were sprinkled with holy water, which would later be taken to the households of the parish, where it was used to banish devils and ensure blessing. The importance of this blessing and distribution of holy water is indicated by the fact that in many places the parish clerk's wages were linked to it, and he was generally known as the "holy-water clerk".[95]

The second additional ceremony on Sundays was the bidding of the bedes. This was a solemn form of prayer in English, which took place before the offertory. The priest from the pulpit called on the people to pray for the Pope, the bishops, the clergy, and especially their own priest, for the king, lords, and commons, for the mayor or other authorities of the town or village, for "all our good parisshens", and for those in special need such as pilgrims and travellers, prisoners, "and all women that be with chylde in this parysshe or any other", and finally for the household which that week was to supply the holy loaf, the basis of another parochial ceremony peculiar to Sundays. In the second half of the bidding the congregation prayed for the dead, especially the parish dead. Recently deceased parishioners or special benefactors of the church

---

[94] E. G. C. Atchley, "Some Notes on the Beginning and Growth of the Usage of a Second Gospel at Mass", *Transactions of the St Paul's Ecclesiological Society*, IV, 1900, pp. 161–76.

[95] For the ritual, *Missale*, cols 29**–33**; for the holy-water clerk, *The Clerk's Book*, *passim*.

or parish were mentioned by name, and once a year every name on the parish bede-roll would be read aloud, at the parish requiem. At the conclusion of these prayers the priest gave warning of any feast or fast days in the coming week.[96]

A further ceremony was added on certain days of the year, the offering days, when people paid parochial dues in coin or wax. A procession was formed (in order of seniority, wealth, or "worship" in the parish pecking order) and the offerings were delivered to the priest at the chancel step. On certain feasts objects to be blessed might be brought up at this point: candles at Candlemas, butter, cheese, and eggs at Easter, apples on St James's day.[97]

The next ceremony which was elaborated on Sunday was the pax: just before his own communion the priest kissed the corporas on which the Host rested, and the lip of the chalice, and then kissed the paxbred, a disk or tablet on which was carved or painted a sacred emblem, such as the Lamb of God or the Crucifix. This pax was then taken by one of the ministers or, in small parishes, by the clerk, to the congregation outside the screen, where it was kissed by each in turn, once more observing seniority. Primers often supplied a short prayer for use at this point, asking for peace in our times and deliverance from enemies, spiritual or bodily.[98]

The pax was clearly a substitute for the reception of communion. At the end of the parish Mass an even more obvious substitute for lay communion was provided. A loaf of bread presented by one of the householders of the parish was solemnly blessed, cut up in a skip or basket, and distributed to the congregation. The offering of this loaf, which was regulated by a rota, was attended with considerable solemnity, the provider processing to the high altar before matins, reciting a special prayer, and offering a candle to the priest at the same time. It was usual for the curate to pray explicitly "for the good man or woman that this day geveth bread to make the holy lofe" when he bid the bedes. This holy loaf was meant to be the first food one tasted on a Sunday; eaten or simply carried in one's pocket, it was believed to have apotropaic powers. If one died without a priest, reception of holy bread was accounted a sufficient substitute for housel.[99]

---

[96] For the bede-roll see below pp. 334–7.

[97] On these blessings in general see Scribner, *Popular Religion*, pp. 5–12, 39–41: for those mentioned, *Manuale ad Usum Percelebris Ecclesie Sarisburienses*, ed. A Jefferies Collins, Henry Bradshaw Society, XCI, 1960, pp. 7–8, 65, 66.

[98] Hoskins, p. 108.

[99] On the method of offering the holy loaf see Stanford CWA, p. 71; for examples of bidding the bedes for the provider see *Church of Our Fathers*, II pp. 295, 7, LFMB, pp. 71–2, 79, and *Manuale et Processionale ad Usum Insignis Ecclesiae Eboraciensis*, ed. W. G. Henderson, Surtees Society, LXIII, 1875, pp. 126, 224.

What all these dramatic Sunday ceremonies have in common is an emphasis on the location and maintenance of blessing, healing, and peace within the community. Absence from these ceremonies was resented and might be taken as a mark not merely of sloth or carelessness, but of heresy.[100] Quite clearly, the use of these ceremonies on Sunday must have reorientated the Mass, giving it a communal dimension, expressed in dramatic and time-consuming ceremonial, wholly lacking at weekday Masses. Parishioners at the Sunday Mass would perhaps have had time for quiet prayer amid the bustle, activity, and loud gossip which countless court present-ments and sermon exempla portray. The sacring at the Sunday Mass would certainly have been especially solemn, surrounded by torches and accompanied by the mutter of elevation prayers from one's fellow parishioners, and the tolling of one of the great bells, so that those abroad in the parish would know, kneel, and share. But the corporate dimension of the sacrament of the altar, its role in building and maintaining community, would have been inescapable at these Masses, as it was not on a weekday. Here again, the recognition of a plurality of Eucharistic experience is vital.

Making the Peace

Of course these ceremonies, so clearly concerned with peace and charity, are as much a testimony to the fragility of those blessings in the communities of late medieval England as they are to their presence. They were used not only to promote harmony, but to impose hegemony, the dominance of particular individuals and groups within the parish and the wider community. The Wife of Bath's rage in parish processions when another woman claimed precedence is well known, and her concern was widely shared; quarrels for precedence seem at times less the occupational hazard of churchgoers in late medieval England than their principal occupation. Thomas Rode and William Moreton at Astbury in Cheshire quarrelled ferociously in 1513, "concerning which of them shold sit highest in church", and which should "foremost goe in procession".[101] In 1494 the wardens of the parish of All Saints, Stanyng, presented Joanna Dyaca for breaking the paxbred by throwing it on the ground, "because another woman of the parish had kissed it before her". On All Saints Day 1522 Master John Browne of the parish of Theydon-Garnon in Essex, having kissed the paxbred at the parish Mass, smashed it over the head of Richard

[100] *Kentish Visitation*, pp. 205, 207; L&P XVIII/2 pp. 205, 306.
[101] Richmond, *Gentleman*, p. 198.

Pond, the holy-water clerk who had tendered it to him, "causing streams of blood to run to the ground". Brown was enraged because the pax had first been offered to Francis Hamden, the patron of the living, and his wife Margery, despite the fact that the previous Sunday he had warned Pond "Clerke, if thou here after gevist not me the pax first I shall breke it on thy hedd."[102]

The procession and the pax were by no means the only moments of the Mass in which such matters of precedence might generate friction, endangering the very unity they sought to affirm, for Eucharistic ritual was felt to be well suited to the demarcation and endorsement of social hierarchy as well as social bonding. The distribution of the holy loaf was no exception. The rotas of providers themselves constituted a list of the "honest men" of the parish, and in some communities the loaf after being blessed was cut into pieces of varying sizes, according to the importance of the recipients, and so dealt out to "every man in his degre", a recipe for friction in the contentious communities of Yorkist and Tudor England. John "Kareles", denounced to the Archdeacon of Lincoln by his neighbours in 1518 for taking too large a piece of the holy loaf, so that other parishioners were bilked of their share, was being accused of pride, of usurping the principal place in the community, not of gluttony.[103]

Yet, as with the ideal of charity and reconciliation before reception of Easter communion, the unitive and harmonizing dimension of the holy bread rituals clearly exercised considerable influence over the lay imagination, an influence vividly illustrated by an incident in late fifteenth-century Bristol. In the early 1460s a dispute arose between the parish and wardens of the small church of St Ewen and a well-to-do merchant, John Sharp, over arrears of rent for a corn shop which Sharp leased from the church. The dispute was bitter and involved the parish in expensive and prolonged litigation. It was finally resolved early in January 1464, when Sharp and the parish came to a settlement. He solemnized this agreement by declaring that he was "advysed of his conscience to depart of sum of his goodes and to leve to this church" in order to have his own name, and those of his wife Elizabeth and his parents and deceased son, entered "yn the general mynd yerly . . . and so after ther dethe to be prayed for evermore yn the commune bed[e] roll." More was to follow. On Sunday, 8 January, it was Sharp's wife's turn to

---

[102] Hale, *Precedents*, pp. 53–4; J. C. Challenor-Smith, "Some Addition to Newport's Repertorium: ii", *Transactions of the Essex Archaeological Society*, VII, p. 175. I am grateful to Michael O'Boy for the latter reference.

[103] *The Clerk's Book of 1549*, pp. 58, 62 (Holy Trinity, Coventry); *Lincoln Visitation*, L p. 6.

provide the holy loaf. Elizabeth Sharp, clearly a woman with a sense of style, duly turned up before matins and "ful womanly bro[gh]t the Cake with Candels in to this Churche, hyr mayden beryng the same after hyr and a fayre twylly towel with werkys at bothe endys and hool". Having duly offered the holy loaf and candles, Mistress Sharp summoned the parson, the leading parish notables, "and others dyvers bothe men and women", who were assembling for matins. Declaring her great joy at the happy resolution of the dispute between her husband and the parish, she announced her intention of symbolizing the restoration of their mutual charity by bestowing her splendid long embroidered towel "after my decesse" for use at Easter as a houseling-cloth, to be held under the parishioners' chins to prevent fragments of the Blessed Sacrament falling to the ground. Till her death she intended to keep custody of the towel, which would therefore be fetched from her house by the parish clerk "every Estur day only yn wurshyp of the sacrament": on her decease it would pass to the parish without condition.[104]

The symbolism of this vividly recorded incident is fairly easily deciphered. The centrality of the bede-roll and the anxiety of the Sharps, husband and wife, to be restored to the community of the "good doers and wellwylleres" of the church is very striking and is buttressed by related symbols.[105] Mistress Sharp chose the appropriate moment of the presentation of the holy loaf for her gesture, and underlined the implicit Eucharistic symbolism in a further gesture of reconciliation and unity. She provided an embroidered towel "to serve the parysshens of an Estur day". This towel was no casually chosen gift: its symbolic identification with herself was emphasized by her retention of custody of it till her death, and it was designed for use on the one day in the year when the whole parish celebrated its unity by receiving communion together. The record of the incident in the church book lays some emphasis on the towel being a single "hool" piece of cloth, and Mistress Sharp explicitly commented that she intended it to replace the parish's existing makeshift arrangement, in which several smaller towels were pinned together. I do not think it fanciful to find here a further underlining of the theme of unity.

Mistress Sharp did not have to invent her own symbolism. Bequests of personal items like the towel were very common: wedding rings to adorn an altar or a saint's robes, a velvet pillow to serve as a book-rest at the altar, embroidered gowns, bedspreads,

[104] Bristol St Ewen's CWA, pp. 60–1.
[105] On the bede-roll and its importance see below pp. 334–7.

or hangings to make frontals or vestments. Above all, again and
again one encounters bequests of linen for use in the Mass. Gifts of
this sort gave those of modest means a way of perpetuating their
personal presence at the heart of the community's worship of the
Sacrament. One did not need to be a millionaire to provide the
parish with a "kerchief to make a corprax" or a "diaper towell for
goddys borde in Ester tyme".[106] In physical terms at least one could
hardly draw closer to the sacrifice which united quick and dead
in one great act of intercession. These bequests might be commemorated in the bede-roll, but offered little other scope for the
public display of one's name. And maybe in these cases the actual
naming of the testator was of less importance than his or her
symbolic proximity to the Blessed Sacrament, the centre of the
community's self-awareness. The same desire was no doubt behind
the action of the Bassingbourn parishioners who clubbed together
to buy a canopy for the Host on Corpus Christi Day, and had
embroidered in the centre a Crucifix, "and the namys off the
gifferes in the iiij corners", surely too small for anyone but the
figure on the cross to read.[107]

If the worshipper kneeling at a weekday Mass was encouraged in
a form of participation which approximated to monastic prayer, a
form of intense affectivity which was essentially private and individualistic, the experience of Sunday Mass, while not excluding
such an emphasis, had a different thrust. The Sunday Mass was
surrounded with lively movement and ceremony, lit by many
candles, accompanied by plainsong and pricksong. The solemn
biddings set the prayer of the parish community within the context
of the greater community of "the gloryous virgyn . . . and all the
company of heven", who glinted in gold leaf and bright paint from
the screens, the tabernacles and the side altars. Participation in this
dimension of Eucharist, even for the élite and the literate, was not
solitary, penitential, interior. Its dynamism and zest are captured
for us in one of the most distinctive and striking of fifteenth-
century carols, described by its editor as "true folksong", and by
Douglas Gray as "vividly combining homeliness and mystery". In
it we catch something of the spirit of English parochial worship
before the solemnities of reform slowed and darkened its music:

> And by a chapell as y Came,
> Met y whyte Ih[es]u to chyrcheward gone
> Petur and Pawle, Thomas & Ihon,

[106] *Test. Ebor.* V p. 119; *Lincoln Wills*, ed. C. W. Foster, 1914–30, I p. 109; Croscombe
CWA, pp. 35–6; *Northants Wills*, II pp. 314, 375, 419.
[107] Bassingbourn CWA, fol. 3b.

And hys desyplys Euery-chone.
  Mery hyt ys in may mornyng
  Mery wayys for to gonne.

Sente Thomas the Bellys gane ryng,
And sent Collas the mas gane syng,
Sente Ihon toke that swete offeryng,
And By a chapell as y Came.
  Mery hyt ys.

Owre lorde offeryd whate he wolde,
A challes alle of ryche rede gollde;
Owre lady, the crowne off hyr mowlde,
The sone owte off hyr Bosome schone.
  Mery hyt ys.

Sent Iorge that ys owre lady knyghte,
He tende the taperys fayre & Bryte -
To myn yghe a semley syghte,
And By a chapell as y Came.
  Mery hyt ys.[108]

---

[108] Greene, *Early English Carols*, no. 323 and notes on p. 428; Carleton Brown, *Religious Lyrics of the XVth Century*, no. 116; D. Gray, *Themes and Imagery in the Medieval English Religious Lyric*, 1972, p. 163.

CHAPTER 4

CORPORATE CHRISTIANS

The religion of the English late Middle Ages has recently been characterized as increasingly "an occupation for the individual as well as, if not more than, the preoccupation of the community". In this perspective, changes in the layout of church buildings, like the introduction of pewing, are taken to indicate the growth of "introspection and non-participation" in church services.[1] A vision of the replacement of corporate by private devotion, of the laity kneeling separately at Mass, conning their primers or meditational guides, or with their eyes closed in private supplication, lies behind this picture of the breakdown of that corporate Christianity which other historians have seen as the essential feature of late medieval Catholicism.

Such a line of argument begs many questions: the apparently individualistic use of devotional books, and especially primers, during church services did not necessarily isolate the reader but may well have had the opposite effect of binding the individual more tightly into the shared symbolic world of the community. But certainly among the aristocracy and higher gentry at least there were signs of a privatizing tendency, notably the growing number all over the country who secured for themselves the convenience, and the status symbol, of a private chaplain and therefore a private Mass.[2]

Yet however real such trends may have been, the overwhelming impression left by the sources for late medieval religion in England is that of a Christianity resolutely and enthusiastically orientated towards the public and the corporate, and of a continuing sense of the value of cooperation and mutuality in seeking salvation. At its most obvious this continuing and indeed growing commitment to corporate Christianity is witnessed by the extraordinary and lavish

---

[1] C. Richmond, "Religion and the Fifteenth-Century English Gentleman", p. 199.

[2] Ibid. pp. 199–200; P. W. Fleming, "Charity, Faith and the Gentry of Kent", in T Pollard (ed.), *Property and Politics*, 1984, pp. 36–58, but see also C. Carpenter, "The Religion of the Gentry in Fifteenth-Century England", in D. Williams (ed.), *England in the Fifteenth Century*, 1987, pp. 53–74.

spate of investment by lay men and women in the fabric and furnishing of their parish churches. Between a third and a half of the 10,000 or so parish churches of architectural interest in England are mainly or wholly Perpendicular in style, and hundreds of these date from the later fifteenth or even early sixteenth centuries. Stoke by Nayland, Stoke-by-Clare, Blythburgh, Southwold, Saffron Walden, Chipping Campden, March – many of the most magnificent parish churches of the Middle Ages were constructed or remodelled on a lavish scale by the devotion of late medieval men and women. Nor was this explosion of building and investment confined to the wool-rich eastern counties. Maybe as many as two-thirds of all English parish churches saw substantial rebuilding or alteration in the 150 years before the Reformation.[3] If we can take it as an axiom of human nature that where your money is your heart is also, then the hearts of late medieval and early Tudor English men and women were in their parish churches. And in this process of corporate investment, whatever the other signs of a move towards individualism, the gentry played their part. In Warwickshire, for example, investment in spectacular parish building projects such as the "liturgically useless" west towers which are such a feature of the place and period was one of the principal ways in which the gentry could establish their place in local society. To quote Dr Carpenter, "it would have been political suicide to retreat into private oratories, where religion, the single significant focus of social life, was concerned."[4] And perhaps the most eloquent testimony to the continuing centrality of the parish even among the gentry down to the Reformation is the fact that the majority of the middling and minor gentry in the late Middle Ages seem to have sought burial in their parish church, rather than in the precincts of religious houses.

It is no accident that the parish church should have been the focus of the laity's sense of corporate religion, for in a very real sense it was responsibility for the church which had helped create the distinctive forms and institutions of lay religion. In the course of the twelfth and thirteenth centuries a demarcation of responsibility had emerged between parson and people: he was to maintain the chancel, they the nave. The need to establish and maintain funds for the upkeep of the building and the provision of officials to administer such funds led to the emergence of the office of churchwarden, men with extensive and ever-increasing responsi-

---

[3] Graham Hutton and Olive Cook, *English Parish Churches*, 1976, pp. 117–32; J. J. Scarisbrick, *The Reformation and the English People*, 1984, pp. 12–15.
[4] Carpenter, "Religion of the Gentry", p. 66.

bilities, as benefactions to the church accumulated and investments in livestock and land mounted.[5]

Some sense of the growth of the responsibilities – and therefore the corporate activities – of the laity in the later Middle Ages can be gauged simply by noting the staggering list of objects the lay people of a parish were obliged to provide for the day-to-day conduct of worship by the fourteenth century. Each parish was required to have the following: a lesson-book (legend) for matins, an antiphonal (the book containing most of the musical parts of the services), a gradual, containing the choir music for the Mass, a psalter, a book of sequences, an ordinal or book of instructions on the administration of the liturgy and sacraments, a missal, a manual, containing the occasional services such as baptism, burial, marriage, and the various blessings, a chalice, a principal set of vestments, including chasuble, dalmatic, and tunicle with their girdles, stoles, fanons, and a choir cope, an altar frontal, and three cloths for the high altar, three surplices and a rochet or sleeveless surplice, a processional cross and a cross to be taken to the dying, a censer, a lantern to light and a bell to go before the Blessed Sacrament on its way to the sick, a pyx of silver or ivory to hang the Sacrament over the high altar, a Lenten veil, a set of banners for processions, the church bells with their ropes, a bier for the corpse at funerals, a holy-water vat and sprinkler, a paxbred for the kiss of peace at Mass, a candlestick for the paschal candle, a font with cover, lock, and key, images in the church, and the chief or patronal image in the chancel. The parish was also required to maintain the graveyard wall, all books and vestments once provided, the windows, and all the images.[6]

What was imposed on the laity as their collective responsibility became the focus of their corporate awareness. The maintenance of the church and the provision of its furniture and ornaments became the principal expression of their mortuary piety, and in the two centuries before the Reformation individuals, groups, and the collectivity of the parish poured into the equipping of their churches a rising flood of "money, sheep, cattle, timber, crops of wheat, rye and beans, bushels of malt and loads of stone, beehives

[5] Dorothy Owen, *Church and Society in Medieval Lincolnshire*, 1971, pp. 112–21; Colin Platt, *The Parish Churches of Medieval England*, 1981, pp. 88–91; Charles Drew, *Early Parochial Organisation in England: the Origins of the Office of Churchwarden*, 1954; Emma Mason "The Role of the English Parishioner 1100–1500", *Journal of Ecclesiastical History*, XXVII, 1976, pp. 24–6.

[6] Aelred Watkin (ed.), *Archdeaconry of Norwich: Inventory of Church Goods temp. Edward III*, Norfolk Record Society, XIX, 1948, part II p. xviii; A. Gasquet, *Parish Life in Medieval England*, 1929, p. 33.

and barrels of salt and fish, jewels and rings, silver and pewter plate, gowns of silk, satin and sarsenet". By the mid fourteenth century even obscure village churches were very fully equipped, largely as a result of such lay gifts: a visitation of 358 churches in the archdeaconry of Norwich in 1368 revealed only a handful without all the requirements of daily worship, while most had far more than the basics. Most churches, for example, had three to five sets of vestments, rather than the one required by law, and some churches had a dozen or more. Once the basics were procured for the church the laity set themselves to provide ever more elaborate and profuse services, equipment, and ornaments. Altars, vestments, vessels, and images proliferated. Before the altars and images lights were set, and the maintenance of these lights, especially during times of service, became the single most popular expression of piety in the wills of the late medieval laity. So great was the proliferation that testators were sometimes hard put to it to find an object which the church was in need of or had room to keep. John Almyngham of Blythburgh left £20 to his parish church in 1500, £10 for a pair of organs, and the residue to be spent on a canopy for the high altar, "welle done with our Lady, and 4 Aungeleys, & the Holy Ghost, goyng upp and down with a Cheyne". But he provided that "yf there be no space that the said canope may not be made ther", the money should be spent instead on a tabernacle for the image of St Andrew. The lavish inventories of late medieval town churches like All Saints, Bristol, or St Peter, Cheapgate, or the great wool churches like Long Melford show how far this process of elaboration could go.[7]

All this was part of what has been called the purchase of paradise, the use of the Mammon of iniquity to make friends with God by promoting his service. Such gifts were designed to aid the individual by speeding his or her soul through Purgatory. But they were not in any straightforward sense individualistic gestures, for they were designed to contribute to the dignity and beauty of parochial worship, and in return for his or her bequest the testator expected to be held in perpetual memory within the parish. All who gave gifts to the parish expected to have their names entered by the churchwardens of parson into the parish bede-roll or list of dead benefactors, there to be prayed for by name perpetually, "that they schall nat be forgetyn, but be had yn Remembranns and be prayed for of all this parysche".[8]

This emphasis in obituary provisions for a corporate remem-

---

[7] Scarisbrick, op. cit. p. 3: for what follows, Watkin, op. cit. pp. lix–lxi; *East Anglian Notes and Queries* NS II, 1887–8, p. 180.
[8] Bristol All Saints CWA (c) pp. 3–4.

brance of the testator is a very striking feature of many late medieval wills, and clearly involved much more than a mere concern with securing the maximum number of prayers at a funeral or month's mind. It is the parish as a corporate entity which such bequests have in mind. So Alyce Chester, a Bristol widow leaving a hearse-cloth to her parish in the 1480s, explained that she did so "for the love and honor that sche had un-to all-myghty god and to all Crystyn Sowlys and for the Ese and socour of all thys parysche un-to whom she owyd her good-wyll and love yn her dayes".[9] John Fayrey, a mercer of St Stephen's, Coleman Street "where he is parishioner" left not only a dole for the poor of the parish, but £20 to be spent on a dinner for the parishioners. Sir Walter Luke left money to build a new church house for parish ales and other meetings, provided the churchwardens and the parson each year on May Day publicly recited "De Profundis" for his soul "and all the parish to say a pater noster". Sir David Owen left to the parish church of Lodsworth a missal, vestment, and chalice on condition that an annual obit was established "and also that some of the most honest of the same parish shalbe at all tymes at the said Obite yerely for evermore to endure".[10] William Denley, from the Sussex parish of Hunston in 1524, left money for drink for the parish at his funeral, and a bequest for the bells and church ornaments, provided the parish representatives, the churchwardens, attended his annual obit: "yf they be not there, then they shal have noo money." If wardens and parson neglected his obit "then I will the said pariscens, for the tyme beyng, shall take it into their handes ageyn." And to underline these parochial concerns he stipulated that at his funeral there should be a distribution of wheat to "pour householders that dwell in the parishe . . . so that I will have noo common doole to straungers".[11] So single-minded an insistence on the exclusive integrity of the parish is perhaps a little uncommon, though similar provisions appear with increasing frequency among the Kentish gentry in the later Middle Ages,[12] but the stipulation that "oon of the churchewardeynes, or bothe, be at the dirige and masses" is not. Indeed, testators frequently required the presence of a wider representation of the community, as in the will of Elisabeth Fitzjames of Temple Combe in Somerset, who left eight pence to every householder in Combe in 1550 "so that they take payne to goo wt my corpus to see yt buried", or Agnes Chanell of Aldingbourne, who left funds in 1556 so that "the whole parish of

[9] Bristol All Saints CWA (c) p. 14.
[10] *Beds Wills* III pp. 157, 160–1; *Sussex Wills*, III p. 172.
[11] *Sussex Wills*, III p. 17.
[12] P. W. Fleming, "Charity, Faith and the Gentry of Kent 1422–1529", in A. J. Pollard (ed.), *Property and Politics: Essays in late Medieval English History*, 1984, pp. 46–7.

Aldyngbourne shall have either at my buriall or els at my monthes
mynde breade drinke with other refreshinge".[13]

Of course the desire to cut a good figure at the end, to have
"honest and worshipfull folkes, frendes and kynsmen" come "to
do my body worship" is clearly present in all these cases, and such
provisions occur in the wills of the well-to-do, not the poor. So as
well as the desire to leave something to one's "neyghbours to make
mery wt alle", there is clear in many such bequests a less attractive
though equally human concern with the testator's own dignity and
status.[14] But they make sense only in a community which placed
a special value on the religious dimension of community, and
believed that the prayers of the parish assembled precisely as a
parish, either in fact or in the person of its representatives, its
priest and wardens, were more powerful than the sum of its component parts. This emerges most clearly in connection with the
archetypal parish gatherings, the processions, and especially
Rogationtide processions.

Late medieval Rogationtide processions, with handbells,
banners, and the parish cross, were designed to drive out of the
community the evil spirits who created division between neighbours and sickness in man and beast. They were also designed
to bring good weather and blessing and fertility to the fields.
Structured round the singing of the litany of saints, the processions
set the earthly community of the parish within the eschatological
community of Heaven in much the same way as did the ranks of
saints painted on the screens before which the parish assembled for
Mass on Sundays. But the Rogation processions were also rituals
of demarcation, "beating the bounds" of the community, defining
its identity over against that of neighbouring parishes, and symbolizing its own unity in faith and charity. The sense of unity on
such occasions was very strong. Processions from neighbouring
parishes which happened to converge might come to blows, in part
because they believed that the rival procession was driving its
demons over the boundary into their parish.[15] Those who absented
themselves from such processions, and even from their lesser reflections held before Mass each Sunday, were seen as bad neighbours.[16] George Herbert, writing in the 1630s, exactly captured
this dimension of the traditional Rogationtide observances.

Particularly [the country Parson] loves procession, and maintains
it, because there are contained therein 4 manifest advantages:

[13] *Somerset Wills*, III p. 116; *Sussex Wills*, I p. 8.
[14] *Test. Ebor.* IV p. 270, V pp. 102–3, 129.
[15] Owen, *Lincolnshire*, pp. 108–9.
[16] *Kentish Visitation*, p. 207

first, a blessing of God for the fruits of the field; secondly, justice in the preservation of bounds; thirdly, charity in loving walking and neighbourly accompanying one another, with reconciling of differences at that time, if there be any; fourthly, mercy in releeving the poor by a liberall distribution and largesse, which at that time is or ought to be used. Wherefore he exacts of all to bee present at the perambulation, and those that withdraw and sever themselves from it he mislikes, and reproves as uncharitable and unneighbourly.[17]

The function of these processions as celebrations of communal identity, so much valued by Herbert, is underlined in accounts of early Tudor perambulations by the prominence within them of the motif of eating and drinking. So in the 1520s and 1530s the men of Chilton and the inhabitants of Clare in Suffolk went in perambulation together each year to Chilton Street, "and there at a tree called Perryes Crosse at thende of that streete, the vicare redde a ghospell as the uttermoste parte of their bounds. And then they had there some ale or drinkings."[18] A few miles away at Long Melford the processional year was more elaborate:

On Corpus Christi day they went . . . with the blessed sacrament in procession about the Church Green in Copes, and I think also they went in Procession on St Marks day about the said green, with hand-bells ringing before them, as they did about the bounds of the town in Rogation Week, on the Monday one way; on the Tuesday another way, on the Wednesday another way, praying for rain or fair weather as the time required; having a drinking and a dinner there upon Monday, being fast day: and Tuesday being a fish day they had a breakfast with butter and cheese, &c, at the Parsonage, and a drinking at Mr Clopton's by Kentwell, at his manor of Lutons, near the ponds in the Park, where there was a little Chappel, I think of Saint Anne, for that was their longest perambulacion.

Such religious junketings, funded by small bequests from modest testators, as well as by the largesse of the village notables, were a way of endorsing and underlining the realities of the community and its ordering, throwing the mantle of holy peace and charity over the structures and pecking order of village life. They were opportunities, like other major communal religious celebrations such as the St John's Eve fires, for the exercise of charity by the rich and deference by the poor. As Roger Martin remembered, in

[17] George Herbert, *Works*, ed. F. E. Hutchinson, 1967, p. 284.
[18] G. A. Thornton, *A History of Clare, Suffolk*, 1928, p. 96.

Henrician Long Melford,

> On Saint James's even there was a bonefire, and a tub of ale and
> bread then given to the poor, and before my doore there was
> made three other bonefires, viz. on Midsummer even, on the
> even of Saint Peter and Paul, when they had the like drinkings,
> and on Saint Thomas's even, on which, if it fell not on the fish
> day, they had some long pies of mutton, and Pease Cods set out
> upon boards . . . And in all these bonefires, some of the friends
> and more civil poor neighbours were called in, and sat at the
> board with my grandfather.[19]

This dimension of holy neighbourliness was as much a feature
of urban as of rural life, and was regularly commented on by
sixteenth-century writers. William Warner, the Elizabethan verse
chronicler, wrote that "At Baptist-day with Ale and cakes bout
bon-fires neighbours stood", while John Stowe explained that in
London "These were called Bone-fires, as well of amity amongst
neighbours, that being before at controversie, were there by the
labour of others reconciled, and made of bitter enemies, loving
friends." Such promotion of charity prompted many bequests
to "neyhboures . . . to make merry withall", with, perhaps, an
impeccably evangelical aim in mind. But the festive atmosphere
and the general promotion of neighbourliness on these occasions
seemed to some observers to threaten the religious solemnity of
the ceremonies, and a medieval Lincolnshire preacher warned his
Rogationtide congregation "not to come and go in processyon
talkyng of nyse talys and japis by the wey, or by the feldes as ye
walke . . . but ye scholde come mekely and lowly with a good
devocion and follow yowre crosse and yowre bells".[20]

It is no surprise then to find late medieval and early Tudor
testators making provision for the association of their own obsequies with these crucial focal moments of the community's self-
awareness. The bequests ranged from small sums of six or twelve
pence "to be distributed in brede and ale, and gyffen to the
parishioners . . . from tyme to tyme in the days of Rogacions callyd
Crosse weke" or "yerly . . . in the crosse weke at the crose before
his dur when the procession cumeth . . . and upon Seint Thomas
nyght after the fest of Seint John Baptyst at the bonefyre",[21] up to
much more elaborate provision. John Absolon, a Kentish yeoman,
charged his wife Eleanor to continue the drinking he had given

[19] W. Parker, *The History of Long Melford*, pp. 70–3.

[20] C. Phythian-Adams, "Ceremony and the Citizen", p. 112; Owen, *Lincolnshire*, pp.
108–9.

[21] *Lincoln Wills*, I PP. 70–3, II pp. 75–7; *Testamenta Cantiana: West Kent* ed. L. L. Duncan,
1906, p. 23.

the parish "in the Rogacion weeke comyng in procession unto Upperdoone", where the priest, after singing the Gospel at the boundary, was to say the "De Profundis" with a collect "for me and all christen soules". The provision of a landmark in the form of a wooden or stone Cross at the "stational" points on the boundaries where the Gospel was proclaimed was an even surer way of ensuring perpetual parochial recollection, for such land-marks, as in the case of "Perryes Crosse" at Clare, were usually known by the name of the founder. John Cole, a Suffolk yeoman, left money to make a new Cross "accordinge to Trapettes crosse at the Hamelanesende and sett upp at Short Groves ende, where the gospell ys sayde upon Ascension Even", and he assigned funds "to fynde a drinkenge upon Ascension Even everlastinge for the parisshe of Thelnetham to drinke at the crosse aforenamed".[22]

Rogationtide observances were, with the exception of the annual Easter communion, the most explicitly parochial ritual events of the year, and the eagerness of testators to associate their own memories with such occasions in perpetuity is eloquent testimony to the importance they attached to the parish community. But wherever one turns in the obituary provisions of late medieval Christians there is an assumption of the close interconnection between the individual and the parish. This is nowhere clearer than in the provision of chantry priests and services within fifteenth- and early-sixteenth century parish churches.

At one level, the foundation of a chantry at a side altar in a parish church was the ultimate act of religious individualism, for it tied the celebration of the Eucharist to the interests of a single individual and his family. Clearly, the central function of a chantry priest was intercession for the soul of his patron, but the cult of the commemoration of the dead was inextricably bound up with the late medieval sense of community. Testators establishing permanent chantries, or the very much more common temporary chantries for a few years at a named altar in their local church, conceived of themselves as providing benefits not only for them-selves and the other dead prayed for there, but for the living community of the parish. A number of chantry chapels served, and were intended to serve, as parochial chapels of ease.[23] Most, however, were intended to supplement the existing services avail-able within the parish church, to contribute "to the increase of divine service". A chantry founder might specify that his priest

---

[22] *Testamenta Cantiana: West Kent*, p. 18 (1538): *Wills and Inventories from the Register of the Commisary of Bury St Edmunds*, ed. S. Tymms, Camden Society, XLIX, 1850 (hereafter = *Bury Wills*) p. 118 1527.
[23] C. Kitching, "Church and Chapelry in 16th century England", *Studies in Church History*, XVI, 1979, pp. 279–90.

say the morrow Mass, the one said at dawn each day for the convenience of labourers whose work began then. Chantry priests were often expected to assist at the parish services, attending in surplice in the choir at matins, Mass, and evensong, and singing the Gospel at the parish Mass when required. Like the others in the London church of St Mary at Hill, the priest of the Causton chantry was expected to attend in choir all the parish services, and after evensong each night to lead the singing of the "Salve Regina . . . or elles help the Syngers after his cunnyng".[24] John Lang of Croft in Lincolnshire established a priest to say mass for him at St Nicholas's altar in the parish church in 1516: his feoffees were to find "an able preiste, and in especiall a syngyng man yf he may be goten, for the mayntenyng of the servyce of god on the olyday". Robert Ashtroke, endowing a priest for ten years in 1534 to "syng and say masse" for him at the Jesus altar of his parish church of High Wycombe, stipulated that "the same priste shall helpe to mayntayne the servyce off God in the quere . . . and that there be no preiste admitted to the saide servys but that can syng at lest his playn songe substancyally".[25]

Just as founders of chantries conceived their foundation as directly benefiting the parish, so parishioners expected as a matter of course that this would be so. The chantry priests in St Mary at Hill were appointed, as was commonly the case in London, by the parishioners, and could be removed if they did not fulfil their obligations to the parish as well as to their founder. The laity of Kent during Archbishop Warham's 1511 visitation lodged a number of complaints against chantry priests who would not assist in parish worship, by reading the Gospel, saying the morrow Mass or distributing holy bread on Sundays.[26] And as they expected benefit from such foundations, they were prepared to add their own means to those of the founder to secure the continuance of them. Both parishes and gilds in late medieval England frequently supplemented or revived failing chantry foundations with fresh funds, because they were seen as a communal and not merely a private benefit. The churchwardens of St James's, Bristol, devised an elaborate and long-term investment strategy to revive the Spicer chantry in their church in the 1470s.[27] The St Mary gild at Chesterton was founded to revive a chantry in the parish church,

---

[24] C. R. Burgess, "For the Increase of Divine Service: Chantries in the Parish in late Medieval Bristol", *Journal of Ecclesiastical History*, XXXVI, 1985, pp. 48–65; London St Mary at Hill CWA, pp. 4–9, 3, 12.

[25] *Lincoln Diocese Documents*, ed. A. Clark, EETS, 1949, p. 166.

[26] *Kentish Visitation*, pp. 76–80, 88, 193.

[27] Burgess, "Increase of Divine Service", p. 60.

the income of which was no longer sufficient to maintain a priest.[28] Founders of modest means might count on this sort of community involvement to extend or augment their foundations, and a fascinating example of this convergence between individual initiative and communal response, involving both gild and parish, took place at Eye in Suffolk in the early 1490s.

John Fiske, a husbandman, left 88 marks to the gild of the Blessed Virgin at Eye to maintain a gild priest, to pray for him and all the members. Fiske hoped that the town would augment his benefaction by an endowment of land to establish his priest in perpetuity, but stipulated that if this had not happened within four years, the money was to be used to secure prayers for his and his parents' souls. The people of Eye did at first respond, and a number of testators left small sums to add to Fiske's bequest, but interest soon flagged, in part because a suitable parcel of land was not found. Shortly before the expiry date of the bequest the vicar, Thomas Golding, fell into conversation by his fireside with one of the town's leading men, John Fanner, and they agreed that it would be a disgrace if the parish "shuld lose this service the whiche should be greate rebuke unto all the town". Fanner offered to sell some suitable land at less than the market price, and the vicar paid a deposit on the spot. On the following Sunday he told the parish what he had done:

> Howe saye ye now, said I unto them, if I have bought a ground for you so that ye maye stande in the churche yard and see it . . . And if it be a bargaine because it is for the comon wele, speake all Una Voce and saye ye this was a godly hearinge. Every man woman and childe seide yea, yea. Dyverse men gave 10 marke a piece, women fower marks, 20s and 40s, 20d and 40d, so that I gathered on Candlemas daye above £20.[29]

This vividly recorded incident highlights the extent to which late medieval Christians identified individual spiritual welfare with that of the community as a whole, an identification in which personal initiative and corporate action in pursuit of salvation could converge without any sign of incongruity or tension.

Gild and Parish

The incident at Eye involved an individual testator, the parish priest, the parish at large, and the Trinity gild, working to a single

---

[28] Westlake, *Parish Gilds*, nos 15, 25, 111, 203, 209.
[29] HMC 10th report Appendix iv pp. 527–8; Colin Richmond, *John Hopton*, 1981, pp. 175–6.

end, for the parish was by no means the only expression of communal religious feeling in late medieval England. Religious gilds or devout fraternities, dedicated to a saint or some aspect of the veneration of Christ, such as Corpus Christi, had proliferated especially in the latter half of the fourteenth century, and new foundations continued into the 1530s to the very eve of dissolution. They were probably urban in origin and the towns of late medieval England harboured literally dozens of them. At a conservative estimate London had something in the region of 150, King's Lynn over seventy, Bodmin over forty, Great Yarmouth at least nineteen. Many gilds in towns were craft organizations, with important social and economic functions over and above any religious activities, but the overwhelming majority of gilds were essentially religious in character, designed to regulate not trade or manufacture but the devotional lives of their members. By the end of the Middle Ages they were as much a rural as an urban phenomenon and most villages had at least one gild, so that the patterns of religious belonging represented by the gilds were available to the majority of the adult population.[30]

The essential features of gild activity are fairly represented in the gild of St John the Baptist at Terrington in Norfolk. It was founded in 1384 "out of devotion" in honour of God and St John the Baptist by six local men who each contributed a bushel of barley. They elected an "alderman or keeper" to administer the gild and its funds and see to the maintenance of the gild light. The gild had three basic functions. The first was to maintain a great torch or candle in honour of St John, presumably before his image in the parish church, whose patron he was. This torch was to be lit every Sunday and holy day at the elevation in the Mass, thereby honouring the Sacrament as well as St John: there was in any case a link between the cult of St John's head and that of the Blessed Sacrament, since in the late fifteenth and early sixteenth century the image of St John's head had Eucharistic associations, and the Terrington gild held its annual Mass and meeting on the feast of the beheading of St John.[31] The second function of the gild

---

[30] For gild activity in Bodmin see CWA passim; on the role of gilds more generally, in addition to Westlake, see Toulmin Smith, Firth, and Palmer, already cited, and Scarisbrick, Reformation, chapter 2; C. M. Barron, "The Parish Fraternities of Medieval London", in C. M. Barron and C. Harper Bill, The Church in Pre-Reformation Society, 1985, pp. 13–37; B. Hanawalt, "Keepers of the Light: Late Medieval English Parish Gilds", Journal of Medieval and Renaissance studies, XIV, 1984, pp. 26–37; G. Rosser, "The Town and Gild of Lichfield in the late Middle Ages", Transactions of the South Staffordshire Archaeological and Historical Society, XXVII, 1987, pp. 39–47, and his "Communities of Parish and Guild in the Late Middle Ages", in S. J. Wright (ed.), Parish, Church and People, 1988, pp. 29–55.

[31] W. H. St John Hope, "On the Sculptured Alabaster Tablets called St John's Heads", Archaeologia, LII, 1890, pp. 669–708.

was the procurement of prayers and alms from all the members for the repose of the souls of deceased brothers. All were to attend the funeral of dead brethren, offering a farthing at the Mass and another as a dole to the poor afterwards, and from the common fund of the gild thirty Masses were to be said within three months for each deceased member. The gild evidently attracted many members, and within five years of its foundation had enough funds to pay a chaplain to celebrate regular Masses for living and dead brethren in the parish church. The third function of the gild was the promotion of charity and a communal sense. Members met together once a year for Mass on the feast of the beheading of John the Baptist, when they solemnly offered the gild torch and transacted business such as the election of officers and the revision or scrutiny of gild statutes. The proceedings ended with a gild dinner or feast.[32]

With some variations all late medieval gilds were modelled along these lines, and served essentially the same functions – the maintenance of lights before images and the Blessed Sacrament, the procurement of attendance by the whole gild at funerals of deceased members, and of intercessory prayers and Masses, where possible daily celebrations by a gild chaplain, and finally the exercise of sociability and charity at a communal feast associated with a saint's day. Other functions might also develop round this core, but they were essentially developments of each of these three emphases. The funds established for the maintenance of lights were usually invested in the purchase of livestock, land, or tenements. These assets were hired or farmed out to members, who then paid the gild an "increase" on the stock at the annual settlement of accounts. Many successful gilds, attracting gifts and bequests, thereby became major elements in village economy, with patronage to dispense; membership of a gild could have very direct financial advantages and in some communities might actually be essential. The gild's central intercessory activities on behalf of deceased members were usually extended to providing decent burial for members too poor to pay their own funeral expenses. The burial of the dead was, of course, one of the corporal works of mercy, here exercised as an act of charity among gild brethren. Gilds also provided even their better-off members with funeral accoutrements, especially impressive torches and candles to dignify their burials. The mutual charity embodied in the gild feast, sometimes underlined by an ordinance requiring the brethren to greet new members with a kiss, "in tokenynge of loue, charite, and pes",[33] was in many gilds

[32] *Norfolk Gilds* II pp. 129–31.
[33] Toulmin-Smith, *English Gilds*, pp. 6, 9.

extended to providing financial relief for members who fell into hardship or illness, provided that their misfortune was not the result of extravagance or loose living. The concern of many sets of gild ordinances with the preservation of peace and the prevention of litigation among members was also an extension of this concern with the promotion of mutual charity.

There is, at first sight, a temptation to oppose parish and gild, for they seem to represent different types of religious allegiance. Membership of the parish was involuntary, the result of "the accident of geographical proximity". Membership of a gild, in contrast, was a matter of deliberate choice: "active personal commitment was the essence of gild membership."[34] Brotherhood, as John Bossy has pointed out, implies otherhood, and the ordinances of many gilds lay great emphasis on the preservation of the secrecy of gild affairs, excluding members who revealed the gild's "councils" to outsiders. In the fourteenth and early fifteenth centuries especially, this sense of identity against the wider community was marked by the fact that many gilds had a distinctive livery, or at least a hood, worn by members at gild functions, though this feature of gild life was much less in evidence at the end of the Middle Ages. The striking emphasis on the "norisshyng of loue and charitee" among the brothers and sisters of the gild, and the fact that gilds often had their own paxbreds for use at the kiss of peace at their services, suggest a strongly developed sense of identity within the gild. Most of them, moreover, had entrance fees and an annual subscription, and although these were usually modest they meant that, unlike the all-inclusive parish community, membership by and large was not open to the very poor. The ordinances of the St Christopher gild at Norwich revealingly stipulate that at members' funerals "two pouere men shul ben hirede of the almesse siluer, to holden the torches about the dede."[35] An emphasis on the preservation of the gild's good name and moral purity, requiring the expulsion of members guilty of flagrant moral or criminal offences, is another feature of gild ordinances which appears to distinguish the groups from the inclusive community of the parish. In urban communities there might be many gilds within a single parish, and the more popular gilds might draw their membership from several parishes, thereby apparently threatening the integrity and cohesion of the parish community.

There is some truth in all these points, but too much should not be made of the distinctions between membership of the parish

[34] Rosser, "Parish and Gild", pp. 35–7.
[35] Toulmin-Smith, *English Gilds*, p. 24.

and membership of a gild. Though some urban gilds did have a membership drawn from outside the parish, especially if it was associated with trading, like the Stratford gild, or possessed of special spiritual privileges, like the Boston indulgence, the majority were essentially parochial in character, a feature which was true even of some of the trade gilds, for craftsmen in the same trade tended to congregate in a single area. What was true even of most urban gilds was emphatically so in the villages. The Suffolk gild of St Peter, Bardwell, whose membership in the early sixteenth century comprised most of the adult population of the village, was typical in having only three non-parishioners on its books, all of them women in the neighbouring village of Barningham: they were almost certainly Bardwell-born girls who had been allowed to retain membership of the gild after "marrying out" into another village.[36] And the very fact that gild ordinances so often show a preoccupation with the moral and religious probity of the brethren suggests that these were not enclaves of the exceptionally pious, but of the man and woman in the pew, moral warts and all.

It is in any case clear both from the evidence of gild ordinances themselves and from the many surviving churchwardens' accounts of the fifteenth and early sixteenth centuries that the majority of gilds worked within and for the structure of the parish, not against it, and that indeed many parochial activities and functions depended for support, organization, and funding on the gilds and their members. Many gilds were expressly founded to maintain the fabric or ornaments of the parish churches, or to provide services within it for the common good. The founders of the gild of the Trinity, St Mary, and All Saints, based in the parish church of All Saints, Roughton, in Norfolk, recorded that the gild had been founded to improve the parish church:

> Because our holy mother church of Roughton was poorly furnished and unmeetly ordered in respect of ecclesiastical ornaments . . . books, vestments and lights, and was a thing of shame and grief to all . . . who beheld it . . . we, and likewise others and the rest of the parishioners of the same town, being of small ability and very poor, have all with one assent and consent ordained a certain gild.[37]

Similarly, the "poor men's gild" in the Norwich parish of St

[36] London, St Botolph's *Parish Fraternity Register*, introduction; F. E. Warren (ed.), "The Gild of St Peter in Bordwell", *Proceedings of the Suffolk Institute of Archaeology*, XI, 1903, pp. 81–110.

[37] Firth, "The Village Gilds of Norfolk", *Norfolk Archaeology*, XVIII, 1914, p. 172.

Augustine was founded "in helpe and amendement of here pouere parish chirche". The Assumption gild at Pampisford in Cambridge-shire was founded to raise a fund "for the use and repair of the church which is in poor condition". The Holy Trinity gild at Bottisham in Cambridgeshire was founded to maintain a light before the patronal image in the parish church, whose dedication it adopted, to repair the church fabric, vestments, books, and ornaments, and to assist the poor in the town by contributing on their behalf their parochial dues, thereby preventing their falling under ecclesiastical censure. Such examples could be multiplied, but even when no such purpose is expressly avowed, wherever one turns in late medieval parochial records the central role of the gilds as integral elements of parochial life is evident. Perhaps the best-known example of this sort is the rebuilding of Bodmin parish church between 1469 and 1472. Bodmin had in the region of forty gilds, five of them trade gilds, the rest purely devotional. The gilds organized the fund-raising for the rebuilding by a penny or half-penny levy on their members.[38] But such examples could be multiplied: the sixteenth century rebuilding of Louth steeple was not only partly funded by the gilds, but they acted as bankers, lending the churchwardens large sums of money to solve the church's cash-flow problems.[39] The Chesterton Resurrection gild paid £29 to equip the parish with bells, and spent £11 on a new Easter sepulchre for the Holy Week liturgy: the gild's name sug-gests that it was founded for this express purpose.[40] Almost all churchwardens' accounts for the hundred years before the Reformation show that each of the various "gilds" and "stores" within the parish not only maintained its own light in the parish church, but made regular payments into the church accounts for the support of the fabric and services.

Indeed, the most characteristic activity of the gilds was the maintenance of lights before images or the Blessed Sacrament in the parish church, and when one attends to the records of such lights it quickly becomes clear that the boundaries between parochial and gild activities were not in most places very sharply defined.

Every parish church in England had many lights – they burnt before the great Rood, before the Sacrament, before each of the images in the church. In addition, extra lights were lit during the

[38] Westlake, *Parish Gilds*, nos 3, 292; Toulmin-Smith, *English Gilds*, p. 40; Bodmin CWA, pp. 5–6.
[39] Louth CWA, pp. 17, 33.
[40] Westlake, *Parish Gilds*, p. 141.

canon of the Mass, and annually dozens of lights were set round the Easter sepulchre in which the Sacrament was reserved from Good Friday till Easter Day. In many parishes there was also a corpse or bier light, lit at the obsequies of parishioners, especially those too poor to find their own wax. All these lights had to be maintained, both financially and in the literal sense of tending. Some were maintained by collections – "paschal wax" collections for the paschal candles and sepulchre lights were common. But most lights were maintained by a "stock" or "store", administered either by the churchwardens themselves, or by appointed or elected light wardens, who cleaned the containers and renewed the wax as was necessary. In some parishes this was evidently an office of burden imposed on some sort of rota, and occasionally paid. Between 1518 and 1521 the Buckinghamshire Lollard Henry Phip was chosen "Roodman" by the parish, and was obliged, greatly to his disgust, to tend the light before "his Block Almighty".[41] Such stocks were funded either by gilds or free donations, or donations of "devotion" from parishioners. Often the light wardens raised money by holding a "drinking" for which they brewed the ale: the capital sum needed to fund these entertainments was often advanced out of central parish funds, emphasizing the close links between the lights and the parish.

There was clearly a distinction between lights maintained by gilds and those which were simply maintenance funds with a single official to run them. Joan Anson of Rowston in Lincolnshire in 1529 left twopence each to the Trinity "gild" and the Christopher "gild" in her parish church, and a penny each to the Weaver's "light" and the St Sunday "light". In 1521 Thomas Jackson of Spalding left bequests of 3s 4d and of threepence to two gilds in his parish church, and five bequests of a shilling to "the v devocions in the sayd church . . . that is to say the devocion of corpus Christi, the devocion of the holy goste, the devocion of St George." The word "devocion" here probably indicates a light maintained by voluntary contributions. In 1528 a testator at Long Sutton in Lincolnshire left fourpence each to the four principal gilds "within the churche of Sutton", and twopence each to the various lights of the church. Lights, stores, stocks, and "devocions" then were evidently not the same as gilds. Yet at Long Sutton, and in many other communities, many of these lights were apparently linked to and maintained by groups or minor gilds – "the plough light, the yeomen's light, the maydens light".[42] Such groups of "maydens",

[41] Foxe, *Acts and Monuments*, IV pp. 237–8.
[42] *Lincoln Wills*, II pp. 115–6.

"wives", "bachelors" occur regularly in churchwardens' accounts as benefactors of the church, like the "light that the childer fyndys" in the parish of the York merchant, Anthony Middleton, in 1519, or the young men and maidens' stores who paid for the replacement of the parish chalice when it was stolen at Morebath in the 1530s.[43] Were such groups simply subscribers to the lights, or behind each light was there an incipient or functioning gild with its own religious and social observances? It is often unclear. Thomas Wolett of Temple Ewell in Kent in 1500 left a bushel of barley "to each Light of which I am a brother". At St Andrews, Canterbury, each year the Easter collections to maintain the Rood and sepulchre lights were recorded as coming not only from the "brothers and sisters of the crosse light" but from "bredern and halff brederne and all the parychs", where there seems to have been a sliding scale of involvement in operation.[44]

This is not simply a matter of obscurity in the sources: it is evident that the nature of the "stores" and "lights" was itself often in flux. In 1535 William Gybbyns, a Rutland farmer, left 3s 4d to the Lady light in the chancel of his parish church on condition that "any of the parishe will give more therto that itt maye be made such a stocke that the chirche boxe be nomore chardged with that light".[45] Here, evidently, is the beginning of a "stock" or "store" initiated by an individual testator, and those who contributed to such a store on a regular basis would thereby become "brethren or sisters" of the light, benefactors of their parish by relieving the central funds of a particular burden. The next stage might be the formation of this brotherhood into a gild, as happened at St Bride's, Fleet Street, where a small group of parishioners clubbing together to maintain a light before the patronal image were soon joined by others, raising enough money not merely for the light but to "augment divine worship" by maintaining a chaplain to celebrate a daily Mass on the altar before the image of St Bride, and eventually forming a gild with its own livery.[46] Many gilds were formed in this way to augment divine service within the parish by providing extra clergy, maintaining lights and altars, and providing parochial benefits such as the morrow Mass. This close association between the activities of gild and parish is evident in the will of John Thompson, a Lincolnshire yeoman who left land to find a priest to sing Mass regularly for him in the parish church

[43] *Test. Ebor.*, V pp. 102–3; Morebath CWA, pp. 64–5.
[44] *Testamenta Cantiana: East Kent*, ed. Arthur Hussey, 1907, p. 117; Canterbury St Andrew's CWA, pp. 5, 14.
[45] *Lincoln Diocese Documents*, p. 191.
[46] Westlake, *Parish Gilds*, no. 195.

at Frieston. He had in mind the chaplain of the local Trinity gild, and made the gild his feoffees, on condition that "the sayd paryshoners will make out the resydue of ther devocion in suche wyse that the sayd preste may continew and have competent wages and salarye."[47] Thompson here assumes that his chantry benefaction will be perceived as a benefit to the whole parish, that the local gild is the appropriate body to administer it, and that his money and the gild's will be augmented by the "devocyon" of the parishioners: there is no sense of any tension between individual, gild, and parish.

The point in all this is that many of the gilds were not bodies with identities fixed and distinct from that of the parish as a whole. They were often more or less informal parts of the structure of the parish, contributing in a variety of ways to its worship and social life, and often growing naturally out of *ad hoc* arrangements to meet specific parochial needs. The parish gilds, indeed, are often indistinguishable from the parish itself. At Bassingbourn in the early sixteenth century the Holy Trinity gild chaplain Sir John Hubbard was one of the linchpins of parochial life, acting as scrivener and parish secretary, keeping the churchwardens' accounts, and directing the village play of St George, which toured twenty-seven neighbouring villages to raise funds for the church building.[48]

As gilds might come almost casually into existence, so they might melt away once again into the body of the parish at large. Robert Claygate, of Birling in Kent, left 6s 8d to the "brotherhode of Seynt James in Bierling as long as the brotherhode is kept there": if the gild should fail "I wull that the encrese of the said vi s viii d be disposed to the reparacon of the chirche of Bierling."[49] When the Henrician attack on lights after 1538 destroyed the essential *raison d'être* of many of the gilds, they appear to have been absorbed relatively painlessly back into the parish. For the gilds were perceived as the outcome, not of separating tendencies, but as manifestations of parochial piety, distinctive only in being voluntary and therefore particularly meritorious, in short, as manifestations of parochial "devotion", like the Resurrection gild at Chesterton, begun "of devocon and comen assente of the inhabitants", or St Anthony's and St John Baptist's gilds at Fincham, or the gild of the Blessed Virgin and the Trinity at Holkham, all begun "by the devotion of the parishioners of the said town".[50]

[47] *Lincoln Wills*, II pp. 27–8.
[48] Palmer, "Village Gilds of Cambridgeshire", pp. 366–70.
[49] Duncan, "Parishes of West Kent", p. 5.
[50] *Norfolk Gilds* II pp. 116, 117, 122; Palmer, "Village Gilds of Cambridgeshire", p. 364.

The close identity of the "voluntary" membership of the gild with the "involuntary" membership of the ecclesiastical structures of parish and diocese is witnessed by the chance survival of a set of visitation records from the deanery of Wisbech dating from the mid fifteenth century. It is clear from these records that the Ely diocesan courts were enforcing the discipline and authority of the parish gilds of the deanery as if they were part and parcel of the official structure of the Church. Thus at Wisbech itself in 1479 the aldermen of the gild of St Lawrence presented Thomas Joley for refusing to obey them, while at Leverington John Caly was presented for retaining certain goods left to the gild of St Mary. In the early 1460s there was a series of presentations of men, presumably the executors or beneficiaries of wills, who refused to surrender to gilds bequests of money or kind. At Wisbech in 1462 a parishioner was presented for refusing to obey the ordinances of the gild of St Peter and Paul, while at Tydd St Giles in 1464 Richard Ocham and Thomas Hunston were presented because they had promised to join the gild of St John the Baptist "before a year had elapsed" but had not done so. Membership of the gilds might in principle have been voluntary, but membership contracted or promised clearly was held to have much the same binding character as membership of the parish, and to fall under the same courts which regulated parochial obligation and punished parochial misdemeanour.[51]

This is not to say that the gilds were never self-consciously exclusive bodies, nor that they did not often give cohesion and identity to groups seeking to differentiate themselves from, or perhaps more accurately within, the parish at large. The "Bachelors", "Young mens", "Maydens", or "wyves" stores so often found mentioned in the accounts of fifteenth- and sixteenth-century parishes, especially in the West Country, were clearly institutions giving some form of religious and social expression to peer groups within their communities, and such groups often sought permanent and formal recognition by inscribed gifts of vestments, vessels, or furnishings to the church. In the Cornish parish of St Neot in 1528 the young men gave a window depicting the legend of St Neot, with an inscription recording their donation, while the "wives of the western end of the parish" gave a similar window with the *Pietà* in 1523. Peer groupings subdivided by physical neighbourhood were also represented in the Bodmin gilds, for donations to church funds were recorded there from gilds identified by their location in

[51] W. Palmer, "Fifteenth-Century Visitation Records of the Deanery of Wisbech", *Proceedings of the Cambridge Antiquarian Society*, XXXIX, 1938–9 pp. 69–75.

the parish – "De gilda Sancte Anne apud le bore . . . Sancti David in forestret . . . virginibus de fforestre . . . virginibus de Berestret",[52] At Garboldisham in Norfolk the young men's gild paid for a "ceiling of honour" before the Rood-loft, boarding in the roof and painting the boards with the names of Jesus and Mary: an inscription proclaimed that "betwex syn th[i]s and the Rode loff, the Yongling han payd for this cost. That Lord that deyd for alle Mankynde have mercy upon hem at her Ende." Here was clear advertisment of the separate identity of the "Yonglings" as a group.[53] But such separation was within, not against, the parish, and gild endorsement of the corporate identity of the town's un-married young men or matrons was certainly not a means of separating them from the community at large, but of accommo-dating them within it.

There was, to be sure, an entrepreneurial element in the activities of the gilds, which sought to increase their prestige and wealth, often enough in competition with other gilds in the same com-munity. Within one community gilds might vary greatly in size, popularity, and property, and there was undoubtedly at times a sense of competition. There were two gilds in the Norfolk village of Bressingham in the 1530s, St John the Baptist and St Peter's. St Peter's gild was a modest affair, meeting in the gild-holders' houses, with only a couple of small parcels of land left by a brother in the 1460s. The St John's gild was far and away the more im-portant, with a herd of thirty cows, a gildhall, and their own chaplain. But the secret of their success lay not simply in their possession of cattle, but in the fact that by 1517 they had used their wealth to purchase for their members a series of pardons, in which all who joined the gild shared – the "Pardon of the Beads", granted for recitation of the rosary, from a number of Charterhouses, from Syon, from the Crutched Friars in London. This sort of disparity should not mislead us into seeing the succesful gild as promoting itself over the rest of the community. The parish was under St John's patronage, and this was, clearly, the main parochial gild, using its material resources to maximize the spiritual benefits available to all who joined the parish gild.[54]

In many communities membership of some of the wealthier gilds might, of course, be a source of prestige and of power, and these gilds, even when they were in effect the parish or patronal one,

[52] G. McN. Rushforth, "The Windows of the Church of St Neot, Cornwall", *Transactions of the Exeter Diocesan Archaeological Society, XV*, 1927–37, pp. 182–4; Bodmin CWA, pp. 5–6.

[53] Blomefield, *Norfolk*, I pp. 268–9.

[54] Blomefield, *Norfolk*, I pp. 67–8.

might be instruments not of integration but of domination within the parochial community at large. This is evidently so in the case of those gilds which became synonymous with town governments – St George's, Norwich, Holy Trinity, Coventry, St Anne's, Lincoln. But many smaller urban gilds, while not monopolizing economic and political power in the community, were clearly exclusive rather than integrative. We have already encountered the Jesus gild at St Lawrence, Reading, founded by a group of wealthy townsmen sometime in the second half of the fifteenth century. The Reading Jesus gild had an altar prominently placed before the north pier of the chancel arch. It was confined to ten members, though their wives were allowed to become members in their own right on payment of an annual subscription of 6s 8d, and its exclusive membership was clearly coveted. Yet even so exclusive an institution was seen as adding to the common religious amenities of the parish, not merely by the provision of the Jesus Mass, one of the most popular of late medieval devotions with the laity, but by contributing directly to parish expenses. By the 1540s the gild was paying the parish sexton's wages, in return for his acting as clock-winder and bell-ringer for the gild.[55]

Even the financial exclusiveness of the gilds should not be taken as marking too sharp a distinction between them and the parish at large. It is true that entrance fees of 6s 8d, which is the sum often mentioned, would have precluded the very poor from membership. Ordinances for the annual processions, stipulating that the brethren process in a grave and dignified way, two by two behind the gild candle, clearly envisage a group in their Sunday best and perhaps wearing the gild hood. Ragged clothes would have been out of place here, and the Cambridge gilds of All Saints and St Peter's both imposed fines of wax on brethren who did not come to the annual mass dressed in "his best clothyng".[56] The tell-tale regulation in many gilds that a member unable to attend the feast might send in his place a poor man or woman as an act of charity, and provisions for poor men to be hired to carry the gild candles or banners in processions, and for doles at gild funerals, all presume that such poor men and women are not brethren or sisters in their own right.[57] Clearly, contemporaries were aware of these social and economic bars to membership. In 1492 a Cheshire gentleman, Geoffrey Downes, completed the endowment of a local chapel of ease at Pott Shrigley with two chantry priests to serve the local

---

[55] Reading St Lawrence CWA, pp. 29–33, 169–73.
[56] CUL MS Mm. i. 36 fols 361–71.
[57] Toulmin-Smith, *English Gilds*, pp. 24, 26, 31,

community. There was a gild attached to the chantry, so that local people wanting to share in its benefits might do so, and the usual 6s 8d was fixed as the gild entry fee. But Downes insisted that if anyone was "not in power to pay soe much att on onys, y't if hee will pay every year 2d or 4d dureing the time unto 6/8 bee fully paid" then they should be admited. And if there be "a poor man or a poor woman that bee known have not Goods ... I will that y'e bee Bro'r or Sister as is aforesaid, as well as ony other". Downes's charitable provision is very unusual, and his recognition of the excluding power of poverty is eloquent testimony to the plight of the very poor where no such charity was forthcoming.[58]

But one should not overestimate the social divide thus formalized by gild membership. The very common provision in ordinances for the gild to pay the funeral expenses of members fallen on hard times suggests that on the lower edges of respectability the gulf between those who could and those who could not afford gild membership was not so very great. The members of the village gilds and stores which abound in the records of late medieval parishes seem indistinguishable from the mass of the parishioners, and in many places the majority of the adult population were members of one or other of the local gilds, many of more than one. The modest social character of many gilds was reflected in that of the Trinity gild at Roughton in Norfolk, founded by parishioners "of small ability and very poor", or the Trinity gild at Wymondham, whose members were liable to "lettying of lordes".[59] The gild of All Saints meeting in All Saints' church in Cambridge set its entrance fee at the relatively modest sum of 2s 6d, and an ordinance of 1504 which established a sixpenny dole to the poor of All Saints' parish at members' funerals expressly stipulated that "if there be any pore Brothyr or Sister, to have part theroff".[60]

And in any case, membership of the parish itself was not so uncomplicatedly all-inclusive as has sometimes been suggested.[61] If, as I shall argue,[62] the bede-roll, rather than the parish register, is the parochial document par excellence in pre-Reformation England, then some of the same economic and social restrictions applied to parochial membership as to gild membership. Parishioners got their names onto the bede-roll by making a gift to the fabric or

[58] The Cheshire Sheaf, 1880, p. 52.
[59] C Firth, "Village Gilds of Norfolk in the Fifteenth Century", Norfolk Archaeology, XVIII, 1914, p. 188.
[60] CUL MS Mm. i. 36 fol. 371.
[61] Rosser, "Parish and Guild", passim.
[62] See below, "Death and Memory" pp. 327–37.

"work" of the church, or by donating an ornament, vessel, or light, thereby qualifying for enrolment among the "good-doers and well-wyllers" of the parish church. This tendency to identify parochial membership in such a way as to exclude the "poverty of the parish" was especially marked in prosperous urban communities. In a characteristic gesture, a parish meeting of St Nicholas, Bristol, decided in 1489 that a new and splendid set of black vestments bequeathed to the church for requiem Masses should never be loaned out of the parish but restricted to local funerals. But the meeting went on to decree that they should be used only for those parishioners "that hath been gode doers to the church in gevyng of land bokes vestyments Juelles or other Speciall gode dedys... Other elees to such pareschens That at the leest will paye to the propters vj s viij d for the occupienge of the Saide vestymentes."[63]

But in rural communities the gap between rich and poor might not be so firmly fixed, and the notion of what it was to be a parishioner more generously conceived. It is clear from the surviving bede-roll of a small and poor village community like Morebath on Exmoor that the sum required to qualify as a "gode doer" to the parish might be very small – Sir Christopher Trychay, the priest at Morebath from the early 1520s to the mid-1570s recorded donors who gave twopence as carefully as those who gave flocks of sheep or butts of bees. In larger and richer parishes the pennies of the poor might well be eclipsed by the splendour of the competitive giving of the showy and well-to-do. But this is no more than to recognize that the sacred communities of parish and gild reflected the realities of the secular order, and that the gilds did not do this very much more strikingly than the parish. To belong to a gild, indeed, was more often than not simply one of the conventional ways of being an active parishioner.

[63] Bristol St Nicholas CWA, p. 48.

CHAPTER 5

THE SAINTS

The Saints in their Images

The cult of the saints, according to Emile Mâle, "sheds over all the centuries of the Middle Ages its poetic enchantment", but "it may well be that the saints were never better loved than during the fifteenth and sixteenth centuries".[1] Certainly reminders of them were everywhere in late medieval England – engraved on drinking-cups and bowls, carved on lintels and gable-ends, their very names given to children at baptism. Their images filled the churches, gazing down in polychrome glory from altar-piece and bracket, from windows and riches. In 1488 the Norfolk country church of Stratton Strawless had lamps burning not only before the Rood with Mary and John, and an image of the Trinity, but before a separate statue of the Virgin, and images of Sts Margaret, Anne, Nicholas, John the Baptist, Thomas Becket, Christopher, Erasmus, James the Great, Katherine, Petronella, Sythe, and Michael the Archangel.[2] This is a very characteristic late medieval list: larger churches could swamp it. At Faversham in Kent the parish church had at least four images of the Virgin, including Our Lady of the Assumption in the chancel, Our Lady of Pity in the south aisle, Our Lady in Jeseyn (childbirth), and Our Lady and Saint Anne, as well as images of Sts Agnes, All Saints, Anthony, Barbara, Christopher, Clement, Crispin and Crispinianus, Edmund, Erasmus, George, Giles, Gregory, James the Great, John (two images), John the Baptist, Katherine, Leonard, Loy, Luke, Mary Magdalene, Margaret, Michael, Nicholas, Peter and Paul, Thomas the Apostle, Thomas Becket, Ronan,[3] and Master John Schorne. All these images had lights before them, and several were housed

---

[1] Emile Mâle, *Religious Art in France: the Late Middle Ages*, 1986, p. 147.

[2] H. Harrod (ed.), "Extracts from Early Norfolk Wills", *Norfolk Archaeology*, I, 1847, p. 117.

[3] "Tronen" in the text. The relics of St Ronan were venerated in Canterbury Cathedral, hence his Kentish cult. Cf D. H. Farmer, *The Oxford Dictionary of the Saints*, 1978 (hereafter = ODS) p. 349.

in their own chapels or on their own altars. All attracted bequests for the maintenance of the lamps before them, and in the cases of the more popular saints like Erasmus, James, Michael, Peter and Paul, and Becket, daily Masses at their altars.[4]

Lists of this sort could be compiled for literally hundreds of churches on the eve of the Reformation, and they show the luxuriant flourishing of devotion to the saints. It was a devotion in part imposed by the church, for over fifty days in the year apart from Sundays were *festa ferianda*, days solemnly dedicated to the saints on which all except the most essential agricultural work was forbidden. The bulk of the sermons in Mirk's *Festial* were designed for use on these days. Parishioners were expected to fast on the eve before, and to attend Mass, matins, and evensong on the day: there was a growing attempt on the part of the authorities to persuade the laity to desist from servile work at noon on the eve of such days.[5]

But such pressure from above was more than matched by enthusiasm from below. In the two generations before the Henrician Reformation the parish churches of England benefited from a flood of investment in building and ornaments,[6] and the making of new images and the gilding, painting, and embellishing of old ones was a prominent part of this manifestation of popular devotion. Between 1498 and 1521 the wardens' accounts for the small Cambridgeshire parish of Bassingbourn record bequests and payments for the painting of the tabernacle or canopy of the image of St James, the painting of the Rood-loft, the carving and painting of new images of St Katherine and St Margaret with their tabernacles, the painting of St Christopher and St Nicholas, the washing of the images of "allablaster" and "the ymage off our Lady peyntyng in the Chapell". In 1521 a serious money-raising effort was launched to provide a splendid new image of St George, completed in 1523 by the "George maker", Robert Joes of Walden.[7] The men and women of late medieval England were busy surrounding themselves with new or refurbished images of the holy dead, laying out large sums of money to provide lights, jewels, and precious coverings to honour these images.

We know which saints were most loved and trusted in the late Middle Ages. The laity left bequests in their wills to honour their

---

[4] *Testamenta Cantiana: East Kent*, pp. 86–91; see also, for another example, pp. 119–29.

[5] Barbara Harvey, "Work and *Festa Ferianda* in Medieval England", *Journal of Ecclesiastical History*, XXIII, 1971, pp. 289–308.

[6] Ronald Hutton, "The Local Impact of the Tudor Reformation", in C. Haigh (ed.), *The English Reformation Revised*, 1987, pp. 115–6.

[7] I have used the transcript of the Bassingbourn Accounts in CUL Add. 2792: fols 27a, 30a, 32a–b, 34a, 43a, 57b–59b.

images with lights, to maintain masses at their altars, or to commission pilgrimages. Every region had its own distinctive saints, its
own shrines, its own observances, yet comparison of the names of
saints mentioned in wills in different counties reveals a striking
similarity from region to region, and it is possible to generalize
about the character of devotion to the saints in the country as a
whole. But we are not dependent only on mentions of such images
in wills: in East Anglia and in Devon the images themselves survive
in their hundreds, in the form of panel paintings of the saints on
Rood-screens. Attention to these surviving images reveals a good
deal about the meaning and function of that cult. Most of these
screens date from the three generations before the Reformation, and
they therefore encapsulate the devotion of the late medieval cult of
the saints at its most fully developed.[8]

It is important at the outset to grasp that almost all of the
surviving screens are apt seriously to mislead the unwary about the
place of the saints in lay perceptions, for though many retain their
saints' images, all have been stripped of their principal image, the
great Crucifix with Mary and John on either side. This image,
which gave the Rood-screens their name and purpose, filled the
arch which marked the separation between chancel and nave.
Above or behind them on the tympanum was portrayed Judgement
Day, when Christ, displaying his wounds and the implements of
his Passion, would call the world to account (Pl. 54–5). The liturgy
in the chancel, therefore, especially the main Sunday Mass, was
viewed through the arches of a screen dominated by the Crucifix as
the focus of universal history, and when at the climax of the Mass
the laity raised their eyes to see the elevated Host, they saw also the
great Rood, a conjunction that texts like the *Lay Folk's Mass Book*
underlined. The Rood itself was supported on a beam or loft, on
which burned perpetually one or more lights, so that the Rood-

---

[8] In discussing the East Anglian screen paintings and their saints I have relied very much
on my own notes and observations on the screens themselves, which are, by and large,
poorly documented. The main literature is cited below. For the dating of the Norfolk screens
see Simon Cotton, "Medieval Roodscreens in Norfolk – their construction and painting
dates", *Norfolk Archaeology*, XL, 1987, pp. 44–54; for lists of the saints on Norfolk screens
see W. W. Williamson, "Saints on Norfolk Roodscreens and Pulpits", *Norfolk Archaeology*,
XXXI, 1955–7, pp. 299–346. I have not always accepted Williamson's identification of the
saints, and the lists given in M. R. James, *Suffolk and Norfolk*, 1930, are still worth consulting. For Suffolk screens see W. W. Lillie, "Screenwork in the County of Suffolk, III, Panels
Painted with Saints", *Proceedings of the Suffolk Institute of Archaeology*, XXI, 1933, pp. 179–
202. There is some general discussion in the pamphlet by John Salmon, *Saints in Suffolk
Churches*, Suffolk Historic Churches Trust, 1981. For a good discussion of East Anglian style
and influence see W. G. Constable, "Some East Anglian Roodscreen paintings", *Connoisseur*,
LXXXIV, 1929, pp. 141–7, 211–20, 290–3, 358–63. For Devon see F. Bond and Dom Bede
Camm, *Roodscreens and Roodlofts*, 1909, II pp. 209–54.

beam or loft was often called the "candle-beam". These were
the principal lights of the church, among the last to be abolished
in the Henrician reforms. The screens were first and foremost
Christological images, proclaiming the centrality of Christ's aton-
ing death. The early sixteenth-century Rood-screen rail at Compsal
near Doncaster had an inscription along it which hammered that
point home:

> Let fal down thyn ne & lift up thy hart
> Behold thy maker on yond cros al to tor
> Remembir his woundis that for the did smart
> Gotyn without syn and on a virgin bor.
> Al his hed percid with a crowne of thorn
> Alas man thy hart ought to brast in two
> Bewar of the dwyl whan he blawis his horn
> And pray thy gode aungel convey the[e fro].[9]

These familiar facts are worth insisting upon when considering
the saints painted on the dados or loft-fronts of Rood-screens,
for they represent a powerful iconic and liturgical gloss on the
perception of the role of the saints in late medieval religious practice. The saints stood, in the most literal sense, under the cross, and
their presence on the screen spoke of their dependence on and
mediation of the benefits of Christ's Passion, and their role as
intercessors for their clients not merely here and now but at the
last day. The whole screen was therefore a complex icon of the
heavenly hierarchy, and many screens were clearly designed to
underline this symbolism, perhaps most strikingly at Southwold in
Suffolk, where the magnificent screen contains panels depicting the
Apostles, the prophets, and the nine orders of angels. Over and
above any devotion to the saint in his own right, such images had a
general symbolic significance, brought out clearly on screens like
the one at Ranworth where the chancel screen, with the Apostles, is
flanked at right angles by screens containing twin images of George
and Michael, each treading down the dragon (Pl. 108–9), representing a belief in the communion of saints, the victory of good over
evil, and a sense of being surrounded and assisted by the "whole
company of heaven". The Ranworth Apostles are typical, and the
twelve Apostles occur in more than two dozen East Anglian screens,
as at Trunch, Mattishall, Gooderstone (Pl. 56–7). The Apostles
were the collective symbol of the saints *par excellence* – they repre-

[9] *Archaeological Journal*, XXXV, 1878, p. 393. Something of the original effect can be got
from the screen at Eye in Suffolk, which has a modern Rood by Ninian Comper. This is,
however, incorrectly reconstructed.

sented the whole heavenly hierarchy and the foundations of the Church, as well as being the primary witnesses to the cross and resurrection of Christ, whose image they supported. As we have already seen, such groups of the Apostles were often pressed into service in the church's catechetical task, each carrying a scroll containing one clause of the Apostles' creed. Another popular group with a mixed symbolic and didactic function consisted of the Four Latin Doctors, Ambrose, Augustine, Gregory, and Jerome, whose teaching was seen as providing the basic framework of medieval theology and who are therefore commonly represented on the doors of the screens, as at Cawston in Norfolk, where they are flanked by the Apostles. The Four Evangelists were sometimes similarly grouped.[10]

The screen was therefore no mere scaffolding for the pictures of the saints. The placing of these multiple images of the saints on the Rood-screen is an important indicator of the doctrinal and devotional context of lay devotion to them. But the majority of saints appearing on screens do so as part of no very obvious sequence. They are there because these are the saints late medieval men and women regarded with most affection and confidence, for there is no serious doubt that these screens provide a unique and reliable guide to popular devotional preference. Though occasionally the result of a single bequest by an individual, they more commonly represent a corporate investment by the parish, in which individuals could participate by modest bequests to paint a single panel or "pane" of a screen. It is difficult to say how far such donations procured involvement in the choice of saints on the screens – few contracts or indentures survive, and those which do are seldom specific about the iconography of the screens. But in the case of the Rood-screen built at All Saints, Bristol, in 1483 by Alice Chester, one can see the mechanics of patronage actually at work. Mistress Chester,

> considering the roodloft of this church was but single, and nothing beauty according to the parish intent, she, taking to her counsel the worshipful of the parish, with others having best understanding and sights in carving, to the honour and worship of Almighty God and his saints . . . hath let to be made a new roodloft in carved work, fulfilled with 22 images, on her own proper cost; of the which images be 3 principal, a Trinity in the middle, a Christopher on the north side, and a Michael on the

---

[10] The location of these sequences of saints in Norfolk is set out in Williamson, "Saints", pp. 300–06, 317.

south side: and besides this, the 2 pillars bearing up the loft,
every one having 4 houses set on in carved work; and within
every house an image.[11]

That the iconography of this screen reflected the preferences not
only of Dame Alice but also of "the worshipful of the parish"
seems likely. It is noteworthy that there is no explicit mention of
the involvement of clergy in the planning of the screen at All
Saints, Bristol, though doubtless, like the parishioners at Farnworth
near Broughton in Amounderness who repaired and painted five
saints' images in 1512, the Bristol people sought the "counsell and
help" of their priest. An equally clear case of the reflection on
a single screen of the devotional preferences of a group of lay
benefactors can be found on the other side of England, in the
Norfolk hamlet of Burlingham St Andrew. There Thomas Bennet
and other members of the Bennet family were responsible for
the north side of the screen painted after the break with Rome
had already occurred, in the early 1530s. Their family patron, St
Benedict, duly features among the saints on that side, along with
Becket, Thomas Bennet's name-saint (Pl. 58). Ironically, within
three or four years of the screen's completion Becket was to
become the special target of royal animosity, and his image is
particularly savagely defaced on the Burlingham screen. John and
Cecily Blake were among the donors of the south screen, and
their names duly appear under paintings of their patrons, John the
Baptist and Cecilia (Pl. 59).[12]

"The debt of interchanging neighbourhood"

The saints honoured by all this expenditure were first and foremost perceived as friends and helpers. According to the *Golden
Legend*, in venerating the saints we pay "the debt of interchanging
neighbourhood". As the saints rejoice in Heaven over us when we

[11] The parish of St Stephen, Hackington beside Canterbury, commissioned a new screen in
1519. The indenture merely specifies that it be "made carven & wrought in every forme of
workmanship or better as nowe is wrought & made after the newe Roodloft nowe sett and
being in the parishe Churche of the holie Crosse of Westgate of the Citee of Canterburie",
Archaeologia Cantiana, XLIV, 1932, pp. 267–8. In contrast the Ludlow Palmers' gild,
commissioning an elaborate reredos for their chapel in the parish church in 1524, specified in
detail the saints and incidents they wanted portrayed, though leaving some liberty for the
portrayal of "other divers saints such as he thinketh best" – *Transactions of the Shropshire
Archaeological Society*, 3rd series, III, 1903, Miscellanea pp. i–ii; Bristol All Saints CWA (b)
p. 226.
[12] Simon Cotton and Roy Tricker, *Saint Andrew, Burlingham* (pamphlet, n.d.) pp. 4–5;
Cotton, "Medieval Roodscreens", pp. 44–5. For Farnworth see *Chetham Miscellany* VI,
Chetham Society, n.s. XCIV, 1935, pp. 5–10.

repent, so it is right that we "make feast of them in earth", and in doing so we procure our own honour, "for when we worship our brethren we worship ourselves, for charity maketh all to be common."[13] Julian of Norwich wrote of St John of Beverley, that "oure lorde shewed hym full hyly in comfort of us for homelynesse, and brought to my mynde how he is a kynd neyghbour and of our knowyng."[14] This neighbourliness and homeliness, singled out by Emile Mâle as the most distinctive feature of late medieval French representations of the saints, is very much a feature of English devotion too.[15] The saints that gazed out from the screens and tabernacles of late medieval England were often emphatically "kynd neyghbours, and of our knowyng", country people themselves, like St James the Great at Westhall, with his sensible shoes, hat, and staff, or St Anthony, on the same screen, with his friendly pig. Henry VI had been an unassuming man in his own lifetime, dressing in farmer's boots, wearing the gown and rolled hood of a slightly run-down urban worthy; up to the Reformation his shabby hat could be tried on by Windsor pilgrims suffering from headache. He liked to appear to his clients in just such unassuming garb, dressed like a pilgrim, unshaven, and walking up and down with a friendly face, "giving . . . no little ground of hope and amazement".[16] Testators counted on their friendship with the saints, "the good saints that I have had mynde and prayers moost unto, that is, to St Nicholas, Saint George, Saint John the Baptist, Saint Christofer, St Mary Magdalene, Saint Gabriell, St Erasmus, Saint Fabian, Saint Sebastian", St John the Evangelist "whom I have always worshipped and loved, . . . SS Cuthbert and Katheryn myn advocates", or "my syngular helpers and socourers in this my grete nede".[17]

This sort of affectionate dependence was clearly the result of particular devotion on the part of the client, who "adopted" specific saints in the hope that he or she would be adopted and protected in turn. The relationship was institutionalized in the case of the patron saint of the parish, who could be relied on, *ex officio*, to care for his parishioners. As John Mirk explained, this relationship was essentially feudal, and the saint was bound by a sense of *noblesse*

[13] *Golden Legend*, VI p. 97.
[14] Edmund College and James Walsh (eds), *A Book of Showings to the Anchoress Julian of Norwich*, 1978, II p. 447.
[15] Mâle, *op. cit.*, pp. 148–53.
[16] Ronald Knox and Shane Leslie (eds), *The Miracles of King Henry VI*, 1923, pp. 77–84; John Foxe, *Acts and Monuments* V p. 467; J. W. Mckenna "Piety and Propaganda: the Cult of Henry VI", in B. Rowland (ed.), *Chaucer and Middle English Studies*, 1974, p. 247.
[17] *Somerset Wills*, II pp. 186, 199, 172; Susan Brigden, *London and the Reformation*, 1989, p. 9.

oblige towards those who paid him honour and financial tribute in the shape of tithe and wax:

> This patron kepte his pareschons, praying for hom bysyly to God nyght and daye; for by hor mayne swynke holy chyrche ys holden up and Goddys servantes that byn yn his chyrch, and offerthe hom up befor the hygh mageste of God. For ryght as a temporall lord helpyth and defendyth all that byn parechons or tenantys, ryght soo the saynt that ys patron of the chyrche helpyth and defendyth all that byn paryschons to hym, and don hym worschyp halowyng his day, and offyrne to hym.[18]

In fact, although parishioners occasionally refer to the parish patron in terms which show some sense of a claim upon him – "Seynt Edmonde myn Advowe" – there is little sign in the later Middle Ages of strong individual devotion to the parish patron. Few surviving screens portray them, and they do not occur very often as the recipients of bequests of coin or wax. But one's own name-saint might be seen in much the same light as that attributed by Mirk to the parish patron, and gestures of filial piety towards name-saints were common. Edmund Mynot of Canterbury stipulated that his annual obit should be held on the eve of the feast of St Edmund King and Martyr, thereby symbolically planting himself on his name-saint's doorstep in perpetuity. At Aylsham one of the donors arranged that the normal symbolic sequence of the Apostles on the screen should be disrupted, so that his patron, St Thomas, might stand first.[19]

Occupation provided another link with specific saints, symbolized in the trade or craft gilds, but also, less formally, in the observation of particular saints' days. In the 1540s the Henrician authorities were to encounter dumb resistance to the removal of such days from the calendar, and Bishop Veysey complained that "fishermen and such as live by the sea" in the West Country "will not go to the sea to fish for their living, and for the commodity of their neighbours, upon divers saints days". Blacksmiths would not shoe "any man's horse, whatever need that fall to occupy the same" on St Loy's day, "neither some carriers upon that day will carry hay, or other things necessary to the use of man".[20]

Such relationships with the saints, rooted in parochial dedication, in name, or in occupation, were given, inherited through the

---

[18] *Festial*, pp. 241–2.
[19] *East Anglian*, X, 1903–4, pp. 3–5 (will of William Haste of the parish of St Edmund, Norwich, 11 Jan. 1535); Canterbury, St Andrews CWA, XXXII, p. 203; *Victoria County History of Norfolk*, II p. 545.
[20] D. Wilkins, *Concilia*, III p.846.

accident of geography, birth, or employment, or the choice of parents or godparents. But it was expected as a matter of course that Christians would cultivate relations of intimacy and dependence with other saints in their own right, observing their feast days and eves with voluntary devotions, and honouring their images. John Mirk's parish priest, announcing the feast of St Winifred, was to remind his parishioners that since "ther ar many men that han devocyon to this holy maayden . . . ye that have devocion to this holy seynt, comet that day to the chyrch to worschypp God and this holy mayden and martyr."[21] In the same way, though the feast of St Margaret was but "a lyght holyday, save theras a church us dent yn hor name" nevertheless the priest was to announce the day in advance to the parish "for as I suppos ther byn some of you that haven such a love to hure, that ye wol fast hor evyn".[22]

In the fourteenth century such voluntary devotions to particular saints often took a corporate form, expressed in the foundation of a gild, like the handful of men and women at Great Yarmouth in 1379 who founded a gild in St Nicholas's church to burn a candle at Mass each day in honour of St Peter, or the inhabitants of Spalding in 1358 who joined together to provide a light to burn before a beautiful image of St John the Baptist which had recently been given to their church.[23] By the later Middle Ages in many communities, especially rural villages, the gilds and their dedications must have seemed as immemorial as the parish church itself. Devotion to the gild saint would therefore have been a "given". Doubtless many were satisfied by these traditional pieties, but there is plenty of evidence of new devotions jostling or supplementing the old. Larger communities gave more scope for such innovation, certainly at gild level, and the gilds of Crispin and Crispianus and of St Erasmus at Great Yarmouth look like late medieval creations, the first mention of Erasmus there occurring in 1479 and of St Crispin and Crispianus in 1525.[24] St Erasmus attracted many clients in the late fifteenth century: there was an Erasmus gild in St Matthew's, Ipswich, by 1487, the members of which seem to have had themselves painted with their patron on the Rood-screen.[25]

[21] *Festial*, p. 177.
[22] Festial, p. 199.
[23] Westlake, *Parish Gilds*, pp. 29–30.
[24] A. W. Morant, "Notices of the Church of St Nicholas, Great Yarmouth", *Norfolk Archaeology*, VII, 1872, pp. 223.
[25] Though there is room for doubt about this, since the present location of the panels of donors next to St Erasmus on the screen is not the original arrangement. See Lillie, "Screenwork", p. 189.

Old and New Allegiances

The cult of the saints, then, was in movement, a process in which fashion played a part. Fifteenth-century inventories of Tavistock parish church describe a reliquary there which contained strands of the hair of the Blessed Virgin and of St Mary Magdalene. By 1538 the churchwardens record the additional presence in this reliquary of the hair of St Katherine of Alexandria, whose cult was one of the most popular of late medieval English devotions.[26] Katherine's cult (like her hair!) had been growing steadily for two centuries, but Erasmus was one of a range of saints who rose to prominence in England in the fifteenth century, like St Sitha (Zita of Lucca) and St Roche, new saints replacing old ones in the affections and hopes of petitioners (Pl. 60, 71).[27]

Such movements of fashion were not entirely random, and there were many reasons why a saint's cult might be deliberately promoted. New saints meant new shrines. As we shall see, the custodians of the relics of a saint stood to gain much from their cultus. Moreover, under both the Angevin kings and their Plantagenet successors the cult of the saints often had a political dimension. The victims of political struggles might become martyrs, and popular devotion to such "saints" might be the vehicle for criticism of or resistance to the political status quo.[28] A number of fifteenth-century English cults had a strong political dimension, like the anti-Lancastrian cult of Archbishop Scrope of York, executed for treason by Henry IV, or the anti-Yorkist cult of Henry VI. Scrope quickly became the focus of a popular cult openly hostile to the monarchy – it was part of the cult legend that Henry IV had been stricken with leprosy as an immediate consequence of Scrope's martyrdom.[29] Henry VI's miracula include very overt political miracles, like the healing of a little girl afflicted with the "King's evil", whose parents had refused to bring her to be "touched" by the "usurper", Richard III.[30] Henry VII attempted to mobilize the cult of Henry VI in support of his own dynasty, building a

---

[26] R. N. Worth (ed.), *Calendar of the Tavistock Parish Records*, 1887, pp. 14, 18.

[27] ODS pp. 133, 346, 418–19. There was no life of Erasmus in the first edition of Caxton's version of the *Golden Legend*, but he added one to the second and subsequent editions.

[28] J. C. Russell, "The Canonisation of Opposition to the King in Angevin England", in C. H. Taylor and J. L. La Monte, *Haskins Anniversary Essays in Medieval History*, 1929, pp. 279–90; J. W. McKenna "Popular Canonisation as Political Propaganda: the Cult of Archbishop Scrope", *Speculum*, XLV, 1970, pp. 608–23.

[29] McKenna, "Popular Canonisation" *passim*, and Jonathan Hughes, *Pastors and Visionaries*, 1988, pp. 298–319.

[30] *Miracles of Henry VI*, pp. 109–10.

magnificent chapel at Westminster Abbey to house Henry VI's relics, and promoting his cause at Rome. The process foundered in the late 1520s, but "good King Harry" would almost certainly have been canonized had not bad King Harry's matrimonial affairs strained and eventually broken ties with Rome.[31]

But it would be a mistake to overemphasize the element of financial or political management in the cult of the saints. Here above all the wishes and affections of the laity made themselves felt, as the number of saints' cults unrepresented in the official calendars and service-books testify. Thomas More was speaking for the laity of late medieval England as a whole when he insisted that the cult of the saints needed no promotion by the clergy: "I byleue this deuocion so planted by goddes owne hande in the hertes of the hole church, that is to wit, not the clargie only, but the hole congregacion of all Christen people, that if the spiritualtie were of the mynde to leue it, yet wolde not the temporalitie suffre it."[32]

Many factors affected the pattern of lay devotion to specific saints – geographical or historical accident, such as proximity to a well-known shrine or image, a devotional initiative by an individual, news of striking cures or other favours. At the end of the Middle Ages such factors were reinforced by literary influences, such as the calendars or suffrages found in Books of Hours, especially the cheap printed versions available from the 1490s, the hearing or reading of the popular verse lives which are such a feature of fifteenth- and early sixteenth-century lay piety, and the plays based on these legends, performed in villages from East Anglia to Cornwall.[33]

Geographical and historical accident lay behind much devotion to particular saints. Testators in Kent not very surprisingly often left bequests for lights before St Thomas, and most regions of England had similar flourishing devotion to local saints, like St Richard of Chichester in Sussex and the Thames Valley, Thomas Cantilupe in Hereford and the West Midlands, or Etheldreda in East Anglia.[34]

[31] McKenna, "Piety and Propaganda", pp. 83–4; "Popular Canonisation", pp. 608–23.

[32] *The Workes of Sir Thomas More Knyght*, 1557, fol. 121 g.

[33] C. Davidson, "The Digby *Mary Magdalene* and the Magdalene Cult of the Middle Ages", *Annuale Medievale*, XIII, 1972, pp. 70–87; E. Duffy, "Holy Maydens, Holy Wyfes: the Cult of Women Saints in Fifteenth and Sixteenth Century England", *Studies in Church History*, XXVII, 1990, pp. 175–96; T. J. Heffernan, *Sacred Biography: Saints and their Biographers in the Middle Ages*, 1988; D. L. Jeffray, "English Saints' Plays", in N. Denny (ed.), *Medieval Drama*, Stratford upon Avon Studies XVI, 1973, pp. 68–89; T. Wolper, *Die Englische Heiligenlegende des Mittelalters*, 1964.

[34] For a general survey of local shrines see John Adair, *The Pilgrim's Way: Shrines and Saints in Britain and Ireland*, 1978; R. C. Finucane, *Miracles and Pilgrims: Popular Beliefs in Medieval England*, 1977, esp. pp. 152–72.

Nor is it very surprising to find in East Anglia devotion to a number of saints popular in the Low Countries, just as Cornish and Devonian devotion to the saints of Brittany seems readily accountable. The curious prevalence of devotion to royal saints in East Anglia (notably absent in Devon and the West Country, for example) is directly traceable to the character of Anglo-Saxon Christianity in the region, and the management of royal cults in the pre-Conquest church to strengthen the monarchy or the great religious houses whose royal founders and foundresses formed the centre of such cults.[35] Regional devotion is not always so readily explained. The oddity of a shrine in the parish church of Great Yarmouth to our Lady of Ardenbourg is dispelled only by the fact that many Yarmouth men had fought under Edward III in the battle of Sluys, and Edward had gone to Ardenbourg on a pilgrimage of thanksgiving immediately after the battle. The shrine was therefore a corporate gesture of gratitude and of civic pride in the Yarmouth men who did the king "most worthy service" there.[36]

Devotional initiatives by individuals might take a variety of forms. The cult of St Faith was brought to Norfolk from Conques by Robert Fitzwalter and his wife, who established a daughter house of Conques at Horsham St Faith.[37] Sometimes all that was needed to start a cult was the gift of an image or the bequest of a light in the parish church. Late medieval people responded directly and emotionally to images, and cults could create themselves rapidly even around new ones. John Warde, a Cambridgeshire painter in the early 1530s, made a picture of St Christopher "whereunto he had ioyned a devout interpretacion of St Christopher's life . . . very lyvely in a table". He put it in his pew in church "to learne to be a ryght Christopher". Warde intended the picture purely as an aid to meditation, but within a matter of a month other parishioners had begun to burn candles in front of it.[38] The gild of St John the Baptist at Spalding was founded to provide a light and a chaplain for a beautiful image of St John presented to the parish church by the carver and "a few devout friends". In 1365 five men from Burgh in Lincolnshire went on pilgrimage to Compostella. On the journey back their ship was caught in a ferocious storm, and they

    [35] Jeron in East Anglia, Meriasek in Cornwall; see Susan Ridyard, *The Royal Saints of Anglo-Saxon England*, 1989.
    [36] A. W. Morant "Notices of the Church of St Nicholas, Great Yarmouth", *Norfolk Archaeology*, VII, 1872, p. 223.
    [37] Benedicta Ward, *Miracles and the Medieval Mind*, 1987, p. 39.
    [38] W. Turner, *A New booke of spiritual Physic for dyverse deseases*, 1535, STC 24368, fol. 20v–21r.

vowed to St James that if he delivered them they would build an altar in his honour in their parish church, and maintain service at it. On their safe return home they told their neighbours of this vow, and the whole community joined with them in founding a gild to erect and maintain this altar. In 1501 John Bewde of Woolpit in Suffolk, who had a particular devotion to St James, presented his parish church with a gilded tabernacle for a statue of the saint, and a "stooll . . . coloard and garnyschyd wt scallops and othyr synys of St Jamys", as well as a cloth "to save the sayd tabernacle from soyle". We do not know whether Bewde, who was about to depart for Compostella, was adorning an existing image or attempting to initiate devotion to St James among his fellow-parishioners, as in the case at Burgh; either way he was clearly eager to encourage greater honour to the saint (Pl. 63).[39] And indeed, most of the references to particular saints in late medieval wills are bequests of lights, money, or ornaments to existing images, which had elicited the devotion of the testator. Where early medieval devotion to the saints was focused on their relics, late medieval devotion focused on images. The pilgrimages provided for in late medieval wills are usually to local shrines based not on a relic, but a statue or painting, as in the will of Alice Cooke of Horstead, who paid for a man to go on pilgrimage for her to "Our Lady of Rafham, to Seynte Spyrite [of Elsing] to St Parnell [Petronella] of Stratton, to St Leonard without Norwich; to St Wandred of Byskeley, to St Margaret of Harstead, to our Lady of Pity of Harstead, to St John's Head at Trimingham, and to the Holy Rood of Crostewyte".[40] All over England minor cults, originally no more than a parish devotion, established themselves round such images, though by the end of the Middle Ages new attitudes towards the images may have been added to the old. John Warde's painting of St Christopher was intended simply as an aid to prayer and imitation, and on discovering the beginning of a cult around it he took it away and replaced it with his hat! William Wulcy, the principal donor of the splendid screen at Horsham St Faith, completed about 1528, had the painter place on it many standard early sixteenth-century favourites – St Anne, St Helen, St Roche, St Apollonia. But he also commissioned the images of St Catherine of Siena and St Bridget of Sweden (Pl. 62), both highly unusual choices. In all probability, the presence of these images is due to Wulcy's interest in the devotional writings of both women, which were in circulation among the pious prosperous laity in England through the agency of the

[39] Westlake, *Parish Gilds* pp. 29–30: *Bury Wills* p. 83.
[40] *Norfolk Archaeology*, VII, p. 277.

Brigittine order, based at Syon. The panel painting of St Bridget, seated at her desk writing her revelations at the dictation of the Almighty himself, is copied directly from a Syon pamphlet, the *Dyetary of Ghostly Helthe*, printed by Wynkyn de Worde in 1528 (Pl. 61). Here, the image seems designed not so much to create devotion as to reflect it.[41]

But if new attitudes to images were emerging, the old ones continued to flourish unabated. And, as it happens, we have a detailed picture from an early Tudor parish of the establishment of a parochial cult as the result of the gift of one such image. In 1520 the newly appointed parish priest of the little Exmoor village of Morebath gave to the parish, at a cost to himself of 33s 4d, a splendidly painted and gilt statue of St Sidwell, a saint who had a shrine and healing well at Exeter and for whom the priest, Sir Christopher Trychay, had a particular tenderness. He placed her on the Jesus altar, perhaps as a deliberate attempt to claim for his patron some share in the very common late medieval devotion to the Holy Name. Certainly he set about encouraging lay devotion to the new saint. By 1523 parishioners had begun to adorn her altar with cloths and brass basins for candles; by the late twenties bequests to St Sidwell were flowing in. Women left their rosaries to adorn the statue on festivals, and bequests of jewellery or coin were used to make a silver shoe for it. The men of the village, including the priest's father, left hives of bees or the fleeces of sheep to pay for a candle before the shrine. By the mid-1530s the altar on which she stood was no longer referred to as Jesus' altar but St Sidwell's altar, and the saint had taken her place alongside the church's dedication patron, St George, on a processional banner presented by a parishioner. And at some point the laity began to christen their children into the saint's protection, for in 1558 Sir Christopher recorded the burial of a "Sidwell Scely". The cult, originally his personal devotion, had established itself as a dimension of the corporate religious life of the parish.[42] Between conventional image and inner devotion there was evident here, as at Spalding or Woolpit, a complicated and close relationship. The placing of such images in the church was both an expression of and an incentive to a sense of shared value and piety, and of kinship and neighbourhood between the saints, the parish, and the individual.

The key figure in promoting St Sidwell's cult at Morebath was the parish priest. But it is clear that devotion to particular saints

---

[41] The screen rail has an inscription commemorating Wulcy and his wives; the picture of St Bridget is in *The Dyetary of Ghostly Helthe*, W. de Worde 1520, RSTC 6833.

[42] Morebath CWA, pp. 11–12, 18, 20–3, 195 *et passim*.

was spread as much by lay report and word of mouth as by clerical encouragement or any official propagandist process. Robert Vertelet, a cripple cured at Henry VI's shrine, had dragged himself to Windsor from Winchester because "he had heard of the wide renown of the most devout King Henry, which had been spread abroad everywhere through the frequent occurrence of miracles done by him." The people of Westwell near Canterbury in August 1481 stood helpless round a millpond in which the miller's son was drowning, till someone "chanced to mention the glorious King Henry", and on invoking him the boy's body was recovered and revived. It was the "fame of his miracles" that led Thomas Fuller to invoke Henry in July 1484 when falsely accused of sheep-stealing. The family and neighbours of a Leicestershire child drowned in a well stood helpless round his body till a passing pilgrim suggested recourse to St Richard Rolle.[43] Behind all this was a form of bush telegraph, news caried by pedlars and pilgrims, spread among a lay public eager for pious entertainment and wonder, and, more to the point, eager for any news of possible healing and help in a world largely without medical remedies other than the dubious ministrations of cunning-men, prayer, and the power of the saints (Pl. 64). This sort of lay advocacy could, of course, be counter-productive. John Robyns, on his way from his village of Inkberrow to Stratford-upon-Avon, fell into company with George Luffar, a pious bore full of the recent fame of Henry and his miracles. Under Luffar's relentless eulogy, Robyns's patience eventually gave out, and he roundly cursed "St" Henry. Naturally, he was struck blind and only healed on vowing to go to Windsor himself. The incident, however, allows us to eavesdrop on the sort of pious conversation which must have been commonplace in late medieval England, and which certainly played a significant part in promoting new devotions.[44]

Holiness and Help

But the cult of the saints was more than an instinctive resort to any possible source of material or spiritual aid. It had a developed rationale of its own. The *Golden Legend* gave six reasons for the veneration of the saints. First, the cult of the saints existed to honour God, for "who that doth honour to saints, he honoureth him specially which hath sanctified them." Second, it existed to provide "aid in our infirmity", so that we may deserve that the

[43] F. M. M. Comper, *The Life of Richard Rolle*, 1933, p. 312.
[44] *Miracles of Henry VI*, pp. 34–9, 74–6, 89–98, 112–13; *Golden Legend*, VI pp. 96–7.

saints aid and help us. Third, in celebrating their glory "our hope and surety may be augmented and increased". Fourth, "for the example of us following". Fifth, "for the debt of interchanging neighbourhood". And sixth, it exists to procure our own honour, "for when we worship our brethren we worship ourselves, for charity maketh all to be common." The saints, the *Legend* went on, were "our dukes and leaders", to be honoured and imitated, for they are the friends of God. Their bodies, having been the temples of the Holy Spirit, were sources of power, the alabaster box of spiritual ointment from which healing flows. Somewhat more pithily, Mirk characterized the attractions of the saints for a late medieval English mind in his sermon on St Andrew, who was to be worshipped, he claimed, "for his hygh holynes of lyvyng, another for gret myracles doyng, the thrid for gret passyon suffryng".[45]

The honour and imitation of the saints as examples of "hygh holynes of lyvyng" certainly had an important place in the hierarchy of values enshrined in the late medieval cult, but it was perhaps not its most striking feature. Many of the "new saints" of the fourteenth and fifteenth centuries were clerics like John of Bridlington or Osmund of Salisbury or, like Henry VI, saintly rulers, characterized by an unspectacular gentleness and charity. Their appeal lay in their tenderness and approachability, their charity towards their clients. But if the evidence of wills and the surviving images is to be credited, the majority of the saints most favoured in the fifteenth and early sixteenth century had vivid and spectacular legends, in which "gret myracles doyng" and "gret passyon suffryng" were especially prominent. St Erasmus, a Syrian bishop martyred under Diocletian, whose cult was one of the most popular and fastest growing in late medieval England, provides the classic example here. One late medieval English account of his passion lists fifty-two separate tortures, from being scourged with brambles and boiled in oil to having his guts wound out with a windlass and the cavity so created filled with salt (Pl. 65). Erasmus's legend is a compendium of most of the major motifs of the late medieval cult of martyrs: he is meek but resolute in his faith, beset by demonic enemies who "swelled upon him for anger", and his enemies are struck down by God's vengeance – the fires stoked to burn Erasmus scorch up the stokers, the red-hot metal coat put upon his flesh explodes and kills the torturers. There are links here with late medieval portrayals of the Passion of Christ, and one or other of these motifs occur in the legends of most of the favourite saints of the late Middle Ages – pierced flesh and

---

[45] *Festial*, p. 6.

exploding torture machines in those of Sebastian, George, and Katherine (Pl. 66), boiling oil or metal in those of George and John the Evangelist, and so on.[46]

This emphasis on the bizarre, the spectacular, and what the American constitution calls "cruel and unusual punishments" is perhaps most striking in the case of the extraordinary popularity in late medieval England of the cult of early Roman virgin martyrs. This devotion was of long standing, at least as far as the paradigmatic cases of St Katherine, St Margaret, and, to a slightly lesser extent, St Barbara are concerned. These three attracted enormous devotion throughout the Middle Ages, and suffrages addressed to them are included among even the briefest sequences of such prayers in almost all Books of Hours. The privileged place of Katherine and Margaret in late medieval piety is attested by the fact that their statues stood on either side of the shrine image of Our Lady at Walsingham (Pl. 67).[47]

By the late Middle Ages Katherine, Margaret, and Barbara had been joined by a whole galaxy of more or less cloned and identical virgin saints. The surviving Rood-screens of Devon and East Anglia provide our single most vivid source for this process of inflation. With the exception of symbolically inclusive groups like the twelve Apostles, the four Evangelists or the Four Latin Doctors, the group of saints most commonly found on these screens are the virgin martyrs.[48] They are frequently grouped together on the screens. At North Elmham nine of them occupy the whole of the south side of the screen – Barbara, Cecilia, Dorothy, Sitha, Juliana, Petronella, Agnes, and Christina (Pl. 68). At Westhall in Suffolk, also on the south screen, there are eight of them – Etheldreda, Sitha, Agnes, Bridget, Katherine, Dorothy, Margaret and Apollonia. At Litcham there are also eight – Sitha, Cecilia, Dorothy, Juliana, Agnes, Petronilla, Helena, and Ursula, occupying the whole north screen, while at Belstead in Suffolk Sitha, Ursula, Margaret, and Mary Magdalene share the north screen with a solitary male figure. No doubt this grouping together of women saints reflected the seating arrangements for men and women in the church, and at Gateley, where no iconographic scheme is discernible, the female saints are nevertheless grouped on the north screen. But there is more to the grouping than that, for

[46] C. Horstmann (ed.), *Sammlung Altenglische Legenden*, 1878, pp. 198–203.

[47] *Reynes Commonplace*, no. 116 and pp. 322–3. Katherine and Margaret also occur together in a charm against the toothache collected by Robert Thornton; see Horstmann, *Yorkshire Writers*, I p. 375.

[48] Duffy, "Holy Maydens, Holy Wyfes", *passim*.

the legends of these women saints are all characterized by extreme examples of the features already noted in the legend of Erasmus, together with others particularly connected with their femininity – an emphasis on their virginity and the attempts of their persecutors to defile or degrade it. This is readily established by a crude outline of the legends of these virgin martyr saints, as they occur in the *Golden Legend*.

Agatha was the daughter of a wealthy Sicilian family, and from her girlhood dedicated herself to God. The base-born pagan consul Quintianus attempted her seduction, with the help of Aphrodisia, the madam of a local brothel, and her nine harlot daughters. All in vain: Agatha remained chaste in word and deed, so the prefect had her tortured on the rack, had her breasts twisted off, and dragged her naked over red-hot broken pot-shards. Miraculously comforted in prison, she eventually expired amid an earthquake which precipitated a revolt against the prefect by the people (Pl. 69). Quintianus was bitten and battered to death by his own horses.

Agnes was a thirteen-year-old virgin, vowed to Christ. The son of the local prefect fell in love with her, but she rejected him with scorn, boasting of her heavenly spouse. The prefect told her she must choose to serve the gods in the temple of Vesta or be put into service in a brothel. She refused pagan worship, so was stripped and marched off to the brothel. Her hair grew instantly to cover her nakedness, and she was robed in light. When the pining prefect's son crept in by night to have his way with her, he was strangled by demons, but restored at her intercession. Flames refused to burn her, so she was despatched with a dagger through the throat. Her younger sister, Emerentiana, rebuking her murderers, was in turn stoned to death, whereupon an earthquake and thunder slew her killers.

Barbara was a virgin of such beauty that her pagan father Dioscorus enclosed her in a tower to protect her virtue. Many princes sued for her hand, but Barbara rejected them all. Converted to Christianity, Barbara destroyed her father's domestic gods, and had the workmen alter the building specifications of her father's showy new bath-house to include three windows instead of two, in honour of the Trinity. Her father, strongly disapproving, dragged her by the hair to an unjust judge. She was subjected by him to horrible tortures, which included the usual stripping and scourging, as well as burning with lamps and, of course, she had her breasts cut off. Her father eventually beheaded her on a mountain, but was himself struck by lightning and reduced to ash.[49]

[49] *Golden Legend*, III pp. 32–9, II pp. 245–52, VI pp. 198–205.

There is no need to labour the point further. The most famous of these legends, that of Katherine of Alexandria and her exploding wheel, will be familiar to most people. Katherine had to defend her virtue and her Christian beliefs against the emperor Maxentius, converted the fifty philosophers he sent to argue with her, and Maxentius' wife, not Katherine, had her breasts torn off. But all the stereotypes familiar from the legends I have outlined are found in their full-blown form in Katherine's, which was one of the most frequently represented subjects in late medieval English churches.[50] That of Margaret of Antioch, lusted after by the governor Olibrius, tortured, and, most spectacularly, swallowed in prison by the Devil disguised as a dragon, whom she exploded by making the sign of the Cross, was hardly less familiar (Pl. 70).[51]

The great and growing attraction of these legends in late medieval England is easily documented, quite apart from the screen paintings in which they so often appear. Literary evidence of their popularity is abundant, perhaps most strikingly in the verse *Legendys of Hooly Wummen* of the Suffolk Austin canon, Osbern Bokenham. Bokenham composed thirteen saints' lives in verse, and his book reads like programme notes to one of the East Anglian screens we have been considering, with which he must have been very familiar. He wrote lives of Margaret, Anne, Christina, Ursula and the 11,000 Virgins, Faith, Agnes, Dorothy, Mary Magdalene, Katherine, Cecilia, Agatha, Lucy, and Elizabeth. All except Lucy appear on surviving East Anglian screens, most of them on many. Some of these verse lives were commissioned by local laity, like John and Katherine Denston, residents and benefactors of the nearby parish of Long Melford, Katherine Howard of Stoke-by-Nayland, and Agatha Flegge, from the neighbouring county of Essex. The names of these women are themselves testimony to the cult of the saints.[52] Bokenham's verse lives were examples of a popular genre, whose leading exponent was the Bury monk John Lydgate. They were designed to appeal to the sententious, moral, and slightly credulous tastes displayed in many contemporary devotional and moral compilations, such as the Cambridge University Library manuscript Ff 2 38, rich in "popular romances which are pious, lively and full of incidents and marvels . . . ideally suited to the edification and entertainment of well-doing, devout readers of modest intellectual accomplishments", precisely the sort of people, in fact, who were the patrons of the Rood-screens.[53]

[50] *Golden Legend*, VII pp. 1–30; ODS pp. 69–70.
[51] *Golden Legend*, IV pp. 66–72.
[52] M. J. Serjeantson (ed.), *Legendys of Hooly Wummen*, EETS, 1938, pp. xiii–xxi.
[53] F. McSparran and P. R. Robinson, introduction to the facsimile edition of *Cambridge University Library Manuscript Ff 2 38*, 1979, pp. vii, ix.

The combination of pious wonder and simple entertainment value for a growing middle-class audience goes some of the way towards explaining the devotional appeal of these bizarre and sometimes lurid stories. The saints at their centre were easily recognizable, and therefore easily portrayed, by their colourful emblems – Katherine's wheel, Barbara's tower, Agatha's breasts, Agnes's leaping lamb, Dorothy's basket of roses and apples. Such motifs were irresistible assets in the adornment of churches made possible by the ever-increasing devotional investment of prosperous lay people, as the gallery of saints on the bench-ends of Wiggenhall St Mary or the windows of Long Melford testify.[54] The harping on the supernatural and the bizarre in these pious legends reminds us that we are in the mental world not only of the *Golden Legend*, but of Mandeville's travels and of verse romances, containing generous helpings of the weird, the wonderful, and the slightly salacious. But the fundamental values implicit in the stories, with their emphasis on sexual purity, their scornful rejection of marriage, and their defiant resistance to the wishes and commands of parents and secular governors seem strange features of a cult whose surviving remains, such as the images on painted screens, were paid for by the solid and prosperous laity of East Anglia or Devon. What was their appeal to these sober and not unworldly men and women of pre-Reformation England?

Recent writing on the devotion to these women saints has focused very much on the ambivalence of the themes of virginity and defilement, and the apparent hatred of women manifested in the outrages on the female body they describe. Their peculiarity and problematic character as examples to be followed have been explored in connection with the piety of individuals like Margery Kempe, obsessed as she was by the apparent contradictions between sexual experience and holiness. There were saints popular with late medieval men and women whose appeal probably lay in their suitability as patterns for imitation; St Zita of Lucca, the model domestic servant and pattern of woman in the kitchen, is a case in point.[55] But I suspect that only a handful of men and women actually perceived these holy maidens as exemplars, just as very few can have thought of St George, St Sebastian, St Roche, or St Michael the Archangel as exemplars.

It is certainly true that chastity was a virtue specially valued, at least in principle, by late medieval English Christians. A number of the prayers prescribed for daily use in the *Horae* are concerned with

---

[54] James, *Suffolk and Norfolk*, pp. 212–13; Woodward, *Norwich School*, pp. 74–127.
[55] Atkinson, *Mystic and Pilgrim*, pp. 184–91; for St Zita see ODS pp. 418–19.

the preservation of chastity, and one of the most widely used of all medieval prayers, the "O Intemerata", invariably included in all *Horae* and primers, is an elaborate appeal to Mary and John the Evangelist precisely in their character as inviolate virgins.[56] But the dynamic of such prayers was not designed primarily to present the chastity of the saint as a model, but as providing the basis of their intercessory power. Virginity as a symbol of sacred power, a concrete realization within this world of the divine spirit, has a very ancient pedigree within Christianity. It is already clearly articulated in the second-century Acts of Paul and Thecla, providing the paradigm for much in these later legends.[57] What it gave to the ordinary Christian man and woman was not so much a model to imitate, something most of them never dreamt of doing, but rather a source of power to be tapped. In the case of the late medieval legends, this is represented by the promises which are attached to the pious remembrance of the saint's passion. In Bokenham's account of the legend of St Dorothy the saint kneels as she awaits death and prays:

> For tho that remembre wold hyr passyoun,
> That hem save from every trybulacyoun
> He wold vouchesaf, & specyally from shame
> Of hateful povert & eek of fals name.
> Also that he wold trew contrycyoun
> And of all here synnys plener remyssyoun;
> And yf wummen wyth chyld of hyr had mende,
> That the tham hastly wold sucour sende;
> And that noon hous where were hyr passyounarye
> Wyth feer ner lyghtnyng shuld neuyr myskarye."

And a voice from Heaven declares

> "Come loue, come spouse, & be ryht glad,
> For that thou hast askyd is grauntyd the,
> And for alle that thou preyst sauyd shal be."[58]

A set of verses in Latin added to another version of Dorothy's legend assures the reader that in whatever house the name or image of Dorothy is honoured no child will miscarry, no danger from fire will befall, and no one will suffer that most feared of all ills in the

---

[56] Texts of these prayers in *Hor. Ebor.* pp. 34, 67–8. On the "O Intemerata" see A. Wilmart, *Auteurs spirituels et textes dévots du Moyen Age Latin*, 1932, pp. 474–504.

[57] Peter Brown, *The Body and Society: Men, Women and Sexual Renunciation in Early Christianity*, 1989, pp. 156–9.

[58] *Legendys of Hooly Wummen*, p. 134.

late Middle Ages, sudden and unprepared death without the benefit of shrift and housel, the last sacraments. These promises are a feature of the legends of Margaret and Katherine too, and received official sanction in the matins lessons of the Sarum breviary, while John Mirk's preacher was to tell his parishioners on St Margaret's day that

> ych man that made a chirch yn hur name other fownde any lyght there yn the worschyp of her, and all that wryttyn her passyon othir redyth hit or callyth to hyr yn gret dystress, that God schuld do hom succoure radly, and graunt hom the joye that evyr schall last, and yche woman that callyth to her yn tyme of travelyng of child, that scho may be sownde delyverd, and the chyld come to crystendome.[59]

Here, surely, is the principal explanation for the popularity of these women saints on the screens of late medieval parish churches, for to contribute to such a screen was a guaranteed way to enlist the help of uniquely powerful intercessors. The saint's heroically maintained virginity was important not primarily as an example to be followed in all its craggy contradiction, but rather as the source of their special intercessory relationship with Christ. The members of the gild of St Katherine in the church of St Andrew, Cambridge, explained their devotion to "the glorious Virgin, Katherine, their advocate" not in terms of her example, but of the "endless miracles" Christ had performed in her honour. Margery Kempe was more aware of the disturbing and potentially disruptive dimension of these saints' legends than most, but the pinnacle of even her spiritual ambition was revealingly disclosed by Christ's promise to her: "Dowtyr, I be-hote the same grace that I be-hyte Seynte Kateryne, Seynt Margarete, Seynt Barbara . . . in so mech that what creatur in erth un-to the Day of Dom aske the any bone & belevyth that God lovyth the he xal have hys bone or ellys a better thyng."[60]

These virgin saints and their male counterparts were invoked by the prosperous and pious donors of the East Anglian screens not as exemplars calling away from marriage and money-making, nor as patterns of perpetual chastity or defiant disobedience to patriarchy and government, but as the helpers of those who would "have their boon or else a better thing", as protectresses of the marriage bed,

---

[59] Horstmann, *Sammlung Altenglische Legenden*, pp. 193–7. There are similar examples in *Legendys of Hooly Wummen*, p. 199, in Horstmann (ed.), *Altenglische Legenden Neue Folge*, 1881, pp. 240–1, 258, 452, and in H. N. MacCracken (ed.), *Minor Poems of John Lydgate I*, EETS, 1911, pp. 189–90; Francis Proctor and Christopher Wordsworth (eds), *Breviarium ad Usum Insignis Ecclesiae Sarum*, 1886, III col. 1116; *Festial*, p. 202.

[60] *The Book of Margery Kempe*, p. 52.

auxiliary midwives, fire-insurance underwriters, and guarantors
against what Dorothy calls "hateful pouert".

And though the virgin martyrs provide a particularly clear and
distinctive collective example of this dimension of the cult of the
saints, these privileges and promises were of course by no means
confined to them. Similar promises were a feature of the charms
associated with the so-called Charlemagne prayers, and were also
attached to the legends of St Erasmus, St Paul, and St George. The
verse account of the Erasmus legend in MS Harley 2382 informs
the reader that

> With devote pater noster or other prayere,
> And with an almesdede, lasse other more,
> Of mete or of money yeven to the pore,
> Or els candel-light more or lasse
> Brennyng at evesong, matynes or masse.
> Who thes thynges doth for this martires sake,
> Thes rewardes folowyng truly shal he take:
> One is: that he shal have to his levyng
> Resonable substance to his endyng;
> Another is this: that any of his foone
> Hyndryng or harme shal thei do hym none,
> Yf his cause be trew – this is certan –
> Thurgh the prayere of this holy mane,
> And that he wol axe resonably,
> That wolle God hym graunte of his mercy;
> Another is this – that hym shal plese:
> He shalle be delyvercd of al his disese;
> Another is this, as the boke seith;
> He shalle dye in ryghtfulle byleve & feithe,
> And sotheely, or the soule fro the body twyne,
> He shalle have contricion & shrift of his syn,
> And he shalle receyve, or he be ded,
> Cristes owne body in forme of bred,
> And he shalle have afore his endyng
> The holy sacrament of anoyntyng.
> And he shalle come to thilke joy & blisse
> In the which truly this hoily martir ys.[61]

Moderate prosperity, safety from enemies, healing from disease, a
holy death comforted by the church's sacraments, and eventual
salvation: this is a very comprehensive list of the aspirations of late

[61] See above, note 46.

medieval men and women.[62] All these blessings recur again and
again in the promises and explanatory rubrics attached to many
of the devotions circulating in manuscript collections and the
printed *Horae*. The cult of the saints was here firmly embedded in
the wider pattern of late medieval piety. Erasmus's cult offered
unusually comprehensive benefits, just as his sufferings embraced
the full gamut of those found singly or in smaller groupings in
other legends. But Erasmus was himself only one of a number
of "helper" saints to whom one or other of such powers were
attributed. An East Anglian Book of Hours of about 1480, now in
the Fitzwilliam Museum, contains a verse devotion to nine martyrs
with special powers to help clients – Giles, Christopher, Blaise,
Denis and George, Margaret, Barbara, Katherine, and, curiously,
Martha, the sister of Lazarus.[63] This line-up could well be taken for
a description of a screen in one of the smaller churches of East
Anglia, and an identical group, with the single addition of the
virgin martyr Christina, occurs in another East Anglian source,
a set of verse prayers to the ten saints by John Lydgate. The
prayers are prefaced by a note that "These holy seyntys folwyng ar
pryvyledged of our lord Ihesu that what man or woman praieth to
them rightfully shal have his bone." This is clearly an English
equivalent to the continental devotion to the auxiliary saints,
the "Fourteen Holy Helpers". Apart from the saints of the major
English or regional shrines, the male saints most commonly found
on the same screens as the virgin martyrs include a high proportion of these holy helpers, such as George, Sebastian, Roche, and
Blaise.[64]

It seems clear, then, that the English laity looked to the saints not
primarily as exemplars or soul-friends, but as powerful helpers and
healers in time of need, whether bodily need or the last spiritual
extremity of death and the pains of Purgatory. This emphasis on
the centrality of healing and help in the cult of saints was hardly
surprising in the case of saints with well-known healing shrines, or
whose legends singled them out as naturally suited for such a role –
Roche (Pl. 71), who had suffered from the plague, as plague healer,
Erasmus as healer of bowel complaints. It was clearly a growing
preoccupation, perhaps under the impact of successive waves of
epidemic disease, and it is very common to find devotions to helper
saints, and especially plague saints like Sebastian or Roche, copied
into flyleaves or blank spaces of *Horae* by their late medieval lay

    [62] See below, chapter 8, "Charms, Promises and Pardons", pp. 266–98.
    [63] Fitzwilliam Museum MS 55, an East Anglian *Horae* of *c*.1480 (the provenance is
established by a full-page illustration copied from the souvenir cards given to pilgrims to the
Rood of Bromholm, as well as by the calendar and suffrages) fol. 139v.
    [64] *Minor Poems of John Lydgate*, pp. 120–4.

owners.[65] So powerful was this trend that it spilled over to absorb
even saints who one might think had no particular appropriateness as holy helpers. Round about 1500 the owner of a Sarum
Horae now in the Fitzwilliam Museum inserted into it a recipe (with
a long medieval pedigree) for choosing one of the Apostles to help a
sufferer from epilepsy. Twelve candles, each inscribed with the
name of an Apostle, were to be burned on the altar during a Mass
of the Holy Ghost. The sick person was to vow to fast on bread
and water on the eve of the Apostle whose candle burnt longest,
and the one so honoured could be expected to bestow healing on
his client. The practice seems to have been widespread.[66]

Nevertheless, though any saint could be expected to help the
sufferer in spiritual distress, or the soul passing to or already in
the pangs of Purgatory, the saints most often invoked for aid in
physical illness or worldly difficulty were specialists: Barbara and
Katherine in childbirth and against sudden and unprepared death,
Anthony against ergotism, Roche and Sebastian against the plague,
Erasmus against intestinal disorders, Master John Schorne (Pl. 72)
or St Petronilla against the ague.[67] These specialisms were easily
ridiculed by satirists like Erasmus or reformers like Bale:

> With blessynges of Saynt Germyne,
> I wyll me so determyne,
> That neyther foxe nor vermyne,
> Shall do my chuckens harme.
> For your duckes saynte Lenarde,
> For horse take Moses yearde,
> There is no better charme.
> If ye cannot slepe but slumber,
> Geve otes unto saynt Uncumber,
> And beanes in a serten number,
> Unto saynt Blase and Saynt Blythe.
> Geve onyons to saynt Cutlake,
> And garlyke to saynt Cyryake,
> If ye wyll shurne the head ake,
> Ye shall have them at Quene hythe.[68]

No doubt resort to a specialist saint was often based on nothing
more profound than the appropriateness of the saint's emblem or
some detail of their legend. One of the most frequently portrayed

[65] Typical examples are Fitzwilliam MS 51, *passim*, and Cambridge University Library Kk
6 10 fol. 163r-v.

[66] Fitzwilliam MS 51, fol. 139v.

[67] J. Huizinga, *The Waning of the Middle Ages*, 1965, pp. 165–8: *Records of Buckinghamshire*,
II p. 67.

[68] John Bale, *Comedy concernynge thre lawes*, Anglia V, 1882, quotation at pp. 175–6.

saints on late medieval screens was St Apollonia. An elderly African matron who leapt into the pyre prepared for her after being tortured by having her teeth smashed with a club, Apollonia's legend had been modified to bring it into line with those of the virgin martyrs – she was always portrayed as young and beautiful, and her teeth were now said to have been pulled out one by one. Portrayed with a pair of pincers holding a giant molar, she was the obvious saint to apply to for relief from the miseries of toothache, and one need search no further for her great popularity (Pl. 73).[69]

But there is also some evidence that resort to a specialist saint might be the result of a deeper and more sympathetic intuition than such simple application to the recognized expert. It might also spring from a sense of empathy and intimacy, as in the case of the mariner, Henry Walter, grievously wounded in a sea battle in the reign of Richard III. Walter had atrocious abdominal wounds, which festered so badly that the stench became intolerable to his shipmates, who put him out of the ship into a small boat on his own. After fifteen days of suffering he had a vision of Henry VI, whose miracles were at that time much in the public eye. Interestingly the royal saint, dressed as a pilgrim, had a fifteen days' growth of beard like Walter's own, apparently as a mark of solidarity in suffering. But the vision was not yet complete. As a mariner Walter had a special devotion to St Erasmus (who, under the name St Elmo, protected ships in storms). On gazing round he saw that "the holy martyr Erasmus (for whom he chanced to have a special devotion) lay near him, as if with the pain of his sufferings renewed, just as he is often represented in churches, being tortured by his executioners." (Pl. 65).

The scene Walter was recalling was indeed familiar from its many representations in paintings and carved altar-pieces: Erasmus was portrayed lying on a table while his entrails were wound out on a nautical windlass. Thus, while Walter tossed in agony in his boat, the saint lay alongside him, sharing his suffering. Erasmus's windlass here provided a vivid symbolic representation of Walter's own torments, just as Henry's fifteen-day beard mirrored Walter's state of physical neglect after fifteen days of suffering. From this vision "the man conceived great gladness of heart, and from that time entertained no little confidence that he could hope for recovery." The whole incident illuminates vividly that sense of the saints as "kynd neyghbours and of our knowyng" of which Julian of Norwich wrote. In this case at least the power of the specialist saint was no mere arbitrary exercise. Instead it sprang from the fact

[69] ODS pp. 21–2.

that they themselves had shared the sufferings of their clients, an extension of the interpretation of Christ's intercessory work offered in the Epistle to the Hebrews and in much late medieval devotion to the Passion.[70]

The same sense of symbolic resonance in the cult of specialist saints is conveyed by the series of paintings over the Lady altar at Ranworth, in Norfolk (Pl. 74). This altar had a special significance for the women of the parish. It was the custom after childbirth for women, when they came to be churched, to present themselves and their babies before the principal image or altar of Our Lady, and to offer a candle in thanksgiving for their safe delivery. The iconography of the Ranworth Lady altar refers directly to this custom, for all four of its paintings deal with childbirth and babies. It portrays the "Holy Kindred", or the extended family of Jesus, in the form of the three daughters of St Anne, the three Marys, and their children. Mary Salome is portrayed with her sons, the Apostles James and John. Next to her is her sister, the Blessed Virgin, with the Christ child. Next to her is Mary Cleophas, with her four sons, James and Joses, Simon and Jude. And completing the sequence of four paintings is an image of Margaret of Antioch, whose bursting out of the dragon's belly in her prison had made her the patron of women in childbirth or "our lady's prison", as it was often called. The invocation of St Margaret against the dangers of childbirth was, as we have seen, commonplace and officially endorsed in liturgy and preaching. The Ranworth screen suggests that it could transcend mere mechanical custom, to be integrated into a sensitive and symbolically appropriate sense of the sacred dimension of human family life.[71]

Late medieval Norfolk, and especially the area round Ranworth, was the focus of a flourishing devotion to St Anne. Her cult was a popular one in the late Middle Ages in England as elsewhere, and she and her daughters provided a symbolic affirmation of the rootedness of the Incarnate Christ within a real human family. At a time when much in the cult of the saints militated against a positive valuation of human sexuality and the realities of marriage and childbearing, the cult of Anne provided an image of female fruitfulness which was maternal rather than virginal, and her thrice-married state, rivalling the career of the Wife of Bath, was an unequivocal assertion of the compatibility of sanctity and married

[70] *Miracles of Henry VI*, pp. 77–84.
[71] I have discussed the Ranworth screen and the cult of St Anne more fully in "Holy Maydens, Holy Wyfes", pp. 194–6; for Reformation debate about this custom of offering a candle to the Blessed Virgin at churchings in the Canterbury diocese see L&P, XVIII (ii) p. 302.

life. She represented both the notion of the family and the principle of fertility, whose three holy daughters gave birth in their turn to six Apostles and the Saviour of the world – at the end of Bokenham's life of St Anne he prays to the saint on behalf of the couple who had commissioned the poem, and who longed for a male heir:

> Provide, lady, eek that Ion denston
> and kateryne his wyf, if it be plese the grace
> Of god above, thorgh thi merytes a sone
> Of her body.[72]

The screen is not the only local evidence of the popularity of this cult. There was also a statue and light of St Anne at Ranworth, while four miles away at Acle, the late fifteenth-century church-reeve Robert Reynes copied a number of items connected with this cult into his commonplace book, including genealogical material and a stanzaic version of St Anne's legend designed for reading at the gild feast of a St Anne fraternity, of which there were a number in the area.[73]

It is no surprise, therefore, to find St Anne's daughters represented together on the Ranworth screen. But their placing on the Lady altar alongside the familiar image of Margaret conquering the dragon shows a desire to present a complex and positive icon of childbearing and childhood to the women who brought their offerings of thanks to Mary and Margaret. The latter, whose spectacular torments and miraculous preservation spoke of holiness and otherness, was a symbol of transcendent power, the sacred beyond the limits of the experience of ordinary people. Her power to help sprang from her divinely protected and heroic virginal integrity. The figures in the other paintings are even more sacred beings – Christ and his six cousins, all of them Apostles, and Anne's three holy daughters. But here they are mothers and children of flesh and blood: one of the toddlers blows bubbles from a pipe, another clutches a toy windmill. The screen spoke to the women of Ranworth simultaneously of the divine indwelling in the concrete reality of the family, of the sanctity of marriage and procreation and God's blessing on ordinary things, and at the same time of the transcendent power of God to help those in extremity, symbolized by Margaret's virginal intercession. As in the case of Henry Walter and St Erasmus, the specialist saint is given a richly

---

[72] K. Ashley and P. Sheingorn, *Interpreting Cultural Symbols: St Anne in Late Medieval Society*, 1990, pp. 95–110; *Hooly Wummen*, p. 45.
[73] Meredith, *The Mary Play*, pp. 9–12 and references cited there.

human symbolic context which prevents her being seen as a mere
mechanical dispenser of power and favour.

Coins, Candles, and Contracts

The relationship between client and saint, however personal, was
governed by a well-established pattern of custom and expectation.
The saint, for his part, desired honour from his clients. This might
take the form of the repetition of suffrages and hymns to the saint,
and many of these were provided in *Horae* and printed primers.
Clients also attended matins, Mass, and evensong on his feast, or
fasted on his eve or even more regularly, like the Tuesday fast in
honour of Henry VI, held to be a sure protection against the
plague.[74] Above all, the saint desired pilgrimage to his shrine, and a
promise to visit the saint's relics and there offer a coin or a candle
was held to be the most likely way to attract his interest and
help. The commonest way of signifying such a vow was to take a
silver coin and bend it: this constituted a formal promise to take the
coin and offer it at the shrine. So when in 1485 a little girl, Ann
Plott, was run over and crushed by a recklessly driven cart in the
Isle of Sheppey, a neighbour "snatched out her purse and bent a
penny over the lifeless corpse, as if to implore the pity of our Lord
and the prayers of his most devout servant King Henry by this
promise of an offering". Similarly, when Joan Walran, a child
living at Lambourn in Berkshire, was accidentally strangled by a
strap hanging from a cellar door, the neighbours "took a penny,
and humbly calling upon the servant of God, hung it round the
girl's neck".[75] The coin was clearly especially efficacious if bent
over or hung on the afflicted part, and there were refinements of
this notion. When one child swallowed a silver groat the owner of
the coin vowed it to Henry and the child immediately coughed it
up. The coin's value to the saint could be increased if the pilgrimage
to make the offering were undertaken barefoot or roughly clad, or
if the pilgrim undertook to abstain from meat or wine till the
pilgrimage was accomplished. But the saint might intervene to
increase its value himself. When one wealthy client vowed to bend
a coin to Henry VI he was unable to find a silver one in his purse,
though he knew there were silver coins there; he duly bent a gold
coin. Instead of or in addition to a coin a candle might be vowed,
and this form of vow was held to be especially efficacious if the

---

[74] *Miracles of Henry VI*, p. 178.
[75] On coin-bending in general see Finucane, *Miracles and Pilgrims*, pp. 94–5; *Miracles of Henry VI*, pp. 114–18, 159–62.

candle was made round a wick measured to the exact length and breadth of the afflicted person's body. The length of string thus measured was folded and coated with wax to make the candle – if it was very long the candle was rolled into a spiral or *rotula*. This custom was looked on with some suspicion by the clergy as semi-magical: the recorder of Henry VI's miracles refers to it as "more moderno laicorum", a phrase clearly designed to distance himself from the practice.[76]

Behind such notions, particularly coin-bending, lay some notion of a contract, in which the pledged coin was an "earnest penny", cash on the nail designed to strike a deal with the saint. The hard-headed businessmen of the London Mercers' Company treated such vows as a legitimate business expense: when the ship *Carrygon* had to jettison its cargo in a storm in 1479 the captain and crew vowed pilgrimages in return for deliverance from drowning: the Mercers' Company's books duly record the fulfilment of the pilgrimages.[77] Such emergency vows were commonplace. Sir Richard Guylforde's chaplain, returning from the Holy Land in the winter of 1506–7 was caught with his fellow-passengers in "the gretyst rage of wynde that ever I saw in all my lyfe". Pilgrims and mariners assembled on deck "and devoutly and ferefully sange Salve Regina and other antymes . . . and we all yave money and vowed a pyllgrymage in generall to our Blessed Lady de Myraculis at Venyse, besydes other particuler vowes that many pylgrymes made of theyr singuler devocions."[78]

The saint thus retained might act very promptly. The Kentish man, Edward Crump, was sceptical about saints and miracles, probably under the influence of Kentish Lollardy. When he became afflicted with agonizing burning pains all over his body, his pious and orthodox wife urged him to have recourse to King Henry. He agreed and sent her to the closet to fetch a silver penny to bend; by the time she got back to his bed he had been cured. The saint might actually suggest such a payment to the sufferer. Katherine Bailey, a Cambridge woman blind in one eye, was kneeling at Mass in the Austin Friars' church one day when a mysterious stranger bent over her and told her to bend a coin to King Henry. She had no purse with her, but made a mental promise to do so at the earliest opportunity. When the priest raised the Host at the sacring she could see it with both eyes and went home cured. Henry himself

[76] *Miracles of Henry VI*, p. 88.

[77] Brian Spencer, "King Henry of Windsor and the London Pilgrim", in *Collectanea Londiniensia*, ed. J. Bird, H. Chapman, and J. Clark, 1978, p. 235.

[78] H. Ellis (ed.), *The Pylgrymage of Sir Richarde Guylforde*, Camden Society, LI, 1851, p. 65.

liked to intervene directly in this way. In another case he reminded
a potential client that his father had died in battle in his service, thus
re-establishing a feudal bond between them, as well as the one
implied in the coin-bending. When he raised from the dead Alice
Newnett, a plague victim from Mere in Wiltshire, he appeared to
her in a vision while she was being stitched into her shroud, and
imposed as a condition that she should remain in her shroud for a
time after her raising, presumably to underline the splendour of the
miracle by emphasizing the fact that she really had died.[79]

If the saint could seek out the devotion of his or her clients, he or
she might punish or at least complain if slighted or if a client's
devotion faltered. Few late medieval saints were as grimly vengeful
as the twelfth-century William of Norwich, who punished with
death a cleric vowed to his service who resorted to medicine when
ill, rather than sticking to an intincture of water in which the saint's
teeth had been washed.[80] Nevertheless, even in the fifteenth century
saints could be stern. A Salisbury cleric who irreverently sat down
on Osmund's tomb was immediately stricken with excruciating
pains (we are not told where) which persisted till he begged the
saint's pardon.[81] Cures secured on payment of the earnest penny,
by bending a coin, might be reversed if the promised pilgrimage
and offering were not promptly performed. Mirk told the story of a
former votary of St Katherine whose zeal had cooled. She was
granted a vision in which the saint passed her by and refused
to look at her: she renewed her former devotion.[82] By contrast,
single-minded faithfulness would be rewarded. Mistress Adowne,
the mother of a three-year-old boy afflicted with paralysis in 1487,
successfully enlisted St Henry's help by "commending her child in
Christ's name to his prayers only, making mention of no other
saints at all".[83]

Bargains are two-way affairs. Although the living clients of the
saint came to him or her as suppliants, there can be no doubt that
the semi-contractual character which the cult of the saints often
took on could give people a sense of grievance and anger if the saint
did not deliver the desired benefits. Perhaps the most spectacular
manifestations of such feelings were associated with images. As we
have seen, the image of the saint played a crucial and central role in

---

[79] *Miracles of Henry VI*, pp. 182, 136, 179–80.
[80] A. Jessopp and M. R. James (eds), *The Life and Miracles of St William of Norwich*, 1896,
pp. 174–8.
[81] A. R. Malden (ed.), *The Canonization of Saint Osmund*, Wiltshire Record Society, 1901,
p. 41.
[82] *Festial*, p. 240.
[83] *Miracles of Henry VI*, pp. 171–6.

late medieval devotion, both at parochial level and at shrines. The saint was believed to be in a very direct relationship with his or her image. Few people would have been likely to make a simple identification of the saint with the image, and the people of Morebath were happy, when they commissioned a new image of St George, to trade in the old statue in part exchange, thereby making clear their perception of the distinction between George and his icons.[84] But the identification of homage to the image with homage to the saint might be taken to mean that possession of the image gave one some sort of leverage over the person represented. One of the best-known stories from the miracles of the Virgin was that of the woman who took the wooden *bambino* from the arms of a statue of the Madonna and held it to ransom for the release of her own child. Mirk tells a similar and even more circumstantial story in his sermon for the feast of St Nicholas. One of Nicholas's specializations was the protection of property from theft. A Jew, hearing of this, bought a statue of Nicholas to protect his premises while he went on a journey. Thieves nevertheless broke in and robbed him. On his return he reproached and scourged the statue "as hyt had ben Seynt Nycolas hymselfe", and promised the saint a beating every day "tyll I have my good ageyne". His property was in due course returned by a frightened and penitent thief, who told how Nicholas had visited him in a dream. The saint, bruised and bleeding from his beating, angrily insisted on immediate restitution to the Jew, who duly became "a trew crysten man"![85] The story neatly brings together the notion of the saint as a human figure, both potentially vengeful and susceptible to pressure and the bonds of obligation and even coercion.

Gift, Grace, and Fellow-feeling

But these emphases are comparatively rare in late medieval sources. For the most part, the saints were perceived as part of the economy of grace. They were dispensers of gifts and miracles, and the essence of their cult lay in its assurance of the possibility of rescue from the iron laws of cause and effect, the painful constrictions of poverty, disease, and the sometimes harsh ordering of society which burdened men and women. The saints were often portrayed as embodying precisely those elements of tenderness and compassionate humanity which were the distinguishing marks of late

---

[84] Morebath CWA, p. 32.
[85] *Festial*, p. 14; for the story of the widow who held the carved Christ-child hostage see *Golden Legend*, V pp. 106–7.

medieval devotion to the name and person of Jesus. Like their master and exemplar, the saints were gentle, loving, merciful. One of the principal attractions of the cult of Henry was the gentleness and readiness to forgive he had displayed in his life. The prayers provided in the *Horae* for his devotees present him consistently as merciful, clement, one "ever compassionate to the miserable and afflicted".[86]

There was about late medieval religion a moralistic strain, which could be oppressive. Churches contained not only the chancel-arch representation of the Day of Doom, with its threat of a terrifying reckoning down to the last farthing, but wall-paintings and windows illustrating the deadly sins, the works of mercy, the Commandments, Christ wounded by sabbath-breaking, the figures of the three living and the three dead, or the related *danse macabre*. Clerics could and did press the saints into service to reinforce such moralism, as in the use of the legend of Erasmus to encourage Sunday observance.[87] But this heavy emphasis on the duties and obligations of the Christian life, the need to do good and to be good, was never a dominant feature of the popular veneration of the saints. Instead the brightly painted and beautiful images spoke of the overflowing abundance of God's grace, even to the undeserving, from whom they required only love. This was fundamental to the ever-popular legends of the miracles of the Virgin, with their recurrent stories of intervention to rescue from the rigours of judgement scoundrels, thieves, and unchaste priests, whose only virtue was their sometimes vestigial love for her.[88] What was true of the Virgin applied, to a lesser degree, to all the saints. They too could be appealed to as loving friends, who would not be too hard on poor weak flesh and blood. In the cases of saints like Archbishop Scrope or Henry VI, this emphasis was related directly to their own histories: the victims of persecution or judicial murder could be expected to have a special tenderness for those who suffered similar injustice. The fact that Henry VI had been wrongfully imprisoned and treated, as his biographer Blacman

[86] Fitzwilliam MS 55 fol. 141b and cf. Bodleian Library, James MS 46 fols 108 to the end, where hymns and prayers of this sort to St Henry have been added.

[87] Erasmus's legend emphasizes that he suffered all his passion on a Sunday and links his cult with observance of the day. He is probably the mysterious "St Sunday" who occurs so regularly in late medieval English wills.

[88] The cycles of paintings of the miracles of the Virgin at Eton and the Winchester Lady chapel provide good examples of this type of miracle. They are listed by M. R. James, "The sculptures of the Lady Chapel at Ely", *Archaeological Journal*, XLIX, 1892, pp. 345–62, and illustrated from the Eton frescoes in James and Tristram, "Wall Paintings in Eton College Chapel", *Walpole Society*, XVII, 1929, pp. 1–44.

commented, "like a thief or an outlaw",[89] together with his well-known readiness during his lifetime to forgive malefactors, meant that he could be called on to rescue those whom human law had judged beyond the pale. When Thomas Fuller was unjustly condemned to death for sheep-stealing, he invoked Henry's help because "he considered him to be the most speedy succour of the oppressed, as the fame of his miracles showed." Henry appeared and placed his hand between Fuller's windpipe and the rope. Though apparently dead, the victim revived in the cart taking him for burial, and was duly released.[90]

Such examples of fellow-feeling were relatively specific, adapted to the particular circumstances of the saint's legend and their client's needs. But a sense of neighbourly community was one of the most striking aspects of the cult of the saints in general. It is witnessed to in the thirteenth and fourteenth centuries by the proliferation of gilds dedicated to maintaining the corporate worship of particular saints, by providing candles before their images and holding processions on their feast days. This communal emphasis was maintained and elaborated to the end of the Middle Ages. It was perhaps most firmly attested in the custom of parochial subscription to provide images in churches, and especially the clustering of images of the saints on the screen which separated nave from chancel. The serried ranks of celestial neighbours gazing back at the parish as it gathered to witness the sacrifice that created and sustained their sense of belonging together was a vivid and speaking embodiment of the all-inclusive circle of Christian communion.

The accounts of the healing miracles of the saints are often strikingly communal in character. Again and again we catch a glimpse in these stories of the sufferers surrounded not only by their families, but by friends, neighbours, and even passing strangers, who involve themselves in concerted acts of intercession to the saint. To secure healing, neighbours suggested recourse to a specific saint, accompanied the family of the client on pilgrimage, vowed fasts or bent coins. The neighbours of an Oxfordshire man, John Hill, secured his recovery by observing a *quatriduum* or four days of fasting and devotion on his behalf, in honour of Henry VI. In August 1481, when Richard Question's grandson got trapped in the mill-race at Westwell in Kent, a "multitude" of neighbours gathered, "asking one another what was to be done". When someone mentioned St Henry, "they were soon all invoking his memory with one voice." When John Wall, of White Roothing in Essex,

[89] M. R. James (ed.), *Henry VI: a reprint of John Blacman's Memoir*, 1919, p. 43.
[90] *Miracles of Henry VI*, p. 94.

was crushed by a falling wagon the whole town "stretched out their hands on high and besieged the hearing of the Heavenly King and . . . especially the memory of King Henry".[91] When Joan Walran, a toddler left to play in an empty house, accidentally hanged herself on a dangling strap, the parents summoned their "fellow townspeople and neighbours", and on the mention of Henry "all were soon wonderfully united in mind, encouraging each other to hope for aid through an appeal to that bountiful patronage." When similar neighbourly supplication "with one accord" brought about the resuscitation of a child drowned at Rye, the *miracula* specifically commented on the healing power of the charity represented by such corporate invocation of the saint.[92]

Not surprisingly, therefore, exclusion from the cult of the saint could be experienced as an exclusion from community. The anguish of the Cambridgeshire "cunning-woman", prevented by an apparition of St William from approaching his shrine because of her magical practices, was due at least in part to a sense that her sin had cut her off from her neighbours, with whom she had made the pilgrimage to Norwich. Though "de consortio eorum", of their company, she was unable to make her offering "cum sodalibus", with her fellows, till shriven and given a penance at the shrine.[93]

Striking examples of communal invocation could be multiplied from the surviving accounts of any late medieval healing saint. They abound in the miracles of St Osmund, for example. But the cult of the saints was not merely seen as an exercise of communal charity: the saint was perceived as a creator of such charity. The healing mediated by the saint restored more than health to the sick: it restored them to the community of the living. This point underlies the accounts of the healing of blind people in the fifteenth-century accounts of the miracles of both Henry VI and Osmund of Salisbury, where the point is specifically made that after healing the sufferers were enabled to see the Host at the sacring of the Mass. Gazing on the elevated Host at the parish Mass, in itself the act of the individual worshipper, was perceived in late medieval piety as a moment of intense communal devotion. Bequests of torches to be lit at this moment in the parish Mass were one of the most common of all bequests, and Lollards were frequently spotted by their neighbours precisely because of their refusal to join in the community's

[91] Ibid., pp. 36–7, 70.
[92] Ibid. pp. 114–18, 138–9.
[93] *St William*, pp. 279–82; the phrase "cum sodalibus" perhaps suggests that the group she came with was a gild.

corporate act of reverence at this moment of the Mass.[94] Restoration of sight therefore was a restoration to a share in this intense moment of spiritual communion in the Body of Christ.

Other, even more explicit links between healing and the restoration of Eucharistic community abound. Perhaps the most striking of these occurred early in the fifteenth century at St Osmund's tomb. A lunatic, John Bemyster, was brought chained and bound to the saint's shrine in the Lady chapel in the cathedral, while a Mass of the Virgin Mary was being celebrated. His head and hands were placed in one of the niches of the tomb, so as to be as near the saint as possible. He remained in this position till the "Agnus Dei", the moment in which Christ is invoked as giver of peace, and the paxbred was passed about among all present to be kissed as a sign of peace. At this point Bemyster's bonds fell away, and he was found to be whole and in his right mind. The whole incident has strong and perhaps deliberate echoes of the account in Mark's Gospel of the healing of the Gerasene demoniac, whose cure concludes with the injunction to "go home to your friends."[95]

This healing of community might take very concrete and literal forms, for the saint might restore charity within a community itself broken by hatred and violence. When Robert Clerk stabbed John Luyde of Duryngton with a long dagger, the intercession of the bystanders secured St Osmund's help to stop the flow of blood. The miracle healed more than the stab-wound, for both victim and assailant subsequently made the pilgrimage to St Osmund, to offer the dagger together to the saint. In the same way, when Richard Wodewell carelessly threw a heavy metal quoit in the village of Larkestoke and brained a little girl standing by to watch the game, he had to seek sanctuary in the cathedral from her friends and family. He invoked St Osmund and the girl recovered. She duly brought the quoit to the shrine as an offering, and Wodewell and the child's family joined together to testify to the saint's goodness.[96]

Pilgrimage

Most of the healing and rescue stories we have been considering either took place at shrines or involved vows of intercessory

<hr/>

[94] *Miracles of Henry VI*, p. 136; A. R. Malden (ed.), *The Canonization of St Osmund*, 1901, p. 67; Foxe, *Acts and Monuments*, IV p. 225. In the same way, failure to invoke the saints in childbirth might cause neighbours to round on a woman as a heretic; see *Acts and Monuments*, IV p. 206.
[95] *Canonization of St Osmund*, pp. 57–8; Mark 5/19.
[96] *Canonization of St Osmund*, pp. 64–6, 68.

or thanksgiving pilgrimages to shrines. Though the heyday of the great national shrine at Canterbury was perhaps over by the fifteenth century, a decline attested in dwindling takings from pilgrim offerings, there is plenty of evidence that regional and local shrines, as well as the classic pilgrimages to Rome, Jerusalem, and Compostella, remained the focus of devotion up to the very moment when they were outlawed.[97] And even the traditional shrines retained their power to attract devotion in times of crisis or calamity. With the pestilence rife in southern England in September 1471 Sir John Paston reported from the West Country and from London troops of anxious suppliants on the roads to Canterbury, "nevyr so moche peple seyn in pylgrymage her-to foor at ones, as men seye".[98]

The primary purpose of pilgrimage had always been to seek the holy, concretely embodied in a sacred place, a relic, or a specially privileged image. Such localization of the holy in sacred places was often criticized in the later Middle Ages, not least by Thomas à Kempis in the *Imitation of Christ*.[99] In fact the practice of pilgrimage, travel to seek the sacred outside one's immediate locality, had important symbolic and integrative functions, helping the believer to place the religious routine of the closed and concentric worlds of household, parish, or gild in a broader and more complex perception of the sacred, which transcended while affirming local allegiances. Pilgrimage also provided a temporary release from the constrictions and norms of ordinary living, an opportunity to review one's life and, in a religious culture which valued asceticism and the monastic life above the married state, an opportunity for profane men and women to share in the graces of renunciation and discipline which religious life, in theory at least, promised. The penitential dimensions of late medieval pilgrimage have perhaps been underplayed in recent discussions. Pilgrimages were often undertaken precisely as penance, and the element of hardship in them was of the essence. As John Heywood's pilgrim says, it was the "dayly payne" of the pilgrim which moved God to mercy:

who sekyth sayntes for Crystes sake –
And namely suche as paynes do take
On fote to punyshe thy frayle body –

---

[97] There is a good general discussion in Finucane, *Miracles and Pilgrims*, pp. 191–202. For some of the problems in assessing the evidence see Spencer, "King Henry", pp. 237–9 (pilgrim badges). For a local survey of shifting fashions, using material from Norwich Cathedral and its shrines, see John R. Shinners, "The Veneration of Saints at Norwich Cathedral in the fourteenth century", *Norfolk Archaeology*, XL, 1988, pp. 133–44.

[98] N. Davis (ed.), *Paston Letters and Papers of the Fifteenth Century* I 1971, p. 443.

[99] *Imitation of Christ*, Book IV, chapter 1.

> Shall therby meryte more hyely
> Then by any thynge done by man.

But late medieval men and women were also well aware of the symbolic value of pilgrimage as a ritual enactment and consecration of their whole lives, helping to interpret them as a journey towards the sacred, an awareness amply attested in works like *Piers Plowman*, the *Pilgrimage of the Life of Man*, and in the remarkable pilgrimage paintings of Hieronymus Bosch. This seems to have been the notion at work behind the late medieval burial recently discovered in Worcester Cathedral, where the corpse was laid out in his pilgrim's gear, staff and cockle-shell by his side, his (little used) boots on his feet.[100]

The continuing popularity of pilgrimage is reflected both in the large number of surviving pilgrim badges from the period, and in the multiplication of pilgrimage literature in English in the fifteenth century, from narrative and autobiographical accounts of the wanderings of Margery Kempe or Sir Richard Guylforde, through manuals of advice produced by experienced pilgrims like William Wey, to comic accounts of the miseries and dangers of the more strenuous pilgrimages.[101] The palmer in John Heywood's play *The Four PP*, written in the early 1530s, recites a formidable litany of mostly English shrines and saints, presupposing at least a nodding acquaintance on the part of his audience with a veritable gazetteer of sanctity. He had been, he claimed,

> At Saynt Toncomber and Saynt Tronion,
> At Saynt Bothulph and Saynt Anne of Buckston,
> On the hylles of Armony, where I see Noes ark,
> With holy Job, and St George in Suthwarke,
> At Waltham and at Walsyngham,
> And at the good Rood of Dagnam,
> At Saynt Cornelys, at Saynt James in Gales,
> And at Saynt Wynefrydes well in Walles,
> At Our Lady of Boston, at Saynt Edmundes Byry
> And streyght to Saynt Patrykes purgatory.
> At Rydyboe and at the blood of Hayles,
> Where pylgrymes paynes ryght muche avayles,
> At Saynt Davys; and at Saynt Denis,
> At Saynt Matthew and Saynt Marke in Venis,

---

[100] *The Plays of John Heywood*, ed. R. Axton and P. Happe, 1991, p. 113. There is an influential discussion of pilgrimage as a "liminal" phenomenon, by Victor and Edith Turner, in *Image and Pilgrimage in Christian Culture*, 1978; H. Lubin, *The Worcester Pilgrim*, Worcester Cathedral Publications I, 1990.

[101] There is a survey in Jonathan Sumption, *Pilgrimage*, 1975.

At mayster Johan Shorne, at Canterbury,
The great God of Katewade, at Kynge Henry,
At Saynt Savyours, at our lady of Southwell,
At Crome, at Wylsdome and at Muswell,
At Saynt Rycharde and at Saynt Roke,
And at Our Lady that standeth in the oke.
To these with other many one,
Devoutly have I prayed and gone,
Prayeng to them to pray for me
Unto the blessed Trynyte.[102]

Heywood's list is by no means exhaustive, but it registers for us something of the sheer exuberant variety of the practice of pilgrimage just before the flood of Reformation overwhelmed it. In a well-known passage from a letter of 1533, Hugh Latimer complained how the country people passed by his house on the Fosse Way, coming "by flocks out of the west country to many images".[103] Such devotion was no peculiarity of West Country men. A fifteenth-century Sussex testator made provision for five pilgrims to go from London to Rome, to the Brigittine house at Syon "when pardon is used to be had", to "Walsyngham to be there at the daie of Assumpcion of our lady", to St James in Hales (Compostella), and to Becket's shrine at Canterbury "to be ther upon seynt Thomas daye".[104]

These arrangements were more than usually elaborate, but bequests for surrogate pilgrimages are a common occurrence in wills from all over England up to and beyond the break with Rome.[105] Many of these bequests were designed simply to gain vicarious merit by paying for "diverse pilgrimages to holly seyntes", or to gain by deputy indulgences "in suche holy places where as moost pardon is".[106] Margery Kempe undertook her many pilgrimages very largely to gain the indulgences available at shrines, for example, the Portiuncula Indulgence at Assisi on Lammas Day 1414, when there was "gret pardon of plenyr remyssyon, for to purchasyn grace, mercy, & foryevenes for hir selfe, for alle hir frendys, for alle hir enemys, & for alle the sowlys in Purgatory".[107] Indulgences at shrines of this sort were greatly valued. Margery

---

[102] *Plays of John Heywood*, pp. 112–13.
[103] Quoted in Finucane, *Miracles and Pilgrims*, p. 199.
[104] *Sussex Wills*, III pp. 210–11.
[105] *Test. Ebor.*, IV p. 199, V p. 155; *Somerset Wills*, II pp. 28–30; Duncan "West Kent Parishes" p. 253 (many examples cited here); *Wells Wills* pp. 97, 100; *Bury Wills* p. 83; "Early Norfolk Wills", p. 115; *Norfolk Archaeology*, VI, p. 277ff; Cratfield CWA, p. 19.
[106] *Lincoln Wills*, II pp. 75–7; *Beds Wills*, III pp. 130–3.
[107] *The Book of Margery Kempe*, p. 79.

was given money by neighbours and strangers to pray for them at pilgrimage sites, and donations must have played a key part in financing many pilgrimages. Though most of the miracles described in shrine legends and saints' lives were miracles of healing, pilgrimages "of devotion", aimed primarily at gaining spiritual benefit, were clearly at least as common. An English chronicler writing in the 1460s gives a vivid account of a shipman returned at Michaelmas 1457 from a pilgrimage of devotion to Compostella, where he had procured three Masses for the souls of his parents and for himself. The shipman was haunted for three nights in his lodgings at Weymouth by the ghost of his uncle, who commanded him to return to Compostella, to procure a Mass there to release him from Purgatory. The shipman complied, "wherefore," adds the chronicler, "I counseylle every man to worship Seynt James."[108] Despite that final injunction the cult of the saint and the practice of pilgrimage has here been wholly integrated into a more general late medieval concern with pardon from Purgatory and the celebration of Masses for the dead. It is difficult to see any distinctive role for St James in the story, though it turns on the need to have Masses said at his shrine.

Many bequests for surrogate pilgrimages were clearly linked to a very specific search for healing or other favours, and many were obviously designed to discharge vows of pilgrimage undertaken by the testators themselves in earlier days, but for one reason or another unfulfilled. Accounts of the saints often contained dire warnings of the dangers of failing to fulfil vows undertaken during moments of crisis, and the non-performance of such vows could clearly lie heavy on the conscience, at least as the moment of final reckoning drew near. Agnes Parker, a Norfolk widow making her will in 1507, recorded that "Item, *I owe* a pilgremage to Canterbury, another to St Tebbald of Hobbies, and another to St Albert of Cringleford."[109] Margaret Est, a widow of Norwich in 1484, appointed "my right trusty and well belovyd Cosyn Thomas Thurkeld, shoemaker in Berstrete" as her executor, having got from him a promise

> to go for me s[er]teyn pylgremage, that is to sey, in my lyf to the holy seynt Wandrede; and aft my dissease he xall go unto seynt Thomas of Canterbury, and ther to prey for me to relesse me of my vowe whiche I made thirdyr myself. And from thens

---

[108] J. S. Davies (ed.), *An English Chronicle 1377–1461*, Camden Society, LXIV, 1856, p. 72.
[109] *Norfolk Archaeology*, VI, p. 277.

the same Thomas xall go for me on pylgrymage unto the Abbey
of Chelksey [Chertsey] ther as Kyng herry lyth, yf my goodys
wyll stretch so ferr for his costs. And so be hys pylgrymages that
I may be relessyd of myn avowes.[110]

Though it is notoriously difficult to come to firm conclusions
about pilgrim numbers, by the eve of the Reformation there is
evidence of the comparative neglect of traditional shrines, like
those of St Hugh at Lincoln, Cuthbert at Durham, or Becket at
Canterbury.[111] There is plenty of evidence, however, that this did
not represent an abandonment of belief in the saints, but was an
aspect of that search for new and more powerful helpers which we
have noted as such a feature of late medieval devotion to the saints.
There is a quantifiable curve of popularity and decline in the fame
and effectiveness of every medieval shrine, which has no apparent
relation to distance or proximity to the Reformation. In the fifteenth century more recent healing shrines, like those of Master
John Schorne and, especially, Henry VI at Windsor, were evidently
booming. There are, for example, almost a third as many surviving
pilgrims' badges from Henry's shrine, which lasted only fifty years,
as from Becket's shrine, which was visited for three centuries (Pl.
75).[112]

Transfer of allegiance from the older healers to the new seems
to have been an explicit theme of some of the miracle stories
associated with the newer shrines. Perhaps the most striking
example of a transfer of allegiance is the case of Miles Freebridge,
a nine-month-old cockney baby whose elder brother gave him a
pilgrim badge representing "that most worthy martyr St Thomas
of Canterbury" to play with. Naturally the child swallowed the
badge and choked. All attempts to remove it having failed, and the
child's life being despaired of, the father and bystanders invoked
Henry VI, whereupon the badge dislodged itself. The grateful parent
took the badge to Windsor, where it was hung over Henry's tomb,
one of the spoils of holy war.[113] There are a number of similar cases
among St Henry's miracles; he even seems to have moved in on
St Anthony's monopoly of cures for ergotism or "St Anthony's
fire" (Pl. 76).[114] Other saints were equally competitive. The early
sixteenth-century verse life of St Walstan, hung over his shrine at
Bawburgh for the edification of pilgrims, told of a Canterbury

[110] Norfolk Wills, IV, p. 338.
[111] Finucane, Miracles and Pilgrims, pp. 191–202.
[112] Spencer, "Henry VI", p. 238.
[113] Miracles of Henry VI, pp. 164–7.
[114] Ibid. pp. 98, 106–9.

weaver crippled with a "bone ach" who petitioned Becket at his shrine to no avail, till a patriotic Norfolk pilgrim in Canterbury suggested he try St Walstan. On vowing a pilgrimage to Bawburgh he was immediately healed. He walked without crutches to Norfolk and left a wax model of his leg as an *ex voto* over Walstan's shrine.[115]

As the presence of stories of this kind in the official *miracula* of saints like Henry or Walstan suggests, transfers of allegiance were, naturally enough, encouraged by the custodians of the bene-ficiary shrines and by the promoters of new cults. Since fashions in devotion to the saints changed, such changes could be managed. The custodians of shrines like that of St Edmund at Bury or St Werburge at Chester commissioned openly propagandist verse lives, explicitly linking devotion to the saint with loyalty to the interests of the monastery where the relics rested. Henry Bradshaw's life of Werburge reminded the various beneficiaries of the saint's power of the blessings they had received, each stanza concluding "Wherefore to the monastery be never unkynde". The printer Richard Pynson published a number of these propagandist legends to promote pilgrimage to particular shrines.[116] Edmund and Werburge, like Cuthbert at Durham, were the foundations on which were reared mighty ecclesiastical corporations, whose con-tinuing power and wealth depended on continuing loyalty to the patron. But even humble local shrines like that of Walstan of Bawburgh or John Shorne's at North Marston stood to gain pres-tige and wealth as the saint's cult expanded. Bawburgh and North Marston parish churches were both substantially rebuilt or enlarged with pilgrim offerings.[117]

There was ample scope for fraud and abuse here. As the Messenger in Thomas More's *Dialogue* remarked:

> Some prieste to bringe up a pilgrimage in his parisshe, may devise some false felowe fayning hym selfe to come seke a saint in hys chyrch, and there sodeinly say, that he hath gotten hys syght. Than shall ye have the belles rong for a miracle. And the fonde folke of the countrey soone made foles. Than women commynge thither with theyr candels. And the person byenge of some lame begger iii or iiii payre of theyr old crutches with xii pennes spent in men and women of wex, thrust thorowe divers

---

[115] M. R. James, "Lives of St Walstan" *Norfolk Archaeology*, XIX, 1917, pp. 238–67, at pp. 262–3.

[116] C. Horstmann (ed.), *Life of St Werburge of Chester by Henry Bradshaw*, EETS, 1887, pp. 189–93. On Pynson and these saints' lives and shrine legends see chapter 2 above, "How the Plowman learned his Paternoster", pp. 78–9.

[117] W. H. Kelke, "Master John Shorne", *Records of Buckinghamshire*, II, 1869, pp. 60–74; W Sparrow Simpson, "Master John Shorne", ibid. III, 1870, pp. 354–69; "Lives of St Walstan", pp. 240–1.

places some with arrowes, & some wyth rusty knyves, wyll make hys offerynges for one vii yere worth twyse hys tithes.[118]

More himself cited a number of examples of fraud at shrines in both England and Germany, though he believed that God's determination to vindicate true miracles, together with the common sense of intelligent lay people, would ensure that they were always exposed. Whether or not they were all discovered, pious frauds certainly occurred. When the Lollard priest Richard Wyche was burned on Tower Hill in June 1440 the parish priest of the neighbouring church of All Hallows, Barking, tried to cash in on the event. Wyche was widely regarded as a saint. A pilgrimage based at All Hallows began, at which the parish priest took "the offeryng of the symple peple". To promote the pilgrimage "and for to excite and stire thaym to offre the more fervently", he took ashes and mixed them with fragrant spices, which he then spread on the site of the burning "and so the symple people was decyved, wenyng that the swete flavour hadde comme of the asshis of the ded heretic."[119]

Such pious frauds succeeded by imitating the conventions of the cult of saints, conventions which formed a code immediately understood by "symple people". Candles left before an image or a grave, abandoned crutches, wax models of a man or woman, or of a foot, a breast, an eye, or an arm, model ships, all these were immediately intelligible claims that here there was power to heal or rescue, and they formed a standard part of the furniture of a shrine. Thomas More, a stout defender of shrines, nevertheless saw the funny side of all this. In his *Dialogue concerning Heresies* he purports to give an account of the shrine of St Valery in Picardy, where the saint specialized in genital disorders, impotence, and infertility, and where "all theyr offrynges that honge aboute the walles / none other thynge but mennes gere and womens gere made in waxe". The York fabric rolls itemize the objects clustered round a real sixteenth-century shrine, the tomb of Richard Scrope in York Minster. They included nine assorted images of men and women, two cows, sixteen eyes, thirteen legs, ten hearts, ten teeth, four breasts, as well as a fleet of model ships and an assortment of anchors, boat-hooks, and horse harness. Many of these were of silver or gold, instead of the more usual wax.[120] We know what

[118] More, *Workes*, p. 134.
[119] McKenna, "Popular Canonisation", pp. 609–10.
[120] Thomas More, *Complete Works*, VI, 1981, p. 228. More describes some of the cult practices at the shrine, including the silver rings, large and small, through which male pilgrims had to pass the afflicted member, and the alarmed wife who prevents her new husband having a candle made to measure, since she feared his virility would waste away as the candle burned! J Raine (ed.), *Fabric Rolls of York Minster*, Surtees Society, XXXV, 1859, pp. 225–6; Jonathan Hughes, *Pastors and Visionaries*, p. 325.

such collections of ex votos looked like, for the custodians of Henry VI's shrine at Windsor produced a propaganda print showing the saint (or his image) surrounded by *ex votos* – crutches, fetters, ships, and human figurines – and by kneeling clients, some of them pierced with arrows or knives, as in the fraudulent shrine described in More's *Dialogue*. On the wall behind him hangs a tablet or hand-board on which is pasted an account of his legend and miracles (Pl. 77).[121] Tables like this, usually in verse, are often referred to in accounts of shrines, and the complete text of the one that formerly hung over the tomb of St Walstan of Bawburgh has survived.[122] The Henry VI print was the visual equivalent; both were designed to give the pilgrim to the shrine a key to the stories behind the various *ex votos*, and thereby to stimulate devotion. Pilgrim badges, cheap prints of the saint's legend or image, and ampullae containing holy water from the shrine shared this function, as well as communicating some of the virtue of it to those unable to visit the shrine, or to the pilgrim himself once he had left.

A number of the objects and figures represented in the Henry VI print can be identified from the miracle collection compiled for his canonization, like Benedicta Barrow with the knife which had buried itself three inches in her neck during a fall, Thomas Fuller or Richard Beys carrying the nooses with which they were unjustly hanged, Reginald Scarborough with the arrow which had pierced him during archery practice in his village, William Sanderson's ship, grounded and sprung on a sandbank, which sailed miraculously on to London despite the loss of fifteen rivets.[123]

The display of *ex votos* touches the very nerve and centre of the meaning of the cult of the saints in the late Middle Ages. The miracle stories associated with the shrines of the saints in fifteenth- and sixteenth-century England opened a window of hope on a daunting world of sickness, pain, and natural calamity. Men and women fled to the protection of the saints from a world in which children fall from trees or tumble down wells, crawl into fires, or jump in play onto sharpened sticks or untended metal spits. Workmen are crushed or ruptured by heavy loads or blinded by branches, women die in the agonies of prolonged childbirth. We catch glimpses of a whole gallery of devastating diseases – bone cancer, gangrene, epilepsy, paralysis – of homes wrecked by insanity, and entire families or villages decimated by plague or famine. The sick and the halt clustered round the shrines, sleeping

[121] Reproduced as the last item in the supplement to E. Hodnett, *English Woodcuts 1488–1535*, 1973. See also V. M. Radford, "The Wax Images Found in Exeter Cathedral", *Antiquaries Journal*, XXIX, 1949, pp. 164–8.
[122] Printed by James, "Lives of St Walstan", pp. 249–67.
[123] *Miracles of Henry VI*, pp. 62–5, 89–98, 149–56, 181–2, 177.

on or near it for days and nights at a time, touching the diseased parts of their body to sacred stone or wood (Pl. 78).[124] Chaucer's pilgrims have printed on our imaginations the notion of pilgrimage as a holiday outing, but to the shrines of late medieval England there also came a heart-rending stream of desperate men and women. Some of them at least went away cured, like Robert Vertelet, a cripple who dragged himself from Winchester to Windsor, or Hervey Acke, who crawled from the parish of St Helen's Bishopsgate in London. Both men left their crutches at the shrine.[125] Such *ex votos* were the most eloquent of all possible testimonies to the reality of healing, assurances of the triumph of life in a world which must often have seemed dominated by suffering and death. Even for the healthy pilgrim, drawn to the shrine by an itch for travel, by simple devotion, or by the desire to obtain indulgences, the ranks of crutches and fetters, boats and legs and hearts, and the sight of the sick themselves, waiting with varying degrees of hope or impatience, were an assurance that God was in his Heaven and the Devil did not always have the last word.

Indeed, the public promotion of such an assurance was very much a feature of successful healing shrines. Beneficiaries of the saint's intercession were expected to make their healing known, at least to the superintending clergy at the shrine, and if possible to produce corroborating witnesses. The clergy would then organize a public "Te Deum" and description of the miracle. The case for the canonization of St Osmund, prepared in the early fifteenth century, relates how during a period of interdict the saint healed a lunatic woman. Because of the interdict the "Te Deum" could not be sung, nor the bells rung, according to custom when a miracle happened.[126] A sermon might also be preached to pilgrims, relating any recent miracle, and addenda were pasted up next to the tablets placed over the tomb describing the saint's legend and miracles.

But the laity themselves saw to it that the saint's favours should not be forgotten. *Ex votos* might be elaborate, like the wax model of an ox-cart and barrel provided "by means of subtle craftsmanship" by two grateful carters after Henry had saved a cargo of expensive wine which they had spilt.[127] In the immediate aftermath of a healing, beneficiaries were anxious to give testimony. Henry Walter, the mariner cured of gangrene by Erasmus and Henry, solemnly swore out a circumstantial account, displaying his scar at Windsor, "in the presence of the venerable assembly of the magistrates and

[124] I have collected this list from the miracles of St Osmund and Henry VI.
[125] *Miracles of Henry VI*, pp. 75–6.
[126] *Canonization of St Osmund*, p. 40.
[127] *Miracles of Henry VI*, p. 105.

certain others".[128] William Fuller, the man unjustly hanged at Cambridge, went both to Chertsey, Henry's first resting-place, and, after Henry's translation, to Windsor, to give public testimony.[129] When Margaret Denys was restored after drowning at Rye in Sussex, her parents and forty neighbours who had witnessed the miracle brought the child to Windsor to give thanks on the feast of Pentecost, thereby ensuring the maximum publicity.[130] Such testimony was most effective if given on the spot, immediately after a miracle had occurred at the shrine, and there is little doubt that miracles publicized in this way, with the ringing of the church bells, the singing of the "Te Deum" by the clergy, and the excited chatter of other pilgrims and bystanders, might have had a snowball effect, one miracle breeding another like it: Robert Vertelet and Hervey Acke, both cripples on crutches, were healed at Windsor on the same day.[131]

St Walstan of Bawburgh

These generalities can be brought into sharper focus by looking briefly at one late medieval local saint's cult. Walstan of Bawburgh occurs in no liturgical calendar so far discovered, no Office or Mass survives for his feast, and his legend contains folkloric and legendary material which makes his very existence, to say the least, uncertain. Yet he was a figure of some consequence in the popular religious imagination in Norfolk between the late thirteenth and the early sixteenth century. His shrine at Bawburgh, five miles from Norwich, was the focus of an annual pilgrimage, "all mowers and sythe folowers sekynge hym ones in the yeare" on his feast day, 30 May.[132] His appeal was certainly to a wider social spectrum than that clientele might suggest. Well-to-do laity evidently had a devotion to him as well, for his image occurs on no fewer than eight surviving Norfolk screens, all of them within a seventeen-mile radius of the shrine, a striking demonstration of both the localization of his cult and its importance in the Norwich area in the fifteenth and early sixteenth centuries, when the images were painted (Pl. 79).[133] Walstan's cult was already well established at

---

[128] Ibid. p. 83.
[129] Ibid. p. 98.
[130] Ibid. pp. 137–40.
[131] Ibid. pp. 75–6.
[132] "Lives of St Walstan", p. 241.
[133] St Walstan is represented on the screens at Barnham Broom, Burlingham St Andrew, Denton (on a chest made up of panels probably from the old Rood-loft), St James's Norwich, Litcham, Ludham, and Sparham. The screen at Beeston next Mileham has been savagely defaced, but one of the figures on the dado of the south screen there appears to have been carrying a scythe, and is almost certainly St Walstan.

Bawburgh by 1309, when the chancel was rebuilt and the rest of the church redecorated by pilgrims' offerings. The proliferation of his image on screens in the fifty or so years before the Reformation indicates its continuing appeal. From the same late period there survives a copy of the verse legend which was hung over his tomb at Bawburgh, to be read by or to pilgrims, and it provides a fascinating insight into the practice of devotion to the saints in early Tudor England.

According to his legend, Walstan was born at Blythburgh in Suffolk. He was a king's son, and his mother, Blida, herself had a minor cult in late medieval Norfolk, though nothing whatever is now known about her. Receiving the calling of God through an angel, Walstan determined to renounce his kingdom, and, after obtaining his parents' blessing, to "follow Christ in wilfull povertie". Giving his clothing away to two poor men, he was miraculously clothed by God "as a pilgrim shuld be", and set out for Norfolk, where he took employment as a reaper.[134] Walstan, unlike the virgin martyrs so popular in medieval East Anglia, was no rebel. He secured his parents' blessing before setting out, and in his new life set himself to work hard and "To please God & men if that he may".

> All manner of worke to doe he doth his devour
> to mow, to reap, & to lay in bond,
> also husbandry requireth from hour to hour.
> in all labour thanketh God of his sonde
> All catell & corne encrease in his hond.

Walstan's life as a labourer is characterized by an almost Franciscan humility and poverty. He works barefoot in the stubble, and when his master and mistress, taking pity on him, provide him with shoes and a haversack and bottle to feed himself, he gives them away to poor men. When his angry mistress forces him to tread barefoot on thorns, he is miraculously preserved from harm, while the thorns "punish and prick" her. Walstan forgives her and returns to his work.[135]

Miraculous fertility blesses all he does: when he "goth forth to feld to semination" the seed in his sower's apron is multiplied by an angel. His employers, impressed by his diligence and obvious holiness, as well as by the abundance his work has brought to their farm, offer to make him their heir, but he declines and asks instead only the offspring of their cow, heavy with calf at that moment,

[134] "Lives of St Walstan", p. 251.
[135] Ibid. pp. 252–3.

and a cart, pledging his service to them night and day so long as he
lives.

Like the corn-fields, the cow proves prodigally fruitful, bearing
twin bullock calves, "might never cow fairer foster and bare".
Walstan works on till the calves are full-grown (Pl. 80). Then, one
Friday while he was mowing in the fields, an angel warns him
of his approaching death. The next day the vision was repeated
at midday. His fellow-labourer is unable to hear the angels, but
on placing his foot on Walstan's scythe "heaven open he say
& Angells singing". He vows never to work after midday on
Saturdays, a form of sabbath observance much encouraged by the
late medieval church.[136] Meanwhile his parents had issued a proclamation in Norwich, requiring anyone who knows of Walstan's
whereabouts to disclose them. His master, panic-stricken at the
thought of having a king's son as labourer, rushes to find him, but
Walstan reveals his own impending death on the Monday, and asks
his employer to bring the curate to the field,

> that the Sacrament I may receive soo,
> & take holy councell of that Clerke,
> to be delivered from all workes darke
> & receive of holy altar the sacrament,
> & ere l die to make my testament.[137]

Having received housel and shrift, and made his will, thus dis-
charging the last obligations of a Christian as they were understood
in the late fifteenth century, Walstan knelt down and begged a
petition of God:

> for the succoring of many a man
> both Priest, Labourer, & also knight;
> that what man or woman labour ne might
> because of sicknes or ache of bones
> by Walston to be holpen more times than once.
>
> If beast also in sicknes shuld fall
> that Mans labour better should be
> In Walston's name, man, to God doe call
> a ready remedie thou shalt soon see.
> A voyce from heaven then heard he
> answering to him & said thus
> "Thine asking is graunted, come dwell with us."

[136] Ibid. p. 254.
[137] Ibid. p. 255.

His last request is that his two bullocks be harnessed to the cart and his body placed on it. The oxen take the corpse towards Bawburgh, miraculously crossing a river. They twice piss *en route*, and in each case a miraculous well springs up on the spot, which "as you may see / both to man & beast doth great remedie". Arriving at Bawburgh church, the oxen pass miraculously through the wall. The Bishop of Norwich and his monks hurry to the scene to conduct the funeral. The year given for his death in the legend is 1016, and he is said to have lived as a labourer thirty years.[138]

The legend continues by reciting eleven miracles performed at the shrine. They form a neat epitome of most of the main types of miracle found in late medieval saints' cult – a manacled lunatic healed at the shrine during the celebration of Mass, like the one described earlier at Osmund's tomb, a Bawburgh woman, accidentally shot by men practising archery in the street, and so grievously wounded that when she ate cockles they fell out of the hole. Brought to the tomb and laid out by it, she calls on Walstan, is healed, and vows an annual pilgrimage. A priest with a rupture is healed by bathing the wound with the water which stood in a vessel on the tomb. A Bawburgh man drowned in a pit is raised when his body is laid before the tomb and his neighbours call on God and St Walstan. A knight, Sir Gregory Lovell, paralysed with "bone ache", who had fruitlessly spent "both silver & gold" on physicians, sent for water from St Walstan's well and recovered. A similar miracle is recorded about the son of "a blunt man called Swanton by name". A maid of Bawburgh who swallowed a pin was able to cough it up when her friends took her to a Mass before the shrine. A cripple who had made an unsuccessful pilgrimage to Canterbury is healed when, prompted by a pilgrim there from Norfolk, he vows to go to Bawburgh. He duly makes the journey, and leaves a leg of wax at the shrine. A weaver of Carlton crawls to Bawburgh, helped by his wife. After keeping vigil by the tomb, he is healed and leaves his crutches there.[139]

Though Walstan is consistently portrayed in these miracles as meek and tender, especially towards the poor, he could also be jealous for his honour. A woman of Crowthorpe, afflicted with a back ailment, makes an unsuccessful pilgrimage to Bawburgh. In her anger and disappointment she rashly vows never to go there again. The next day, on attempting to reap corn in the fields she is unable to relinquish either the sickle or the ears of corn in her hands, and is only released on returning to the tomb.[140]

[138] Ibid. pp. 255–8.
[139] Ibid. pp. 258–65.
[140] Ibid. p. 260.

Most of these miracles happen to local people, and, despite single miracles for a knight and a priest, most of them are of lowly status – "a blunt man", a maidservant, a thatcher, a weaver. In several Walstan's role as patron of the harvest is prominent, a role evident even in the revenge miracle of the faithless woman of Crowthorpe, for she is "frozen" in the act of reaping. It is on display more edifyingly in the miracle of the harvester of Flegge, crushed under a laden cart of wheat but miraculously preserved from harm. The man left a votive cart of wax at the shrine, and the account of the miracle underlines the fact that "St Walston a petitioner for Labourers he was."[141]

It is in this role that he is invariably portrayed, wearing the crown and ermine of his birth, but barefoot and carrying his scythe, sometimes with his oxen at his feet. His annual feast was one for harvesters, and the theme of fertility and increase so prominent in his legend was reflected in the belief that "both Men and Beastes which had lost their Prevy partes, had newe members again restored to them, by this Walstane", a fact which led the reformer John Bale to compare him to Priapus and describe him as "the god of their feldes in Northfolke and Gyde of their Harvestes." (Pl. 81).[142]

Clearly, pagan, Christian, and folkloric elements are very closely interwoven in the Walstan legend. Neither a tenth-century king of Blythburgh nor a bishop of Norwich in 1016 is possible, and it is impossible now to determine what, if any, historical basis there is for the cult. Walstan's wells remain, though one has dried up, but his shrine has long since disappeared from the north aisle of Bawburgh. The fairytale themes of the missing heir, a prince disguised as a farmer's boy, with a tenderness for and an understanding of the lives of the poor – all this is readily appreciated. The appeal of a holy man who can bring healing and fertility to man and beast, and who can bless the harvest and the harvesters, is no less obvious. And over these elements the clerical custodians of the shrine who produced the verse legend have cast the moral emphases and pastoral preoccupations of the late Middle Ages. Walstan is deferential to parents and employers, diligent and meek, charitable to the poor. He encourages devout observance of the sabbath. Though a saint, he is as glad as the most worldly user of the primers to have advance warning of his death, responsibly makes his will, and provides for his funeral arrangements. He seeks the

---

[141] Ibid. p. 264.
[142] John Bale, quoted in Blomefield, *Norfolk*, II p. 389.

counsel and comfort of his parish priest, and secures the sacraments of housel and shrift.

Yet despite the clerical colouring, he remains a saint of the common people. His legend has taken on a characteristic late medieval moral tone, but the heavenly guarantee given at his death of the power of his intercession for "priest, labourer and also knight", for man, woman, and beast, comes straight out of the wonder-world of helper saints like Katherine, Barbara, and Erasmus. His miracles are miracles for the poor, and his power to make all fertile erupts through even the pietistic proprieties of the official account of his story. The social status of the bulk of his clientele is revealed not only in the dramatis personae of the official miracles, but in the provision at the end of the legend for those who "be unlearnd nor can nor read nor spell" of a short doggerel prayer to Walstan:

> You knight of Christ, Walston holy,
> our cry to thee meekly we pray;
> Shield us from mischeife, sorrow & folly,
> engendring and renewing from day to day,
> replenishd with misery, Job doth truly say,
> & bring us to health blessed with [Jhesus] right hand
> him to love & know in everlasting land [143]

One could have worse summaries of the objectives of late medieval religion, and of the place of the cult of saints within it.

---

[143] "Lives of St Walstan", p. 265.

C: Prayers and Spells

CHAPTER 6

"LEWED AND LEARNED":
THE LAITY AND THE PRIMERS

The relationship between the privacies of personal religion and the corporate religious drama of the liturgy was complex, and, as we have seen, by no means a one-way traffic. To grasp the inwardness of late medieval lay piety attention to the liturgy is vital, but is not enough. Beyond and even within the liturgy, there flourished another world of devotion, sharing much ground with the official worship of the Church but distinct from it, a world vividly glimpsed in the *Book of Margery Kempe*. The undistorted reconstruction of this world of private prayer and devotional feeling is fraught with difficulties, not least as one attempts to penetrate below the level of the aristocracy and gentry to that of the common man and woman. Yet the prayers of late medieval English men and women do in fact survive in huge numbers, jotted in the margins or flyleaves of books, collected into professionally commissioned or home-made prayer-rolls, devotional manuals, and commonplace books, above all gathered into the primers or Books of Hours (*Horae*), which by the eve of the Reformation were being produced in multiple editions in thousands, in formats ranging from the sumptuous to the skimpy, and varying in price from pounds to a few pence. A study of these books and the related collections of prayers from which they were compiled or which were derived from them, will take us deep into the heart of late medieval lay religion.[1]

---

[1] The standard handbook to the English primers is Edgar Hoskins, *Horae Beatae Mariae Virginis or Sarum and York Primers with kindred books*, 1901; in using the printed primers I have identified the book being used by reference to the numbering in Hoskins, as well as by the new STC number. For the contents of the *Horae*, the magisterial work of V. Leroquais, *Les Livres d'heures manuscrits de la Bibliothèque Nationale*, 3 vols, 1927, with its 1943 *Supplément* is indispensable. Virginia Reinburg's 1985 Princeton doctoral dissertation, *Popular prayers in Late Medieval and Reformation France* explores the French *Horae*, and I am very grateful to Dr Reinburg for allowing me to read her dissertation. She has also contributed to the valuable collection edited by R. S. Wieck, *The Book of Hours in Medieval Art and Life*, 1988. See also J. Backhouse, *Books of Hours*, 1985. Apart from Helen White's *The Tudor Books of Private Devotion* there is little in English on the printed Latin *Horae*, though Jonathan Hartan's *Books of Hours and their Owners*, 1977, has a short account on pp. 169–74. In discussing prayers which occur routinely in *Horae* I have used the text printed in *Hor. Ebor.*

The Primer and Lay Prayer

The early history of the primer, as Books of Hours were often called in England, is complex and essentially monastic. Arising out of the pious practice of individual monks who added the private recitation of the fifteen gradual Psalms (120–34), and the seven penitential Psalms (6, 32, 38, 51, 102, 130, 143) to the public liturgy of the seven monastic Hours, the primer acquired an identity as a separate book and absorbed other material, most notably the so-called Little Office or Hours of the Blessed Virgin Mary. From a voluntary devotion, these observances came to be considered in time an obligation on all religious. As the devout laity sought increasingly to emulate monastic piety, the Hours of the Blessed Virgin offered a convenient and religiously satisfying way of sharing in the monastic round of prayer. The Little Hours included some of the most beautiful and accessible parts of the psalter, notably the gradual Psalms, whose humane and tender tone was accentuated by the Marian antiphons, lessons, and collects celebrating the beauty, goodness, and merciful kindness of the Virgin, with which the Office surrounded them. Offering the lay devotee some approximation to the order and tranquillity of monastic piety, it possessed the vital qualification for lay devotion of being relatively uncomplicated, varying very little with the liturgical seasons, unlike the calendrical complexities of the Offices recited by the clergy. It is not surprising, therefore, that although it was one of the last elements to be added, the Little Office came to dominate the primer. In addition to the Little Office and the gradual and penitential Psalms, almost all primers included the Litany of the Saints, the Office for the Dead (consisting of vespers, called "Placebo" from the opening word of the Office, and matins and lauds said as one office, known as "Dirige"). With these were usually grouped the Psalms of commendation (119 and 139), essentially an extension of the "Dirige". Many editions also included Psalms 22–31, the so-called Psalms of the Passion. A version of the calendar, placed at the beginning of the book, completed the basic shape. Few primers, however, confined themselves to this basic shape, especially after the advent of printing, when publishers were competing in a cut-throat market in which Books of Hours were being offered for sale in their thousands. Most books therefore included an additional range of popular devotions, over and above the core prayers derived from the liturgy. These included a range of morning prayers, devotions for use at Mass, most commonly elevation prayers such as the "Ave Verum Corpus", suffrages to the saints and angels, prayers to the Virgin Mary, and, above all, prayers to Christ in his Passion.[2]

Given the range and variety of the primer, it is no great surprise to find that devout, literate, lay people increasingly gave it the central place in their devotions. What is perhaps more remarkable is the social breadth of its appeal. The very notion of a Book of Hours conjures up images of richly gilt initials, jewelled covers, exquisite miniatures, and many of the surviving early manuscript *Horae* were clearly designed for an aristocratic, or at least wealthy, readership. Nor did this orientation disappear with the advent of printing. When Edgar Hoskins produced his exhaustive analysis of the contents of the pre-Reformation printed Sarum Hours, he took as his base text the edition of 1494 printed by Wynkyn de Worde.[3] This book, though without the elaborate full-page and initial illuminations which were so much a feature of manuscript Hours, is nevertheless printed on vellum, has hand-coloured initials and borders, and claims in its colophon the patronage of Henry VII's queen, Elizabeth. It was clearly expensive, and one of the two Cambridge University Library copies belonged to the Earl of Surrey. Yet even before the dramatic shift in the sociology of book ownership produced by printing, many editions of the primer were produced for a wider and less affluent clientele. Books of Hours were among the first books to be efficiently mass-produced; by the fifteenth century stationers' shops all over Europe had geared themselves to production-line methods.[4] The basic text was produced by teams of copyists, then ornamented to a greater or lesser degree, normally by the colouring of capitals and simple floral ornaments, with the insertion at appropriate points of standardized full-page illustrations, themselves often mass-produced by hack painters of indifferent talent. Such pictures were designed not merely to ornament the books into which they were tipped or bound, but to serve as an additional devotional resource, providing material for devout meditation. But despite the contribution they undoubtedly made to the selling power of these mass-produced *Horae*, the pictures were sometimes omitted altogether, and there

---

[2] The standard discussion of the evolution of the primer is the prefatory essay by E. Bishop in H. Littlehales, *The Prymer or Prayerbook of the Lay People in the Middle Ages*, 1891, reprinted in Bishop's *Liturgica Historica*, 1918, pp. 211–37.

[3] *Hoskins* no. 7: RSTC 15875.

[4] Lucien Febvre and Henri-Jean Martin, *The Coming of the Book*, 1984, pp. 18, 27, 70, 88, 90, 92, etc.

are many surviving manuscript Books of Hours, plainly produced in a small format to economy standards.[5]

The advent of printing dramatically widened the accessibility of the *Horae* even further. Between Caxton's first recorded printing of a Book of Hours and the appearance of the first Protestant primers in the 1530s, at least 114 editions of the Latin *Horae* were published for lay English use. Precise numbers for editions of books of this sort are impossible to assign, but 500 is probably a conservative estimate, in which case there were something like 57,000 of these books in circulation in the two generations before the Reformation. Many of these editions were up-market productions, finely printed and richly decorated. But many were small ones, cheaply produced, with few or no illustrations, and they cannot have cost more than a few pence.[6]

There is abundant evidence of very wide use of the primers among the laity. Gentry wills had long included bequests of "my best Primer", "a little prymer", "a prymar covered in blew".[7] The remarkable expansion of lay literacy among the mercantile and artisan classes in the fourteenth and fifteenth centuries placed such books literally within the grasp of the middling and lower sorts, a fact abundantly evident in their wills. A fifteenth-century London grocer could leave "my primer with gilt clasps whereupon I am wont to say my service", while Roger Elmsley, servant to a wax-chandler, left his godchild "a primer for to serve God with".[8] An Italian visitor to fifteenth-century England, commenting on the notable devotion of the laity, wrote that "any who can read tak[e] the Office of our Lady with them, and with some companion recit[e] it in the church verse by verse in a low voice after the manner of the religious." The "Instructions for a devout and liter-ate layman" drawn up for the religious guidance of an unidentified town-dweller of the early fifteenth century prescribe the daily recitation of the Little Hours of the Blessed Virgin in the parish church before Mass. In early fifteenth-century King's Lynn, Margery Kempe was accustomed to "seyn hir Mateyns" in the church when she went to hear Mass, "hir boke in hir hand". A century later, Jean Quentin's *The Maner to lyve well*, translated into English for "all persones of meane estate" and published as

[5] For the production and character of MSS *Horae* for the English market see N. Rogers's unpublished 1982 Cambridge M Litt thesis, "Books of Hours Produced in the Low Countries for the English Market in the Fifteenth Century".

[6] For example Hoskins, nos 46, 68: STC nos 15919, 15940.

[7] Hoskins, pp. xv–xvii: Maskell, *Monumenta Ritualia* III pp. xlvii-xlix: *Horae Ebor* pp. xxxviii–xl.

[8] Margaret Aston, *Lollards and Reformers*, 1984, pp. 101–33, quotes at p. 124. On the spread of literacy see also Janet Coleman, *Medieval Readers and Writers 1350–1400*, 1981, pp. 18–57; J. H. Moran, *The growth of English Schooling: Learning, Literacy and Laicisation in the*

a preface to a number of inexpensive Latin primers from 1529 onwards, instructed its readers "Whan ye have arayed you /say in your chambre or lodgyng: matyns / pryme & houres . . . ," and the recitation of the Little Office was also enjoined in courtesy or etiquette books. By the early sixteenth century, in urban congregations at least, one was probably almost as likely to find a primer as a pair of beads in the hands of the worshippers in church (Pl. 82).[9]

What is so remarkable about all this is that we are dealing here not with an English but with a Latin book. In the fourteenth and early fifteenth centuries English versions of the primer had circulated, but the panic over Lollardy had made them suspect. Fewer than a dozen-and-a-half pre-Reformation primers in English survive, none of them dating from after the mid fifteenth century. The mere possession of one might be grounds for suspicions of heterodoxy in the early sixteenth century.[10] The growing popularity of the primer among "persones of mean estate" is therefore something of a puzzle. The driving force behind the new literacy was practical, not scholarly. Men (and even some women) engaged in business or administration, or anxious to secure more immediate control of their own affairs by learning to read and write letters, bills, wills, and ledgers, or in search of amusement in the form of the rhymed tales of chivalry, romance, morality, or miraculous piety which circulated so widely in the fifteenth century needed English, and perhaps some French.[11] Fluent mastery of Latin would have been outside the scope of most lay people, as indeed it was for many clergy and religious. How then did they say their prayers in Latin? The question should alert us to the complexity of the use of and response to sacred texts, such as the prayers of the primers, before the Reformation. Indeed, before we can seriously attempt to answer it we need to consider the extent to which primers were both more and less than texts.

That the primers were more than texts can be readily gathered from handling a few of them, manuscript or printed. The

Pre-Reformation York Diocese, 1985; N. Orme, English Schools in the Late Middle Ages, 1973; M. B. Parkes, "The Literacy of the Laity", in D. Daiches and A. K. Thorlby (eds), Literature and Western Civilisation: the Medieval World, 1973, pp. 555–77.

[9] A Relation, or Rather, a True Account of the Island of England about the year 1500, ed. A Trevisano, Camden Soc, XXXVII, 1847, p. 23; W A Pantin, "Instructions for a Devout and Literate Layman", in J. J. G. Alexander and M. T. Gibson (eds), Medieval Learning and Literature, 1976, p. 399; The Book of Margery Kempe, pp. 216, 221; This prymer of Salysbury use is set out a long wout ony serchyng / with many prayers / and goodly pyctures in the kalender . . . Paris, F. Regnault 1531, Hoskins, no. 98, RSTC 15973, fol. 15b, and Hoskins, p. xv; Foxe, Acts and Monuments, V p. 29; London Consistory Court Wills pp. 100–1.

[10] One, from the library of St John's College Cambridge, is edited in Littlehales, The Prymer; W. Maskell, Monumenta Ritualia Ecclesiae Anglicanae, III pp. 1–lxvii; Foxe, Acts and Monuments, IV pp. 230, 236.

[11] J. Coleman, English Literature in History pp. 18–57; F. McSparran and P. R. Robinson, Cambridge University Library MS Ff 2 38; see above, pp. 68–84.

ornamentation that most primers contained would have established
for their readers the fact that they were, in the first place, sacred
objects. Paintings or woodcuts of the Trinity, of the life of the
Virgin, of the saints with their emblems, above all scenes depicting
the suffering and death of Christ, served in themselves as focuses of
the sacred, designed to evoke worship and reverence. They were
often conceived as channels of sacred power independent of the
texts they accompanied. The fifteenth century had seen the circulation of devotional woodcuts which the faithful were encouraged to
meditate on, to kneel before, to kiss. These images often had
indulgences attached to them, encouraging a devotion which
might be mechanical or meditative, but at any rate not verbal. One
typical image of Christ as the Man of Sorrows, surrounded by the
Implements of the Passion – nails, scourges, lance, cross, vernicle
and so on – carried the promise that "To them that before this
ymage of pyte devoutly say fyve Pater noster fyve Aveys & a Crede
pytously beholdyng these armes of Christ's passyon ar graunted
32,755 yeres of pardon." It circulated widely as a separate woodcut, sold at pilgrimage centres or hawked about by preaching
friars, pardoners or simple pack-men (Pl. 85). The image, with its
spectacular promise of indulgences, found its way into the primers,
and its presence there alerts us to the fact that many who used these
books must have been as interested in the religious power of the
pictures as in the meaning of the text.[12] Nor were the pictures
the only emblems of sacred power. The use of rubric print, and
the frequent punctuation of the text with the sign of the cross,
particularly in prayers of exorcism and invocation, also served to
establish the sacred character of the primers as objects in their own
right, by approximating them in appearance to the books used on the
altars of the parish church and in other ceremonies of the liturgy.

The fact that many of the texts contained in the primers were
held to be powerful and holy in their own right also helped sacralize
the books in which they occurred. In addition to the Psalms and
other scriptural passages in the Offices of the Blessed Virgin and of
the Dead, the primers usually contained at the beginning of the
book four Gospel passages. These were the opening chapter of
St John's Gospel "In Principio", the Annunciation story from
Luke's Gospel "Missus est", the story of the Magi from Matthew's
Gospel "Cum Natus est", and the final section of Mark's Gospel
"Recumbentibus", containing Christ's promise to give his disciples
power over demons, serpents, poison, and disease. The reading
of Gospel passages, especially of the great feasts, had from time

[12] On this image see below, pp. 238ff.

immemorial acquired a special significance in lay devotion. Priests could earn alms by reciting these Gospels for the laity, as a protection for home or person, in much the same way as they said votive Masses; this equation of saying a Mass and reading a Gospel was exploited by clergy anxious to maximize their incomes. There was a long tradition of ecclesiastical legislation to prevent "doubling" or "trebling" of Gospels at Mass, and the Tudor jest-book *A Hundred Merry Tales* has a joke about a priest who would say two Gospels for a groat, "as dog-cheap a mass as any place in England". All four of the Gospel passages found regularly in the primers were charged with special significance for medieval Christians, for they formed the Gospels read at Mass on four of the major festivals, Christmas Day, Epiphany, the Feast of the Annunciation (Lady Day), and the Ascension. They thus offered a sort of microcosm of the liturgical year, but their power extended beyond their association with the festivals on which they were read. They were found together in some editions of the Sarum processional, and were the Gospels read aloud at the stations in the course of the Rogationtide processions, to scatter demons and bring grace, blessing, and fertility to the community and its fields.[13]

They were well suited to this purpose. The opening of St John's Gospel, "In Principio", was one of the most numinous texts used in the late medieval Church. It was prescribed as part of the ritual for the blessing of holy bread at the main Mass of Sunday, and was recited as an additional or last Gospel by the priest after Mass each day. There was a widely held belief that anyone who crossed themselves during this recitation would come to no harm that day. This belief was strengthened by the fact that in the early fourteenth century Pope Clement V had granted an indulgence of one year and forty days to everyone who attended to the last Gospel and who kissed something – a book, a sacred object, even their thumbnail – at the words "Verbum caro factum est." This indulgence was publicized in the standard instructional texts on devout hearing of Mass, and contributed to the awe associated with the text. William Tyndale in the 1520s was to complain contemptuously that

> Thousands whyle the prest patereth Saynt John's Gospel in Latine over theyr heedes crosse them selves wyth I trow a legyon of crosses behynde and before and wythe reverence on the very arses and (as Jack off napis when he claweth him selfe) ploucke

---

[13] E. G. C. Atchley, "Some Notes on the beginning and Growth of the Usage of a Second Gospel at Mass", *Transactions of the St Paul's Ecclesiological Society*, V, 1900, pp. 161–76; *A Hundred Merry Tales*, p. 129; *Ceremonies and Processions of the Cathedral Church of Salisbury*, ed. C. Wordsworth, 1901, p. 17.

up theyr legges and crosse so moch as their heeles and the very
soles of their fete and beleve that if it be done in the tyme that he
readeth the gospell (and else not) that there shall no mischaunce
happen them that daye because only of those crosses.

It was also read at the end of the baptismal service, immediately
after a passage from St Mark's Gospel describing the exorcism of a
demoniac boy, designed to protect the newly baptized' child against
epilepsy, and it was used in ceremonies of exorcism, and, in Henry
VII's reign, in the ceremony of touching for the king's evil. It is no
surprise, therefore, to find that it was widely used as a charm
against all evils. Inscribed on parchment, it was frequently worn
round the neck to cure disease, and lay people also often hung it on
the necks or horns of ailing cattle.[14] The Lucan Annunciation story,
"Missus est", was in some places used as the last Gospel, and was
also believed to be powerful against the Devil in this way, but of
course had its own distinctive potency. The Annunciation was
arguably the single most frequently depicted Gospel scene, the
Crucifixion apart, and the greeting of the angel to Mary formed the
basis of the Hail Mary.[15]

The story of the Magi represented something less accessible
but hardly less potent in the late medieval imagination. Caspar,
Melchior, and Balthazar, the "Three Kings of Cologne", directly
led by God and delivered by dreams from Herod's malice, were
very frequently invoked as intercessors and protectors. Their names
often occur in incantatory prayers for deliverance from evil, and
they were invoked as protectors against the bites of mad dogs or
the falling sickness. Their star-gazing gave some legitimacy to
astrology, and they may have been associated in lay perceptions
with the "wise" or "cunning" men and women who were the
common resort in illness or ill fortune. Their extraordinary and
mysterious-sounding names almost certainly contributed to their
imaginative power for late medieval lay Christians. Prayers to them
were an invariable element in the small group of morning prayers
included in most Books of Hours.[16] The Marcan passage, with
its divine promise of victory over demons, disease, and evil,

[14] More, *Works*, VIII part 3, 1973, p. 1507.
[15] *Missale*, p. 629; *Manuale*, p. 38; *Manuale et Processionale ad Usum Insignis Ecclesiae
Eboracensis*, ed. W. G. Henderson, Surtees Society, LXIII, 1875, p. 19; K. Thomas, *Religion
and the Decline of Magic*, 1973, p. 39; *Malleus Maleficarum*, trans. M. Summers, 1971, pt. II,
ch. 6, p. 390.
[16] On the Magi see item no. 91 in C. Louis (ed.), *The Commonplace Book of Robert Reynes
of Acle*, 1980, and the literature cited in the note, and Horstmann's edition of their legend,
EETS os LXXXV, 1886; *Liber de Diversis Medicinis*, ed. M. S. Ogden, EETS, 1938,
pp. 42–3, 99.

formed the Gospel for the Mass of Ascension Day. It thus came as the culmination of the Rogationtide exorcism of the parish and community by beating the bounds, in which the demons which infested earth and air were banished with cross, bells, banners, and by declaiming these passages of the four Gospels to the points of the compass.[17]

In each case, therefore, these Gospel texts carried an element of the numinous greater than might seem immediately warranted by their function as texts. For many people, it was probably these texts, not the Gospels as a whole, which were associated with the names of Matthew, Mark, Luke, and John, and they were probably seen not principally as authors, but as the guarantors of blessing, an emphasis preserved in the traditional childhood prayer "Matthew Mark Luke and John, bless the bed that I lie on." When the parishioners of Bramfield in Suffolk had the evangelists painted on their magnificent Rood-screen, they had them identified with scrolls containing not the opening words of their Gospels, but the *incipits* of these four passages used in the processionals and primers (Pl. 83–4).[18] Virtue inhered in these passages quite apart from actual comprehension of their message, and their presence in the primers suggests that these books were themselves seen as sacred objects, focuses of power, as much as books to be read and understood. There is a clear parallel here with the way in which the book of the Gospels might be kissed, censed, and venerated in the course of the liturgy, or, like relics and the Blessed Sacrament, used as the focus of oath-taking. Sir John Fastolf sealed the promise of land to a servant by taking an oath not on the Gospels, but on his primer.[19]

Nevertheless, the primers were books of prayers, to be recited, rather than sacred objects mediating grace or power simply by being handled or contemplated. Given their widespread and steadily growing appeal, what sense can we make of the undoubted fact that many who used them can have had only an imperfect grasp of the meaning of the prayers they contained?

The most obvious point to make here is that the available models of prayer – supremely in the day-to-day liturgy of the parish churches, but also in monastic piety and the great literary models of devotion – were all in Latin. The highest form of prayer was uttered by the priest at the sacring, the moment of consecration at the Mass. It was part of the power of the words of consecration that

[17] For the use of another passage from Mark, "Respondens unus de turba", to fend off the falling sickness from newly baptized children see *Manuale*, p. 38.

[18] The painter, it should be noted, has given Matthew Mark's text, and vice versa.

[19] Norman Davis (ed.), *Paston Letters and Papers of the Fifteenth Century* vol. I, p. 224.

they were hidden, too sacred to be communicated to the "lewed", and this very element of mystery gave legitimacy to the sacred character of Latin itself, as higher and holier than the vernacular. Moreover, since the words of scripture and the liturgy came from God, they were held to convey power even to those who did not fully comprehend them. One author, writing to help lay men and women participate properly in the Mass, compared the beneficial effect of such uncomprehending hearing at mass to that of a charm upon adders![20]

So it was also with the prayers of the primers: they were "good words", full of "vertu" which "availed" by God's grace, independently of the reader's or hearer's comprehension. Often their intrinsic "vertu" was emphasized by rubrics claiming that these precise words had been revealed as specially powerful or pleasing to God or the saints. The hymn "Ave Rosa Sine Spinis", printed in many *Horae*, whose popularity is attested by the fact that it supplied a motto on some of Henry VIII's coins, was usually prefaced by an English rubric which claimed that "this prayer shewed our lady to a devoute persone, sayenge that this golden prayer is the most swetest and acceptablest to me. And in her apperyng she had this salutacyon and prayer writen with letters of golde on her brest."[21]

Such canonizations of specific "golden" forms of words were common. One of the most popular of all prayers in fifteenth- and early sixteenth-century England was the Passion devotion on the Last words of Jesus known as the "Fifteen Oes of St Bridget". Circulating both in manuscript and, at the end of the fifteenth century, in printed versions, the prayers were often accompanied by a legend which emphasized the extraordinary power of the prayers in releasing souls from Purgatory, which claimed that the prayers had been directly revealed to "a woman solitary and recluse". In the versions of the legend copied by the Norfolk artisan Robert Reynes, and by the highly literate clerical compiler of the collection of devotions and prayers contained in the Bodleian Lyell MS 30, it is revealed to a woodland hermit by a group of distraught and outraged "ffendys" that "in this wode woneth an olde woman ful of many holy wordes and seyth an Orison so plesyng to God of hevene Wher through we takyn ful oftyn gret harme for with that orison sche getyth to God ful many soules that were in our power fast be foren."[22] One did not tamper with "holy wordes" and "orison[s] so plesyng", nor was it necessary to understand them fully to benefit from them. In fact the "Fifteen Oes" were translated

[20] LFMB, p. 140.
[21] *Hor. Ebor.*, p. 136; Hoskins, p. 124.
[22] Bodleian Library, Tanner MS 407 fol. 43; Lyell MS 30, fols 41v–43.

more than once, and a vernacular version said to have been commissioned by the Lady Margaret circulated widely in its own right, as well as being included in many *Horae*.[23] But Reynes probably copied the legend of the "Oes" before that translation was given wide currency by Caxton, and there are other clear signs that the indulgenced or otherwise privileged devotions which appeared in their dozens in printed primers were very often recited for the virtue of the words in themselves, and not for their power to move or persuade to intenser devotion. One of the most common items in printed *Horae* were the eight verses of St Bernard, "to be saide a noon aftur masse or ellis at heryng of a masse". These verses from the Psalms, the accompanying legend claimed, would preserve from damnation anyone who said them every day. St Bernard had exacted knowledge of these verses from the Devil, who had at first refused to disclose which they were, until Bernard threatened to recite the whole psalter each day. To prevent this flood of supererogatory prayer, the Devil disclosed the verses. Though Lydgate wrote an English paraphrase and elaboration of St Bernard's verses, the legend seems to establish that, for the users of late medieval Books of Hours what mattered was not so much the meaning of the words as their power, guaranteed, depending on one's point of view, either by St Bernard, or the Devil himself.[24]

Other indications point in the same direction. As printed primers became more plentiful and moved down-market, many devotions which in manuscript and early printed *Horae* had stood on their own began to have attached to them a prescribed number of Paters and Aves. The recitation of the Lord's Prayer and Hail Mary had been the basis of the church's catechetical activity since the thirteenth century, and was the essential lay expedient during those parts of worship which were unintelligible to the "lewed", and were occasionally explicitly recommended as substitutes for Latin prayers of the sort we have been discussing.[25] The prescription of Paters and Aves after every Latin devotion in a primer, therefore, is a strong indication that the readership envisaged was expected to have at best only a partial comprehension of the Latin "holy wordes", and consequently to be in need of supplementing their recitation with prayers which they could be expected to understand.[26]

---

[23] On the "Oes" see H. C. White, *Tudor Books of Private Devotion*, 1951, chapter 13, and below, pp. 249–56; for their separate circulation in print see RSTC 20195.

[24] Hoskins, p. 114.

[25] On the laity and the Paternoster, see above, chapter 2, "How the Plowman learned his Paternoster".

[26] For a representative example of this sort see *Hore b(ea)tissime marie virginis ad usum Sarum*, Christopher Endoviensis (Antwerp) for Francis Byrckman (London), 1525; Hoskins no. 67: RSTC 15939.

Yet it would be a mistake to emphasize too strongly the element of incantation and imperfect understanding which was undoubtedly a feature of some lay use of the primers. Even for those with little or no Latin, there were degrees of possible comprehension of the texts. Much of their contents, especially those liturgical or quasi-liturgical sections which made up their central core, would have been familiar even to lay people, and their meaning well understood. This can be most clearly demonstrated from the prayers for the dead which, after the Little Office of the Blessed Virgin, formed the single most important element in the primer. These consisted essentially of the Office of "Placebo" and "Dirige", recited at every funeral, together with the seven penitential Psalms and litany, which usually preceded "Placebo", and the Commendations (and often the Psalms of the Passion), which usually followed "Dirige". Given the centrality of intercession for the dead in the piety of late medieval men and women, these were the most commonly used of all prayers, and ordinary men and women eagerly sought their recitation as part of their own mortuary provisions. Langland, who seems to have made a living as a lay chantry clerk both in London and in the country, tells us that these prayers were his bread and butter:

> The lomes that y labore with and lyflode deserve
> Is *pater-noster* and my prymer, *placebo* and *dirige*,
> And my sauter som tyme and my sevene psalmes.
> This y segge for here soules of suche as me helpeth.[27]

But such matters were not left to the professionals. Even for those who could not read at all, simple repetition must have made the Office of the Dead familiar as no other prayer was. Every gild prescribed attendance at the funeral of every deceased brother or sister as a condition of membership and imposed fines for avoidable absence, and both gild and parish celebrated corporate Diriges for their members. Literate lay people certainly participated in these services by following them in their primers, and some gilds, like that of St Katherine in the parish of Sts Simon and Jude, Norwich, expressly stipulated that they should do so, requiring that

> at the Dirige, every brother and suster that is letterede shul seyne, for the soule of the dede, placebo and dirige, in the place wher he shul comen to-geder: and every brother and sister that bene nought letterede, shul seyne for the soule of the dede, xx sythes, the pater noster, with Aue maria.[28]

---

[27] William Langland, *Piers Plowman: an edition of the C Text*, ed. D. Pearsall, 1978, Passus v lines 45–8.
[28] Toulmin-Smith, *English Gilds*, p. 20.

The detailed specification of mortuary prayers in many wills reveals the familiarity of many lay people with this part of the primer above all. The presence of those who could recite the whole of the Office for the Dead at one's obsequies was clearly much valued: Anne Buckenham, a Suffolk testator of the 1530s, was prepared to pay for it, offering twopence a head to "everie laye manne that ys lettered beinge at Dirige and masse". In 1540 Margery Rokebye of Yafforth in Yorkshire left twopence "to everye scholer, that can say Direge for my sowle", and such bequests appear to have been common in the region.[29]

The acceptance of alms at funerals was not done lightly, for it implied a formal acceptance of "charity", probably involving some loss of face and position. The provision of doles for lettered laymen tells us much about the downward spread of literacy, for the difference between lettered and unlettered was not simply coterminous with social or economic distinctions. John Estbury, in founding his Berkshire almshouses, envisaged that some of the pauper inmates would be literate, and required them to recite each day in the parish church the Little Office of the Blessed Virgin, the seven penitential Psalms, "Placebo" and "Dirige", and the Psalms of the Passion, thereby prescribing for his paupers daily recitation of the major part of the primer.[30] Similar provision for lettered paupers to recite both the Little Office and the "Dirige" were laid down for the almshouses established at Hadleigh in Suffolk by the will of Archdeacon Pykenham,[31] while a number of fifteenth- and sixteenth-century testators assumed that poor men could be found capable of reciting all or part of the primer Offices for the Dead – "a poore man that will saye everie Fridaye in the yeare the vij psalmes with the letany" or the "De Profundis and Miserere Psalm".[32]

These poor men may not all have been readers. Sir William Bulmer, a Yorkshire testator of the early 1530s, thought that those inmates of his almshouse who didn't know the "De Profundis" and "Miserere" Psalms when they first arrived would in due course learn them by dint of constant repetition. No doubt many more or less literate users of the primers who nevertheless had little Latin used the text as not much more than a set of cues to launch them on prayers they knew by heart from hearing and recitation, rather than from reading. In a culture where the whole of the liturgy was celebrated in Latin most lay people would pick up a wide range of

[29] *Richmond Wills*, pp. 18, 24, 26.
[30] J. Footman, *The History of the Parish Church of St Michael and All Angels, Chipping Lambourn*, 1854, pp. 186–7.
[31] *Proceedings of the Suffolk Institute of Archaeology*, vii, 1891, pp. 379–80.
[32] *Bury Wills*, pp. 137–8; *Test. Ebor.* V pp. 313–19.

phrases and tags, with a depth of understanding perhaps not much more profound than Chaucer's Sumouner's grasp of legal Latin – "Ay 'Questio quod juris' wolde he crie" – but enabling them to recognize the general purport of particular prayers, and to use them with some degree of confidence. Indeed, even professed religious and the exceptionally devout laity seem to have managed with just such a partial grasp of Latin. Early in the fifteenth century it was felt necessary to produce for the ladies of the royal Brigittine monastery at Syon, all of whom were certainly literate in English and possibly French, a translation and exposition of their breviary "forasmoche as many of you, though ye can synge and rede, yet ye can not se what the meanynge therof ys". Yet ignorance of Latin was not held to be a complete barrier to intelligent use of the primer. A smattering coupled with constant repetition might supply what was missing. Bishop John Fisher reported that his patroness, the Lady Margaret Beaufort, had never studied Latin, in which, nevertheless, "she had a lytell perceyvynge specially of the rubrysshe of the ordinal for the sayeng of her servyce whiche she dyde well understande."[33]

The story of William Malden, converted to Protestantism in the late 1530s, throws a fascinating light on the use of the Latin primer at the other end of the social scale from the Lady Margaret, among the tradesmen and the poor of urban England, and on the relationship between English and Latin literacy. On the promulgation of the 1538 royal Injunctions a group of poor men in Malden's home town of Chelmsford pooled their resources and bought a copy of the New Testament, "and on sundays dyd set redinge in [the] lower ende of the churche, and many wolde flocke about them to heare theyr redinge". Malden himself, a teenager at the time, began to join these Bible-reading sessions every Sunday, though at that stage he could not himself read. His father was a theological conservative, and to draw the boy away "wolde have me to say the lattin mattyns with hym". Deprived of hearing the New Testament, the boy decided to learn to read English for himself. He had been provided with a primer to say his matins with his father, which he describes as an English primer. Since he quotes part of the Hours of the Cross from it in Latin, it was almost certainly one of the bilingual primers which had begun to appear in the 1530s, orthodox in content but introducing the Trojan horse of the vernacular into traditional liturgical observance. By "plying" this

[33] A. Jefferies Collins (ed.), *The Bridgettine Breviary of Syon Abbey*, Henry Bradshaw Society, XCVI, 1969, p. xxxii; John Fisher, *English Works*, ed. J. B. Mayor, EETS, 1876, p. 292.

primer on Sundays, and following the English translations of the Latin service he taught himself to read.[34]

This is a fascinating story, for it demonstrates not only the use of the primer by the urban middle classes, but the extraordinary fact of the son of a tradesman literate in Latin before he could read English. Yet this fact should not surprise us. The primer, as its name suggests, was the basic learning book for most people, even before it was available in English, and Malden's father presumably learned to ply his primer in much the same way as his son, though without the benefit of an English translation. In such a use of the primer the Latin obviously had an autonomous authority of its own, just as it had primacy as written text. How could these users of the Latin text have understood it?

In addition to constant repetition in the liturgy, there were a variety of ways in which "lewed" men and women could gain a working understanding of their Latin primers. Fifteenth- and early sixteenth-century England saw a proliferation of prayers and meditations in English, paraphrasing or elaborating devotional themes characteristic of the prayers of the primer.[35] Lydgate, for example, produced verse translations of the calendar, the "Fifteen Oes", the Marian antiphons from the Little Office such as the "Salve Regina", and a number of popular devotions from the primer, like the indulgenced hymn on the five joys of Mary, "Gaude Virgo Mater Christi". He also contributed to the flood of devotional poems on the Passion and on the compassion of the Virgin, which formed the central theme of most of the non-liturgical material in the primers.[36]

Lydgate's "Primer" verses were no doubt intended for the edification of the well-to-do and aristocratic lay clientele of his monastery at Bury and around the Lancastrian court, but such material in fact proliferated at every level of society. The commonplace book of Richard Hill has many similar pieces, as does Cambridge University Library Ff 2 38, a manuscript collection of didactic, edifying, devotional, and entertaining material which is perhaps our best surviving guide "to the religious and literary tastes and preoccupations of the bourgeosie in the late fifteenth century". In addition to a group of Passion poems and celebrations of the titles of the Virgin, similar to the "Ave Rosa Sine Spinis" which we

---

[34] J. G. Nicholls (ed.), *Narratives of the Days of the Reformation*, Camden Society, LXXVII, 1859, pp. 348–50.

[35] A. Barratt, "The Prymer and its influence on Fifteenth-Century English Passion Lyrics", *Medium Aevum*, XLIV, 1975, pp. 264–71.

[36] H. N. McCracken (ed.), *The Minor Poems of John Lydgate*, EETS, 1911, pp. 238ff, 288ff, and 260ff, 291–6, 297–9, 250ff.

have already discussed, this collection has verse paraphrases of the magnificent series of lessons from the book of Job used in the "Dirige", and of the penitential Psalms: the material implies not only a poet "but also an audience familiar with the primer".[37]

As these examples suggest, a good deal of this supplementary primer material was in verse, which could be memorized comparatively easily. But prose devotions duplicating, expanding, or explaining the Latin prayers of the primers were also very widely used, and penetrated far down the social scale. Robert Reynes had a series of prayers and other devotional matter clearly related to the primer in his commonplace book, notably a circumstantial and lengthy version of the legend normally attached to the "Fifteen Oes". He omitted the prayers themselves, a fact best explained by the likelihood that he already had access to them, perhaps in his primer.[38]

Much of this supplementary devotional material was copied by owners directly into their primers, just as they often stuck devotional pictures into them. The same owners copied both vernacular and Latin prayers, suggesting at least a minimal competence in both languages (Pl. 86). In this way comparatively simple Books of Hours could be expanded to include a wider range of Latin and English devotions and these collections seem in turn to have affected subsequent printings of the primers, which became more and more comprehensive as they incorporated material earlier found only in manuscript. One typical fifteenth-century English Book of Hours was supplemented in this way in the early sixteenth century with a poem on the vanity of the world and the need to love "gentel Ihesu", a Latin prayer to the Virgin, often found in printed primers, beginning "O Gloriosa O Optima", a threefold invocation of the name of God in Greek, taken from the Good Friday liturgy and headed "A good prayer ayenste the pestilence", a Latin prayer of thanksgiving to Christ for his Passion, and a prayer to the angel guardian.[39] In the early 1490s Edmund Appleyard, a Londoner who doubtless used his manuscript Book of Hours at the "Diriges" organized by the Jesus Gild at St Paul's, of which he was a brother, copied a series of English prayers to the Blessed Sacrament, arranged for every day of the week, onto the blank reverse sides of the illustrations preceding each of the Hours in the Little Office. The fortunate early sixteenth-century owner of one of

---

[37] Dyboski, *Songs*, nos 24, 29, 63, 66a, 66b, 67a, 68, 69; F. McSporran and P. R. Robinson (eds), *Cambridge University Library MS Ff 2 38*, 1979, pp. vii, ix, and items 2, 7, 8, 15, 29, 30.
[38] *Reynes Commonplace*, pp. 264–8.
[39] CUL MS Dd vi 1 fols 142v ff.

Simon Vostre's beautifully printed Sarum primers added a series of devotions on the five wounds of Christ and the sorrows of the Virgin. And of course Thomas More's famous prison prayer, "Gyve me thy grace good lord / to sett the world at nought" was copied into the margins of the Little Office of the Blessed Virgin Mary in his printed primer.[40]

Examples of this sort could be multiplied indefinitely: what they reveal to us is a wide spectrum of lay people using and supplementing the Latin devotions of the primers with familiarity and freedom. Their Books of Hours, in which they copied the details of births and deaths just as later generations would do in the family Bible, were very much their own, and the devout scrawls which embellish or disfigure so many of the surviving *Horae* are eloquent testimony to their centrality in the devotional lives of their owners. If their Latin contents were not always fully understood in a way readily accessible to twentieth-century perceptions, they were certainly appropriated and used meaningfully by their first possessors (Pl. 87).[41]

One final element contributing to lay understanding of the Latin material in the *Horae* remains to be discussed. Most of the *Horae* were, to a greater or lesser extent, illustrated. Before the advent of printing only the wealthiest owners would have had books with a consistent and programmatic series of illustrations matching image and text. The more modest mass-produced manuscript books had a relatively simple visual scheme, which we have already touched on in discussing the primers as devotional objects. The seven Hours of the Little Office often had illustrations related to the life of the Virgin, but might instead be preceded by illustrations of the conventional Hours of the Passion – Christ brought before Pilate at Prime, mocked, scourged, and led out to Calvary at Terce, Crucified at Sext, and so on. Such images can hardly be said to illustrate the Little Office: they took on a devotional importance of their own, and in time the hours of the Little Office were often interspersed with the so-called Hours of the Cross, a set of devotional verses with appropriate antiphons and collects developing the sevenfold division of the Passion embodied in the pictures.[42]

A more direct correspondence between pictures and text was

---

[40] E. S. Dewick, "On a manuscript of a Sarum Prymer which belonged to a brother of the Jesus Gild at St Paul's, London", *Transactions of the St Paul's Ecclesiological Society*, V, 1905, pp. 170–1; CUL Inc.5.D.1.29 (this is Hoskins no. 17, RSTC 15887).

[41] For a representative example of a primer used to record family history, as well as additional prayers over a period of a century or so, see CUL MS Ii VI 2. (Pl. 86, 87).

[42] The standard layout of illustrations to the Little Office in the MS *Horae* is discussed in R. S. Wieck (ed.), *The Book of Hours in Medieval Art and Life*, 1988, pp. 60–73.

achieved in the representations of saints with their attributes which
often accompanied the suffrages to the saints at Lauds in the Little
Office. These marginal or initial images, which became an even
more consistent feature of printed *Horae* than of the manuscript
books, would have enabled the devotee to find the particular prayer
he wanted to use, and to be quite certain whose aid he was invoking once launched on the prayer – James with his cockle-shell
and hat, Sebastian bristling with arrows, George and the dragon,
Anthony with his pig, Martin dividing his cloak, Barbara with her
tower, Apollonia with her pliers and tooth. Such images helped
link the private prayer of the primer with the corporate worship of
the parish church, where essentially the same images looked down
from the windows, or flickered on pillar, tabernacle, and bracket in
the candlelight maintained by the wills of fellow-parishioners and
gild brothers or sisters.[43]

In the rest of the book the correspondence between images and
text was more complicated. The treatment of the penitential Psalms
illustrates this complexity. Since their recitation was part of the
normal intercession for the dead, the illustration might portray
Judgement Day, with Christ seated on the rainbow and Mary and
John the Baptist interceding for souls before him. This was the
conventional imagery of Doomsday, and a similar Christ would
have gazed sternly down from the chancel arch in most parish
churches, once again effecting a link between the prayer of the
primer and the parish church. But especially in the printed primers,
it became more common to preface these Psalms with a depiction
of David watching Bathsheba, often portrayed with considerable
voluptuousness, at her bath (Pl. 88). The reference here, of course,
was to the belief that David had composed the penitential Psalms in
his remorse for his unlawful passion for Bathsheba, the murder of
Uriah, her husband, and the subsequent judgement of God in the
death of their child. The message encoded in such an image, often
expanded into a series of pictures with accompanying rhymes in the
Horae of the 1520s and 1530s, was quite different from that carried
in the Doom picture, more particular, but paradoxically, in the
specificity of its application to David, perhaps less pressing and
immediate than the Doom's generalized call to penitence.[44]

Other images universally found in the *Horae* could take on a
similar independent existence. The image of Veronica holding in
outstreched arms the vernicle or veil on which Christ's face was
imprinted always preceded the indulgenced devotion "Salve Sancta

[43] Ibid. pp. 111–23.
[44] Ibid. pp. 97–103.

Facies nostri Redemptoris". But the accompanying rubric, offering 5,000 days of pardon to those reciting the prayer "beholding the glorious visage or vernacle of our Lord" offers the same indulgence to anyone who "cannot say this prayer" provided they say five Paters, five Aves, and a Creed. What mattered was "beholding the glorious visage or vernacle", not the words. The picture here has broken free of the constraints of any text, and is an icon, not an illustration.[45]

The advent of printing had enormous implications for the iconography of the primers. Though many editions were produced in duodecimo or smaller sizes with few illustrations, aimed at the cheapest end of the book-buying market, the woodcut made it possible for the first time to produce moderately priced but richly illustrated *Horae*, with decorated borders as well as initial and full-page illustrations. This meant that an interpretative scheme could be sustained through whole sections of the text, rather than relying on the impact of single images to "colour" or direct the reading of the text that followed. A beautifully produced edition of the primer published by Thielman Kerver in Paris in 1497 had a fine series of large marginal illustrations of the six days of Creation (Pl. 89) and a smaller set of the fifteen signs of the end of the world, both popular themes in the devotional literature of the day and often illustrated in glass- or wall-paintings. Scattered through the book to illustrate appropriate prayers were a set of individual devotional images, such as a Nativity scene, a Calvary, and the Mass of Pope Gregory. Repeated throughout the book was a set of marginal illustrations of the life of Christ, each Gospel scene being flanked by Old Testament types, derived from the *Biblia Pauperum*. So the illustration of the Resurrection is flanked by pictures of Jonah being disgorged by the whale and Samson carrying off the gates of Gaza. Such typological images had a venerable ancestry, and English users of Kerver's *Horae* could have seen the image of Samson on a misericord in Ripon Minster, or a roof-boss in Norwich Cathedral, or, in the early sixteenth century, the Creed illustrations in didactic works like *The Arte or Crafte to Lyve well* (Pl. 90).[46]

The most successful *Horae* of this kind in England were produced by the printer Philippe Pigouchet for Simon Vostre, deservedly the best-known French publisher of Books of Hours. This partnership produced at least six editions of the Sarum Hours before

[45] See for example Hoskins 37, RSTC 15909; text of the indulgence quoted in Hoskins p. 125.
[46] Hoskins 15, RSTC 15885; M. D. Anderson, *The Imagery of British Churches*, pp. 97–8.

1512, characterized by sensitivity and intelligence in the use of stock illustrations.[47] Certainly, the need to decorate every page dictated the use of much purely ornamental material in borders – occupations and amusements of the seasons, putti, children climbing fruit-trees – all delightfully done if not particularly conducive to recollection at prayer. There was also a certain amount of repetition, the same images recurring without particular appropriateness at several points within one book. But in the most important parts of the *Horae* the imagery advances and assists the use of the text. This is evident at once at the very beginning of the books, where the calendar is ornamented not only with the signs of the zodiac and cuts of seasonal activities, but also the most important saints whose feast days occur in the month, alerting the worshipper to the holy days even before he or she attends to the small print.

Like other publishers, Vostre prefaced the Seven Psalms with a picture of David and Bathsheba, but he surrounded the Psalms themselves with borders depicting the parable of the Prodigal Son, including a shortened version of its text (Pl. 91). The Office for the Dead was prefaced, as was customary, with a picture of Job and his comforters, but the borders depicted the Dance of Death, a vivid series impressing on the reader the personal as well as the generalized applicability of the prayers. At the foot of each page a separate sequence of appropriate illustrations on the themes of death, judgement, and repentance – the Judgement of God on Sodom and Gomorrah, or the story of Job – offered an eloquently compressed reminder of the transience of worldly greatness. The Commendations were surrounded by a different series portraying the universal victory of death, and the Psalms of the Passion had borders depicting the story. The "Rosarium Beate Marie" with which the Bodleian Library copy of Vostre's 1512 *Horae* concludes had margins displaying the miracles of the Virgin.[48]

Not all Vostre's images were so directly related to the text. The fifteen signs of the end of the world which surrounded the litany of the saints had some appropriateness in a prayer of supplication which was also part of the liturgy for the dead, but the story of Joseph which is placed round the series of prayers for use in the morning seems to have no particular application. Other images, such as the series of virtues treading down vices, occurred in

---

[47] This discussion is based on *Officium beate Marie v(ir)ginis ad usum Sarum* (Paris), for S Vostre, 1512, Hoskins 40, RSTC 15913 (Bodleian Library copy). On Vostre's work more generally see Mâle, *Religious Art In France*, pp. 208–9, 253–8, 307–8, 347–8; J. Harthan, *Books of Hours and their Owners*, 1977, pp. 169–74.

[48] The Rosarium is a non-STC item: it is to be found on University Microfilms reel 89.

apparently random placings (Pl. 92). Nevertheless, the user of Vostre's primers was not merely provided with material for endless devotional browsing in the margins of his book, but a host of images and stories, often derived directly from scripture, on which he could reflect at leisure. In many cases, such as the Office for the Dead or the penitential Psalms or the Psalms of the Passion, the images provided added a new dimension to the reading of the prayers of the Hours, offering a direct and sometimes profound commentary on the text being recited.

In the late 1520s and early 1530s the Parisian publisher François Regnault, whose presses commanded the market for Sarum primers in the years immediately before the schism with Rome, produced a highly successful series of primers simpler in scheme than Vostre's, but whose illustrations were similarly a major part of the attraction of the book to the lay purchaser.[49] The title-pages of these *Horae* vary slightly, but characteristically had an emblematic picture of Mary illustrating her prerogatives and titles from the Song of Songs – the fountain, the enclosed garden, the gate of Heaven, the star of the sea, and so on. Beneath it was printed the English metrical prayer "God be in my head", and over it an advertisement that the book contained "many prayers and goodly pictures", the title-page thereby cleverly giving examples of both (Pl. 93). The English material in these primers was prominently placed at the front of the book, and was clearly an important selling-point. That English material is fascinating in its own right, and will be discussed elsewhere. It included a brief treatise on "the maner to live well", a form of confession, English prayers to the Trinity, Christ, and the Virgin, a moralistic text on "the three verities" by Gerson, and sets of verses moralizing the months of the year as reflections of the ages of man and the days of the week. The verses on the months accompanied emblematic illustrations of the stages of man's life, printed opposite each month of the calendar, from the child playing with birds and toys in January to the dying man having a candle placed in his hand by the priest in December.[50]

It might be thought that in a book with so much English material the pictures would be of less importance than in earlier *Horae*, but those in Regnault's books were in fact carefully planned. The decoration of the books follows a common scheme: the cuts are in a

[49] The disastrous end of Regnault's English career is briefly treated in H. S. Bennett, *English Books and Readers 1475–1557*, 1970, pp. 311–12, 221; the following analysis is based on Hoskins nos 98, 109, RSTC 15973 and 15981.

[50] On the vernacular material in Regnault's primers for England see M. C. Erler, "The *Maner to lyve well* and the coming of English in François Regnault's Primers of the 1520s and 1530s", *The Library*, 6th series, VI, 1984, pp. 229–43.

distinctively Renaissance style, reflecting the advances in perspective and realism in the painting of the period, and lacking the
elaborate Gothic framing of Kerver's and Vostre's books, but the
themes of the woodcuts are thoroughly traditional. The Gospel
passages have vignettes of the evangelists. The hours of the Virgin
have a cut of the Jesse tree at the beginning, and then scenes from
the life of Mary – the Annunciation, the Nativity, the adoration of
the shepherds, and so on. The most striking images in the book are
those in the Office for the Dead. This begins with a double-page
picture of the three living and the three dead, then three pictures
illustrating the fall of Adam and Eve and their expulsion from the
Garden, the sin which brought death into the world. The other
illustrations for the "Dirige" picked up texts from the prescribed
lessons from the Book of Job and elaborated them. All had an
English quatrain at their foot, expanding the text illustrated. The
picture for the fourth lesson of the Office depicts the story of the
English "canon of Paris", whose dead body was supposed to have
declared his soul's damnation for a concealed sin during the singing
of the Office for the Dead. This was a moralistic tale frequently
included in sermons on repentance,[51] and the cut depicts his startled
fellow-canons gathered in choir round the hearse, while above them
a devil drags the lamenting soul to hell. The fifth lesson from the
"Dirige" was illustrated by a striking portrayal of the text "man
that is born of a woman, having but a short time to live, is filled
with many miseries." In an upper room a child is being born to a
woman on a bed, assisted by a midwife. On the stairs outside
the room the grown man, ragged and on crutches, stumbles downwards into a lower chamber where the aged man is expiring, his
wife placing a candle in his hand. Regnault's artists produced a
number of version of this scene (Pl. 94), all of them memorable.
The verses are less so:

> Every man / that borne is of woman
> Fulfylled is of all mysery
> Sure of dethe / but how / where / nor whan
> It is so short as it is seen dayly.

The cut for the seventh lesson illustrates the verses "the grave only
awaits me" and "deliver me, O Lord, and set me beside thee"with
a deathbed scene, the dying man receiving the viaticum while the
frustrated Devil rages and God blesses from Heaven (Pl. 95). The
eighth lesson, a lament for physical decay and sickness, has a
picture of Job on his dunghill, and the final illustration expands the

---

[51] For example in *Middle English Sermons*, pp. 176–7.

opening of the ninth lesson, "why didst thou bring me forth out of
the womb?" with a moralizing emblem of "Mundus et Infans" –
the newborn child surrounded by temptations – a voluptuous
woman carrying a flower that fades, a richly dressed man proffering
a bag of gold, and a grinning bat-winged devil.

> A chylde that is in to this worlde comyng
> Is hardely be set with many a fo.
> Whiche euer is redy to his undoyng.
> The worlde / the fleshe / devylle and deth also.

The rest of the book was punctuated by devotional images matched
to appropriate prayers and texts. The Passion narrative had a
representation of the agony in the garden, the prayers provided for
use at the sacring had an illustration of the Last Supper, while the
"Stabat Mater" had a striking image of the Seven Sorrows of the
Virgin, each sorrow represented in a roundel from which a sword
proceeds, each sword piercing the Virgin's heart: the whole picture
is clearly designed as an aid to systematic meditation on the scenes
represented (Pl. 96). Regnault's *Horae* were produced in both
up-market and cheaper versions with cruder cuts, but the same
iconographic scheme, testifying to the breadth of their appeal,
and they were being produced right up to and beyond the break
with Rome. Their mixture of traditional devotional and didactic
imagery with innovative material and techniques, in particular their
Renaissance style illustrations, alongside an increased use of the
vernacular, demonstrates the vitality of the traditional primer form
and its ability to adapt to a changing religious market. Simpler and
in some ways less sophisticated than the Vostre books, they were
probably more direct and memorable in their impact on unlearned
readers.

The primers, then, were an immensely complex and multilayered
expression of late medieval lay religion, functioning in part as
sacred objects, communicating blessing in much the same way as
the devotional images which filled the churches and which, in the
form of cheap woodcuts and plaster and alabaster plaques, were
to be found in lay households. Because their essential core was
liturgical, and the visual conventions which governed their production were derived from liturgical books, they formed an important
bridge between lay piety and the liturgical observance of the
church, for they enabled lay people to associate themselves with the
prayer of the clergy and religious. They were also repositories of
the proliferating affective devotions which are to be encountered
everywhere in the commonplace books and devotional collections
of the late Middle Ages. These devotions were often linked to and

glossed by conventional illustrations, but they functioned also as texts in their own right, and they were familiar to lay people at all social levels through continuous repetition. Up to the very moment of Reformation the layout and content of the primers was evolving, adapting to the growth in English literacy and the demand for more vernacular devotional material. In the next chapter we will consider the character and content of the Latin and English devotional material of the primers.

CHAPTER 7

THE DEVOTIONS OF THE PRIMERS

The basic shape of the *Horae* was the product of the high Middle Ages: in essence they were scriptural prayer-books, drawn largely from the liturgical arrangement of the psalter. The primer, there-fore, was intended to be in some sense the lay man or woman's breviary. But the late Middle Ages saw an enormous flourishing of extra-liturgical piety which, though often originating in religious communities, quickly found favour with the laity. Hard-nosed city shopkeepers just as much as aristocratic ladies with time on their hands took an active and enthusiastic interest in things of the spirit. This spreading lay devotionalism was reflected in the expansion of the business of producing devotional objects, not merely the *Horae* themselves but the holy images which poured from the alabaster factories of Nottinghamshire or the printing-houses in London, France, and the Low Countries, catering for the demand for cheap religious prints.[1]

It was also reflected in the swelling volume of devotional and edifying texts circulating among lay people for use in their own homes. As we have seen, many owners of *Horae* entered the prayers they had collected into the margins and blank pages of their primers, but they were just as likely to copy them into miscellaneous commonplace books, as Richard Hill and Robert Reynes did. Specialized collections of prayers and devotions also proliferated in the fifteenth century. Such collections could be commissioned, like the prayer-book given by Lady Margaret Beaufort to her second husband, Thomas Stanley, in the late fifteenth century, and now in Westminster Abbey.[2] The prayers preserved in this way clearly

---

[1] For the market for devotional objects see Francis Cheetham, *English Medieval Alabasters*, 1984, pp. 11–53. On the growth of lay devotion see M. Vale, *Piety, Charity and Literacy among the Yorkshire Gentry, 1340–1480*, Borthwick Papers 1, 1976; J. Catto, "Religion and the English Nobility in the Late Fourteenth century", in H. Lloyd Jones *et al.* (eds), *History and Imagination*, 1981, pp. 43–55; H. M. Carey, "Devout Literate Lay-People and the Pursuit of the Mixed Life in Later Medieval England", *Journal of Religious History* XIV, 1987, pp. 361–81.

[2] See above, chapter 2, "How the Plowman learned his Paternoster", pp. 68–77.

reflected lay religious preferences more closely than the inherited structure of the *Horae* could, but it was merely a matter of time before consumer demand resulted in the expansion of the *Horae* to include such material, and the history of printed *Horae* is to a large extent one of growing elaboration of the basic structure by the accretion of such material. Though individual clerics were doubtless involved in the production and editing of these prayers, no real regulation by the Church appears to have dictated or inhibited what was included. Market forces dominated, a fact which permits some degree of confidence in using the resulting compilations as indicators of lay opinion. Lay people wanted prayer-books which, in addition to the core materials of Little Office and "Dirige", enabled them to say their morning prayers, helped them venerate the Sacrament at Mass, or prepared them for its reception at Easter-time. They wanted prayers which helped them cultivate that intense relationship of affectionate, penitential intimacy with Christ and his Mother which was the devotional *lingua franca* of the late Middle Ages, and they wanted prayers which focused on their day-to-day hopes and fears. They wanted books which would provide them with illustrations, indulgences, and other spiritual benefits. And increasingly in the years before the break with Rome, they wanted more vernacular material. All these concerns were reflected in the additional material in the *Horae* of the late fifteenth and early sixteenth centuries, and they offer us a unique window into the religious preoccupations of those who used the books. And since the Passion of Jesus dominated these devotions, as it dominated the piety and art of the period, it is to late medieval devotion to the Passion that we must turn first.

Devotions to the Passion

The presentation of the stages of the Passion as themes for medita-tion and prayer was already implicit in the placing of illustrations of the Hours of the Passion before the Hours of the Little Office. It developed its own devotional momentum in the course of the fourteenth and fifteenth centuries. This was the age when, as Emile Mâle wrote, "the Passion became the chief concern of the Christian soul."[3] The liturgical centrality of the Crucifix in the surroundings of late medieval English men and women was matched by a similar emphasis on the Passion as the centre of their private devotion. In England as elsewhere the Bernardine tradition of affective medita-

[3] Emile Mâle, *Religious Art in France: the Late Middle Ages*, 1986, p. 83.

tion on the passion, enriched and extended by the Franciscans, had become without any rival the central devotional activity of all seriously minded Christians. The most common method of such meditation was that prescribed in the *Meditationes Vitae Christi*, normally then attributed to the Franciscan St Bonaventura. Translations of this work circulated freely in late medieval England, and the best of them, by the Carthusian Nicholas Love, was probably the most popular vernacular book of the fifteenth century. In it the events of the Passion were distributed according to the primer pattern of the liturgical hours, to facilitate systematic meditation. The devout soul was encouraged to saturate her or his mind with detailed imaginings of the Passion itself:

> It behoveth [a man] to set thereto all the sharpness of his mind, with open eyes of [the] heart . . . and making himself present in all that befell in the Passion and Crucifixion, effectively, busily, thoughtfully and perseveringly, and passing over naught lightly or with tedious heaviness, but with all the heart and with ghostly gladness.[4]

There was more than the arousal of mere emotion to all this. Behind such affective devotion was a Christology which traced itself back at least to St Anselm, and which found in Christ's suffering not merely a theme for grateful and penitent reflection, but the ultimate manifestation of his human nature, and therefore his credentials as Saviour of humankind.

The theory of atonement contained in Anselm's *Cur Deus Homo?* involves the notion that Christ, as perfect man, on behalf of sinful men, makes to God the satisfaction due to him for the dishonour done to his majesty by sin. It is thus central to the Christological claim of the *Cur Deus Homo?*, that the God-man Jesus is representative of humanity, that he is our brother:

> To whom could he most fitly assign the fruit of and retribution for his death . . . or whom could he more justly make heirs of a debt due to him of which he himself had no need, and of the overflowings of his fulness, than his kindred and brethren, whom he sees burdened with so many and so great debts and wasting away in the abyss of misery.[5]

"Kindred and brethren" – that is also a central note of the affective tradition in the late Middle Ages. It is made explicit by Langland in

---

[4] Horstmann, *Yorkshire Writers*, I p. 198.
[5] Anselm, *Cur Deus Homo?* Book 2 chapter 19, in *S Anselmi Opera Omnia*, ed. F. S. Schmitt, 1946–61, II, pp. 130–1.

Passus XVIII of *Piers Plowman*, where Christ is describing the Judgement:

> And thanne shall I come as a kyng, crowned with aungeles
> And have out of helle alle mennes soules.
> "Fendes and fendekynges bifore me shul stande
> And be at my biddyng wheresoevere [be] me liketh.
> Ac to be merciable to man thanne, my kynde it asketh,
> For we beth brethren of blood, but noght in baptisme alle.
> Ac alle that beth myne hole bretheren, in blood and in
>   baptisme,
> Shul noght be dampned to the deeth that is withouten ende.[6]

"Myne hole bretheren, in blood and in baptisme": it was to emphasize this kinship that the affective tradition was designed. Emphasis on the suffering humanity of Jesus gave medieval men and women confidence to see in him a loving brother, and to claim from him the rights of kin. It was this sense of close kinship with the suffering Christ which underlay the English form of the devotion to the Holy Name of Jesus, a cult which emphasized the sweetness, gentleness and accessibility of the human Saviour. The fervent and affectionate prayer "O Bone Jesu", invariably found in the printed Sarum *Horae*, and directly derived from St Anselm's *Meditations*, was the classic expression of this sense of solidarity:

> O good Jesu, o sweet Jesu, o Jesu, son of the Virgin Mary, full of mercy and truth . . . who for us sinners deigned to pour out your blood on the altar of the cross: I invoke your holy name. This name of Jesu is a sweet name . . . for what is Jesu but Saviour . . . O good Jesu, call to mind what is yours in me, wipe away all that I have made alien.[7]

The perception of Jesus as brother, kin, recurs again and again in the devotional literature of pre-Reformation England:

> Thou my suster and my moder
> And thy sone my broder
> Who shulde thenne drede?[8]

It was summed up on the eve of the Reformation by Luis de Vives, the humanist whose prayers were a staple resource for the compilers of Tudor devotional manuals: "O Brother of ours, O natural son of the Father, whose sons thou makest us by adoption,

---

[6] Langland, *Piers Plowman*, B Text Passus xviii lines 372–9.
[7] *Hor. Ebor.* pp. 83–4.
[8] M. S. Luria and R. L. Hoffman, *Middle English Lyrics*, 1974, p. 173.

O Head of our Body, we see that thou art king of Heaven: forget
not thou thy earth, whereinto thine inestimable love to us did bring
thee down."[9]

The affective dimension of all this, the dwelling on the details of
Christ's suffering reflected in the realism of late medieval images of
the Crucifix, or in the visual listing of the instruments of the
Passion in the Images of Pity, or in the brutal realism of such plays
as the Towneley *Coliphizacio*[10] were vital elements in an understanding of redemption in which the humanity shared by Saviour
and sinner was central. The Crucifix was the icon of Christ's
abiding solidarity with suffering humanity. As Ludolf the Carthusian
wrote, in the life of Jesus which supplied so much of the imagery of
the affective tradition,

> O Good Jesus, how sweet you are in the heart of one who thinks
> upon you and loves you . . . I know not for sure, I am not able
> fully to understand, how it is that you are sweeter in the heart of
> one who loves you in the form of flesh than as the word, sweeter
> in that which is humble than in that which is exalted . . . It is
> sweeter to view you as dying before the Jews on the tree, than
> as holding sway over the angels in Heaven; *to see you as a*
> *man bearing every aspect of human nature to the end*, than as God
> manifesting divine nature, to see you as the dying Redeemer than
> as the invisible Creator.[11]

The enormous imaginative power of this form of meditation, and
its spread into the world of the "lewed" laity, is evident from the
accounts Margery Kempe has left of her visionary experiences,
which seem in places little more than literal-minded paraphrases of
the relevant sections of the *Meditationes Vitae Christi* or of Richard
Rolles's almost equally influential *Meditations on the Passion*, works
read to her by the spiritual directors she found in such abundance in
fifteenth-century East Anglia.[12]

All this was amply reflected within the *Horae*. They were not, of
course, meditational manuals, but the Passion of Christ was as
dominant here as in the rest of late medieval religion. Most of the
Horae contained the so-called Hours of the Cross, and the full text
of the Passion narrative from St John's Gospel, the central text of
the Good Friday liturgy. Some editions also printed an indulgenced

---

[9] *A Booke of Christian Prayers* in *Private Prayers Put Forth by Authority in the reign of Queen
Elizabeth*, ed. W. K. Clay, Parker Society, 1851, p. 514.

[10] Happe, *English Mystery Plays*, pp. 465–83.

[11] C. A. Conway, *The Vita Christi of Ludolph of Saxony . . . a descriptive analysis*, Analecta
Cartusiana no. 34, 1976, p. 56 (my emphasis).

[12] C. W. Atkinson, *Mystic and Pilgrim*, pp. 144–7.

summary of the Passion narrative, reputedly compiled at Avignon for the dying Pope John XXII, which had an attached prayer invoking the Wounds of Christ.[13] But the most striking embodiment of this Passion piety was the group of prayers found almost universally in the printed *Horae*, and frequently also in manuscript prayer collections and handwritten supplements to *Horae*, itemizing the incidents of the Passion, especially the Wounds of Christ or his Seven Words on the Cross.

The Mass of St Gregory and the Wounds of Jesus

Devotion to the Wounds of Jesus was one of the most popular cults of late medieval Europe, and in England it was growing in popularity up to the very eve of the Reformation.[14] It is hardly surprising, therefore, that all of the printed *Horae* contain a selection of prayers to the Wounds. Several of these had rubrics, often in English, ascribing them to Pope Gregory the Great. None is in fact his work, but the attribution is crucial to an understanding of the way in which the use of these prayers spread among the laity, for it indicates their link with a devotional image, the picture known variously as the Mass of Pope Gregory, the Man of Sorrows, or the Image of Pity. According to the legend, Pope Gregory, while celebrating Mass in the church of Santa Croce in Gerusalemme in Rome, had experienced a vision of Christ, seated on or standing in his tomb, displaying his Wounds and surrounded by the Implements of the Passion. The legend almost certainly derives from an early medieval Byzantine icon displayed in the church of Santa Croce, which had a chapel dedicated to St Gregory. The image became an object of pilgrimage, and from the fourteenth century was widely copied, first in Italy and then in France. With its symbolic itemization of the stages of the Passion, depicting lance, spear, scourges, nails, and so on, the image provided an ideal *aide-mémoire* for non-literate and even literate devotees seeking to practice affective meditation. More importantly, perhaps, the poignancy and strangeness of the central image of the dead Christ, often supported by angels, together with the lavish indulgences which Popes bestowed on those who prayed before it, combined to fire the popular imagination.[15]

---

[13] On the Hours of the Cross see Wieck, *The Book of Hours*, pp. 89–93. For the shortened Passion narrative see *Hor. Ebor.* p. 123.

[14] Pfaff, *New Liturgical Feasts*, pp. 84–90.

[15] On the Mass of St Gregory and its related images see Emile Mâle, *Religious Art*, pp. 94–100 and the literature there cited. See also Erwin Panofsky, "Imago Pietatis", in *Festschrift für Max J. Friedlander*, 1927, pp. 261–308.

Endlessly reproduced, both in the form of cheap block-prints to be pinned up in the houses of the poor, and as an illustration for Passion prayers and devotional poems such as Stephen Hawes's "See me, be kinde", the Image of Pity was an obvious and early candidate for inclusion in the *Horae*. There it took a variety of forms, sometimes depicting the Pope saying Mass with Christ as Man of Sorrows appearing above the altar, sometimes simply displaying the Image of Pity itself, detached from the Gregory legend. In both forms it normally had a rubric offering enormous indulgences (up to 32,755 years of pardon) for those who devoutly repeated before the image five Paters, five Aves, and a Creed.[16] Any prayer accompanying the image, whatever its detailed content, became in effect a prayer to the Wounds which the Imago Pietatis so vividly presented. This assimilation of disparate material to the cult of the Wounds is clearly at work in the prayer which most often accompanied this image and indulgence, "Adoro te, Domine Jesu Christe, in cruce pendentem". This is a restrained and dignified prayer in seven short sections, each divided from the next by a Pater and an Ave, and ending with a collect.

I adore you, Lord Jesus Christ, hanging upon the Cross, and bearing on your head a crown of thorns: I beseech you, Lord Jesus Christ, that your cross may free me from the avenging Angel.

I adore you, Lord Jesus Christ, wounded upon the cross, drinking vinegar and gall: I beseech you, Lord Jesus Christ, that your wounds may be my remedy.

I adore you Lord Jesus, placed in the tomb, laid in myrrh and spices: I beseech you, Lord Jesus Christ, that your death may be my life.

I adore you, Lord Jesus Christ, descending into hell, liberating the captives: I beseech you, never let me enter there.

I adore you, Lord Jesus Christ, rising from the dead, ascending into heaven and sitting on the right hand of the Father: have mercy on me, I beseech you.

O Lord Jesus Christ, the good shepherd, preserve the righteous, make righteous the sinners, have mercy on all the faithful: and be gracious to me, a sinner.

O Lord Jesus Christ, I ask you for the sake of that most bitter suffering which you bore for my sake upon the cross, and above all when your most noble soul left your most holy body: have mercy on my soul at its departing. Amen.

---

[16] Hoskins p. 112.

We adore you O Christ and we bless you,
Because by your holy cross you have redeemed the world.
Lord hear my prayer.
And let my cry come to you.

The prayer:
O most kindly Lord Jesus Christ: turn upon me, a miserable
sinner, those eyes of mercy with which you beheld Peter in
[Caiaphas'] court, and Mary Magdalene at the banquet, and
the thief on the gibbet of the cross: and grant that with blessed
Peter I may worthily lament my sins, with Mary Magdalene
may perfectly serve you, and with the thief may behold you
eternally in heaven. Who live and reign with the Father and the
Holy Spirit, God for ever and ever.[17]

Despite their constant association in the *Horae*, this prayer was
clearly not written for the Image of Pity, for in that image the body
of Jesus is not "hanging upon the Cross", but resting on or in its
tomb. Moreover, though the prayer alludes to Christ's sufferings,
death and, burial, it also invokes his Resurrection and Ascension,
and in evoking the Passion its focus is selective – the thirst of
Christ, and his giving up the Ghost. It is not, therefore, designedly
a prayer to the Wounds.

The prayer has in fact an immensely long devotional pedigree.
It was probably compiled in ninth-century Britain, possibly in a
northern English monastic setting with Celtic affiliations, for it is
found as part of a prayer of fifteen invocations all beginning "Lord
Jesus Christ, I adore you", in the *Book of Cerne*, a devotional
collection compiled for Adeluald of Lichfield sometime before 830.
In this, its earliest recorded form, our prayer consists of five of
the last six invocations in a series of fifteen which begins with
Christ's work in Creation, and progresses through his dealings as
the Word of God with the patriarchs and ancient Israel, through the
Incarnation and ministry, concluding with the second coming. In
the original prayer, then, there is no particular emphasis on the
Passion as such. But the sections of the prayer dealing with the
Passion were soon detached from the rest of the invocation, and by
the mid tenth century, when the Anglo-Saxon pontifical of Egbert
was compiled, the fivefold invocation of Christ in his Passion
which is the basis of the primer text was in use as a liturgical prayer
by the celebrant at the solemn veneration of the cross on Good
Friday. With slight variations, it was prescribed for similar use

[17] *Hor. Ebor.* pp. 81–2, my translation.

in the Good Friday liturgy given in the tenth-century monastic consuetudinary, the *Regularis Concordia*, and in a number of later liturgical books and missals. But the prayer also had a continuing existence as a devotional rather than a liturgical text, and it is this devotional tradition which is represented in the primer versions.[18]

In the primers the prayer has been reshaped to late medieval devotional currents, its character subtly but decisively altered. In the original full text found in the *Book of Cerne* the overall emphasis of the prayer was on the eternal dignity and triumph of Christ as Incarnate God: the prayer emphasized his role in creation and redemption, his power to heal and save, his descent as King of Glory into the underworld to liberate the captive patriarchs, his coming in glory on Judgement Day. Even the invocation of Christ on the cross, crowned with thorns, portrayed the Crucifixion as the victorious action of Christ himself – "Domine Iesu Christe, adoro te in cruce ascendentem". The same word, *ascendentem*, is used later in the invocation to celebrate the Ascension into Heaven, and behind its application to the Crucifixion is the theology found in such English vernacular texts as the *Dream of the Rood*, the Latin hymn "Pange Lingua Gloriosi" used in the modern Roman rite on Good Friday, and the early medieval Crucifixes which display the crucified not as an anguished and defeated figure, but as a tranquilly victorious king, robed and crowned. This triumphal theology of the cross remained in medieval liturgical use of the "Adoro Te", despite the isolation of the Crucifixion and post-Crucifixion invocations from the rest of the prayer. The substitution of the word *pendentem* for *ascendentem* occurs only in the later medieval devotional texts of the prayer, and it transforms its whole theological resonance. The Crucifixion is now something which happens to Christ, rather than his triumphal act: he does not ascend the cross, he hangs upon it, and the final section of the expanded version in the primers increases this understanding of the Passion as passive suffering by a loving victim by directing the devotee's attention to Christ's "bitter sufferings" and the moment of his death, emphases entirely absent in the original and its liturgical derivatives.

This preoccupation with the moment of Christ's death, and with his sufferings, pervades the prayer as reshaped in late medieval piety

---

[18] L. Gjerlow, *Adoratio Crucis*, 1961, pp. 13–28 and references there cited; H. M. J. Banting (ed.), *Two Anglo-Saxon Pontificals*, Henry Bradshaw Society, 1989, pp. xxix–xxxii, 142; T. Symons (ed.), *Regularis Concordia*, 1953, pp. 41–5. The Good Friday observances of the *Concordia*, with the text of the "Adoro Te" prayers, are discussed in K. Young, *The Drama of the Medieval Church*, 1962, I pp. 112–48.

and included in the primers. The reference to the avenging angel, the prayer's play on the opposites of death and life, its plea for delivery from Hell, and its invocation of Christ at the moment at which he gave up his soul, all combine to focus the energy of the prayer on death and judgement. In its primer versions it has become a prayer for deliverance *in articulo mortis*. The striking and slightly odd reference to Peter, Mary, and the penitent thief confirms this. This is no arbitrary grouping, for all three in fact occur together in the *Ars Moriendi*, the standard late medieval handbook on how to die a Christian death. In its discussion of despair, the second temptation a dying Christian faces, the *Ars Moriendi* cites as an antidote from scripture and pious legend a series of great sinners who had repented and were now among the saints. In reducing this part of the *Ars Moriendi* to a picture for a mass audience, the popular block-books derived from the fuller text singled out the most readily identifiable figures: Peter with the cockerel which crowed when he denied Jesus, Mary Magdalene with her jar of ointment, and Dismas, the penitent thief, tied to his cross. One can hardly doubt that this picture reflects the route by which Peter, Mary Magdalene, and Dismas have found their way together into the primer versions of the "Adoro Te" prayer (Pl. 97).[19] That section of the *Ars Moriendi* follows immediately an eloquent appeal to the appearance of the crucified Jesus as the source of the sinner's hope, a passage which draws directly on one of the classical *topoi* of late medieval devotion, St Bernard's famous evocation of the posture of the crucified:"Take heed & see his heed inclyned to salve the, his mouthe to kysse the, his armes I-spred to be-clyp the, his hondes I-thrilled to yeve the, his syde opened to love the."[20] This is clearly a meditation on the Crucifix, not the Image of Pity, but its lingering attention to Christ's wounded body as a hieroglyph of love has an obvious appropriateness to the Image of Pity, designed to serve precisely that function. Prayer and image have come together by a network of association in which the crucified and wounded Christ features as the guarantor of the dying Christian's hope. What began as a quasi-liturgical devotion to the Passion becomes a deeply personal plea for redemption at the moment of death. The combination of the image of the crucified Jesus and deathbed concern is entirely characteristic of the religious ethos of the fifteenth century. And obviously the stupendous indulgences attached to the use of the prayer in conjunction with

[19] On the *Ars Moriendi* see below, chapter 9, "Last Things" pp. XXX
[20] Text from "The book of the craft of dying" in Horstmann, *Yorkshire Writers*, II p. 410. On the passage from St Bernard see Bennett, *Poetry of the Passion*, p. 71.

the image had a special and urgent attraction to someone facing their own imminent death and the prospect of Purgatory.[21]

All this might seem to have little to do with the devotion to the Wounds of Christ as such, of which the Image of Pity is an expression. In fact there is more reference to the cult of the Wounds than at first appears. The prayer from its earliest adaptation for use in the Good Friday liturgy was selected, as we have seen, from the final six invocations of the prayer as found in the *Book of Cerne*. But the invocations selected from the final group of six vary from source to source: what is constant is that *five* invocations are used. There is here a clear reference to the wounds, and this use of fivefold symbolism in connection with the Passion was to become a very striking feature of medieval English piety. Although in the primer versions of the prayer its fivefold structure has been obscured by the addition of the two invocations beginning "O Lord Jesus Christ, the good shepherd" and "O Lord Jesus Christ I ask you", its original fivefold character remained a prominent feature of the indulgence rubric which accompanied the prayer, which explicitly states that two petitions were added by Pope Sixtus IV (who also doubled the indulgence!).[22] And there is a further link in the prayer with the votive Mass of the Five Wounds of Jesus. This was one of the most popular votive Masses of the late Middle Ages and was prefaced in the missal by a legend in which the Archangel Raphael, the angel of healing, appeared to Pope Boniface I, promising deliverance from all earthly evil to anyone who procured the saying of five Masses of the Wounds, and deliverance from Purgatory for any soul for whom five Masses of the Wounds were celebrated. The Gospel prescribed for the Mass was the section of St John's Passion narrative which describes Christ's thirst, his drinking of vinegar and gall, and his giving up the Ghost. Since Christ's drinking of vinegar and gall, and his giving up of the Ghost are both referred to in the prayer, and are indeed the only biblical incidents from the Passion which feature there, it seems likely that users of the prayer would naturally associate it with the Mass of the Five Wounds. The prayer's emphasis on the Christian's plight *in articulo mortis* can only have strengthened this association: the Mass of the Five Wounds is one of the votive Masses most

[21] In fact, although the "Adoro Te" is illustrated by an Image of Pity in Hoskins no. 7 (1494) RSTC 15875, no. 37 (1510) RSTC 15909, and by the more elaborate Mass of Pope Gregory in no. 81 (1527) RSTC 15955, in some books the Image of Pity is replaced by a conventional Crucifix or Calvary scene, as in no. 68 (1525) RSTC 15940 and no. 98 (1531) RSTC 15973, thereby bringing the prayer closer to being a general devotion to the Passion.

[22] *Hor. Ebor.* p. 80: the rubric erroneously identifies the added petitions as numbers 4 and 5, but the main point stands.

commonly specified in obit provisions, and Five-Wounds brasses were common on graves.[23]

Devotion to the Wounds of Jesus was expressed more straightforwardly within the *Horae* in such prayers as the "Ave Manus dextera Christi", a simple invocation of each of the Wounds in turn, concluding with a collect asking that the Wounds of Jesus should inflame the hearts of Christians to love of God.[24] This notion was elaborated in many of the moralized devotions to the Wounds found in the collections of prayers circulating among both clergy and laity in late medieval England, which often make use of the notion that the Wounds of Jesus are caused by particular sins, or, more commonly, that they act as antidotes to particular vices (Pl. 98).

> O Blissful Ihesu for the wounde of your lefte hand kepe me from the synne of envy and yeve me grace . . . to have this verytu of bounte that of all myn even crysten welfare & profit bodely & gostely therof to be as of myn owyn. In honour of thys peyne *Pater Noster*.
>
> Gracious Ihesu for the wound of your ryght foot kepe me from the synne of covetyse that I desire no maner thynge that is contrary to your wylle & yf me grace to have allwey the vertu of freness in dissescioun. In honoure of thys peyne *Pater Noster*.[25]

The side Wound of Christ had a particular fascination and devotional power, for it gave access to his heart, and thereby became a symbol of refuge in his love. Julian of Norwich was shown in her tenth revelation the Wound in Christ's side, and saw there "a feyer and delectable place, and large jnow for alle mankynde that shalle be savyd and rest in pees and in love". Much the same notion is embodied in the fifteenth-century tag attached to a crude drawing of the wounded Christ displaying his heart:

> O! Mankinde,
> Have in thy minde
> My Passion smert,
> And thou shalt finde
> Me full kinde –
> Lo! here my hert.[26]

---

[23] *Northants Wills* II p. 249.
[24] Hoskins no. 137 and p. 124.
[25] Cambridge University Library MS Ii.vi. 43 fol. 23r.
[26] E. Colledge and J. Walsh (eds), *A Book of Showings to the Anchoress Julian of Norwich*, 1978, II pp. 394–5.

73. Helper saints: St Apollonia (right) from the screen at Ludham. She was invoked against toothache.

74. The Lady altar at Ranworth: from left to right, St Mary Salome with her sons James (kneeling) and John: the Blessed Virgin and Christ: St Mary Cleophas with Simon and Jude, Joses, and James: St Margaret.

82. St Anne teaches the Virgin to read her primer, All Saints North Street, York: a reflection of fifteenth-century female piety among the urban well-to-do.

85 (facing page).   The Image of Pity, with an indulgence defaced after the Reformation.

83 (below left).   St Mark and St Matthew at Bramfield, with their primer texts: the painter has given the evangelists each other's texts by mistake.

84 (below right).   St Luke and St John at Bramfield: St John's primer text, "In Principio", was so widely known and used by lay people that the painter did not need to paint it.

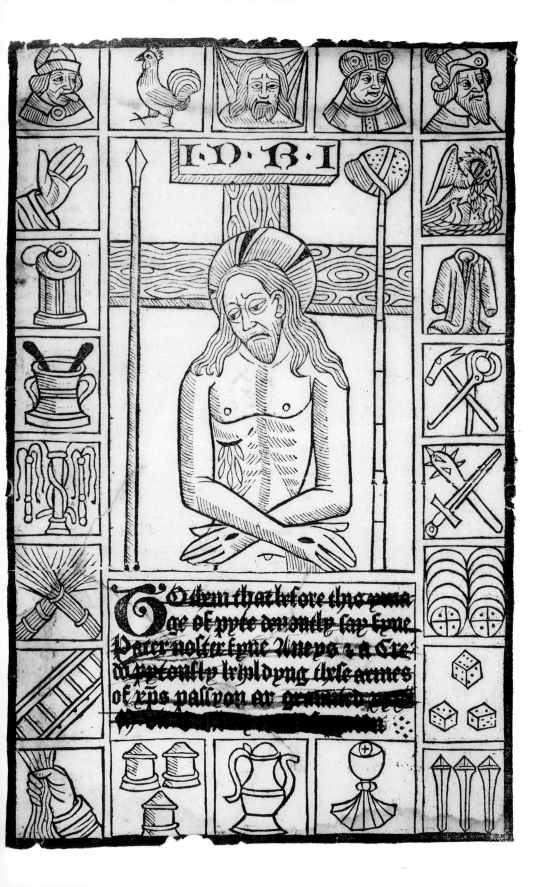

I.M.R.I

To them that before thys ymage of pyte devoutly say .v.pater nosters .v. aves & a crede pyteously beholdyng these armes of crys passyon ar graunted ...

86. Latin and English elevation prayers copied at different times into a family primer now in the Cambridge University Library.

87. Notes on Roberts family birthdays copied alongside prayers into a primer from 1550 to 1574.

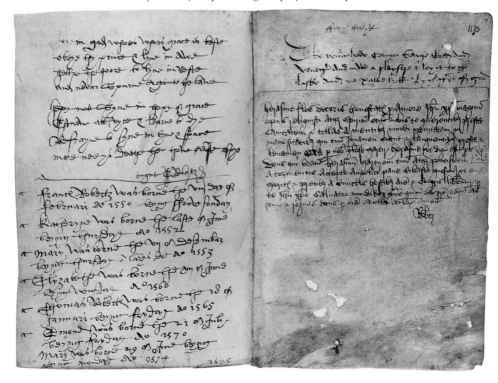

Ominel ne in furoze tuo arguas me:
neqʒ in ita tua cozripias me Miſere/
re mei domie quoniam infirmus ſum

88.   David and Bathsheba: the opening of the penitential Psalms from a printed Sarum primer.

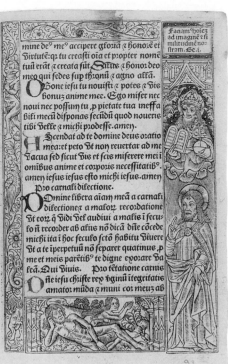

tus Voca me et pone me iuxta te Vt cū an
gelis et sanctis tuis laude te dītz saluato
rem meū i sēcla seculōz. Amē.   Vvhā
thou entrest in to the churche say thus.

Ntroibo in multitudine mie tue introibo in
domū tuā. Adorabo ad templū sctm tuū
et confitebor noī tuo dñe deduc me in iu
sticia tua ppter iimicos meos dirige i cō
spectu tuo viam meam.   Vvhā thou
takest holy vvater say thus.

Er qua bndicta sit mihi sal et vita psta
mihi dñe per hāc creaturā aspersiōis aq
sanitate mētis integritate corporis tutela
salutis securitate spei corroboratione fi
dei nisi et in futuro. Amē.   Vvhā thou
begynnest to praye thē begynne knēelig

Iscedite a me maligni et scrutabor: mā
data dei mei aufer a me dñe oēs iniquita
tes meas Vt merear pura mēte introire in
sancta sctōr. Veni dñe visitare me i pa
ce Vt laeter corā te corde pfecto. Aperi dñe
os meū ad bñdicēdū nomē tuū emūdaq
cor meū a vanis et nequissimis cogitatio
nibus Vt dignus merear exaudiri aū cōspe
ctum diuine maiestatis tue. Dignus es do

mine deus meus accipere gloriā et honorē et
virtutē: qz tu creasti oia et propter nomē
tuū erāt et creata sūt. Salue et honor deo
meo qui sedes sup thronū et agno allā.

O Bone iesu tu nouisti et potes et vis
bonuz anime mee. Ego miser nec
noui nec possum tu p pietate tua ineffa
bili meū disponas secūdū quod noueris
tibi velle et michi prodesse. amen.

Scendat ad te domine deus oratio
mea: et peto Vt non reuertar ad me
vacua sed sicut vis et scis miserere mei i
omibus anime et corporis necessitatibus
amen iesu iesu esto michi iesus. amen.
Pro carnali dilectione.

Omine libera aiam meā a carnali
dilectione et maioru recordatione
Vt eor q vidi vel audiui a malis i secu
lo q recorder ab aīus nō dicā dñe cōcede
michi ita i hoc seculo sctō habitu viuere
Vt a te iperpetuū nō separer quatinus p
me et meis parētibus te digne exorare va
leā. Qui viuis.   Pro tētatione carnis

Osie iesu christe rex virginū integritatis
amator mūda et muni cor meuz ab

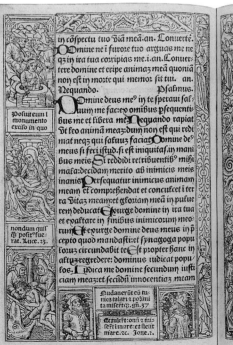

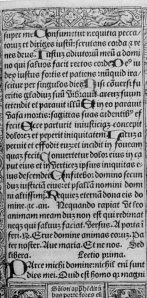

in cōspectu tuo viā meā. an. Conuerte.

O Domine ne i furore tuo arguas me ne
qz in ira tua corripias me. i. an. Conuer
tere domine et eripe animaz meā quoniā
non est in morte qui memor sit tui. an.
Nequando.   Psalmus.

O Domine deus meus in te speraui sal
uum me fac: ex omibus psequenti
bus me et libera me. Nequando rapiat
Vt leo animā meaz dum non est qui redi
mat neqz qui saluuz faciat. Domine deus
meus si feci istud. si est iniquitas in mani
bus meis. Si reddidi retribuentibus michi
mala: decidam merito ab inimicis meis
inanis. Persequatur inimicus animam
meam et comprehendat et conculcet i ter
ra vitaz meam: et gloriam meā in puluě
rem deducat. Exurge domine in ira tua
et exaltare in finibus inimicorum meo
rum. Exurge domine deus meus in p
cepto quod mandasti: et synagoga popu
loruz circundabit te. Et propter hanc in
altuz regredere: dominus iudicat popu
los. Iudica me domine secundum iusti
ciam meaz: et secūduz innocentiaz meam

super me. Consumetur nequitia pecca
toruz et diriges iustū: scrutans corda et re
nes deus. Iustuz adiutoriū meū a domi
no qui saluos facit rectos corde. Deus iu
dex iustus fortis et patiens: nuquid ira
scitur per singulos dies: nisi couersi fu
eritis gladiū suū vibrauit: arcuz suum
tetendit et parauit illū. Et in eo parauit
vasa mortis: sagittas suas ardentibus
fecit. Ecce parturit iniusticia: concepit
dolorez et peperit iniquitatem. Lacuz a
peruit et effodit euz: et incidit in foueam
quaz fecit. Conuertetur dolor eius in ca
put eius et in verticez ipsius iniquitas e
ius descendet. Confitebor domino secun
duz iusticiā eius: et psallā nomini domi
ni altissimi. Requies eternā dona eis do
mine. et an.   Nequando rapiat Vt leo
animam meaz dum non est qui redimat
neqz qui saluuz faciat. Versus. A porta in
feri. Ry. Erue domine animas eoruz. Pa
ter noster. Aue maria. Et ne nos.   Sed
libera.   Lectio prima.

Parce michi domine: nichil enī sunt
dies mei. Quid est homo qz magni

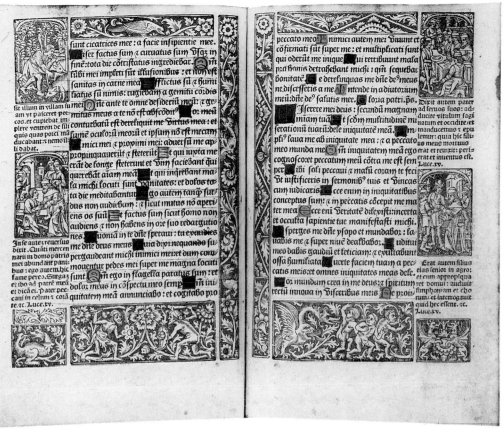

91. The penitential Psalms with a border illustrating the parable of the Prodigal Son, from a Sarum primer by Simon Vostre.

89 (facing page, above).   The days of Creation in a Sarum primer by Theilman Kerver, 1497.

90 (facing page, below).   Scenes from the life of Christ with their Old Testament types above and below, in the margins of Kerver's primer of 1497.

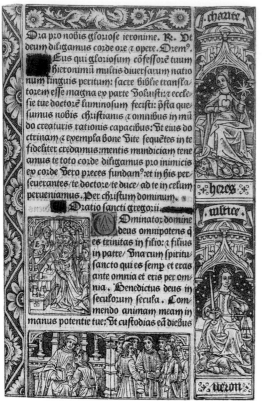

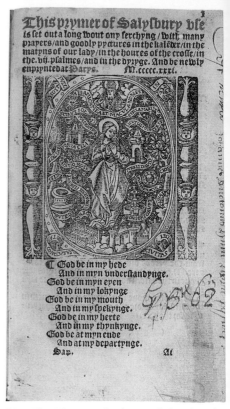

92. The Virtues tread down the Vices in the margin of Vostre's primer. In the text, the Mass of St Gregory, and at the foot, two of the seven sacraments.

93. The title-page of a characteristic primer by Fançois Regnault.

94. The misery of human life, from the Office of the Dead in a primer by François Regnault.

95. Viaticum, from the Office of the Dead in a Regnault primer.

96. The Seven Sorrows of Mary, from a Regnault primer.

97. Comfort against despair, from the *Ars Moriendi*

98. The Five Wounds of Jesus displayed for devotion on a bench-back at Ashmanhaugh, Norfolk.

99. *Arma Christi*: the Five Wounds of Jesus displayed heraldically on a devotional card circulated by the Carthusians of Sheen.

100. Christ in Judgement displays his wounds: a print from the Briggitine house of Syon.

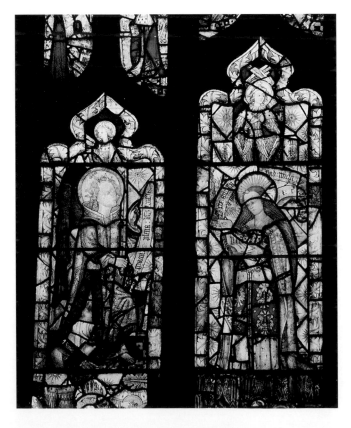

101. The Annunciation, from Bale in Norfolk.

102. The Annunciation, from a font displaying the Joys of Mary, St Matthew's, Ipswich.

103. Mary crowned in Heaven, from the font, St Matthew's, Ipswich.

104. This prayer for victory over enemies, copied for the first owner of a manuscript primer, has been appropriated by a subsequent owner, who has written in his initial.

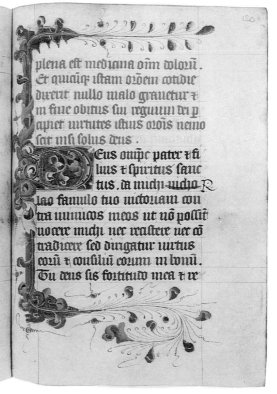

105. From the Nine Orders of Angels, Barton Turf, Norfolk.

106. From the Nine Orders of Angels, Southwold, Suffolk.

107. Michael weighing souls at Martham, Norfolk.

108. St George, north altar screen, Ranworth.

09. St Michael, south altar screen, Ranworth.

110. The "Measure of the Nails" and the Wounds of Jesus with miraculous promises: from a prayer roll once owned by the young Henry VIII, now at Ushaw College, Duham.

111. The *danse macabre* from the borders of a Sarum primer.

As might be expected, the side Wound acquired its own separate indulgenced devotions, and although printers of *Horae* for England seem not to have included the very common icon of it as a well or chalice of life, often found in such books on the Continent, lay people could and did stick such images into their *Horae*, alongside devotions such as the hymn "Salve plaga lateris nostri Redemptoris". These drawings or prints were part of a cult of the "mensura vulneris", in which indulgences and other benefits were attached to devotional acts such as kissing or carrying about with one the drawing or measure of the side Wound.[27]

The cult of the Wounds was, therefore, one of the most important and far-reaching in late medieval England, and it found expression not only in the *Horae* but in countless vernacular sermons, prayers, and verses.

> Jesus woundes so wide
> Ben welles of life to the goode,
> Namely the stronde of his syde
> That ran ful breme on the rode.
> Yif thee list to drinke
> To fle fro the fendes of helle
> Bowe thu doun to the brinke
> And mekely taste of the welle.[28]

That image of the Wounds as wells of grace recurs again and again in medieval English devotion, even finding its way onto jewelry, such as the ring, now in the British Museum, inscribed with an image of Christ surrounded by the Instruments of the Passion, in which the side Wound is labelled "the well of everlasting lyffe", and those in hands and feet "the well of comfort", "the well of gracy", "the well of pitty", and "the well of merci", with the inscription "Vulnera quinqque dei sunt medicina mei."[29]

The symbolism of the Wounds, and their importance in the late medieval religious imagination, is everywhere evident in the wills of the laity, as in that of the York metalworker in 1516 who stipulated that "I wit to be done for my saull and all Cristyn saulles the day of my beryall v masses of the v woundes of our Lord

---

[27] W. Sparrow Simpson, "On the Measure of the Wound in the Side of the Redeemer", *Journal of the British Archaeological Association*, XXX, 1874, pp. 357–74; D Gray "The Five Wounds of Our Lord", *Notes and Queries*, CCVIII, 1963, pp. 50–1, 82–9, 127–34, 163–8.

[28] Gray, *Themes and Images*, pp. 131, 134.

[29] Joan Evans, *Magical Jewels in the Middle Ages and the Renaissance, particularly in England*, 1922, p. 127; and cf. John Longland, *A Sermond . . . 1535* fol. R v "The wounde in the syde and harte of Jesu Christe, is the wele of mercy, the welle of liffe, the well of plentyfull redemptyon."

Jhesu."[30] A Greenwich widow in 1496 asked her parish priest to say "V masses of the V woonds V days to yeder a fore the hie aulter and every masse wyle V smale candells brenyng"[31] and a London mercer desired five poor men to kneel every feast day at his tomb and repeat five Paters and Aves "in honor of the five woondes of our Lord Jesus Chryste".[32] The fivefold symbolism of the wounds was ubiquitous, even where the link with them was not made explicit, as in the Somerset will of 1471 which instructed the executors to give "to 5 poore men 5 gownes, and also every friday by an hoole yere next ensuying my decease 5d".[33] Such fivefold doles were often specifically associated with Friday, and above all with Good Friday, to underline the symbolism of the Wounds.[34]

The devotion to the Wounds developed its own extraordinary iconography, notably the Arms of the Passion images, in which the hands, feet, and side-hole or pierced heart of Jesus were heraldically displayed against the cross. This emblem was carved on bench-ends, painted in glass, cast in brass or carved in slate to be placed on graves. It was also distributed, in the form of cheap woodcuts, by the Charterhouses (Pl. 99). But the devotion to the Wounds was not simply a Passion devotion. Its prominence in wills suggests that the link between this cult and prayer for delivery in death, which is evident in the "Adoro Te" prayer in the *Horae*, is no coincidence. Devotion to the Five Wounds was specially linked to intercession for the dead and deliverance from Purgatory, as, indeed, the legend attached to the votive Mass might anyway suggest.

It is not immediately obvious why this should be so, till one considers the ambiguity of the Image of Pity itself. In many versions of the image a prominent feature is the *ostentatio vulnerum*, the gesture or pose by which Christ displays his Wounds to the beholder. This is a gesture derived not from the iconography of the Passion, but from that of the Last Judgement, for it was believed that when Christ came as Judge he would display his Wounds (Pl. 100), to the elect as pledges of his love for them, to sinners as bitter reproach – "they shall look on him whom they have pierced."[35] Thus the very image which spoke of Christ's tenderness and compassion for the sinner could become a terrifying indictment of the impenitent. Bosch's extraordinary tabletop depiction of the

---

[30] *Test. Ebor.* V p. 79
[31] L. L. Duncan "Parishes of West Kent" (Alis Fischer), p. 270.
[32] *Sussex Wills*, III p. 281.
[33] *Somerset Wills*, I p. 221.
[34] *Lincoln Diocese Documents*, p. 157.
[35] *Early Netherlandish Painting*, 1971, I pp. 123–5.

Seven Deadly Sins, now in the Prado in Madrid, captures this sense of menace perfectly. In the four corners are vignettes of the Four Last Things – Death, Judgement, Heaven, and Hell. Between these, the Seven Deadly Sins are depicted in a circular frieze, making the iris of an eye, the pupil of which is a representation of the Man of Sorrows, pierced anew by the sins of mankind, and displaying his Wounds. Underneath him, and underlining the eye symbolism of the picture, are the terrifying words "Cave Cave Deus Vidit".[36]

This link between the sins of mankind and the Wounds of Jesus was familiar in England.[37] John Mirk, urging his congregation to come to confession in Lent, told how Christ had appeared to a sick man "with blody wondys stondyng before the seke manys bede", urging him to be shriven. When the sick man refused, "Cryst toke out of hys wounde yn hys syde his hond full of blod and sayde: 'Thu fendys-chyld, thys schall be redy token bytwyx me and the yn the day of dome, that I wold have don the mercy and thou woldest not.' And therwyth cast the blod ynto hys face, and therwyth anon thys seke man cryed and sayd: 'Alas! Alas! I am dampnest for ay!' and so deyd."[38]

The convictions behind this macabre story were given resonant expression in the York play of Judgement, where Christ, surrounded by angels bearing the Instruments of the Passion in a *tableau vivant* immediately recalling the Image of Pity, confronts humanity:

> Here may ye see my woundes wide,
> The whilke I tholed for youre mysdede
> Thurgh harte and heed, foote, hande and hide,
> Nought for my gilte, butt for youre nede.
> Beholdis both body, bak, and side,
> How dere I bought youre brotherhede.
> Thes bittir peynes I wolde abide
> To bye you blisse, thus wolde I bleede.
> Thus was I dight thi sorrowe to slake:
> Manne, thus behoved the to borowed be.
> In all my woo toke I no wrake;
> Mi will itt was for the love of the.
> Man, sore aught the for to quake,
> This dredfull day this sight to see.
> All this I suffered for thi sake;
> Say, man, what suffered thou for me?[39]

---

[36] Reproduced in M. J. Friedlander, *From Van Eyck to Brueghel*, fig. 145.
[37] M. W. Bloomfield, *The Seven Deadly Sins*, 1952, pp. 167–8, 189, 203, 205, 224.
[38] *Festial*, pp. 90–2.
[39] Happe, *English Mystery Plays*, pp. 641–2.

This passage comes immediately before Christ, re-enacting the story of the sheep and the goats from Matthew 25, judges mankind on the basis of their response to the plight of the naked, the hungry, the sorrowful, and the sick. The *ostentatio vulnerum* is also an *ostentatio pauperum*: the wounds of Christ are the sufferings of the poor, the outcast, and the unfortunate. Margery Kempe was articulating this entirely conventional insight when she declared that she hardly dared behold "a lazer er an-other seke man, specialy [yf] he had any wowndes aperyng on hym" because it was as if "sche had sen owr Lord Ihesu Crist wyth hys wowndes bledyng".[40] It was for this reason that the cult of the Five Wounds in England repeatedly expressed itself in acts of charity as well as Masses and prayers, and especially by acts of charity in multiples of fives, bestowed on Fridays and above all on Good Friday. By such actual and symbolic charity one could turn the Wounds of Judgement into Wounds of Mercy, forestalling the condemnation threatened in Matthew 25 by attending, while there was still time, to Christ's wounded members, the poor.

Into what appears to be a simple affective devotion to the Passion, there was compressed the essence of the practical soteriology of late medieval religion. It is hardly surprising, therefore, that the symbol of the Five Wounds should have been chosen by the Pilgrims of Grace as the emblem of their loyalty to the whole medieval Catholic system. Bishop Latimer was not the only one in England who deduced from the attack on the monasteries that Purgatory itself, and the doctrinal, devotional, and liturgical system which went with it, had been called in question.

The Seven Words on the Cross

Affective meditation on the Passion provided much of the rationale behind the flowering of the cult of the Wounds; it also encouraged a similar devotional elaboration of the Words of Jesus on the Cross. These were conventionally divided into seven, and prayers and meditations on them multiplied.[41] The one most commonly used in the *Horae* was generally attributed to St Bede, and carried with it the promise that "whos ever seith this preyor folowyng every day knelyng on his knees, the dule no noon ule man shall not have no power to nye hym, no he shall not dye with out confession, and xxx dayes afore his deth he shall seen oure lady aperying to

---

[40] *The Book of Margery Kempe*, p. 176.
[41] The seven words are listed, with the standard interpretations, in Nicholas Love, *The Mirror of the Blessed Life of Jesu Christ*, 1926, pp. 235–7.

hym."[42] Almost inevitably, the prayer explicitly invokes the Seven Words of Jesus as remedies for the seven deadly sins, but its main thrust is the very straightforward application of Jesus' words to the devotee's own behaviour. The opening petitions are enough to illustrate this

> Lord Jesus Christ, who spoke Seven Words hanging on the Cross on the last day of your life, and wished us always to have those words in remembrance: I beseech you, by the power of those Seven Words forgive me all that I have done or sinned concerning the Seven Deadly Sins, namely Pride, Envy, Wrath, Sloth, Luxury, Avarice and Gluttony.
>
> Lord, as you said, "Father, forgive those who crucify me": grant that for love of you I may forgive all those who do me wrong.
>
> Lord, as you said to the thief, "This day you will be with me in Paradise": make me so to live that in the hour of my death you may say to me "This day you will be with me in Paradise."

This rather pedestrian prayer no doubt owed much of its immense popularity to its accompanying promises of miraculous preservation from evil, and of Our Lady's assistance as death drew near, but its somewhat flat-footed moralizing of the Seven Words was congenial to an age which poured much energy into promoting a version of the Christian life structured round teaching on the seven sins, seven virtues, Ten Commandments, and five bodily wits:

> Kepe well X & flee from seveyn;
> Spend well V, & cum to hevyn.[43]

The most powerful prayers structured round the Seven Words, however, are very far removed from such prosiness. The "Fifteen Oes of St Bridget", found in both Books of Hours and private devotional collections, were quite certainly the most distinctive, and probably the most popular, of all prayers in late medieval England. They are English in origin, probably composed either in the devotional world of the Yorkshire hermitages associated with figures like Richard Rolle and his disciples, or in the circle of the English Brigittines.[44] In sheer comprehensiveness and eloquence

[42] *Hor. Ebor.* p. 140: the rubric is normally in Latin, but I have quoted it from Bodleian MS Lyell 30 fol. 49v; see also Wormald, "Revelation of the 100 Paternosters" p. 168, and British Library MS Lansdowne 379 fols 74v–76r for an English version of the whole prayer.

[43] Balliol MS 354 fol. 213v. See above, chapter 2, "How the Plowman Learned his Paternoster", p. 77.

[44] A. Wilmart, "Le grand poème Bonaventurien sur les sept Paroles du Christ en Croix", *Revue Bénédictine*, XLVII, 1935, pp. 274–8; Nicholas Rogers, "About the 15 Oes, the Brigittines and Syon Abbey". *St Ansgar's Bulletin*, LXXX, 1984, pp. 29–30.

they present an unrivalled epitome of late medieval English religion
at its most symbolically resonant. Despite their immense popularity
these are learned prayers, with roots in Patristic and early medieval
theology, as well as the writings of Rolle and the affective tradition.
The central thread running through the collection is reflection on
the Words from the Cross, a fact easy to miss because of the
fifteenfold, rather than sevenfold, arrangement of the prayers, but
they also explore the range of imagery associated with the cult of
the Wounds and of the Passion in general.

All fifteen of the "Oes" are conceived as pleas for mercy to a
merciful Saviour whose understanding of the human condition is
guaranteed by the fact that he took flesh and suffered for us,
and whose suffering forms an enduring bond of endearment and
tenderness between him and suffering humanity. Jesus in these
prayers, as in the affective tradition in general, is loving, tender,
brotherly:

> O Jesu, endles swetnes of lovynge soules: O Jesu, ghostly joy
> passynge and excedynge all gladnes and desyres: O Jesu, helthe
> and tender lover of repentaunt synners, that lykest for to duuelle
> as thou sayd thiselfe with the chyldren of men. For that was the
> cause why thou wast incarnate, and made man in the ende of the
> worlde ["in fine temporum"].[45]

But, true to the Anselmian origin of such a theological emphasis,
the Jesus of the "Oes" is also emphatically God incarnate, whose
actions are of overwhelming significance because they are the
expression of the mind of the Trinity. His human anguish in the
Passion was the product not merely or primarily of human evil, but
"in divino corde ab eterno preordinata", eternally preordained in
the heart of God. Thus, Christ dying on the cross between two
thieves is hailed as "speculum claritatis divine", a mirror of divine
clarity or omniscience, by virtue of which divine sight he sees "in
the mirror of his most serene majesty" all the names and numbers
of the elect, predestined to salvation, and equally "the reprobation
of the wicked in the multitude of the damned". In the light of that
double foreknowledge, moved to profound sorrow "in the abyss of
his mercy" for "lost and despairing sinners", Jesus turns to the
penitent thief and says "this day you will be with me in paradise."
The "Oes" never lose sight of the dialectic between the human and
the divine in the Incarnation, and though their systematic progress

---

[45] In translating, I have followed the text in *Hor. Ebor.*, pp. 76–80; where the quotation is
given in Middle English, I have taken it from the one printed in Hoskins no. 67, RSTC
15939, fols cxlv(r)–cxlix(r).

through the details of the Passion signals their indebtedness to the affective tradition, they never slip into mere emotionalism by slackening the theological tension which gives them their distinctive power.

Many of the prayers turn on the paradox of the divine nature concealed in a form of suffering which exactly inverts some divine attribute. Jesus, the "well of endlesse pity" (prayer vii), calls out "I thirst," Jesus, "swetnes of hertes and goostly hony of soules" (prayer viii) drinks bitter vinegar and gall, Jesus, the maker of all, whom nothing can measure or contain and who holds the earth in the hollow of his hand (prayer iii) is savagely measured out on the Cross and nailed through hands and feet, Jesus, the heavenly physician (prayer iv), has not a single limb nor a single inch of skin left whole and healthy.

The "Oes" also employ in a distinctive and vital way much of the conventional imagery of the cult of the Wounds. The interest in the measure of Christ's wound which we have already noticed is taken up and developed in two of the "Oes":

> O Jesus, Beginning and End, and life and strength in all that comes between: remember that, for our sake, from the crown of your head to the sole of your foot you were plunged deep beneath the water of your Passion. For the sake of the breadth and depth of your wounds, teach me, who am drowned deep in sin, by true charity to keep your broad commandment.

> O Jesus, most profound abyss of mercy: I beseech you by the depth of your wounds, which pierced your flesh to the heart and very marrow of your bones, draw me out from the depths of sin into which I have sunk, and hide me deep in the holes of your wounds from the face of your anger, Lord, until the judgement is past.

The twists and turns of the metaphors of measurement here – beginning, end, middle, height, depth, breadth, submersion and concealment – are very striking. The prayers also rework other conventional Passion imagery. The drying out and discolouring of Christ's body as he dies on the cross, associated with the saying "I thirst," fascinated the English religious imagination, and feature prominently in Julian of Norwich's revelations.[46] In the fifteenth and final prayer of the "Oes" this drying is linked with the Eucharistic imagery of Christ's blood as the fruit of the mystic

---

[46] *A Book of Showings*, pp. 357–65.

vine, crushed to quench the spiritual thirst of mankind:

> O Jesu, true and fruitful vine, remember the overflowing and
> abundant outpouring of your blood, which you shed copiously,
> as though squeezed from a cluster of grapes, when on the Cross
> you trod the wine-press alone. And [remember how] when
> pierced with the soldier's spear, you gave us from your side both
> water and blood to drink, so that little or nothing remained in
> you, and at last you hung on high like a bundle of myrrh, and
> your delicate flesh changed its colour, and the moisture of your
> vitals was dried up, and the marrow of your bones vanished
> away. By that most bitter passion of yours, and by the shedding
> of your most precious blood, o sweet Jesu, wound my heart, that
> tears of penitence and love may be my bread both night and day:
> and convert me wholly to you, that my heart may ever be a
> dwelling place for you, and my behaviour may be always pleasing
> and acceptable to you, and the end of my life so praiseworthy,
> that I may be found worthy to praise you with all your saints for
> ever and ever. Amen.

This is a complex prayer, drawing on scriptural, patristic, and
liturgical sources, as well as on the Bonaventuran tradition of affective meditation. The central image of Christ as the mystic vine,
shedding his blood to quench our thirst, is derived not only from
John 15, but from Isaiah 63, with its vision of a saviour robed in red
as Christ was robed in his own blood on the cross, and who
declares that "I have trodden the wine-press alone," a passage
applied in the liturgy of Holy Week directly to Christ's Passion. At
the same Mass in which this passage was read, the Gospel reading
was the Passion according to St Luke, in which Jesus at the Last
Supper says over the cup not "this is my blood," but "take and
share it amongst yourselves, for I shall not drink of the fruit of the
vine till the kingdom of God has come."[47] In an inversion characteristic of the "Oes" as a whole, the piercing of Christ receives
its mirror image in the piercing of the sinner's heart by remorse,
and the pouring out of Christ's blood and the drying of his body
is matched by the moistening of the sinner's heart by tears of
penitence and love. In a similar inversion, the prayer takes the
conventional notion of the Wound in Christ's side as a refuge for
the sinner, a conceit which is explored in the tenth and eleventh
"Oes", but turns it round. Pierced by sorrow and repentance, the
sinner's heart is to be Christ's dwelling-place, an image which
receives its full burden of meaning from the overall Eucharistic

---

[47] Luke 22: *Missale*, cols 286, 29 (Wednesday in Holy Week).

metaphor of the prayer: the bread of tears and the bloody fruit of Christ the vine are the Eucharist, and it is thus that he will dwell within us. Finally, the apparent clumsiness of the mismatch between the imagery of drinking sustained in the first half of the prayer and the description of the penitent's tears as "bread" in the second half is only apparent, for this is a quotation from Psalm 42, "As the hart panteth for the water-brooks," well-known to the laity from its inclusion in the "Dirige", and the verse before that used here runs "my soul thirsteth for God, for the living God," so that the literary resonance stays firmly within the language of thirst and drinking, while enriching the Eucharistic reference of the prayer by introducing the word "bread".

Despite their enormous popularity, or perhaps as a direct consequence of it, the sophistication and learning of these prayers must have been lost on all but a minority of those who used them, and some elements in them were actually unwelcome. The interest in predestination evident in the first and sixth prayers, which was so characteristic of fourteenth-century English theology, was suspect after the condemnation of Lollardy; all of the fifteenth-century English versions of the "Oes" therefore omitted or drastically modified the predestinarian passages.[48] The liturgical and scriptural references were also coarsened or lost in the process of translation. The passage in the fifteenth prayer on the crucified Christ "treading the wine-press alone", with its direct reference to Isaiah and the Holy Week liturgy, becomes "Whan they pressed thy blessyd body as a rype clustre upon the pressoure of the crosse". This is a clear example of scriptural and liturgical theology giving way to devotional fashion. Though the imagery of the vine had long been applied to Christ and his blood-shedding, the fifteenth century had seen the emergence into new prominence in art and piety of the literalistic image of the cross as mystical wine-press, in which Christ was grotesquely portrayed being pressed or screwed down under the beam of the cross while his blood ran into a wine-vat or a set of barrels. This conceit, in which Christ is a passive victim, was allowed to shape the fifteenth prayer, in place of the original reference to Isaiah, with its overtones of action and triumph.[49]

Yet, at whatever cost in terms of coarsening, the "Oes" were popular, and were used by men and women of such lowly status and learning as Robert Reynes of Acle, and as exalted as the Earl of Suffolk or the Lady Margaret Beaufort. Lydgate rhymed them, and

---

[48] Cf. C. Meier-Ewart, "A Middle English Version of the Fifteen Oes", *Modern Philology*, LXVIII, 1971, pp. 355–61, and note 50 below.

[49] Mâle, *Religious Art*, pp. 110–14.

at least two English prose versions circulated in manuscript. In 1491 Caxton printed a collection of English and Latin prayers dominated by a new translation of the "Oes", and thereafter they were a regular element in printed editions of the *Horae*.[50] Their popularity is easy to understand. The prayers took the devotee through the whole history of the Passion with considerable economy of phrasing, yet with all the vividness of imagery and the warmth and urgency of tone which is so much a feature of late medieval religious sensibility. Drawing many details from the classic sources of affective meditation on the Passion, such as Rolle's *Meditations*, the *Golden Legend*, and the *Meditationes Vitae Christi*, the "Oes" nevertheless gave to familiar themes such as the Wounds or Words of Jesus a depth and resonance lacking in less learned prayers like the "Adoro Te" or the prayer of St Bede. Yet where originality would have been inappropriate, as in the benefits petitioned for at the end of each prayer, the "Oes" settled for conventionality. Like so many other popular prayers of the period, the "Oes" ask for mercy, forgiveness, protection from the temptations of the world, the flesh, and the Devil in the hour of death, devout reception of Christ in the Sacrament, and "plenary remyssyon and forgyvenesse" of sins. Though the prayers professedly originate from the devotions of a "woman, solitary and recluse", there is no sign in them at all of that growing gulf between individual and official religion which some historians have held to be characteristic of the period. They are resolutely churchly in tone, and presuppose the Church's sacramental and penitential system, a presupposition spelled out in the very first prayer, with its concluding plea:"For mynde of thys blessyd passyon, I beseche the, benygne Jesus, graunte me afore my dethe very contrycyon, true confession, and satysfaccyon, and of all my synnes clene remyssyon. Amen."

Indeed, it is in the quest for "clene remyssyon", a phrase redolent of the late Middle Ages' preoccupation with Purgatory and the system of indulgences, that we touch what was probably the principal reason for the widespread use at every social level of these prayers. Many of the prayers circulating among the laity had accompanying indulgences or legends, designed to impress on the devotee the particular benefits of that devotion. The "Oes" had one of the most striking and circumstantial of all. Though the legend varied in details and degree of particularity, its overall features remain consistent. "A woman solitary and recluse", often identified

---

[50] J. C. Hirsch, "A Middle English Version of the Fifteen Oes from Bodleian Add MS B 66" *Neuephilologische Mitteilungen*, LXXV, 1974, pp. 98–114: H. White, *The Tudor Books of Private Devotion*, 1951, pp. 216–29.

with St Bridget of Sweden, desired to know the exact number of
Christ's Wounds in the course of his Passion. At last Christ told her
that if she recited each day fifteen Paters and fifteen Aves, at the
end of one year "thou shalt have worshypped every wounde and
fulfylled the nombre of the same." Christ then revealed to her the
"Fifteen Oes", promising that if recited each day for a whole year
they would effect the release from Purgatory of fifteen of the
devotee's kinsmen, and would keep fifteen of his or her living kin
in grace. Those who recited the prayers would be granted "bitter
contrition of alle his olde synnes", and fifteen days before their
death "schall see myn holy body and it receyve . . . And I shall yeve
him drynk of myn blood that he shall never thyrst. And I shall put
before him the sygne of my victoryous passoun . . . and before his
deth I shall come with my dere Moder and take his soul and lede it
into everlastyng joye . . . and whatsoever he ask rightfully of me or
of my Moder it schall not be denyed." Every recitation would
bring forty days of pardon, those due to die would have their
lives lengthened, those in danger of damnation would have their
sentence commuted to Purgatory, those in danger of the worst
pains of Purgatory would endure only the pains of this world, and
have Heaven at last. Wherefore, Christ urged, let "every lettered
man and woman read eche day these orisones of my bytter passion
for his sowlen medicine".[51]

These extraordinary promises, restrainedly characterized by
Fr Wilmart as *très indiscrets*, are a curious amalgam of pietism,
presumption, and insecurity. Much in them simply picks up the
themes and even the very language of the prayers themselves, as in
the promises of drinking Christ's blood so as never to thirst again,
or the theme of the soul's medicine, echoing the "Jesu, heavenly
physician" of the fourth prayer. Such promises could readily
enough be accommodated as an emphatic way of reiterating the
prayers themselves. But the circumstantial guarantees of pardon
and deliverance for souls in danger of damnation were a different
matter, and much less easy to accommodate within even the wide
bounds of fifteenth-century orthodoxy. Yet they were clearly
immensely attractive to lay people. Though the legend was usually
drastically pruned in the printed *Horae*, the promise of delivery to
the souls of fifteen kindred in Purgatory was a constant, as was
the promise to grant any request made of God "yf it be to the

---

[51] Latin text in Leroquais, *Livres d'Heures*, II pp. 97–9: translation in Bodleian Tanner MS
407, fols 42r–43v; *Reynes Commonplace*, pp. 264–8; another version in Lyell MS 30, fols
42r–43r; Latin version in Cambridge University Library MS Ii.vi. 43 fols 100v–103r.

salvacyon of your soule".[52] This latter phrase is an anodyne and harmless formula, an escape clause which commits the divine guarantor to nothing. It is the promise of benefit to deceased kindred, therefore, which seems closest to the nub of the matter. We are confronted with a paradox. These beautiful and complex prayers were certainly valued for their content. The circulation of a range of translations and the inclusion of such vernacular versions in the printed *Horae*, which were otherwise largely confined to Latin prayers, testifies to this. Equally clearly, the "Oes" were valued at least as much for their simple instrumental effectiveness in releasing the souls of the devotee's kinsfolk from the pains of Purgatory. There is no easy resolution of this contradiction between devout interiority of devotion on the one hand, and an apparently crudely mechanical view of the power of "good words" on the other. Indeed, as we shall see, that paradox lies close to the heart of late medieval English religion.

Devotions to the Virgin

Given the development of the Book of Hours round the Little Office of the Blessed Virgin, it would not be difficult to argue that the whole of the primer was in some sense a Marian prayer-book. Devotions to Mary proliferated in late medieval England as elsewhere in Christian Europe, and indeed Englishmen were encouraged to think of their country as being in a special way "Mary's Dowry", a notion propagated, for example, by the custodians of the shrine at Walsingham. Her cult came second only to that of Christ himself, and towered above that of all other saints. This is amply reflected in the *Horae*, which reflect a range of attitudes and responses to the figure of the Virgin. It was the Nativity which offered the most accessible context for the celebration of the Madonna, and in modern perceptions of the fifteenth century these devotions are perhaps most often associated with the awe and tenderness of Nativity poems, like the exquisite fifteenth-century meditation on the Incarnation "I syng of a mayden". For all its delicacy of touch and deep personal feeling, that poem was firmly rooted in the worship and teaching of the Church about Mary, and had behind it a battery of "learned" imagery, such as Gideon's Fleece, on which the dew fell when all the ground was dry, often used as a symbol of Mary, and the Advent responsary, "Rorate Coeli" – "Drop down your dew, ye heavens, from above" (Pl. 101).

[52] *Hor. Ebor.*, p. 76 n.2.

I syng of a m[a]yden that is makeles.
kyng of alle kynges to here sone che ches.
he cam also stylle there his moder was
as dew in aprylle, that fallyt on the gras.
He cam also stylle to his moderes bowr
as dew in aprille, that fallyt on the flour.
He cam also stylle ther his moder lay
as dew in aprille, that fallyt on the spray.
Modcr & mayden was never non but che –
wel may swych a lady godes moder be.[53]

But the prayers to the Virgin that made their way into the *Horae*
were mostly in Latin, and less personal than "I syng of a mayden".
Some of them simply elaborate the prayers to Mary used in the
liturgy, such as the "Salve Regina" or the "Ave Maria". Others
celebrated her exalted status and titles and her virtues, such as
purity and tenderness towards sinners.[54] Some are invocations to
her quite specifically as protectress against disease or danger: the
frequently recurring hymn "Stella Celi extirpavit" explores the
"Eva/Ave" idea of Mary's reversal of the evils brought by our
first parents – specifically here disease – and invariably appears
with a rubric explaining that it was effective "contra pestem". Its
popularity is attested by the fact that the shepherds in the N–Town
plays sing it as they travel to Bethlehem, and it was singled out for
reforming attack in the 1530s.[55] A favourite form of Marian piety
was the use of prayers and meditations on her Joys and Sorrows.
The Joys of Mary, most commonly in England counted as five –
Annunciation, Nativity, the Resurrection, Ascension, and her own
Coronation in Heaven – were familiar to every man, woman, and
child from their endless reproduction in carving, painting, and
glass. They were central to the great cycles of Corpus Christi
plays and, with the opportunities they offered for tenderness and
devotional elaboration, were a natural theme for carols and other
verses. As one might expect, therefore, they formed the basis for a
number of prayers in the *Horae*, most characteristically the hymn
"Gaude Virgo Mater Christi". Marian piety lent itself naturally to
vernacular elaboration for devotional purposes, and Latin poems

[53] Carleton Brown, *Religious Lyrics of the XV Century*, 1939, p. 119.
[54] For an example of the elaboration of familiar prayers, see the "Golden" prayer, "Ave
Rosa sine spinis", *Hor. Ebor.*, p. 136, which is based on the Ave Maria; for examples of the
celebration of Mary's titles and virtues see "Gaude Flore Virginali" *Hor. Ebor.*, pp. 64–6, and
the "Ave Maria, Ancilla Sancte Trinitatis", ibid. p. 137.
[55] *Hor. Ebor.*, p. 69; Block (ed.), *Ludus Coventriae*, p. 148; Hoskins, pp. 165, 169–70.
Rosemary Woolf saw its presence in the N–Town play as evidence of the learned ambience of
the original, thereby, in my view, missing the essential point – Woolf, *Mystery Plays*, p. 183.

like the "Gaude Virgo" were widely imitated in English. The London grocer Richard Hill collected many, like this macaronic one, which uses the final line of each stanza of the "Gaude Virgo" as the concluding line of each English verse (Pl. 102–3):

> Gaude Maria, Cristis Moder!
> Mary myld, of the I mene;
> Thou bare my Lord, thou bare my broder;
> Thou bare a louly child and clene.
> Thou stodyst full still withowt blyn,
> Whan in thy ere that arand was done so;
> Tho gracius God the lyght with-yn
> Gabrielis nuncio.
>
> Gaude Maria, yglent with grace!
> Whan Jhesus, thi son, on the was bore,
> Full nygh thy brest thou gan hym brace;
> He sowked, he sighhed, he wepte full sore.
> Thou fedest the flowr that never shall fade,
> Wyth maydens mylke, and songe ther-to:
> "Lulley, my swet! I bare the, babe,
> Cum pudoris lillio . . .
>
> Gaude Maria, thou rose of ryse!
> Maydyn and moder, both jentill and fre,
> Precius prynces, perles of pris,
> Thy bowr ys nect the trynyte.
> Thy sone, as lawe askyth a-right,
> In body and sowle the toke hym to;
> Thou regned with hym, right as we fynd,
> In celi palacio.
>
> Now blessid byrde, we pray the a bone:
> Be-fore thy son for us thou fall,
> and pray hym, as he was on the rode done,
> and for us dranke asell and gall,
> That we may wone withyn that wall,
> Wher ever ys well without wo,
> and graunt that grace unto us all
> In perhenni gaudio.[56]

But the most distinctive manifestation of Marian piety in late medieval England was not devotion to the Joys, but rather to the

[56] Dybosky, *Songs*, no. 69; see also nos 29, 43; *Hor. Ebor.*, pp. 63–5.

Sorrows of Mary. This was of course a European rather than a merely English phenomenon, and was yet another aspect of the devotion to the Passion which expressed itself in such prayers as the "Fifteen Oes". As it developed in the later Middle Ages the cult of the Sorrows of the Virgin, or the Mater Dolorosa, had a variety of functions, high among them that of serving as an objective correlative for the discharge of grief and suffering in the face of successive waves of plague sweeping through Christendom. As one might expect, much of the writing and visual art in which the theme of Mary's sorrows were expressed is over-fervid, even hysterical. But the essence of the devotion was that evident in what is arguably its noblest expression, the "Stabat Mater".[57] Here the Virgin's grief is presented, not as an end in itself, but as a means of arousing and focusing sympathetic suffering in the heart of the onlooker. In this literal compassion, this identification with the sufferings of Christ by sharing the grief of his Mother, lay salvation:

> Eia Mater, fons amoris
> Me sentire vim doloris
> Fac, ut tecum lugeam.

[Come then Mother, the fount of love, make me feel the force of your grief, make me mourn with you.]

> Fac me tecum pie flere,
> Crucifixo condolere,
> Donec ego vixero.

[Make me weep lovingly with you, make me feel the pains of the crucified, as long as I shall live.]

> Juxta crucem tecum stare,
> Et me tibi sociare
> In planctu desidero.

[I long to stand with you by the Cross, and to be your companion in your lamentation.]

> Fac, ut portem Christi mortem,
> Passionis fac consortem,
> Et plagas recolere.

[Grant that I may carry within me the death of Christ, make me a partner in his Passion, let me relive his wounds.]

[57] As the Stabat Mater is not included in *Hor. Ebor.* I have followed the text edited by C. Blume and H. M. Bannister in *Analecta Hymnica Medii Aevi*, 1886–1922, LIV, 1915, pp. 312–18.

This quest for a share in the sufferings of Christ, through identification with Mary, dominated the piety of Christian Europe in the
fourteenth and fifteenth centuries. It gave rise to literally thousands
of treatises, hymns, poems, sermons, and devotional images, and
the Sarum missal, like other pre-Tridentine rites, provided a *Missa
Compassionis sive Lamentationis beatae Mariae Virginis*.[58] Mary was a
natural focus for the attempt to realize for oneself the sufferings
of Jesus, for she had stood by the cross, supported by John the
beloved disciple, when the rest of the Apostles had fled. Her
Mother's grief could be dramatized so as to melt the hearts of those
whom the stark facts of the crucifixion left untouched.

> Quis est homo qui non fleret
> Matrem Christi si videret
> in tanto supplicio?

[Who is there who would not weep, were he to see the Mother
of Christ, in so great anguish?]

That question was dramatized in the vernacular in a thousand
forms:

> I said I coud not wepe I was so harde hartid:
> Shee answered me with wordys shortly that smarted,
> "Lo! nature shall move thee thou must be converted,
> Thyne owne fadder thys nyght is deed!" – lo thus she
>   thwarted –
> > "So my son is bobbid
> > & of his lif robbid."
> > forsooth than I sobbid,
> > verifying the words she seid to me
> > who cannot weep may lern at mee.[59]

Every parish church contained an image of this Mater Dolorosa, for
all were dominated by the Rood across the chancel arch, invariably
flanked by the mourning figures of Mary and the Beloved Disciple.
Other images, however, proliferated to sharpen the point. Of these
the most widespread was the *Pietà*, or image of Our Lady of Pity,
which spread in England in the course of the fifteenth century.
There was a typical one at Long Melford in Suffolk "a fair image of
our Blessed Lady having the afflicted body of her dear Son, as he
was taken down off the Cross lying along on her lap, the tears as it
were running down pitifully upon her beautiful cheeks, as it seemed
bedewing the said sweet body of her Son, and therefore named the
Image of our Lady of Pity".[60] We have the recorded response of an

---

[58] *Missale*, cols 919*–924*.
[59] Carleton Brown, *Religious Lyrics of the XV Century*, pp. 17–18.
[60] Parker, *History of Long Melford*, pp. 70–3.

East Anglian bourgeois woman to one of these images. Margery Kempe tells us that once she entered a church where there was an image of Our Lady of Pity, and

> thorw the beholding of that pete hir mende was al holy occupyed in the Passyon of owr Lord Ihesu Crist & in the compassyon of owr Lady, Seynt Mary, be whech sche was compellyd to cryyn ful lowde & wepyn ful sor, as thei sche xulde a deyd. Than cam to hir the . . . preste seying, "Damsel, Ihesu is ded long sithyn." Whan her crying was cesyd, sche seyd to the preste, "Sir, hys deth is as fresch to me as he had deyd this same day, & so me thynkyth it awt to be to yow & to alle Cristen pepil. We awt euyr to han mende of hys kendnes & euyr thynkyn of the dolful deth that he deyd for vs."[61]

Whatever one may think of its expression, Margery's fundamental response to the Pietà was by no means untypical. Images of Our Lady of Pity exercised a growing attraction throughout the fifteenth and early sixteenth centuries. Lay people in increasing numbers left money in their wills to maintain lights before them and sought burial near them. Crude devotional woodcuts of Our Lady of Pity circulated, modelled on the Mass of St Gregory, with the same border of the Arms of the Passion, to enable the beholder to meet Margery's demand that all Christians should think of "the dolful deth that he deyd for us". Like the Image of Pity proper, such images were often accompanied by lavish (and apocryphal) indulgences.[62]

This cult was abundantly reflected in and fostered by the *Horae* and private collections of prayers. Many of the *Horae* had the Hours of the Compassion of the Virgin, a set of verses with response and collect tracing the progress of the Passion through Mary's eyes, inserted after each of the Hours in the Little Office.[63] The "Stabat Mater" itself, which did not feature in the Sarum missal or breviary, was a very frequent devotion in the *Horae*, with a rubric promising "vii yers of pardon and xl lentys" to all who would devoutly say "thys lamentable contemplation of our blessyd lady stondynge onder the crosse wepyng and havyng compassion wyth her swethe sone Jesus".[64] An apocryphal devotion to the Sorrows of the Virgin ascribed to St Anselm is found in many fifteenth-century manuscript collections, and clearly enjoyed very wide popularity. It told of a vision St John the Evangelist had, in which Mary and Jesus discussed her five Sorrows, and Jesus promised

[61] *The Book of Margery Kempe*, p. 148.
[62] See the example reproduced opposite p. 87 of Douglas Grey, *Themes and Images*.
[63] *Hor. Ebor.*, pp. 47ff.
[64] RSTC 15939, Hoskins, no. 67 fol lxiii (v).

that what man or woman dewoutely schalle have compassyon
of these grete sorowes & hertely that prayeth. # For the first
sorow I wolle hym asoyle of alle maner of synne & amonge my
chylderyn reseyve hym in-to blysse. # He that prayth for the
secunde sorow schalle have before hys dethe veray contricyon wt
parfyte love & charite . . .[65]

But by far the most important of Marian devotions in the *Horae*
was the "Obsecro Te", a lengthy and comprehensive prayer to
Mary, celebrating her Joys as well as her Sorrows, but having as its
central pivot her grief under the Cross as she beheld her dead
Son. This prayer was one of the invariable elements in the *Horae*,
found in virtually every edition, printed or manuscript. It therefore
originated before the emergence of the iconography of Our Lady
of Pity, and it was often illustrated in French *Horae* with tender
images of the Virgin of Humility, suckling the child Jesus.[66] But in
England by the end of the fifteenth century the cult of Our Lady of
Pity was exerting an irresistible centripetal pull, and, at least in the
printed *Horae*, the "Obsecro Te" was often described as a prayer
"Before Our Lady of Pity", and carried a rubric promising

> To all them that be in the state of grace that daily say devoutly
> this prayer before our blessed lady of pitie, she wyll shewe them
> her blessyd vysage and warne them the daye et the owre of
> dethe, et in theyr laste ende the aungelles of God shall yelde theyr
> sowles to heven, & he shall obteyne v hundred yeres & soo many
> lentes of pardon graunted by v holy fathers popes of Rome.[67]

The prayer falls into four sections. In the first the Virgin is greeted
with a litany of tender titles, emphasizing her purity and perfection,
but above all her tenderness towards the erring and unhappy. The
effect is that of a litany:

> I implore you, holy Lady, Mother of God most full of tender
> love, daughter of the High King, mother most glorious, mother
> of orphans, consolation of the desolate, right road for all who go
> astray, health and hope of those who hope in thee. Virgin before
> childbirth, Virgin in childbirth, Virgin after childbirth. Fount of
> mercy, fount of health and grace, fount of tenderness and joy,
> fount of consolation and gentleness.

The second section invokes Mary's aid by reminding her of the

---

[65] *A Worcestershire Miscellany compiled by John Northwood, c.1400*, ed. N. S. Baugh, 1956,
pp. 151–2; *Hor. Ebor.*, pp. 178–9; CUL MS Hh.i.11 fol. 136; CUL MS Ii.vi.43 fols
82v–85v. The promised benefits vary slightly from version to version.
[66] V. Reinberg, "Popular Prayers", pp. 116–24.
[67] *Hor. Ebor.*, pp. 66–7.

joy of her part in the Incarnation, from the Annunciation to her Assumption, dwelling on the mystery of God's work in her, and her exaltation above all creation because of her humble acceptance of God's will for her:

By that holy and inestimable joy which exalted your spirit in that hour when, through the Archangel Gabriel, the Son of God was announced to you and conceived in you. And by the Divine Mystery which the Holy Spirit then worked in you. And by that holy and inestimable tender care, grace, mercy, love and humility by which the Son of God descended to take human flesh in your most venerable womb . . . And by those most holy Fifteen Joys which you had from your Son Our Lord Jesus Christ.

The third section of the prayer moves from the Joys of Mary to her Sorrows, invoking her help in the name of all the pain she endured as witness to her Son's Passion:

By that great and holy compassion and most bitter sorrow of heart which you had when Our Lord Jesus Christ was stripped naked before the Cross, and you saw him raised up and hanging there, crucified, wounded, thirsting with bitter gall set before him, when you heard him cry out and saw him dying. And by your Son's five Wounds, and the sorrow you had to see him wounded: And by the fountains of his blood, and all his passion, and by all the sorrows of your heart, and by the fountains of your tears: that with all the saints and chosen ones of God you may come and hasten to help and counsel me in all my prayers and petitions, and in everything I shall do, say or think, by day or by night, every hour and minute of my life.

The final section of the prayer rehearses the benefits the suppliant seeks through Mary's intercession. They comprise everything conceivable – long life, health, peace, but above all the spiritual gifts a Christian requires to get to Heaven. Despite its length, the list deserves quotation as a summary of the good life as it was then conceived:

and the grace of the Holy Spirit, so that He may rightly order all my actions, and that He may keep my soul, rule my body, raise my understanding, direct my courses, order my behaviour, test my actions, perfect my wishes and desires, instil holy thoughts, forgive my past offences, correct my present ones, and restrain my future sins. May He grant me an honest and honourable life, and victory over my adversities in this world. May He grant me blessed peace, both spiritual and bodily, good

hope, charity, faith, chastity, humility and patience. May He rule
and protect my five bodily senses, make me fulfil the Seven
Works of Mercy, and to hold and believe firmly the Twelve
articles of Belief and the Ten Commandments. May He liberate
and defend me from the Seven Deadly Sins to the end of my life.
And in my last days show me your face and tell me the day and
hour of my death, and receive and answer this suppliant prayer,
and grant me eternal life. Hear and answer me most sweet
Virgin Mary, Mother of God, Mother of Mercy. Amen.

The popularity of this prayer, windy and repetitious though it is, is
not difficult to understand. The litany in the first section, with
its hypnotic insistence on Mary's gentleness and pity, her role as
consolation of the desolate and guide of the wanderer, sets the
tone for the whole devotion, and is taken up again in the final
phrase of the prayer, "mater dei et [mater] misericordiae". The
Mother of Mercy was one of Mary's most resonant medieval titles,
unforgettably carved, painted, or engraved, extending her shelter-
ing cloak over the suppliant faithful and enshrined in the most
haunting of Marian prayers, the "Salve Regina". All over Europe
the singing of the "Salve" each night after compline had become a
popular devotion, and English testators left bequests for lights,
incense, and musical accompaniment to dignify this most tender of
tributes to the Mother of Mercy.[68] The tenderness of Mary as
Mother of Mercy was sometimes contrasted to the justice and
severity of the Father and Son, but not here: the section on Mary's
joys accentuates the "tender care, grace, mercy, love and humility"
of Christ in the Incarnation, and Mary here is a mirror reflecting
qualities found in God. This is emphatically the sense of the passage
on her Sorrows, where the prayer shifts without any sense of
incongruity between those sorrows, and the sufferings of Jesus
which were their cause, and even pairs his sorrows and hers – "per
fontes sanguinis sui . . . et per fontes lachrymarum tuarum". It is no
surprise therefore that this prayer to Mary becomes for its final
section (a third of the whole), a prayer for and to the Holy Spirit.

What is striking about the content of this final section is how
closely it corresponds to the catechetical programme of the late
medieval Church. The twelve articles of belief, the Ten Commandments, the seven deadly sins, the seven corporal works of mercy,
the five bodily wits, the theological and cardinal virtues – clause by

[68] St Mary at Hill CWA, pp. 4–9, 12; Bristol St Nicholas CWA, p. 50; Salisbury St
Edmund CWA, p. 100 (Marian revival). It is worth noting that the text of the "Salve
Regina" in the *Horae* was sometimes accompanied by an image of Our Lady of Pity – *Hor.
Ebor.*, p. 62.

clause, the prayer covers the material found in catechetical and confessional manuals and textbooks, a summary of what every good Christian was expected to know and to do. The churchly quality evident in some of the petitionary sections of the "Fifteen Oes" is even more striking in the "Obsecro Te". Popular piety seems here to have absorbed and interiorized clerical objectives without any sense of incongruity, and the cult of Mary appears to have been successfully harnessed to underline and reinforce a programme of Christian education, both in affective devotion to the Passion and in the elements of the Christian life. In fact, many of the fourteenth- and early fifteenth-century English primers had contained more elaborate catechetical material of precisely this sort, very often in rhyme for easier memorizing. The same fear of Lollardy which led to the disappearance for a century of English primers seems to have led to the exclusion of this material from the Latin *Horae*, though it continued to circulate widely among the laity and to be used by the clergy in their parochial work. The presence of such material in compressed form in the "Obsecro Te", therefore, represents the persistence of an earlier tradition and a testimony to the interconnection of official and popular piety.

The devotions considered in this chapter reflect the democratization of the tradition of affective meditation on the Passion which was the staple of the religious practice of the devout and the religious élite of late medieval England and Europe in general. They are, to that extent, a faithful reflection of the devotional preoccupations found in the hothouse *dévot* world of the Lady Margaret, or the circles of laity associated with Carthusian and Brigittine spiritual direction. That such concerns were by the fifteenth century becoming democratized and spreading to the "middling" people of the towns is evident from the *Book of Margery Kempe*. Their presence on such a massive and dominant scale in the *Horae*, books increasingly aimed at a wider and humbler readership as printing made devotional books cheap, is eloquent testimony to the social homogeneity of late medieval religion.

CHAPTER 8

CHARMS, PARDONS, AND PROMISES: LAY PIETY AND "SUPERSTITION" IN THE PRIMERS

To turn from the Passion devotions of the primers to the morning, evening and other prayers found there is, at first sight, to enter an entirely different world. Many are what one would expect in any practical guide to daily prayer – what to do at Mass, prayers to use at the sacring, prayers for protection in daily tasks. A substantial group of prayers focuses on the moment of death: and the preoccupation with the trials and temptation the dying can expect from the Devil, which is the main theme of the *Ars Moriendi*, features large here. This, indeed, is almost the dominant note struck in the small group of English prayers regularly included in the printed *Horae*, with their repeated affirmations of faith whatever temptation to despair or unbelief might trouble their last moments: "I poore synner make this daye in despyte of the fende of hell protestacyon . . . yf by aventure . . . I fall or declyne in peryll of my soule, or preiudyce of my helthe, or in errour of the holy fayth catholyke . . ."[1]

Behind such prayers lay a vivid and urgent sense of the reality of the demonic, and the Christian's need for eternal vigilance. The sense of defiance in the face of relentless enemies is an insistent and striking feature in prayer after prayer of the *Horae*, many of which take the form of exorcisms or adjurations. This note is struck at once in the series of invocations with which the prayers of the *Horae* generally begin:

> per signum sancte crucis de inimicis nostris libera nos deus noster . . .
>
> Crux triumphalis domini nostri Iesu Christi, ecce vivifici crucis dominicum signum: fugite partes adverse. In nomine Patris et filii et Spiritus Sancti. Amen.[2]

---

[1] *Hor. Ebor.*, p. 87.
[2] *Hor. Ebor.*, pp. 34–5; Hoskins, p. 109.

"Flee, you enemies": this was no mere pious convention. The private devotions of earnest lay people in fifteenth- and sixteenth-century England included many urgent and eloquent prayers for deliverance from their enemies. Richard III had one such prayer copied into his Book of Hours calling on the Saviour who had reconciled the human race to God and made peace between men and angels to free him from the plots of his enemies. In mid-fifteenth-century Yorkshire Robert Thornton prayed to the Trinity to

> give me, your servant Robert, victory over all my enemies, that they not be able to oppose me, nor to harm me, nor to speak against me . . . Christ conquers, Christ reigns, may Christ deign to make me victor over all my adversaries . . . Deliver me Lord Jesus Christ from all enemies, both visible and invisible, [for you] were hung upon a cross, and allowed your side to be pierced with a lance, and with your holy and precious blood have redeemed me, as you freed Susannah from a false accusation, and the three young men from the burning fiery furnace . . . and as you drew Daniel out from the lion's den.[3]

Who were these enemies? Thornton's prayer calls for deliverance from enemies "visibiles et invisibiles", and for liberation "from all my sins, tribulations and anxieties, and from every danger of soul and body". His enemies, therefore, were at least in part spiritual enemies. In a prayer which has many similarities to Thornton's, the early sixteenth-century London grocer, Richard Hill, clearly also had such spiritual enemies in mind, but the terms of his prayer make it clear that he also sought deliverance from earthly foes:

> Deign, Lord Jesus Christ, to establish and confirm peace and concord between me and my enemies, and stretch out your grace over me, and pour out your mercy, and deign to moderate and extinguish the hatred and wrath which my enemies have towards me, as you removed the wrath and hatred which Esau had against his brother Jacob . . . free me as you freed . . . Susannah from false accusation, . . . Daniel from the lion's den, the three young men . . . from the burning fiery furnace . . . by your holy incarnation . . . by your labours and afflictions . . . by the seven words you spoke on the cross . . . I beseech you Lord Jesus Christ my redeemer guide and keep me, your unworthy servant

---

[3] Horstmann, *Yorkshire Writers*, I pp. 376–7. For Richard III's prayer, and a valuable discussion of the type as a whole, see Anne F. Sutton and Livia Visser-Fuchs, *The Hours of Richard III*, 1990, pp. 67–78.

{Richard} from the malicious foe and from all who hate me
and from all dangers of soul and body now and in time to come
(Pl. 104).[4]

Both these prayers, and that of Richard III, draw on the commendation of the departing soul, "Proficiscere anima Christiana",
recited by the priest assisting at the deathbed: this is the source of
the references to David, Daniel, Susannah, and the three young
men. Realization of that indebtedness helps us define the enemies
referred to in such prayers more clearly, for the "Proficiscere anima
Christiana" is immediately preceded in the service of commendation by a set of petitions which name them:

> From the ancient enemy: free and defend his soul, O Lord
> From the stratagems and snares of the devil; free &c
> From the onslaught of malignant spirits: free &c
> From the fear of enemies: free and defend &c.[5]

As that passage suggests, the enemy most feared by late medieval
men and women was the "malicious foe" of Hill's prayer,
mankind's "ancient enemy", the Devil. There was no contradiction
between this identification of the enemy with the spirit of evil,
on the one hand, and Hill's evident preoccupation with concrete
earthly foes on the other, for in late medieval thought the Devil and
his fallen angels were held to be the source of all the evils which
afflicted humanity, including enmity and maleficence between
people:

> thay rerythe warres: thay makyth tempestys in the see, and
> drownyth schyppes and men, thay makythe debate bytwyx
> neghtburs and manslaght therwyth; thay tendyth fyres, and
> brennen howses and townes; thay reryth wyndys, and blowyth
> don howsys, stepuls, and tres; thay make wymen to ouerlaye hor
> children; thay makyth men to sle homsolfe, to hong homsolfe
> othyr drowne hom in wanhope, and such mony othyr curset
> dedys.[6]

Given the scope of the Devil's brief, it is no surprise to find that
private devotional collections and the manuscript and printed *Horae*

---

[4] Balliol MS 354, transcript pp. 203–4, my translation.
[5] *Manuale*, pp. 116–17.
[6] *Festial*, p. 150; *Dives and Pauper*, I p. 152 – the devils have leave of God "to causen
hedows tempest, to enfectyn and envenymen the eyr and causen moreyn and sykness, hunger
and droughte, dessencioun and werre be destruccioun of charite, be myspryde, covetyse,
lecherye, wratthe, envye".

abound in prayers against him and all his works. It is the character of these prayers which is liable to surprise. At one level Thornton's and Hill's prayers are essentially extended intercessions, appealing to God for his help and invoking the incarnation and sufferings of Christ as part of their persuasive technique. But like many of the prayers against the Devil and other evils found in the *Horae* they also come very close to litany or invocation, at times indeed closer to spells or charms than anything else. A rubric regularly prefixed to the very similar prayer used by Richard III promised that if used on thirty successive days by one free from mortal sin, "all his trouble will turn to joy and comfort, whether he says it for himself or for another."[7] If prayers like the "Fifteen Oes" or the "Obsecro Te" take us into the mainstream of late medieval affective piety, and the centrality of the Passion of Jesus as a focus for prayer and meditation, these prayers for deliverance from evil seem to point rather to a devotional underground of dubiously orthodox religion in which the dividing line between prayer and magic is not always clear. Confronting such prayers, we seem worlds away from the élite piety of the disciples of Rolle, of the Carthusians of Sheen and Mount Grace, and of well-to-do lay devotees like the Lady Margaret. In fact, as we shall see, the issues are not so simple: the "popular" religion revealed in these prayers has more in common not only with the élite piety of the devout, but with the official liturgy of the Church, than might at first appear.

Consideration of three frequently recurring "magical" prayers will serve to highlight the complexities of the relationship between popular and élite or official religion in the *Horae*, and therefore in lay piety in general. These are the prayer "Deus propicius esto", for the protection of angels; the related invocation of the Cross "Crux Christi sit (semper) mecum"; and the invocation of the names of God "Omnipotens + Dominus + Christus".

Deus Propicius Esto
God be favourable to me a sinner, and be my guard all the days of my life. God of Abraham, God of Isaac, God of Jacob, have mercy on me, and send to my aid Michael your Archangel, that he may keep, protect and defend me from all my enemies, visible and invisible.

Holy Michael, the Archangel of God, defend me in battle, that I may not perish in the dreadful judgement. Archangel of

---

[7] *The Hours of Richard III*, pp. 68–9.

Christ, by the grace which you have merited I beseech you, through Our Only-Begotten Lord Jesus Christ, draw me today and always from deadly peril. Holy Michael, Holy Gabriel, Holy Raphael, all holy angels and archangels of God, hasten to help me. I beseech you, all you heavenly Virtues, that by the power of the most high God you give me your aid, so that no enemy may be able to condemn or oppress me, neither in my house nor out of it, neither sleeping nor waking.

Behold + the cross of the Lord, begone you enemies. The lion of the tribe of Judah has conquered; root of David, stem of Jesse, saviour of the world, who have redeemed me through your cross and blood, save me, help me, my God. Agios, Agios, Agios. Cross of Christ protect me. Cross of Christ, save me. Cross of Christ, defend me from every evil.[8]

This is, among other things, a prayer to the Archangels Michael, Gabriel, and Raphael. Devotion to the angels was a prominent feature of late medieval piety. They are strikingly depicted in Henry VII's window at Great Malvern, and they dominated the decorative schemes of more than one fifteenth-century parish church, like the nine orders of angels painted on the Rood-screen at St Michael's, Barton Turf in Norfolk (Pl. 105), or at Southwold in Suffolk (Pl. 106), or the fluttering hosts carved in the roof of St Wendreda's, March. Michael, symbol of God's power and providence, was the representative figure here, depicted in armour treading down the ancient enemy in the form of a serpent or dragon, or weighing souls in paintings of the "iudicium tremendum" of the prayer (Pl. 107). He appears in both these activities on several Norfolk Rood-screens, often paired on either side of the doorway with St George, who seems to have served the same function as a visual image of the triumph of invincible goodness over demonic evil (Pl. 108–9).[8] This placing by the doorways between nave and sanctuary, between profane and sacred, is certainly deliberate, and sometimes elaborately contrived. Michael was the guardian spirit of the boundaries between worlds, and in this role he featured largely in depictions of the deathbed, widely believed to be the scene of pitched battles for possession of the soul as the devils threw all their malevolent energies into a last desperate onslaught on the dying Christian. Prayers to the guardian or "proper" angel were a feature of all the *Horae*, and vernacular versions of these in verse and prose were very common.[9]

[8] *Hor. Ebor.*, p. 125.
[9] For the angels in late medieval English art see G. McN. Rushforth, *Medieval Christian*

In the light of all this, the first part of the prayer, asking for the protection of the angels against peril from visible and invisible enemies, becomes readily intelligible. At first sight, the final part of the prayer, invoking the protection of the cross, also looks like a straightforward piece of pious self-exhortation. The presence of the sign of the cross in the text, however, suggests that something more complex is going on. The user of the prayer was expected at this point to make the sign of the cross, either on himself or in the air, as the priest did in ecclesiastical ceremonies, such as the blessing of holy water, and it is clearly envisaged that this act will cause the enemy to flee. This part of the prayer is an exorcism, and the exotic repetition of the Greek Trishagion and the threefold invocation of the cross are clearly designed to add to the incantatory effect. Incantations of this sort were extremely common at the end of the Middle Ages. The early sixteenth-century owner of a manuscript *Horae* now in the Cambridge University Library copied into it a typical example: "Agyos otheos sancte deus Agyos ischyros sancte fortis Agyos athanatos eleyson ymas. Sancte et immortalis miserere nobis Pater Noster Ave Maria + credo in deum."[10] This elaboration of the Trishagion in Greek and Latin, "Holy God, Holy Strong One, Holy Immortal One, Have mercy on us," is taken direct from the "Improperia" or "Reproaches" sung during the annual creeping to the cross in the liturgy of Good Friday. It was one of the most emotionally charged moments in the liturgical year, and it is not surprising to find it being used as "a good prayer ayenste the pestilence". Mirk has a story of a child "pult up ynto the ayre and soo ynto Heven" by angels during the Rogationtide procession, when the devils were being driven from the parish, in order to be

---

Imagery, 1936, pp. 204–16, and, more generally, J Villette, *L'Ange dans l'art d'Occident du XIIe au XVIe siècle*, 1940. Fifteenth- and early sixteenth-century representations of the Angelic Hierarchy can be found in glass at Combe Martin in Devon, Coxwold in Yorkshire, Great Malvern in Worcestershire, Great Snoring, Harpley, Salle, and Martham in Norfolk (more of the Martham angels are at Mulbarton), Hessett in Suffolk, Minster Lovell in Oxfordshire, All Saints, North Street, and St Michael, Spurriergate, in York. St Michael appears on panels on the screens at Barton Turf, Binham (painted over, but clearly visible), Elsing, Filby, Gressenhall, Ranworth and Wellingham in Norfolk, and at Somerleyton and Westhall in Suffolk. At Beeston next Mileham, St Michael has not been painted on the screen, but he and St George have been carved into the spandrels of the panels immediately on either side of the chancel door, Michael to the south, George to the north, as at Ranworth. Both carvings have been savagely defaced. The late medieval lore on the nature and work of the angels is conveniently set out in *Golden Legend*, V pp. 180–99. For a series of English prayers to the angels, see British Library Add MS 19596, fols 55v ff. and see Dyboski, *Songs*, p. 51; Cambridge University Library MS Dd.vi.1 fol. 144r has another such prayer "ad angelum proprium".

[10] CUL MS Dd.vi.1 fol. 143r.

taught these words: when he sang the words, God enabled the parishioners "forto feght wyth the fende".[11] In the inscription copied into the Book of Hours, the words were clearly being used as some sort of spell, depending on the innate power of the mysterious words, for the owner of the *Horae* noted "And ye must say this iii tymes."[12]

Similar presuppositions to these are at work in the "Deus Propicius esto" prayer. In some printings it is described as having been divinely revealed in the year 1485 to "A monk of Bynham", but elsewhere it carries a different attribution:

> Thys p[r]air was scewed un to saynt Augustine be revelation of the holy gooste & who that devoutly say thys prayer or here hyt rede or bereth abowte thaym schall not perische in fyer nor in wather nother batyll or in iugement and he schal dye no sodyne deeth and no wenowme schal poysyn hym that day and what he asketh of god he schal opteyne if yt be to the salvatyon of hys soull and whan thy soull schall deperte from thy body yt scall not entre to hell.[13]

Such apocryphal attributions to important figures, combined with extraordinary promises, were commonly attached to devotions in the late Middle Ages. We have already encountered those in the legend of the "Fifteen Oes", and every devotional collection of the period contained many of them. The Yorkshire gentleman Robert Thornton was a sophisticated and devout collector whose commonplace book preserves many of the spiritual classics of the late Middle Ages, especially those associated with Richard Rolle and his followers. Yet Thornton's prayer against enemies, examined at the beginning of this chapter, was prefaced by just such a set of legendary promises. The prayer is attributed to St Paul "by the Ensencesynge of the haly gaste", and those who recited it daily were promised remission of their sins and protection from an "evylle" death. Neither thieves nor enemies in battle would have power to harm them. Those who carried it about them would win favour "byfore kyng or prynce or any other lorde". A cup of water blessed by reciting the prayer over it would bring safe delivery to women in labour, or, cast into stormy seas, would quell them. Wheaten bread blessed in the same way was a speedy cure for diarrhoea![14]

---

[11] *Festial*, p. 151.

[12] CUL MS Dd.vi.1 fol. 143r.

[13] Hoskins, no. 67. STC 15939, fol. lxxix (v); modernized version printed in Hoskins, p. 124.

[14] Horstmann, *Yorkshire Writers*, I pp. 376.

The same pattern of apocryphal attribution, supernatural promises, and invocations against the "ancient enemy" occurs in the *Horae* devotions associated with the so-called letter to Charlemagne, the "Crux Christi" and the "Omnipotens + Dominus + Christus". A typical version of the rubric before the "Crux Christi" runs "Thys epystell of our sauvyour sendeth our holy father pope Leo unto the emperour Carolo magno of the wyche we fynd wryteyns who that bereth thys blessyn upon hym and says ut ones of a day schall opteyne xl ycre of pardon and lxxx lentys. And he schall not peryshe wyrt soden deeth."[15] The "epystell" which follows is an elaborate invocation of the cross, close in phrasing and content to the final section of the "Propicius esto":

Cross + of Christ be with me. Cross + of Christ is what I ever adore. Cross + of Christ is true health . . . May the Cross + of Christ banish all evil. Cross + of Christ . . . be ever over me, and before me, and behind me, because the ancient enemy flees wherever he sees you . . . Flee from me, a servant of God, o devil, by the sign of the holy Cross + behold the Cross of the Lord + begone you enemies, the lion of the tribe of Judah, the root of David, has conquered.[16]

The *Horae* rubric about the letter to Charlemagne before this prayer is a brief and relatively bowdlerized version of a legend which is found in literally dozens of forms in manuscript. Sometimes declared to have been brought direct from Heaven by an angel to Charlemagne on the eve of a battle against the Saracens to free the Holy Land, or forwarded to him via the Pope, usually Leo, but sometimes Pope Gregory or Pope Sylvester, the promise varies only in degrees of extravagance. Whoever carried it about them and recited it, or a prescribed number of Paters and Aves, would overcome their enemies, spiritual and physical, would not perish in battle and would not be robbed or slain by thieves. They would be immune to the dangers of pestilence, thunder, fire, and water, and would not be troubled by the evil spirits who turned all these to mischief. Pregnant women could ensure safe delivery and the survival of their children long enough to receive baptism by writing the prayer on a strip of parchment and placing it or wearing it round their bellies, and the prayer preserved against attacks of epilepsy, a disease then commonly associated with demonic possession.[17]

[15] Hoskins, no. 67, RSTC 15939, fol. lxxvii (v); modernized version in Hoskins, p. 124.
[16] Hoskins, no. 67, RSTC 15939, fol. lxxviii (r)–lxxix (r).
[17] C. F. Buhler, *Early Books and Manuscripts*, 1973, pp. 564–575; "Prayers and Charms in Certain Middle English Scrolls", *Speculum*, XXXIX, 1964, pp. 27–80; W. R. Jones, "The Heavenly Letter in Medieval England", *Medievalia et Humanistica*, ns VI, 1975, pp. 163–78.

The close correspondence between the benefits promised in the letter to Charlemagne and the conventional range of demonic activities listed by Mirk makes clear that the devotion, for all its extravagance, is essentially a prayer of exorcism. The prayer which makes up the epistle itself is not always the "Crux Christi", but the most usual alternative, the extraordinary invocation of the names of God beginning "Omnipotens + Dominus + Christus" is just as clearly an exorcism:

> Omnipotens + Dominus + Christus + Messias + Sother + Emmanuel + Sabaoth + Adonay + Unigenitus + Via + Vita + Manus + Homo + Ousion + Salvator + Alpha + et Oo + Fons + Origo + Spes + Fides + Charitas + Oza + Agnus + Ovis + Vitulus + Serpens + Aries + Leo + Vermis + Primus + Novissimus + Rex + Pater + Filius + Spiritus Sanctus + Ego sum + Qui sum + Creator + Eternus + Redemptor + Trinitas + Unitas + Clemens + Caput + Otheotocos + Tetragrammaton + May these names protect and defend me from all disaster, and from infirmity of body and soul, may they wholly set me free and come to my help.

> These names of the kings, that is, Jaspar, Melchior, Balthasar. And of the twelve Apostles Peter, Paul, Andrew, James, Philip, James, Simon, Jude, Thomas, Bartholomew. And of the four Evangelists, namely Mark, Matthew, Luke, John: may they assist me in all my necessities and defend and liberate me from all dangers, temptations and difficulties of body and soul, and from every evil, past present and future, keep me now and in eternity.

> O Lord Jesu Christ, I your unworthy servant [name] commit myself this day and always to the protection of your angels and saints: commit me to the protection of all your saints, as once, on the Cross, you committed the holy virgin Mary your mother to saint John the Evangelist, so that you may deign to keep me your unworthy servant [name] today and always, to bless, protect and save me from sudden and unprovided death and from every deceit of the devil, and from every enemy both visible and invisible. Amen.[18]

Once again, this prayer, like the preliminary legend, survives in countless permutations.[19] It appears in printed English *Horae* without the Charlemagne legend, being presented simply as "A prayer of the names of Christ". The legend, in any case, was

---

[18] *Hor. Ebor.*, p. 126.
[19] R. Scot, *The Discoverie of Witchcraft*, 1584, pp. 232–6; *Proceedings of the Society of Antiquaries*, 1877, pp. 302–3; Bodleian Library Lyell MS 30 fols 54v–55r.

attached to a range of texts, and indeed the place of these two prayers in the manuscript versions was often taken not by a text, but an image. The object which Charlemagne was to carry with him into battle was a representation or measure of the side Wound of Christ, or a cross which, multiplied fifteen or twenty-one times, gave the measure of Christ's body. Sometimes it is a drawing giving the measure of the nails of the Crucifixion. In these cases the references to Charlemagne often disappear altogether, while the other details of the promise remain, with their assurance of safety from death in battle or by fire or water, their protection for pregnant women, their guarantee of freedom from "unprovided" death, that is, death without the benefit of housel and shrift (Pl. 110, 112).[20]

What are we to make of all this? Here, it seems, are prayers which reveal a great ocean of popular belief infinitely remote from Christian orthodoxy: the apocryphal legend of the Emperor, the angel, and the Pope, the grotesque and materialistic promises attached not merely to devout use but to the simple possession of texts or images, and the use of a catena of sacred names, coupled with forty-seven signs of the cross to conjure away evil spirits, all seem to point to a magical rather than an orthodox religious outlook. Even Robert Thornton, whose learning and devotion are everywhere evident in his manuscript collections, copied a charm against the fever based on portions of the "Omnipotens + Dominus + Christus" which involved writing it on (presumably unconsecrated) Mass wafers which were then swallowed, and on parchment which was then burned.[21] The version of the Charlemagne legend included in the *Horae*, it is true, has generally been shortened and cleaned up, the promises reduced to the narrowly "spiritual" dimensions of indulgences and a guarantee of the Sacraments at death, yet the full-blown version of the legend was so widely known and so universally used that it is hard to believe that the users of the *Horae* could have been expected not to know it.

And the context which they would have supplied for it seems a bizarre mixture of piety and magic. The version copied into his commonplace book by the rural Norfolk church-reeve, Robert Reynes, combined the names of God with the "Christus vincit . . . fugite partes adverse" texts associated with invocations of the cross, but also contained among the names of God the magical words ANAZAPTA and AGLA, and the benefits promised were

---

[20] Buhler, *Early Books*, pp. 564–76.
[21] *Liber de Diversis Medicinis*, p. 63.

attributed to "the grace of God *and the vertue of these names*". An early fifteenth-century version written in Worcestershire claimed that "in this wrytyng ar to names ho-so nemyth hem tht day he schal not dye they he were hongud on a tre."[22] Most of the texts we have been considering occur regularly on medicinal or magical rolls, long strips of parchment inscribed with the prayers and their attached promises, evidently worn round the waist by women in labour and others in danger. The names of God and other exotic-sounding names, the manual signs and invocations of the cross, together with other texts possessing "vertu", such as the prologue to St John's Gospel, were regularly used in conjurations of spirits for purposes of divination, from the fourteenth to the eighteenth century.[23] Significantly, the Charlemagne legend and its promises never found their way into French printed *Horae*, and where any version of the prayer was included in printed *Horae* in France it was invariably shorn of its talismanic character. Though the full-blooded version of the legend does occur in surviving French *Horae*, it has generally been copied into the books, in untrained, non-scribal hands and often apparently from memory, by lay owners themselves. This suggests some effective French ecclesiastical concern about such prayers. English clerical control over the Sarum *Horae* seems to have been slacker, perhaps because most were printed in France or the Low Countries, and so a range of such texts made their way into print. Their presence in the Sarum and York *Horae* seems on the face of it to point to a demand among their readers for a folk religion which owed more to the survival of pagan and magical ways of thinking than to orthodox Christian piety. They cater, it would seem, for the same primitive level of folk belief represented in the night prayers of the shepherds in the Wakefield *First Shepherds* play:

> For ferde we be fryght, a crosse lett us kest –
> Cryst-crosse, benedyght eest and est –
> For drede,
> *Iesus onazarus*
> *Crucyefixus*,
> *Marcus, Andreus*
> God be oure spede![24]

[22] Bodleian Library Tanner MS 407 fol. 36r–36v, *Reynes Commonplace*, pp. 247–8; *A Worcestershire Miscellany*, p. 154.

[23] Scot, *Discoverie of Witchcraft*, pp. 401–20; W. Sparrow Simpson, "On a Seventeenth Century Roll Containing Prayers and Magical Signs", *Journal of the British Archaeological Association*, XL, 1884, pp. 297–332, and "On a Magical Roll Preserved in the British Library", *Journal of the British Archaeological Association*, XLVIII, 1892, pp. 38–54.

[24] V. Reinberg, *Popular Prayer in Late Medieval and Reformation France* pp. 288–300; *The Wakefield Pageants in the Towneley Cycle*, ed. A. C. Cawley, 1958, p. 50.

There can be no doubt that the guardians of official Christianity – theologians, pastors, inquisitors – did find such prayers and invocations in the mouths of the unlettered problematic, even in England. The *Doctrinal of Sapyence*, a manual for priests published by Caxton in 1489, tackled the Charlemagne prayers directly:

> Ther ben summe that make wrytynges and bryvettes full of crosses and other wrytynges. And sayen that alle they that bere suche brevettys on them may not perysshe in fyre ne in water: ne in other peryllous place: And ther ben also somme brevettis and wrtytynges whyche they doo bynde upon certeyn persones for to hele them of somme sekenesses and maladyes: And for admonycyon. ne for predycacyon. ne for excommynycacyon that may be doo to them they wyl not leve it: Alle they that make suche thynges / or doo mak it. or bere it. or do it to be born / And have trust and affyaunce therin. And they that selle it. gyve or leve it synnen ryght grevously. But yf they be symple people and so ignoraunt of symplesse / that by ignoraunce they be excused.[25]

There is here a clear association of the use of such prayers and charms with "symple people . . . ignoraunt of symplesse", and this is a view which has been taken up by historians of popular religion. For Jean Delumeau, the peasantry of late medieval Europe "were in fact polytheistic and deeply magical, making use of pagan rites and deflecting christian sacraments to this-worldly ends". Keith Thomas's discussion of late medieval English attitudes is more carefully nuanced, and he recognizes the sophistication of much lay religious belief and practice, but his overall view is not substantially different. Many theologians, he argues, were strongly "rationalist" in temperament, viewing "cautiously" the rites and ceremonies inherited from "a more primitive era", and regarding even the sacraments "as symbolic representations rather than as instruments of physical efficacy". Moreover, "the late medieval Catholic laity were not *all* ignorant peasants: they included educated urban dwellers who were intellectually more sophisticated than many of the clergy", and they had "a realistic social outlook". It was thus "only at popular level" that sacraments and other ecclesiastical rituals, prayers, and popular devotional practices "were credited with an inexorable and compelling power".[26]

The printing of the Charlemagne prayers and related invocations and charms in the *Horae* does not bear out these generalizations,

[25] *The Doctrinal of Sapyence*, fol. 4v.
[26] Natalie Davis, "Some Tasks and Themes in the Study of Popular Religion", p. 308; Thomas, *Religion and the Decline of Magic*, p. 53.

and neither does the provenance of many of the surviving manuscript versions. There certainly are indications that such devotions
were attractive to peasant Catholics of "symple" outlook. Robert
Reynes, the Norfolk country church-reeve, provides a good example.
The religious items in his collections all indicate just such an
unsophisticated and credulous faith as Delumeau and Thomas
describe: verse legends of the saints, or the signs of the end of the
world and its attendant horrors; a circumstantial version of the
legend of the "Fifteen Oes", charms for making angels appear in a
child's thumbnail, the Charlemagne prayers. Yet such items can all
be found just as readily in sources whose overall sophistication and
orthodoxy cannot be doubted. The clerical compilers of the great
collections of late medieval devotions found in Lyell Ms 30 in the
Bodleian, and Ii vi 43 in the Cambridge University Library both
preserved a number of charms and invocations of the Charlemagne
type, as did the devotional compilation prepared at the beginning of the fifteenth century by the Worcestershire cleric John
Northwood.[27] The versions of the "Deus Propicius esto" and the
"Omnipotens + Dominus + Christus" in the 1536 York Horae
were said to have been arranged and printed in the form of a
"treatyse concernynge the helthe of mannes soule" at the request of
Sir George Darcy, son of Lord Thomas Darcy who was to be
beheaded in the following year for complicity in the Pilgrimage
of Grace.[28] And perhaps most strikingly of all, the collection
of private prayers commissioned by the Lady Margaret for her
third husband, Thomas Stanley, and now at Westminster Abbey,
includes four distinct versions of the Charlemagne legend and its
accompanying invocation of the names of God.[29] Lady Margaret's
prayer-book is highly representative: though not a Book of Hours,
it contains not only many of the illustrations commonly found in
the Horae, but a very large number of the prayers most commonly
found there, such as the "Obsecro Te", the Prayer of St Bede, and
the "O Bone Jesu". This is not the devotional underground, it is
the devotional mainstream, and the prominence within it of the
Charlemagne legend and other related invocations and prayers
suggests that any attempt to explain this dimension of late medieval

[27] Bodleian Library Lyell MS 30 fols 13v–15r, 51v–55rv. For a list of some of the many
other MS versions, see A. De La Mare, Catalogue of the Collection of Medieval Manuscripts
Bequethed . . . By James Lyell, 1971, pp. 63–4; Cambridge University Library MS Ii. vi. 43
fols 20v–22r; A Worcestershire Miscellany Compiled by John Northwood c.1400, ed. N. S. Baugh,
1956, p. 154.
[28] Hor. Ebor., p. 125.
[29] Westminster Abbey, MS 39; the relevant section is printed in Proceedings of the Society of
Antiquaries, 2nd Series VII, 1877, pp. 302–3.

piety in terms of pagan survivalism among the uneducated peasantry is misconceived. These prayers were clearly a manifestation of popular religion, but it was a popular religion which extended from the court downwards, encompassing both clerical and lay devotion, which could place the Charlemagne prayers, without any apparent sense of incongruity, alongside classic devotional texts such as the "O Bone Jesu" or the "Anima Christi".

And in any case, it would be a mistake to see even these "magical" prayers as standing altogether outside the framework of the official worship and teaching of the Church. The world-view they enshrined, in which humanity was beleaguered by hostile troops of devils seeking the destruction of body and soul, and to which the appropriate and guaranteed antidote was the incantatory or manual invocation of the cross or names of Christ, is not a construct of the folk imagination. Such ideas were built into the very structure of the liturgy, and formed the focus for some of its most solemn and popularly accessible moments. This will become clear if we consider three such moments: the Rogation processions, the administration of baptism, and the blessings of salt and water every Sunday and of wax candles at Candlemas.

The Rogationtide processions took place on the three days leading up to Ascensiontide and were one of the principal focuses of parish identity. Everyone was expected to turn out for them, when the parish notables were expected to provide food and, especially, drink for their poorer neighbours. All the church banners were carried through the parish, and the processional crosses, and a standard of a dragon, carried with a long cloth tail before the procession on the first two of these "Cross-days" or "gang days", and carried, shorn of its tail, after the procession on the last day, as a symbol of the Devil's overthrow. For that was the principal purpose of the processions, to drive out of the parish, with bells and banners and the singing of the litany of the Saints, the spirits "that flye above in the eyer as thyke as motes in the sonne". At the centre of the ritual was the solemn reading of portions of the Gospel at stations on the boundaries of the parish, often marked by large wayside Crosses: the virtue of the words of the Gospel brought cleansing and fertility to the fields, and it was considered fortunate to hear these Gospels. This aspect of the ritual struck the reformers as particularly superstitious, and they bitterly condemned this "saying of the gospels to the corn in the field in the procession week, that it should the better grow".[30] Above all the ceremonies

---

[30] William Tyndale, *Answer to Sir Thomas More's Dialogue*, Parker Society, 1850, pp. 61–2.

centred on the carrying of the cross into the fields and lanes. Rogationtide was "Cross-tide", for the cross was the triumphal banner of Christ the conquerer, and the "spyrytes that flyethe on lofte in the eyer dredythe moch . . . cristis baners that ben the crossis a reysed." As John Longland declared, "wher soo ever the devyll . . . doo see the syne of this crosse, he flees, he byddes not, he strykys not, he cannot hurte."[31]

The baptismal liturgy was even more explicitly concerned with the expulsion of the Devil, not merely by the act of baptism itself, but by the elaborate prayers and ceremonies which preceded the immersion of the child in the font. These ceremonies centred on the exorcism and blessing of salt and of the baptismal water, and finally of the child, whose liberation from the power of Satan was symbolized by the imposition of the sign of the cross on head, breast, and hands. In a typical prayer, after putting salt in the child's mouth and invoking the protection of the angels on her, the priest addresses the devil:

> Therefore, cursed devil, know now your doom, and give honour to the true and living God, to his Son Jesus Christ, and to the Holy Spirit, and depart from this servant of God [Name], because that same God and Lord Jesus Christ has deigned to call her to his holy grace and blessing and to the baptismal font by the gift of the holy spirit. And do not dare to violate, o cursed devil, this sign of the holy Cross + which we now make on her forehead. Through Him who shall come to judge the living and the dead and the world by fire. Amen.[32]

As in the Rogationtide processions, everything about the baptismal rites emphasized the objective power of holy words, gestures, and things over the Devil. The blessed water in the font was kept under lock and key to prevent its removal and use in magical rites. The rubrics of the Sarum *Manual* forbade its use in the asperging of the people in other parts of the liturgy. This was not a simple matter of preventing superstition: the water itself was clearly considered to be both powerful and holy, and the priest was strictly charged to prevent anyone except the child from even touching the baptismal water. The chrisom or cloth tied over the anointed spot on the child's forehead was to be returned to the priest by the mother when she came for her churching, and he was to burn it, or keep it for "the uses of the church". The godparents were required to wash their hands before they left the church in case any of the holy oils

[31] Owst, *Preaching in Medieval England*, pp. 210–12; John Longlande, *A Sermond*, sig. G iii (r).
[32] *Manuale*, p. 27.

remained from contact with the child. The service ended with the priest reading over the child the Gospel "Respondens unus de turba" from St Mark, describing the casting out of a demon by Jesus because "according to the greatest scholars it was good for the falling sickness." This reading was followed immediately by the prologue of St John's Gospel, a text which, as we have already seen, was regularly used in exorcism, healing, and against thunder and storms.[33]

The same insistence on the objective power of sacred things and formulae, and especially of the sign of the cross, to banish the Devil characterized the service of blessing of salt and water, performed before Mass each Sunday. Both salt and water were exorcized with repeated signs of the cross, and the words of the exorcism attribute to the substances so hallowed actual power. The salt is to be "salvation of body and soul to all who take you", and "wherever you are sprinkled, let every delusion and wickedness, and every craftiness of devilish cunning, scatter and depart when called upon." The water was to acquire "effectual power" to cast out demons and drive away disease. It was to have such power not merely for people, but over inanimate objects, so that "whatever in the houses or places of the faithful shall be sprinkled with it, may be freed from all pollution, and delivered from harm." In all this, the instrument of blessing was the invocation of God's name, "per invocationem sancti tui nominis". By the repetition of that name every invasion of the unclean spirit was to be turned away, and "the dread of the venomous serpent driven far away".[34] Similarly, in the Candlemas ceremonies, candles were solemnly blessed "by the virtue of the holy Cross", and thereby acquired the power, wherever they were lit or set up, to send the Devil and all his ministers "trembling away". Here at the heart of the liturgy, and not simply in the uninformed minds of ignorant peasants, was the assertion of "an inexorable and compelling power" inherent in the name and cross of Christ.[35]

Unlike baptism, where the objects used in the sacrament were jealously guarded against lay misuse or contamination, the blessings of salt, water, and wax were intended to provide the laity with sources of "inexorable and compelling power" which they themselves could use against demons, diseases, and distress of every kind. One of the principal perquisites of the parish clerk was the holy-water fee he exacted when he carried supplies of it to every

[33] *Manuale*, pp. 25–43.
[34] *Manuale*, pp. 1–4.
[35] *Manuale*, pp. 7–9.

household. There it was sprinkled on the hearth to fend off evil, in byres and fields and even the marriage-bed to promote fertility. Ailing animals were fed blessed salt or given holy water to drink. The candles blessed in the Candlemas ceremonies were lit during thunderstorms, to drive away the demons which were believed to be especially active when the air was thus agitated. They were placed near women in labour, and in the hands of the dying, to keep the Devil at bay. The blessing of these "sacramentals", as such sacred objects were called, put into lay control powerful spiritual weapons.[36]

And in fact, the blessing ceremonies in which these holy objects were made, together with the baptismal and Rogationtide services, created a set of paradigms for the use of the sacramentals which seemed to be fairly closely adhered to even in the "magical" abuses which worried theologians and confessors. The texts of the blessing ceremonies clearly presuppose that their effects would by no means be confined to the merely spiritual – holy water, salt, bread, candles, as well as the herbs blessed at Assumptiontide or the meat, cheese, and eggs at Easter, were for the healing of bodies as well as souls. The application of the sacramentals to this-worldly concerns, which some historians have seen as a mark of the superficiality of late medieval Christianity, was amply legitimated by the liturgy itself.

It is in this overall context that the "charms" and incantations of the *Horae* and the private prayer collections need to be read, for they have clear and close similarities to the sacramentals. Their use of the sign of the cross, their direct address to the devils they seek to exorcize, in fact their whole rhetorical strategy is borrowed from this area of the Church's official practice. It is worth considering here the "charm" against thunder and storms provided in some of the Sarum *Horae*:

> The triumphal superscription ["Titulus triumphalis"] Jesus of Nazareth, King of the Jews. Christ conquers; may Christ reign: may Christ vindicate us, and from all thunder, tempest and every evil free and defend us. Amen. Behold + the Cross of the Lord, flee you enemies: the lion of the tribe of Judah, the root of David, conquers.[37]

---

[36] The best short introduction in English to the significance of sacramentals in this period is R. W. Scribner, *Popular Culture and Popular Movements in Germany*, 1987, pp. 1–49. The standard work is the two-volume study by A. Franz, *Die Kirchlichen Benedictionen in Mittelalter*, 1909. There is a useful brief account of the official theology of sacramentals by H. Leclercq in *The Catholic Encyclopedia*, XIII, pp. 292–3.

[37] Hoskins, p. 115.

This charm may have been intended to accompany the lighting of the Candlemas candles used to banish thunder, and the employment of the sign of the cross prescribed in the prayer was probably intended to accompany the use of holy water, scattered in the air crosswise to the four corners of the earth in a gesture borrowed from the baptismal liturgy. It incorporates phrases and gestures which we have already encountered in other charms, and the "Titulus Triumphalis", Ihesus Nazarenus Rex Iudaeorum, or its initials INRI, regularly appeared on protective amulets and similar magical objects, as well as on rosaries, chalices, and other religious objects.[38] Yet the prayer is neither more nor less than the translation into action of the teaching of countless Rogationtide sermons on the power of the cross and the nature of the Devil. All this, as we have seen, had impeccable ecclesiastical precedent and rationale. That is not to suggest that all such invocations remained within the bounds even of fifteenth-century orthodoxy. My point is simply that the rhetoric and rationale at work in such incantations cannot sensibly be called pagan. Instead, they represent the appropriation and adaptation to lay needs and anxieties of a range of sacred gestures and prayers, along lines essentially faithful to the pattern established within the liturgy itself. This is not paganism, but lay Christianity.

Even the least promising aspects of such invocations can be traced back to liturgical use. Consider here the extraordinary catena of divine names so often turned to magical use, and much in evidence in the Charlemagne prayers. This list, in which God is described as "Egg, Calf, Serpent, Ram, Lion, and Worm", seems the least likely of candidates for orthodox liturgical origin. In fact, it is a hymn dating back at least to the eleventh century, and occurring in a variety of liturgical contexts. It was used as the hymn at compline on Whit Sunday and the three days following, and as the sequence at the nuptial Mass, where its presence would have ensured that every man and woman in England would be familiar with it. Even more significantly, from the 1480s it was employed as the compline hymn on the Feast of the Holy Name of Jesus. The historian of the "new feasts" in late medieval England found it "hard to imagine" this hymn being sung "with a straight face", yet its presence in the liturgy of the Feast of the Holy Name was an extraordinary testimony to, and legitimation of, the widespread equation of this magical sequence of names with the Church's solemn use of the name of Jesus.[39]

[38] J. Evans, *Magical Jewels of the Middle Ages*, 1922, pp. 128–9; Louth CWA, p. 153.
[39] *Sarum Breviarium*, II col. 236; *Manuale*, p. 52; Pfaff, *New Feasts*, p. 71.

This is strikingly brought home by one of the documents we have already considered in this chapter. In late fifteenth-century England the cult of the Holy Name of Jesus was spread, and at length established as a feast, through the patronage of the Lady Margaret Beaufort. The text of the Office of the feast was probably composed by a former dean of her chapel. It is not surprising, therefore, to find that a large section of the prayer-book commissioned by the Lady Margaret for Thomas Stanley is made up of a series of devotions "de nomine Ihesu", in honour of the Holy Name. In the light of the inclusion of the Charlemagne sequence of names in the Office of the Holy Name, the presence in Stanley's prayer-book alongside these prayers to the Holy Name of Jesus of no fewer than four versions of the Charlemagne charm becomes more readily intelligible. Neither the Lady Margaret nor those responsible for assembling the book drew any hard and fast distinction between "orthodox" devotions to the Holy Name, such as the "O Bone Ihesu", and the "magical" invocations we have been considering. That fact alone has far-reaching implications for the concept of "popular" piety in late medieval England.[40]

The point to be grasped here, of course, is that the reliance on the "vertu of these names" in the Charlemagne charm was close to the way in which the late medieval Church understood the power of the Holy Name of Jesus itself. The daily Offices began "Our help is in the Name of the Lord." Mark 16, one of the four Gospel passages regularly included in primers and used in the fields at Rogationtide, was constantly quoted in justification of ecclesiastical conjuration and exorcism, and promised that "*in my Name* they shall cast out devils . . . they shall take up serpents . . . They shall lay hands on the sick and they shall recover." This teaching was reiterated in the Office of the Holy Name, where the third lection for the first nocturne of matins insisted: "This is the Name which bestows sight on the blind, hearing on the deaf, makes the crippled walk, gives speech to the dumb and life to the dead: the virtue of this name has put to flight all the power of the devil from the bodies of the possessed."[41] This insistence on the salvific power of the Holy Name is evident in the New Testament, and has been a perennial feature of Christian practice and piety. It underlies not only the form which many exorcisms take, but the devotion of respectable modern Church of England matins congregations singing St Patrick's breast-plate:

---

[40] Westminster Abbey, MS 39; and see N. Ker, *Medieval Manuscripts in British Libraries, I* London, 1969, pp. 412, 413.

[41] *Sarum Breviarium*, III col. 623.

> I Bind unto myself the Name
> The Strong Name of the Trinity
> By Invocation of the Same
> The Three in One and One in Three.[42]

But faith in the "vertu" of the Holy Name was particularly strong in the late Middle Ages, and its mere repetition seemed full of power and blessing, a belief magnificently testified by the decoration of the roof of Blythburgh church, where the Holy Name is the principal motif, a splendid visual equivalent to the hypnotic litany of the Name enshrined in a devotion like the Jesu Psalter or Richard of Caistor's prayer.

This sense of the symbiotic relationship between the official practice of the Church, orthodox devotions like that to the Holy Name, and even apparently superstitious practices and prayers is evident in a number of late medieval discussions of magic, perhaps most strikingly in the *Malleus Maleficarum*, the magisterial treatment of this whole area. Though it spelt out at some length the conventional warnings against sorcery and reliance on the Devil in conjurations, and laid down strict conditions for the lawful use of charms and incantations, the *Malleus* nevertheless recognized that many popular "magical" practices, though fallen into the hands of "indiscreet and superstitious persons", were in their origin "entirely sacred", and were legitimate when "applied by pious men", even lay men or women. It brought arguments from St Thomas to justify the use of charms and benedictions invoking sacred names and things, and therefore "let us by all means invoke the name of God . . . by the Triumphant Inscription, by the three nails, and by the other weapons of Christ's army against the Devil and his works. By these means it is lawful to work, and our trust may be placed in them, leaving the issue to God's will." Again drawing on St Thomas, the *Malleus* even permitted the use of written charms, such as passages from the Gospels or other "sacred words", to be hung round the neck or placed by the sick or given them to kiss. Even if the lay user of such charms could not understand the words thus written the practice might be legitimate, for "it is enough if such a man fixes his thoughts upon the Divine Virtue, and leaves it to the Divine Will to do what seems good to his Mercy."[43]

The scope given by this, the most exhaustive manual against witchcraft and superstition produced in the Middle Ages, to the sort of practices and prayers I have been discussing, was enormous. It expressly legitimated the use as charms not only of prayers, but

[42] *The New English Hymnal*, 1986, p. 361.
[43] *Malleus Maleficarum*, pp. 381–7.

of the names of God and such symbolic objects as the Five Wounds, the Nails, or specific sayings of Jesus, comparing their power to that of relics, for "the words of God are not less holy than the relics of the saints." This broad approach was no doubt in part dictated by realism in the face of popular practice: it was certainly amply reflected there. The *Malleus* had cited St Thomas to the effect that the incidents of the Passion or the words of Jesus might be invoked as "lawful means" of working the signs promised in the last chapter of St Mark. These signs were as concrete, miraculous, and concerned with life's ills and dangers as anyone could desire – casting out demons, drinking poison unharmed, healing the sick, taking up serpents unharmed. Therefore charms against unstaunchable wounds, invoking the Wounds of Jesus or the nails or lance that caused them seemed legitimate. Joshua's prayer that made the sun stand still and Christ's word that made the sea stand still might be invoked to make thieves unable to move if they touched the devotee's goods. Phrases from the Gospels such as "Jesus passed through the midst of them" might be used to ensure safe passage through perils, or "not a bone of him shall be broken" to heal a toothache. Christ's harrowing of Hell and breaking of its gates might even be invoked to open jammed locks.[44] To a twentieth-century eye this is clearly a form of sympathetic magic; to its users and to the ecclesiastical authorities it might seem a perfectly legitimate application of the principles set down by St Thomas or the *Malleus*, and an extension of the practice of the liturgy. Was this "Medicina pro Morba Caduco et le Fevr", for example, a prayer, or a spell?

> What manere of Ivell thou be
> In Goddis name I coungere the.
> I coungere the with the holy crosse
> That Iesus was done on with fors.
> I coniure the with nayles thre
> That Iesus was nayled upon the tree.
> I coungere the with the croune of thorne
> That Iesus hede was done with skorne.
> I coungere the with the precious blode
> That Iesus shewyd vpon the rode.
> I coungere the with woundys fyve
> That Iesus suffred be his lyve.
> I coungere the with that holy spere
> That Longenus to Iesus hert can bere.

---

[44] Evans, *Magical Jewels*, p. 128; Scot, *Discoverie of Witchcraft*, pp. 233, 244; Carleton Brown, *Secular Lyrics of the XIV–XV Centuries*, 1952, pp. 58–61.

I coungere the neuertheless
With all the vertues of the masse
And all the prayers of Seynt Dorathe.
In nomine Patris et Filii et Spiritus Sancti. Amen.[45]

Some charms confused the matter further by inserting a clause that made what clearly operated as a binding conjuration into a prayer of supplication. Thus one charm against thieves conjures potential robbers in no uncertain terms by the Trinity, the "vertu of every masse / that ever was seyde", by herb and stone and tree, "that they stand still as stone / they have ne powere away to gon / By the vertu of the holy trinite / Tylle they have lyve of me". But it concludes as a straightforward petition – "Lord iesu, Graunte me thys / as ye ben in heven blys."[46]

Pardons and Promises

The charms and invocations found among the popular prayers of the *Horae* and related prayer collections are not the only texts which raise problems for any understanding of the nature of popular religion in the late Middle Ages. The indulgences or pardons and other promises in the rubrics which accompanied not merely the charms, but even such impeccably mainstream devotions as the "Obsecro Te" and the "Fifteen Oes" raise similar questions about the relationship between official and popular piety.

These rubrics offered essentially two types of promise. The first of these consisted of indulgences, ranging from a sober forty days to a spurious 40,000 years; the second type consisted of promised benefits in this world or the next – the conversion of fifteen kinsmen and the release of fifteen souls from Purgatory, prefaced to the "Fifteen Oes", the promise of immunity from death by poison, battle, judicial process, fire, or water attached to the "Deus Propicius Esto", or the promise prefixed to the "Obsecro Te" that the Blessed Virgin would appear to the devotee to give them warning of the day and hour of his or her death, and would guarantee them salvation.[47]

Before the indulgence rubrics can be understood, it is necessary to define exactly what an indulgence or pardon was believed to be.

---

[45] T, Silverstein (ed.), *Medieval English Lyrics*, 1971, p. 126; on the whole question see D. Gray, "Notes on Some Middle English Charms", in B. Rowland (ed.), *Chaucer and Middle English Studies*, 1974, pp. 56–71.

[46] CUL MS Add. 5943f 170r.

[47] *Hor. Ebor.*, pp. 66, 76; a representative group of these promises are conveniently gathered in Hoskins, pp. 124–7.

The pardon concerned was remission not of sin, but merely of the penance or temporal punishment believed to be still due to God after a sin had been repented, confessed, and forgiven. The origin of the concept lay in the ecclesiastical penance imposed on penitents by confessors in the early Middle Ages, which was often prolonged and severe, involving arduous and dangerous pilgrimages or lengthy fasting. Such penances often exposed the penitent to public shame, and were found burdensome and off-putting. Compassion and pastoral realism led to the gradual evolution of commutation of such severe penances, and the emergence of the system by which a comparatively mild penance, involving prayer, fasting, or alms-giving, was imposed by the priest in confession. The unfulfilled balance of a penitent's debt of penance was believed to be made up from the treasure of merits acquired by Christ and by his saints, in a transaction rather resembling the transfer of credit to an over-drawn current account from an abundant deposit account. This transfer was often conceived of as an exercise of the power of the keys, and therefore lay in the hands of the bishops and the Pope. The imposition of the earlier form of penance had been by days or years, and individual indulgences were therefore measured in the same way – the standard grant was forty days. On rare occasions, such as the declaration of the Jubilee at Rome, or the displaying of some mighty relic at some other pilgrimage site, they might be total or plenary. In every case the indulgence could only be obtained by a Christian in a state of grace, that is, one who had truly repented, sincerely confessed, and been duly absolved of all grave sins, and the pardon was awarded in return for the per-formance of specific pious acts, such as pilgrimage or the recitation of particular indulgenced devotions.

Despite some theological problems implicit in the notion, indulgences in the late Middle Ages were almost universally believed to be applicable to souls in Purgatory, to shorten their torments. Inevitably, this belief promoted interest in the gaining of indulgences, and there is abundant evidence that they were eagerly sought by every class of English society in the later Middle Ages. The well-to-do purchased letters or bulls of pardon by contributing to charitable causes, such as the notorious rebuilding of St Peter's, or by associating themselves with particular religious orders or gilds. Those who had them took great comfort *in articulo mortis* in the possession of such pardons, often specifying that they be displayed on or near the grave, and some of the later medieval *Manuals* preserve special forms of absolution for those who pos-sessed them.[48] Margery Kempe, for all her mystical intimacy with

---

[48] *York Manuale*, p. 129.

Christ and repeated visionary assurances that she would never have to endure the pains of Purgatory, showed herself once again a woman of her time by taking the liveliest possible interest in clocking up the "great pardon and plenary remission" of all the pilgrimage sites she visited. One of the most spectacular signs of divine favour granted to her was the ability to gain the indulgences attached to the Holy Places in Jerusalem without needing to make pilgrimage there, and apparently the right to grant these indulgences to others.[49]

Margery's appetite for pardons was very widely shared. Indulgences were considered an indispensable incentive in connection with a variety of fund-raising activities, for example, the building or restoring of churches and religious houses. But the incentive might be attached not merely to ecclesiastical projects, but to secular causes, such as the repair of bridges and roads.[50] Wealthy Londoners sought burial in the indulgenced "Pardon Churchyard" in the cloisters of St Paul's, and evidence of the quest for pardons at the highest level was found in the later Sarum *Horae*, many of which printed details of an indulgence of 300 days at each recital, secured from Pope Sixtus IV by Edward IV's queen, Elizabeth, for all who used a particular devotion in honour of the Virgin three times a day at the Ave or Angelus bell.[51] Perhaps the most macabre testimony to the demand for indulgences was the custom of granting forty days' indulgence to anyone who brought a faggot to the burning of a heretic, whereby, according to Foxe, "many ignorant people caused many of their children to bear billets and faggots to their burning." Nor was this appetite confined to ignorant people. At the burning of the Suffolk Protestant Nicholas Peke one of the officials proclaimed the indulgence "To as many as shall cast a stick to the burning", upon which "Baron Curson, Sir John Audley, knight, with many others of estimation, being there present, did rise from their seats, and with their swords did cut down boughs, and throw them into the fire, and so did all the multitude of the people."[52]

Set against this background, the proliferation of indulgenced devotions in successive editions of the *Horae* is readily understandable. The indulgences were prominently advertised on the title-pages or colophons of Sarum primers, and clearly constituted one

---

[49] *The Book of Margery Kempe*, p. 75.
[50] See below, "The Pains of Purgatory", pp. 367–8.
[51] Hoskins, p. 126. The indulgence was granted on 2 January 1480/1 – *Calendar of Entries in the Papal Registers relating to Great Britain and Ireland*, XIII, Part 1 pp. 90–1.
[52] Foxe, *Acts and Monuments*, IV p. 581, V p. 254.

of their principal selling-points. Equipped with his or her primer and an hour or two to spare for pious browsing, the devout lay person could clock up an impressive tally of days of pardon. But it would be a mistake to see this as a merely mechanical process: the indulgences were not intended as an incentive to mindless parroting of the maximum number of prayers. They could not be gained without inner devotion. John Mirk told his congregation that every fifty years the Pope of Rome "yn more confort of all Godys pepull" granted a plenary indulgence to all who came to Rome. But because not all could go to Rome, "the Pope of Heven, Ihesu Cryst, of his specyall grace grantythe all men and woymen full pardon of hor synnys yn hor deth-day" in return for three things – "full contricion with schryft, full charite wythout feynyng, and stabull fayth wythout flateryng". And indeed, Mirk adds, "wythout thes thre, ther may no mon have pardon at Rome ne elleswhere."[53] The indulgence rubrics which preceded most of the extra prayers in early sixteenth-century *Horae* reflect this same insistence. The indulgence granted at Queen Elizabeth's request by "our holy fathers the Archbishops of Canterbury and York with other ix bishops of this realm", for example, was offered "to all them that be in the state of grace able to receive pardon". The forty days of pardon attached to the "Gaude Virgo, Mater Christi" was offered "to all them that say thys prayer in the worschyp of our blessyd lady, beyng penitente and trewly confessed of all theyr synnes". The indulgences were for "them that devoutly say these prayers".[54]

There were, of course, wrong perceptions and misunderstandings of all this. Many of the indulgences promised were for tens of thousands of years, and were clearly apocryphal. Other rubrics betray a fundamental confusion about what an indulgence was. The indulgence attributed to Alexander VI, attached to a prayer in honour of St Anne, St Mary, and the child Jesus, was for "V thousand years of pardon for deadly sins, and XX years for venial sins" implying that the indulgence could actually remit sins.[55] This confusion was rare in the printed *Horae*, but fairly frequent in prayers circulating in manuscript, even those in comparatively learned collections like the Bodleian manuscript Lyell 30. A variant of a common rubric in that collection runs:

> Whoo ever saith this orison every day: ther is graunted to hym yaf he be in the state of everlastyng dampnacion, God woll turne

[53] *Festial*, p. 74.
[54] *Hor. Ebor.*, p. 63; Hoskins, pp. 124–7.
[55] Hoskins, p. 125.

everlastyng peyne into the peyne of purgatori. And yef he be in
the state of the peynes of purgatory; God woll change thilke
paynes of purgatori & him will cut purgatori to everlastyng ioy.
To all thilke that seyn this orison, xx dayes contynewyng there is
graunted to hym playn remission as hit is retyn at Rome in the
mynster of Seynt Peter under a bul of led.[56]

As that reference to the "bul of led" in St Peter's suggests, the
purpose of these extraordinary rubrics was to impress on the devotee
the great power and authority of the prayers they accompanied. So
in some of the printed *Horae* the "O Bone Ihesu" is recommended
to the user not merely by that same promise of the commutation of
the fires of Hell to those of Purgatory, and of Purgatory for the
joys of Heaven, but by the fact that its use brought St Bernard
"a singular rewarde of perpetuall consolation of our lorde Jesu
Crist". And should anyone doubt the ecclesiastical credentials of the
prayer, it was, the rubric claimed, "wrytten yn a thabell that
haungeth at rome" near the high altar in St Peter's where the Pope
"ys wonte to say the office of the masse". Not all the rubrics went
in for this sort of overkill. Often the incentive is strategically vague,
like the rubric to the "Ave Maria Ancilla Trinitatis": "this prayer
was showed to saint Bernard by the messenger of God, saying that
as gold is most precious of all other metal so exceedeth this prayer
all other prayers, and who that devoutly says it shall have a singular
reward of our blessed Lady and her sweet son Jesus."[57]

In all this, we are clearly in the same mental world as that
reflected in many of the miraculous and fabulous exempla used to
illustrate and flavour parochial preaching. Mirk's story of the child
"pullt" up to Heaven to be taught the "Sancte et Immortale"
prayer, with which he then banished the Rogationtide devils, is a
case in point, but any collection of late medieval sermons would
yield dozens. These exempla, with their circumstantial details of
miraculous happenings, were not pious frauds; they were pious
fictions, whose use was governed by clear sets of conventions, and
they were used and reused in sermon after sermon. They were
collected into encyclopaedias and preaching dictionaries, and topped
and tailed with different place and personal names as circumstances
and pastoral needs demanded.[58] The legends and indulgences

---

[56] Bodleian Library Lyell MS 30 fols 51r–51v; also in CUL MS Dd.vi.1 fol. 144r.
[57] Hoskins, p. 124.
[58] On exempla and their use see G. R. Owst, *Literature and the Pulpit in Medieval England*,
1961, especially chapter 4 "Fiction and Instruction in the Sermon Exempla"; for a collection
in English see *An Alphabet of Tales*, ed. M. M. Banks, EETS, 1904–5.

attached to the prayers of the laity seem equally conventional and stereotyped in character, and should probably be seen in much the same way.

Yet there is no escaping the peculiarity of the gulf between the beauty, coherence, and power of many of the prayers collected in the *Horae*, and the tawdry oddity of many of the promises and indulgences promised in the rubrics. Should we therefore assume a two-tier readership, reflecting a high and a low, an élite and a popular piety? Were there some users of these prayers who sought in them that devout and recollected interiority which devotions like the "Fifteen Oes" seem to demand, and others, a rabble of indulgence hunters spawned by cheap printing, with cruder palates and coarser perceptions, who thumbed through their primers in search of marvels and quantifiable dividends, temporal as much as spiritual?

There may be something in this, for indulgences and apocryphal attributions did multiply as successive editions of the primers rolled from the presses.[59] But once again we should resist any simplistic division of late medieval religion into high against low, élite, churchly, or official against popular. The "Fifteen Oes" were among the best and most theologically sophisticated of the prayers of the *Horae* and among the most widely used. Yet the legend attached to them, with its tale of visionary solitaries, demons in the woods, and its extravagant and circumstantial promises in multiples of fifteen, was as suspect as anything to be found in the whole repertoire of late medieval religion. As we have seen, the crudest of supernatural promises, the most grandiloquent offers of indulgences, the most apocryphal of legends, are to be found in collections used by educated, pious, and orthodox lay people and clerics. No easy stratification along these lines seems possible. Even the distinction between official and unofficial piety, which might seem promising, given the undoubted concern of many of the ecclesiastical author-ities to prune the wilder extravagances of folk religion, is not here very helpful. Strange legends and extravagant promises were not confined to the periphery of unofficial or lay religion, for they were strikingly represented in the most clerical and official of books, the missal, in the material prefixed to the votive Mass against the pestilence, "pro mortalitate evitanda", the Mass of the Five Wounds, and in the instructions for the celebration of the Trental of St Gregory.

---

[59] It is worth comparing the indulgences, and the claims made about them, in Hoskins, no. 7, RSTC 15875, with later books such as Hoskins, nos 37 (RSTC 15909), 43 (RSTC 15916), or 67 (RSTC 15939).

The "Missa pro Mortalitate Evitanda" or Mass against the pestilence, generally known, from its opening word, as the Mass "Recordare", was apparently compiled and authorized by Pope Clement VI at Avignon during the Black Death there in 1348–9. With its appeals for mercy to "pie Jesu" and its reliance on the intercession of the Mother of Mercy, it is a very characteristic product of the later Middle Ages. In our present context, however, its real interest lies in the prefatory rubric which explained Clement's authorship, promised 260 days of indulgence to all who heard the mass "truly contrite and confessed", and, most spectacularly, guaranteed that all who heard it on five consecutive days, kneeling with a burning candle in their hands, would not succumb to sudden death. And it concludes, in a sentence which immediately recalls the *Horae* references to prayers authenticated by "buls of led" in Rome, "Et hoc est certum et approbatum in Avinione et in partibus circumvenis."[60]

The Mass of the Five Wounds, whose enormous popularity we have already noticed, was preceded by a more circumstantial if less historically reliable rubric. This attributed the text of the Mass to the Archangel Raphael, who had revealed it to an unspecified Pope Boniface, when he lay close to death. The Archangel commanded the Pope to rise and write the Mass down, and then to say it five times, on which he would recover. Thereafter, anyone in trouble in this world who said it five times, or caused it to be said, "without doubt, would be set free". If said for a soul in Purgatory five times, they would be released to Heaven. These promises Raphael assured the Pope were delivered with the authority of God, to which the Pope added his apostolic authority, and granted to all those "truly contrite and confessed" who said five Masses a "seventh part of the remission of all their sins", and to those who caused it to be said, forty days' remission of mortal sins and a year's remission of venial sins.[61]

The Trental of St Gregory was an even more complex devotion, much and increasingly favoured by fifteenth-century English testators. It involved the saying of thirty Masses spread out over a year, three each in the octaves and using the Masses of the Nativity, Epiphany, Purification, Annunciation, Easter, Ascension, Pentecost, Trinity, the Assumption of the Virgin and her Nativity, together with daily recitation of "Placebo" and "Dirige". The devotion was accompanied by a legend, in which Pope Gregory's deceased mother appeared to him, monstrously disfigured by her torments in

[60] *Missale*, col. 886*.
[61] *Missale*, col. 750*.

Purgatory, the result of unconfessed sins. She asked her son to celebrate the Trental of thirty masses, and when this was done, she reappeared so radiantly beautiful that he mistook her for the Blessed Virgin. The story, duly versified in English, was immensely popular. It linked up with the lay habit of recitation of the primer Office for the Dead and this, combined with the fact that the Trental represented a sort of recapitulation of the whole liturgical year and seemed to produce such dramatic and guaranteed effects, led to an enormous demand for its celebration.[62] Rigorous Catholic opinion, represented by the author of *Dives and Pauper*, strongly disapproved of the "Pope Trental" on both theological and historical grounds. Nevertheless, detailed instructions for its celebration found their way into the missal.[63]

In each case, these votive Masses and Mass devotions represent the point of maximum influence of the laity over the Church's liturgy. It is of the nature of a votive Mass that it is celebrated on a particular occasion, for a specified need, and normally at the instigation of lay clients. Popular and official piety here join hands. The cult of the Five Wounds, had the Reformation not intervened, might well have passed from the status of a popular but voluntary devotion, to that of a feast, whose observance was binding on the whole of the English Church, as the closely related cult of the Holy Name did in the 1480s. The pious legends attached to these Masses were emphatically expressions of a popular religion often operating at or outside the boundaries of formal orthodoxy, and they certainly originated in private usage. A late fifteenth-century version of the York missal owned by the Fitzwilliam family contained, attached to the Mass of St Anthony, a set of promises which do not seem to have become general, and which were decidedly more extravagant than any that found their way into print. The rubric guaranteed to all who said or heard the Mass, and fasted on bread and water, immunity that year from ill fortune, famine, dropsy, cancer, the spasm, leprosy, asthma, and unclean spirits, as well as the more usual guarantees of protection against misfortune by fire, water, tempest, and pestilence, and the prosperity of their goods.[64] Such promises bear all the marks of the quest for healing and victory over evil, deliverance from sudden and unprovided death, and the longing for assurance of salvation, so widely felt and

[62] R. W. Pfaff, "The English Devotion of St Gregory's Trental", *Speculum* XLIX, 1974, pp. 75–90. On the Trental, see below pp. 370–5.
[63] *Dives and Pauper*, ed. P. H. Barnum, EETS, 1976, II pp. 186–92, and see below, chapter 10, "The Pains of Purgatory".
[64] *York Missale*, II pp. 233–4.

so clearly reflected in the *Horae* devotions we have been considering. Since the Mass was the most powerful of all prayers and the source of all blessings, it is not surprising to find such longings attaching themselves to its celebration. The boundaries between private devotion and official religion were fluid, and the fact that legendary material so closely tailored to lay religious aspirations but so loosely grounded in orthodox theological teaching could find a lodging, and even some official countenance, in the missal itself is eloquent testimony to the freedom of movement between official and popular piety. Unlike the *Horae*, the missal was the Church's own book; the presence of such material there is the clearest demonstration one could have of the interpenetration of popular and official piety at the end of the Middle Ages, and of the unwisdom of any attempt to drive a wedge between them.

And what is true for the mixture of official and unofficial religion is equally so of any attempted distinction between devout, reflective, interior piety on one hand, and the cruder, materialistic, and wonder-seeking piety reflected in some of the legends and rubrics prefixed to the prayers of the *Horae* and private collections. In this area too, hard and fast distinctions are impossible to draw, a difficulty made clear in the history of the Passion devotion known as the "Revelation of the Hundred Paternosters".

This survives in a manuscript devotional book of the fifteenth century now in the British Library. The contents of this collection, a mixture of Latin and English, are absolutely standard and include many of the prayers we have been discussing, such as the "Adoro Te" and the prayer of St Bede. It also includes the usual crop of indulgences and supernatural promises attached to these devotions. The manuscript evidently originated from the sort of *dévot* circle associated with Syon, Sheen, and the Lady Margaret Beaufort. There is a slightly higher than average proportion of vernacular material in it, and it includes the Jesu Psalter, the long prayer of invocation of the Holy Name associated with Syon and found also in the prayer-book commissioned by Lady Margaret for Thomas Stanley.[65] The "Revelation of the Hundred Paternosters" itself is a Passion devotion in the form of an extended meditation on the seven blood-sheddings of Christ, from his Circumcision to the piercing of his side after his death by Longinus. The devotion divides the meditation into seven, for the days of the week and against the seven deadly sins. The devotee was to meditate each day on the appropriate scene of Christ's suffering, described in

[65] F. Wormald, "The Revelation of the Hundred Paternosters: a Fifteenth-Century Meditation", *Laudate*, XV, 1936, pp. 165–82.

prose which draws very directly on classic meditational sources, particularly Richard Rolle's *Meditations on the Passion*. He was then to recite a short prayer against one of the deadly sins, and say a hundred Paternosters.

This devotion is a very characteristic late medieval mixture of intense affective piety and mechanical repetition, but there can be no doubt of its essentially meditative character. The text emphasizes the need for recollection, charging the user "afore or thou begynne thys prayer gadre thy mynde & thy wyttes from all outeward thinges and besynnes as thou maist and thynk most on the same thyng to the which thou shalt praye." The devotion originated among, or at least was taken up by, the English Carthusians, who played a crucial role in propagating serious inward religion in late medieval England. They were also key figures in the transmission of both continental and earlier English devotional and spiritual writing. The élite and devotional credentials of the Hundred Paternosters are therefore impeccable. Yet the discussion of the benefits of the devotion which concludes the text once again confronts us with the disconcerting combination of spiritual and brutal materialist priorities which characterizes so much in the *Horae* devotions. The document describes how "in late dayes" not only one or two but "many persones" have used the devotion, and thereby proved for themselves "and felt hit by experience" that "In the love of god & all thinges to the belongiyng shall the bettre folowe & succede bodily & gostely."[66]

The story told to illustrate this point gives a fascinating insight into the network by which such devotions spread among the laity. It describes how the instructions for the devotion were sent from the London Charterhouse to Mount Grace in Yorkshire. One of the monks there sent it in turn to a devout country parish priest. This priest copied out the devotion, and distributed it to various friends, "of whom ther was a good husband mon harde of the grete vartu and grace of the forsaid prayers he used hit dayly as deuoutly as he coude". Shortly after this, a farm labourer beat one of the husbandman's oxen so severely that the beast lay on the ground, unable to rise or eat, over a whole weekend. All attempts at medication failed, and the husbandman was at his wits end "for he was but a pore man". In desperation, he turned to the devotion of the Hundred Paternosters, "and used forthe the prayer aforsaid as deuoutly as he coude". The beast was duly discovered heartily eating and entirely well, and the grateful husbandman knew that "god had sauyd his oxe by the grace and vartu of the foresaid holy

---

[66] "Revelation", pp. 180–2.

prayers." And so, "withyn ii dayes after he cam to oure hous of Mountgrace & told me of all hys fortune in his mater and desired Right tenderly to have a copy in writing . . . which copy I wrotte for hym and he caused others to do the same."[67] This is a fascinating story for a whole range of reasons, not least because it allows us to see how an elaborate form of affective meditation on the Passion could pass from the monastic stillness of the Charterhouses, through the zeal of a devout parish priest associating himself with Carthusian piety, to a range of pious lay people, including the literate but poverty-stricken husbandman who is the central figure in the anecdote. The multiplication and distribution of copies of the devotion is initially a monastic initiative, but once the devotion begins to make its way among the laity, its partisans, like the grateful husbandman, seize the initiative and themselves procure and distribute copies. These are the processes behind the circulation of the multitude of prayers and devotions which fill so many late medieval manuscript collections, and which ultimately found their way into the *Horae*.

But in the present context, the particular interest of the story lies in the extraordinary mixture of high and low, spiritual and materialistic motivation underlying the use of the prayer. It is emphatically a form of affective, interior recollection, and is so used even by the husbandman at first. But in the face of calamity, he unhesitatingly turns to the devotion for a power which can heal his ox as readily as it edified his spirit. So much might be allowed to a simple man, "ignorant of symplesse". But his clerical mentors, even in the exalted atmosphere of the Charterhouse, see nothing amiss. Instead, the miracle is eagerly seized on as demonstration of what many had already experienced for themselves, that the prayer brought with it blessings, by virtue of which "all thynges to the belongyng shall the bettre succede bodily & gostily."

There is no clear divide between popular and élite piety here. We are firmly in the world in which prayers of the depth and quality of the "Fifteen Oes" can go unblushingly side-by-side with exotic promises and barefaced fantasy, a world in which the pragmatic instincts of even the devout led them to grope for financial and material equivalents for the things of the spirit. In the merchant community of King's Lynn, even a "worschepful clerk . . . a doctoure of divinite" might set a price on his devotional aspirations, telling Margery Kempe that he "had levyr than xx pound" have such a sorrow for the Passion as Margery Kempe had. In the same way, when a wife whose husband was ailing tried to persuade

[67] *The Book of Margery Kempe*, pp. 164, 202.

Margery to stay and pray by his bedside, the conversation took on the character of marketplace haggling, the wife declaring that she would not "for xl s" that her husband died while Margery was away, and Margery replying that she would not stay at home even if "ye wolde yeve me an hundryd pownde".[68]

This is the world reflected in these *Horae* prayers and devotions, in which religion was a single but multifaceted and resonant symbolic house, within which rich and poor, simple and sophisticate could kneel side by side, using the same prayers and sharing the same hopes. That the Lady Margaret in her chapel, John Fisher at her elbow to guide and exhort her, had a fuller and more balanced grasp of Christian fundamentals than Robert Reynes, conjuring angels on his daughter's thumbnail in rural Norfolk, we need not doubt. But they did not have a different religion. Lady Margaret and her like did not live perpetually in the heights of a spiritualized and other-worldly Christianity, and the rural husbandman, seeking divine intervention in the face of the ruinous sickness of a beast, was not locked out from the comforts of interior affective devotion. Late medieval Catholicism was a broad Church.

[68] *Book of Margery Kempe*, pp. 164, 202.

D: Now, and at the Hour of Our Death

CHAPTER 9

LAST THINGS

Everybody knows, or thinks they know, that the late Middle Ages were obsessed by death. In his classic treatment of the *mentalité* of late medieval Europe, Johan Huizinga claimed that "no other epoch has laid so much stress as the expiring Middle Ages on the thought of death. An everlasting call of *memento mori* sounds through life."[1] Huizinga's account of the morbidity of the period is now widely considered to be too highly coloured, but his fundamental assertion has not been challenged, and Galpern's recent and deservedly influential study of French popular religion argued that "Catholicism at the end of the Middle Ages was in large part a cult of the living in the service of the dead."[2]

On the face of it, this claim is irrefutable. Wherever one turns in the sources for the period one encounters the overwhelming preoccupation of clergy and laity alike, from peasant to prince and from parish clerk to pontiff, with the safe transition of their souls from this world to the next, above all with the shortening and easing of their stay in Purgatory. It is a preoccupation which shows no slackening up to the very moment of Reformation, and in England, as everywhere else in Europe, it was the single most influential factor in shaping both the organization of the Church and the physical layout and appearance of the buildings in which men and women worshipped.

It shaped the organization of the Church because belief in the supreme efficacy of the Mass in relieving the pains of those in Purgatory had fuelled an enormous inflation of the number of priestly ordinations in the later Middle Ages, and contributed to the emergence of a non-beneficed clerical proletariat employed, when they had employment, as parochial or gild chaplains or as chantry priests, increasingly on short-term rather than permanent contracts to the laity.

[1] Johan Huizinga, *The Waning of the Middle Ages*, 1965, p. 134.
[2] A. Galpern, "The Legacy of Late Medieval Religion in Sixteenth-Century Champagne", in C. Trinkaus and H. Oberman (eds), *The Pursuit of Holiness*, 1974, p. 149.

It shaped the physical surroundings of worship because belief in the efficacy of good works, and above all of gifts to adorn churches or beautify the worship of God, led to a massive channelling of resources into the decoration or rebuilding of churches, chapels, and colleges in the later Middle Ages. The extensive and often sumptuous rebuilding of so many of the churches of East Anglia in the fifteenth century was an expression not simply of the bourgeois prosperity brought by the wool trade, but of the concern of rich graziers or cloth-merchants to use their wealth as post-mortem fire insurance. The flinty splendours of Blythburgh, Long Melford, or Lavenham were certainly a testimony to the desire of the Masons, Cloptons, Hoptons, Martins, Springs, and Branches for a permanent reminder to their neighbours of their family wealth and status. But first and foremost, their benefactions were prompted by a concern to erect before God a permanent witness to their piety and charity, which would plead for them at the Judgement Seat of Christ. The major benefactors of Long Melford church had their names inscribed on the outside of the clerestory, above the arches their money had raised, for all to see, but the primary object of the exercise was to prompt the grateful prayers of the parish. There is no need for excessive scepticism in the face of John Clopton insistence at the end of one such inscription requesting prayers for his and his family's souls that "may Christ be my witness, this is displayed not to earn praise, but that the soul may be remembered."[3]

The influence of the cult of the dead was ubiquitous. Yet it would be a mistake to deduce from its ubiquity that late medieval English religion was morbid or doom-laden. It was certainly not the case in England, as Huizinga thought was generally so in late medieval Christianity, that it knew only "lamentation about the briefness of all earthly glory" and "jubilation over the salvation of the soul". All that lay between these extremes, he argued "– pity, resignation, longing, consolation – remained unexpressed . . . absorbed by the too much accentuated and too vivid representation of Death hideous and threatening. Living emotion stiffens amid the abused imagery of skeletons and worms."[4] Graves and worms and epitaphs abounded in the late medieval English imagination, but the range of attitudes and responses to death and the afterlife were more complex and more humane than Huizinga's stark polarities suggest. Even the more measured formulation of "a cult of the living in the service of the dead" will not quite do as a description of the place of mortuary preoccupation in fifteenth- and early sixteenth-century

[3] N. Pevsner, *The Buildings of England: Suffolk*, 1974, p. 345.
[4] Huizinga, *Waning*, pp. 145–6.

England. This country certainly produced figures like John Fisher, of whom it was reported that when he said Mass "he always accustomed to set upon one ende of the altar a dead man's scull, which was also set before him at his table when he dyned or supped." English popular audiences, no doubt, flocked to performances of *Everyman*, that sombre exploration of the loneliness of the inescapable pilgrimage of death, or the Towneley play of Lazarus, with its gloating evocation of the processes of corruption

> Youre rud that was so red,   youre lyre the lylly lyke,
> Then shall be wan as led   and stynke as dog in dyke;
> Wormes shall in you brede   as bees dos in the byke,
> And ees out of your hede   thus-gate shall paddokys pyke.[5]

But late medieval responses to the prospect and reality of death were more complex and more varied than these examples might suggest. Even the wills of fifteenth- and sixteenth-century Englishmen and women testify not to a morbid obsession with death but to a vigorous relish for life. Their detailed and often loving listing of cherished possessions, their attempts to order lasting relationships among family and friends even from beyond the grave, and their circumstantial and businesslike prescription of elaborate exequies all provide abundant evidence not of morbidity, but of a practical and pragmatic sense of the continuing value of life and the social relations of the living, with a determination to use the things of this world to prepare a lodging in the next. If it is true that much of the religious activity of the period had death and the other world in mind, it is also true that the thought of mortality was endlessly harnessed by preachers and dramatists, not to call people away from social involvement but to promote virtue and sociability in this world. The cult of intercession for the dead can be seen as an incubus dominating the religion of the living, but it makes just as much sense to see it as a means of prolonging the presence of the dead within the community of the living, and therefore as the most eloquent of testimonies to the permanent value of life in the world of time and change.

The Image of Death

Still, there can be no questioning the imaginative power of death for the men and women of the late Middle Ages. This was the age of the *danse macabre*, that extraordinary and chilling portrayal of the

---

[5] Happe, *English Mystery Plays*, p. 405; B. Bradshaw and E. Duffy (eds), *Humanism, Reform and the Reformation: the Career of Bishop John Fisher*, 1989, p. 206.

universal power of death, in which pope and emperor, knight and peasant, lawyer and merchant, sergeant-at-law and monk, all find themselves confronted with a grinning corpse, not the abstract image of Death, but the image of themselves as they are soon to be. And all, however wretched their present lives, draw back from death, which makes even the relentless toil of the farm labourer seem desirable. The *danse macabre*, first portrayed round the cloisters of the cemetery of Les Innocents in Paris, was taken up by printers and by provincial wall-painters, and it rapidly established itself as one of the most haunting and most popular images of the age (Pl. 111).[6] It had arrived in England by the 1440s, when it was painted in the cloisters of the "Pardonkirkhay" at St Paul's. Lydgate translated the verses which accompanied the images, and a number of printed editions of the Sarum *Horae* had marginal illustrations of the *danse*. The *danse* at St Paul's had been swept away by 1549 (its rubble used in the building of Lord Somerset's new house in the Strand) and it never had the impact of the original at Les Innocents, but it was evidently impressive nonetheless. At Long Melford three long cloths hung before the Rood-loft, painted with "the dawnce of Powlis", and by the early sixteenth century a testator in faraway Ludlow could prescribe for his memorial brass two images depicting himself and his wife, and a third representing

the mortal after the daunce of powles having a scripture in his hand in this manner

"Man behold so as I am now, so shalt thou be
Gold and silver shall make no plea
This daunce to defend, but follow me."[7]

That insistence on the irresistibility of death was not in itself a particularly Christian emphasis, and indeed Huizinga saw in it evidence of a profound collapse of Christian faith. Certainly its essence was a message of transience, rather than transcendence, like the fashionably dressed cadavers who leered at the congregation from the late fifteenth-century screen in Sparham parish church, the woman carrying a posy of summer flowers, the man a burning torch labelled "Sic transit gloria mundi" (Pl. 114).[8] The universal

---

[6] On the *danse macabre* see E. Male, *Religious Art in France: the Late Middle Ages*, 1986, pp. 328–48; J. M. Clark, *The Dance of Death in the Middle Ages and Renaissance*, 1950; R. Eisler,"Dans Macabre", *Traditio*, VI, 1948, pp. 182–227.

[7] Parker, *History of Long Melford*, p. 86; H. T. Weyman, "Chantry Chapels in Ludlow Church", *Transactions of the Shropshire Archaeological and Natural History Society*, 3rd series, LV, 1904, pp. 359–60.

[8] The screen is described in C. L. S. Linnell, *St Mary's Sparham*, 2nd, ed., 1976.

appeal of the *danse macabre* and related imagery has been attributed to the impact of the Black Death, but in fact reflections on the inescapable fate of all flesh were common long before: the later Middle Ages saw the unfolding of the theme, not its invention. Many of the scraps of verse on the theme of mortality which are found in such numbers in sermons or commonplace and devotional collections on the eve of the Reformation had been in circulation in English for at least 300 years, and often had a long prehistory in Latin before that. They are certainly characterized by gloom about the human condidition

> With wind we blowen,
> With wind we lassun,
> With weopinge we comen,
> With weopinge we passun.
> With steriinge we byginnen,
> With steriinge we enden;
> With drede we dwellen,
> With drede we wenden.[9]

But it would be quite mistaken to see in this simple nihilism or even pessimism. The mood enshrined in such verses, as in the *danse* itself, was profoundly congenial to the ascetic ethos of much medieval piety, and from its first appearance it was seized on by preachers and moralists. This was Adam's legacy to all his race: "forto be borne yn sykenes, forto lyven yn travayle, and forto dye yn drede."[10] It quickly became one of the most important weapons in the armoury of anyone seeking to drive home the brevity of life, and the need to prepare for death while there was still time; this concern is what lies at the heart of the dramatic power of *Everyman*, for example. The tradition reflected a profoundly Augustinian other-worldliness, but it was hortatory and didactic as much as expressive, not the articulation of despair about the worth of human existence so much as part of a concerted attempt by religious and moral teachers to persuade the laity of the transience of earthly pleasures and goods, and the need to seek eternal salvation at all costs.

> He that hath thoughte
> ful in wardly and ofte
> How hard it is to flyt

[9] F. J. Furnivall (ed.), *Political, Religious and Love Poems from the Archbishop of Canterbury's Lambeth MS no. 306*, EETS, 1866, p. 227.
[10] *Festial*, p. 1.

> Fro bedde on to pytte
> Fro pytte on to pyne
> Whoche neveyr schal have fyne
> for alle thys world to wynne
> Wold not do a synne.[11]

To judge by the relentless regularity with which such sentiments were expressed from the pulpit and in the morality tradition, the laity needed some persuasion. They were not easily detached from the things of this world. There is therefore an element of shock tactics in the deliberate evocation of the horrors of death. Preachers spared no detail in order to bring their audiences to a sense of their own sinful frailty:

> Go to the buryeles of thy fader & moder; and suche schalt thou be, be he never so fayr, never so kunnynge, never so strong, never so gay, never so lyght. Loke also what fruyt cometh of a mon at alle yssues of his body, as at nose, atte mouthe, at eyghen, and atte alle the other ysghues of the body, and of the pryvey members, and he schall have mater to lowe his herte.

Man from his beginning was "a foule thing, litel and pore, . . . a stynkynge slime, and after that a sake ful of donge, and at the laste mete to wormes".[12] Such rhetoric found its visual equivalent in the rise to popularity, particularly among ecclesiastics, of the so-called *transi* or cadaver tombs, which portrayed the deceased as a decaying corpse, the skin stretched tight over grinning teeth, starting bones, and empty eye-sockets, the stomach bursting open to reveal a seething horror of worms and unclean creatures. The physically explicit character of these tombs had abundant parallels in devotional literature:

> I was ful fair now am i foul
> my faire fleische begynnyth forto stinke.
> Wormes fynden at me greet prow,
> i am hire mete i am hire drinke.
>
> I ligge wounden in a clout
> in boordis narwe i am nailid
> allas that evere i was proud.
> now alle mi freendis ben to me failid.

---

[11] *Reynes' Commonplace*, pp. 249–50, Tanner MS 407 fol. 36v, a version of a common poem, from the mid thirteenth century. See Carleton Brown, *Religious Lyrics of the Thirteenth Century*, no. 71, and notes to 13 and 71; Silverstein, *Medieval English Lyrics*, p. 21.

[12] Owst, *Preaching*, p. 341. And for an example of the difficulty of detachment, see the anguish of Humanum Genus in *The Castle of Perseverance*, ed. P. Happe in *Four Morality Plays*, 1987, when his goods are taken by Garcio – lines 3005–18.

In mi riggeboon bredith an addir kene.
min eighen dasewyn swithe dymme.
mi guttis roten myn heer is grene.
mi teeth grennen swithe grymme . . .

I rede every man that wiis wil be.
take kepe herof that i have seid.
thanne may he sikir of heven be.
whanne he schal in erthe be laid.[13]

Commenting on the English cadaver tombs of the fifteenth century, Lawrence Stone considered that "this emphasis upon the corruption of the flesh as opposed to the salvation of the soul marks a profound psychological change in the human outlook," and expressed himself puzzled that this strange preoccupation with "the material finality of death" should have been particularly marked among "the higher ecclesiastics of the age".[14] The puzzle is due to a wrong estimate of the significance of the whole cult of the cadaver: the emphasis on the corruption of the flesh was not perceived as being in any sense "opposed to the salvation of the soul". On the contrary, for all its gross physicality, its function was spiritual, to bring home to the spectator the reality of his own mortality, and thereby to bring him to a sense of the urgency of his need for conversion. More immediately, it was designed to evoke fellow-feeling and pity for the occupant of the tomb, and thereby to secure the help of the spectator's prayers, as in the brass Thomas Morys, grocer, commissioned for his and his wife's grave in 1506, showing their images "lyke ii deade cakas as pitiouslye made as canne be thoughte holdinge upp owr handes in ower wyndedinge sheats".[15] John Baret's cadaver tomb at Bury St Edmunds makes both these motives clear (Pl. 113). At Baret's head is the inscription:

He that wil sadly beholde one with his ie
May se hys owyn merowr and lerne for to die.

From the rest of the border of the pedestal, Baret himself speaks in appeal:

Wrappid in a selure as a ful rewli wrecche
No more of al myn good to me ward wil strecche
From erthe I kam and on to erth i am browht
This js my natur, for of erthe I was wrowht;

[13] J. C. Hirsch, "Prayer and Meditation in Late Medieval England", *Medium Aevum*, XLVIII, 1979, pp. 61–2.

[14] L. Stone, *Sculpture in Britain: the Middle Ages*, 2nd ed., 1972, pp. 213–14.

[15] Malcolm Norris, *Monumental Brasses*, 1977, p. 206.

Thus erthe on to erthe to gedir now is net
So endeth each creature Q'd John Baret
Qwerfor ye pepil in weye of charite
Wt yor god prayeris I prey yu help me
For lych as I am right so schal ye all be
Now God on my sowle have mercy & pite. Amen.[16]

As in the *danse macabre*, the corpse on the cadaver tomb was intended to speak to the living of their own not so remote fate. "Gode men," begins the sermon for funerals in Mirk's *Festial*, "as ye alle se, here is a myrroure to us alle: a corse browth to the chyrch."[17] The macabre treatment of death was rarely indulged in without this broader didactic purpose. Thomas More was a forceful exponent of the tradition: his *De Quatuor Novissimis*, written in 1522, excels in its attention to the grisly physical minutiae of human mortality, even in the very act of dying:

> lying in thy bedde, thy hed shooting, thy bak akyng, thy vaynes beating, thine heart panting, thy throat ratelyng, thy fleshe trembling, thy mouth gaping, thy nose sharping, thy legges coling, thy fingers fimbling, thy breath shorting, all thy strength fainting, thy lyfe vanyshing, and thy death drawyng on.[18]

Yet More was deeply suspicious of the cult of the macabre for its own sake. Neither the "daunce of death pictured in Poules" nor "the sight of all the dead heades in the charnel house" nor the "plain grievous sight of the bare bones hanging by the sinews" were of any value, he thought, unless they let sink into our hearts the "very fantasye and depe imaginacioun" of our own deaths, for it was that imagining which would bring us to consider our position before God, and thereby to a proper remembrance of the four last things, "deth, dome, pain, and ioy".[19]

It was the religious complex of these last things, death, judgement, Hell, and Heaven, that formed the essential focus of late medieval reflection on mortality, coupling anxiety over the brevity and uncertainty of life to the practical need for good works, to ensure a blissful hereafter. As Richard Hill recorded in his commonplace book,

Whan I thynk on thyngis thre
Well carefull may I be:

---

[16] N. Pevsner, *The Buildings of England: Suffolk*, 1974, pp. 144–5.
[17] *Festial*, p. 294.
[18] More, *Workes*, p. 77 F.
[19] Ibid., p. 77 D.

One is, that I shall henne;
An other is, I wot not when.
Offe the thirde is my most care,
For I shall dwell I wot not wher.
Man, remember whens thou com & wher thou shalt;
& to thyn evyn Cristyn do no wronge;
For man with-out marcy, of marcy shall misse;
And he shall have mercy, that marcyfull is.[20]

Behind that insistence on mercy lay a vision of judgement based on the parable of the sheep and goats in Matthew 25. On the Day of Doom, declared countless medieval preachers, Christ would assemble all the world before him, showing his wounds all fresh, new and bleeding. And he would "heghly thonke hom, and prayse hom that has don mercy to hor even-cristyn, and schall say thus to hom: My fadyrs blessyd chyldyrne comethe unto the joy that ever schall last. For when I was hongry, ye fedden me." But those who had withheld their goods from the poor he would banish to "the fyre of helle that ys ardeynt", because "ye wold do no mercy, and therfor ye schull have no mercy."[21]

Depicted above every Rood-loft and dramatized as the climax of all the cycles of Corpus Christi plays, that daunting vision haunted the popular imagination. The whole machinery of late medieval piety was designed to shield the soul from Christ's doomsday anger – "Ye cursed kaitiffes, fro me ye flee / In helle to dwelle with-outen ende."[22] And the general judgement of doomsday would be anticipated for the individual at death. Preparedness at the moment of death was, therefore, everything. But being prepared was the essence of the problem: death might strike at any moment. "O Death, thou comest when I had thee least in mind," declares Everyman, "for all unready is my book of reckoning."[23]

Such a vision must have seemed at times oppressive. But it was at this point that the relentless moralism of late medieval eschatology gave way to something else. It was fundamental to late medieval perception of human nature that, almost by definition, Everyman – every man and every woman – would be unprepared to meet the "Domesman", Christ, their good works inadequate, their sins overwhelming. Though the laity were endlessly exhorted to virtue, and to use their goods while they lived for the benefit

[20] Dyboski, *Songs*, p. 141; for another and earlier version see Furnivall, *Political, Religious and Love Poems*, p. 22.

[21] *Festial*, p. 4.

[22] Happe, *English Mystery Plays*, p. 645.

[23] G. A. Lester (ed.), *Three Late Medieval Morality Plays*, 1990, p. 69, lines 119, 134.

of the poor and sick, and thereby of their own souls, preparedness
for the moment of death could not be equated with a life of
successful endeavour after charity, for in that pursuit almost no one
was entirely, or even very successful. Everyman finds his good
works too weak and feeble to help him when he calls on them to
accompany him to the grave. His soul is saved not by them, but by
the grace of repentance, mediated through the Church's sacramental
system, confession and penance, anointing and viaticum. Shrift,
declares Everyman, is mother of salvation.[24]

The Hour of Death

It is no surprise, therefore, to find that "mors improvisa", sudden
and unforeseen death, was universally dreaded. The certainty of
death was made more terrible by the uncertainty of the hour of its
coming, which might catch the unsuspecting soul unawares and
sweep it to Hell. Death "giffes noo respit certayn to levyng creature, but takis thaym sodaynly". The wills of the period abound in
references to this suddenness and uncertainty, and to lay concern
for providing against it, "evermore havyng in remembraunce the
deylye casualtyes of dethe, the daye, and houre thereof no man is
worthy to knowe witout especyall grace of God Almyghtie". Such
"especyall grace" might reasonably be expected only by the saints,
yet direct divine forewarning of the hour of death was precisely
what many sinners yearned for. One of the most consistent features
of the many revelations and promises attached to the prayers and
devotions of the *Horae* and related manuscript devotional collections was the assurance that the devotee would never die in sin, or
"shall die no sudden death", or even that the Virgin would appear
to them and give them warning of approaching death.[25]

For time was what was needed. Everyman pleads with death for
another twelve years, but the speaker summoned away by death in
one of the most poignant of fifteenth-century mortality poems had
a more modest demand:

> Farewell this world, I take my leve for ever,
> I am arrested to appere affore Godis face.
> O mercyfull God, Thow knowest that i had lever
> Than all this worldis good to haue an owre space
> For to make aseth for my great trespace.[26]

[24] Ibid. p. 86, line 552.
[25] Hoskins, pp. 124–7; *Hor. Ebor.*, pp. 66, 76; Bodleian Library, Lyell MS 30 fols 49v,
51,116, 160v, etc.
[26] T. Silverstein (ed.), *Medieval Lyrics*, p. 112.

An hour is too little time for much in the way of amendment of life, too short a space for a wholesale distribution of goods to the poor: what is being asked for here is Everyman's boon, repentance sealed in the last sacraments of "schrift, housel, and anneling" – confession, communion, and anointing. The vernacular rhymes used by the laity at the elevation of the Host at Mass were often concerned, oddly as it seems to us, with securing this grace in the hour of death:

> Ihesu, lord, welcome thow be
> In forme of bred as I the se;
> Ihesu! for thy holy name,
> Schelde me to day fro synne & schame;
> Schryfte & howsele, lord, thou graunte me bo,
> Er that I schale hennes go,
> And verre contrycyone of my synne,
> That I lord never dye ther-Inne.[27]

In the same way, the laity sought the intercession of those saints with special influence in the hour of death or those credited with the ability to fend off sudden death – St Katherine, St Barbara or St Erasmus, who was believed to be able to guarantee housel and shrift to his devotees in the hour of death. When Richard ap Meredith was pierced by a spear in an affray at Barnet in 1489 the bystanders prayed to St Henry VI not for Meredith's recovery, but for his life to be prolonged sufficiently for him to make his last confession.[28]

Behind all this lay a more than merely conventional sense of "the incerten stroke of dethe and the souden knokkynge and flagicion of allmyghtty God".[29] There can be no doubt of the crucial importance attached to proper preparation for death by ordinary men and women, which underlay the expression of such sentiments in wills. "Forasmoche as the lif of man in this wretched world is shorte, uncertain and transitory," declared John Burgoyne in 1540, "it is necessary and requisite, for every true Christen man furst to provyde and ordeyn for the lif everlasting in hevyn."[30] The making

---

[27] Mirk, *Instructions for Parish Priests*, pp. 9–10; Robbins, "Levacion Prayers in Middle English Verse" *Modern Philology*, XL, 1942, pp. 131–46;

> O Iesu, for thy Holy Name
> Schelde me thys day fro sorro and schame.
> And lete me lyfe in trewth and ryght
> Before my dethe have hosyll and schryfte.

[28] Knox and Leslie, *Miracles of Henry VI*, pp. 56–7.
[29] *Test. Ebor.*, V pp. 198–201, VI p. 44; *Lincoln Wills*, II p. 15.
[30] *Beds. Wills*. III pp. 153–5.

of a will was itself one aspect of this provision, thought of not merely as a secular but as a religious duty. Even more important was the securing of time for repentance and the last Sacraments of the Church. One of the most consistent anxieties expressed by the laity in 1511 in the diocese of Canterbury was over priests who were absentees or slept out of the parish, so that "whan they have nede of a preest they goo to seke theym a preest, wherby many have died without shrifte or hoselle."[31]

A vivid insight into the way in which this preoccupation with "housel and shrift at my last ending" (Pl. 115) shaped late medieval perceptions of death is afforded by one of the entries in Robert Reynes's commonplace book, a version of the well-known series of the "signs of death". Derived from medical literature, these verses had a wide popular circulation from at least the thirteenth century. In their early versions they made a grim *memento mori*, without any very direct religious point, other than the general one of the transience of life:

> Whanne mine eyhnen misten
> And mine eren sissen,
> And my nose koldeth,
> And my tunge foldeth,
> And my rude slaketh,
> And mine lippes blaketh,
> And my mouth grenneth,
> And my spotel renneth,
> And my her risith
> And min herte griseth
> And mine honden bivien,
> And min fet stivien –
> All too late, all too late,
> Whanne the bere is ate gate.

Such sentiments were very likely to appeal to a late medieval man like Reynes. Indeed, his parish church had a striking verse inscription under one of the chancel windows, dating from the time of the Black Death and lamenting the universal sway of "lamentable death". Yet by the time Reynes copied a version of the rhyme for his own devotional use, its original starkness had been softened somewhat and harnessed to practical provision for the last hour. From a gruesome reminder of the finality of decay and death, the signs had been shaped into an exhortation to seek shrift as death approached:

[31] *Kentish Visitation*, pp. 62, 64, 115, 119.

Whan thi hed qualyth, *memento*
Whan thi lyppys blakyth, *confessio*
Whan thi nose scharpeth, *contricio*
Whan thi lymmys starkyth, *satisfaccio*
Whan thi brest panteth, *nosce te ipsum*
Whan thi wynde wantyth, *miserere*
Whan thi eyne fylmyn, *Libera me domine*
Whan deth folowyth, *venite ad judicium.*[32]

That men and women *in articulo mortis* should have set such store by the ministrations of the clergy is not in itself perhaps very remarkable, but it is a fact which has hardly, if at all, been allowed to impinge on discussions of late medieval perceptions of death and mortality. Astonishingly, for example, there is no real discussion of the Offices of the Visitation of the sick, anointing, burial, or "Dirige" in the most important modern historical treatment of death and dying, Ariès's *The Hour of Our Death.*[33] Yet the constantly reiterated concern to secure shrift and housel in the hour of death clearly represents a strong lay conviction, and not merely the mechanical acceptance of ecclesiastical directives. Significantly, there was no comparable emphasis on the desirability of the sacrament of Extreme Unction, for anointing was feared by the laity. In part this was on account of its frightening finality. The Church forbade anointing till death was imminent, so that reception of this sacrament effectively constituted a death sentence. But there was more to lay reluctance than this. It was widely and erroneously believed that the solemn anointing of all the senses involved in the reception of Extreme Unction was a sort of ordination or consecration, cutting the recipient off from the normal activities of life, even should they recover. They would have to live thereafter as a sort of animated corpse, as it was widely thought that "stinking Lazarus" had done after Jesus had raised him from the tomb. Despite all the authorities could do to reassure them, many lay people believed that an anointed person could never again eat meat, or have sexual relations with his or her spouse (Pl. 116).[34]

Ars Moriendi

Horror and fear are the emotions most commonly associated with late medieval perceptions of death and the life everlasting, and preachers, dramatists, and moralists did not hesitate to employ

---

[32] Luria and Hoffman, *Middle English Lyrics*, p. 224; *Reynes Commonplace* pp. 245–6.
[33] P. Ariès, *The Hour of Our Death*, 1981.
[34] W. Maskell, *Monumenta Ritualia*, I pp. ccxxiii–ccxxix, 95.

terror – of death, of judgement, of the pains of Hell or Purgatory – to stir their audiences to penitence and good works. But the priest at bedside or graveside had different priorities, and the texts of the services for the visitation of the sick and for burial were directed towards reassurance and support. The reality of evil and the peril of Hell were not shirked, any more than the personal sinfulness of the dying or dead parishioner, but the consistent emphasis of the services was on the power and will of God to save, and on the all-sufficiency of the merits of the crucified Christ for the sinner, from whom nothing but repentance and faith was required.

The note of reassurance was struck at the very outset of the *Ordo Visitandi*, not in words, but by a single, eloquent gesture. The priest was directed to hold up before the face of the dying person the image of the Crucifix "that in the image they may adore their redeemer and have in mind his passion, which he endured for their sins". It was this gesture which provided the trigger for the most remarkable theological achievement of the English late Middle Ages, the "showings" of Julian of Norwich. She has left an account of the incident which marked the beginning of her visions, when she lay "atte the poynte of dede" and her parish priest was sent for, "and a childe with hym, and brought a crosse". Holding the Crucifix before her, the priest said, "Dowghtter, I have brought the the ymage of thy savioure; loke there oponn and comforthe the there with in reverence of hym that dyede for the and me."[35] This was the standard opening of the service of visitation, and many texts devised to guide the clergy in their deathbed ministrations do little more than elaborate it. It was generally believed that the Devil's favourite ploy to disturb and terrorize the dying into despair was to convince them of the depravity of their own sins, and especially those not confessed and absolved. The *Ars Moriendi*, the immensely influential fifteenth-century tract compiled as a commentary and elaboration of the *Ordo Visitandi*, used a well-known devotional passage from St Bernard on the Crucifix to highlight the comfort of the cross: Christ there hung with arms extended to embrace, with head bowed to kiss the sinner, his pierced side exposing his heart of boundless love. And it reminded the dying man of the examples of great sinners who had by reliance on the cross become great saints – Peter, Mary Magdalene, the good thief on Calvary.[36] In a briefer English treatise of guidance for priests at the deathbed the priest was instructed to exhort the sick person:

[35] *Manuale*, p. 98: Colledge and Walsh (eds), *A Book of Showings*, I p. 208.
[36] Horstmann, *Yorkshire Writers*, II pp. 409–10.

Put alle thi trust in his passion and in his deth, and thenke onli
theron, and non other thing. With his deth medil the and wrappe
the therinne . . . and have the crosse to fore the, and sai thus; – I
wot wel thou art nought my God, but thou art imagened aftir
him, and makest me have more mind of him after whom thou
art imagened. Lord fader of hevene, the deth of oure lord Jhu
Crist, thi sone, wiche is here imagened, I set betwene the and my
evil dedis, and the desert of Jhu Crist I offre for that I shuld have
deservid, and have nought.[37]

But comfort was not the exclusive task of the priest, or the
only deathbed priority. He was to interrogate the dying person,
to discover whether or not they rejected heresy and desired to
die in the faith of Holy Church, whether they recognized and
truly repented their own sinfulness, and whether, setting aside all
merits of their own, they put their trust wholly in the passion of
Christ. He was to make sure that they were in charity with their
neighbours, forgiving any who had wronged them, and intending
in so far as they could to make reparation to any whom they had
wronged.[38]

The intensity of this deathbed scrutiny was left to the discretion
of the priest, but it was only after satisfying himself as far as
possible on all scores that he might proceed to absolve and anoint
the penitent. Pastoral practice here was expected to be tough.
The *Ars Moriendi* insists on the importance of bringing the dying
Christian to a knowledge of his or her condition, in order to evoke
from them a declaration of faith and repentance, even if they were
therby disturbed and frightened. It was better to trouble the sick
person to a "holsom fere and dred" than to allow them to be
damned because of "flaterynge and false dissimilacioun" on the
part of friends and relatives unwilling to "distroble" them by
emphasizing their imminent death. By the same token, all who had
to do with sick people, whether doctors, friends, or relatives, were
to see to it that the sick person was warned in good time of the
approach of death, and thereby brought to fulfil their duties by
receiving the last Sacrament, making their will, and disposing as
best they could for their dependents and households. Brief texts
advising lay people how to assist neighbours and friends on their
deathbeds, including brief interrogatories and forms of prayer,
circulated in manuscript, and both Caxton and Wynkyn de Worde
printed such guides.[39]

---

[37] Maskell, *Monumenta Ritualia*, III pp. 357–8; for the many surviving manuscripts of such
treatises for priests see Joliffe, *Check-List* pp. 122–6.
[38] Horstmann, *Yorkshire Writers*, II pp. 412–13.
[39] Ibid., pp. 418–20.

Behind these deathbed interrogations lay the belief that at the last the Devil would take advantage of the weakened state of dying sinners to launch a concerted attempt to pluck them from the arms of God, coming "in before you with a foule sort of ugsum souldiours / and assayle you in many sondry wyse".[40] In later medieval popular belief this attack was quite precisely analysed, and it was believed to be fivefold. The Devil would try to make the dying person sin against faith by slipping into heresy, superstition, or infidelity, to sin against hope by succumbing to despair on account of their great sins, to sin against charity by becoming impatient under their sickness, refusing to accept it from God and abusing those who tended the deathbed, to forfeit salvation by trusting in their own good deeds rather than solely in the merits of Christ, and finally to reject Heaven and the eternal world by clinging to the goods and relationships of the present world.

The desire to equip the clergy and laity for this final struggle gave rise to one of the central pastoral preoccupations of the late medieval Church, concern to inculcate the so-called *Ars Moriendi*. The "art of dying" was one which every human being had to master; hence arose the need to set out for the guidance, not only of clergy but of all Christians, the rationale underlying the deathbed pastoral practice of the late medieval church. This was formulated early in the fifteenth century by order of the Council of Florence, in the *Speculum artis bene moriendi*, a tract largely based on a work by Gerson, itself modelled on the Office for the visitation of the sick. Aimed at clergy and laity, "not only at lewed men but also to religiouse men", it sought to provide a general guide to the business of dying well. It was only for "uncunnyng of dying" that "the passage of deth owt of the wrecchidnesse of the exile of this world" seemed "wonderfull harde & ryght perlouse & also ryght ferefull & horrible". The treatise sought to rectify this by removing needless terrors about death itself, by preparing the Christian for the struggles against the Devil which characterized the last moments of all, and by providing prayers and guidance about conduct both to the persons dying and to those assisting them, including the priest. Appearing sometime between 1414 and 1418, it was quickly translated into English, circulated widely in manuscript and, with the advent of printing, was given even wider currency in both full-length and shortened versions by Caxton and others. The most influential chapter of the *Ars Moriendi* was devoted to the final

---

[40] R. Whitford, *A Dayly Exercyse and Experyence of Death*, ed. J. Hogg, Salzburg Studies in English Literature, 1979, p. 93.

deathbed temptations and their remedies. Reduced to the vivid
form of eleven pictures with a brief accompanying text, this scheme
became the basis for an immensely popular and influential block-
book, circulating in England as in the rest of Europe, and accessible
even to the illiterate.[41]

It is easy to see why this block-book captured the popular
imagination. For late medieval men and women the suffering of the
deathbed, as the sinful soul even of the most righteous drew near to
its judge, was "the moost grete necessyte & dystresse that euer unto
hym may come in this worlde".[42] The block-book gave vivid
expression to this conviction. It portrayed the deathbed as the
centre of an epic struggle for the soul of the Christian, in which the
Devil bent all his strength to turn the soul from Christ and His
cross to self-loathing or self-reliance. Against these temptations the
cross and the armies of the redeemed were marshalled to assist
the dying Christian. The bedroom became a crowded battlefield
centred on the last agonies of the man or woman in the bed.
The stages of this struggle were vividly resolved into striking
images. The temptation to despair was pictured as a theatrical troop
of demons enacting in the sickroom a pageant of all the deadly sins
(Pl. 117), the consolation offered by the thought of great penitents
portrayed by the presence by the bed of the good thief on his cross,
of Peter with his cockerel, and of the converted Paul tumbling from
his horse. The dying man's impatience and loss of charity was
vividly captured in a petulant flurry of bedclothes and tumbling
medicine-bottles and bowls (Pl. 118), and the final triumph of his
redemption in a complex scene in which the baffled devils retreat,
the relatives and helpers gathering in prayer and placing a taper in
the corpse's hand, while above the bed the ransomed soul is borne
by its angel to paradise (Pl. 119). It was a sequence which accepted
the reality of spiritual struggle and the deadly seriousness of the
business of salvation, while offering a message of reassurance
rooted in a vivid sense of the communion of the saints. At one
level the curiously passive figure of the dying Christian in the
block-book pictures is remote and lonely, so much so that some
commentators have thought of him as a spectator rather than a
participant in the drama. At another, he is the focal point for a
powerfully communal vision of the world, in which every individual is surrounded by a host of helpers and opposers, every lonely

---

[41] Discussed and illustrated in Mâle, *Religious Art in the Late Middle Ages*, pp. 348–55;
Ariès, *The Hour of Our Death*, pp. 107–10; they were adapted and absorbed into other
popular treatises on the Christian life – the *Ars Moriendi*, with the block-prints, forms part of
The Arte or Craft to Lyve Well and to Dye Well (1505), RSTC 792.

[42] *Ordynarye of Crysten Men*, sig. kk iii(v).

step in the drama of dying in reality a participation in a communal
effort, in which living friends and relatives and dead patrons and
intercessors join hands to assist.[43]

The deathbed regimen of the late medieval Church made a deep
impression on the laity. Concern with securing the ministrations of
a priest and the comfort of the last Sacraments at the hour of death
manifested itself in every aspect of late medieval piety. As we have
seen, lay people in parishes with non-resident clergy worried about
this problem above all.[44] Hence the recurrence of rubrics in the
printed primers promising that devout users of particular devotions
"shall not perish with sudden death". In some Sarum primers users
of the prayer to the Virgin beginning "Obsecro Te" were promised
that Mary would appear to them and "shewe them her blessed
vysage and warne them the day et the owre of dethe", so as to
enable them to receive the Sacraments. Those who recited daily the
hymn "Ave Maria, ancilla Trinitatis" were promised that they
would not "depart owte of thys worlde wytheout penaunce and
mynystracyyon of the holy sacramente". For Mary was above all
the saint of the deathbed, one who guaranteed even her most
wayward and sinful clients the grace of shrift and housel, rescue
from the rigours of judgement at that moment of truth. Her
miracles included stories of how she had even raised from the dead
sinful devotees who had died unshriven of a mortal sin, so that
they could die properly confessed. Another told of a sinful client
whisked in his sleep to the Judgement Seat of God. He appeals in
vain for help to Truth and Righteousness, for he has been the
Devil's servant many a year,

> and our Lord said: Bring forth the balance, and let all good and
> evil be weighed; and then Truth and Righteousness said to the
> sinner, Run with all thy thought unto the Lady of mercy which
> sitteth by the judge, and study to call her to thine help. And
> when he had so done, the Blessed Virgin Mary came in to his
> help and laid her hand upon the balance whereas were but few
> good deeds. And the devil enforced him to draw on that other
> side, but the Mother of Mercy won and obtained and delivered
> the sinner. And he came again to himself and amended his life.[45]

---

[43] On the dying man as spectator of rather than participant in the deathbed struggles, see
A. Tenenti, *La Vie et la Mort à travers l'art du XVe siècle*, Cahiers des Annales, VIII, 1952,
p. 55; Nancy Lee Beaty, *The Craft of Dying: a study of the literary tradition of the Ars Moriendi*,
1970, pp. 1–53; Sister Mary Catherine O'Connor, *The Art of Dying Well: the Development of
the Ars Moriendi*, 1942.

[44] See above, pp. 310–3.

[45] *Golden Legend*, V pp. 107–10, IV pp. 247–54; Hoskins, p. 124; *Hor. Ebor.*, pp. 66, 137.

The fortunate sinner is given a second chance, Everyman's boon of time for amendment, and the warning needed to make a good end. That scene, and the part played in it by Mary's prayers, was precious to late medieval people: like the sinner in the story, in their last hour they "studied to call to their help" the Lady of Mercy. A conventional iconography developed, showing Michael, the other great saint of the deathbed, weighing souls in the scale of justice, the naked soul in one pan, straining devils tugging at the other. Behind the Archangel a gentle (and often diminutive) Virgin decides the struggle by laying her rosary on the sinner's side. The frequency with which this scene recurs in the late Middle Ages leaves no room for doubt about the importance of the beliefs and hopes it represented. Versions of it were turned out by the Nottingham alabaster factories (Pl. 120), carved on church porches and altar-pieces, and painted on the walls of sickrooms to console the dying (Pl. 121). In the 1530s the parishioners of Wellingham had the scene vividly painted in pride of place on their new chancel screen (Pl. 122). [46]

The same concern manifested itself in the cult of the other saints too. The early sixteenth-century text of the legend of St Walstan, displayed over his shrine at Bawburgh, told how the saint, being supernaturally warned of his approaching death, sends for the parish priest,

> that the Sacrament I may receive soo
> & take holy councell of that Clerke,
> to be delivered from all workes darke
> & receive of the holy altar the sacrament,
> & ere I die to make my testament. [47]

Perhaps the most striking and certainly the oddest manifestation of this concern with protection against sudden and unrepared death was the St John's fast or the Wednesday fast. This was a custom promoted in a doggerel pamphlet printed by Wynkyn de Worde in 1500. It was still flourishing in the late 1530s, when Bishop Shaxton of Salisbury recorded that the ringleader of the opponents of the Reformation in Salisbury, "a blind ignorant man and willful", was "a faster of St John's fast upon the Wednesday". The fast involved abstention from meat every Wednesday of one's life, "in the worshypp of John baptyst and Kathryn, Crystofre and

---

[46] The room in the Commandery at Worcester which contains a wall-painting of the weighing scene was probably the infirmary of the hospital of St Wulstan; see *The History of the Commandery, a Pre-Reformation Hospital*, pp. 14v, 15. For the Nottingham image see Cheetham, *English Medieval Alabasters*, Pl. III and p. 134.

[47] M. R. James (ed.), "Lives of St Walstan", p. 255.

margarete". In return one was guaranteed access to a priest and reception of the last Sacraments before one died. The promise was backed up by a series of miracle stories illustrating its efficacy:

> In Irelonde I rede / of a full grete wonder
> A quarrey was fall / and a man laye there under.
> And was there fyve dayes / and at last was shryve
> For he dyd on wednesday / forbere flessh al his lyve.
>
> There was a ship of dertmouth / saylyng to saynt Iame
> They cast out a deed man / than came agayn the same
> & founde the body upon the stronde / that over borde was cast
> That spake & had his rightes / for wednesday fast . . .
>
> At the batayll of durham / I rede there was a hede
> Fyfty yere under erthe / that laye so longe deed
> A squyer herde a voyce / that rode the water by
> For wednesdayes fast / after a preest I crye.
>
> There was a man of lawe / besyde wodestoke
> That fell from his horse / his necke was to broke
> For he fasted the wednesdaye / ever spake the heed
> Until I have a preest / shall I never be deed.[48]

At a somewhat profounder level, the conviction that the Devil would assail the faith of the dying Christian, and concern for preservation in faith, hope, and charity at that moment, manifested itself in a series of four English prayers printed regularly in the Sarum and York *Horae*. These were in most cases the only English prayers occurring in primers before the 1520s, which were otherwise exclusively in Latin. The fact that they are all concerned with a good death is eloquent testimony to the centrality of this pre-occupation for the purchasers and users of the primers.[49] The first of these prayers is concerned with devout reception of the Sacrament on one's deathbed:

> O glorious Jesu, o mekest Jesu, o moost swetest Jesus, I praye the that I may have true confessyon, contrycyon and satisfaction or I dye, and that I may se and receyue they holy body God man Savyour of al mankynde, Cryst Jesu without synne, and that thou wylt, my Lorde God, forgyve me all my synnes for thy

---

[48] RSTC 24224: *Here begynneth a lytel treatyse that sheweth how every mon & woman ought to fast and absteyne them from flesshe on the Wednesday*, W. de Worde, 1500; L&P XIV (i) no. 777.
[49] *Hor. Ebor.*, p. 85.

gloryous woundes and passyon, and that I may end my lyfe in
the true fayth of holy churche, and in perfyte love and charytc
with all myn even crysten.

The prayer continues with a series of invocations to the sacramental
presence of Christ; it was probably intended for direct use by or
with dying people. The second and third of this group of deathbed
prayers were intended for daily use while in health, pre-emptively
expressing contrition and complete dependence on the passion of
Christ "crucifyed and wounded, and out of thy herte rennynge
plentously blode and water for the redemcyon of me and all
mankynde". The last prayer in the group seeks to guard against
succumbing to the temptation of despair or infidelity in the agony
of death:

> I poore synner make this daye in despyte of the fende of hell
> protestacyon that yf by aventoure ony temptacyon, decepcyon,
> or varyacyon comyng by sorowe, peyne or sekenesse, or by ony
> feblenesse of body, or by ony other occasyon what somever it
> be, I fall or declyne in peryll of my soule, or preiudyce of my
> helthe, or in errour of the holy fayth catholyke, in which I was
> regenerate in the holy font of baptym:
> Lord God in good mynde, in which I holde me now by thy
> grace, wherfore with all my herte I thanke the, of that erroure
> wyth my power I resiste, and here renounce, and of the same one
> confesse in protestyng that I wyll lyve and deye in the fayth of
> holy chirch our moder, and thine espouse.[50]

Clearly, prayers and preoccupations of this sort made an impression on the laity. Avelyne Carter, a Norwich widow, incorporated
them wholesale in her will in 1508. Declaring her determination
with God's help "to lyve and dey in the Fayth of Holy Church",
she went on:

> and therfor yf yt fortuneth me by Reason of Sykness, ille
> Custome, Alienacon of Mynde, Tribulacon, Temptacyon or
> any Vexacyon of the Devyll, to do, wyll, sey, or thynck, or
> otherwise thanne holy Church hath ordeyn'd, as God forbyd, I
> now at this Tyme, for that Tyme, revoke yt, and forsake yt,
> and hartly pray Almyghty God of forgyvenes, onto whome I
> mekely comend my Soule, and to our blyssyd Lady St Mary, St
> Lawrence, my Adwer, and all Saints.[51]

[50] *Hor. Ebor.*, p. 87.
[51] Blomefield, *Norfolk*, IV p. 270.

The same concerns find vivid illustration in the surviving account of the deathbed of a London woman, Alice Gysbye. Falling ill with a great swelling in her throat on the Sunday before Embertide, she called on her neighbours "saing neyghbors for goddes sake praye for me / for I am very syke / and I thynke I shall never eskape yt". These were her last coherent words: through the week her condition worsened, but her curate deferred bringing her the Sacrament. When, finally, agitated neighbours fetched a priest from a local alehouse and he brought her the Host, she was too far gone to respond. The priest and neighbours "dydd cry and call meny tymes unto the seid Alice to loke upon the sacrament then standing by hir, and knocked hir upon the breste but [she] didd nother looke upon the sacrament nother dydd make any knowledge or countynaunce to yt". Women standing by called out "What wyll ye dye lyke a hellhound and a beast / not remembring your maker", and later that day one of her friends pleaded at her bedside "Alice I am here, I pray you speke to me and remember the passhion of Christ and speke for your soule helth."[52]

This was 1538, at the zenith of the reformist phase of the Henrician Reformation, and perhaps contemporary worries about heresy added special urgency to the traditional concerns of Alice Gysbye's neighbours. But in its essentials this scene was enacted at many less fraught deathbeds, for it is clear that there was a well defined set of attitudes and gestures which dying Christians were expected to manifest at this, the most solemn and important moment of their lives. The deathbed was a communal event, not a private one.

There was a practical side to all this. Since the deathbed was normally the occasion for will-making, the dying property-owner was likely to be surrounded by family, business associates, and executors, concerned with the disposal of property – what preachers and moralists were prone to dismiss as "a rabble of fleshly frendes, or rather of flesh flies".[53] The textbooks were unanimous in urging the banishing of all such concerns from the deathbed, but in fact they had a definite religious content. Justice and charity alike demanded that the dying Christian should be reconciled not only to God, but to neighbour also. To have hope of Heaven the Christian must die in charity, reconciled to enemies, if possible having paid, or being purposed to pay, all debts. Any unfinished business of this sort would have to be expiated in Purgatory, and so the wills of

---

[52] R. Wunderli and Gerald Brose, "The Final Moment before Death in Early Modern England", *Sixteenth Century Journal*, XX, 1989, pp. 268–9.
[53] Horstmann, *Yorkshire Writers*, II p. 417; More, *Workes*, p. 78.

propertied men and women regularly reflect this eleventh-hour concern to set right all that was amiss in their familial and business relationships, and to make amends to "all thos persones that ever I toke any good wrongfully". Where such debts could no longer be repaid in kind – if the person wronged was already dead – money might be set aside for intercession for their souls, a spiritual repayment.[54] But the bonds of simple neighbourliness also found religious expression at this moment above all. The sick and their families were supported by the company, prayers, and encouragement of friends and neighbours, and lay people who knew the right prayers or had a reputation for sanctity, and could thus assist the dying person to make a good death, were especially welcome. Margery Kempe was in considerable demand among her neighbours to attend and pray by deathbeds.[55] This was not an entirely one-sided transaction, for in return, the dying person was expected to affirm the common framework of value and belief by manifesting orthodox faith and the approved signs of piety. Richard Whytford evoked a typical early Tudor deathbed, with "the people about, some wepynge and mournyng / some cryenge, and callynge upon the sycke / to remember our lorde god and our most swete sanyor Jesu Christ / our blessyd lady with other holy sayntes".[56] We glimpse the same picture of family and neighbours surrounding the dying person, a pail of holy water to hand so that they "and other that ben aboughte them" might be often sprinkled, "that fendes may be voyded from hem", in the *Ars Moriendi* (Pl. 123).[57]

The approved attitudes expected from the dying Christian in this conventional scene were on display in the last words of another Londoner, Jane Monford, to her neighbours: "I thanke god nowe I have receaved my maker, and I doo aske all the world forgyvnes, and I pray you bear me recorde that when I shall dy I doo dye a true Christian."[58] The distinctive emphasis on repentance and reconciliation, trust in the Passion, and doctrinal orthodoxy manifested in devout reception of the Sacraments and witnessed by devout neighbours was no doubt heightened by the circumstances of the 1530s and the spread of heresy, but it was not created by

[54] *Instructions for Parish Priests*, p. 64; S. Thrupp, *The Merchant Class of Medieval London*, 1948, pp. 176–7; for some striking examples, "Extracts from Early Norfolk Wills", ed. H. Harrod, *Norfolk Archaeology*, IV pp. 329–31; *Lincoln Wills*, II p. 142; *Somerset Wills*, II pp. 3–4, III p. 175; Whiting, "For the health of my soul", p. 70; J. C. Cox and R. M. Serjeantson, *A History of the Church of the Holy Sepulchre, Northampton*, 1897, pp. 242–3.
[55] *The Book of Margery Kempe*, pp. 172–3.
[56] Whytford, *A Dayly Exercyse and experyence of Dethe*, p. 93.
[57] Horstmann, *Yorkshire Writers*, II p. 417.
[58] R. Wunderli and Gerald Brose, "The Final Moment", pp. 268–9.

them. John Dalton, a Hull merchant making his will in 1497, besought God that he might die "the true son of holy kirk, of heart truly confessed, with contrition and repentance of all my sins that ever I did since the first hour I was born of my mother into this sinful world". The same model of the ideal deathbed was operative in John Fisher's funeral sermon for Henry VII, preached ten years before Luther's revolt, in which Fisher described the king's "true byleve that he had in God, in his chirche & in the sacramentes therof, which he receyved all with mervaylous devocion, namely in the sacrament of penaunce, the sacrament of the auter, & the sacrament of anelynge". Fisher dwelt in particular on Henry's humility before the Blessed Sacrament "with suche a reverence, with so many knockynges & betynges of his brest", and on his devotion on the day of his death towards the Crucifix. "The ymage of the crucyfyxe many a tyme that day full devoutly he dyd beholde with grete reverence, lyftynge up his head as he myght, holdynge up his handes before it, & often embracyncge it in his armes & with grete devocion kyssyng it, & betynge ofte his brest", so that "all stode aboute hym scarcely myght conteyne them from teres & wepynge."[59]

One of the most striking features of the deathbed regimen displayed in late medieval sources was its Christocentricity. Peter Heath, writing of the wills of late medieval merchants of Hull, has asserted the contrary, claiming that the invocation of Christ's name was mingled in such wills "with too many other invocations": yet the particular example he cites, that of John Dalton in 1497, demonstrates the very clear theological priorities which the Church had imprinted on the sensibilities of the educated laity:

> I recommend in humble devotion, contrition and very repentance of my defaults and sins, praying and crying to our saviour, Jesus Christ. And in this I commend and will my soul to our Lord Jesus Christ when it shall depart from my body and to our Lady Saint Mary, St Michael, St John the Baptist, St John the Evangelist, St Katherine, and St Barbara and all the holy company of saints of heaven.[60]

Dalton here is following to the letter the instruction of the *Ars Moriendi* to pray first for deliverance by the Saviour, Christ, "and afterwards ... lett him cry to oure blessed lady seynt Mary ... to angellis ... and specially to tho seyntis which he loved & wor-

---

[59] Peter Heath, "Urban Piety in the Later Middle Ages", in R. B. Dobson (ed.), *The Church, Politics and Patronage*, 1984, p. 213; Fisher, *English Works*, pp. 272–4.

[60] Heath, *op. cit.*, pp. 213–14.

shipped moste specially in his hele, that thei will helpe hym than in his laste & most neede."[61] The late medieval Christian was encouraged to seek the support of the saints at the hour of death as in life, and deathbed devotion abounded to saints associated with the boundaries between life and death – John the Baptist and John the Evangelist, who were both intercessors at the Judgement, or St Peter. The angels featured prominently in the iconography of the deathbed, battling the Devil and receiving the soul. Michael was an especially important figure, since in late medieval iconography he epitomized the victory of God over all that was demonic. He was "the provost of Paradyse", and presided over the weighing of souls. Images of Michael were frequently placed alongside the door from nave to chancel, for he stood at the door between this world and the next. So Michael in particular and angels in general were invoked as particularly powerful protectors "whanne drede of helle schal agaste the outgoinge of my soule from the bodi".[62] But, in the words of John Bossy, the medieval believer "knew who his saviour was", and was taught to place his trust first and foremost in the Passion of Christ. The precise theological balance of the *Ordo Visitandi* and the *Ars Moriendi* is exactly reproduced in a number of striking preamble formulas of fifteenth- and early sixteenth-century wills, as in that of John Olney of Weston:

> Atte the begynnynge I bequethe my soule into the mercy off mythfull Ihesu, prahyng hym, for his precious passioun, that he resseyve me yn-to the brode bosum off his mercy; prahyng forthermore to his modur, hour lady Seynt Mary, modur of mercy, to seynt Iohn Euangelist, seynt Iohn Baptist, and to hall seyntes off hevene, that they be menez for me, and helpers to me att my most nede.[63]

That "forthermore", like "afterwards" in the *Ars Moriendi*, expressed a qualitative and not merely a sequential priority. The distinction between the saving action of God in Christ and the intercessory help of the saints is registered again and again, as in the will of Robert Constable, a northern gentleman:

> "Fyrst I bequeth my sole to Almyghty God, beseching the most blissed Virgine our lady Seynt Mary, wt all the holy Seyntes in

---

[61] Horstmann, *Yorkshire Writers*, II p. 415.

[62] J. E. Stocks, *Market Harborough Parish Records to 1530*, 1890, pp. 216–17 (will of 1521 with the "provost of paradise" phrase); see the series of prayers to angels in British Library Add MS 10596 fols 55 v ff.

[63] *Earliest English Wills*, p. 47; there is a very similar formula in the will of Lord John Scrope, 1498, *Test. Ebor.*, IV pp. 94–5.

heven, to prey for my seyd soule, that it shall pleas Almighty God of his aboundant grace and pety to receyve it to His mercy."[64]

The will of Richard Gravely, a London grocer, started with

"Ferst y bequeth my sowle to our lord God Almyghty, maker of hevene and of yerth, praeyng and besekyng our lady seynt Mary . . . & all the company of hevne to pray for me to our lord Ihesu our savyour, that y may have mercy and foryevenysse of synne."[65]

Such formulas are more elaborate than the conventional openings of most wills, but they are an important indication of the theology concealed under simpler bequests of the soul to Christ and the saints. The more subtle preambles are to be found in the wills of devout people throughout the century before the Reformation, and they frequently echo the very wording of the *Ars Moriendi* and the pastoral textbooks provided for clergy at the sick-bed. The results can be very striking. The injunction to "put alle thi trust in his passion and in his deth, and thenke onli theron, and non other thing . . . medil the and wrappe the therinne," and the instruction that the dying person should say "Lord I put the deth of oure lord Ihesu Crist betwene me and myn evil dedes, betwene me and thi Iugement,"[66] themselves derived from the liturgy, are deliberately recalled in the phrasing of many wills. As might be expected, the correspondences are closest in the wills of clergy. In a fascinating group of wills made at the turn of the fifteenth and sixteenth centuries by priests associated with Archbishop Rotherham and his College of Jesus at Rotherham, each of the testators uses identical words, beseeching the Trinity to have mercy "of me a synfull creature", praying Christ "of his infinite mercy to put his most excellent passion betwix my soull and his reightwise judgement", asking forgiveness for sins not duly confessed or for which no penance had been done, and invoking the prayers of Mary and the saints.[67] This carefully articulated schema, which moves from the merits of Christ to the sacraments of the Church and the prayers of the saints no doubt reflects the preoccupation with orthodoxy so evident among the higher clergy in the early Tudor period, but it is also frequently echoed in the wills of pious and well-to-do lay folk. In just this way John Estbury committed his soul to the Trinity in 1507, and went on to repudiate his own merits, placing his trust entirely in God:

Whom I beseche ever of his mercy and grace for that I have offended hym in my synfull lyving here in yerthe, specially in

[64] *Test. Ebor.*, IV p. 195.
[65] *Earliest English Wills*, p. 80.
[66] Horstmann, *Yorkshire Writers*, II, p. 413.
[67] *Test. Ebor.*, V pp. 28–32, 196–8.

brekyng of his commaundmentes and mesusyng of such goodes
as I have occupied under his sufferaunce; and ever to putt betwixt
my synfull soule and his rightfulnes at the day of my dredful
Judgement his infynite mercy; and also I beseche our blessid lady
seynt Mary wt the speciall helpe of all the holy company of
heven and of my advowers Peter and Pawle, seynt Frideswide,
seynt barbara, seynt brigett, seynt Kateryne, & King Henry if he
be soo at our Lorde accepted, to be mediators for my soule, and
all my frendes here in yerthe to pray for me.[68]

The self-consciously "correct" theology of this preamble is evident
even in the qualification attached to his invocation of the intercession of the uncanonized Henry VI "if he be soo at our Lorde
accepted". Indeed, a careful theological schema seems to be at
work in many of these wills. Colin Richmond has commented on
the "remarkable opening" of the unmistakably personal will of
Sir Roger Townsend, a successful Blythburgh lawyer who died
in 1492, but the distinctive tone of Townsend's will is clearly
derived from his internalization of the theology underlying the late
medieval church's deathbed ministrations, of which it might be
taken as a convenient epitome. Townsend commits his soul to God,
his maker and redeemer,

besechyng him for the merytes of his bitter and gloriouse passion
to have mercy oon me and to take me into his mercy which is
above all workes, unto whom it is approposed to have mercy . . .
of the wych numbre of contrite synners I mekely and humbly
besechith him that I may be oon and one of the predestinate to be
found and the rather thorow the meanes of our most blessid lady
modre and mayde and of all the aungells of hevyn and patriarks
prophets apostels maters confessours virgyns and all the hooly
company of hevyn and in speciall of them that I have moost in
remembraunce. Now I hertly pray themme of their soccour and
help that I may be partyner of the sacramentes and merites of all
hooly church and to end my lyff in the same to passover and so
fynally to be oon of the Numbre at the dredfull day of dome that
shall stond and be oon of his right hand.[69]

Death and Memory

The language of memory pervaded the cult of the dead: the
obsequies celebrated for each departed soul on the seventh and the
thirtieth day after burial, and on the first anniversary, were called
the week's, month's, and year's "mind" or remembrance. The focal

[68] Footman, *History of . . . Lambourn*, pp. 73–4.
[69] Richmond, *John Hopton*, pp. 244–5.

point of the Church's liturgy of supplication for the dead, All Souls' Day, was properly called the "Commemoration" of All Souls. It was, of course, the desire for prayer which lay at the root of this preoccupation with remembering. The dead needed to be remembered, for the dead were, like the poor, utterly dependent on the loving goodwill of others. For all the stories of apparitions and Purgatory spirits walking to disturb their survivors, it was orthodox teaching that the living hold no direct converse with the dead.[70] For medieval people, as for us, to die meant to enter a great silence, and the fear of being forgotten in that silence was as real to them as to any of the generations that followed. But for them that silence was not absolute and could be breached. To find ways and means of doing so was one of their central religious preoccupations. For what late medieval English men and women at the point of death seem most to have wanted was that their names should be kept constantly in the memory and thus in the prayers of the living.

For the well-to-do, this presented few problems. If not many of the wealthy were building and endowing perpetual chantry foundations in the parish churches of the fifteenth and early sixteenth centuries, they still lavished money on long-term mortuary provisions. Like other forms of conspicuous consumption, these were certainly designed to display the testator's wealth and social status, and for that reason they were attacked by preachers and moralists. They had a less suspect religious rationale, however, which was, quite simply, to make it impossible for the living to forget or ignore the founder's name and his or her continuing spiritual need. One form of such provision was to create a class of pensioner whose sole occupation was to remember the benefactor – the chantry priest (perpetual or temporary) is an obvious example, but the creation of almshouses or the endowment of existing institutions provided another. The poor men of John Estbury's Berkshire almshouse, founded before his death in 1507, were required not only to recite daily parts of the Little Hours of the Blessed Virgin, the penitential Psalms and the Office for the Dead in the parish church at Lambourne, but to gather each midday after Mass round Estbury's tomb and recite the Paternoster and Ave Maria, before which the senior bedesman announced aloud and in English that they prayed "For John Isburies sowle, the sowls of his parents, auncestors, frendes, and all christian sowles".[71] Nor was such provision confined to religious services. It was a common mark of familial piety to adopt the monastic custom of reciting the

---

[70] *Arte or Crafte*, fol. lxxxx [*sic*].
[71] *History of . . . Lambourn*, p. 187.

"De Profundis" for dead benefactors (especially parents) during grace at meals.[72] Wealthy testators could exploit this pious custom to keep their own memories alive. John Alger, prebendary of St Stephen's, Westminster, left his brethren a silver-gilt loving-cup in 1536 on condition that each day at grace they said "God have mercy of Maister Algars sowle."[73] At Bury St Edmunds John Baret got even better value for money by prescribing that his chantry priest, who lodged in the town, should pray for his soul at every meal wherever he dined, "and yif he gyvve gracys and say De Profundis, he to reherse my name, John Baret, opynly, that they th[a]t here it may sey, *God have mercy on his soule*", thereby conscripting the other diners as Baret's bedesmen.[74]

The best remembrance was that in which the whole parish community participated. "Synguler preyere," wrote the author of *Dives and Pauper*, "is good in chambre & in oratorie and betere in chirche, but comoun prayere of a comonte in chirche is beter."[75] And here again wealth could command attention. Chantry chapels in the parish church, like the Clopton chapel at Long Melford or the Greenway chapel at Tiverton, could be festooned with inscriptions beseeching the prayers of all who read them. Considerable ingenuity was exercised to ring the changes on this simple idea. We have already encountered John Baret's cadaver altar-tomb at Bury, with a *memento mori* rhyme invoking the prayers of the parish. He had purchased a bull of pardon, and this he commanded to be framed and set by the tomb, "th[a]t it may be redde and knowe to exorte the pepill rathere to pray for me".[76] But the physical reminder even of a deliberately shocking memorial like a cadaver tomb, in any case the prerogative of the very rich, was less effective than the integration of the name and remembrance of the testator into the parish liturgy. The fifteenth-century London merchant, William Cambrigge, built a chantry chapel dedicated to St Stephen in the parish church of St Mary at Hill. Naturally, his chapel had its own liturgical round, and in addition his priest was required to play a full part in the worship of the parish, but another bequest secured

---

[72] *Festial*, p. 85.
[73] *Somerset Wills*, III p. 33.
[74] *Bury Wills*, p. 21.
[75] *Dives and Pauper*, I p. 196.
[76] Whiting, "For the health of my soul", p. 69; *Bury Wills*, p. 19. For a similar display on a monument of an indulgence as an inducement for memorial prayer, Wordsworth and Littlehales, *Old Service Books*, p. 289 (c). There was a distinctive genre of "Pardon Brasses" designed to secure prayers of this sort, the best known of which is probably that of Roger Legh of Macclesfield (d. 1506), which promises 26,000 years' and 26 days' pardon! See also R. M. Serjeantson, "The Restoration of the Long-lost Brass of Sir William Catesby", *Associated Architectural Societies Reports*, XXXI, 1911–12, pp. 519–24.

the perpetual recognition of Cambrigge's status as a major parochial benefactor during the Christmas liturgy itself, when the clergy and choir held a candlelight procession at evensong on St Stephen's day to sing an antiphon at his tomb. Testators who could afford it might make provision for candles to burn over their graves during the parish Mass on Sundays and holidays, and pay the clergy to draw the attention and the suffrages of the parish by reciting the "De Profundis" with an appropriate collect, and sprinkling holy water on the grave before Mass began. It was common for chantry clergy celebrating trentals in parish churches to be required to name the benefactor for whom the Mass was being offered, and to lead the congregation in the recitation of a Pater or the "De Profundis", at the lavabo of the Mass.[77]

A simple way to link the perpetual memory of one's own name with the worship of the community was to give to the church a missal, vestment, vessel, or other ornament with an appropriate inscription. A favourite choice was a chalice with one's name on lip or foot, so that as the priest raised it at the sacring he would read it, and in any case he symbolically raised one's name to God. A wider audience could be achieved with altar frontals and even Mass vestments "with a scriptur on the back . . . desiring the parishens to pray for my soule". The advent of printing, far from banishing such gestures, increased the scope for them: the magnificent *Missale* printed by Pynson for Archbishop Morton in 1500, "perhaps the finest book printed in England before 1501", had a printed inscription asking for prayers for Morton, turning every church where the book was used into an informal chantry.[78] Inscribed books, vestments, and vessels were normally intended initially for use in temporary chantries, but after the chantry lapsed they passed – and were intended to pass – into parochial use, thereby ensuring a more extended if diffused perpetuation of the chantry.[79] A similar (and considerably less expensive) symbolic extension of specific mortuary provision into parish worship was the common stipulation that endowed torches, designed to burn around the testator's tomb or at his obsequies for a specified number of years, should thereafter be bestowed on the altar during Mass.[80] For the very wealthy, even closer association of one's own memory with the Eucharistic mystery might be possible. One Bristol testator gave a

[77] London, St Mary at Hill CWA, p. 16; "Churches of West Kent", p. 246: *Test. Ebor.*, V p. 10; *Sussex Wills*, III pp. 159–60.
[78] "Inventories of St Stephen's, Bristol", pp. 168, 169 (three inscribed chalices); *Sussex Wills*, III p. 172; *London Consistory Court Wills*, pp. 44–5 (inscribed chalice and vestment); *Testamenta Cantiana: West* p. 19 (altar frontal), 24 (vestments). For the Morton Missal see Bennett, *English Books and Readers*, p. 47.
[79] Burgess, "For the Increase of Divine Service", pp. 61–4.
[80] *Sussex Wills*, III pp. 159–60.

silver-gilt tabernacle shrine to stand on the high altar, on which were carved representations of himself and his wife in adoration.[81] Best of all was the identification of one's own burial with the mystical burial of Christ's body in the Holy Week liturgy. As we have seen, a number of fifteenth-century testators were buried in tombs on the north side of the chancel, designed to serve as the base of the Easter sepulchre in Holy Week, the focus of the most solemn annual expression of the parish's worship of the Sacrament. There was more to all this than an appreciation of the symbolism of death and resurrection. Since the sepulchre itself invariably attracted multiple bequests of lights from lesser testators, the occupant of the tomb reaped a harvest he had not sown.[82] A similar gesture was intended by testators who left a sum of money to pay for the paschal candle and sepulchre lights, relieving poorer parishioners of the cost, on condition that the priest on Easter Day announce it, "and they shall pray at the same time specially for his soul."[83]

As these examples suggest, bequests for the vessels and ornaments of Eucharistic worship, or the altar, were a much favoured way of securing remembrance. But the provision of the accoutrements of funeral and anniversary worship might achieve much the same effect. At Louth in Lincolnshire a former vicar, Thomas Sudbery, provided a silver-gilt processional Cross to be used on major feasts, at the funerals of the "brethren of the lampe light" (a Eucharistic guild) and at his own annual obit, with the express purpose that each time it was used "the devocyon of goode pepull shall the rather be sturode to pray for his saull."[84] With greater panache the Bristol widow, Alice Chester, "consyderyng that non herse-clothe was yn the Churche of any Reputacyon", for the "love and honor that she had un-to all-myghty god and to all Crystyn Sowlys, and for the Ese and socour of all thys parysche" gave a black and gold hearse-cloth for use at funerals, inscribed "Orate pro animabus Henrici Chester et Aliciae uxoris eius", thereby transforming every funeral into a commemoration of herself and her husband.[85]

The accoutrements of one's own funeral, of course, were the most accessible of all, and towards the end of the fifteenth century the furnishings of the grave itself were undergoing adaptation to promote the remembrance of the dead. It was a conventional mark of status in most communities in late medieval England for prosperous

[81] Bristol All Saints CWA (c) p. 29.
[82] Duncan, "Churches of West Kent", p. 248; *Lincoln Wills*, II p. 89; *Visitation of the County of Suffolke*, I p. 36.
[83] Bristol St Nicholas CWA, pp. 40, 45.
[84] Louth CWA, p. 94.
[85] Bristol All Saints CWA (c) p. 14.

parishioners to stipulate burial within the church, a development which preachers like Mirk disapproved of.[86] Many testators stipulated burial near a favoured image or altar, thereby soliciting the intercession of the saint. An examination of the printed calendars of Kentish wills for the early sixteenth century suggests, for example, that a growing number of testators sought burial near the image of Our Lady of Pity. But as more churches were pewed, testators began to ask for burial "afore my seat", "against my pue and seat there", "where as I was wont to sit", indicating a desire to retain their place in the community quite literally.[87]

Alongside this development, the provision of monumental inscriptions went through a social shift. From the 1460s onwards regional workshops began to produce relatively cheap brasses, and a visible and enduring remembrance over one's burial place ceased to be the exclusive prerogative of the gentry or the very rich.[88] The object of these brasses, of course, was to solicit prayer for those who lay beneath them.

> Though we be gone, & past out of mynde,
> As ye wold be prayed for, pray for us.[89]

Given the growth of literacy among the middling sort of people, and the widespread demand for devotional material in English, served by the presses of Caxton, Wynkyn de Worde, and Richard Pynson,[90] it is not surprising to find that a growing number of these inscriptions were in English rather than Latin.

After the Reformation, funerary inscriptions would as a matter of course record not the desire for prayers but the Christian virtues of the deceased, forming an obvious contrast with pre-Reformation inscriptions, which were essentially supplicatory and emphasized the need of the dead.[91] But the contrast, though real, was not absolute. It was part of orthodox teaching about the cult of the dead that holy souls in Purgatory deserved our prayers, not simply because they were our loved ones, but because they were good, and their very presence in Purgatory was a proof of their faith, hope, and charity. If the best alms were those given to the deserving poor, then the holy dead were the most deserving of all.[92] This

---

[86] *Festial*, pp. 297–8.

[87] *Testamenta Cantiana: West*, pp. 19, 20, 29.

[88] *Bulletin of the Monumental Brass Society*, XXXIX, 1985, pp. 140–2 (précis of a paper by Sally Badham, "London standardisation and provincial idiosyncracy").

[89] Norris, *Monumental Brasses*, p. 175.

[90] See above, chapter 6, "Lewed and Learned" and chapter 2 "How the Plowman Learned His Pater Noster", pp. 77–87.

[91] See above, p. 302.

[92] *Kalender of Shepherdes*, p. 175.

perception was reflected in some inscriptions, which recorded the meritorious works of the deceased, so as to evoke not merely the pity, but the admiration and gratitude, of the living, and thereby assure their intercession. In the process, they move decisively towards the eulogistic inscriptions of a later period. Here is the inscription of John Terry, a former mayor of Norwich buried in St John Maddermarket in 1524:

> Devote Crystene Peple desirouse to knowe
> Whose Body restyth under thys stone so lowe,
> Of John Terry merchant, the tyme hys lyfe ledde
> Mayr et Alderman of this cyte in dede,
> Vertuose in lyvynge, to the Comonwelthe profytable,
> And to Ryght and Conscyence ever conformable
> The same to preserve and also to ayde,
> And eyke to be mayntened, cc 1 [£200] have payed:
> Among the Cytizens, in love for ey to remayne,
> Therewyth for a Tyme to earne ther Nede and Payne
> And over that cc 1 to purchase Lande or Fee,
> To comfort and releve por Fowks at necessyte.
> When herafter yt chancyth the Kyngs Tasks to be layde,
> The Rentts of the same for them to be payde,
> For the wyche Dedis, Gode that ys but one,
> Extend His Pety upon the same John
> Wyche thys World departyde in January the fyrste Day,
> And hys Sowle in Marcy to have that beste may,
> The Yere of owre Lorde God Mccccc xx and foure,
> The Trynyte his sowle kepe from all Dolour.[93]

It would, I think, be pushing the evidence, such as it is, too far to argue for any straightforward chronological development here: inscriptions listing the good works of the deceased can be found from the 1430s. If there are more such inscriptions in the early sixteenth century, it almost certainly has more to do with growing literacy than with any shift in theology. But there is no doubt that there was a tendency in much mortuary provision to personalize the memory of the dead to a greater extent than before. The opportunity for testators to leave an image of themselves, however stylized, almost certainly reflected, and probably contributed to, a desire for a personal continuance among the living. This desire is vividly evident even now in a number of surviving painted images, for memorials were not necessarily confined to brasses or associated

---

[93] Blomefield, *Norfolk*, IV p. 291.

only with graves. John and Katherine Goldalle left paintings of themselves (alongside the Four Latin Doctors) on the pulpit they had erected at Burnham Norton. The Four Latin Doctors seem to have been a favourite choice for such commemorations: John Wayment and his wife kneel before them on the doors of the screen they paid for at Foxley in Norfolk (Pl. 124), and John Bacon was painted with his wife and children, kneeling proudly in their Sunday best, rosaries in hand, before the Latin Doctors on the north screen dado in the parish church of Fritton in 1520 (Pl. 125).[94] The overall trend is evident elsewhere in the cult of the dead, as in requests for burial under one's accustomed pew, or in the even more common custom of leaving intensely personal items – gowns, cloaks, wedding rings, bed linen – for conversion into vestments or ornaments for images, and thus to be used on the altar or in the course of the liturgy.

But the most straightforward, and the cheapest, way of securing the perpetual recollection of one's name in the course of the worship of the parish was to have it entered on the bede-roll. This was a form of immortality which appealed especially to those of modest means. The recitation of the bede-roll at the annual obits and other solemn meetings of the gilds was an important element in their appeal to the hundreds of thousands of poor and middling people who joined them. Every parish also kept such a roll, recited in full at the annual requiem for the benefactors of the church, and in a somewhat truncated version every Sunday at the bidding of the bedes at the parish Mass, when the congregation was exhorted to pray for all those whose names were contained there, as well as more generally for all the souls in purgatory "and in special for them that have most need and least help".[95] The bede-roll offered those with limited means the possibility of being prayed for both "namely" and "perpetually", and testators very frequently made special provision to have their own and their spouses' or parents' names set in the rolls, "there to be prayed for every Sonday yn the yere, as other be".[96]

There was far more to this than a simple desire for perpetual intercession; inclusion on the bede-roll ensured that, of course, but it did more. Its specific cataloguing of all those who "have honoured the church wyth light, lampe, vestmente, or bell, or with any ornamentes" gave parishioners a vivid sense of the permanence

[94] N. Pevsner, *Buildings of England: North-West Norfolk*, 1962, pp. 105, 167.

[95] Rock, *Church of Our Fathers*, II pp. 286–306.

[96] Bramley CWA, p. 30; *Wells Wills*, p. 164; Ashburton CWA, pp. 41, 47; Tavistock CWA, pp. 9, 12–13, 21; "Reculver and Hoath Wills", ed. A. Hussey, *Archaeologia Cantiana*, XXXII, 1917, pp. 79–80; *Lincoln Wills*, II pp. 56–7; Firth, "Village Gilds of Norfolk", pp. 179–80.

and security of their own place, large or small, within the community of the parish. The bede-roll was a social map of the community, often stretching over centuries, and promising a continuing
place in the consciousness of the parish in which he or she had once
lived, not as one of the anonymous multitude of the dead, but as
the named provider of some familiar object. The parishioners of St
Mary's, Sandwich, were bidden to pray, among others for

> the sawlys of John Goddard of this parsschc, of whose goodys
> was gevyn ii bokys, a grayell and a martologe. Also for the
> sawlys of Symon Chapman and Julyen his wyf, of whos goodys
> was gevyn a hole vestyment for a priest of cloth of gold of Luke
> lynyd with grene tartary, and a chalys syluyr and gylt. Also for
> the sawlys of Stephyn Gerard and Margery hys wyff of whoos
> goodys was gevyn a good newe masse boke. Also for the sawlys
> of Raff Archere and hys wyf, the whyche gaf be hys lyf daiis a
> crysmatory of syluyr, and the kuveryng of the fonte, and the
> ymage of seynt Jamys withyn seynt Jamys chapell.[97]

In prosperous mercantile communities like Sandwich the pennies
of the poor might dwindle to apparent insignificance compared
to such lavishness, but churchwardens and parish clergy were
extraordinarily conscientious in recording every benefaction, however modest. A memorandum in the accounts of St Andrew's,
Canterbury, requests prayers for "the sowlle of Mesteres Whyttloke
the w[hic]h gave to the reparacion of the Cherch 6/8d". In the tiny
Exmoor parish of Morebath the Henrician priest, Sir Christopher
Trychay, painstakingly compiled a roll headed "Orate pro animabus
sequentibus", naming the giver of every gift received by the parish
during his time as vicar, in sums ranging from 26 s 8 d down to
twopence.[98].

Such meticulous recording was by no means exceptional: most of
the surviving fifteenth- and early sixteenth-century inventories of
church goods list not merely the objects, often in considerable
descriptive detail, but also the donors, where these were known. A
gift to one's parish really did ensure a sort of immortality. At All
Saints, Bristol, the bede-roll grew so detailed and so long that
by the late fifteenth century it stretched to 150 folio pages and
became impossible to read out on one occasion: two separate
and increasingly drastic attempts were made to reduce it to more
manageable proportions.[99] We are not dealing here with some

---

[97] Rock, *Church of Our Fathers*, II p. 305.
[98] Canterbury St Andrew's CWA, p. 211; Morebath CWA, pp. 19–28.
[99] Bristol All Saints' CWA (c) p. 4.

obsessive bureaucratic tidy-mindedness but with a religious act. This degree of comprehensiveness was aimed at so that the dead might receive the prayers which were their due, in charity and in justice. But the names of the dead were also preserved because the bede-roll was integral to the parish's sense of identity, both in conserving a sense of a shared past and in fostering a continuing commitment to the religious ideals and the social and religious structures embodied in the parish church.

The place of the bede-roll in conserving the parish's sense of a shared past is obvious enough. At one level it served as a simple inventory. The fact that it was "browght forth & redde openly before the wholl parysche" helped preserve the church's goods, themselves the concrete embodiments of the charity and piety of past generations of parishioners. Though it was usually kept up to date by the clergy and always read from the pulpit by them, it belonged to the parish as a whole, and symbolized the people's common responsibility for the spiritual well-being of deceased parishioners. The whole parish, not merely or primarily the clergy, was to see that nothing was lost or embezzled, and that no one's spiritual needs were forgotten, since it was the welfare of souls, and not merely property, which was at stake. That duty was often exercised on behalf of the parish by the church and store wardens, and it was they who normally paid the clergy for reading the bede-roll, but it was recognized that in doing so they acted for the parish. Where they failed, or were thought likely to fail, testators could appeal directly to their fellow-parishioners. In the 1470s Avery Cornburgh established a chantry in Romford church, the incumbent to be a Doctor or Bachelor of Divinity, and to preach in the surrounding parishes. Cornburgh died in 1480, and had the details of the foundation carved on his grave in Romford church, together with this admonition to the parishioners:

> Moreover this call to your remembrance anon,
> That in the beadroll of usage every Sonday redd;
> The souls of this Avery, Beatrice and John
> Be prayed for in speciall; se that owr will be spedd
> And that the curate of this church curtesly be ledd
> And for his labor have in reding of that roll
> Forty pens to pray for them and every Christian soul.[100]

But the reading of the bede-roll was designed not merely to recall the devotion of the dead and elicit the suffrages of the living on their behalf. It was also designed to present for imitation a pattern

---

[100] *Transactions of the Essex Archaeological Society*, IV, 1869, pp. 15–20; Stanford CWA, p. 71.

of piety, and to instil in the hearers a sense of the parish and its worship as a continuing reality. In this respect it was one of the principal expressions of the late medieval church's understanding of salvation. The preamble to the bede-roll of All Saints, Bristol, read on the Sunday before Ash Wednesday each year, is worth quoting at length:

> Hit hath ben of a lawdabyll Custom and of longe Contynewans y-usyd that on this day . . . they Namys of good Doers and well-wylleres, by whon lyvelodes, Tenementes, Byldynges, Jewellys, Bookys, Chalys, Vestymentes with dyverys other Ornamentes and goodes as folowith hath ben gevyn un-to this Churche, unto the honour and worschippe of all-myghty God, and encresyng of Dyuyne seruyce, to be rehersyd and schewyd yerly vn-to yowe by Name bothe man and woman, and whate Benefettys they dud for hem self and for her ffrendys . . . by her lyfetymys and whate they lefte for hem to be don aftyr her dayes that they schall not be forgetyn but be had yn Remembranns and be prayed for of all this parysche that ben nowe and of all them that bethe to cum and all-so for an exampyll to all ye that bethe nowe levyng that ye may lyke-wyse to do for yourself (and for your frendes) whyle ye be yn thys world that aftyr this transitory lyf ye may be had yn the Nombyr of Good Doers rehersyd by Name and yn specyall prayoures of Crysten pepyll yn tyme cummyng that by the Infynytyf mercy of allmighty God by the Intercessyon of our blessyd lady and of all blessyd seyntes . . . yn whose honour and worschippe this Churche ys dedycatt ye may cum to the evyr-lastyng blysse and Joye that our blessyd lord hath redemyd yowe vn-to. AMEN.[101]

Here the parish community has become something more than the total of its past and future members: it has been set in the full perspective of eternity itself. The mercy of God to which "Good doers and well-wylleres" aspire is to be gained not only by their pious gifts and alms and the prayers of their fellow parishioners, but by the intercession of the saints "yn whose honour and worschippe this Church ys dedycatt". Enrolment on the bede-roll has taken on an eschatological significance, far greater than the simple presentation of the individual's name for the charitable prayers of the hearers. The presence of the parishioner's name on the bede-roll is more than an assurance of continuing intercession: to have one's own name or that of parent, spouse, or child enrolled was to affirm one's unity in salvation with the parish community, and to seek to perpetuate that unity beyond the grave (Pl. 126).

---

[101] Bristol All Saints' CWA (c) pp. 3–4.

CHAPTER 10

THE PAINS OF PURGATORY

Purgatory featured only in passing in the Church's ministrations at the deathbed, and implicitly in the practice of praying for the dead. It loomed large, however, in lay awareness, and provided the rationale underlying the immense elaboration of the late medieval cult of intercession for the dead. The whole structure of mortuary provision of Masses, alms, pilgrimage, and the adornment of churches and images, which to a greater or lesser degree characterized almost all the wills of fifteenth- and early sixteenth-century English men and women, was raised on the belief that such largesse would hasten the soul's passage through the pains of Purgatory.

It is not difficult to understand the motivation for the large-scale channelling of resources in this direction. Late medieval men and women were circumstantially well-informed about what they might expect in Purgatory, not only from the vivid evocations offered in sermons and, on the eve of the Reformation, apologetic works like More's *Supplication of Souls*, but from many accounts of visions and revelations about the afterlife which circulated among the laity and found their way into devotional commonplace books and collections. The best-known examples include the *Gast of Gy*, the vision of Tundale, and the pilgrimage of the knight Sir Owen (both the latter concerned with St Patrick's Purgatory), and the revelations of St Bridget of Sweden, but there were innumerable less well-known revelations, such as the one of the Monk of Eynsham, which was printed in English in the 1480s, or the one dated 1422 "schewed to ane holy womane now one late tyme" which circulated in manuscript.[1]

The prognosis for sinners which emerged from these works was, to put it mildly, not encouraging. Visitors to Purgatory saw souls in every posture of physical torment – suspended by meat-

---

[1] For a survey see George R. Keiser, "The Progess of Purgatory: Visions of the Afterlife in Late Medieval English Literature", *Analecta Cartusiana*, CXVII, 1987, pp. 72–100; there is a good bibliography in R. Easting (ed.), *St Patrick's Purgatory*, EETS, 1991.

hooks driven through jaws, tongue, or sexual organs, frozen into ice, boiling in vats of liquid metal or fire "als it had bene fysche in hate oyle".[2] Often the punishment was carefully matched to the crime: the sexually promiscuous were tormented in the loins, the gluttonous forced to drink scalding venom or nauseous filth, the backbiters and liars had their tongues or lips sliced away. But always it was detailed vividness which seemed the essence of such visions. Bridget of Sweden, whose revelations circulated very widely in fifteenth-century England, witnessed the judgement passed on a newly dead soul guilty of lies and pride:

> Than methought that thar was a bande bonden abowte his hede so faste and sore that the forhede and the nodell mete togiddir. The eyn were hingande on the chekes; the eres as thai had bene brent with fire; the brayne braste out at the nesethirles and hys eres; the tonge hange oute, and the teth were smctyn togyddir: the bones in the armes were broken and wrethyn as a rope; the skyn was pullid of hys hede and thai were bunden in hys neke; the breste and the wombe were to slongen togiddir, and the ribbes broken, that one myght see the herte and the bowelles; the shuldirs were broken and hange down to the sides; and the bonys were drawen oute as it had bene a thred of a clothe.[3]

This, it should be emphasized, is Purgatory, not Hell. Immediately after describing these torments Bridget tells how this soul's guardian angel reminded the "domesman" that the soul's last thought before death had been "Wald god gyfe me spase of lufe, I wald gladly amend my trespas and nevir syn more." To such thoughts Christ replied, "sall not hell be gyven", and therefore "for my passion it sall be saved and com to blis eftir that it is purged in purgatory."

The retailing of such horrors was not simply intended to harrow and terrify but to convert and chasten. The vernacular instructional and devotional collection published by Wynkyn de Worde in 1505 under the title *The Arte or Crafte to Lyve well and to dye well*[4] included an eschatological treatise on the pains of Hell and Purgatory, the fifteen signs of Judgement Day, the coming of Antichrist, and the joys of Heaven. Its treatment of the sufferings of the damned and of the souls in Purgatory was headed "The nedyll of the fere dyvyne for to deye well". The treatise explained that "truely the fere of god

---

[2] *Brome Commonplace Book*, pp. 82–106. Easting, *St Patrick's Purgatory*, pp. 3–75 contains an edition of two versions of the Knight Sir Owen legend; Horstmann, *Yorkshire Writers*, I pp. 383–92.

[3] *Liber Celestis*, p. 298.

[4] *The Arte or Crafte to Lyve Well*, W. de Worde 1505, RSTC 792.

chaseth and putteth out the synne of our soules", and that "there ne
is thynge that more may ne sholde cause or produce the fere of god
in our hertes than often to thynke and ymagen the paynes eternalles
of helle."[5] Late medieval devotional literature abounded in moral-
ities in verse and prose which presented the sufferings of the
damned as a warning to the living to mend their ways, such as the
legend of the adulterous Falmouth Squire, or the rhyme of Sir
William Basterfeld:

> I myght not fast, I wold not praye,
> I thought to amend me in myn age,
> I droffe ever forth fro dey to dey,
> Therefore I byde here in this cage.
> Thys cage is ever-lastynge fyre,
> I ame ordeynde ther-in to duelle;
> It is me gyven fore myne hyre,
> Ever to bryne in the pytte of helle;
> I am feteryd with the fendys of helle,
> There I abyde as best in stalle.
> There is no tonge my care cane telle.
> Be were ye have not sych a fall![6]

Accounts of the pains of Hell and Purgatory, therefore, were often
in fact circumstantial treatises on the nature and avoidance of the
deadly sins, which were their cause. This is true even in the most
vivid of the accounts of the pains of the damned. The *Arte or
Crafte to Lyve well* provided one of the most detailed accounts of
the torments of Hell, illustrated in woodcuts, of the early Tudor
period. They are expounded at Christ's command, at a feast in the
house of Simon the Leper, by Lazarus, who had witnessed them at
first hand during his three days in the grave; the description could
thus claim a particularly overwhelming authenticity. Following the
convention, each of the sins is punished in a vivid and appropriate
way, and this matching of punishment to crime is the real point of
the visions. The usurous are boiled in molten gold, the gluttonous
fed with, and fed on by toads and serpents, and, perhaps most
vividly, the proud are bound to great iron wheels, covered with
burning hooks (Pl. 127–8). The restless revolution of the wheels,
endlessly raising and lowering the souls of the proud, is a gruesome
metaphor of their sin, for in life they will "evermore be lyft up
above these other, and lyve in dyscorde without peas . . . and for

---

[5] *Arte or Crafte*, fols lxiv–lxv.
[6] C Horstmann (ed.), *Altenglische Legenden Neue Folge*, pp. 366–70.

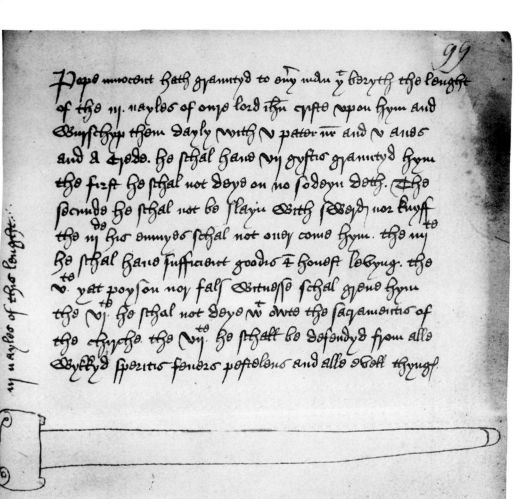

Pope innocent hath grauntyd to ony man ý beryth the lenght of the iij. naylis of oure lord ihu cryste vpon hym and wurschyp them dayly with v pater nr and v anes and a crede. he schal haue vij gyftis grauntyd hym the first he schal not deye on no sodeyn deth. The seconde he schal not be slayn with swerd nor knyf the iij his enmyes schal not ouey come hym. the iiij he schal haue sufficient goodis & honest lesyng. the v. yet poyson noy fals wrtnesse schal greue hym the vj he schal not deye wᵗ owte the sacamentis of the chyrche. the vij. he schal be defendyd from alle wyckyd speritis fenvis pestelens and alle evell thynigf.

iij naylis of the lenght

112.   The "Measure of the Nails" with miraculous promises, from the commonplace book of Robert Reynes.

113.   John Baret's cadaver tomb, Bury St Edmunds.

114. The Sparham *memento mori* panels.

115. "Housel and shrift at my last end":
viaticum from a Sarum primer by François
Regnault.

116. Annointing, from the font at *Great Glenham*, Suffolk.

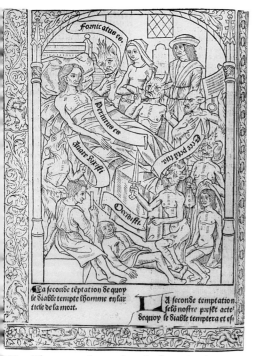

117. The temptation to despair, from the *Ars Moriendi*.

118. Impatience, from the *Ars Moriendi*.

119. The moment of death, from the *Ars Moriendi*.

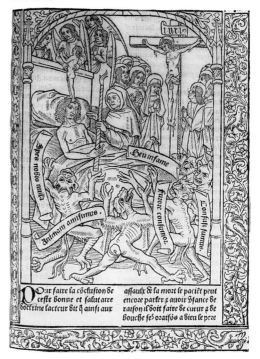

126.   "Good doers and well-willers of this church": John Chapman and his wife pray at Swaffham, Norfolk.

127 (above left). The torments of the Ireful, from the Vision of Lazarus: the vice of ire or anger was normally depicted as a man brandishing a sharp weapon – hence the punishment.

128 (above right). The torments of the proud, from the Vision of Lazarus.

129. "Full of good hope and of grace": Purgatory from a Sarum primer, 1531.

130.   Givers and receivers: rich and poor from the Works of Mercy window, at All Saints, North Street, York.

131.   The attack on St Thomas Becket. Destruction of his images was ordered in November 1538: this screen at Burlingham St Andrew, Norfolk, had been completed only in the mid-1530s.

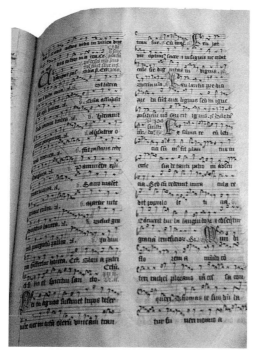

132. The attack on St Thomas Becket: at
Ranworth, the service for St Thomas has been
"deleted" from the great antiphonal with the
slenderest of token pen-strokes.

133. Tudor conformity: the owner of this
manuscript primer went on using its indulgenced
prayers for the dead, but obediently deleted every
mention of the Pope's name.

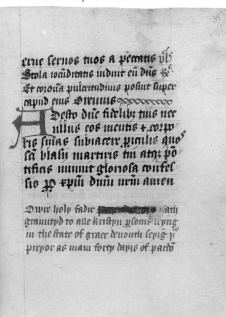

The Ship of the Romish Church.
Burning of images.
Ship over your trinkets & be packing you papists.
The Temple well purged.
The Papists packing away their Paltry.
The Cōmunion Table.
BIBLIA

134. The Edwardine destruction of traditional religion, from Foxe's *Acts and Monuments*.

135. Token conformity: the parishioners at Foxley, Norfolk, obediently cut down their Rood-loft and its Crucifix. But they kept the pieces, and repaired them in Mary's reign, as this join shows.

136. Marian restoration: the parishioners of Ranworth must have concealed their liturgical books illegally; here the name of St Thomas has been restored to the calendar in Mary's reign.

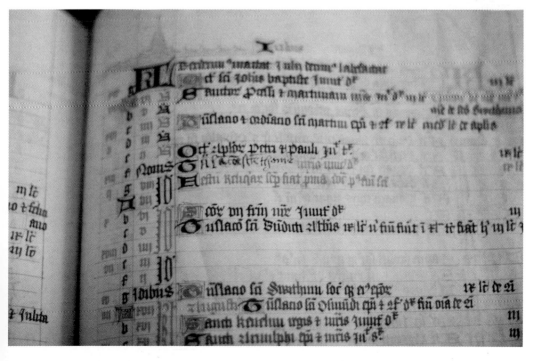

137. Marian restoration: the loft and Rood of the sumptuous screen at Ludham had been destroyed in Edward's reign: the parishioners had a new "Rood" painted on the Tympanum boards in Mary's reign. The Marian authorities ordered three dimensional carvings to replace such makeshift arrangements.

138. At Ludham in Elizabeth's reign, the Marian "Rood" painting was covered with canvas, and the royal arms painted over it.

139. Iconoclasm: the Mass of St Gregory, detested by
the reformers both as an image and as an expression of
traditional eucharistic belief, on a panel at Wyverstone.

140. Iconoclasm: St Anne at Kersey: the figure of the
Virgin has gone, and St Anne's head and hands have
been battered away.

141. Iconoclasm: at Ringland the faces, hands and feet of the Apostles have been gouged off the wood.

thys cause theyr herte is in contynuall moevynge the whiche is never fedde with honoure".[7]

The vision of Lazarus, with its pseudo-scriptural claim to provide information on the afterlife straight from the horse's mouth, clearly had great popular appeal, and as we have seen it was adapted for inclusion in the best-selling devotional and practical almanac, the *Kalender of Shepherdes*. This version of the vision of Lazarus makes even clearer the essentially didactic and moral purpose of the original, and of the genre in general. The *Kalender* retains the particularly vivid woodcut illustrations of the torments which accompanied the French original, but brief generalized expositions of the deadly sins entirely replace the circumstantial descriptions of the pains of Hell found in the *Arte or Crafte*. What mattered to the editors and presumably the readers of the *Kalender* was clearly not the horror stories about the hereafter, but the urgency – and the possibility – of avoiding punishment by right conduct in this life.[8]

What was true of visions of Hell was even more true of Purgatory. Late medieval Christians feared Hell but hoped for Heaven. Through a lifetime of observant piety, but more especially through the deathbed ministrations of the Church, even the half-hearted might hope for salvation. Hell was for hell-hounds, the infidel, and the reprobate. But that being so, Purgatory rather than Hell became the focus of Christian fear. Though every Christian might hope for Heaven, only the saints could hope to go there directly. All who died in a state of venial sin, all who had forgotten or concealed such sins in confession, all who had not yet fulfilled every part of the penance imposed in confession for sins repented, confessed, and absolved, all who had had insufficient penance imposed on them by over-indulgent confessors, all who fell short of that fullness of charity which lay at the root of salvation . . . all these were bound to spend some time in the pains of Purgatory. Such was God's mercy that even deathbed repentance or repentance based merely on fear, if accompanied in fact or in desire by resort to the Sacraments, would save from damnation. But it was a further and an infinitely large step from avoidance of Hell to the vision of God which was the bliss of Heaven, the goal and fulfilment of human life. That vision of God was granted only to those who were in charity, who truly loved him for his own sake and not his benefits, who rejected their sins from love of God and not the fear of Hell, and who had been purged by penance of every trace and

---

[7] *Arte or Crafte*, fol. lxiii(v).
[8] *The Kalender of Shepherdes*, pp. 67–73.

scar of sin, thereby making amends to God and peace with their "evenchristen" for all the damage their sins had done.

This might have been a negative vision, the relentless insistence that all but the exceptionally pious must endure unspeakable pain before they came to bliss. But that was not in fact the thrust of late medieval preaching and teaching on the subject. The natural school of charity and the proper place for purging was not Purgatory, but here on earth, now in the time of grace, for after death would be the time of justice: penance for sins was far more easily done in life than after death. One day of sickness or tribulation patiently borne while we are still in this world was equivalent to a year's torment in Purgatory, and by meek suffering and good works Christians might purchase "so mekill perdone in this werlde that sall fordo all the paynes of purgatorye and lightly brynge tham to blysse of heuene".[9] This was a preacher's commonplace, and preaching source-books provided a host of illustrations of the point, like the tale of the spirit of a monk who appeared to reproach a friend for leaving him twenty years in torment without offering prayers, only to discover that in earthly time he had only just died and his friend was still vesting for the Mass which, in fulfilment of his promise, he was preparing to say "incontynent as thou wert expired".[10]

Here lay a crucial clue to the horrible vividness and particularity of the accounts of Purgatory circulating in fifteenth- and early sixteenth-century England. These accounts were designed to move the Christian to action on his own behalf while still in health, to complete his penances, to live a mortified life, to be generous in charity. These were the good deeds which would accompany Everyman, to plead for him,

> For after dethe amendes may no man make,
> For than mercy and pyte doth hym forsake.[11]

Late medieval preachers and moralists feared that the laity might become presumptuous, relying on deathbed confession and posthumous good works to hurry them through Purgatory, conceived as a soft option to Hell, and an alternative to the rigours of mortified living in this world. John Fisher complained that "Many there be that wayle and be contryte and also confesse theyr synnes, but scante one amonge a thousande can be founde that dooth dewe

---

[9] Horstmann, *Yorkshire Writers*, I pp. 390–1; *Arte or Crafte* fol. lxxxxxvi [*sic*]. Clive Burgess is almost the only recent writer on the subject who has done justice to this dimension of belief in Purgatory, and the element of comfort and hope which it brought to Christian eschatology; see his very valuable "A Fond Thing Vainly Invented", in S. Wright (ed.), *Parish, Church and People*, 1988, pp. 56–85.

[10] *Arte or Crafte*, fols lxxxxxvi–lxxxxxi(v) [sic]; cf. *Golden Legend*, VI p. 114.

[11] G. A. Lester, *Three Late Medieval Morality Plays*, p. 102, lines 912–13.

satysfaccyon."[12] Fisher feared that such incomplete repentance was
not genuine at all, and this was a fairly general attitude. *The Arte or
Crafte to Lyve well and to dye well* is generally less austere in tone
than Fisher's sermons, but agreed that "penaunce is helthe in the
man hole, and it is sick and feeble in the man unstedfaste." The
author argued that while we may be obliged to carry out the testa-
mentary dispositions which spring from the panic piety of a
belatedly penitent sinner on his deathbed, "we presume not that he
fortuneth or deyeth well." And even if such repentance proved real,
the sinner would have a rude awakening in Purgatory, finding that
"the sayde payne of purgatory is more grevous an hondred thousand
double than that of this present world."[13] So the souls in Purgatory
in Thomas More's *Supplication* offer a "friendly warning" to the
living that

> we that have so dyed have thus found it, that the goodes dis-
> posed after us, geat our executoures great thanke, & be toward
> usward accompted afore god much less then halfe our owne, nor
> our thanke nothing lyke to that it would have been if we had in
> our health geven half as much for gods sake with our own
> handes.[14]

The miseries of Purgatory, then, like the physical horrors of the
processes of death itself, were evoked not to curdle the blood and
oppress the spirit, but to stir the living to present action. Mortified
lives of penance would make Purgatory superfluous, almsgiving
and good works in time of prosperity would be better than last-
minute fire insurance.

Purgatory: Ante-room of Heaven or Outpost of Hell?

In the noblest, most circumstantial, and most theologically sophisticated of all medieval visions of the other world, Dante's *Commedia*,
Purgatory is unequivocally a place of hope and a means of ascent
towards Heaven. It thus has nothing in common with Hell. Before
Dante begins the ascent of the Mount he is reclothed in the rushes
of repentance, his face washed free from the grief and horror
of Hell with the cleansing dew which distils in the clean air of
Purgatory. He constantly greets those he encounters with phrases
which speak of their redemption and happiness, "spiriti ben nati"
or "anime fortunate". From this Purgatory the devils are barred
by protecting angels, and although all the souls whom Dante

[12] Fisher, *English Works*, p. 25.
[13] *Arte or Crafte*, fol. lxxxxxiv–lxxxxxv [*sic*].
[14] More, *Workes*, p. 337.

encounters are suffering, their sufferings are eagerly embraced and impatiently returned to, for they lead the soul through a pedagogy of love to the vision of God. Here, as in other medieval visions, the punishment fits the crime, the proud are brought low by the burden of immense rocks on their shoulders, the gluttonous waste away from famine, the avaricious are pinioned to the earth by their longings for the things of earth. But in Dante's poem the appropriateness of the torment is related primarily to the processes of healing, not to those of punishment. The souls are being taught to unbind the chains they have made for themselves, "solvendo il nodo", loosening the knot of their sin by appropriate counter-measures. As each soul passes from a lower to a higher stage in the healing process the mountain shakes, and everyone on it rejoices and is inspired to a new and deeper surrender to the cleansing process. For in Purgatory as in Heaven every soul lives and moves within the love that moves the sun and the other stars: charity is the life of Purgatory.

English perceptions of the nature of Purgatory in the late Middle Ages were less coherent or at least less carefully nuanced, and altogether grimmer. In the first place, there was general agreement that, at least as far as its activities and staff were concerned, Purgatory was an out-patient department of Hell, rather than the antechamber of Heaven. Purgatory, according to the *The Ordynarye of Crysten Men*, "is one parte of hell and the place of ryght mervaylous payne".[15] In Purgatory, declared Fisher, "is so great acerbite of pynes that no dyfference is betweene the paynes of hell and them, but only eternyte, the paynes of helle be eternall, and the paynes of purgatory have an ende".[16] There were other similarities to Hell. The collect used in celebrations of the Trental of St Gregory asked for deliverance "out of the hands of evil spirits".[17] The ministers of punishment in Purgatory, according to Thomas More, are "cruell damned spirites, odious, envious and hateful, despitous enemies".[18] This conviction was given lurid imaginative expression. In the vision of Sir Owen, the revelation to the Monk of Eynsham, and the "Reuelacyone schewed to ane holy woman", as well as in the revelations of St Bridget, devils "ranne ouer all lyke as madde men and were also full cruell and wodde apone tho wrechys".[19] In addition to mocking and reproaching

---

15 *Ordynarye*, sig. L1 ii(r).
16 Fisher, *English Works*, p. 10.
17 *Missale*, cols 883*–884*.
18 More, *Workes*, pp. 337–8.
19 E. Arber (ed.), *The Revelation of the Monk of Eynsham*, 1869, p. 57.

them, they scourge them, roll them in spiked barrels, boil them till they melt, choke them with scalding pitch, and rend their flesh with irons.

There were alternative views. The *Arte or Crafte to Lyve well and dye well* agreed that "it is one selfe fyre in hell and in purgatorye", but was equally clear, following St Thomas Aquinas, that "the soules of purgatorye be not punysshed by the devylles of whom they have had tryumphe & vyctorye for they ne may exercyse theyr malyce upon the soules of purgatorye as they done upon soules dampned." They might show themselves to the souls in Purgatory, to frighten and distress them, but their activities were contained and countered by the good angels, who came to console the holy souls.[20] Even more emphatically, the *Gast of Gy* insisted that the soul entering Purgatory was led "with his goode aungel, and wickid aungels schul wend away from hym". The difference between the pains of Hell and those of Purgatory was not simply one of duration but of kind (Pl. 129), for in contrast to the despair of Hell "the peyne of purgatorie is full of goode hope and of grace."[21] This was a fundamental theological perception. All who entered Purgatory were *ipso facto* redeemed and, however prolonged their probation, certain of salvation. As More makes the souls in Purgatory say, "in surety of salvation we be felowes with angels."[22] But even about this point there was uncertainty. The sodomite encountered in purgatory by the Monk of Eynsham was in doubt about his salvation (a doubt, it must be said, shared by the reader), and St Bridget considered that such uncertainty was the worst pain of Purgatory, reserved to punish certain souls for the misuse of their "great wytt and discrecion" in their lifetimes.[23] This view, which ran directly counter to the teaching of St Thomas and of preaching source-books such as the *Golden Legend*, was theologically incoherent, but it persisted in certain quarters right up to the Reformation. The Brigittine writer, Richard Whytford, agreed that "all the soules beynge in payne ben communely sure, and certayn of their saluacyon", an assurance which "dothe cause them to suffre the paynes with good wyll in the charyte of our lorde". Nevertheless, in deference to the foundress of his order, he considered that "it may be, that some one, or few soules haue nat that

---

[20] *Arte or Crafte*, fol. lxxxxxv.
[21] *The Gast of Gy: a Middle English Prose Tract*, ed. R. H. Bowers, *Beiträge zur Englischen Philologie*, XXXII, 1938, pp. 23–5; there is a version of the same legend in verse in Horstmann, *Yorkshire Writers*, II pp. 292–333.
[22] More, *Workes*, p. 327.
[23] *Revelation of the Monk of Evesham*, pp. 61–2; *Liber Celestis*, p. 261.

knowledge / but that God (for some specyall offence / and for a specially payne and punysshment therof) doth hyde, and kepe that knowledge from them."[24]

So strong an emphasis on the pains of Purgatory, whatever its pedagogic and corrective intentions, must clearly have developed an impetus of its own. Every week the parish priest bid the people pray "for all the saules that abydes the mercy of god in the paynes of purgatory".[25] Those pains were a vivid reality to his listeners. Fifteenth- and sixteenth-century wills abound in instructions which make clear the testators' urgent concern that the alms-giving and intercession which would shorten their torments should begin at the earliest possible moment. Wills ask for "Diriges" and doles "as hastily as possible . . . after my departing frome this world" or "as sone as I am deade w'toute eny tarying", trentals "to be done for me from the houre of my dethe unto the tyme of my buriall", scores of Masses "to be song wher they may be sonest getton".[26] A Somerset testator in 1504 asked that her "ghostly fader" and other clerks present at the administration of Holy Unction should watch for the earliest moment "as by mon erthly it may be perceyved that my soule shuld be fro my body separate", and so might begin "Dirige" and Mass "as soone as the lawe of holy church ordeyneth after the apperyng of the daylight". Each was to recite a trental of Masses and "Diriges" from the howre of myn Avete" to "the hour of the burying of my body . . . never cessing".[27] Not everyone was content that matters should be delayed even till they were dead, like the Sussex testator who wished doles to begin "when ye see me in the panges of death", or Sir John Manyngham, who wished the friars to begin two trentals of Masses for him "if tyme and season may be, whan I lye in the article and poynt of deth laboring towards the everlasting life".[28]

But despite the evident anxiety of such testators to minimize their time in Purgatory, in this respect also the note of hysteria is on the whole absent from English wills of the later Middle Ages. Whatever one may think of the doctrine of God which could accommodate the torture-house methods of purgation He was held to favour, the men and women of Yorkist and Tudor England seem to have set themselves to cope with the problem in a sober and

[24] Whitford, *Dayly Exercyse*, pp. 83–4.
[25] LFMB, p. 72.
[26] *Test. Ebor.*, IV pp. 27, 206, 216, V pp. 57–8; H. T. Weyman, "Chantry Chapels in Ludlow Church", *Transactions of the Shropshire Archaeological and Natural History Society*, 3rd series, IV, 1904, pp. 355–6; *Bury Wills*, pp. 73–81; *Beds Wills*, III pp. 13, 19–21, 40.
[27] *Somerset Wills*, III p. 72.
[28] *Sussex Wills*, III p. 112; *Beds Wills*, III pp. 43–7.

businesslike way. This was especially true of the well-to-do, whose wills often contain detailed and sometimes extremely elaborate instructions for the provision of Masses, "Diriges", and doles. Display and a sense of social rank certainly account for some of this – the desire to be buried "conveniently and according to my degree and the office the which I had".[29] Yet the well-to-do had special cause to make elaborate provision, for they believed the Gospel teaching about the difficulty of a rich man entering Heaven, and felt the need to "make use of their wealth to buy their way out of being punished for its possession".[30] "I knowe well," declared John Clopton in 1494, "that prayers is a singular remedie for the deliverance of soules in purgatory, and specially the offering of the Blessed Sacrament of our Lorde's body", and he proceeded to dispose of fifty marks to secure 2,000 Masses within the first month after his decease. Such lavish provision was by no means un-common, but it argues no hysteria. Clopton's will is an immensely elaborate document, providing for every conceivable form of intercession for the health of his soul. Yet the tone of voice is far from panic-stricken. Clopton felt himself to be at peace with the world, declaring that "as ferr as I canne remembre, I am clere of all wronges done to any person." His will was designed to speed his peacemaking with God, and no expense was spared, but having seen to that, he went on in just as meticulous detail to settle his worldly affairs and attend to the reward of his servants.[31]

Indeed, the religious provisions of many wills of the period were couched in much the same terms as building contracts or shopping-lists. John Duddely, of Clymping in Sussex, specified in 1500 that he should be buried "muche after the rate, considering the charge therof, that my wiffe's was done, savyng where my wife had vi torches I will have viii", and he left £6 3s 4d annually for a priest to sing Mass for his own soul and those of his benefactors and friends "if he may no better chepe be had". When Edmund Hunt, a Nottingham man, left the substantial sum of forty shillings in 1488 for wax for the parish light (before the Sacrament), he also gave strict instructions to the churchwardens "to by wax where it is best chepe".[32] Investment in intercession for the health of one's soul was indeed a serious business, and was so treated by testators. Its urgency, however, was the result not of hysteria, but of a businesslike attempt to follow through the consequences of belief in

[29] *Test. Ebor.*, IV p. 9.
[30] C. Carpenter, "The Religion of the Gentry", pp. 71–4.
[31] *Visitation of the County of Suffolke*, I pp. 34–40.
[32] *Sussex Wills*, I p. 53: *Test. Ebor.*, IV p. 34.

Purgatory and to minimize the suffering that one's sins might have let one in for.

Christendome and Kindred

Late medieval English preachers and writers on the afterlife, for all their emphasis on the pains of Purgatory and the role of the demons in administering them, believed, with Richard Whytford, that the souls there "suffre the paynes with good wyll in the charyte of our lorde". In that phrase Whytford acknowledged the central element in understanding the distinction between Hell and Purgatory; for him as for Dante souls in Purgatory abide in the charity of God. As we shall see, this perception was central to the practice of the cult of the dead in England, though in this area as in others there were elements in popular tradition about Hell and Purgatory which obscured the distinction. The *Arte or Crafte to Lyve well* emphasized that in Hell there was no love: it was a place of hatred and discord, in which even natural ties of affection fall into ruin: "undoubtedly there is one ryght mervayllous hate in hel . . . for the fader ne schal haue compassyon ne pyte of the sonne ne the moder of the doughter / nor the chyldren on the faders & moders."[33] Being beyond the reach of love, the dead in Hell were beyond the reach of prayer. One English preacher considered that prayers offered for the souls of the damned might indeed produce "alegyng of peynes, but no redempcion".[34] But this was an unusual position. Orthodox theology and popular belief coincided in the conviction that prayer for the damned was wasted on them, and in one verse legend about Hell the damned soul of a father pleads with his son to cease his prayers for him since

> Fore euer the more thou prayst fore me
> My peynes schall be more and more.[35]

By contrast, a recurrent motif in treatments of Purgatory is the centrality of both natural and supernatural bonding between the living and the dead. The souls in Purgatory were part of the church of the redeemed, and prayer for the dead was one of the

---

[33] *Arte or Crafte*, fol. lxxxi(v).

[34] *Liber Celestis*, pp. 441–2; *Speculum Sacerdotale*, p. 225.

[35] *Altenglische Legenden Neue Folge*, p. 370, though this legend in fact undermines the intuition of the breakdown of relationship and the unbridgeable gulf between the damned and redeemed by the affectionate language the damned father continues to use towards his child – "Fare wele, he seyd, my dere sone"; the standard view on the uselessness of prayers for the damned is concisely set out in *Golden Legend*, VI pp. 123–4.

principal expressions of the ties that bound the community together. Remember, dear friends, plead the souls in More's *Supplicacion* "how nature and christendome [i.e. baptism] bindeth you to remember us".[36] John Fisher elaborated the same point. We should pray for the holy souls in Purgatory because "They be of the same fayth, hope and charyte, that we be of. They have ben made parteners of the same sacraments." So much for "christendome", the supernatural bond which Fisher thought should have primacy in moving us to pray for the dead. But to this there was added, "that which peradventure ye wyll the more regarde", the natural ties of affection, blood kinship, and obligation. "Euery one of us hath sum of his frendes and kynsfolk there . . . sum of hys kyndrede, or som of his alyaunce, or some of his frendes to whom he had in this worlde tofore some favour and frendeshyp." Therefore we must "do lyke frendes . . . let us be louing vnto them as we pretentyd louve before unto theym."[37]

Friendship and kindred, therefore, are constantly recurrent notions in the cult of Purgatory, for the souls there were "your late acquaintance, kinred, spouses, companions, play felowes, & frendes".[38] In this cluster of relationships kin had a special place. The dead in Purgatory continued to care for their families on earth. The ghost of Gy appears not merely to secure prayers for himself, but also to warn his wife in time of the need to do penance for the sins he and she had committed together.[39] But although writers and preachers invariably emphasized the reciprocal benefits to be gained by the living who prayed for the dead, the relationship was by no means equal. Some theologians believed that the souls of the dead could pray for others, but all agreed that they were powerless to help themselves, and so were at the mercy of their kindred who, as inheritors of their property, could use it in good works to secure their speedy release or could divert it to other uses, and so leave them in torment. According to the *Ordynarye of Crysten Men* the souls in Purgatory continually call out "have pity have mercy / have mercy on me / at the leest ye my sonnes and doughters / nyeces and nevewes / cosyn and cosyns and ye other unnto whome I have left my goodes."[40] One of the principal horrors of death, much dwelt upon, was that the deceased became an object of fear and loathing, hastily banished underground out of the sight and the society of his or her living kin, and all too likely thereby consigned

[36] More, *Workes*, p. 339.
[37] Fisher, *Two Sermons*, pp. 19–22.
[38] More, *Workes*, p. 288.
[39] *Gast of Gy*, pp. 34–5.
[40] *Ordynarye*, sig. L1 ii(v).

to oblivion – "a stynkyng stoke of yerthe, an ys hyed to be putte ynto the erthe, and last ther, and sone foryetyn".[41] The dead were widely conceived of as anxious about the neglect of the living, and on occasion menacing towards those they feared would neglect them: the visionary in the "Reuelacyone schewed to ane hooly woman" is greeted ferociously by the spirit of her dead friend, "Cursede mote thou be and wo worthe the bot if thou hast the to be my helpe." The neglected dead could be angry and dangerous.[42]

This neglect of the dead by their survivors was thought to be so widespread that the first pain of Purgatory, according to Thomas More, was the anguish and shame of the newly arrived soul "to loke his olde frendes in the face here [in Purgatory] whom he remembered him self to have so foule forgotten while he lived".[43] There was a literature of cynicism, which dwelt on the rapacity of executors or the fickleness of spouses and children:

> Do sum good, man, by thy lyffe,
> Whilis thow hast thy mynde;
> Thy children will for-gete the sone
> Thy wyffe will be vnkynd,
> Thy executowrs be covytes,
> And take all that they fynde;
> Yff thow wilt not, while thow may,
> They will bryng the behynde.[44]

But even where the neglect was perceived more benignly as the result "not of evil mind . . . but of negligence . . . and . . . forgetfulness",[45] concern for an enduring place in the memories, and therefore the prayers, of surviving kindred features large in the preoccupations of fifteenth- and early sixteenth-century testators. However thorough and elaborate one's provision of Masses, alms, and prayers for the welfare of one's own soul, in the last resort one was at the mercy of the executors. Most wills left much of the detailed charitable and ritual provision "for the health of my soul" to the executors "affter theyr discretion . . . as by theym shall be thowte moste nedefull and meritorye".[46] But often such general provision is supplemented by more specific appeals to the

[41] *Festial*, p. 84.

[42] Horstmann, *Yorkshire Writers*, I p. 384; and see the stories, much used by preachers, in *Golden Legend*, VI pp. 116–17.

[43] More, *Workes*, p. 335.

[44] Dyboski, *Songs*, p. 138; and see, for example, the Towneley Play of Lazarus in Happe, *English Mystery Plays*, pp. 405–6.

[45] More, *Workes*, p. 334.

[46] *Lincoln Wills*, II p. 14; see also ibid. pp. 3, 9, 12, 15, 16, 19, 26–7, 64, 65, etc.

executor's love or sense of justice, "most singulerly trusting in hir love and conscience", to act on the testator's behalf "as she thinkethe best in conscience", or as the testator would do "as I should do for you if I shoulde be the longer lyver", or as they must answer "at the dredfull daie of dome" or "be fore the hyghe Judge of hevyn".[47] Testators might appeal explicitly to the bonds of kinship or affection[48] and, where such appeals seemed likely to fail, attempt to bind an undutiful son "upon pain of my curse".[49] Such anxieties were no doubt rooted in simple realism about the rapacity or inertia of human nature. The *Golden Legend* provided a hair-raising story of a negligent executor haunted by the ghost of the kinsman whose trust he has betrayed; the executor is whisked off to Hell himself as punishment. The story seems to have been popular with preachers, which suggests that it was felt to provide a necessary deterrent to a common neglect.[50] Ecclesiastical court proceedings bear abundant testimony to both rapacity and inertia, and it was by no means unknown for executors to leave their obligations at least partially unfulfilled till they themselves were faced with imminent death, and were forced in turn to trust their own executors to make good their neglect.[51]

But such cases were in all probability a minority. Executors were bound by natural affection, by charity, by conscience, and by social pressure. Most of them seem to have discharged their religious responsibilities to the full,[52] if not quite to the extent portrayed in the verse account of the model son and executor, the Boy of Bristol:

> Al the catel his fader hade
> He sold it up and money made
> and labored morow and eve.
> He sought about in that country tho
> Where any almes myght be do,
> And largely he dud hem yeve,

[47] Barfield and Parker, *Thatcham, Berkshire*, II p. 80; *Beds Wills*, III p. 40; *Lincoln Wills*, I pp. 46, 90, 205; *Sussex Wills*, I p. 8; *London Consistory Court Wills 1492–1547*, ed. I. Darlington, London Record Society, III, 1967, pp. 58–9.

[48] *Test. Ebor.*, V p. 24–5.

[49] *Somerset Wills*, II pp. 3–4.

[50] *Golden Legend*, VI p. 127; *Festial*, p. 270; *Speculum Sacerdotale*, pp. 227–8.

[51] For unfulfilled or partially fulfilled bequests, see *Kentish Visitation*, pp. 91, 94, 110, 196–8, 207, 213–16, 247–8, etc; for executors fulfilling duties belatedly in their own wills see *Sussex Wills*, III p. 52 and Carpenter, "Religion of the Gentry", p. 58.

[52] But for a suggestion that aristocratic families found such obligations burdensome, and sought to evade them or failed to implement them, see M. Hicks, "Chantries, Obits and Almshouses: the Hungerford Foundations 1325–1478", in Barron and Harper-Bill, *The Church in Pre-Reformation Society*, pp. 123–42.

> Wayes and brugges for to make
> And pore men for goddis sake
> He yeaf them gret releve.
> Whoso axed oght, he made her pay
> And XXXti trental of masses he let say
> For his fadres sake.
> He let never til he had bewared
> Al the tresour his fader spared,
> Aseth to god for to make.[53]

If one's kin did not remember, no one else could be expected to do so,[54] and the textbooks emphasized the pathetic plight of myriads of anonymous and forgotten souls in purgatory "for as much as many falleth from this worlde that have not any kynesmen nor frendes . . . that euer prayeth for them", and so are doomed to be "longely holden in the sayd paynes". There was therefore special merit in praying not only for one's kin but for these friendless sufferers. The *Golden Legend* had a vivid winter's tale of a man who lived by a churchyard and regularly prayed for all the dead in it. When one day he was pursued through the churchyard by enemies, the grateful dead rose up in regiments to protect him, bearing the implements of their earthly trades, a benevolent reversal of the *danse macabre*. Provision for prayers not only for one's own soul, and those of one's relatives and benefactors, one's "good frendys", but also of "all crystyn soulys" was a pious convention of many wills on the eve of the Reformation, and the primers regularly provided a prayer for the dead in a churchyard, offering as many days' indulgence as there were corpses buried there.[55]

There was, then, a very obvious practical dimension to the emphasis on the role of kin in securing intercession, not least in the mere brute fact that one's property and therefore one's charitable buying power passed at death to one's heirs. But there was more to the matter than this. The first consolation of Purgatory, according to the *Arte or Crafte to Lyve well* was that good angels show the souls there "the suffrages the whiche ben done for them by theyr kynnesfolke / by theyr frendes / and coseynes".[56] It was not merely that news of such prayers had power to cheer. The theology of purgatory turned on the notion of satisfaction, the payment to God by works of mercy, by penitential practices, and by prayer, of the

[53] *Altenglische Legenden Neue Folge*, p. 317.
[54] *The Book of Margery Kempe*, pp. 46–7.
[55] *Arte or Crafte*, fol. ci; Hoskins, pp. 117–18; *Golden Legend*, VI p. 117, elaborated in *Festial*, pp. 269–70.
[56] *Arte or Crafte*, fol. lxxxv (v).

debt due after sin had been forgiven. In the surrogate repayment of such a debt, kindred were crucial.[57] Ties of blood gave kindred both the obligation and the power to discharge the penances of the dead. The repayment of financial debts and the restoration of property unjustly gained or retained by the deceased was one of the primary duties of executors; this same principle was extended to supernatural debts. The souls in Purgatory "may be socoured by the ablaycyons of theyr frendes to thende that the sayd soules ben loysed and qnyte off dettes for the whiche they ben bounde ayenst god".[58] The legend of the Boy of Bristol turns on the young man's sale of all he possesses, and his willingness to exchange his own freedom for that of his father by becoming a bondsman, to rescue his sinful father's soul from the prison of Purgatory by works of charity. The *Golden Legend* tells the story, much used by English preachers, of a woman who sold her soul to the Devil, and was thereby supernaturally prevented from confessing her sins or doing penance for them. But though her heart is hardened and she cannot weep for her sins, she confides in her son on her deathbed, and his surrogate grief and willingness to do penance on her behalf bring her the gift of repentance. The demons, fearful of losing their prey, frighten her to death before a priest can be fetched, but her son "confessid hym for hire and receyued penaunce of vii yere in fastyngis". At the end of the seven year penance the soul of his mother appeared to him "bryght and schynyng as the sone thonkynge hym of hire delyveraunce".[59]

The motif of the child whose prayers, good works, and penances secure release for the soul of the unshriven parent was a potent one in late medieval thinking about the cult of the dead, and the popular and influential legend of the Pope Trental, in which St Gregory the Great rescued his sinful and unshriven mother's soul from Purgatory, or perhaps even Hell, by an elaborate sequence of Masses, fasts, and other mortuary observances, was based on it.[60] But the intercessory powers and obligations of kinship extended wider than the relationship between parent and child. A fifteenth-century chronicle tells of a shipman of Weymouth who goes on pilgrimage to Compostella to have Masses said there for his parents. On his return he is haunted by the ghost of his uncle, who tells him

---

[57] See above, p. 195.
[58] *Arte or Crafte*, fol. lxxxvii.
[59] *Golden Legend*, VI p. 121; *Speculum Sacerdotale*, p. 227.
[60] For the "Pope Trental" see Horstmann, *Minor Poems of the Vernon MS*, I pp, 260–8; R. W. Pfaff, "The English Devotion of St Gregory's Trental", *Speculum*, XLIX, 1974, pp. 75–90; R.-J. Herbert, "Les Trentains Grégoriens sous forme de cycles liturgiques", *Revue Bénédictine*, LXXXI, 1979, pp. 108–22. See also *Arte or Crafte*, fol. lxxxvii.

that he has been trying to speak with him for nine years, and who demands that he return as a penniless beggar to Compostella to have Mass said and to distribute alms for him, for "yef thou haddest lete say a masse for me, I had be delievred of the payn that I suffre". The nephew duly sets out once more for Compostella.[61] One of the attractions of the enormously popular prayers on the passion known as the "Fifteen Oes" of St Brigid was the prefatory rubric, which promised that if anyone said them daily for a year "he shall delever xv soules out of purgatory of hys nexte kindreed, and converte other xv synners to gode lyf, and other xv ryghteous men of hys kynde shall persever in good lyf."[62]

So wholesale a package of benefits, affecting so wide a circle of kinsmen, argues for a vivid and extended conviction of the religious reality of the ties of blood. Moreover, the spiritual effect of such ties was believed to function mechanically, even when hidden from the living and forming no part of their intentions. According to the spirit who revealed the secrets of Purgatory in the "Revelacyone schewed to ane holy woman" of 1422, prayers offered in ignorance for a soul damned were not wasted, though they could not help the intended beneficiary; instead "the helpe and the mede turne to the nexte of his kynne in purgatorye and hastelye spede tham owte of thaire pergatorie."[63] The practical influence of this complex network of belief and assumption about the spiritual dimensions of kinship is evidently at work in the will of the Norwich widow, Margaret Est, in 1484, whose "belovyd Cosyn" Thomas Thurkeld had undertaken to go on pilgrimage on her behalf to the shrines of St Thomas of Canterbury, King Henry at Chertsey, and to St Wendreda, "And so be hys pylgrymages that I may be relessyd of myn avowes."[64]

Ways of Deliverance: Shortening the Pains of Purgatory

Purgatory was God's prison; the "sely souls" there were bound in the chains of their own sins. But "four keys" hung at the girdle of every Christian in a state of grace, "for to open purgatory".[65] Charity and duty alike moved the living to "do lyke frendes" to the dead, to help them by prayer, by works of penance, by alms-deeds, and above all by securing Masses for the repose of their souls.[66]

---

[61] J. S. Davies (ed.), *An English Chronicle 1377–1461*, Camden Society, LXIV, 1856, p. 72.
[62] *Hor. Ebor.*, p. 76.
[63] Horstmann, *Yorkshire Writers*, I p. 385.
[64] *Norfolk Wills*, IV p. 338.
[65] *Kalender of Shepherdes*, p. 177.
[66] Fisher, *Two Fruytfull Sermons of St John Fisher*, ed. Sr M. D. Sullivan, Notre Dame University PhD thesis 1961, p. 22.

Preachers and moralists were consistent in urging men and women to "do for themselves" in this matter, to send "our substance before us by our own handes" by alms to the poor and other good works, while they were still in good health,[67] rather than leaving such matters to the deathbed or in the chancy hands of executors. There is no way of knowing what proportion of the laity took this advice to heart. What is certain is that the overwhelming majority of pre-Reformation wills show that in the immediate prospect of death most men and women sought to make use of these keys on their own behalf, and to see that others did so for them when they were gone. Their wills therefore provide, well into the 1530s, a detailed picture of the ways in which lay people appropriated the teaching and the priorities of the late medieval Church.

The will, then, was more than a way of disposing of property. It was in principle a religious document, the last opportunity to set one's fundamental religious orientation and orthodoxy solemnly on record before the confusions of the deathbed and the spiritual onslaught of demons. For the exceptionally pious or articulate, the will might fulfil this function by serving as a solemn and explicit declaration of faith. For most, its religious character lay in its concrete practical expression of the testator's belief in the importance of providing for prayer and good works for the health of one's soul. Most wills, indeed, were highly conventional, their basic structure, their language, and even many of their detailed provisions dictated not by but to the dying testator by the scribe who was often the local priest. But this fact need neither detract from their value as evidence about the nature of traditional religion in England before the solvents of Reformation began to bite in the 1530s, nor mislead us into dismissive assumptions about the merely external or second-hand religion they represent. In traditional societies social rituals are the underlying and living skeletons of the body corporate, not the fossils of life long since passed away. The formulaic character of most late medieval wills offers evidence not of shallowness, but of overwhelming social consensus in religious convictions and priorities.

Before considering the two main religious preoccupations evident in the wills made before 1540, almsgiving and prayers, one other dimension of these wills needs to be noted. The essence of the deathbed pastoral care of the Church was to see that the Christian died in faith, hope, and charity. To die in charity meant, among other things, to die discharged of one's debts, and forgiving all injuries. Spiritual or material debts left undischarged would detain a

<hr>

[67] More, *Workes*, p. 336.

soul in Purgatory, and it was a folkloric commonplace that the spirits of Purgatory might trouble the living till their debts were paid. The detailed business of the settlement of debts was, in most cases, done before the will was made, or left to the executors, as in the case of Richard Hall of Bucknall in 1512, who left a sheep worth twenty pence to his parish priest "that he maie dispose it for the helthe of my soule as I have shewed him in confesson", and then left the residue of his goods to his wife "to the paienge of my debtes and to dispose for the heyll of my soule as my executrix".[68] Occasionally, testators troubled with a bad conscience made explicit directions for an act of recompense, like the London merchant who recalled how forty years before he had helped a kinsman in Derbyshire unjustly to distrain a poor man's oxen "in my wanton dayes whanne I lakkyd discrecyon": he asked his executors to trace the man or his executors and restore the cost of the beasts, or else to consult "some sadde doctours of dyvynyte" to find the best way of spending the money "for the wele of the soule of the said man . . . and for the discharge of my consciens".[69]

Provisions of this sort for the discharge of material debt were relatively uncommon, but most testators made arrangements for the discharge of spiritual debt. The whole notion of penance, of course, turned on the idea of a debt discharged by pious activity, and every bequest for a soul in Purgatory could be understood in this light, but there are more explicit examples of the notion of debt as well. These included the fulfilment of vows of pilgrimage, many testators making arrangements for relatives, executors, chantry clergy, or feed bedesmen to discharge for them "certeyn pilgramages which as yet I have not goon".[70]

But by far the most widespread expression of concern about spiritual indebtedness is to be found in the almost universal provision of bequests to the high altar of one's parish church, for "tithes and offrynges neglgently forgotten".[71] This was no mere form of words. Four times a year the parish priest solemnly pronounced the Greater Excommunication or General Sentence to his parishioners. This formidable curse listed a comprehensive range of offences against the Church, its personnel, and precepts, and then pronounced that all guilty of such offences were

---

[68] *Lincoln Wills*, I p. 50.

[69] S. L. Thrupp, *The Merchant Class of Medieval London*, 1948, p. 176.

[70] "Wills at Somerset House relating to Derbyshire", ed. S. O. Addy, *Journal of the Derbyshire Archaeological and Natural History Society* XLIV, 1923 (hereafter = *Derbyshire Wills*) pp. 63–5.

[71] *Lincoln Wills*, I p. 113. Virtually every will in the three Lincoln volumes contains this or a similar clause.

departed fro God and al holi chirche, and . . . they have no part of the passion of our Lord Jesu Christ, ne of no sacrament that is in holy chirche, ne no part of the prayer among cristine folke, but that thei ben accursed of God and holi chirche, fro the sole of the foot unto the crowne of the heed, slepinge and wakynge, sythynge and standinge, and in all their wordes and werkes.[72]

Since much of the General Sentence was aimed at those who laid hands on the property or challenged the jurisdiction of the Church, including its monasteries, Henry VIII was to forbid the reading of it. There is no doubt that it made an impression on even quite sophisticated lay people. As "sheriffe of the shyer" and com-missioner for benevolences in the North and East Ridings, Sir Marmaduke Tunstall had ample opportunity of offending against the Church and its property, and thereby falling foul of the Greater Sentence. On his deathbed in 1518 he asked that one of his "most trusty servants" should be dispatched to every religious house in the region, "desyryng theme in the waye of charitie of forgive me and absolve me . . . and also to pray for me, consyderuyng the sentence and censurs of the churche ar dredefull and many waise unadvisedly a man may fall and trespasse therein, as I fere me that I have done".[73] Few of the laity had Sir Marmaduke's opportunities for offending against the precepts of the Church, but anyone might, deliberately or by oversight, fail to pay their tithes, and this offence too incurred the rigour of the General Sentence. Unpaid tithe, like other debts, hindered or cut off the benefits of prayer and alms-deeds, and left the soul longer in purgatory. The routine bequest to the high altar was thus part of a necessary settling of accounts before any of one's other mortuary provisions could be of any benefit.[74]

The Works of Mercy

As we have already seen, the eschatology of the medieval Church was dominated by the parable of the sheep and the goats from chapter 25 of St Matthew's Gospel. At the Day of Doom Christ will judge men and women not by their professions of piety, but by their actions towards the poor and weak. That moment formed the climax of all the great cycles of Corpus Christi plays

---

[72] Printed in Maskell, *Monumenta*, II pp. 286–301.
[73] *Test. Ebor.*, V pp. 88–93, 108.
[74] Giles Constable, "Resistance to Tithes in the Middle Ages", *Journal of Ecclesiastical History*, XIII, 1962, pp. 172–85.

> Caitiffs, as oft as it betid
> That needful aught asked in my name,
> Ye heard them not, your ears ye hid,
> Your help to them was not at home.
> To me was that unkyndness kid,
> Therefore ye bear this bitter blame;
> To least or most when ye it did,
> to me ye did the self and same.[75]

Therefore the seven corporal works of mercy – feeding the hungry, giving drink to the thirsty, clothing the naked, visiting the sick, relieving the prisoner, housing the stranger, and burying the dead – loomed ever larger in late medieval perceptions of the Christian life, and hence of preparation for judgement. Every Christian was expected to relieve the poor:

> For man with-owt marcy, of marcy shall misse;
> And he shall have marcy, that marcyfyll is.[76]

The emphasis here is on motivation – mercy – and that is representative of late medieval religious teaching in general. But enormous importance was also attached to the mere fact of giving alms, however defective the intentions of the giver. Mirk tells the story of a hard and unfeeling rich man who throws a loaf at an importunate poor man, simply for lack of a better missile. After his death he is saved from damnation by the Virgin, who produces the loaf and routs the Devil with this solitary, and grudging, good deed.[77] The inexorable association between alms-giving and salvation is precisely, though more positively, caught in the popular theology of the "Lyke-wake Dirge":

> This ae night, this ae night
> Every night and alle;
> Fire and fleet and candle light
> And Christ receive thy saule.

> When thou from hence away are paste,
> Every night and alle;
> To Whinny-muir thou comest at laste
> And Christe receive thy saule.

> If hosen and shoon thou ne'er gavest nane,
> Every night and alle;
> The whinnes shall pricke thee to the bare bane;
> And Christe receive thy saule.

[75] Beadle, *York Plays*, p. 279.
[76] Dyboski, *Songs*, p. 141.
[77] *Festial*, p. 104.

From Whinny-muir when thou mayst passe,
Every night and alle;
To Brigg o' Dread thou comest at laste;
And Christe receive thy saule.

From Brigg o' Dread when thou mayst pass,
Every night and alle;
To purgatory fire thou comest at laste;
And Christe receive thy saule.

If ever thou gavest meat or drink,
Every night and alle;
The fire shall never make thee shrinke;
And Christe receive thy saule.

If meate or drinke thou never gavest nane,
Every night and alle;
The fire will burn thee to the bare bane;
And Christe receive thy saule.

This ae nighte, this ae nighte,
Every night and alle;
Fire and fleet, and candle lighte,
And Christe receive thy saule.[78]

Since one's funeral was the last occasion on which one might distribute meat and drink, shoes and stockings, if only by proxy, doles to the poor in the form of money, clothing, or bread and beer became an invariable feature of the burials of all but the destitute, a last chance to turn away the dreadful "Ite Maledicti" which awaited those who had ignored the cry of the poor. Even where such "common doles" are not expressly stipulated in a will, they can be presumed to have been as routine as the requiem Mass offered for every dead Christian. The common practice of paying the bell-man to go round the parish between a death and the burial, invoking the prayers of the people for the deceased, was also a signal for the poor and the local clergy to gather at the burial. There were fixed tariffs of reward to those present, from the fourpence given to priests and literate clerks who could recite "Dirige", to the penny or halfpenny given to the unlettered poor, who would merely recite a Pater or an Ave. In 1511 the parishioners of St Mary's, Dover, complained that the weekday services in their church were cancelled "if there be any mynde within the towne where our curate may get a grote".[79] By the 1520s testators who disapproved of such common doles might

---

[78] W. Beattie (ed.), *Border Ballads*, 1965, pp. 176–7.
[79] *Kentish Visitation*, p. 132.

feel it necessary to stipulate that the bell-man should give warning that there would be no dole at the burial.[80]

But in fact, doles to the poor do feature in huge numbers of wills to the end of the 1530s, and in many cases the basic practice was the focus of symbolic elaboration, behind which lay the framework of the works of mercy (Pl. 130). This could range from the direct invocation of the language or the corporal works, as in Richard Dekyn's request that his widow "dispose for my soule in werkes of mercy and charite, as she wold I did for her in caas like", to much more detailed provisions designed to hammer home the point. So John Mangeham, a London fishmonger, requested burial in 1514 "directly afore the wyndowe of the vij werkes of mercy" in his parish church of St Mary at Hill, and went on in his will to exemplify those works in practical terms as part of his mortuary provision – twenty shillings for poor parishioners and forty shillings in the form of a general penny dole on the day of burial "except I do deale it wyth myne hondis or I depart this present lyeffe", forty shillings' worth of linen cloth to make shirts and smocks for poor men, and an unspecified sum to "redeme and pay the fes of xij presoners lyeng in the kynges bench, the Merchelsee, Newgate or Ludgate".[81] In 1502 Elizabeth Greystock, a Yorkshire widow, ordered that her "houseold stuff" be disposed of "for my soule and all Christen soules in doynge of masses, acquitinge of powere prisoners oute of prison, releving of ympotent people, blynde and lame, and in other dedes of mercye and charitie".[82] Even apparently simple bequests to "the hearse light", "the common torches", or lights to burn "at pore men's buryalls" are probably conscious references to the seventh corporal work of mercy.[83]

The provision of doles at one's burial was not a matter of mere last-minute provision for something better done earlier. There were special and powerful reasons for kindness to the poor "coming together to my burial". There was a clear *quid pro quo* involved in all such gifts: in return for the gift the recipient was to pray for the giver. In 1500 Edmund Thwaites, leaving provision for a penny dole at his burial "to every person that at that day wil take almous, to help my saul with their prayer", was merely making explicit the rationale of all such giving, for the prayers of the poor were believed to be especially powerful with Christ, who had identified himself with them. As Mirk explained:

[80] *Lincoln Wills*, II p. 89.
[81] *Somerset Wills*, I p. 222; London St Mary at Hill CWA, p. 19.
[82] *Test. Ebor.*, V p. 3.
[83] *Northants Wills*, II p. 422; Duncan, "Parishes of West Kent", p. 249.

Ye schull know well that yn the day of dome pore men schull be domes-men wyth Cryst, and dome the ryche. For all the woo that pore men haven, hit ys by the ryche men; and thogh thay have moche wrong, thay may not gete amended, tyll thay come to that dome; and ther thay schall have all hor one lust of hem . . . Wherfor, syrs, for Goddys love, whyll ye ben here, makyth amendes for your mys-dedys, and maketh hom your frendes that schall be our domes-men.[84]

This was intended as general advice about life lived in the prospect of general judgement at the end of time, but it had a special appropriateness at the point of death and burial, when the soul of the individual faced its own particular judgement. To gather the grateful poor round one's corpse at this moment was to spike the Dooms-man's guns, to enlist one's judges as one's advocates. There emerged a widespread practice of paying poor men to stand around the corpse with candles in their hands. This was an extremely dramatic gesture, particularly as testators wealthy enough to pay for it often provided cloaks and hoods of black, white, or russet for the "weepers" to wear, thereby fulfilling another of the works of mercy and adding to the dignity and spectacle of the burial. Moralists like More sometimes deprecated the element of display in the practice, satirizing such "honorable burying" with "so many torches, so many tapers, so many black gowns, so many mery mourners laughyng under black hodes".[85] More was articulating a perception often found among well-to-do Londoners in the late Middle Ages. Some wealthy testators there expressed similar reservations about "comen torch-bearers",[86] but such objections were comparatively rare. They were dismissed even by so austere a writer as the author of Dives and Pauper, who vehemently endorsed "candelis, clothis, mete and drynk, elmysse dede and holy prayeris" as "ceremonyys that turnen to gret profyt bothin of the qwyke and of the dede".[87] Although the practice of employing the poor to bear torches or tapers round one's corpse undoubtedly lent itself to the vanity of ostentatious display, the primary object of the practice was religious.[88] The burning of candles round a corpse was an act with profound resonances. Blessed candles had apotropaic power to banish demons. They were also understood as particularly eloquent examples of a whole vocabulary of light and darkness, symbolizing the desire that Christ "that is the lughte of the worlde wyll gyve

[84] Somerset Wills, I pp. 36–7; Festial, pp. 4–5.
[85] More, Workes, p. 79.
[86] Thrupp, Merchant Class, p. 180.
[87] Dives and Pauper, I p. 216.
[88] C. Gittings, Death, Burial and the Individual in Early Modern England, 1988, p. 29.

clere lyght unto the soule by the derke way and unknowen by the whyche he shall walke".[89] Held in the hands of the poor, candles were both a prayer in themselves and a means of ensuring the powerful intercession of their bearers. Hence it was often stipulated that the poor men who held them should actually touch the candles as they stand, "berying each of them a taper in ther handes", "ilkon a torche in his hande", "without any candlesticks being hired for the same".[90]

The association of the poor with the religious language of light was not the only symbolic extension of the basic practice of alms-giving at funerals. Since the poor were in a special sense the images of Christ, gifts to them could be made into a deliberate act of homage to the Crucified. Bequests to poor men and women in groups of twelve or thirteen, in honour of Christ and his Apostles, were common. Even more frequently, bequests were made in multiples of the number five and thereby, especially if associated with Friday, equated the poor with the precious Wounds of Christ, as did Walter Dolman, who asked his wife to distribute each Friday while she lived "vd to v por men in the worship of our Lord v woundes and they to pray for us".[91]

The Rejection of Penny Doles

The rationale behind the distribution of alms at funerals, month's minds, and anniversaries was straightforwardly religious, to "refresh the poverte . . . to pray for my soul". All who came seeking "the alms of Christ" were conceived of as entering into some sort of contractual obligation to intercede on behalf of their dead bene-factor. The formalizing of the practice, however, the fact that alms were given as a matter of course at every funeral, meant that testators increasingly feared that the recipients of their charity might not honour their part of the bargain, that doles would be given but no prayers said, or that the recipients would not after all be God's poor. "Forasmuch," declared Elizabeth de Vere in 1537, "as I have had experience that to general doles as well the Riche as the poore and nedye personnes do resorte, I will therefore that no suche common doles be made for me."[92] Some of the wealthy

[89] *Arte or Crafte*, fol. lxxxvi(v).

[90] *Beds Wills*, III p. 89; *Test. Ebor.*, III p. 214, IV pp. 7, 10, 21, 27, 52, 201, V p. 55, VI p. 211; *Somerset Wills*, I p. 6, III p. 163 (where the poor men are to be replaced by innocent children, another common provision); *Sussex Wills*, I pp. 7–8.

[91] *Somerset Wills*, I p. 221; *Sussex Wills* III pp. 208, 304.

[92] *Sussex Wills*, I pp. 201–2; "Testament and last will of Elizabeth, widow of John de Vere" printed in *Transactions of the Essex Archaeological Society*, ns XX, 1933, pp. 9–10.

testators of late medieval London were concerned to exclude beggars and "rynners about in town" from their doles.[93] By the beginning of the sixteenth century a growing number of testators sought to ensure that a closer control was exercised over their funeral doles, and that those who received any benefaction intended as a work of mercy should "take it by way of charyte, elles not none penny".[94] The norm probably remained a general and un-discriminating distribution, so far as the means of the deceased allowed, and a few testators reacted against the growing concern with a return for charitable investment by stipulating gifts to "evere pore creature that cometh", or spelt out their desire that "every poore man, woman and childe asking almes be gyven for Godd's sake a peni wyth out any excessive charge or objection maid agenst any of them".[95] But a significant number of testators sought to guard their investment by setting conditions or limitations. A common restriction was to "pore men of my parysche",[96] who would know the testator and whose good will and prayers could therefore be more securely relied upon. Marmaduke Constable, forbidding "any maner of dole" at his obsequies in 1523, fulfilled the dominical command to give alms by providing gifts for "the most nedfull poore people" in eight parishes, fourpence to house-holders, twopence to others.[97] Henry Coby of Southover in Sussex in 1521 made a similar provision for poor householders "and noon other dole to be delt". Richard Clerke of Lincoln in 1521 forbade any penny dole, but left a groat apiece to 100 persons "that be in povertie and age, dwellers in the towne ther as I shal departe".[98]

The targeting of alms on the local poor obviously reflected both the central religious importance of the parish community in late medieval and early modern England and a concern that poor relief should be applied with more discrimination. It is possible to see here some of the preoccupations embodied in some of the less attractive aspects of the Tudor poor laws. They were not, however, peculiar to the Tudor period, for Margery Kempe, hardly a social innovator, was firmly of the opinion that "it was mor almes to helpyn hem that thei knewyn wel for wel dysposyd folke & her owyn neyborys than other strawngerys whech thei knew not." This view that charity begins at home is very much the sort of

[93] Thrupp, *Merchant Class*, p. 180.
[94] *Lincoln Wills*, II pp. 93–4.
[95] *Test. Ebor.*, IV p. 270, V p. 29.
[96] *The Fifty Earliest English Wills in the Court of Probate, London*, ed. F. J. Furnivall, EETS, 1882, p. 40.
[97] *Test. Ebor.*, V pp. 166–70.
[98] *Sussex Wills*, III p. 111; *Lincoln Wills*, II p. 89.

sentiment one expects in a hard-nosed mercantile community like fifteenth-century King's Lynn, and it was to become common in Tudor England. Those charitable provisions which reflect it frequently make explicit mention of the need of the recipients, as in Myles Roos's stipulation in 1529 that every house in his home parish of Naseby All Saints should have a cheese "and the poorest house the best cheese",[99] or Robert Peche's provision in Aldingbourne for bequests to five of his poor neighbours "as it shall seme to my overseers most nede".[100] But there was also by the early sixteenth century a discernible concern among some testators with the deserts or worthiness of the recipients of charity, reflected generally in bequests to poor householders, but also more particularly in provision for "suche as be honest", in requests to testators to bestow alms where it is "most nedefull and meritorye", or in bequests like Henry Tawyer's fund for the relief of poor men who have had sudden or wrongful loss of goods, excluding "comyn ale gohers or comyn gammers".[101]

It is tempting to see in moves to restrict the indiscriminate charity associated with funerals a move towards more secular or even proto-Protestant attitudes, reflecting doubt about the religious value of alms or the prayers of the poor. But I think that this would be a mistake. Few of the wills which make such restrictions show any lack of confidence in traditional Catholic belief or practice, many of them providing for the full range of Masses and prayers, including such unequivocal manifestations of the full-blown doctrine of Purgatory as the "Scala Coeli" indulgence.[102] Indeed, some of them may reflect not a weakening grip on the orthodox doctrine of the value of the prayers of the poor, but a firmer grasp of its technicalities.

The notion that penances, prayers, and good deeds performed on behalf of the dead shortened the pains of Purgatory depended for its coherence on the notion of a sharing of merit within the mystical body of the Church, a "bearing of one another's burdens", in which the debts of the dead could be paid by the living. But such an exchange, it was held, could only take place in charity. Only those who shared the divine life of grace and love could give or receive in this transaction – "for the comunycacyon the whiche is rote of the merytoryous werke . . . is of charyte whiche is rote of all good dedes".[103] It was for this reason that the damned were unable to

---

[99] *Northants Wills*, II p. 369; *Book of Margery Kempe*, p. 56.
[100] *Sussex Wills*, pp. 7–8.
[101] *Northants Wills*, II pp. 337, 398.
[102] On the Scala Coeli indulgence, see below pp. 375–6.
[103] *Kalender of Shepherdes*, p. 175.

benefit from the prayers of the living, and by the same token, the living could do no good to the dead if they themselves were in a state of mortal sin and so cut off from the divine life. It was the prayers of "true Cristen peple", those "yn charyte and out of dedly synne", which alone availed for the relief of souls.[104] It was true that a Mass said by a sinful priest was nevertheless effective, but that was because the sacraments worked *ex opere operato* not *ex opere operantis*: the true author of the act here was not the individual priest, but the whole Church, which subsisted perpetually in grace and charity. The effectiveness of all lesser prayers and good works depended on their being "devout prayers", and the state of the soul of those who instigated or offered them was crucial. As Fisher declared, "The more that any prayer is grounded in charyte, the sooner it shall be herde of hym whose commandment is all charyte."[105]

The implications of this were not ignored. Two representative popular manuals at the beginning of the sixteenth century, the *Arte or Crafte to Lyve well* and the *Kalender of Shepherdes*, both insisted that prayers or alms-deeds offered for a dead soul by someone in a state of mortal sin availed nothing. Even more disturbingly,

> yf a cursed man beynge in deedly synne gyve an almesse to a poore man that is in the state of grace and that the sayd pore myn [*sic*] by the sayd almes were moved to pray god for the soule of hym for whome the almes was gyuen, by the sayd synnes truely the sayd almes sholde nothynge proufytte the sayd soule.[106]

This meant, among other things, that if one's executor was in mortal sin, none of the mortuary provisions initiated by him, apart from the requiem Mass, would be of any benefit to one's soul. It also meant that any activities organized by one's executor for the "welth of my soul" was more effective if undertaken in a spirit of charity than if done merely mechanically as a matter of duty. Some testators marked their awareness of this by giving the executor discretion "therwith to doo hir free wyll for the well of my soule and all Christen soules", or even more explicitly in the case of Margery Cowper, a widow of Diss, who asked in 1504 for an annual obit from her son, adding "but never the lesse, I constrayne him not to do it, but at his own voluntary will be it done."[107] Thus it was vital that all involved in one's obsequies, whether as

---

[104] *Speculum Sacerdotale*, p. 225; *Festial*, p. 269.
[105] Fisher, *English Works*, p. 170.
[106] *Arte or Crafte*, fol. lxxxviii(v).
[107] *London Consistory Court Wills*, pp. 58–9, 63; Blomefield, *Norfolk*, I p. 27.

executor, officiant, or recipient of alms should be "true Cristen peple", in grace and charity with God and neighbours, and moved by charity in praying for one's soul. As the *Kalender of Shepherdes* put it, "And therefore it is a grete welth when suche as gyveth almesse / or that maketh a masse to be sayd / and he to whome it is gyven or the masse commysed be in charyte."[108] Widespread awareness of these considerations appears most clearly in the very frequent injunction in wills that the priests celebrating the obsequies should be "honest", a "sad and devoute prest", "a discrete prest of good condicion", "a well disposyed prest and vertuous", or "the best lyver that may be y-geten".[109]

What was true of the priest had also to be true of the poor, though their spiritual state was less easy to specify. Nevertheless one Bedfordshire testator in 1504, leaving twenty pence a year for twenty years, stipulated that it should be distributed as a penny dole among twenty poor men and women of his parish every Good Friday. Each of the recipients was to have received his Easter communion, and in return for the dole was to say, devoutly, five Paters, five Aves and a Creed for the benefactor's soul. This, if he got it, was a good twenty pence-worth, but it may well throw further light on another dimension of the very common Good Friday doles. Perhaps they were designed not only as homage to the Passion of Christ, but to ensure that the recipients of the benefactor's charity were in the best possible spiritual state, and therefore in the best possible position to benefit him with their devout prayers.[110]

By the early 1500s, then, popular works such as the *Kalender of Shepherdes* were teaching very emphatically that the recipients as well as the dispensers of funeral alms, or the clergy who conducted intercession and Masses, must be in a state of grace and motivated by charity, if the soul for whom these things were offered were to benefit. Some testators clearly had such considerations in mind in making their mortuary provisions, and this suggests that the growth of concern evident in some wills to target the honest poor may have reflected a stricter level of Catholic orthodoxy about the nature and effectiveness of prayer and the doctrine of the treasure of merit, rather than a drift towards Protestantism or secularism.

---

[108] *Arte or Crafte*, fols lxxxviii(v)–lxxxix; *Kalender*, pp. 175–6.

[109] From hundreds of examples, *Northants Wills*, II p. 412; *Sussex Wills*, III pp. 82, 110, 159, 161, 208, 338, 348; *Somerset Wills*, II pp. 11–16, III p. 111; *Test. Ebor.*, V p. 55; *Earliest Wills*, pp. 87–8.

[110] *Bedford Wills*, III pp. 62–3; see also the will of Giles Fenis, in April 1551, providing for five celebrations of the first Edwardine prayer-book communion by five separate priests, with a dole of eightpence to "as mayny poore folkes as receave the same holly communyon the same tyme", *Sussex Wills*, I p. 38.

Bridges and Highways

A significant number of medieval wills left money not only for works which were palpably works of mercy, designed directly to relieve the poor, the sick, or the imprisoned, but also for more general and apparently more secular purposes. The upkeep of roads, causeways, and bridges was one of the commonest forms of such secular bequests, and the increase in the number of them during the Reformation, when more overtly religious bequests were declining, has sometimes misled historians into thinking they discerned the emergence of a secularizing or Protestant cast of mind.

This is not the place to explore this question in any detail, but it is important to register that the testators providing for such works made no distinction between them and works of mercy, with which indeed they frequently lump them. William Kypas, making arrangements for his property to be sold by the churchwardens, in default of heirs, "i part to a prest to syng for my soule and all cristen soules, the ijde parte to the highe wayes of Aswardby, and the iijde parte to be geven in almos to pour people" clearly thought these all cognate types of bequest, as did Margaret Jakson of Bicker, leaving land to be sold "and the money so receyed to be delt the more part emonges pore pepull and the other to the mendinge of the churche ways that I and my frendes bi whom it come may be prayd for".[111] This linking of "almoes dedes to poore people and amending of foule wayes"[112] to secure prayers was very common, and is perhaps puzzling to a twentieth-century mind, for whom road-mending is neither a devotional nor a charitable activity. It is true that many of the roads and causeways mentioned in wills were, as in Margaret Jackson's will, "church ways", roads linked directly to the parish church from the corners of the parish, along which both the living and the dead came by the shortest route. For the theologically sophisticated, bridges were symbolic as well as practical structures, emblems of the Christian life and of the communication of charity within the community. The Pope and each bishop was a *pontifex*, a bridge-builder. The middle English *Orchard of Sion*, a translation of a work by Catherine of Siena, devotes five chapters to an elaborate exploration of the notion of Christ as a bridge. These were sophisticated refinements of symbolism, but the religious dimensions of bridges and bridge-building were accessible even to the unlettered. Many bridges had small

---

[111] *Lincoln Wills*, I pp. 79, 130.
[112] *Sussex Wills*, I p. 34 (will of Richard Culpepper).

hermitage chapels built on or by them, and charitable contributions to the hermit secured his prayers for the donor and went to maintain the bridge.[113]

But even where no overtly symbolic significance can be attached to such works, those who provided finance for them conceived themselves to be performing a religious act. All contributions to the comfort of one's neighbours were understood as a dimension of the promotion of charity, the divine life in the community. This was expressed in the fact that indulgences were frequently granted to those who contributed to these projects. Just how wide this understanding of the religious, charity-enhancing, character of such benevolent activity was can be gauged from glancing through the registers of any bishop of the period. Between April 1513 and March 1516, for example, Richard Mayhew, Bishop of Hereford, granted indulgences for contributions to Charing Cross, Bedlam, and St Thomas Hospitals in London, to several Roman hospitals, to hospitals in Lincoln, Thelisford, and Burton, to the repair and equipping of St John's Hospital in Ludlow after a fire, to the repair or extension of a number of religious houses, parish churches, and chapels, to the Jesus gild at St Paul's in London, and to several other gilds for the aid of elderly and destitute members, to those who gave succour to John Jeakyn, ruined by cattle disease, Richard Corbet, who had lost all his goods by fire, and Meredyth ap Richard and his children, who were destitute because he had lost the use of his hands, to the completion of a road up Dunmore hill and to the upkeep of the bridge and chapel of Mudiford, and the bridge and chapel at Bridgnorth.[114] All of these activities were seen as religious, and contributions to them as pleasing to God. Indulgences could be granted for such acts because all of them were expressions of charity, and all therefore constituted part of that network of prayer and well-doing by which the debt of satisfaction which remained after sin had been forgiven could be paid. Such secular works as repairing "foul wayes" therefore found their way into wills not as the harbingers of incipient secularism or Protestantism, but because they too could speed the soul through purgatory.

Prayers and Supplications

Corporate intercession for the dead, being one of the most central aspects of late medieval religion, was highly regulated, highly formalized. At its heart lay the saying or singing of the Office

---

[113] For bridges and piety see C. Kerry, "Hermits, Fords and Bridge-Chapels", *Derbyshire Archaeological Journal*, XIV, 1882, pp. 54–71.

[114] A. T. Bannister (ed.), *The Register of Richard Mayhew*, 1919, pp. 285–7.

for the Dead, "Placebo" and "Dirige", and the celebration of requiem Masses. Most funerals took the same form. "Placebo", that is, vespers or evensong for the dead, was recited in church (or occasionally in the home of the deceased) on the night before the funeral, and "Dirige" (matins, with its nine readings from Job, to which was tacked on lauds) recited immediately before the Mass, "Dirige" was said in the presence of the corpse at funerals; at week and month minds and at anniversaries the deceased would be present symbolically in the form of a draped hearse surrounded by candles. To ensure the proper recitation of these lengthy and complicated services of Psalms and readings, clerks and literate lay people attending were often given a special dole, normally of a groat. The celebration of the "Dirige" would have been particularly solemn at the funerals of gild-members (in many places the majority of the adult population), and some gilds paid for "Diriges" and Masses "by note" (i.e. sung).

These devotions, together with the seven penitential Psalms, especially the "De Profundis", and the litany of the saints, were the central prayers of intercession for the dead, feeding souls and making them "strong to suffren here peyne wyth the more paciens".[115] The obsequies of most people would have followed this essential pattern with little variation, except that those who could afford it made provision for more than the regulation single requiem. Requests for five Masses in honour of the Wounds were common, though the commonest multiple was the trental, thirty masses celebrated on thirty consecutive days, where this could be managed. Nervous testators anxious to shorten their stay in Purgatory might if they were influential enough have all their requiem Masses compressed into a shorter period, though clearly the celebration of a trental in a day or a week required the clerical resources of a monastery (and possibly more than one) or a large town.[116] The cost of a trental was upwards of ten shillings: for five or six pounds one could "wage" an "annualer", a priest who would sing for one's soul for a whole year.[117] Bequests for short-term chantries of this sort, usually for periods from one to seven years, formed an important element in the religious economy of many communities, the soul-mass chaplains providing a daily round of Masses valued by the parishioners at large, and often required by their founders to

[115] *Festial*, p. 296.
[116] *Beds Wills*, III p. 40.
[117] There is a representative example in the will of William Crofts, of Waley in Bolsover, a yeoman, 28 November 1546, providing for an "honest priest" to sing for his soul, "a yere after my departure, that is to say, one quarter of a year at Bolsover where I shall be buried, halfe a year at Brampton, where I was born, and another quarter a yere at Chesterfelde, and the same priest shall have for his wages and labour that yere a hundred shilling, or under as my maister can hyer him", *Derbyshire Wills*, p. 69.

assist the parish priest at the main Sunday services or to organize the music.[118]

One of the reasons why temporary chantries were valued in parish churches was that they often provided, not merely more Masses, but particular Masses. As we have already seen, a feature of late medieval intercessory practice was the specification by many testators of votive Masses, other than the requiem, as part of their mortuary provision. Parishioners at St Mary's, Dover, in 1511 complained that the chantry priest there "wille not syng Jesus masse ooneys a weke, as othre his predecessors have doone afore hym of anncyent and laudabille custom".[119] The Jesus Mass or the Mass of the Wounds were very commonly found in such specific provisions. Testators too poor to secure regular celebrations of such a "running" or regularly repeated Mass out of their own resources could contribute a mite towards its general upkeep by membership of a gild, which frequently maintained such Masses, or by single donations, like Thomas Drure of Holy Cross parish, Daventry, who in 1528 left "a farthinge every Fryday to fynd a lyght at Jhesus mass".[120] Even for testators providing for a small fixed number of masses, rather than an annual series, it became common to specify Masses other than the requiem, as in Thomas Capell's desire that his confessor should sing for him "five . . . of a trentall for my sowll, the fyrst masse shalbe of the nativitie of or Lord, the 2 of the Epiphanie, the 3 of the resurrecon, the 4 of the Holy Ghost the v of the Assumpsion of our lady". Such specific provisions could become extremely elaborate, with a programme of Masses carefully worked out for all the days of the week. Lay people frequently showed a remarkable familiarity with the fine detail of the missal, specifying in addition to the votive Masses variant collects and other prayers to be used by their chantry priests and annualers.[121]

The most striking elaboration of this sort was the devotion known as the Trental of St Gregory or the Pope Trental. This was a series of thirty Masses, to be said over the period of a year, three Masses on each of the ten major feasts of Christ and Mary – Christmas,

---

[118] Cf. the will of Robert Ashtroke of High Wycombe, in March 1534, who provided a priest to sing at the Jesus altar in his parish church for ten years, at an annual stipend of £6 13s 4d, "and the same prieste shall helpe maytayne the servys of God in the quere . . . and that there be no preiste admissted to the saide servys but that can syng at lest his pleyn song substancyally". *Lincoln Diocese Documents*, p. 166; C. Burgess, "For the increase of divine service", *passim*.

[119] *Kentish Visitation*, p. 112.

[120] *Northants Wills*, II p. 311.

[121] *Northants Wills*, II pp. 287–8; *Test. Ebor.*, IV pp. 27–8, 167, V pp. 182–8; *Beds Wills*, III pp. 14–15, 165–9.

Epiphany, Candlemas, Annunciation, Easter, Ascension, Pentecost, Trinity, Assumption, and the Nativity of Mary. The Masses were to be said within the octave of the feasts to which they related, and at each Mass the priest was to use a special set of prayers linking the captivity of the souls in Purgatory to the subjection of the Holy Land to Islamic rule. The priest was also to recite "Placebo" and "Dirige" every day of the year in which the trental was performed, and the penitential Psalms, the litany of the saints, and the rosary on the days of the special Masses. In some versions of the trental he was also to say three Masses of requiem every week, unless hindered by a major festival. After every Mass throughout the year he was to recite the "De Profundis". In addition to these Masses and prayers, the priest was to fast on bread and water and either "forbere his shirt" or wear a hair shirt every Friday, every vigil, and on all the ten feasts of the trental.[122] The Pope Trental was validated by a verse legend, which told how Gregory's mother, to all appearance a devout and godly matron, had succumbed in youth to lust and had an illegitimate child. To cover her shame she murdered the baby and secretly buried it, never confessed this sin, and so died unshriven. The Pope, thinking his mother a saint, had a vision of her at Mass, when she appeared as a grisly demon, oozing flame at every orifice. Confessing her sin, she asked him to say the thirty Masses in their right order:

> Who-so sayth these masses, with-out fayle,
> ffor synfull sowles they shall a-vayle;
> All a yere, with-outen trayne,
> They delyvere a sowle out of payne.

The Pope dutifully complied, and in due course his mother appeared once more, but now so radiant that he mistook her for the Virgin Mary,

> Comely crowned as a qwene,
> Twenty Angellys her ladde be-twene.[123]

The Pope Trental was already established in England as "the gyldene trental" by 1410, when it was the object of an extended and hostile discussion in Dives and Pauper, but its popularity continued to grow in the century that followed. There were also a number of variants on the basic theme, like the "xiij masses . . . thatt were

---

[122] See above, note 60, and C. Eveleigh Woodruff (ed.), Sede Vacante Wills, Kent Archaeological Society, Records Branch, III, 1914, pp. 9, 125–7; Dives and Pauper, I pp. 186–9.
[123] Horstmann, Minor Poems of the Vernon Manuscript, I pp. 260–8.

shewd to bishope Innocente be revelation of an aungell" described by a Northampton testator in 1534.[124]

In a perceptive discussion of the Pope Trental Professor Pfaff has suggested that its attraction as a form of intercession for the dead lay in "an idea – the recapitulation of the liturgical year – and a story". This is certainly right, but it is important to grasp that the story behind the Pope Trental was important not merely because it was vivid or distinctive, but because it was a striking example of a recognizable genre – the revelation of the secrets of the other world by a suffering spirit, who asks for Masses and prayers, and who reveals a specially privileged form of devotion. It was of course a commonplace that the spirits of the dead troubled the living, like Gregory's mother, to secure relief from their suffering, "for when any soule apereth to any man, euermore he wylneth and prayth forto haue massys songen for hym."[125] Stories of such appearances were the stuff of every funeral and All Souls sermon, and of pious anecdotes like that of the Shipman of Weymouth. A number of the classic visions of Purgatory contain revelations that particular prayers are efficacious. In the *Vision of the Monk of Eynsham* a goldsmith who is in Purgatory because sudden death caught him unprepared, reveals that the daily tracing of the words "Ihesus Nazarenus" on brow and breast will protect against unprepared death.[126] In the *Gast of Gy* the whole Office for the Dead is explained and commended, but the penitential Psalms with the litany are declared to be "the devoutist orisouns to the soulis in purgatory" because the seven Psalms act as antidotes to the seven deadly sins.[127] This much could be understood as devout commentary on the official prayers for the dead. In the "Revelacyone schewed to ane holy woman" of 1422 the specified devotion is far more elaborate, and the promises attached to it far more extravagant. Indeed, the spirit of Purgatory in the "Revelacyone" discloses two privileged sets of Masses. The more effective consisted of 300 Masses – a hundred of the Trinity, a hundred of the Blessed Virgin, fifty of St Peter, and fifty of requiem, together with 300 repetitions of the Psalm "Miserere mei deus" and the hymn "Veni Creator". The spirit guaranteed that whatever sins had been committed by the soul for whom these prayers were offered "thare sall no maner of payne in purgatory halde hym that ne hastyly he sall be delyuered

---

[124] *Northants Wills*, II p. 376; the masses specified here were for Advent, Christmas, Epiphany, Septuagesima, Palm Sunday, Easter, Ascension, Holy Cross, a composite mass of the Blessed Virgin Mary, the Trinity, the Apostles, and the Holy Angels.

[125] *Festial*, p. 270.

[126] *Vision of the Monk of Eynsham*, pp. 53–4.

[127] *Gast of Gy*, pp. 29–30.

fra thame, and many other saules be delyuerde, for his sake."
Recognizing that few were "of powere to do" so many Masses, the
spirit revealed in addition a series of thirteen Masses – one of
requiem, three of the Trinity, two of St Peter, two of the Holy
Ghost, three of Our Lady, and two of All Saints, each group of
Masses to be accompanied by the devout repetition for five days of
the "Miserere" and "Veni Creator".[128]

The attraction of the Pope Trental to the late medieval laity
was not primarily its encapsulation of the liturgical year or its
colourful story, but the fact that it contained a supernaturally
authenticated scheme of intercession guaranteed to bring the torments of Purgatory to a swift and certain end. It belongs firmly to
the same mental world as the "Revelacyone" and the legend of the
revealing of the "Fifteen Oes" to a woman "solitary and recluse",
together with a guarantee of release to fifteen souls in Purgatory for
a year's recitation.[129]

Inevitably such detailed and unqualified claims to influence
the fate of the souls in Purgatory troubled the theologians. The
visionary in "Ane Revelacyone" asks "what prophete it was for a
saule to say mo messis of the trynyte and of oure lady and of saynt
Petir, thane it was of requiem?" No answer was vouchsafed to
this question, but it was one which would not go away, and the
problem it raised was indicative of the tendency of lay practice,
in search of supernatural solace and certainty, to stray beyond the
strict bounds of orthodoxy. The explanation of how the universal sacrifice of the Mass could be appropriated to the benefit of
a single soul had long been debated. It was generally resolved by
distinguishing between the essential sacrifice which constituted the
Mass, on one hand, and which was efficacious for all the quick and
the dead who share the divine life of charity, and the particular
prayers which formed the proper of each Mass, on the other,
which, like any other prayers, could be directed to specific purposes
or persons. Thus might "a masse of requyem profyte more unto
the delyueraunce of soules of purgatorye than an other masse".[130]
This did not, however, explain how, for the relief of souls in
Purgatory, a Mass of the Trinity, or of Jesus, or of the Virgin, or
any combination of them, could be more efficacious than a requiem
Mass, since the prayers of the requiem were better suited to the

---

[128] Horstmann, *Yorkshire Writers*, I pp. 384–6. There is a helpful commentary on this
whole area by Keiser, "Progress of Purgatory", but his simple chronological framework for
the growing elaboration of such devotional schemes needs to be handled with some caution.
[129] See above, chapter 7, "Charms, Pardons and Promises".
[130] Thus, following St Thomas, *Arte or Crafte*, fol. lxxxix.

purpose. Mirk's solution to this problem locates the effectiveness of special votive Masses or sequences in their devotional power over the deceased in his lifetime, implying that the growth in charity which such affectivity represented and promoted continued after death. So "to a soule be hymself the masse that he loveth moste in hys life, that helpeth him moste whan he is dede; as yef a man or womman loue a masse of the Trenite, or of the Holy Gost, or of our ladyes, that masse schulde moste helpon hym, whan he is ded."[131] The *Arte or Crafte to Lyve well* offered a similar solution, but suggested also that the value of many votives was their ability to enlist the help of the saints. The "defawte" of Masses other than the requiem as intercession for the dead was compensated for not only by "the ryght grete devotion of hym that hath mayd it to be said", but also by "the intercessyon of the saynt whom a man shall employe and are the suffrage wherof the masse is sayd".[132] That the latter concern was an important part of much mortuary provision is clear – lights before the images of the saints are one of the major categories of late medieval pious bequest, testators often sought burial near the image of their patron saint, and many temporary chantry priests were directed to sing their Masses at particular altars. But none of this really addresses the assumptions underlying intercessory sequences like the Pope Trental. Here the attraction lay in a complex web of factors: the authority of Pope Gregory, the horse's mouth testimony of a spirit out of Purgatory, a sequence of Masses and prayers summing up the whole Christian mystery and extending over the whole liturgical year, and, not least, the formidable penitential regime of hair shirt and fasting imposed on the celebrant, ensuring as fully as was humanly possible that one's "annualer" was in a permanent state of grace and devotional intensity, and thereby his prayers were rendered more powerful with God.

The most sustained pre-Reformation English critique of this dimension of the popular cult of the dead was the discussion of the "gyldene trental" in *Dives and Pauper*. Though the author never explicitly challenges the fundamental premise of the Trental, that a sequence of prayers or Masses might have special value to souls in Purgatory, he clearly detested every aspect of such devotions, in which was "mychil symonye, mychil ypocrisie and mychil folye". The legend, he thought, was a patent forgery, for St Gregory's mother was a holy woman, not a child-murderer and fornicator.

---

[131] *Festial*, p. 296.
[132] *Arte or Crafte*, loc. cit.

The contract by which the annualer singing the Trental bound himself was simoniacal, hindering his celebration of the ordinary Mass of each day. It was also a profound breach of charity, since every priest, by virtue of his office "is bondyn to syngyn for alle cristene, and for the mo that he preyyth for in his messe by the weye of cherite the mor he plesith God and the mor ben tho soulys holpyn". The author saw no point in having the specified Masses rather than any others, especially since the requirement to spread them over the liturgical year delayed the deliverance of the souls in torment for longer than necessary, when they might have had "thretty messis as goode as tho to helpe of the soule withynneyn thretty dayes and so betere and sonere helpyn the soulys out of pyne". Moreover, far from the Trental encapsulating the liturgical year, the author thought it subverted it. The obligation to say three Masses of each feast within its octave would prevent due observance of the normal calendar, and would often in any case be impossible, as when the feast of the Annunciation fell on Good Friday. The penitential regime of the Trental would also require the priest to fast on the greatest feasts, like Easter and Christmas. All this led the author to suspect that the Devil, not any good spirit, had devised the Trental to delay souls in the flames, not to speed their delivery.[133]

Dives and Pauper made much of the fact that the Pope Trental was a wholly unauthorized devotion, but in fact, as it gained in popularity among the laity (and among some clergy, since a higher stipend might be paid for this demanding form of "annual") it gained at least tacit official approval. Instructions for its celebration began to be copied into missals, and were included in pre-Reformation printed editions of the Sarum missal.[134] Clearly Masses with a guaranteed power to relieve the dead met a felt need. An answer to this need with fewer theological problems emerged in the early sixteenth century in the celebration of Masses "at Scala Coeli". According to legend, while celebrating a requiem at the Church of St Mary at Scala Coeli (in the monastery of Tre Fontane, near St Paul's outside the walls in Rome), St Bernard was granted a vision of the souls for whom he prayed ascending to heaven by a ladder – the "Scala Coeli". This legend was the basis for an indulgence, applicable to the dead, attached to requiem Masses celebrated in the church. In due course this indulgence was made available in specially nominated churches outside Rome. In May 1500 Henry VII secured the "Scala Coeli" indulgence for requiem

[133] *Dives and Pauper*, II pp. 186–92.
[134] Pfaff, "St Gregory's Trental"; *Missale*, col. 883*.

Masses celebrated in his new chapel in Westminster Abbey, and, in accordance with his will, it was secured for the cemetery chapel at the Savoy in 1512. The prestigious gild of St Mary at Boston in Lincolnshire procured the indulgence in 1510, and its popularity spread rapidly; by the 1520s bequests for Masses "at Scala Coeli" were common. Though the devotion was, like the Pope Trental, rooted in a foundation legend involving a vision of spirits from Purgatory, the "Scala Coeli" indulgence had none of the Trental's theological difficulties, and it had the vast advantage of papal and royal sanction behind it. Its hold over the popular imagination made it a particular target of the Henrician reformers in the late 1530s, and a recurrent topic in Latimer's preaching.[135] The continuing vigour of the Pope Trental, and the fact that so hawk-eyed an observer of popular abuses as Bishop Latimer thought demand for "Scala Coeli" masses a major cause for concern, is eloquent testimony to the continuing hold of belief in Purgatory over the minds and imaginations of the laity in early Reformation England.

[135] *Calendar of Papal Registers: Papal Letters*, XVIII no. 102, 118; *Lincoln Wills*, I p. 258 and I–III *passim*; *Beds Wills*, III pp. 130–33. For the reformed attack see below, chapter 11, "The Attack on Traditional Religion I", pp. 392–3.

PART II

THE STRIPPING OF
THE ALTARS, 1530–1580

In the wracks of Walsingham
Whom should I choose,
But the Queen of Walsingham
To be guide to my muse?
Then thou, Prince of Walsingham,
Grant me to frame
Bitter plaints to rue thy wrong,
Bitter woe for thy name.
Bitter was it so to see
The seely sheep
Murdered by the ravening wolves
While the shepherds did sleep.
Bitter was it, O, to view
The sacred vine
(While gardeners played all close)
rooted up by the swine.
Bitter, bitter, O, to behold
The grass to grow
Where the walls of Walsingham
So stately did show.
Such were the works of Walsingham,
While she did stand;
Such were the wracks as now do show
Of that holy land.
Level, level, with the ground
The towers do lie,
Which with their golden glittering tops
Pierced once to the sky.
Where were gates no gates are now,
The ways unknown
Where the press of peers did pass
While her fame far was blown.

Owls do shriek where the sweetest hymns
Lately were sung;
Toads and serpents hold their dens
Where the palmers did throng.
Weep, weep, O Walsingham,
Whose days are nights,
Blessings turned to blasphemies,
Holy deeds to despites.
Sin is where Our Lady sat,
Heaven turned is to hell.
Satan sits where Our Lord did sway;
Walsingham, O, farewell.

From Bodleian Library MS Rawl.
Poet. 291 fol 16, perhaps by Philip,
Earl of Arundel, printed in *The New
Oxford Book of Sixteenth Century
Verse*, ed. E. Jones, 1991, pp. 550–1.

CHAPTER 11

THE ATTACK ON TRADITIONAL RELIGION I: FROM THE BREAK WITH ROME TO THE ACT OF SIX ARTICLES

The Henrician religious revolution had been preceded by a vigorous campaign against heresy, in both its familiar Lollard and its newer Lutheran forms. Specifically, the heretics of the late 1520s were pursued for their attacks on the traditional cultus — the observation of fasts and holidays, the invocation of saints, the veneration of images and relics, pilgrimages, and the cult of intercession on behalf of the dead in Purgatory.[1] Henry long retained an aggressive dislike of the views of proponents of "the new learning" on these issues, and the renunciation of Roman obedience was not at first intended as a retreat from the attack on heresy. However, as the stoutest defenders of traditional doctrine and practice all too often proved to be also the least enthusiastic supporters of the supremacy, heterodox views gained ground and increasing countenance from the authorities. The pattern of later developments was already evident before the final break with Rome, in the spring of 1533, when the radical preaching of Hugh Latimer plunged the town of Bristol into bitter conflict over the meaning and legitimacy of traditional piety.

By March 1533 Latimer was already a man "nott unknowne". As an early Cambridge supporter of the divorce he attracted royal favour and a West-Country living. But in 1532 he had been accused of preaching against the veneration, adornment, and lighting of

---

[1] John Foxe, *Acts and Monuments*, IV, Appendix, the process against Bilney and Arthur (unpaginated), V Appendix ii, the articles against Thomas Phillips (unpaginated); see also Richard Rex, "The English Campaign against Luther in the 1520s", *Transactions of the Royal Historical Society*, 5th series, XXXIX, 1989, pp. 85–106.

images, the invocation of saints, and the doctrine of Purgatory, and
he was forced by Bishop Stokesley of London, and by Convocation,
to make a circumstantial and humiliating recantation. But then as
now, there is no such thing as bad publicity, and as the best known
West-Country incumbent Latimer was invited by the Mayor of
Bristol to be the town's Lenten preacher. Once again he chose to
preach "of pylgremages, worshyppyng of seyntes, wurshypyng off
ymages, off purgatory, &c. yn the whyche he dyd vehemently
perswade towarde the contrary, that the peple ware nott a lyttle
offendyd".[2] Outraged local clergy mobilized Convocation against
Latimer and organized a series of counter sermons. By Easter
the town was torn by "infamy, dyscorde, stryfe and debate".[3]
The most prominent of the conservative preachers, William
Hubberdyne, further inflamed matters by making no secret of his
view that "all Brystow was knaves and eretykes". The chancellor
of the diocese inhibited both Hubberdyne and Latimer, but matters
were taken out of his hands by Thomas Cromwell, who had
Hubberdyne arrested. A commission of inquiry set up at the
request of citizens worried about the civic strife reached no very
firm conclusions. Latimer clearly emerged the victor, however, for
he was recruited by Cromwell as a Reformation publicist, and the
most decisive outcome of the Bristol debates was the ominous
association of traditional piety with disaffection to the Crown and
loyalty to the Papacy.[4]

The prior of the Dominicans at Bristol, John Hilsey, himself a
future evangelical propagandist, was one of those mobilized against
Latimer, but reported that on closer acquaintance "I have percevyd
that hys mynd ys muche more agenst the abusyng off thynges than
agenst the thynge hytt selfe." This was probably true enough at this
stage. Latimer was still feeling his way towards his mature reformed
views, and his careful explanation of his position on Purgatory, for
example, is at least as close to Dante or St Catherine of Genoa as to
Luther. But in practical terms there was no doubt that the whole
thrust of his attack on the abuses of popular devotion was towards
abolition, not reform. As he himself admitted to Archbishop Warham
in 1532, "It cannot be, I own, that the blameable abuse of these
observances can be duly censured, but that straightway the use of

---

[2] John Hilsey to the chancellor of the diocese of Worcester, 2 May 1533, printed in Foxe,
Acts and Monuments, VII, Appendix (unpaginated).
[3] Thomas Wright (ed.), *Three Chapters of Letters Relating to the Suppression of Monasteries*,
Camden Society, XXVI, 1843, pp. 7–10.
[4] G. R. Elton, *Policy and Police*, 1972, pp. 112–17.

them shall become less frequent," a prospect he viewed with ill-disguised enthusiasm.[5]

Traditional piety was meanwhile encountering even less measured attack. Iconoclasm had been a growing feature of the 1520s, and eastern England in the early 1530s saw a minor epidemic – the destruction of the Rood of Dovercourt, of a highway Cross at Coggeshall, of images of St Petronella at Ipswich and Great Horkesley, of a St Christopher at Sudbury, and a Crucifix and other images at Stoke.[6] By October 1533 it was even being reported in London that images were being taken from their places and cast out of the churches as "stocks and stones" of no value, and that some "will prick them with their bodkins to see whether they will bleed or no".[7] While Stokesley was bishop such "damnable abusions" were still treated as sure tokens of heresy, and where the culprits could be found they were harshly dealt with, but increasingly the break with Rome meant a change of priorities. The orthodoxy which mattered most to the regime was adherence to the new doctrine of royal supremacy. The great champion of the cult of the saints and the doctrine of Purgatory, Thomas More, went to the Tower at the end of April 1534; it was a decisive moment. In Easter week of the same year Cranmer reached an agreement with the staunchest conservatives among the bishops, Longland, Stokesley, and Gardiner, for a ban on contentious preaching for a year. Preachers were to set forth the supremacy and denounce the power of the Pope, but were to preach "neyther with nor against purgatory, honouring of saynts, that priests may have wives; that faith only justifieth; to go on pilgrimages, to forge miracles, . . . considering that thereupon no edification can ensue in the people, but rather occasions of talk and rumour, to their great hurt and damage".[8] Such an apparently even-handed embargo was comprehensible enough in view of the notoriously divisive effects of the battle of pulpits at Bristol, where, as Hilsey had remarked "ower kryynge owne agenst another ys not frutfull", and in principle it muzzled radicals as much as conservatives. In reality it represented a dramatic retreat from the earlier Henrician regime's vigorous enforcement of orthodoxy.

The ban was, in any case, disingenuous. Cromwell's role as vice-gerent in spirituals gave him plenty of scope to forward the evangelical cause. His reforming convictions meant that the

---

[5] John Hilsey to the chancellor of the diocese of Worcester, 2 May 1533, printed in Foxe, *Acts and Monuments*, VII, Appendix (unpaginated); Latimer, *Remains*, pp. 236–9, 354.
[6] Foxe, *Acts and Monuments*, IV p. 707.
[7] L&P, VI no. 1311.
[8] L&P, VII nos 463–4; G. Burnet, *History of the Reformation*, 1850, II p. cccxlvii.

band of publicists for the supremacy which he gathered around him were equally dedicated to the attack on the forms of the old religion. Within weeks of the preaching ban one of Cromwell's men, William Marshall, the translator of Marsiglio of Padua, issued an English *Primer*.[9] In a dramatic and eloquent break with all earlier primers, Marshall's book, which was heavily dependent on Luther's writings, omitted the Litany of the Saints and the "Dirige", and contained no other prayers for the dead, while the preface launched an all-out attack on the legends of the saints and on traditional primers "garnished with glorious titles and with red letters, promising much grace and pardon" which have "sore deceived the unlearned multitude". Marshall called for "sharp reformation" of such abuses, a call whose significance was perhaps to be read in the light of the colophon of the book, which claimed that it was printed "cum gratia et privilegio regali".

This primer produced a public outcry, and within a year Marshall published a second edition which restored both the litany and the "Dirige", and which insisted that in omitting them "I dyd not of any perverse mynde or opinion, thynkyng that our blessed lady, and holy sayntes, myghte in no wyse be prayed unto, but rather bicause I was not ignoraunte of the . . . vayn superstitious maner, that dyverse and many persons have . . . used in worshyppyng of them." But although the "Dirige" was included, Marshall denounced as blind superstition "that we have rung and sung, mumbled, murmured and piteously puled forth a certain sort of psalms . . . for the souls of our christian brethren and sistern that be departed out of this world." The preface to this revised primer was a systematic attack on some of the most treasured items in the traditional books, including almost all collects addressed to saints, anthems like the "Salve Regina", the rubrics and promises before the "Fifteen Oes" and similar prayers, and those before the Masses of the Five Wounds and "Recordare", "which promises and pardons have flowed and come from the cursed and wicked bishops of Rome . . . and are but lies and vanities, as is recognised by the holy Church of England, both spiritual and temporal". In particular he attacked the cult of Our Lady of Pity – "why might not a man smell a little idolatry here, in that there appeareth in this title a certain respect, a reverence, more to one image than to another?" This was as comprehensive an onslaught on the time-honoured forms of Catholic piety as had yet appeared in England, and far

[9] *A Prymer in Englyshe, with certeyn prayers & godly meditations*, Hoskins, no. 115: RSTC 15986; C. Butterworth, *The English Primers 1529–1549*, 1953, pp. 61–2. Marshall's Primer was reprinted in E. Burton (ed.), *Three Primers put forth in the Reign of Henry VIII*, 1834.

less circumspect than even any of Latimer's preaching to date. It was issued, however, with every appearance of representing royal policy, for the colophon page carried a claim to a royal patent for six years.[10]

Moreover, Marshall called in his preface for Convocation to take action against the pardon rubrics of the traditional primers. This was apparently a direct echo of a speech made in Convocation the preceding December by a Northamptonshire abbot, claiming that the people were being led astray by the false claims of the traditional primers. Taken together, these attacks on the primers perhaps suggest a concerted policy on the part of Cromwell and his associates. At any rate, clear confirmation that Marshall's primer was favourably regarded by Cromwell and Cranmer and enjoyed quasi-official status was to come two years later with the incorporation of whole paragraphs and many phrases and sentences from it into the *Bishops' Book*.[11]

In the spring of 1535 another reformed primer, by Robert Redman, was issued "Cum gratia et privilegio regali". Redman's primer was much more traditional in content than Marshall's, representing a translation rather than a reformation of the Sarum primers, but like Marshall's book it too omitted all the pardon rubrics, and its preface was clearly designed to endorse the radicalizing of the Henrician revolution, arguing that "some people have ben greatly deludyd of longe tyme about the veneracyon of Sayntes and such lyke thinges", but that now "almyghty god of hys eterne providence hathe put in the myndes of his electe princes, and true pastours of his flocke to purge the fylthynes of false doctryne."[12]

It was evident then, by the early summer of 1535, that Cromwell was lending his backing to increasingly open criticism of traditional Catholic devotional practices and the doctrines which underpinned them. Alarmed conservatives broke through the ban on contentious preaching to denounce "these new books and new preachers" and the Judases who were leading the people astray.[13] Any remaining doubts about official endorsement of the new books and preachers were dispelled when the royal visitation of the smaller monasteries began, in July 1535. The visitors, whose brief seems to have been to provide Cromwell with the ammunition he needed to damn the

---

[10] Burton, *Three Primers*, "Admonition to the Reader", pp. 1–9.

[11] Butterworth, though he does not connect the speech with Marshall's primer, is certainly right in his insistence that the Abbot was criticizing a Catholic and not a Protestant book (*English Primers*, pp. 70–1). For the use of the primer in the *Bishops' Book* see Burton, *Three Primers*, pp. xlvi–li.

[12] Butterworth, *English Primers*, pp. 90–1.

[13] L&P, VIII nos 626, 1000.

monasteries, not to reform them, displayed a particular interest in their role in the promotion of pilgrimage and the cult of the saints. The general injunctions for the visitation stipulated that religious "shall not show no reliques, or feyned miracles, for increase of lucre".[14] The commissioners therefore sent Cromwell a stream of mocking reports and inventories of the contents of the monastic reliquaries, to convict the monks of superstition and pious racke-teering; before long they were sending the relics themselves. From Bath Abbey in August Richard Layton wrote "I send you vincula S. Petri, which women put about them at the time of their delivery . . . I send you also a great comb called St Mary Magdalen's comb, and St Dorothy's and St Margaret's combs." From Bury St Edmunds John ap Rice reported: "Amongst the reliques we founde moche vanitie and superstition, as the coles that Sant Laurence was tosted withall, the paring of S. Edmundes naylles, S. Thomas of Canterbury penneknyff and his bootes, peces of the olie crosse able to make a hole crosse of . . . , with suche other."[15] What is striking about the relic lists compiled by the visitors is the number which were clearly for use and not only for ostentation. Everywhere one turns in the *comperta* and other records of the visitation one finds evidence of large-scale resort by the people to the monastic shrines as centres of healing and help. At Westminster was Our Lady's girdle "which women with chield were wont to girde with", at Bruton in Somerset St Mary Magdalene's girdle "sent to women travailing". At Burton-on-Trent was an image of St Moodwyn with her red cow and her staff, "which wymen laboryng of child in these parties were very desirous to have with them to leane upon, and to walk with yt, and have greate confidence in the same staff". At Basedale in Yorkshire was the "singulum of S. Bernard . . . sometimes lent for pregnant women", and there was another such "singulum for pregnancy" at Kirkstall, while at Rievaulx the girdle "helpful to lying-in-women" was that of St Aelred. At Newburgh the lying-in girdle was called after St Salvator, at Holy Trinity, York, it was the girdle of a former holy prior, while at Kelham the finger of St Stephen was sent to "lying-in women". Not all these working relics were for pregnancy. At Bury there were "reliques for rayne and certain other superstitiouse usages, for avoyding of wedes growing in corne", as well as "divers skulles for the hedache". At Haltemprise, in addition to the usual girdle of Our Lady "healthful for childbirth

[14] G. Burnet, *History of the Reformation*, 1850, II p. lxiii.
[15] L&P, IV no. 42; Thomas Wright, *Three Chapters of Letters Relating to the Suppression of Monasteries*, Camden Society, os XXVI, 1843, p. 85.

(as is thought)", there was a pilgrimage to Thomas Wake for sufferers from fever, while at Arden there was a shrine of St Bridget where offerings were made for cattle lost or ill.[16]

In attacking monastic "superstition", then, Cromwell's men were striking at institutions with a central place in popular religious practice, perhaps most unexpectedly in the domestic intimacies of pregnancy and childbirth. In such widespread evidence of the integration of the monastic shrines into the fabric of popular religion, however, the visitors saw, or chose to see, nothing more than evidence of large-scale exploitation of simple believers. Yet they could hardly be unaware of the large numbers of devotees affected, and potentially alienated, by their actions. Pilgrims often arrived in large numbers even while the commissioners were at their work, and Richard Southwell reported from Walsingham in July 1536 that the offerings made there "from the satredaye at night tyll the Sondaye next followynge" amounted to £6 13s 4d, "over and besyde waxe".[17] Cromwell had reports from St Asaph in April 1538 that on a single day that month the pilgrims to the shrine of Darvelgadarn amounted to "fyve or syxe hundrethe...to a man's estimacion". When one of Cromwell's agents stripped the shrine of St Anne at Buxton not only of its image, but of the "cruchys, schertes, and schetes, with wax offeryd" which were the testimonies of the people's devotion, he found it necessary to "lokk...upp and seal...the bathys and welles...thatt non schall enter to washe them".[18]

Traditionalist outrage at such sacrilege was muted. The Treasons Act was a formidable instrument, and complaint against the King's proceedings liable to backfire on the complainer. As early as March 1534 Cromwell had made a memorandum "to have substantial persons in every good town to discover all who speak or preach" against the Henrician religious revolution, and his postbag bears eloquent testimony to the network of denunciation and reprisal which resulted.[19] In May 1535, for example, the vicar of St Clement's, Cambridge, having had a few beers in the Pump tavern, called the King a despoiler of the Church. Sensing his companion's

---

[16] L&P, IX no. 42; Wright, *Monasteries*, pp. 58–9, 85, 143–4; Charles Wriothesley, *A Chronicle of England 1484–1559*, ed. W. D. Hamilton, Camden Society, ns XI, XX, 1875–7, I p. 31; J. W. Clay (ed.), *Yorkshire Monasteries Suppression Papers*, Yorkshire Archaeological Society Record Series, XLVIII, 1912, pp. 16–18.

[17] Wright, *Monasteries*, pp. 138, 224–5 – an account of the destruction of the shrine of Our Lady of Caversham by Dr London, where "even at my being ther come in nott so few as a doseyn with imagies of wexe".

[18] Ibid., pp. 190, 143–4.

[19] L&P, VII no. 420; the whole Cromwellian machinery of denunciation and enforcement is explored definitively in G. R. Elton, *Policy and Police*, 1972.

disapproval, the priest said "Neighbour Richardson, there be no one here but you and I," but neighbour Richardson denounced him to the mayor all the same, and his words were duly reported to Cromwell.[20]

Nor was there much doubt that the attack on images and pilgrimage was part of the royal will, or, what amounted to the same thing, Cromwell's policy. In September 1535 both the Imperial ambassador and the Lord Chancellor complained to Cromwell about a book lately printed "touching taking away images". This was a translation of Bucer's *Das Einigerlei Bild*, a key Reformation iconoclastic tract, which had been produced in 1530 to justify the destruction of all images at Strasbourg. The treatise allowed that in principle images were legitimate as long as they were not worshipped. However, "syth it is so that in churches every were / ymages are honoured / and namley roodes", such is the strength of "old rooted custome" that "though thou prech never so ofte / nor never so ernestly" there will always be some "whiche wyll hold on styl to put of their cappes unto them orels to lowre and make curtesy to them" and those "snarled" in the Devil's bonds "wyll never refrayne from worshippynge of ymages". This was well beyond the declared policy of the Henrician regime, but not perhaps beyond the unspoken objectives of Cromwell and Cranmer. The treatise's translator was none other than Cromwell's client, William Marshall, and as in his primers the colophon claimed "the Kynges most graciouse privylege".[21]

In drawing Cromwell's attention to Marshall's translation, Audley recorded that he had encountered among the people "some discord and diversity of opinion touching worshipping of saints and images, creeping at cross, and such ceremonies . . . which discord it were well to put to silence". He wanted the treatise suppressed and steps taken to see that both preachers and people should "abstain from opinions of such things". But Cromwell did nothing to suppress the treatise, and it ran to a second and more radical edition the following year. Moreover, both he and Cranmer were actively protecting radical preachers who were stirring up precisely the sort of divisions among the people of which Audley complained.[22] Well might conservatives lament that "these new preachers now-a-days . . . have made and brought in such divisions

---

[20] L&P, VIII no. 727.

[21] L&P, IX nos 357–8; *A Treatise declaryng & shewing . . . that pyctures & other ymages . . . ar in no wise to be suffred in the temples or churches of Cristen men*, 1535, STC 24238–9. For a discussion of the work and its original see M. Aston, *England's Iconoclasts*, 1988, pp. 203–10.

[22] *Miscellaneous Writings and Letters of Thomas Cranmer*, ed. J. E. Cox, Parker Society, 1846 (hereafter = *Remains*), p. 311; L&P, IX p. 1059.

and seditions among us as never was seen in this realm, for the devil reigneth over us now." At Folkestone, when a preacher "turned a hundred men's hearts to his opinion" that the Virgin Mary "could do no more for us than another woman", the town bailiff wanted to pull him out of the pulpit, but the vicar was afraid to do it, because he had heard that the preacher "had a licence from the king to preach in all places".[23]

Concern about the privileged position of such preachers was not confined to rank-and-file officials of church and state. On 29 October 1535 Archbishop Lee of York despatched to Cromwell the first of a series of complaints about contentious preachers. Reminding Cromwell of the royal prohibition of 1534 "which expired last Whitsuntide", he pointed out that "yet some preach against purgatory, &c . . . wherwith the people grutche, which ooderwies all the Kinges commandement heer obeye diligentlie, as well for the settinge forthe of his title . . . as also of the abolition of the primatie of Rome." He reported that, to prevent controversy, he himself had recently inhibited a friar who was preaching in defence of Purgatory. Lee wanted an official pronouncement about such contested matters: the fact that he wanted it to include the opinions of "tholie auncient doctours of the church" leaves little doubt that he hoped for a conservative resolution. In any case, his letter was a clear enough hint to Cromwell that licensed radicals were an increasing nuisance. A further letter in November, complaining against one of Cromwell's protégés, who had "rayled and jested" in a sermon against fasting, made Lee's own anger clear.[24]

Lee shrewdly played on Henry's and Cromwell's nervousness about public acceptance of the supremacy and the break with Rome, suggesting that attacks on traditional religious practices agitated an otherwise docile and obedient people. This point evidently went home, and on 7 January 1536 Henry circulated a letter to all the bishops about contentious preaching. Professor Elton has described this circular as having "a strong reformist air", but this hardly does justice to the fact that its principal target was indiscreet and divisive reformist preaching, at least as much as its papalist opposite. The King complained that he sought to ensure that the people should be fed with wholesome doctrine, not "seduced with filthy and corrupt abominations of the bishop of Rome or his disciples and adherents, ne yet by the setting forth of novelties and the continual inculcation of things not necessary

<hr />

[23] L&P, IX no. 230.
[24] L&P, IX no. 742.

brought and led to inquietnes of mind and doubt of conscience". In his covering letter, Cromwell stressed again the need that the people

> maie be taught the truthe, and yet not charged at the beginning with over manney Novelties, the publication wherof onles the same be tempered and quallified with moche wisdom doo rather brede contention Devision and contrarietey of opinion in the unlerned multitude, then either edifie, or remove from them and oute of their hartes . . . the corrupte and unsavery teachinge of the bishoppe of Rome.[25]

Nevertheless, despite this admonition, radical preachers continued to assail traditional religion, under the protection of Cromwell, Cranmer, and Hugh Latimer, whose appointment as Lenten preacher to the King in 1534 and to the see of Worcester in 1535 hardly bears out the regime's official protestations of concern about the divisive effects of pulpit radicalism. Lee returned to the attack again in April 1536, when he told Cromwell that following the King's command he had given orders that "no prechers shalbe suffred that withowte discretion preche novelties" who "as you right wieselie considered, doo rather sowe seedes of dissention than doo anye good". After this judicious application of soft soap, Lee came to the point of his letter. He had silenced several contentious preachers, "and some of them saie they wooll get licence of the king to preache. If they obteigne anye suche licence, I then ame discharged for them that have such licence; but I trust that you woll suffre no such licence to passe, but that I shall knowe therof." Some others of them, he added bitterly, "saie theye have licence of my lord of Cantorborie: but I trust theye have no suche, and if they have, none shalbe obeyde here, but onlie the kinges and youres".[26]
Lee was not the only conservative bishop battling to keep government-backed radicals out of the pulpits of his diocese. John Longland, who had used the royal circular to tighten up his campaign against heresy in the diocese of Lincoln,[27] wrote to Cromwell twice in May 1536 to complain of such preachers, including Latimer's protégé Thomas Garrett and John Swynnerton, who held the King's licence, but whose preaching, on "doubtful matters . . . forbidden to be touched . . . offends the people". When rebuked, "he answers that he knows the king's mind." Longland, less timid

[25] L&P, X no. 45; R. B. Merriman, *The Life and Letters of Thomas Cromwell*, 1902, II pp. 111–12; Elton, *Policy and Police*, pp. 244–5.
[26] Wright, *Monasteries*, pp. 123–5.
[27] M. Bowker, *The Henrician Reformation: the Diocese of Lincoln under John Longland*, 1981, pp. 143–5.

or less diplomatic than Lee, made no bones about saying that it was the reformed character of Swynnerton's views that he detested, declaring that he resorted to "light people . . . who leave their worldly labour and read English books all day . . . and assemble many times together". Such turbulent preachers were stirring the poor, and against them "Lincolnshire much grudgeth."[28] Similar complaints from the conservative sheriff of Gloucester against the "disorderly and colorable preaching of certain of the bishop of Worcester's preachers", who had attacked intercession for the dead and the doctrine of Purgatory, pilgrimages, and oblations to saints "to the disquiet of Christian people", reached Cromwell in June.[29]

By June 1536 influential conservatives were increasingly restive at the official support or protection being extended to attacks on pilgrimage and the cult of the saints, on Purgatory and the whole framework of intercession for the dead which was so central a part of the religion of late medieval England. On 8 June a new Parliament assembled, charged with sorting out the fiasco of the succession caused by the fall of Anne Boleyn. Anne's execution was of course a potential Protestant disaster, and traditionalists everywhere rejoiced. At the beginning of the month a rumour was running round the pubs of Dover that on the day that Anne was beheaded the tapers round Queen Katherine's grave had spontaneously kindled themselves, and that "this light contynuyng from day to daye" was a token of the restoration of the old order. Soon the King would command "to pray for Quene Katherine as it was accustomed to be don: and . . . after the same a grete hepe of heretiks and newe invencions should be hanged and brent."[30]

If traditionalists hoped for support from Cromwell or his royal master, however, they were to be bitterly disappointed. With the calling of Parliament, Convocation also assembled. In a message conveyed through Cromwell Henry informed the clergy that they were to seek means to resolve the religious divisions which had sprung up, and especially "to set a stay for the unlearned people, whose consciences are in doubt what they may believe".[31] Yet in what can only have been intended as a deliberate official endorsement of the radical preaching which was causing so much disquiet, Latimer was appointed to open Convocation's proceedings on 9

[28] L&P, X nos 804, 891.
[29] L&P, X no. 1099: one of the clergy principally complained of was Thomas Garrett, who had already fallen foul of Longland. A fuller list of Garrett's usual preaching themes is in L&P, XI no. 1424.
[30] Sir Henry Ellis (ed.), *Original Letters Illustrative of English History*, 1824–46, 1st series, II pp. 68–71.
[31] Foxe, *Acts and Monuments*, V p. 379.

June with a Latin sermon which was a *tour de force* of offensiveness,
a manifesto calculated to outrage the overwhelming majority of his
hearers. Latimer had neither forgiven nor forgotten his treatment
at the hands of Convocation in 1532, and he gleefully dwelt on
their ineffectiveness and his own escape. "For what have ye done
hitherto, I pray you, these seven years and more?... What fruit
is come of your long and great assembly? What one thing that
the people of England hath been the better of a hair...?" It
was true that the people were now better instructed, there was
more preaching, reform had begun, but all this was the work of
Cromwell and the King, not the clergy:

> Whether stirred other first, you, or the king, that he might
> preach, or he you by his letters, that ye should preach oftener? Is
> it unknown, think you, how both ye and your curates were, in a
> manner, by violence enforced to let books be made, not by you,
> but by prophane and lay persons; to let them, I say, be sold
> abroad, and read for the instruction of lay people?

But there was more to the sermon than the understandable desire to
administer salt to the clergy's smart and to settle a personal score.
It was clearly a quasi-official call to specific reformation, and
Latimer's targets form a comprehensive list of the main features of
popular devotion – the cult of the saints, images, lights, relics, holy
days, pilgrimage, pardons, and Purgatory. Images, he insisted,
were "only to represent things absent", and he denounced those
who preached that they should be gilded or "in this scarceness and
penury of all things" be "clad in silk garments . . . lighted with wax
candles . . . yea, and at noon days". Steadily he worked through
the abuses – too many holidays, hindering industry, and thereby
depriving poor men of necessary meat and drink for their families
since "they cannot labour . . . except they will be cited" into the
Church courts, encouraging drunkenness, strife, dancing, dicing,
and idleness. Then there was pilgrimage to "these images that are
so famous, so noble, so noted . . . Do you think that this preferring
of picture to picture, image to image, is the right use, and not the
abuse of images?" Many relics were fraudulent, "pigs bones instead
of saints' relics". Then there were the many abuses connected
with shrines: "the solemn and nocturnal bacchanals, the prescript
miracles, that are done upon certain days in the west part of
England . . . I think ye have heard of St Blasis heart which is at
Malvern, and of St Algar's bones, how long they deluded the
people." There had been, he argued, many attempts to prune such
abuses in the past, but in vain, so that now there remained no
remedy but abolition – "if ye purpose to do anything, what should

ye sooner do, than to take utterly away these deceitful and juggling images . . . ?" Latimer accepted the value of prayers for the dead but rejected "purgatory pick-purse, . . . this monster purgatory"; the dead, he insisted in the bidding prayer to his sermon, "sleep in the sleep of peace and rest from their labours . . . faithfully, lovingly and patiently." We may pray for them, but the whole system of pardons and "venality and sale of masses", and of privileged mortuary devotions like the popular "Scala Coeli" indulgence, were born of none other but "our most prudent lord the Pope", and were designed to pocket "dead men's tributes and gifts". They too should all be swept away.[32]

The first few sessions of Convocation were taken up with transacting the King's business, in particular with declaring his marriage to Anne Boleyn null and void, but on the first available opportunity, 23 June, the fourth sitting day, the clergy of the Lower House retaliated against Latimer's sermon by presenting to Cranmer a book containing a "declaration of fautes and abuses . . . worthy special reformation". This consisted of a list of sixty-seven errors and abuses "commonly preached, thought and spoken" to the "disquietnes of the people and damage of Christen sowles". A number of these condemned propositions were couched in the familiarly ribald language of Lollard polemic, as in the reported question of "light and lewd persons" about the Blessed Sacrament, "Is it anything else but a piece of brede, or a litle pretie pece rownde Robyn?" or the claim that holy water is "moore savorer to make sawce with . . . because it is mixed with salt . . . yea, if there be put an onyon therunto, it is a good sawce for a gygget of motton". But many of the "mala dogmata" were clearly derived from or aimed at Latimer's sermon, and represented a comprehensive rejection of his reform programme. So they denounced those who condemned the cult of the saints or denied their intercession, and specifically the claim that it was idolatrous to set lights before images "or in any place in the church in the tyme of divine service, as long as the sonne giveth light", a clear swipe at Latimer's railing against lights at "noon day". They reaffirmed the value of the veneration of images and relics, defending "rich and costly ornaments". They condemned attacks on Purgatory, and on the procurement of "diriges, commendations, mass, suffrages, prayers, almes dedes or oblations" for the dead, and insisted on the value of pilgrimages. They condemned the attack on holidays, or the suggestion that servile work might be done on them. And tackling head-on Latimer's claim that the only way to reform was to abolish, they

---

[32] *Sermons of Hugh Latimer*, ed. G. E. Corrie, Parker Society, 1844, pp. 33–57.

condemned those who "woll nedes have the thing itself taken away, and not enough the abuses to be reformed". Similarly, taking up his taunt about the clergy's helplessness in the face of the circulation of religious books by "prophane and lay persons", they condemned the "many sclanderous and erroneous bokes, that have ben made, and suffered to go abroad indifferently". Daringly, they specifically condemned those which carried the words "Cum privilegio", and which were therefore "the moore gladly bought" by the unsuspecting, as being thought to have the King's express approval, though, they added diplomatically, "it was not so indede." They reproached the bishops for failing to condemn such erroneous books, and they complained of the "apostates, abjured persons" who had been suffered to preach without licence.[33]

Just over a fortnight after this resounding response to Latimer's manifesto, Convocation agreed on a set of articles of belief designed to put an end to the "diversity of opinions" which had "grown and sprongen" up in the realm, not only about doctrine but also "touching certain honest and commendable ceremonies, rites and usages". These Ten Articles were the first official doctrinal formulary of the Church of England; they reflected the struggle between radical and traditionalist within the Convocation. Only three, not seven, sacraments were treated - baptism, penance, and Eucharist – and a form of justification by faith was affirmed, but the articles specifically approved the veneration of images and the cult of the saints, and the practice of intercession for the dead. The terms in which these were approved, however, were carefully qualified. Images were "representers of virtue and good example", and were meant to be the "kindlers and firers of men's minds". They might therefore stand in the churches, but preachers were to ensure that the people were warned against idolatry. As for "censing of them, and kneeling and offering unto them, with other like worshippings", which had "entered by devotion and fallen to custom", the people were to be instructed that such worship was in reality not offered to the images, but only to God and in his honour "although it be done before the images, whether it be of Christ, or the cross, or of our Lady, or of any other saint beside". This was by no means reforming rhetoric, for the qualifications here were almost precisely those advanced in such impeccably Catholic works as the early fifteenth-century treatise *Dives and Pauper*, and despite its careful wording this article expressly legitimated "censing,

---

[33] Printed in J. Strype, *Ecclesiastical Memorials*, 1822, I/2 pp. 250–6; see also James Gairdner, *Lollardy and the Reformation*, 1908–13, II pp. 308–10.

kneeling and offering" before images. Similarly, though it was insisted that in praying to saints the people must not think that "any saint is more merciful . . . than Christ; or, that any saint doth serve for one thing more than another, or is patron of the same", the Articles expressly stated that "it is very laudable to pray to saints in heaven . . . to be intercessors and to pray for us," and "likewise, that we must keep holydays unto God in memory . . . of his saints, upon such days as the church hath ordained."

But if the traditional reliance on the saints was reaffirmed, the denial of the patronage of the saints for specific needs or benefits represented a substantial break with popular practice, and the Article on Purgatory similarly modified traditional teaching, while retaining the belief that the dead benefit from the prayers of the living. It was, the Article maintained, of the "due order of charity for a Christian man to pray for souls departed . . . and to cause others to pray for them in masses and exsequies, and to give alms to others to pray for them, wherby they may be relieved and holpen of some part of their pain," but "the place where they be, the name wherof and kind of pains there, also be to us uncertain by Scripture." Therefore, we must leave all that to God, and in the meantime

> it is much necessary that such abuses be clearly put away, which under the name of purgatory hath been advanced to make men believe that through the bishop of Rome's pardon souls might clearly be delivered out of purgatory, and all the pains of it, or that masses said at Scala Coeli, or otherwise . . . or before any image, might likewise deliver them from all their pain, and send them straight to heaven.

In this rejection of the name Purgatory, and the specific attack on the "Scala Coeli" indulgence, one may see the hand of Latimer, since both of these were recurrent preoccupations of his, but the Article fell very short of Latimer's wishes, and his sermon was evidently not the only factor determining the handling of ritual matters in the Articles. Article nine tackled questions of popular devotion which he had not referred to, but which had featured in the list of "mala dogmata" sent up by the lower clergy, as points being questioned by lewd and light persons. They had been concerned at attacks on sacramentals such as holy water, holy bread, blessed candles, ashes, and palms. All these "laudable customs, rites and ceremonies" were defended in the article, together with the Good Friday and Easter ceremonies of creeping to the Cross and the setting up of the sepulchre, as well as baptismal and other exorcisms. However, though these practices were retained, they were given a didactic and symbolic explanation, rather than the apotropaic significance which was often explicit in the liturgical texts, and which was certainly a dominant part of popular understanding of the ceremonies. So the sprinkling of holy water was explained not in terms of the water's power to banish demons or bring blessing, but "to put us in remembrance of our baptism and the blood of Christ sprinkled for our redemption," holy bread was presented not as a curative but "to put us in remembrance of the sacrament of the altar," candles at Candlemas not as defences against the power of evil or the disorder of the elements but "in memory of Christ the spiritual light". Such explanations were henceforth to be regularly impressed on the laity, and were "right necessary to be uttered from henceforth in our mother tongue always on the same day" that they were performed. And it was insisted that "none of these ceremonies have power to remit sin, but only to stir and lift up our minds unto God."[34]

Eight days after these Articles were signed by Cromwell and the members of Convocation, the assembly returned to the agenda mapped out in Latimer's sermon, with an Act "for the abrogation of certain holydays". The Act complained of the excessive number of feast days, growing "dayly more and more by mens devocyon, yea rather supersticyon", causing the decay of industry and the encouragement not only of sloth and idleness, but also of sins of excess and riot, "being entysed by the lycencyous vacacyon and lybertye of those holydayes". Moreover crops were being lost in harvest from a superstitious reluctance to work on feast days. Therefore the king, in his capacity as supreme head, decreed that from henceforth the feast of the Church dedication should be kept everywhere on the first Sunday in October. The patronal festival or "Church Holyday" was no longer to be kept as a feast day at all, "but . . . it shall be lawful . . . to go to their work, occupacyon or mystery." All feast days falling in harvest, from 1 July to 29 September, as well as all those occurring in the Westminster law terms, were abolished, excepting only feasts of the Apostles, the Blessed Virgin, and St George. Ascension Day, the nativity of John the Baptist, All Saints' Day and Candlemas were also to continue to be observed. The clergy might continue to celebrate the traditional Masses and offices on the abrogated days, but they were not to "do the same solempnely, nor . . . ryng to the same in the maner used in hygh holydayes, ne to command or indict the same to be kepte or observed as holydayes".[35]

---

[34] The Articles are printed in Burnet, *Reformation*, II pp. cxxix–cxxxiii.
[35] D. Wilkins, *Concilia*, 1737, III pp. 823–4.

This Act constituted the first overt attack by the Henrician regime itself on the traditional pattern of religious observance in the parishes, and it was bound to have a very large impact. At one stroke the Crown decimated the ritual year, not only wiping out a multitude of local festivals but removing many major landmarks from the Sarum calendar at large. In July the principal abrogated feasts included those of St Martin, St Swithin, St Margaret, St Mary Magdalene, St Anne, and the main feast of Becket, the translation of his relics. Those abolished in August included the immensely popular "new feasts" of the Transfiguration and the Holy Name of Jesus, as well as the feasts of St Laurence and St Augustine. From September the Act swept away the feasts of St Giles, St Cuthbert, and Holy Cross Day. The abrogated days commonly falling within the law terms included those of St John of Beverley, St Dunstan, St Augustine of Canterbury, St Edmund, St Edward the Confessor, St Alban, St Etheldreda, Sts Crispin and Crispinian, St Winifred, St Cecilia, St Clement, St Katherine, and St Agatha.

Henry anticipated trouble from this Act, not least because the harvest period which contained the greatest concentration of abrogated days had already begun. He therefore wrote to the bishops on 11 August, ordering them "as you will answer unto us for the contrary" to see that the clergy did not "indict or speak of any of the said days and feasts abolished, wherby the people might take occasion either to murmur, or to contemn the order taken therin . . . but to pass over the same with such secret silence, as they may have the like abrogation by disuse, as they have already by our authority in convocation". The drawback with this tactic was evident at Beverley on the Sunday before St Wilfrid's day (12 October), when in bidding the bedes the parish priest obeyed the royal command and failed to announce St Wilfrid's day. His parishioners challenged him in the pulpit about his omission "for it was wont always to be a holiday here". When the priest explained that the day had been abrogated "by the King's authority and the consent of the whole clergy in Convocation" there was an uproar. After Mass was over "the whole parish was in a rumour and said that they would have their holydays bid and kept as before." The disorder created by the Pilgrimage of Grace, in which the parish joined, meant that between then and the following January the old observance continued.[36] The abrogation of holy days was clearly an issue with many of the pilgrims, and it was prominent among the

[36] L&P, XII part 1, no. 201.

grievancess of the Lincolnshire rebels in October 1536, perhaps because one of the abolished feasts, St Anne's day, was a major festival, marked by the performance of religious plays. When the parson of Byrchforde, Sir Nicholas Leche, tried to persuade the people that they might work on the abrogated days "he feared he should have been slain by the commons."[37]

But it was not only among the rebels that there was such resistance. Many clergy continued to announce the abrogated days, or celebrated them with ostentation, like the parish priest of Rye, who kept "high and holy in the church" the feasts of St Anne, the Transfiguration, and the Holy Name, with "solemn singing, procession, decking of the churches".[38] Even in Kent, under the watchful eye of the Archbishop, matters were no better. Cranmer complained bitterly that the whole diocese was "very obstinately given to observe and keep with solemnity the holydays lately abrogated". He blamed the clergy for stirring up the people and instituted a series of exemplary punishments. But he was furious to discover that Henry's own court observed St Laurence's day in 1537. While dictating a routine letter to Cromwell he took the pen from his secretary's hand and wrote himself, "but my Lord, if in the court you do keep such holydays and fasting . . . when shall we persuade the people to cease from them?"[39]

It was in any case all too easy for the clergy, while keeping the letter of the King's command, to flout its spirit. The parish priest of Broughton announced the feast of the Holy Name, St Laurence's day, and Relic Sunday, and told his parishioners that though he could not now command them to keep holy days, yet they should come to church to receive the indulgences traditionally granted on those days. The curates and sextons of churches in the region round Bishop's Stortford kept Holy Cross Day (14 September) "high and solemn, with singing and ringing", with consequent dissension between them "and those who went to their bodily labour".[40] Dissension about the abrogated days was evidently widespread. A group of neighbours sitting drinking in William Browning's house at Bledney fell to arguing about religion on St Mark's day, one of the abrogated feasts. John Tutton of Mere called Thomas Poole of Bledney a heretic because he had worked that day, and when Poole replied that it was the King's command, Tutton denounced Cromwell and all his "witholders" as "stark heretics", and declared,

[37] L&P, XI nos 553, 970, XII part 1, no. 70 (para. xi).
[38] L&P, XII part 2, no. 567.
[39] L&P, XII part 2, no. 592.
[40] L&P, XI no. 514.

"Shall I obey the King's commandment, and it be naught? Marry I will not."[41]

In the aftermath of the Pilgrimage, such sentiments were doubly worrying. In the late spring and early summer of 1537 Norfolk was full of unrest, and a plot to raise the commons against their landlords was uncovered at Walsingham. Though economic grievances lay at the root of much of this disturbance, the religious changes of the previous year played their part. Harry Jarvis, a husbandman of Fincham, deplored the failure of the Pilgrimage of Grace to his neighbours. He wished the Yorkshiremen had prospered, he told them, "that the suppressed holydays might have been restored."[42]

From the other side of England, Cromwell's monastic visitors for Cornwall, with its myriad local cults, reported widespread unrest about the abrogated days, and they seem to have secured a dispensation to allow the celebration of Cornish patronal festivals, to the "marvelous pleasure" of the people. The issue did not go away. In April 1537 Cromwell was to be alarmed by news from Cornwall that the parish of St Keverne had commissioned a banner of the five Wounds, like those carried in the Pilgrimage of Grace, on which was portrayed "the commonalty kneeling, with scripture above their heads, making this petition to the picture of Christ that it would please the King's grace that they might have their holydays". His informant thought that all that was needed to defuse the potential trouble was to concede the holy days. The West Country was to remain obdurate on this issue, and in 1539 Bishop Veysey of Exeter circulated an angry admonition to the clergy of his diocese, complaining not only of the people's continued observance of the abrogated days, but of the widespread abstention from work from noon on the eves of feast days, and the observance by fishermen, blacksmiths, and other craftsmen of the feast days of their occupational patrons, a practice which had of course been implicitly condemned by the Ten Articles.[43]

Discontent was to be found in high places, as well as in country parishes and alehouses. It emerged during the investigations of the Pilgrimage that the Archbishop of York had made no secret of his disgust at the abrogation, not least because he resented the imposition of Westminster law terms as a rule for religious observance in his archdiocese.[44] The abrogation also agitated the

---

[41] L&P, XII part 1, no. 567.
[42] L&P, XII part 2, no. 150.
[43] L&P, XI no. 405, XII part 1, nos 1001, 1126; Wilkins, *Concilia*, III p. 846.
[44] L&P, XII part 1, no. 786.

Church and town authorities at the cathedral shrines. In June 1537 Richard Sampson, the conservative Bishop of Chichester, requested a licence to celebrate the Cathedral's "church holiday", the feast of the translation of the relics of St Richard of Chichester on 14 June. In the same month the mayor of Salisbury and "others of the discreetest of his brethren that have been mayor" wrote for guidance about the traditional watch kept on the eve of the feast of St Osmund, and to know whether they were to be allowed to keep his festival.[45]

Though this general atmosphere of uncertainty and disgruntlement would only become explicit with the passage of time, Cromwell was well aware of the likelihood of clerical resistance to the reform measures of 1536, and in his role as vice-gerent in spirituals issued in August 1536 a set of injunctions, designed to enforce conformity. These Injunctions insisted on clerical obedience to the legislation abolishing the Pope's jurisdiction, ordered incumbents to provide Bibles in both Latin and English, and to encourage their parishioners to read them, though without contention. Clergy were to preach on the Ten Articles, and to see to it that the abrogated days were not observed. Parents and masters were to be encouraged to catechize every member of their family in the Creed, the Lord's Prayer, and the Ten Commandments in English. All this was a straightforward attempt to consolidate the reform measures so far enacted, and to secure a better-educated laity with a grip of the fundamentals of the faith in their own language. More negatively, the Injunctions further sharpened the regime's growing hostility to the cult of the saints, by attacking the "superstition and hypocrisy" which had crept into the people's hearts through the excesses of such devotion. Clergy were not to "set forth or extol any images, relics or miracles for any superstitious lucre, nor allure the people by any enticements to the pilgrimage of any saint, otherwise than is permitted in the Articles lately put forth". The people were to be taught to look only to God for help, and to redirect the money spent in pilgrimages to providing for their own families, and for alms to the poor. The tone of all this is more overtly hostile than that of the Ten Articles, and one can recognize in these provisions the preoccupations and ideas of radicals like Latimer.[46]

All this reform activity of 1536 took place against the backdrop of the Pilgrimage of Grace, and the relatively modest steps in the direction of reform represented by the Ten Articles, the Act

---

[45] L&P, XII part 1, nos 4, 52.
[46] *Visitation Articles and Injunctions of the Period of the Reformation*, ed. W. H. Frere and W. M. Kennedy, Alcuin Club, XIV–XVI, 1908–10 (hereafter = VAI), II pp. 1–11.

abrogating holy days, and the Injunctions of August 1536 were quickly perceived as part of the struggle between the old religion and the new which was one major strand in the Pilgrimage. Harry Jervis's imprudently expressed regrets about the failure of the Pilgrimage were by no means out of the ordinary in East Anglia. John Bale, intent on challenging his Suffolk parishioners' attachment to the "Popish baggage" of ceremonies and saints' lives, was scandalized to find them adamant that neither for King nor Council would they use the Paternoster or the Creed in English, and also that they would "take the Northern men's part, for that was the . . . juster".[47]

The rising in the north was, of course, terrifying confirmation of the jeremiads of conservatives like Lee and Longland, that the people "grudged" against the preaching of radicals like Bale or the wandering preachers licensed by Latimer or Cromwell. Accounts of support expressed by men and women up and down the country for the religious dimension of the northern men's cause stung Henry into action. On 19 November 1536 he issued a circular to the bishops bemoaning the "contrariety of preaching" which had sown division among the people. He reminded them of his circular of January 1536, which had been aimed at "a certain contemptuous manner of speaking against honest, laudable and tolerable ceremonies, usages and customs of the Church". This admonition had been little regarded, and so he had issued the Ten Articles, with the consent of all the clergy in Convocation, "for avoiding of all contention". Despite all this, "light and seditious persons" had continued to speak in a "fond and contentious manner" against "the honest rites, customs and ceremonial things of the church", so that "our people be much more offended than before" and "*principally upon that ground*, and for the reformation of those follies and abuses, *they have made their commotion and insurrection*." Under threat of deprivation, Henry now ordered the bishops to travel around their dioceses, expounding the Articles every holiday, and commending and praising:

> honest ceremonies of the church . . . in such plain and reverend sort, that the people may perceive that they be not contemned, and yet learn how they were instituted, and how they ought to be observed and esteemed, using such a temperance therein, as our said people be not corrupted by putting over-much affiance in them . . . and that our people may thereto the better know their duties to us, being their king and sovereign Lord.

[47] L&P, XI no. 1111.

This was a striking recognition by the King that religious discontent and an attachment to traditional religion lay at the heart of the Pilgrimage. The nub of the letter, though, was yet to come. Some bishops had been harbouring and encouraging radical preachers. Now, the letter went on, "we straitly charge and command you, that . . . you shall [not] keep or retain any man of any degree, that shall in his words privately or openly, directly or indirectly speak in those matters of these ceremonies contentiously or contemptuously." Any such person "that will not better temper his tongue" was to be arrested and sent to the council, as "an offender and seducer of our people". The bishops were also instructed to hunt out any clergy who had presumed to marry and arrest them. There are several surviving versions of this letter: one, more ferocious than the others, imputes to the episcopal recipient positive disobedience in harbouring and encouraging radical preaching, "so little regard ye took" of earlier royal instructions. It is not difficult to identify Latimer or Shaxton as the likely recipient of this version.[48]

It was under this sort of pressure that the *Bishops' Book* was compiled early in 1537, designed to be an authoritative explanation and expansion of the teaching of the Ten Articles for use in preaching and catechizing. Behind the drafting a fierce struggle between radical and traditionalist bishops took place. There was energetic lobbying on barge journeys up and down the Thames, as Stokesley of London and Tunstall of Durham did what they could to stiffen the resistance of less resolute bishops, exhorting them to "stand for the old customs" of the Church, supplying evidence of the value and antiquity of rites and ceremonies, from the Greek fathers and liturgies, since these could not be charged with "popery".[49] The document eventually authorized in the summer of 1537 shows that the pressure against radicalism had given defenders of traditional orthodoxy like Lee, Stokesley, and Tunstall a certain advantage, and the *Book* is accordingly in some ways less reformist than the Ten Articles. Where the Articles had mentioned only three sacraments, the *Bishops' Book* discussed all the traditional seven, and Lee told the York clergy that the other four had been "found again". Despite the growing reservations of Latimer and of Cranmer himself, the teaching of the Ten Articles on Purgatory and prayers for the dead was reaffirmed. But the drafting had not gone all one way. On the question of images the *Bishops' Book* was decidedly more radical than the Ten Articles, unequivocally stating that "we be utterly forbidden to make or

---

[48] Wilkins, *Concilia*, pp. 825–6; L&P, XI no. 1110.
[49] Strype, *Ecclesiastical Memorials*, I part 1, p. 502, I part 2, p. 381.

have any similitude or image, to the intent to bow down to it or worship it." Though it allowed for the use of images, it argued that their use in church was a concession to the dullness of men's wits and the surviving traces of "gentility" or paganism, and more particularly said that it would be far better to have no representations whatever of God the Father. From the annotations subsequently made by Henry VIII it is clear that he thought the tone of all this too drastic. It is equally clear from Cranmer's notes that the Archbishop thought the *Bishops' Book* did not go far enough, making too many concessions to the people's infirmity. Henry was happy to see images venerated so long as they were not "honoured as God". Cranmer, in contrast, thought images should have "no manner of honour" neither that due to God nor "such as is due to his reasonable creatures".[50]

For all the ambivalences of the Ten Articles and the *Bishops' Book*, it was inevitable that, in the charged and tense atmosphere of 1537 both conservatives and radicals should seize on the new formularies to vindicate their position. Cranmer found that in Kent influential members of the gentry were resisting reform, discouraging both Bible-reading and reformist preaching, and were appealing to "the new book" in doing so. As he wrote to "a Kentish Justice":

> Whereas your servants report that all things are restored by this new book to their old use . . . calling those that of late hath preached the abuses of them, false knaves and men worthy of no credence . . . if men will indifferently read these late declarations, they shall well perceive, that purgatory, pilgrimages, praying to saints, images, holy bread, holy water, holy days, meats, works, ceremony and such other, be not restored to their late accustomed abuses; but shall evidently perceive that the word of God hath gotten the upper hand of them all.[51]

Despite Cranmer's reformist reading of what had been achieved, the Kentish Justice was by no means alone in choosing to understand the Articles and the *Bishops' Book* as a welcome set-back for the reformist cause. For radicals convinced that "purgatorye ys pissed owte", that images were "idols and mawmets", and that pilgrimages were useless, the enactments of 1536 might be at one and the same time an incentive to further reform and an unsatisfactory half measure.[52] The parson of Thwaite in Suffolk, Sir

[50] Cranmer, *Remains*, pp. 100–3; for discussion of the *Bishops' Book* and images see Aston, *England's Iconoclasts*, pp. 239–43.

[51] Cranmer, *Remains*, pp. 350–2.

[52] L&P, XI no. 1424.

John Gale, was in trouble at Easter 1537 for denying the value of holy bread and holy water, and for refusing to make any for his parishioners. With the help of one John Augustine, he broke up the candle-prickets and ironwork before the images of Our Lady and St Erasmus in the parish church, and turned the statue of St Erasmus to face the wall, compounding matters by refusing to declare the Ten Articles, "for the one half of them were naught".[53]

Gale's disgust was understandable: the officially endorsed propaganda of this year has an air of caution and studied deference to tradition which was worlds away from the reforming polemic found in earlier manifestos such as Marshall's primer. Robert Redman reissued his English primer in 1537, in a version which seemed consciously to respond to the injunctions of 1536. It now included English versions of the Sunday Epistles and Gospels, based on Tyndale's New Testament, and an English version of the Ten Commandments. The preface dwelt on the work of "electe princes & true pastors" engaged in purging "the fylthynes of false doctrine", and emphasized the fact that when the first edition of the primer had appeared the previous year "it semed to men of authorite nat inconvenyent to passe amonge the commen people." All the more striking, therefore, is the revised primer's insistence on the need for deference and respect for tradition: "It is a poynte of presumptuous perversite and arrogance proudly to reject that thing which the religious contemplacion of good and godly men have eyther taughte . . . or left to the instruction of the unlernyd multitude." Therefore those who "frowardly . . . refuse" the traditions of our elders gave clear tokens of "rashness and temeryte . . . with an extreme zeale, but not accordynge to knowledge". The ancient devotions to saints and other traditional prayers contained, it was true, many things "that seme not to have theyr hole grounde in the scriptures," yet "dothe christain charite require that everything should be construed to the beste".[54]

This studied moderation was clearly in line with official policy in the wake of the Pilgrimage and its attendant discontents elsewhere. Yet it was a product not of any deep conviction of the value of the golden mean, but of caution in the face of possible rebellion, and despite it the attack on traditional religion represented by the dissolution of the monasteries and the dishonouring and dismantling of their shrines proceeded throughout 1537 and the early part of 1538. "Pilgrimage saints go down apace," observed John Hussee in March 1538, and their fall was a continual source of

[53] L&P, XII part 1, no. 818.
[54] *This Prymer in Englyshe and in Laten*, Hoskins, no. 128, RSTC 15997, preface.

trouble and grievance. On the feast of the Assumption 1537 Thomas Emans, a Worcester serving-man, entered the despoiled shrine of Our Lady of Worcester, recited a Paternoster and an Ave, kissed the feet of the image, from which jewels, coat, and shoes had been taken away, and declared bitterly for all to hear, "Lady, art thou stripped now? I have seen the day that as clean men hath been stripped at a pair of gallows as were they that stripped thee." He told the people that, though her ornaments were gone, "the similitude of this is no worse to pray unto, having a recourse to her above, then it was before." That careful distinction between the image and its heavenly original suggests that Emans was choosing his words to reflect the permitted use of images in the Ten Articles and the Injunctions, but there is no mistaking the outraged piety behind his dangerous gesture, and the same outraged loyalty manifested itself elsewhere.[55] In the same year the workmen and officials who oversaw the dissolution of the priory of St Nicholas, Exeter, attempted to take down the Rood-screen and loft, on which were images of saints to which there was popular devotion. Local women formed a mob, one of the supervising aldermen had to hide for his life in the priory buildings, and a workman broke a rib escaping through an upstairs window. In January 1538 a woman at Walsingham was carted about the market-place in deep snow and set in the stocks for spreading rumours that the image from the despoiled shrine, now in Cromwell's keeping at Chelsea along with many others awaiting destruction, had begun to work miracles. Roger Townsend, the magistrate who had hunted down the rumour-monger and devised her punishment in order to discourage "other lyght persons", had been instrumental in uncovering the "Walsingham conspiracy" the previous year, and he was clearly still afraid of the popular undercurrent of traditionalist religious feeling. He told Cromwell that though he was aware that he was probably acting without the law he felt something had to be done since "I cannot perceyve butt the seyd Image is not yett out of sum of ther heddes."[56]

To offset such dangerously persisting loyalties Cromwell staged an elaborate series of set-piece exposures of "feigned images" such as the Rood of Boxley, a long-disused image which had movable eyes and which quickly became the proof *par excellence* of the "juggling tricks" of monks to deceive the people. There was more to all this than the mere removal of "abused images". Cromwell's ecclesiastical lieutenants had come round to the thinking of Bucer's

[55] L&P, XII part 2, no. 587.
[56] Ellis, *Original Letters*, 3rd series, III pp. 162–3.

treatise against images, expressed by the Bishop of Rochester at the burning of the Boxley Rood that "the idolatrie will neaver be left till the said images be taken awaie." Latimer, who characteristically dismissed popular feeling for Our Lady of Worcester as inspired by fear of the loss of tourist trade, wrote to Cromwell in June 1538 urging the burning of the image of "our great Sibyll", together with "her older sister of Walsingham, her younger sister of Ipswich, with their other two sisters of Doncaster and Penrice", which would make "a jolly muster in Smithfield".[57] He had already cheerfully presided and preached on 22 May at one such jolly muster, the roasting alive of the Papalist friar John Forest over a slow fire made of the famous Welsh pilgrimage image of Darvell Gadern. This ritual wedding of the anti-papal cause with that of radical iconoclasm triggered less official action: on the night of Forest's execution the miracle-working Rood of St Margaret Patten's in the City was "broken all in peeces with the house he stoode in by certeine lewd persons, Fleminges and Englishe men, and some persons of the sayde parishe". On this occasion, however, no one was roasted alive.[58]

The implications of all this for religion in general were not lost on observers. John Husee warned Lady de Lisle in March 1538 against the use of traditional devotions: it would cause "less speech", he wrote, "if it might be your pleasure to leave part of such ceremonies as you do use, as long prayers and offerings of candles," and he cautioned her against even private keeping of abrogated feast days; "leave the most part of your memories, and have only mass, matins and evensong of the day." In a word, she must for safety's sake conform herself "partly to the thing that is used and to the world as it goeth now, which is undoubtedly marked above all other things".[59]

There were plenty of enraged traditionalists who had no intention of conforming to "the world as it goeth now". Popular observance of the abrogated saints' days continued: at St David's the reforming bishop, Barlow, found the people "wilfully solemnising the feest" of St David, and forcibly removed the relics which had been set out in the cathedral, but such disobedience was very widespread and often vocal. From Candlemas 1538 onwards the Vicar of Newark was preaching angry sermons urging his parishioners to kiss and offer to images, "saying they were heretics who would

[57] *Sermons and Remains of Hugh Latimer*, ed. G. E. Corrie, Parker Society, 1845, pp. 393–5, 403.
[58] *Wriothesley's Chronicle*, I pp. 75–81.
[59] M. St. Clare Byrne (ed.), *The Lisle Letters*, 1981, V 1120, 1131.

take any images down". He praised the gilds, those traditional corporate expressions of the cult of the saints and of intercession for the dead, denounced English books, especially those published "with the King's privilege", and urged the continued use of sacramentals like holy water, not as permitted by the Ten Articles and the *Bishops' Book*, as mere reminders of spiritual truths, but as powerful means to "drive away the devil".[60] Thomas Coveley, the Vicar of Tysehurst, was in trouble in June 1538 for his staunch defence of the "old fashion", which he was convinced would triumph again soon. He preached vigorously in praise of miraculous images, and urged his parishioners to "do as they have done", offering candles to St Loy for their horses and to St Anthony for their cattle. Bible-reading was the preserve of "botchers, bunglers and cobblers", and was to be discouraged, "It is but trick and go. Lightly it came and lightly it will begone again." He steered particularly close to the wind in defending traditional fasting practices. On 11 March Henry exercised the supremacy in an unprecedented way by issuing a proclamation dispensing the nation from observance of the traditional Lenten fast, on the grounds of scarcity of fish. Coveley implicitly denounced this royal act – and the supremacy itself – when he upbraided those parishioners who took advantage of the dispensation. "Ye will not fast lent, ye will eat white meat, yea, and it were not for shame, ye would eat a piece of bacon instead of a red herring. I daresay there be a hundred thousand worse people now then there were this time twelvemonth within England."[61]

Like the abrogated holidays the issue of the Lenten fast readily became a shorthand token for one's attitude to reform in general, and one of Cromwell's agents reported from Nottingham and Lincolnshire in the spring of 1539 that though the better sort were obeying the King's instructions about abrogated feast days, "the poor will not labour on those days as yet," and "the people here did little practice the King's gracious liberty to eat white meats in Lent time."[62] John Tyle, a baker of Windsor and part of a nest of traditionalists under the King's very nose, insisted in April 1538 that "By the grace of God, no eggs shall come into my belly before Easter." He complained that so many people were breaking the Lenten fast that there was a price revolution in eggs.[63] The parish

---

[60] L&P, XIII part 1, no. 604; *Tudor Royal Proclamations*, ed. P. L. Hughes and J. F. Larkin, 1964 (hereafter = TRP), I no. 177.
[61] L&P, XIII part 1, no. 1199.
[62] L&P, XIV part 1, nos 295, 839.
[63] L&P, XIII part 1, no. 686.

clergy of Windsor were just as dedicated as Tyle to the preservation of traditional customs, and conservative clergy everywhere used their influence in the confessional against the reform, as in the case, reported to Cromwell in the summer of 1538, of the "pryvie operation of certayn prystes within the cyte of Sarum, in ther confessons concernyng forrbyddyng of whytmeate in Lent, the redyng of the New Testament in Englisshe, and the cumpany of such as be of the new lernyng".[64] Conservative feeling was strong in Salisbury: in July and August 1538 the back streets of the town were agog with rumours that Heaven had been stirred by the mass destruction of the monastic shrines, and an angel had appeared to Henry VIII, bidding him go on pilgrimage to St Michael's Mount in Cornwall and offer a noble there on pain of death. Queen Jane's ghost had also appeared with the same message, and so it was said "God save the King, I trust we shall go a pilgrimage again." This was wishful thinking, but some of this conservative talk was clearly seditious, as in the case of William Ludeham, hermit at the chapel of St Thomas in Chesterfield, who was arrested for saying that since a man who plucked down the King's arms was liable to be hanged, drawn, and quartered for treason, "What shall he do then that doth pluck down churches and images, being but a mortal man as we be?"[65]

In this fraught atmosphere, at the end of September 1538 Cromwell issued a second set of Injunctions, several of which were little more than an emphatic reaffirmation of the positive provisions of the 1536 set, as in those calling for quarterly sermons, or for the instruction of the laity in the Creed, Ten Commandments, and Paternoster in English.[66] Curates and parishioners between them were now to provide "one book of the whole Bible of the largest volume", Coverdale's reworked and toned-down version of the Matthew Bible, and conservative clergy were warned against discouraging anyone from "prively and apertly . . . reading or hearing of the said bible", admonishing them nevertheless "to avoid all contention, altercation therein, and to use an honest sobriety in the inquisition of the true sense of the same". Cranmer was to supplement this passage in the Injunctions with a declaration to be read by curates to the people, warning them against "gevyng to moche to your own minds, fantazies, and opinions" in interpreting scripture, and forbidding "any open reasonyng in your open tavernes or alehowses", a recognition of the inflammatory potential of religious disputes. The rest of the Injunctions, though, provided more than enough fuel for the fires of controversy.

[64] Wright, *Monasteries*, p. 216.
[65] L&P, XIII part 2, no. 62, XIII part 1, no. 1345.
[66] VAI, II pp. 34–43.

The 1536 Injunctions had attacked pilgrimage and the cult of images and relics, but in a muted way. It was the abuse of such things "for superstition or lucre", and the economic ill consequences of leaving one's work to go about on pilgrimage, which had been criticized. The Injunctions of 1538 are far starker, their language more dismissive of the traditional cultus. The people were to be exhorted to works of charity, mercy, and faith, which alone are prescribed in scripture,

> and not to repose their trust and affiance in any other works devised by men's phantasies beside Scripture; as in wandering to pilgrimages, offering of money, candles or tapers to images or relics, or kissing or licking the same, saying over a number of beads, not understood or minded on.

This is the language of condemnation and contempt, designed not to moderate but to discredit the traditional cult, and these and "such-like superstition", far from being pleasing to God, are roundly said to incur "great threats and maledictions of God, as things tending to idolatry and superstition, which of all other offences God Almighty doth most detest and abhor".

Theological condemnation was translated into direct action. The seventh Injunction commanded that "such feigned images as ye know of in any of your cures to be so abused with pilgrimages or offerings of anything made thereunto, ye shall . . . forthwith take down and delay." The Injunctions hit out at traditionalist critics of the recent policy of the regime by demanding that any clergy who had "declared anything to the extolling or setting forth of pilgrimages, feigned relics, or images, or any such superstition" was publicly to recant, acknowledging such things to have crept into the church by "abuse and error".

In one fell swoop, these Injunctions outlawed not merely pilgrimage, but virtually the entire external manifestation of the cult of the saints, and also what was in many regions the single most common feature of mortuary piety, by forbidding the burning of candles before any image and commanding the quenching of the lights which, financed by the piety of gilds and the individual bequests of almost every adult with property to dispose of, burned in their dozens during divine service in every church and chapel in the land. From henceforth

> no candles, tapers, or images of wax to be set before any image or picture but only the light that commonly goeth across the church by the rood-loft, the light before the sacrament of the altar, and the light about the sepulchre, which for the adorning of the church and divine service ye shall suffer to remain.

In a further attack on the cult of the saints as a whole, the seventeenth Injunction claimed that in processions during which the litany was recited, the list of saints invoked was sometimes so long that "they had no time to sing the good suffrages following, as *Parce nobis Domine*" and therefore "it must be taught and preached that better it were to omit *Ora pro nobis*, and to sing the other suffrages." In short, the saints were to be squeezed out of the litany. And just as the Injunctions condemned the recitation of the rosary, so they struck at the cult of the Virgin Mary by forbidding the ringing of the Ave bell or Angelus. In 1481 Edward IV's queen, Elizabeth Woodville, had consolidated an already established custom by securing a papal indulgence of a hundred days for all who, on hearing the Ave Bell at morning, noon, or evening, knelt and recited at least one Ave Maria.[67] This charming custom was now condemned as having been "brought in and begun by the pretence of the Bishop of Rome's pardon", and the bell was silenced.

The radical implications and intent of the second royal Injunctions can hardly be doubted, and they need to be read in the light of the propagandist literature produced in Cromwell's household at this time. He kept about him "sundry and divers fresh and quick wits" to popularize the cause of reform. One of them, William Gray of Reading, composed a ballad in celebration of the stripping of the shrines, "The Fantassie of Idolatrie". The ballad is clearly an inside job, drawing heavily for its details on reports sent by the monastic visitors to Cromwell. It therefore constitutes both a progress report from Cromwell's household on the attack on the cult of the saints and a manifesto revealing its real objectives.[68]

The ballad begins with an exposition of the second Commandment, interpreted as forbidding all religious images:

> Idols and images
> Have none in usage
> (of what mettel so ever they be)
> Graved or carved;
> My wyle be observed
> Or els can ye not love me.

There follows a burlesqued catalogue of the shrines, accounts of whose destruction had filled Cromwell's postbag for the last two years:

[67] *Calendar of Entries in the Papal Registers Relating to Great Britain and Ireland: Papal Letters*, XIII part 1, pp. 90–1.
[68] Foxe, *Acts and Monuments*, V pp. 404–9.

> To Walsyngham a gaddyng,
> To Cantorbury a maddyng,
> As men distraught of mynde;
> With fewe clothes on our backes,
> But an image of waxe,
> For the lame and for the blynde.

The set-piece unmasking of celebrated relics like the Blood of
Hailes or images like the Boxley Rood are made the most of:

> He was made to jogle,
> His eyes would gogle
> He would bend his browes and frowne;
> With his head he would nod
> Like a proper young god,
> His shaftes wold go up and downe.

The ballad extended its attack beyond the pilgrimage saints to
the even more ubiquitous helper saints whose cult was focused
on images to be found in most parish churches, and to whom,
consequently, there was no extended pilgrimage:

> To Saynt Syth for my purse;
> Saynt Loye save my horse;
> For my tethe to Saynt Apolyne:
> To Saynt Job for the poxe;
> Saynt Luke save myne oxe;
> Saynt Anthony save my swyne!

Now these idols have fallen and in their helplessness at the hands of
their abusers are exposed as frauds:

> For when they bored holes
> In the roodes back of poles,
> Which, as some men saye, dyd speake,
> Then lay he still as a stocke,
> Receyved there many a knocke,
> And did not ones crie "creake".

The consequence of all this was inescapable, and led to direct
action.

> Thus were we poore soules
> Begyled with idolles,
> With fayned myracles and lyes,
> By the devyll and his docters,
> The pope and his procters:
> That with such, have blerid our eyes . . .

With dyvers other trickes,
Whiche sore in mens' consciences stickes:
But to Christ let us all pray!
To plucke it up, by the hard rote
(Seeing there is none other bote),
And utterly to banyshe it away.

There is no hint in Gray's ballad of any idea that there might be a legitimate use of images, as laymen's books, of the sort envisaged by the Ten Articles. All were the tools of the Devil, and all must go down. Read in the light of Cromwellian propaganda such as the "Fantassie of Idolatrie", the Injunctions become the spearhead of a radical onslaught on one of the main pillars of late medieval piety, "utterly to banish it away".

Inevitably, traditionalists were scandalized by these "sinister Injunctions . . . clear gone out of the faith", and many rated them at no more than "a rhyme, a jest or a ballad". Six months after they had been issued it was reported to Cromwell that "from Sarum westward the Injunctions are not observed," and this neglect was by no means confined to the West Country. In December 1538 the King issued a circular to Justices of the Peace and other officers, complaining of the "cankered hearts" of many of the clergy who "to bring our people to darkness" read the Injunctions "so confusely, hemmyng and hacking the word of God, and such our injunctions . . . that almost no man can understande the trewe meanyng".[69]

Such clerical temerity was no doubt encouraged by the contradictory signals emanating from the Court. The Injunctions began to circulate early in October 1538, and they clearly represented a decided advance of the Reformed cause in England. Yet on 16 November Henry issued a proclamation whose overall conservative position was unmistakable, and which certainly represents the conservative outcome of a power struggle within the regime itself.[70] The main body of this proclamation exists in a draft corrected extensively in Henry's own handwriting, and clearly reflects his own traditionalist attitudes. It repudiated the "contentious and sinister opinions . . . by wrong teaching and naughty printed books" which had increased of late in England, and specifically the books "set forth with privilege, containing annotations and additions in the margins, prologues and calendars, imagined and

[69] L&P, XIII part 2, no. 1037, XIV part 1, nos 542, 894; Elton, *Policy and Police*, pp. 258–9; Burnet, *Reformation*, pp. ccclxxxiv–ccclxxxv.
[70] Elton, *Policy and Police*, p. 258.

invented . . . by the makers, devisers and printers of the same books". This was an unmistakable reference to the Protestant primers set out apparently with royal countenance by protégés of Cromwell such as William Marshall. The proclamation forbade the import of English books without special licence, and required that any translation appearing must have the author's name on the title-page. It forbade annotated translations of the scriptures, or the printing or sale of any English scriptural translations without prior examination by a Privy Councillor or bishop. The proclamation went on to outlaw Anabaptists and sectaries, who were to leave the realm within ten days, and outlawed debate on the Blessed Sacrament.

Turning to traditional religious ceremonies and customs, the proclamation condemned those who "arrogantly attempt of their own sensual appetites and froward rash wills to contemn, break, and violate divers and many laudable ceremonies and rites hitherto used and accustomed in the Church of England, and yet not abolished . . . whereby daily riseth much difference, strife, and contention". The ceremonies specifically mentioned as having come under attack indicate how extensive the reforming onslaught on the traditional framework of ceremonial religion had been – holy bread, holy water, procession, creeping to the cross on Good Friday and Easter Day, the setting up of lights "before the Corpus Christi", probably a reference to the Easter sepulchre, the Candlemas cere- monies, the ceremonies at the churching of women and surrounding the chrisom-cloths used in baptism, and tithes and other traditional offerings. These ceremonies were interpreted along the lines laid down in the Ten Articles and the *Bishops' Book*, and were to be used "without superstition . . . [as] good and laudable ceremonies to put us in remembrance of higher perfection, and none otherwise". No one was to "repose any confidence of salvation in them, but take them for good instructions until such time as his majesty doth change or abrogate them". In a clause which was clearly the original ending of the proclamation, the marriage of clergy was attacked, and married clergy were ordered to be expelled from office and deemed to be laymen.

This proclamation was a devastating set-back for the reformed cause as it had been promoted by Cromwell and his circle. They seem to have secured some amelioration, for in its final form the proclamation had two additional clauses, not found in the draft amended by Henry. The first of these emphasized the need for the clergy to instruct the laity in the "true meaning and understanding of Holy Scripture, sacramentals, rites and ceremonies", warning against "superstitious abuses and idolatries" and the contentions which had arisen about the ceremonies. They were to make a sharp distinction between "the things commanded by God" on the one hand, and the "rites and ceremonies aforesaid" on the other. They were to read, and the people to hear without contention and strife, the "very Gospel and Holy Scripture".

The final clause of the proclamation was an attempt to regain the high ground for the reforming cause with a sweeping attack on the memory and cult of St Thomas Becket, whose shrine at Canterbury had been pillaged early in September, and his bones scattered. Denounced here as a maintainer of the enormities of the Bishop of Rome, and a rebel against the King, he was no longer to be esteemed as a saint, and his images and pictures were to be "put down and avoided out of all churches, chapels and other places" (Pl. 131). His name was to be erased from all liturgical books, and his Office, antiphons, and collects to be said no more. This abolition of his festivals was said to be, like the earlier abrogations, "to the intent that his grace's loving subjects shall be no longer blindly led and abused to commit idolatry".[71]

Here was a proclamation which unmistakably spoke with two voices, reflecting profoundly different senses of the limits and objectives of the Henrician reforms as they impinged on the religion of the people. The divisions it revealed were mirrored in the regime's other public actions at this time. On 24 November Bishop Hilsey staged another of his by now famous exposés of "feigned relics", with a set-piece sermon at Paul's Cross on the Holy Blood of Hailes. On the same day four Anabaptists were made to carry faggots, also at Paul's Cross. Similar conflicting signals were sent by the utterances of the bishops. In the wake of the royal Injunctions individual bishops were encouraged by Cromwell to endorse the Crown's actions by issuing their own Injunctions. At long last, writes Sir Geoffrey Elton, "the bishops had been fully mobilised".[72] The resulting utterances, however, while following the lines set out in the royal Injunctions, differed radically in tone and in target, and it was clear that not all the bishops were being mobilized in the same direction. Edward Lee, Archbishop of York and a man whose conservative convictions had already brought him into conflict with Cranmer, issued a lengthy set of thirty Injunctions, for the most part simply echoing the royal ones, encouraging Bible-reading, vernacular instruction in the Creed, Commandments, the Lord's Prayer, and Ave Maria. He went beyond the Injunctions in commanding that the Epistle and Gospel

---

[71] TRP, I no. 186, pp. 270–6.
[72] Elton, *Policy and Police*, p. 255.

of the day should be read in English, and where there was a preacher, that one or other should be preached on. The fact that other bishops also ordered this, combined with the appearance of a number of primers with the English Epistles and Gospel in 1537 and 1538 suggests that this was an informal part of the policy of Cromwell.

All this was compliant enough, even enthusiastic. Lee's handling of the sections of the Injunctions dealing with the attack on the traditional cult of saints and their images, however, was more cautious. Curates were instructed "diligently" to inform their congregations

> according to the King's Highness' Injunctions, that they may in no wise yield worship to any images, lowtinge or bowing down, or kneeling to the said images, nor offering to them any money, or wax light or unlight, or any other thing, for so much as offering is to be made to God only, and to no creature under God.

Nevertheless, the people might still "use lights in the rood-loft, and afore the sacrament, and at the sepulchre at Easter . . . so that they none use to the honour or worship of any image, nor by way of offering made, either to any image, or to any saint represented by the same." Reiterating the teaching of the Ten Articles, Lee insisted that the people were to be taught "that images be suffered only as books, by which our hearts may be kindled to follow the holy steps and examples of the saints represented by the same; even as saints lives be written . . . for the same purpose". Moreover, a distance must be preserved between the image and the thing imagined, "although they see the image of the Father represented as an old man, yet they may in no wise believe that the heavenly Father is any man, or that he hath any body or age." And finally, "All images, to which any manner of resort is used by way of pilgrimage, or offering, they must depose and sequester from all sight of men, and suffer them no more to be set up."[73]

Lee's Injunctions are as significant for their silences as for their inclusions: there is no hint of the further abolition of images promised in the royal Injunctions, no suggestion that the invocation of saints is undesirable, no hint that the litany of the saints might be curtailed, no mention of the Ave Bell which the royal Injunctions had commanded to be suppressed. The language used about the cult of images is carefully neutral, and the order for their removal

[73] VAI, II pp. 44–52.

confined to those to which "resort is used by way of pilgrimage or offering". Even these images are not called "feigned" or "abused", and Lee never uses the word "idolatry", so fundamental to the Reformed attack on images. Accordingly he also omits the word "delay" which, in the royal Injunction, probably implied the destruction rather than the simple removal of the images. Lee was ready to welcome the positive provisions of the 1538 Injunctions for the better instruction of the people, but his compliance with the royal attack on the traditional cultus was resolutely minimalist and carefully avoided criticizing the old ways. In this light the constant reiteration of the phrase "according to the King's Highness' Injunctions" looks as much like an attempt to distance Lee himself from the reforming measures as an eagerness to show compliance with the royal will.

By contrast, Nicholas Shaxton's Injunctions for Salisbury are patently a reforming document, openly contemptuous of the traditional cultus. Where Lee had contented himself with a reaffirmation of the broad lines of the Ten Articles, Shaxton goes well beyond the detail even of the royal Injunctions of 1538 in his attack on popular religious practice. He clearly had in mind very specific West-Country local observances, of the sort already attacked by Latimer in Convocation, in cautioning his clergy that "ye suffer no night watches in your churches or chapels, neither decking of images with gold, silver, clothes, lights, or herbs; nor the people kneel to them, not worship them, nor offer candles, oats, cakebread, cheese, wool, or any other such things to them." Images were laymen's books, and only so might be used, for "otherwise there might be peril of idolatry, especially of ignorant lay people, if they either in heart or outward gesture worship them or give honour to them, which ought only to be given to God, the Lord of all saints." Similarly, the clergy must instruct their parishioners "not to be envious about works invented by their own foolish devotion, as, to go about pilgrimage, and say with vain confidence this prayer and that prayer, with other superstitious observations, in fastings, praying, and keeping of old foolish customs". In a gesture which must have warmed evangelical hearts by its poetic justice, Shaxton ordered that the Bibles which were required to be provided under the royal Injunctions should be paid for if necessary out of the "stocks given for maintaining lights before images (with which I dispense for this better use)". And he attacked head-on the cult of relics, the source of "intolerable superstition and abominable idolatry". Ignorant people were being deluded by false relics, many of which had already come into his hands, "namely of stinking boots, mucky combs, ragged rochets, rotten girdles, pyld purses, great bullocks' horns, locks of hair, and filthy rags, gobbets of wood, under the name of parcels of the holy cross, and such pelfry beyond estimation". He commanded that all such relics were to be sent to him at his house at Ramsbury, together with any documentation concerning them, and those that were judged "undoubtedly true relics" would be returned, with instructions how they might be used.[74]

It was clear therefore that the intensity and scope of the Henrician assault on popular religion would vary greatly from region to region, diocese to diocese, and that in the dioceses of conservatives like Lee of York or his namesake of Lichfield and Coventry, or Longland of Lincoln, a minimalist reading of the provisions of the second royal Injunctions would prevail. There were plenty for whom even a minimal enforcement was too much. Despite the unequivocal repudiation of any cult of images in the royal and episcopal Injunctions, the cult continued. The parish of Great Dunmow erected a new tabernacle for the image of Our Lady in the chancel, though when the vicar of Highley in Herefordshire "new-gilded" a wonder-working image of the Virgin, "to which much offering was made in times past", he was duly denounced to Cromwell.[75] Sir Thomas Tyrrell, parson of Gislingham in Suffolk, was in trouble at the Ipswich sessions in January 1539 because, despite his parishioners' timid refusal to assist him, he had celebrated the feast of Thomas Becket on 29 December, and had devoted his sermon the following Sunday to exhorting his people to continue to go on pilgrimage. When they asked where they might go, "seeing that Our Lady of Walsingham, Our Lady of Grace [at Ipswich] and Thomas Becott were put down", he told them to go to Jerusalem, adding that "if he were disposed to go a pilgrimage he knew whither to go".[76]

These were unlucky clergy, with enemies or pro-reformers in their parishes ready to denounce them. In many more places community feeling was solidly the other way, and it was the reformers who found themselves in trouble. In September and October 1538, at Barking, a few miles south of Gislingham, there was a revealing series of confrontations between traditionalists and reformers in the parish church. The local parson, Richard Redman, was reputed to be no great enthusiast for royal religious policy. Preachers in his church had not declared the supremacy nor attacked the Pope, and neither the first nor second royal Injunctions had been published by

[74] VAI, II pp. 53–60.
[75] W. T. Scott, *Antiquities of an Essex Parish*, 1873, p. 37; L&P, XIII part 2, no. 1243.
[76] L&P, XIV part 1, no. 76.

him. His churchwardens and "greatmen" were similarly such as had "no knowledge or goodwill to the truth", and he employed as parish priest one John Adryan, a favourer of "Romly" traditions who had evidently crossed swords with John Bale, whose radical views had so antagonized the parishioners of nearby Thorndon. So the Pope's name had not been erased from the liturgical books in the Barking chapelries of Darmsden and Needham Market, and there was opposition there to English books. Every defeat of the reforming party was greeted with glee in this part of Suffolk.

But there was a snake in the grass of this traditionalist Eden. Robert Ward, an Essex man and former friar who had been in trouble in 1535 and the following year for his vehemence against ceremonies and superstition, had moved into Suffolk, and was a regular participant in services at Barking.[77] He was something of a self-appointed watchdog against the "old ways", and on 15 September, the octave of the feast of the Nativity of the Blessed Virgin, which fell on a Sunday in 1538, he attended matins, sitting in choir next to the parish priest. When Adryan invoked the Virgin's prayers, "Divina solatia impetret nobis Virgo Maria", Ward said "with a submiss voice", "That is naught." There was clearly a history of friction between the men, and Adryan, nettled, declared aloud that "I believe the Church better than you." Ward reminded him that it was "the Popish church" which "did make and maintain that", and bade Adryan "Say forth your matins and make no more din." But while Adryan was completing the service "with murmuring cheer", Ward took the opportunity to scour through the missal to see if the Pope's name had been duly scraped out. Evidently it had in most places, but he managed to find a rubric in the marriage service which referred to a matter debated "in Palatio Domini Papae", and an undefaced collect headed "pro Papa". Adryan, spotting what Ward was doing, provocatively emphasized those parts of matins which he thought Ward would find theologically offensive, pausing to ask each time "Is this naught also? Ye will say this is heresy." At the end of the service he confronted Ward with the missal, asking "Is there anything in that book which is naught?" This interchange ended in violence with the two men wrestling for possession of the missal. One of the "greatmen", Nicholas Fowler, came up to Ward "with threatening words and great oaths", saying "It were alms that thou were hanged and all such as thou art. Camest thou hither to control our priest?" A headstrong man prone to violence, he had to be restrained by other

---

[77] On Ward see John Fines, *A Biographical Register of Early English Protestants*, 1986, II *sub* Ward, Robert.

parishioners from stabbing Ward, and Ward and some supporters left to avoid further violence. A group of parishioners went back to the parsonage with Adryan, where he held forth on the necessity of the intercession of saints.

The matter did not rest there. Ward clearly had some following in the parish, and a week later Adryan was in dispute with one of them, Hugh Buck of Barking. Meeting Adryan on his way to church, Buck asked him "How shall a man have knowledge of eternal life?" Adryan replied with an impeccable appeal to the tradition – "Thy father and mother taught thee." But Buck would have none of this: his parents, he said, had taught him only his Pater, Ave, and Creed in Latin, "and partly idolatry", and when Adryan replied that "they bade thee love thy Lord God above all thing" he insisted "Nay, that was taught me since." Here with a vengeance was a stark repudiation of the religion of his fathers, and the conversation degenerated into another argument about the old religion, in particular the intercession of the saints, in the course of which Buck insisted that Christ died for Mary as well as for others. This was in fact an impeccably orthodox proposition which Adryan, now thoroughly rattled, was unwise enough to challenge. By the time he got to church he had thought better of this, and preached on the Virgin's intercession, insisting that she was "a mean to God to pray for us and with us". While acknowledging that Christ died for her as for us, he nevertheless insisted that "we are sinners and she is no sinner."[78]

The confrontation at Barking was especially fully reported, but incidents like it were occurring up and down the country. At St Germans in Cornwall Friar Alexander Barclay preached in honour of the Blessed Virgin. At a supper in the Priory there afterwards one of Cromwell's correspondents, William Dynham, "moved suche questions as I thought myght do good to the audyence", evidently sounding them out on their views of the recent reforming measures. This provoked Barclay to rashness, as it was probably meant to do, and he declared that "I wolde to God that at the beste the lawes of God might have asmuche auctoryte as the lawes of the realme." Men, he said, were nowadays too busy "in pullinge doune of ymages without especiall comaundement of the Prynce". Dynham countered that only images to which idolatry had been paid had been pulled down, and gave the specific example of the Rood of Grace in St Margaret Patten's in the City of London, destroyed by parishioners on the day of Friar Forest's roasting to death. The rest of the company were clearly uncomfortable

---

[78] L&P, XII part 2, no. 571.

by now, unable to endorse this particular act of iconoclasm, yet unwilling to appear critical of royal policy, so that, as Dynham reported to Cromwell, though they "somewhat dispraised" the act "yet for the intente and good facte therof toleratyd". Barclay was clearly nettled by this spinelessness, and intervened, demanding "What followed therof", and when asked what he meant, reminded them that a week after the destruction of the Rood there had been a judgement on the parish, for "many tenements and some people were burnt." Dynham was triumphant: "What, Barclay . . . here is somewhat marvyl . . . Wulde you infecte this audience with that opynyon that God for such cause plageid them: your kankrid harte is disclosed."[79]

There were "kankrid hartes" everywhere. Myles Coverdale reported in the spring of 1539 that the area from Newbury in Berkshire to Henley-on-Thames was deep in popery. At Newbury the Pope's name and titles stood still in the "great Matins book", at Henley the legend of Becket with the "feigned story of his death" stood still in the glass of the windows. And not only this, but "all the beams, irons and candlesticks, wherupon tapers and lights were wont to be set up unto images, remain still untaken down, whereby the poor simple unlearned people believe that they shall have liberty to set up their candles again unto images, and that the old fashion shall shortly return." In these parts "and I fear me in many more," Coverdale thought, there were "an innumerable sort of . . . popish books", keeping the people in error and containing devotions to Becket, probably a reference to the continuing widespread circulation of traditional primers, and he persuaded the curate of Newbury to try to call in all such books.[80]

He was certainly right in thinking that the situation at Newbury was typical of many areas. All over the country there were examples of service books unreformed, or reformed half-heartedly: clergy and churchwardens erased the Pope's or Becket's name by lightly gluing strips of paper over them.[81] The great antiphonal of the parish of St Helen's, Ranworth, a few miles from Norwich, which survived the destruction of Edward's and Elizabeth's reigns, and is still to be seen in the church for which it was made, was probably typical of many country liturgical books. In it the services for Thomas Becket have been neither properly erased nor removed, but merely crossed out with the faintest of diagonal pen-lines, making continued use of them perfectly possible, as was indeed to

[79] Ellis, *Original Letters*, III pp. 113–15.
[80] Myles Coverdale, *Remains*, ed. G. Pearson, Parker Society, 1846, pp. 498–9, 500–2.
[81] Elton, *Policy and Police*, pp. 237–8.

happen at Ranworth in Mary's reign (Pl. 132–3).[82]

Even under the eye of Cranmer himself there was resistance to the Injunctions as time-honoured devotional customs persisted. Well into 1539 at Ashford in Kent there was a Crucifix in the north aisle which was an object of local veneration, before which, as Henry Goderick, the reformist parson of nearby Hothfield reported, "there stands a box to receive offerings, and people daily blaspheme God by making a reverence to it." Goderick mounted a campaign against such idolatry, preaching against it in Ashford church several times. An "erroneous table", containing devotions and an account of the Rood, had been set up beside it; when Goderick crossed out particularly objectionable words like "honour" and "reverently", the Ashford clergy wrote them back in again. He had recourse to two local justices sympathetic to the reformist cause, and one of them, Henry Goldwell, expanded on the particular evils of crucifixes: "I have found that when there is any crucifix in a church or chapel except that in the roodloft, that there be more fashions of idolatry used to the crucifix apart than to that in the roodloft." This was to echo the language of Bucer's iconoclastic tract with its polemic against the peculiar dangers of the image of the cross. But crucifixes were not Goldwell's only worry, for he particularly disliked the very common images of Our Lady of Pity, "having her son in her arms after he was taken down from the cross; which I do not perceive to be a true story by the Scripture, yet to these images the people have much mind". He conceded that offerings to the Images of Pity in Kent had probably largely ceased in obedience to the Injunctions, but Goldwell and Goderick between them reported many examples of evasion of the spirit of the Injunctions. Thus the prohibition against setting up tapers before the images of saints had not in fact extinguished the lights in many places, for the people were evading the prohibition by setting them up instead in the Rood-loft, between "the tapers suffered to stand for the adorning of the church". At Ashford after the proclamation against Becket had come out, the parishioners had not destroyed his image in the church, as they were required to do, but instead had "transposed it", taking his archiepiscopal Cross from his hand and putting in its place a wool-comb, thereby transforming Becket into St Blaise. Goderick thought this a common device, and that many people believed that "they might transpose and let the images stand with new tokens in their hands," and he was almost certainly right. The parishioners of the Suffolk

[82] The feasts of St Thomas, deleted from the calendar of the Ranworth antiphonal under Henry VIII were carefully restored under Mary.

church of Earl Stonham similarly could not bear to destroy their fine wall-painting of the martyrdom of St Thomas, so they commissioned a painter to "transpose it" into the martyrdom of St Katherine.[83]

What Cranmer called the "stiff opinion of the people in the alteration of ordinances and laws in the church" was not confined to the widespread observance of abrogated feast and fast days, or their persisting affection for images and lights. Already in 1537 the Archbishop had had cause to complain bitterly that in Kent "the people dare not apply themselves to read God's word", for fear of influential conservative gentry.[84] Bible-reading in English became a contentious issue in many parishes, and a badge of support for the wider attack on traditional ways. The case of William Malden of Chelmsford is well known. After the Injunctions of 1538 a group of poor men clubbed together to buy a New Testament, and "on sundays dyd set redinge in [the] lower ende of the churche, and many wolde flocke about them to heare theyr redinge". Malden, a teenager, was one of those who listened, but his father, a staunch conservative, forced him away each Sunday, gave him a primer, and made him join in the rival activity of reciting Our Lady's matins.[85] At Enfield in Middlesex John Hanon similarly began to read the Gospels aloud, but was resolutely opposed by many in the parish, led by the parson, who thought the English New Testament "the book of Arthur Cobler", and a "green learning that will fade away". Hanon was duly warned off by the parish constable: "This must be left, for I am sent for to warn you by the honest men of the parish for to leave your reading, for you cause other to hear you: it were better that they prayed on their beads than to come about you." Coverdale reported similar victimization of Bible-readers in the Thames Valley, where at Henley one of the local gentry "did forbid five of his neighbours his house for holding with the gospel, and said that he had evil will for receiving such men of the new learning". Thus "poor men are not only discouraged from the truth of God, but it appeareth also that the king's most gracious commandment is not put in execution."[86] In August 1539 disappointed radicals could lament the general resistance to reform: "Who is there, almost, that will have a Bible, but he must be compelled thereto?" asked George Constantine. The clergy were loath to teach the Creed, the Commandments, and the Lord's Prayer in English, and, he added, "how unwilling the people to

[83] N. Pevsner, *The Buildings of England: Suffolk*, 1974, p. 195.
[84] Cranmer, *Remains*, pp. 349–55.
[85] J. G. Nichols (ed.), *Narratives of the Days of the Reformation*, 1859, pp. 348–50.
[86] Coverdale, *Remains*, pp. 501–2.

learn it! Yea, they jest at it, calling it the New Pater Noster and New Learning."[87]

These local jangles, enacted in parishes in every county in the land, were made all the worse by the divided councils about the King, for the public acts of the regime were increasingly clearly the consequences of divided policy. In February 1539 the proponents of reform seemed to have won a victory, with the issuing of a proclamation about the "laudable ceremonies" dealt with in the Ten Articles. Ostensibly a reiteration of the conservative proclamation of 16 November, which had dwelt on the value of the ceremonies and sacramentals, this new proclamation insisted that they were of didactic and symbolic value only: "And so it shall be well understood and known that neither holy bread nor holy water, candles, bows, nor ashes hallowed, or creeping and kissing the cross be the workers or works of our salvation, but only as outward signs and tokens whereby we remember Christ and his doctrine, his works and his passion." The proclamation pointed firmly in a reformist direction, and "straitly charged" that the spiritual significance of all such ceremonies should be "truly and plainly" declared to the people whenever they were used. The Protestant drift of the proclamation was underlined by its final section, pardoning Anabaptists and Sacramentaries.[88]

But any reformer who took encouragement from this proclamation was to be rudely disillusioned before the spring was out. Henry was on the whole committed to the reform of the cult of the saints and of images, but he was ferociously opposed to any deviation from traditional teaching on the Mass. The inclusion of an attack on the Mass in Bucer's Strasbourg treatise against images illustrates how difficult it was for reformers to keep the two issues safely separate. An incident at Easter 1539 in Salisbury Cathedral demonstrated the dangers which beset over-zealous reformers. The reforming bishop of Salisbury, Shaxton, had been locked in conflict with the town and the Cathedral clergy for several years, and had built up round himself a deeply unpopular group of Protestant officials. On Easter day 1539 one of these men, Shaxton's baillie, John Goodall, passed through the Cathedral at three in the afternoon. The choir was full of people, venerating an image of Christ on an altar at the north side of the choir. This was an immemorial part of the liturgy of the Easter sepulchre, and this very altar and image were explicitly provided for in the rubrics of the Sarum *Manuale*. The image of Christ was in fact a monstrance, containing the Blessed Sacrament, which had been "buried" in the sepulchre

[87] L&P, XIV part 2, no. 400.
[88] TRP, I no. 188.

on Good Friday and "raised" that morning, to the singing of the antiphon "Christus Resurgens", the high point of the Easter liturgy and one of the major focuses of lay piety everywhere in England. Goodall can hardly have been ignorant of what was going on: such images were very common, and the public veneration of the Sacrament and the image of Christ which contained it a feature of Easter worship in every parish in England. He chose to mis-understand the people's actions, however, and peremptorily ordered them to stop kissing the image, commanding one of the clergy to remove it, citing the 1538 Injunctions' prohibition against "kissing and licking" images as his authority. When the priest refused to cooperate, "and the people fast pressing to kiss it", Goodall had one of his servants pick up the image, with its precious contents, and take it away.

Chaos and outrage ensued at so breathtaking an act of sacrilege. Goodall's servant was clapped in gaol, and the mayor and cor-poration denounced Goodall himself to the Privy Council as a Sacramentary. Shaxton sprang to his defence, claiming that the incident was a genuine mistake, and that Goodall's opponents at Salisbury were enemies of the King's Injunctions, their ringleader a Justice of the Peace who was a pillar of the old religion, "a faster of saint John's fast on the Wednesday", and therefore a "blind ignorant man and wilful".[89] Attempts to prosecute Goodall in the Star Chamber collapsed, but the incident was a warning of the way in which excessive zeal for the reformist cause could land its promoters within a hair's breadth of fatal heresy charges.[90]

The danger was all the more real because Henry was still deeply worried by the religious divisions which had sprung up in the realm, and by the rumble of discontent from the conservative mass of the population. A draft proclamation "for uniformity in religion", dating from April 1539 and heavily corrected in Henry's hand, makes it clear that he blamed the rising tide of "murmur, malice and malignity" among the people in large part on unfettered Bible-reading. He had hoped that the English Bible would be read "with meekness . . . and not to maintain erroneous opinions". Instead, the people disputed "arrogantly" in churches, alehouses, and taverns, and slandered each other "as well by word as writing, one part of them calling the other papist, the other part calling the other heretic". Such name-calling was to stop, and to prevent further dispute none except curates, or licensed graduates of the Universities, were to expound scripture. Moreover, though lay people might continue to read the Bible, this was to be done, as

[89] L&P, XIV part 1, no. 777.
[90] Elton, *Policy and Police*, p. 106.

Henry himself insisted, "quietly and with silence . . . secretly"; there was to be no more of the "open" reading "with any loud or high voices, and specially during the time of divine service or of celebration and saying of masses". Instead, the people were "virtuously and devoutly to hear their divine services and masses", and to use their time "in reading or praying with peace and silence, as good Christian men ought to do".[91]

This draft proclamation was to be overtaken by events and was never issued. But it was a clear indication that Henry had decided to throw his weight on the side of traditional religion. On Ascension Day he celebrated the feast with an extravagant display of old-fashioned piety. He went in procession to Westminster, where the high altar in his chapel was decorated with images of the Apostles, for an elaborate sung Mass. Eager conservatives, noting the presence of the images, recalled that on Good Friday Henry had crept to the cross "from the chapel door upward", and had himself served the priest at Mass. It was noted too that Henry made a point of receiving holy bread and holy water every Sunday "and doth daily use all other laudable ceremonies", so that "in all London no man upon pain of death dare to speak against them."[92] On 7 June 1539 the elaborate celebration of "Diriges" and requiem Masses for the repose of the soul of the Empress Isabella in every church in London, with a three-line whip for the attendance of the two archbishops and eight bishops present in London at the "Dirige" in St Paul's, was yet another endorsement of traditional piety, and was so perceived in the country at large. As one defender of prayers for the dead observed, in a discussion at Malmesbury later the same year, "I trow excepte dyrygys and massys dyd goode on to the soles departed, the Kyngys grace wolde nott have causyd suche solemnyte to have byn done for the Empres as he dyd."[93]

But in any case Henry had decided to tackle the problem of religious disunity in characteristically draconian form. The victory for traditional piety which the draft proclamation undoubtedly represented, and which was signalled by events like the Empress's "Diriges", was even more dramatically consummated within three days of the celebration of those "Diriges", with the passing on 10 June of the Act of Six Articles. Though it would be a year to the day before his final fall, this Act marked the beginning of the end for Cromwell. More immediately, it dislodged from office some of the key figures behind the radical onslaught on traditional piety: Latimer and Shaxton resigned their bishoprics. The cause of reform and of traditional religion had reached a crisis.

[91] TRP, I no. 191.
[92] Byrne (ed.), *Lisle Letters*, V p. 478.
[93] *Wriothesley's Chronicle*, I pp. 97–9; L&P, XIV part 2, no. 804.

CHAPTER 12

THE ATTACK ON TRADITIONAL RELIGION II: TO THE DEATH OF HENRY VIII

The Act of Six Articles marked a decisive turning-point for the progress of radical Protestantism under Henry. In the summer of 1539 the most outspoken advocates of reform, like Shaxton and Latimer, who both resigned their sees rather than enforce the Act in their dioceses, were being widely denounced by the common people as "false knaves and whoresons". But the full scale of the reversal of evangelical fortunes was not at first evident. Cromwell remained all-powerful in the Council, and in the spring of 1540 was to be created Earl of Essex. Anxious debate about the efficacy of traditional ceremonial continued to disturb rural alehouses, and clues to the King's beliefs, like the Empress's dirge, continued to be scrutinized.[1] Disgruntled conservatives, deploring the fate of the abbeys, the desecration of relics, and the continued boldness of radical preachers like Robert Barnes, considered that the Act had failed to settle the religious question. "Jesus," lamented one of them, "I had thought that schism and diversity of opinions had been pacified in the last Parliament."[2] But this radical immunity was illusory: by Easter 1540 Barnes, Jerome, and Garrett had been forced to make public recantations. Cromwell, fighting off conservative enemies within the Council, for once did nothing to bail out these evangelicals, and there were significant indications that the process of religious settlement would bring the proponents of further reform little joy. A week before his ennoblement he had announced to Parliament the establishment of an episcopal commission to secure "concord in religion". Opposing the "forwardness and carnal lust" of the more imprudent reformers (the reference is presumably to clerical marriage, outlawed by the Six Articles) to the

[1] L&P, XV no. 587.
[2] L&P, XIV part 2, no. 750.

"inveterate corruption and superstitious tenacity" of traditionalist opinion, Cromwell deplored the division and name-calling of heretic and papist, and declared the King's determination to secure the promulgation of true doctrine. Despite the careful balancing act represented by the speech, there was no mistaking Cromwell's own sympathies, for he praised the King's solicitude for the salvation and consolation of the people in giving them the scriptures in English, and he declared that one of the primary objectives of the commission would be to distinguish "the pious observation of ceremonies... from the impious", a distinction for which few conservatives would have much sympathy. For all that, the make-up of the commission was overwhelmingly traditionalist in character, an ominous straw in the wind, which Cromwell seems not sufficiently to have recognized till too late. At the end of June he had two of the Commission's staunchest members arrested, including Richard Sampson, Bishop of Chichester, but Cromwell himself fell within a fortnight of their arrest, and with him, temporarily at least, the fortunes of the reform. His execution was the prelude to the burning of a clutch of his evangelical clients, Barnes among them.[3]

The impact of the fall of Cromwell in undermining the confidence of the reformed attack on traditional religion can be gauged from the change in tone between the first and second parts of Richard Taverner's postils on the epistles and Gospels, both published in 1540. Taverner was one of Cromwell's evangelical clients: in 1536 he had published a translation of the Confession of Augsburg, dedicated to Cromwell, and in 1539 he had produced a revision of the emphatically reforming Matthew Bible, which was to run to thirteen editions. In or before 1540 he was commissioned to edit a series of postils or homilies on the Epistles and Gospels at Mass for each Sunday, to be published alongside translations of the texts themselves. This book was clearly designed to help the clergy to fulfil the injunction laid on them by the bishops in 1538 to "read the Gospel and Epistle of that day out of the English Bible... and they that have such grace... make some declaration, either of the one, or of both."[4]

Taverner's text was emphatically a reforming one, substantial sections of which were to be adopted word for word into the

---

[3] S. Brigden, London and the Reformation, 1989, pp. 299–324: The Rationale of Ceremonial, ed. C. S. Cobb, 1910, pp. xlix–1; G. R. Elton, "Thomas Cromwell's Decline and Fall", in Studies in Tudor and Stuart Politics and Government I, 1974, pp. 215–20.

[4] The Epistles and Gospelles wyth a brief Postil upon the same from Advent tyll Lowe Sunday which is the Wynter parte, 1540, RSTC 2967; E. Cardwell (ed.), Postils on the Epistles and Gospels Compiled and Published by Richard Taverner in the Year 1540, 1841.

Elizabethan *Book of Homilies*. Not surprisingly, there is in it clear evidence of the hostility to traditional ceremonial which was so marked a feature of the reforming party up to 1540. The sermon for Rogation Day, for example, consisted in large part of an attack on traditional Rogationtide observance – "those uplandyshe processions and gangynges about, which be spent in ryotyng and in belychere", during which "the banners and badges of the crosse be so unreverently handled and abused, that it is merveyle God destroye us not all in one daye." With the characteristic insistence of his party that abuse does indeed take away use, Taverner advocated the abolition of the Rogationtide ceremonies, since "they are now growen into such abuse, that there be farre greater causes to take them awaye and utterly to abbrogate them with the other holydayes, than there were in tyme past for holy fathers to ordeyne them." It would be better to abolish the litanies and processions altogether and instead to "gather and assemble" the people in church to make their supplications, "than after suche an hethen and unruly fashion to mocke God and his holy signes".[5]

This was a tone of voice familiar since Latimer's Convocation sermon of 1536, but in 1540 it was all too likely to rebound on the head of those who used it. This was in part due to the fact that the summer of 1540 was one of drought, agues, and pestilence, prompting a royal command to bishops to procure general processions with the litany to be held weekly "in everie parish in the hole realme".[6] But political circumstances, as well as acts of God, made the tone and content of Taverner's postils particularly inopportune. The first part of Taverner's collection, though undated, clearly appeared before Cromwell's fall, and its preface has the confident tone of a man favoured by authority and speaking for it, even threatening clergy who did not make good use of the book with royal wrath and the ending of all hope of preferment. The preface to the second part of the collection, however, evidently published after the calamity, has a positively panic-stricken air about it, and contains a strident defence of Taverner's own orthodoxy and rectitude. Though there were many, he said, whose "carnal liberty" led them to wrest all they read to the "worste sense", Taverner insisted there was nothing in his book "contrary eyther to the kynges maiesties lawes and proclamations, or to the determination and sentence of the catholike churche". None could learn from it "to despise God's laws and mans, nor the decent and laudable ceremonies and rytes of the churche". To make assurance

---

[5] *Epistles and Gospelles wyth a brief Postil . . . from after Easter tyll Advent*, 1540, RSTC 2968, fol. xxxii.
[6] *Wriothesely's Chronicle*, I p. 123.

doubly sure, however, Taverner denounced the heresies of the Anabaptists, reminded the reader that even St Augustine had not been ashamed to write a book of retractations, and declared his own readiness in advance to "submyt my selfe to the iudgement of the church", and to withdraw anything found to be amiss. "Erre in my wrytynges I may, but an heretique I can be none."[7]

On 12 April 1540 Cromwell had brought to Parliament a plan to resolve the religious uncertainties which prevailed in the wake of the passing of the Six Articles. The King, he reported, was determined both to "set forth true doctrine" and to "separate pious from impious ceremonies, and teach the true use of them". He had therefore decided to establish a commission of bishops and theologians to determine these matters, meeting in two groups, one to consider doctrine, the other to determine the "rationale of ceremonies".[8] The best-known outcome of this determination, duly enshrined in an Act of Parliament on 6 June[9] was the so-called *King's Book*, a conservative reworking and rewriting of the *Bishops' Book*, which was to be issued in 1543. But the episcopal commission also produced a report on traditional ceremonies, which, for reasons now difficult to recover, was never published.

Though the committee appointed to draw up a *Rationale of Ceremonial* contained some committed reformers, such as Goodrich and Holgate, the group as a whole was predominantly traditionalist in character, and this bias is fully borne out by the text eventually produced. This was, in effect, a systematic and detailed defence of traditional ceremonial. It dealt specifically with the consecration of churches and cemeteries, with the ceremonies of baptism, this section representing a detailed exposition of the Sarum baptismal rite, the ceremonies of the pontifical, the solemn celebration of the daily hours in church, the ceremonies of the Mass, once again providing here a devotional exposition of the meaning of the various actions of the liturgy, the celebration of feast days and the observance of fasts, the use of clerical vestments and tonsure, of bells, and the bearing of lights at Candlemas, ashes on Ash Wednesday, palms on Palm Sunday, as well as all the traditional Holy Week ceremonies, in particular those surrounding creeping to the cross on Good Friday, and the Easter sepulchre. Rogationtide and other processions were defended, as was the blessing of holy bread and holy water.

---

[7] *Epistles and Gospelle . . . from Easter till Advent*, "the preface of Richarde Tavener to the reader, declaryng howe his boke is to be read" (unpaginated).

[8] *Rationale*, pp. xlviii–xlix.

[9] 32 Henry VIII cap. 36.

The text bears some signs of concession to evangelical sensibilities. Most notably, the exposition of the Mass says virtually nothing about the doctrine of the sacrifice of the Mass, passes over the prayers of oblation in the canon without mention, and describes the Mass as "a remembrance of the passion of Christ, whose most blessed body and blood is there consecrated". An insertion in the section on baptism, apparently in Gardiner's hand, permits the interrogatories to the godparents and their declaration of faith to be in English. In line with the Ten Articles and the *Bishops' Book*, the emphasis throughout is on the didactic and symbolic meaning of the ceremonies, rather than their apotropaic powers. In one of the two surviving manuscripts of the rationale, indeed, an additional section has been added denying any such powers, and ordering that since

> plenary remission of sin and everlasting life is purchased unto us by the merits of Christ's passion only, therefore all such exorcisms and prayers which attribute remission of sins, redemption, propitiation, salvation, or other like to any other creature than to Christ shall be from henceforth omitted and in no wise used.[10]

The same manuscript contains a final clause emphasizing that these rites and ceremonies, "with other good and laudable now used in the ministration of sacraments" were to continue to be used, unless otherwise ordered by "rulers and governors upon good considerations to take away, alter or change", provided that the people put no trust of salvation in them, but used them without superstition "taking them for good tokens and signs to put them in remembrance of things of higher perfection, and for a decent and convenient order to be had in the church".[11]

Nevertheless, the *Rationale of Ceremonial* represents a decisive reaffirmation of the value of the traditional ceremonies which had been under such intense evangelical pressure over the previous five or six years. It was, significantly, silent on the use of images, though a defence of the veiling of images in Lent presupposes their continued use in churches. In the more conservative of the two surviving recensions of the document this silence about images is rectified in a separate document on "the Right use of Images", in the same scribal hand as the main text of the *Rationale*, and bearing corrections and additions in a number of hands, including those of Cranmer, and, more extensively, of the leading conservative, Bishop Tunstall.[12] This little treatise stuck very close to

[10] *Rationale*, p. 42.
[11] Ibid., p. 43.
[12] Ibid., pp. 44–52.

the teaching of the Ten Articles on images, permitting their use as "unlearned men's books", emphasizing that the honour done to them in censing, kneeling, or offering before them, was done to God and the saints they represented, not to the images themselves. As in the Ten Articles, this caution as to the need for a right understanding of the practice of censing, kissing, and offering to images was of course a mandate for the continuation of these practices. The treatise also expanded the Ten Articles' denial that "any saint doth serve for one thing more than another, or is patron of the same". But it reaffirmed this point in the context of a vigorous defence of the legitimacy of praying to

> any saint particularly as our devotion doth serve us, so that it be done without any [vain] superstition, as in esteeming one [saint] to be patron for one thing and another saint for another [thing,] as St Appolonia for the toothache [S Blase for the throat] St Legeard for the eyes, St Loye for horses, St Anthony for... hogs, St Rooke for the plague, St Barbara for thunder and gun-shot, and such other.

Yet even in condemning such superstition, the document goes on to add that it might be practised innocently, by such as have "good minds, but they lacked right judgement".[13] In general, and as one would expect from Tunstall's involvement with the drafting, the treatise on images represents a benignly reforming attitude towards traditional ceremonies and devotional practices, and a marked retreat from the abolitionist approach favoured by Latimer, Shaxton and, almost certainly, Cranmer. When the revised version of the *Bishops' Book*, the so-called *King's Book*, appeared in May 1543 it was marked by a similar permissive attitude to ceremonies and images; its treatment of the second Commandment was dramatically more traditionalist than its equivalent in the *Bishops' Book*. It explicitly approved the setting up of images of Christ and the saints in churches, and explained the "reverent use" of them, including the use of incense before them, while attacking vows or pilgrimage to particular images.[14] It is probably no coincidence that the parish of Cranbrook in Kent defiantly set about erecting a new Rood-screen at about this time.[15] For the time being at least, conservatives like Tunstall, Gardiner, and Longland were in the ascendant. The dominant mood was reflected in Thomas Becon's *A Potation or Drinking for this Holy Time of Lent*, first issued in the spring of 1542, and reissued the following year. Becon's works

[13] Ibid., pp. 49–50.
[14] T. A. Lacey (ed.), *The King's Book or a Necessary Doctrine and Erudition for any Christian Man, 1543*, 1932, pp. 87–9.
[15] L&P, XVIII part 2, p. 315.

were a fair barometer of the state of "advanced" opinion at this time, but this pamphlet contained a detailed "rationale" of the ceremonies of Holy Week, particularly those of Palm Sunday, and displayed little discomfort with any of them though, significantly, he makes almost no mention of the place of the Blessed Sacrament in the Palm Sunday procession. There was certainly no hint in the work that reformers might seek the abolition or even the substantial modification of the traditional ceremonial.[16]

The resurgence of traditionalism did not, however, go wholly unchecked, for Henry, deprived of Cromwell's energy and drive, inevitably tended to turn to Cranmer in religious matters. He, for all his caution, did what he could to push the cause of reform forward. While the episcopal commissions were still at their work, in May 1541, the King issued another proclamation on Bible-reading, reiterating his concern that it should never provoke disputation or "exposition of mysteries" by laymen, yet lamenting that "divers and many towns and parishes" had wholly neglected to provide Bibles for the use of the people, and ordering a copy of the Great Bible to be placed in every parish church by the feast of All Saints.[17] This was followed by a proclamation late in July on the fraught question of abrogated feast days. Issued on the feast of Mary Magdalene, the proclamation restored her day and those of St Mark and St Luke, "considering that the same saints been often and many times mentioned in plain and manifest Scripture". But this concession to traditionalist feeling was offset by the abrogation of both feasts of the Holy Cross, which sometimes fell in and sometimes outside Westminster terms or harvest time, and were therefore still often observed. The fast on St Mark's day, part of the Rogation observances kept then, was abolished, as was the fast on the eve of St Laurence, which, despite the abrogation of the feast itself, had continued to be widely observed, not least and much to Cranmer's forcefully expressed dismay in Henry's own court. The proclamation went on to abolish the boy bishop and misrule ceremonies traditionally kept on the feasts of Sts Nicholas, Catherine, Clement, and the Holy Innocents, when

> children be strangely decked and appareled to counterfeit priests, bishops and women, and so be led with songs and dances from house to house, blessing the people and gathering of money, and boys do sing mass and preach in the pulpit, with such other

---

[16] *The early Works of Thomas Becon . . . Published in the Reign of Henry VIII*, ed. J. Ayre, Parker Society, 1843, pp. 85–121; D. S. Bailey, *Thomas Becon and the Reformation of the Church in England*, 1952, pp. 36–8, 41–3.

[17] TRP, I no. 200.

unfitting and inconvenient usages, rather to the derision than to any true glory of God, or honor of his saints.

From henceforth, all such superstitions were to be "left and clearly extinguished".[18]

The autumn of 1541 was to see one further blow to traditional religion. On his progress into Yorkshire Henry evidently saw widespread evidence of the retention of abrogated customs and devotions. The staunch traditionalism of Bishop Longland of Lincoln seems to have shielded his diocese from most of the winds of change, and even the shrine of St Hugh in Lincoln Cathedral had not been demolished until 1540. Traditionalist feeling was particularly strong in connection with the cult of the saints, and evidently many "abused" images and shrines still stood, in defiance of Henry's Injunctions and proclamations. Cranmer himself was currently locked in controversy with traditionalist members of the Canterbury chapter on this very issue, and one of them, Robert Serles, a zealous defender of images, chose this inauspicious moment to appeal over Cranmer's head to the King. He made his way north into Yorkshire, and on 19 September appeared before the King and the Privy Council at Hull, where the whole issue of images was discussed. Serles had disastrously misjudged his moment, and, despite the overwhelmingly conservative cast of the Councillors accompanying the King, was despatched south with a sealed letter to Cranmer, which ordered the Archbishop to put him under arrest.[19] His intervention evidently had the effect of galvanizing Henry into action, but not at all as Serles had hoped, and at a further meeting of the Privy Council at Hull on 22 September, the King issued a letter directed, through Cranmer, to the bishops, expressing his displeasure that "our good intent and purpose notwithstanding, the shrines, coverings of shrines, and monuments of those things do yet remain in sundry places of this realm . . . the same being means to allure our subjects to their former hypocrisy and superstition." The bishops were therefore to begin with their cathedrals and remove from them any "shrine, covering of shrine, table, monument of miracles, or other pilgrimages", and then to see that the clergy did likewise in the parishes.[20] This letter elicited an interesting complaint from John Bird, first bishop of the new diocese of Chester, who explained that in his backward region "popish idolatry is like the longer to continue by reason that divers colleges and places, claiming to be exempt from the bishop, have . . . taken down the idols and images accustomed to be

[18] TRP, I no. 203.

[19] Sir William Dugdale, *Monasticon Anglicanum*, ed. J. Caley, H. Ellis, and B. Bandinel, 1830, VI part III, p. 1286; J. Ridley, *Thomas Cranmer*, 1962, pp. 230–2.

[20] VAI, II pp. 67–9; L&P, XVI nos 1192, 1258.

worshipped, but keep them and suffer the ignorant people to offer as before."[21]

Bird was no doubt right in claiming that the people of Chester diocese, "for lack of doctrine and preaching" were "much behind the King's subjects in the South", but the resistance to change which he found there was sufficiently widespread for the matter to be taken up in Convocation in February 1542, probably at Cranmer's instigation. Notoriously, the main issue in this session of Convocation was the attempt by Gardiner and his supporters to revise the text of the Great Bible. Cranmer fended off this attack and struck back by promoting a debate on the many places in the realm where, contrary to the Injunctions, lights and candlesticks still stood before images, which were themselves still decked with silken coats and other ornaments. There were also complaints about the many breviaries, missals, and other liturgical books which remained unreformed, containing still undefaced the titles of the Pope and the services for the feasts of Thomas Becket. The clergy must be induced to erase these superstitions and to apply themselves to instructing their flocks in the Creed, the Lord's Prayer, and the Ten Commandments in English. Cranmer was eventually to gain his point, and in the following year it was agreed to make representations to the King to have all church books examined and purged of "all manner of mention of the bishop of Rome's name, from all apocrypha, feigned legends, superstitious orations, collects, versicles and responses" and that "the names and memories of all saints, which be not mentioned in the Scripture, or authentical doctors, should be abolished and put out of the same calendars, and that the service should be made out of the scriptures and other authentic doctors."[22] This last was a proposal which, if carried out, would have swept away not merely the externals of the cult of the saints, but much of the fabric of the medieval liturgy. A committee led by Goodrich of Ely and Salcot of Salisbury, both reformers, was appointed for this purpose, though inevitably, as the pace of traditionalist recovery mounted, its deliberations bore no fruit.[23]

In any case, 1543 was to bring its own catastrophic set-back for the cause of reform, the notorious Act, passed on 10 May, "for the advancement of true religion".[24] This measure, masterminded by Gardiner, blamed the "ignorance, fond opinions, errors and blindness" of many of the King's subjects, especially "the youth", on

[21] L&P, XVI no. 1377.

[22] Wilkins, Concilia, III pp. 861–3.

[23] F. Procter and W. H. Frere, A New History of the Book of Common Prayer, 1925, pp. 30–1.

[24] 34 & 35 Henry VIII cap. 1; see the discussion in S. E. Lehmberg, The Later Parliaments of Henry VIII, 1977, pp. 186–8.

the spread of heretical preaching, argument, and disputations, but especially on books, ballads, plays, and songs. Severe penalties were therefore to be imposed on those who had or kept any books containing doctrines contrary to those authorized since 1540. The Act targeted unauthorized versions of the scriptures, in particular Tyndale's New Testament, and it forbade altogether the reading of scripture in private or in public by "women . . . artificers, prentices, journeymen, serving men of the degrees of yeomen or under, husbandmen or labourers", though noble and gentlewomen might read the Bible in private. Persistent clerical offenders against this Act might be burned, laymen were subject to forfeiture of goods and perpetual imprisonment. The Act reaffirmed the Act of Six Articles, and provided for proceedings against offenders by a panel consisting of the bishop of the diocese sitting with two Justices of the Peace.

The battle raging in Convocation and the Parliament house was a reflection of the one being waged every bit as bitterly in the localities. Serles's abortive attempt to enlist the King's support for the traditionalist cause was not simply a reflection of Cranmer's warfare with the prebendaries of his cathedral. It reflected the open warfare which had been dividing parishes all over east Kent throughout the late 1530s, and which was to continue throughout the rest of the reign. The combined influence in the county of Cromwell and of Cranmer as diocesan had secured the promotion and protection of radical preachers and the appointment of Protestants to key positions. Kent, with an established Lollard tradition in many parishes, was destined to have more than its fair share of Protestants. Despite the Act of Six Articles, Cranmer continued this policy into the 1540s. He had made his brother Edmund Archdeacon of Canterbury and appointed as his own Commisary his niece's husband, Christopher Nevinson, an advanced Protestant who used his position to the full to shatter the local framework of traditional religion. The new cathedral foundation at Canterbury provided another institutional foothold for reform, with implications for the diocese as a whole, and although the majority of the prebendaries there were strong traditionalists, Cranmer enlisted the King's support in appointing a small group of reformers, including Nicholas Ridley. Three of the six preachers at the cathedral were strong Protestants – John Scory, Michael Drumme, and Laurence Ridley, Nicholas's cousin.[25]

In the spring of 1543 a consortium of influential Kentish gentry and the conservative prebendaries at Canterbury sought to bring

[25] Ridley, Cranmer, pp. 227ff; P. Clark, English Provincial Society from the Reformation to the Revolution, 1977, pp. 60ff; Michael L. Zell, "The Prebendaries Plot of 1543: a reconsideration", Journal of Ecclesiastical History, XXVII, 1976, pp. 241–53.

about Cranmer's downfall as a heretic and a supporter of heretics.
Notoriously, the plot backfired. Henry placed Cranmer himself in
charge of the enquiry which ensued, with the consequent rout of
his enemies. Ever meticulous, Cranmer collected a vast quantity of
testimony on the struggles between radicals and traditionalists in
the diocese, including the material prepared by his enemies for
use against himself, and the dossier he compiled has survived in
Parker's library at Corpus Christi College, Cambridge. It provides
a unique window into the parochial divisions triggered by the
recent religious innovations. The situation in Kent was hardly
typical, for in few dioceses was the cause of reform so consistently
backed by the bishop and his officials, and few counties had so
many itinerant radical preachers. The dossier has therefore generally
been read for the light it throws on Protestant radicalism in Kent,
and to chart the advance of Protestantism in Kentish parishes.
However, when all due allowance has been made for the polemical
intentions of those who collected much of the material, it is just as
remarkable for the light it throws on the strength and character of
traditionalist beliefs under pressure. The struggle between the old
and the new ways was more intense and more existential than in
most other parts of England, but the issues involved were not in
essence different from those raised by the progress of reform, or the
lack of it, in parishes up and down the country.[26]

Cranmer's protégés distinguished themselves precisely in their
attacks on parochial religion. Though their preaching naturally
included expositions of the Protestant doctrines of justification by
faith or the non-sacrificial nature of the Mass,[27] the bulk of the
material in Cranmer's dossier concerns religious practice rather than
doctrinal abstractions. Nevinson, as the archbishop's commisary,
was a key figure in diocesan visitation, and he used the platform
thus provided to condemn and suppress popular usages. He forbade
the distribution of sacramentals such as holy water and Candlemas
candles to the people, tried to prevent blessed candles being placed
in the hands of the dying, limited outdoor processions, attacked
auricular confession, and sought to prevent absolution being given
to those who could recite their Pater and Ave only in Latin. He
used the 1538 Injunctions as the basis for a systematic campaign to

---

[26] In what follows, I have followed the modernized spelling of the very full calendar of
Corpus Christi MS 128 contained in volume XVIII part 2 no. 546 of L&P Henry VIII, but I
have collated all the material with the manuscript; when supplying material not given in the
calendar I have followed the spelling in the manuscript. Page references, unless otherwise
stated, are to the calendar.

[27] L&P, XVIII part 2, pp. 304–5.

remove images wherever he could. He was warmly supported by the archbishop's brother, Archdeacon Cranmer, who himself removed the lights and robes adorning a Rood in St Andrew's, Canterbury, and then "did violently break the arms and legs of the rood".[28] The lead thus given was taken up by other radical clergy. John Bland, vicar of Adisham from 1541, travelled well beyond his parish, preaching a series of radical sermons at Faversham and leading a destructive onslaught on the imagery in the church at Ospringe. Richard Turner, curate at Chartham, refused to use holy water, would give his parishioners no blessed candles, and when he baptized babies omitted the prescribed anointings. Chartham was unlucky with its priests, another of whom, James Newnham, would not use the Virgin's name in the "Confiteor", refused to offer incense or other honours to the Crucifix, and led a series of iconoclastic attacks on churches in Canterbury and the surrounding villages, personally destroying the images of the Virgin and the Apostles from Northgate parish church and casting the rosary beads of the parson of Pevyngton into the fire. When the owner protested he mockingly paid him a penny compensation. In his own parish he removed an image of the Blessed Virgin, though, as indignant parishioners complained, it had never been abused with offerings, "except candles at the purification of women".[29]

It is clear that the radicalism of the clergy at Chartham, as elsewhere, did not by any means carry the whole parish with them. Bland was one of the best-known preachers of Protestantism, but at the accession of Mary his parish revolted against his teaching, led by members of the Austen family who, as churchwardens, sworn men, and parish "bosholder" or constables, dominated parish life. They demanded compensation from Bland for the iconoclasm he had carried out and which would now have to be put right, and denounced him as a heretic "and hast taught us nothing but heresy". Bland had a following in the parish, but their time was past and they were outnumbered. Traditional religious practice rapidly re-established itself in the parish.[30] The ferocity of feeling at Adisham in 1553 is eloquent testimony to the frustrations built up in a traditionalist community dominated in the 1540s by a radical minority with the ear and backing of the archbishop and the Crown. Similarly, while it is true, as Peter Clark has observed, that Richard Turner's Protestant sermons attracted large

[28] Ibid., pp. 291, 301, 313.
[29] Ibid., p. 302.
[30] Foxe, *Acts and Monuments*, VII pp. 287–91; *Archdeacon Harpsfield's Visitation 1557*, ed. L. E. Whatmore, Catholic Record Society, XLV–XLVI, 1950–1, I p. 1.

audiences at Chartham, many of those who came were scandalized by what they heard and saw. The churchwardens denounced what they considered the outrageous behaviour of their clergy to the commissary, who, of course, took no action.[31] Some Chartham parishioners grumbled that it would become the archbishop to preach like the clergy of "the old fashion", exchanged stories of miraculous images with conservative clergy from other parishes, offered candles to the Rood at Candlemas, since candles before other images were now forbidden, and withheld their tithes. When, in defiance of the King's letter from Hull, a pilgrimage image of St Margaret was set up again by the vicar of Milton, Cranmer made a note to discover "how many of Chartham were of counsel therof".[32]

Adisham and Chartham were not the only parishes where the clergy outstripped the laity in radicalism. The parson of Lenham in the late 1530s was Thomas Dawby, a convinced Protestant who vigorously encouraged Bible-reading among the laity, attacked clerical celibacy, and ridiculed traditional reverence for the Blessed Virgin. He removed eight images from the church which, the parishioners complained, "never were abused by any pilgrimage", and induced his successor at Lenham to steal the key of the church from the sexton's house "and take down one image more of Our Lady of Pity, and break her in pieces; which is the fairest image in the church and never abused". He tried unsuccessfully to persuade the parish to make a clean sweep of all the images in church, "caused divers to break their fast that were disposed to keep it" on the eves of feast days, refused to sing the litany of the saints, or to recite a Latin Gospel or sprinkle holy water during the rogation processions. He would not say the "De Profundis" for dead parishioners, and harassed lay people who used primers or breviaries to say the Office. More dangerously for himself, he "asked an honest man why he made reverence when he came before the sacrament". His attacks on images in 1542 were rebutted by laymen who pointed out that the images stood still at Cranbrook, where a "goodly roodloft" was even then being built, and where some of the gentry who supported the old ways were "of the King's Council". Dawby had no regard for such "Pope-holy knaves", and declared that he looked forward to the day when all such were swept away and no candles would burn even before the sepulchre. Conservative preaching at Lenham by Robert Serles gained the approval of many but provoked a pulpit controversy, "and many

---

[31] L&P, XVIII part 2, pp. 301–2, 313.
[32] Ibid., p. 303.

words were multiplied and great variance among the people."[33] In general, the impression left by the dossier is that radical priests more often than not found themselves at variance with their parishioners, though some do seem to have carried large numbers of the community with them. It was reported in September 1543 that at Pluckley, where the priest refused to provide holy water "accordynge to the laudable customs of the churche", omitted the litany of the saints in procession, and rebuked parishioners who used traditional forms of prayer for the dead, "the great part of his parish do not receive holy bread", a reliable indicator of reformed opinions.[34]

Conversely, sturdily conservative clergy might find themselves afflicted with radicals in the congregation. The Canterbury parish of All Saints Northgate had a nest of radical Protestants in it, in particular several generations of the Toftes family, who harboured the notorious Joan Boucher, and provided a base for preaching and iconoclastic sorties by radical clergy from elsewhere in the diocese. The Toftes and their associates had down most of the images in the church, taking the statue of the Virgin and its tabernacle home to burn, and led loud Bible-reading sessions during services in the church. Margaret Toftes the younger, a termagant who refused to creep to the cross on Good Friday and wanted to burn the church down round the "idols" within it, told the parish clerk that "her daughter could piss as good holy water as the priest could make any." Her mother-in-law, Margaret Toftes the elder, when attacked by traditionalists, invoked the support of Commisary Nevinson and predicted that "When my Lord of Canterbury's Grace comethe down to Canterbury, we trust to have a day against you."[35]

On the basis of the many references to it in Cranmer's dossier, it would be easy to categorize Northgate as a radical parish, but there is more than a hint of beleaguerment in Margaret Toftes's threat. The priest of Northgate, William Kempe, was a dyed-in-the-wool traditionalist, who omitted to read the royal Injunctions to the parish, discouraged Bible-reading, and ignored the command of the Ten Articles to declare the "right use" of sacramentals like holy water, holy bread, holy candles, ashes, and palms, "for lack whereof the most part of the parish be as ignorant in such things as ever they were, and many of them do abuse holy water: insomuch that againste tempests of thunder and lightning many run to the

---

[33] Ibid., pp. 315–16.
[34] Ibid., pp. 299, 306–7: Corpus Christi MS 128 p. 50 (16v).
[35] L&P, XVIII part 2, p. 307.

church for holy water to cast about their houses to drive away ill
spirits and devils, notwithstanding his Majesty's proclamations in
the same." Kempe had the support of those in his parish who
thought that "the doctrine that was taught 20 or 30 years ago was
as good as the doctrine that is set forth these days." The parish as a
whole was, therefore, according to Cranmer's informants, "blind
and ignorant". Paradoxically, Cranmer notes that the witnesses to
this sad state of affairs were "the parish". He is clearly using the
notion of the parish here in two quite different senses: censoriously
about the blind and ignorant majority, untouched by reform and of
a mind with their priest, and approvingly to mean the influential
Protestant minority who, by using his and Nevinson's authority,
had gained the whip hand.[36]

Conflict between traditionalists and reformers in Kent closely
reflected the concerns evident in the Convocation debates of 1542,
the Act for the Advancement of True Religion, and the conservative reworking of the *King's Book*. Kentish clergy and conservative
Kentish magistrates were certainly still active in discouraging Bible-
reading, as the "Kentish Justice" had been to Cranmer's dismay in
1537, and the Act of 1543 enormously strengthened their hand. But
it is clear that many of the traditionalist positions brought them
dangerously near the wrong side of the law, even in the triumphant
conservatism of 1542 and 1543. Some had failed to delete the
Pope's name and titles from their liturgical books. Many of them
continued to encourage the observance of abrogated feasts and fasts,
and rebuked parishioners for taking advantage of royal dispensations to eat eggs and cheese in Lent. Clement Norton, vicar of
Faversham, told his parish that if the king were to be asked he
would say that he had intended such dispensations only for the sick.
Norton was an incorrigible traditionalist who continually sailed
close to the wind. Despite the royal demotion of church dedication
days, the suppression of relics and of papal indulgences, he continued to insist that "the crysom cloth with a bell . . . be hanged out
upon the Dedication day . . . to put the people in remembrance of
pardon which they should have that time."[37] Many clergy seem to
have resisted the royal injunction to teach the people the Pater,
Ave, and Creed in English; the parson of Ripple told his people "I
am commanded to show you the paternoster in English: you may
do as you will in learning of it, but it is against my opinion. For I
liken the paternoster in English to the hard shell of a nut and the
paternoster in Latin to the sweet kernel."[38]

[36] Ibid., pp. 300, 309.
[37] Ibid., pp. 293–4, 299, 300–1.
[38] Ibid., p. 296; by contrast, Nevinson was instructing the clergy to refuse absolution to
any who came to confess unable to say their Paternoster and Creed in English.

One of the commonest accusations against the conservative clergy in Cranmer's dossier is the failure to "declare the good use of the ceremonies" such as the blessing of holy water, the distribution of ashes, palms, or blessed candles, or the Holy Week creeping to the cross. Omission of the declaration commanded by the Ten Articles and reiterated even in the *King's Book* was clearly very widespread. Edmund Shether, one of the six preachers, gleefully told a Sandwich congregation in June 1542 that "no man nowadays sayeth that holy water signifieth of Christ's blood. O these are very glorious words; but it is not fit, good christians, that such new fangles and phantasies should be brought into the Church of God."[39] What was at stake was not a simple matter of newfangled ways, nor obedience to the Ten Articles. Nevinson, Scory, and the reformed party were trying to stamp out the apotropaic use of sacramentals, and the declaration of the ceremonies, by substituting a merely symbolic or didactic explanation of their use, was a means of obscuring or denying their power. In conducting visitations Nevinson consistently tried to persuade curates into refusing to allow their people to take home holy water and blessed candles. Clergy who complied thereby denied their parishioners a resource against storm, sickness, demons, and sudden death. In contrast, clergy who omitted the declaration endorsed the traditional use; many actively encouraged it, and Clement Norton even prescribed the drinking of holy water as a specific against piles.[40]

But perhaps the most significant issue in the Kentish parishes was the place of images in the churches. This was a question increasingly close to the archbishop's own heart. As his annotations to the *Bishops' Book* show, he was uneasy even about the didactic use of imagery as "laymen's books", and in the early 1540s he used the Injunctions of 1538, and the subsequent royal letter from Hull, as an excuse to remove all images, and not simply those "abused" by pilgrimage and offerings. Thus he had the image of Christ over the "morrow-Mass" altar in Christ Church taken down, though no offerings had ever been made to it. Protestant radicals in the diocese were now openly campaigning against the liturgical use of images, as in the creeping to the cross or the Palm Sunday ceremonies. Before long Cranmer himself would openly embrace their opinion.[41] Meanwhile, the battle to retain or to remove images in the parishes raged. Accusations flooded in of "abused" images retained or restored.

[39] Ibid., pp. 294, 295, 296, 299, 301, 305.
[40] Ibid., pp. 291, 293, 296, 308.
[41] See below, pp. 443–4.

At Eastwell (near Ashford) there was an image of Our Lady still standing "whereunto was continual oblation in times past of money; which image had also a coat fixed with pence".[42] The parson of Milton by Canterbury removed an image of St Margaret from his church because there had been a "common pilgrimage" to it. On St Margaret's day 1542(?) John Cros, former cellarer of Christ Church, came to the church "and did set the same image again with a garland of flowers on the head of it, and did strowe the church and said mass there". The parish priest of Sholden set up again four "abused" images. But such restorations were by no means always the work of conservative clergy. When the priest and churchwardens at North Mongeham set about defacing the images in accordance with what they took to be royal command, they were stopped by another parishioner, Thomas Bleane, who bade them let well alone "saying that such ways should continue but a while, and that they should see shortly". Bleane evidently had his way, at least within his own immediate sphere of influence, since Cranmer's dossier notes that "an image with three crowns standeth near unto his own seat till this day."[43]

In 1541 John Tofer, the absentee parish priest of St George's, Canterbury, prompted by Nevinson, sent a letter from London to his curate and the churchwardens, instructing them to remove the patronal image of St George. They seem to have delayed doing so, and Tofer himself, though no radical, supervised the removal on his return to Canterbury. Shortly afterwards the curate and churchwardens were summoned before Commisary Nevinson, asked if the image had been "cut in pieces", and were treated to a lecture to the effect that "it is not only the King's majesty's pleasure to have such images abused to be pulled down, but also to be disfigured, and nothing of such images to remain, with the tabernacle." The churchwardens protested, one of them, Gregory Rande, saying that he thought it was not the King's wish that images "where no common offering was" should be removed, and this image should be left "being patron of England and the church dedicate in the name of the holy saint". Nevinson retorted "Why not . . . as well as the crucifix? We have no patron but Christ," at which Rande and his colleagues gave up in disgust: "If you pull down the Crucifix, then pull down all." Nevinson made sure that it was done, sending his summoner to check, but clearly the removal of the image left a sense of outrage and of a local community's integrity violated. The parson, his curate, the churchwardens, and

[42] L&P, XVIII part 2, p. 296.
[43] Ibid., p. 299.

many senior laity subsequently testified against Nevinson's high-handed action, clearly rejected any notion that their patronal image was abused, and thought that the destruction had no excuse except that "he was borne in procession on St George's day in the honour of God and the King, with Mr Mayor, the aldermen, their wives, with all the commons of the same going in procession."[44] There were similar incidents elsewhere in the county, for example, at Elmstead, where the parishioners petitioned Cranmer to replace their patronal image of St James "in his tabernacle at the high altar's end" where he had stood "time out of mind".[45]

An even more striking example of the rallying of a local community in defence of shared sanctities occurred at Chilham, where the vicar, Dr John Willoughby, was a staunch defender of the old ways and a devout believer in pilgrimage. He was rumoured to have hidden one such miraculous image, Our Lady of Courtship Street, in his house. He was also deeply implicated in the prebendaries' plot. His church had been given the empty covering of the Canterbury shrine of St Augustine at the time of the suppression. This was precisely the sort of "monument of superstition" aimed at in the King's letter from Hull, and attracted Nevinson's personal attention to the parish. In addition to the empty shrine, Chilham church had a Rood which before the Injunctions of 1538 had borne shoes of silver, a sure indicator of votive offerings. The shoes were removed, but the Rood remained, and, given Willoughby's known views on the apotropaic powers of particular images, this was sufficient to warrant intervention. In the summer of 1543 Nevinson demanded the Rood's destruction, sending a written order to the vicar. Willoughby received the order on a Saturday, but kept it overnight, then when the parish assembled on the Sunday morning showed it to "Master Pettet, Wylyam Amys, goodman Macstede, holde fader Baker, and alle the holle parysch". The parish leaders invoked the permissive passage on images in the King's Book, saying that it contradicted Nevinson's policy "except where oblations were made". They therefore had the relevant section of the King's Book read aloud, as a counterweight to Nevinson's order, "and then all sayde ther scholde none be pollyd downe ther". The church was locked up to prevent action by Nevinson's officers. Ultimately they sought the backing of one of the most influential of the local conservative Justices of the Peace, and a prime mover behind the plot against Cranmer, Walter Moyle, who asked "wherever the wor one oblacion ther to or no". On being told that there were

---

[44] Ibid., p. 309.
[45] Ibid., p. 317.

none, "then sayde Master Moyle 'Then I warrant yow let him
stonde.'"[46]

The issues which surfaced in these struggles in Kent were
representative, though no doubt more pointed and more fraught
than elsewhere, since the archbishop's backing gave evangelicals an
advantage which was rarely theirs in other dioceses. But Cranmer's
support could only go so far, for the reformers were in fact on very
thin ice. To Protestants like Ridley, the Kentish struggles were over
"beggarly ceremonies". His opponents defended, in the words of
the Ten Articles and the *King's Book*, "*laudable* ceremonies".[47]
Between the two emphases there was not a question of semantics,
but a wholly different understanding of religion. For the moment,
it was the conservative understanding which was in the ascendant.

That conservative ascendancy was made manifest in the publication of *A Necessary Doctrine and Erudition for any Christian Man*, the
so-called *King's Book*. Ostensibly a straightforward revision of
the *Bishops' Book* of 1537 it was in fact, in theological terms,
effectively a new work, and in almost every respect emphatically
more traditionalist than its predecessor. The differences are most
obvious in the sections on images and the seven sacraments. The
sacramental teaching of the *King's Book* stressed the value of all
seven sacraments, made more of the role of the priest, taught the
reality of minor orders, and devoted its longest section to the
sacrament of the altar, the sacrament treated most cursorily in
the *Bishops' Book*. In its treatment of the Second Commandment,
the *Bishops' Book* had uncompromisingly declared that

> we be utterly forbidden to make or have any similitude or image,
> to the intent to bow down to it, or worship it. And therefore we
> think it convenient, that all bishops and preachers shall instruct
> and teach the people . . . that God in his substance cannot by any
> similitude or image be represented or expressed.

In the *King's Book* this passage becomes:

> We be not forbidden to make or to have similitudes or images,
> but only we be forbidden to make or to have them to the intent
> to do godly honour unto them . . . And therefore, although
> images of Christ and his saints be the works of men's hands
> only, yet they be not so prohibited but that they may be had and
> set up both in churches and other places.[48]

[46] Ibid., pp. 303, 319.
[47] Ibid., pp. 301, 306.
[48] For a discussion of these issues see M. Aston, *England's Iconoclasts*, 1988, pp. 239–43.
The *King's Book* will be discussed in detail in a forthcoming Cambridge PhD dissertation by
Colin Armstrong.

Only in its treatment of prayer for the dead was the *King's Book* significantly more radical than the *Bishops' Book*. While still permitting prayers on behalf of the dead, the *King's Book* was far more emphatic in its denial of any knowledge of the state of the departed, of the value of prayers and Masses for a single departed soul as opposed to the "universal congregation of Christian people". It denounced in much stronger terms than before the abuses of the doctrine of Purgatory and the practices it had given rise to.[49]

Despite that significant shift of emphasis, traditionalists saw in the *King's Book* a vindication of their position, even on the issue of prayers for the dead, and in its aftermath testators could confidently ask for "solempne masses of Requiem, dirige, and other orisons and prayer according to the Auncient custome of the Churche of Englande".[50] In March 1544 William Stapleton of Wighill, a member of a conservative family deeply implicated in the Pilgrimage of Grace, made a will "beseching the holie churche to pray for me as God hath appointed it aftre the maner as it is sett forthe by the Kinges Booke to Godes glory".[51]

Cranmer felt to the full the adverse tide which had set against him, and he was not the man willingly to fall foul of the law, yet he pressed on in the direction of reform. His English translation of the litany for use as a form of intercession on Wednesdays and Fridays, first used in 1544, drastically reduced the place of the saints, compressing what had once been the major part of the litany into a mere three petitions. In the following October he reported that he was at work on a series of translations of the processional and the canticles used in Divine Office, as well as Mass texts like the Creed and the Gloria. All of this had the backing of the King and was not in itself necessarily out of harmony with conservative reforming measures as embodied in the *King's Book*.[52] But it is clear nonetheless that Cranmer shared the convictions of many of his less prudent protégés. During the Kentish disturbances several of them had attacked not only the veneration of images, but related Holy Week ceremonies such as the Palm Sunday procession and the Good Friday creeping to the cross. By January 1546 Cranmer was prepared to try to mobilize the King against even these hitherto sacrosanct ceremonies, which the whole policy of declaration existed to regulate. Taking advantage of Gardiner's absence on an embassy in Brussels, he persuaded the King of the evils of many such observances, notably the tolling of the "deadbell" on All Saints' night (the eve of All Souls), the covering and uncovering of

[49] *The King's Book*, pp. 163–4.
[50] *The Visitation of Suffolke*, ed. J. Jackson Howard, 1866, I p. 177.
[51] *North Country Wills*, Surtees Society, CXVI, 1908, CXXI, 1912, I p. 194.
[52] Cranmer, *Remains*, p. 412.

images in Lent, the raising of the veil before the Rood on Palm Sunday at the singing of "Ave Rex Noster", and the ceremony of creeping to the cross. Most of these provisions affected the cult of images, but the tolling of the All Souls' bell was attacked not merely because it was an expression of traditional belief in Purgatory, but of belief in the apotropaic power of sacramentals, for the tolling of a consecrated bell was held to rout the demons and evil spirits loose on that night. Cranmer and his advisers expected trouble in particular from the abolition of creeping to the cross, since "it shall seem to many that be ignorant, that the honour of Christ is taken away." In the draft letter Cranmer prepared for Henry to sign he took pains to make this particular measure seem to be the King's initiative, not his, making the king write "forasmuch as you make no mention of creeping to the cross, which is a greater abuse than any of the other".[53] In the event, however, nothing came of these somewhat convoluted moves. Gardiner warned Henry of the likely diplomatic fallout from overtly reforming measures in England, and the King let the matter drop.[54]

Despite Cranmer's failure to secure the abolition of these ceremonies, the cause of reform was by no means wholly in eclipse in Henry's last years. The publication on 29 May 1545 of an official primer in English, carrying the King's authorization "and none other to be used throughout all his dominions" was a notable blow at one of the strongholds of traditional religion. Ever since the mid-1530s Cranmer and his associates had seen the potential of the primers as a means of carrying Protestant convictions to the widest possible audience of devout lay people, catching them off-guard as it were, on their knees. Marshall's *Goodly Primer* of 1535 was the most dramatic early example, but others had followed. John Hilsey's posthumously published *Manual of Prayers or the Primer* of 1539, produced "by the commandment of the right honourable Lord Thomas Crumwell" was less iconoclastic than Marshall's, but showed if anything more clearly the desire of the reformed party to harness the traditional materials of the primer to a reformed message. Hilsey's book contained many of the traditional materials, and was less hostile than Marshall to prayers for the dead and honour to the saints. Nevertheless Hilsey drastically reworked many of the traditional elements. He shortened and altered the "Dirige", including introductions to the Psalms which emphasized their value as prayers for the living rather than the dead, eliminated

---

[53] Ibid., pp. 414–15.
[54] Ridley, *Cranmer*, pp. 250–1.

six of the nine readings from Job, substituting three passages from St Augustine attacking traditional funeral customs and folk beliefs about the spirits of the dead, and three New Testament passages, from I Corinthians 15 and I Thessalonians 4. Hilsey included the "Fifteen Oes", but prefaced them with a denunciation of the traditional rubrics, "goodly printed prefaces, promisinge to the sayers thcrof many thinges both folyshe and false". And Hilsey's book contained a good deal of didactic material – short passages scattered through the book as prefaces, as well as a long treatise on the presence of Christ in the Sacrament, an exposition of the Ten Commandments, and a series of passages illustrating the duties of the various estates of life.[55]

Most primers were the product not of government commission but of free enterprise, and most remained largely traditional in character, though English became the dominant language, Latin being relegated to the margins. Yet from the late 1530s even primers produced in traditional style show signs of adaptation to reformed emphases, most obviously in the exclusion of Becket and papal saints from the calendar and the conformity of the calendar in general to the laws abrogating feasts and fasts. The inclusion in many otherwise traditional primers of the prayer "Hail Holy King, father of Mercy", a Protestant adaptation of the ancient Marian prayer "Salve Regina, Mater Misericordiae", is another case in point.[56] The issuing of patents and privileges to printers in order to secure some sort of conformity, and a proclamation of 1538 banning the import of religious books, did something to regulate the character of the commercially produced primers. As we have seen, official forms of bidding the bedes, translations of the Epistles and Gospels, and other reformed measures were reflected in these semi-official primers. But it was only a matter of time before the Tudor state attempted a stricter regulation of this vast and potentially influential area of religious publishing, and the so-called King's Primer published by Richard Grafton on 29 May 1545 was the result.[57]

[55] The manual of prayers, or the prymer in Englysh & Laten . . . Set forth by Jhon by Goddes grace, at the Kynges callyng, bysshoppe of Rochester at the commaundemente of Thomas Crumwell, Wayland 1539, RSTC 16009, Hoskins no. 143. Hilsey's Manual was reprinted in E. Burton (ed.), Three Primers, 1834, pp. 305–436. There is a very detailed list of the contents in Hoskins, pp. 225–33. For a good discussion of the character of the book see H. White Tudor Books of Private Devotion, 1951, pp. 103–18; C. Butterworth, English Primers, 1953, pp. 181–94.

[56] It appears to have been first printed in 1538; see Hoskins, p. 176.

[57] The Primer, in Englishe and Latyn, set foorth by the Kynges maiestie and his Clergie to be taught, learned and read: and none other to be vsed thoroughout all his dominions, London, 1545: RSTC 16034–40, Hoskins nos. 174–9. I have used the copy in Magdalene College Old Library, which does not appear to be in STC.

The *King's Primer* had been preceded by a proclamation, on 6 May, emphasizing the need for a book which would provide the basic texts for the programme of lay religious education in English required by the Injunctions of 1536 and 1538. It also deplored the "almoost innumerable sortes" of primers in circulation, "whiche minister occasion of contencions & vaine disputations, rather than to edifye". There was now to be "one uniforme ordre of al suche bokes throughout our dominions", and booksellers, readers, schoolmasters, and teachers of young children were forbidden to "bye, sell, occupie, use, nor teach prively or apartly" any other primer.[58] The *Primer* itself carried a further preface, ostensibly by Henry, stressing the need for the people to understand the prayers they used, and relating the publication of the *Primer* to the other reform measures of the reign.

In many ways the *King's Primer* looks a very traditional book. It begins, as usual, with the calendar and then the basic materials of lay religious instruction, English versions of the Lord's Prayer, Hail Mary, Creed, Commandments, and graces before and after meals. There follow the Little Hours from matins to compline, the seven penitential Psalms, the litany and suffrages, the "Dirige", the Commendations, Psalms of the Passion, the Passion narrative from St John, a set of "Praiers of the Passion", and finally a lengthy and rather heterogeneous mixture of prayers. It is the calendar which alerts one to the reformed character of the book, for it jettisons most of the saints normally commemorated. Even Marshall's *Goodly Primer* had preserved the traditional calendar more or less intact, but where Marshall has twenty-seven feast days in March, the *King's Primer* has only four. A similar reforming spirit appears elsewhere. The "Dirige" looks traditional, but has in fact been cut down to a third of its length, Psalms of praise and thanksgiving being retained, Psalms of mourning, complaint, and supplication being excluded. Even the "De Profundis" Psalm, the prayer most closely associated with the rites of the dead in Catholic piety, has been omitted. Though the "Dirige" still contained prayers of intercession on behalf of the dead, the doctrinal implications of all this are obvious. In the rest of the book a consistently reforming emphasis is evident. Prayers and references to the Virgin were replaced with verses of scripture such as the Beatitudes. The litany included in the *Primer* is the English one published the previous year by Cranmer. And of course the book contains none of the traditional prayers to the Virgin, the saints or, perhaps most sig-

[58] Ibid., fols ci–cii.

nificantly of all, to the Blessed Sacrament, which were such a feature of the traditional primers.

Instead the book concludes with selection of prayers from many sources. The first six, the "Praiers of the Passion", are grave and dignified prayers which dwell on the unworthiness of humanity and the mercy of God in redemption. Some of them take an incident of the Passion, such as the betrayal by Peter or Christ's prayer in Gethsemane, as the peg on which to hang a moral – our inconstancy and moral weakness, our need to pray in all heaviness of heart. It has been suggested that Cranmer himself composed these prayers.[59] These "Praiers of the Passion" were followed by a more varied collection. Several were by the Spanish humanist Luis de Vives, and several by Erasmus, notably his lengthy prayer "for the peace of the Churche". This prayer, perfectly consistent with Catholic beliefs, nevertheless evoked the chaos and corruption of Christendom where there was "no charite, no fidelitie, no bondes of love, no reverence, neither of lawes nor yet of rulers, no agreement of opinions, but as it were in a misordered quire, euery man singeth, a contrary note". To Cranmer and his associates this must have struck a sympathetic note, as did another of Erasmus's prayers, for the guidance of God to princes to remedy these evils, and for bishops who might be given "the gift of prophecy that they may declare and interpret holy scripture".[60] The other prayers include paraphrases of scripture taken from translations by Richard Taverner of the German reformer Wolfgang Capito. Though this collection of prayers contains much that was Catholic – not only the prayers by Vives and Erasmus, but even medieval favourites like the "O Bone Jesu" – the overall tone was quite different from that of the traditional primers. Sombre and self-consciously scriptural, adapted to the specific circumstances of daily life – prayers against loss of goods, in adversity, for a competence of living – these prayers point away from the lush affectivity of medieval piety, towards the starker and graver tones of Reformation. The *Primer*, published with all the panoply of royal approval, and with every sign of the direct involvement of the King himself, was a portent of things to come. Under the exuberance of traditionalist rejoicing over victory the foundations were slowly but decisively shifting.

[59] Butterworth, *English Primers*, p. 269.
[60] *The Primer*, sigs r iii–s iii(v).

CHAPTER 13

THE ATTACK ON TRADITIONAL RELIGION III: THE REIGN OF EDWARD VI

The death of Henry VIII in January 1546/7 freed the reforming party from the restraint of a King who, for all his cynicism and hatred of the papacy, remained attached to much of the traditional framework of Catholicism. Yet when Cranmer's secretary, Ralph Morice, observed in 1547 that "now your grace may go forward in these matters, the opportunity of the time much better serving therunto than in king Henry's days," Cranmer disagreed. Religious changes in Henry's lifetime had been widely obeyed as Henry's personal diktat. Cranmer was worried that too rapid a progress towards Protestantism in the new reign would be resisted by the people at large as the manipulation of the child-king by a Protestant clique within the Council. His and Somerset's actions with respect to popular religious observance as the new reign opened reflected this worry, and at times seemed to point in two conflicting directions. The essential clue to their real intentions, however, was given by the archbishop in the homily he delivered to the nine-year-old Edward at the coronation ceremony on 20 February, when he told him that "Your majesty is God's vice-regent and Christ's vicar within your own dominions, and to see, with your predecessor Josiah, God truly worshipped, and idolatry destroyed, the tyranny of the bishops of Rome banished from your subjects, and images removed."[1] The detailed programme which Cranmer, as a "messenger from my Saviour Jesus Christ", had in mind for Josiah redivivus can be gathered from the *Homily of Good Works*, published in July 1547:

> And briefly to pass over the ungodly and counterfeit religions, let us rehearse some other kinds of papistical superstitions and abuses, as of beads, of lady psalters, and rosaries, of fifteen oes,

[1] Cranmer, *Remains*, p. 127.

of St Bernard's verses, of St Agathe's letters, of purgatory, of masses satisfactory, of stations and jubilees, of feigned relics, of hallowed beads, bells, bread, water, palms, candles, fire, and such other; of superstitious fastings, fraternities or brother-hoods, of pardons, with such like merchandize, which were so esteemed and abused to the great prejudice of God's glory and commandments . . . Thus was the people through ignorance so blinded with the goodly show and appearance of those things, that they thought the keeping of them to be a more holiness, a more perfect service and honouring of God, and more pleasing to God, than the keeping of God's commandments.[2]

That denunciation was written throughout in the past tense, as though these things were all securely abolished. Some were, of course. The veneration of relics had been outlawed since 1538, indulgences were no longer proclaimed or permitted, and the primers which contained the "Oes" and St Bernard's verses had, at least in theory, been superseded by the *King's Primer* of 1545. Yet the fabric of medieval religion, torn and faded as it was by fifteen years of attrition, held. The people still for the most part prayed upon beads, and the hallowing of bread, water, and candles, as well as the Holy Week ceremonies of the blessing of Palms and of the paschal fire, were all, despite Cranmer's efforts in 1546, still retained in the liturgy. Everywhere the observance of Lent was still enforced. And although the quenching of the lights before the saints and the gradual suppression of their cults had led to the dissolution of many gilds, they were in principle still legal, and in fact many survived into the new reign. Above all, Masses satisfactory were sung, week by week and day by day, in most of the parish churches of England the bede-rolls were still read and, in many places, the traditional bequests for requiems and "Diriges" were still included as a matter of course in wills. What was composed in the form of a celebration of the passing of the old religion was in fact, and unmistakably, a manifesto for the forging of the new.

Cranmer's *Homily* was not published till July 1547, but the drift of the regime was evident from the court's choice of preachers during Lent. On Ash Wednesday itself Nicholas Ridley denounced the images of the saints and the apotropaic use of sacramentals like holy water in a sermon before the court. On the following Sunday William Barlow, Protestant Bishop of St David's, took up these themes at Paul's Cross. Stephen Gardiner, alarmed by such officially endorsed preaching and by a rash of pamphlets

[2] Ibid., p. 148.

and ballads containing scurrilous attacks on traditional doctrine and ceremonies, as well as by acts of iconoclasm in London and elsewhere, bombarded Somerset, Ridley, and others with letters defending the religion of the Henrician settlement, and pleading for an end to change until the King reached his majority.[3] But Gardiner's time had passed, and his attempts to hold back the flood-tide of reform were useless. In the summer of 1547 a royal visitation of the whole country was announced. At first sight the articles and Injunctions drawn up for it seem essentially a reaffirmation of the reform measures achieved in Henry's reign, but on closer scrutiny they can be seen to represent a significant shift in the direction of full-blown Protestantism.[4] The 1547 Injunctions incorporated wholesale most of those of 1538, so that all the main emphases of the Henrician reform were reaffirmed – scripture reading by the laity, vernacular instruction in the rudiments of the faith by the clergy, attacks on pilgrimage, image worship, abrogated fasts and feasts. Some of these elements were extended, as in the provision for the reading of the Epistle and Gospel in English at Mass, and for the shortening of the Latin lections at matins and evensong to permit a chapter of the Bible in English to be read aloud to the people.

But several of the 1547 Injunctions which appear to be little more than a reissue of those of 1538 were in fact significantly more radical. Injunction two, like number six of the 1538 set, condemned "wandering to pilgrimages", kissing of relics, and other "suchlike superstition". But where the 1538 Injunction condemned the recitation of the rosary only if it was done mechanically "saying over a number of beads, not understood or minded on", the 1547 Injunction, by omitting the qualifying phrase, condemned all recitation of the rosary. Similarly, Injunction three, a reworking of number seven of the 1538 set, commanded the clergy to proceed with the destruction of all images abused even by the simple act of censing. The definition of "abuse" was capable of almost infinite extension. The Injunction significantly omitted the sentence describing images as "the books of unlearned men, that can no letters", which seemed to make images indispensable in a culture where most were illiterate. Now they were said to serve "for no other purpose but to be a remembraunce, whereby men may be admonished of the holy lives and conversations of them that the said images do represent".

[3] Foxe, *Acts and Monuments*, VI pp. 58–64; S. Brigden, *London and the Reformation*, 1989, pp. 426–33; P. Hughes, *The Reformation in England*, 1950–4, II pp. 85–100.
[4] TRP, I no. 287; VAI, II pp. 103–13 (Articles), 114–30.

The same Injunction now forbade the burning of lights anywhere except two candles on the altar before the Sacrament, thereby outlawing the Rood lights and, as it turned out, the sepulchre lights, both of which had been specifically permitted in 1538. This sounds a minor change, but was in fact of considerable importance, and would certainly have dramatically changed the appearance of many churches. Many of those maintaining lights before the images of the saints, forbidden in 1538, had not in fact extinguished them, but had circumvented the Injunctions by moving the light onto the Rood-loft. This was the device used by the Morebath Young Men's gild, who had burned a light before the parish patron, St George, until 1538. When, in compliance with this Injunction, the wardens of the London parish of St Thomas Vintry sold off the wax "which was aboute the roode lofte" they had to dispose of over fifty pounds of candles. The quenching of the Rood lights therefore marked the decisive break with the tradition of maintained lights, and the groups who existed to provide them.[5]

Injunction twenty-eight, which was based in part on Henry VIII's 1541 order from Hull against images and shrines, ordered the removal of relics, images, pictures, and paintings which were "monuments of feigned miracles, pilgrimage, idolatry and superstition". It went beyond both the spirit and the letter of the Henrician provision by ordering the destruction of such images not only on the walls of churches but "in glass windows". Even in Zwingli's Zurich the stained-glass windows had been allowed to stand: no one had ever seriously suggested that the people knelt before images in windows to venerate them. This radical extension of the prohibition was heavy with portent for the outlawing of all imagery whatsoever. It was also significant that the Injunction required the clergy to destroy the images not only in the churches, but also to "exhort all their parishioners to do the like within their several houses".[6]

Some of the Injunctions of 1547 had no precedent in those of 1538 or in the acts of Henry's reign. One of the most dramatic changes ordered was the abolition of all processions, in particular the parish procession with which the main Mass of each Sunday and major feast began. On the pretext of eliminating "all contention and strife" which had arisen among the people "by reason of fond courtesy, and challenging of places in procession", and also so that they might hear quietly what was said or sung "to their edifying", there were to be no more processions "in church or

---

[5] Morebath CWA pp. 7, 143, 159–60; *London Churches at the Reformation*, ed. H. B. Walters, 1939, p. 617.

[6] M. Aston, *England's Iconoclasts*, 1988, pp. 254–9.

churchyard or other place". Instead, each Sunday the priests and the choir were to kneel in the centre aisle of the church and sing the English litany. The ringing of bells during the Sunday services was to be "utterly forborne", "except one bell in convenient time to be rung or knolled before the sermon", a provision which was probably intended to silence the sanctus bell, rung to announce and honour the sacring.

By outlawing the Sunday processions, this injunction struck at the heart of one of the principal expressions of medieval communal religion, and one of the most distinctive features of English parochial worship. It is not clear whether it was also intended to abolish Rogationtide processions, during which traditionally the litany of the saints was sung to the clamour of handbells used to banish demons, but in the light of another of these new Injunctions, it seems likely that it was. Injunction twenty-seven represented a frontal attack on popular religious observances, in particular on the apotropaic use of sacramentals. Behind it we can discern the influence both of the troubles in Kent four years earlier, and of the controversy between Gardiner and Ridley a few months before the new Injunctions were issued. It begins misleadingly, apparently as a defence of traditional ceremony, requiring clergy to instruct their people that no man ought "obstinately and maliciously to break and violate the laudable ceremonies of the church, by the King commanded to be observed, and as not yet abrogated". But it immediately proceeds to its real concern, to condemn anyone who uses these ceremonies in the traditional way, to bring healing or blessing

> in casting holy water upon his bed, upon images, and other dead things; or bearing about him holy bread, or St John's Gospel, or making crosses of wood upon Palm Sunday in time of reading of the passion, or keeping of private holy days, as bakers, brewers, smiths and shoemakers, and such others do; or ringing of holy bells, or blessing with the holy candle, to the intent therby to be discharged of the burden of sin, or to bribe away devils, or to put away dreams and fantasies.

They were only reminders of the benefits of Christ, and whoever used them for any other purpose "grievously offendeth God".[7] Finally, in a provision which anticipated the dissolution of the chantries which was to take place at the end of the year, Injunction twenty-nine was devoted to obit provision, requiring clergy to dissuade the dying from providing in their wills for the traditional

[7] VAI, II p. 116.

works and intercessions on which "heretofore they have been diligent to bestow much substance", such as pardons, pilgrimages, trentals of masses, candles and torches, or the decking of images. Instead they were to be encouraged to make bequests to the poor man's chest. The Injunction directed that existing funds from "fraternities, guilds and other stocks of the church", as well as any stocks of money bequeathed to find torches, tapers, or lamps, should also be placed in the poor box, a provision which had implications for the cult of the Sacrament as well as for that of the dead.

The Injunctions formed the basis of a royal visitation, planned for May but put into effect in September, which was to extend into the next year and to precipitate the most sweeping changes in religion England had yet seen. Thirty commissioners, most of them laymen, were named for the whole country, which was divided for the purpose into six regions. They were equipped with the Injunctions and Cranmer's *Book of Homilies*, whose use every Sunday was enjoined on the parish clergy by Injunction thirty-two. The commissioners also had an exhaustive set of articles of enquiry, and had power to make their own articles where they deemed that necessary. The visitation was thorough, in many places aggressive, and it was consistently used to push through a radical reading of the Injunctions. Everywhere they went the commissioners enforced the destruction of images, the extinguishing of lights, the abolition of "abused" ceremonies (Pl. 134).[8]

The visitation rapidly developed its own momentum. The Council had been uneasy about the dangers of disorder in unauthorized iconoclasm: at the beginning of the reign they had even enforced the replacement of images removed by over-zealous London wardens. They were concerned too at the potential for parochial strife involved in deciding which images were or were not abused. But their own actions inevitably encouraged and endorsed iconoclasm. The visitation of St Paul's commenced in the first week in September, and all the images except the Rood, Mary, and John were removed. The policy was extended to St Bride's, Fleet Street, and to other City churches a few days later. By mid-September the wave of image- and window-breaking had got out of hand, and the Council tried to call a halt to it by ruling that images not abused might be retained, and that any such already destroyed should

[8] For the visitation see J. Strype, *Memorials of . . . Cranmer*, 1840, pp. 207–11; R. W. Dixon, *History of the Church of England*, 1895–1902, II pp. 428–34, 478–80; R. Hutton, "Local Impact", 1987, p. 120; P. Hughes, *Reformation*, II pp. 92–4; C. J. Kitching, *Royal Visitation of 1559*, 1975, pp. xv–xvi.

be re-erected. Windows containing images of the Pope or Becket were to be selectively defaced or covered over, not smashed; any doubtful cases were to be referred to one or more of the Privy Councillors. It was a futile and self-contradictory ruling. On 17 November the visitors ordered the removal even of the Rood at St Paul's. To avoid public outcry the work was carried out at night, the Rood fell from the loft, and two of the workmen were killed, an accident seized on by conservative clergy as a judgement of God on sacrilege.[9] But the work went on, statues and niches were pulled down, windows painted over or broken, walls whitewashed and covered with texts against idolatry.[10]

For all the signals emanating from Protector Somerset and his circle favoured radicalism. In December a new Chantries Act was passed, replacing that of 1545 which had lapsed with Henry's death. Unlike the earlier measure, the preamble to this Act stated baldly that what was wrong with chantries was not any maladministration, but their whole end and purpose, "phantasising vain opinions of purgatory and masses satisfactory, to be done for them which be departed".[11] Debate about the motives for and the long-term effects of the dissolution of the chantries continued: the regime itself was divided about it, Cranmer and most of the bishops being opposed to the confiscations involved. The impact of the dissolutions certainly varied from region to region, and from community to community even within the regions. The historian of the dissolutions in the East Riding has emphasized both the scrupulous care of the commissioners to see that "the parishes did not suffer by the dissolution" and the lack of resistance by the people, suggesting that the contribution of the chantries "was not greatly missed".[12] This seems too bland an assessment by far, and in many places it is hard to see the measure as anything short of a disaster for lay religious life. It was designed to eliminate the remaining institutional framework underpinning the daily round of intercession for the dead in many parishes. At the same time, in dissolving all religious gilds and stripping the remaining craft gilds of any property devoted to intercessory activity, the Act destroyed the main form of organized lay religious activity. In the process it deprived parishes all over England of the auxiliary clergy who had so often provided liturgical variety, and the lay control over it, which was

[9] *The Grey Friars' Chronicle of London*, ed. J. G. Nichols, Camden Society, LIII, 1852, pp. 54–5; *Wriothesley Chronicle*, II p. 1.

[10] Brigden, *London*, pp. 426–33.

[11] H. Gee and W. J. Hardy, *Documents Illustrative of English Church History*, 1896, p. 328.

[12] C. J. Kitching, "The Chantries of the East Riding", *Yorkshire Archaeological Journal*, XLIV, 1972, pp. 178–85.

such a feature of late medieval religious culture. The Act put an end to the morrow mass, Lady Mass, and Jesus Mass priests, and the army of chaplains who assisted at the singing of the services on Sundays and holidays, who read the Epistle or Gospel on high days and Rogationtide, and who helped the curate to shrive and housel the people at Easter. In the West Country, "despite the fair words of the Act," it was almost wholly negative, not a reform but an abolition, and little or nothing was done to replace the charitable and pastoral services provided by many of the chantry priests. Some communities were devastated by their disappearance. At Ashburton in Devon, where the burgesses of the town formed collectively the gild of St Lawrence, the town "lost at a blow control over its market, the endowments of its parochial school, the funds used for supplying water to the town and caring for the sick, [and] most of the clergy serving its parish church", where there had been at any one time up to seven stipendiary priests on chantry and gild foundations.[13] Elsewhere, the promise in the Act to provide for auxiliary clergy where the dissolutions created clerical shortages was indeed honoured in some places, but ignored in others equally or more needy. So many of the people of the Lincolnshire fens, cut off in winter from their mother churches, now found the chapels which gave them their only access to the Sacraments closed, and their clergy pensioned off.[14] The disappearance of the gilds also robbed the parishes of the intermediate structures which enriched and underpinned, and to a large extent funded them, and which frequently played a key role in organizing the festal dimension of the parish's liturgical year.[15]

The Edwardine Chantries Act justified the dissolutions, not on economic grounds, but on the basis of religious principle. Yet it involved the confiscation by the Crown of immense resources. Commissions were therefore issued for a survey of all the possessions of the chantries, prior to confiscation. This involved the drawing up of inventories of plate, vestments, and lights, as well as lands. In the same year separate instructions were issued to the bishops for the compilation of inventories of the church goods of

[13] N. Orme, "The Dissolution of the Chantries in Devon", *Transactions of the Devonshire Association*, CXI, 1979, pp. 75–123; H. J. Hanham, "The Suppression of the Chantries in Ashburton", *Transactions of the Devonshire Association*, XCIX, 1967, pp. 111–37.

[14] R. B. Walker, "Reformation and Reaction in the County of Lincoln", *Lincolnshire Archaeological and Architectural Society Reports*, IX, 1961, pp. 51–2.

[15] See above, chapter 4, "Corporate Christians", pp. 141–54; A. Kreider, *English Chantries: the Road to Dissolution*, 1979, esp. pp. 186–208; J. J. Scarisbrick, *Reformation and the English People*, 1984, pp. 19–39. The dissolution is discussed, benignly, in A. G. Dickens, *The English Reformation*, 2nd ed., 1989, pp. 230–42.

every parish in the land.[16] The object of this survey was ostensibly to preserve parochial resources "entirelie to the churches, without embeselinge or privat sales". One may legitimately reserve one's position on this declaration of good intent by the Privy Council, but whatever the facts, the coincidence of the two sets of inventories was unfortunate, and, as in Lincolnshire in 1536, persuaded many that the regime was about to strip the parish churches, as it was stripping the chantries and gilds.[17]

These fears came to a head in the West Country, in the hundred of Penwith in Cornwall. William Body, a protégé of Cromwell and a layman, had leased the archdeaconry of Cornwall, with all its offices and rights, from Wolsey's bastard son Thomas. As lessee of the archdeaconry he was responsible for carrying out the parochial surveys and enforcing religious change. His activities appear to have confirmed the universal suspicion that the surveys were a prelude to sacrilegious attacks on the parishes themselves. Body compounded these fears by his own crass behaviour. To save himself the trouble of travelling round the archdeaconry, he summoned all the wardens and sworn-men of the parishes to a single meeting in December 1547, "whereas the letter [from the Council] purported that there should be severall ensrch be taken in every place apart". It was a blunder, for as they assembled, alarmed wardens and parishioners compared notes and fed each other's fears, and their anger grew. Local gentry had to intervene to calm the "tumulteous assembly of the parisheoneres of Penwith". To appease the people the Council disciplined Body: he was to be committed to ward for a week, and bound over to appear before them. In the meantime, a copy of the Council's letter was to be shown to the "substanciall persones of everie parish" to reassure them that the inventories were simply designed for the "preservacion of the church juelles".[18] The fears Body's tactlessness aroused were perfectly rational. The parishes were indeed to be stripped of almost everything of value in 1553, and Body's assistants in the 1547/8

[16] W Page (ed.), *The Inventories of Church Goods for the Counties of York. Durham and Northumberland*, Surtees Society, XCVII, 1896, pp. ix–xviii.

[17] In 1549 this exercise was repeated and, in addition to the inventories themselves, the Crown ordered a brief summary simply listing the bells and plate of each church, suggesting that the Crown was less concerned about preserving the accoutrements of worship than cataloguing the saleable goods of the parishes. The Suffolk certificates specifically identify those items of value which had been alienated or sold. Wardens seem to have justified such sales by itemizing repairs to their churches or local highways, and by contributions towards the Crown's military expenses from the proceeds, all of which suggests that everyone understood that the Crown considered the goods of the churches its own property. See, e.g., *East Anglian*, ns I, 1885, pp. 49–51, 67–70, 83–4, 102–4, 114–16, 128–9, 142–3, 159–61.

[18] *Acts of the Privy Council*, ns II p. 535; A. L. Rowse, *Tudor Cornwall*, 1941, pp. 253–4.

survey elsewhere in the West Country seemed to let the cat out of the bag by informing the churchwardens and parishioners that "the said Jewells and plate should be safflie kept and to be forthe commynge at all tyme that the Kynges Ma[jes]tie requyred." This might have been no more than an insistence that the wardens be accountable at all times for the goods entrusted to their keeping, but it might also have meant that they should be ready at any time to surrender them for the Crown's needs. This was certainly what was most commonly believed, and an avalanche of sales ensued, designed to pre-empt government confiscation. But whatever the object of the exercise, for the time being the Council backed off.[19]

They were not, however, idle. On 6 February 1548 the Council issued a proclamation ostensibly designed to tackle the growing "diversity of opinion and variety of rites and ceremonies" caused by those who "rashly . . . and of their own and singular wit" persuaded the people away from the "old and accustomed rites and ceremonies". The proclamation forbade any innovation or alteration in the ceremonies not abrogated in Henry's reign or by the Council. This seemed a straightforward endorsement of the Henrician settlement, as modified by the 1547 Injunctions, but, as so often with Somerset's regime, protestations of moderation and traditionalism concealed a deeper radicalism. The Council had already passed an order on 18 January, abolishing the use of candles, ashes, and palms, and the copy of the proclamation sent to Bonner (in any case in disgrace because of his resistance to the royal visitation and the Injunctions) contained a paragraph not in the printed schedule, but embodying the decision of 18 January. That paragraph stipulated that despite the command to observe existing ceremonies, no one was to be troubled who refused to bear a candle on Candlemas day, or palms on Palm Sunday, or who refused to creep to the cross, or who would not take holy bread or holy water, or for omitting any ceremony which Cranmer had or for the future might declare to be omitted or changed: Cranmer's word was to have the force of the royal Injunctions.[20] Under pretext of protecting the traditional ceremonies, the revised proclamation effectively abolished them. Cranmer had at last achieved the programme campaigned for by the Kent radicals in the early 1540s, which he had pressed on Henry in vain in 1546.

The progress of the visitation facilitated, perhaps even necessitated, further radicalization. As the visitors sought to enforce the

[19] B. F. Creswell (ed.), *The Edwardian Inventories for the City and County of Exeter*, Alcuin Club, XX, 1916, pp. 32–3; for the sales see below, chapter 14, "The Impact of Reform: Parishes", pp. 483–7.
[20] TRP, I no. 299; VAI, II p. 184.

Injunction against abused images they ran into fierce opposition. On 21 February the Lords of the Council wrote to Cranmer, and reported that although the Injunction against abused images had in many places been "well and quietly obeyed", yet in many others "much strife and contention hath arisen, and daily riseth, and more and more increaseth", since some men were "so superstitious, or rather wilful" that they wished to retain images which had manifestly been abused. The dangers from this growing conflict had to be prevented, and since the only places in the realm where there was no conflict were those where all the images had been removed, they therefore ordered that all images in every church and chapel, abused or not, should now be taken away.[21]

The idea that the total removal of images would bring peace to the parishes can hardly have been advanced with any great seriousness; at any rate, it was soon to be belied. Protestantism was soon to establish a foothold among the city fathers of Hull, and the town was not perhaps the most obvious place for discontent at iconoclasm. But as a comparatively new town, with few religious amenities, Hull had been particularly hard hit by the Henrician and Edwardine dissolutions. Perhaps for this reason the public destruction of the extraordinary patronal image of the parish church of Holy Trinity, with its three heads, and the images of the Virgin, St James, St John, St Lawrence, and St Anne, black with the smoke of the people's offerings, caused "much murmuring", though the parishioners did nothing to stop the destruction, and indeed "did not even dare to express their disgust".[22]

In more traditional communities reaction was more straight-forward. In the Lent of 1548 William Body was busy once more about the removal of images in the parish churches of the Lizard peninsula. This time his overbearing manner proved too much for the restraint of the men of the West. On 5 April 1548 a mob led by a local Mass-priest and some yeomen from St Keverne attacked Body's lodgings at Helston and murdered him. The leaders of the mob proclaimed in the market-place their rejection of all religious innovation, demanding that the Henrician settlement should stand until Edward's twenty-fourth birthday, and declaring that "whoso would defend Body, or follow such new fashions as he did, they would punish him likewise". Though the unrest escalated, the crowd growing over the next few days to more than 3,000, it

[21] Cranmer, *Remains*, p. 510.

[22] George Hadley, *A New and Complete History of the Town of Kingston upon Hull*, 1788, pp. 88–9; Claire Cross, "Parochial Structure and the Dissemination of Protestantism in Sixteenth Century England: a Tale of Two Cities", *Studies in Church History*, XVI, 1977, pp. 269–78.

was eventually quelled, and the ringleaders were sent for trial to London. Significantly perhaps, though he had not struck a blow against Body, the only leader actually executed there was the chantry priest, Martin Geoffrey. But violent reaction to the stripping of local religious institutions was by no means confined to the West Country. There was a similar incident on the night of St James's day 1549 at Seamer near Scarborough in Yorkshire, when Thomas Dale, the parish clerk of Seamer, and William Ambler, a local yeoman, raised the countryside by setting Staxton beacon alight, and denounced the "laying aside" of God's service and the substitution of "new inventions, neither good nor godly". At the head of a mob which was said to have grown to 3,000 they dragged from their beds Richard Savage, a former mayor of York, Matthew White, one of the chantry commissioners, and his unfortunate wife, and one of the servants of Sir Walter Mildmay, another of the commissioners, and put them to death on the moors above Seamer. The grievances aired by Dale and Ambler were varied, ranging from rejection of the religious changes of the reign to resentment of the local gentry, who "oppress us and ever favour these novelties". But there is little doubt that a major reason for the support they got was that the dissolution of the two local chantries deprived the people of a chapel of ease, the parish church being a mile away.[23]

In the meantime, the radical decisions of January and February 1548 were implemented almost everywhere, starting in London. At Candlemas that year the bearing of candles "was left off throughout the whole city of London", ashes were omitted on Ash Wednesday, palms abandoned on Palm Sunday "and not used as afore". At Easter the new Order of Communion was introduced, interpolating into the medieval Mass penitential and devotional material derived from Protestant sources, and requiring communion in both kinds for the laity. At Whitsun at St Paul's, where the clergy had hidden the image of the Virgin to protect her from the iconoclasts, English versions of matins, Mass, and evensong came into use. The reformers also abolished one of the most distinctive of the cathedral's symbolic observances. It had been the custom at Whitsun for a great censer, emitting clouds of sweet smoke and sparks, to be swung from the roof of St Paul's, and for doves to be released, re-enacting the descent of the Holy Ghost on the Apostles. Such

[23] Rowse, *Tudor Cornwall*, pp. 257–9; W. Page (ed.), *The Certificates of the Commissioners appointed to survey Chantries, Guilds, Hospitals, &c in the County of York*, Surtees Society, XCI, 1892, pp. xvi, 515; Dixon, *History*, III pp. 94–5; Dickens, *English Reformation*, p. 237. For a similar but much less serious incident in Lincolnshire see R. B. Walker, "Reformation and Reaction", p. 52.

gestures had no place in the world of the reformers, dominated
as that was by texts, and this "sensyng of Powlles" was now
suppressed.[24]

Glossing all these changes came a flood of polemical Protestant
literature, much of it scurrilous, rejoicing in the destruction of
image and chantry, but above all attacking the Mass, the Pope's
whore who infects all her lovers:

> A good mistress missa
> Shall ye go from us thissa?
> Well yet I must ye kissa
> Alack from pain I pissa.[25]

It was true that in December the Council had issued a proclamation
against defamers of the Sacrament, but actions spoke louder than
words, and official promotion and endorsement of sacramentarian
preaching made clear the backing that radical Protestants could now
expect. Indeed, much of this satire seems to have been tuned to
the reforming timetable of Cranmer and his associates, like the
publication of Luke Shepherd's *John Bon and Mast Person*, a satirical
dialogue attacking traditional Eucharistic teaching. It was set
on Corpus Christi eve, and although it landed its publishers in
trouble, it was perhaps timed for publication to coincide with
Cranmer's suppression of the feast in 1548.[26]

The changes which were dividing the parishes of London were
also being pushed ahead in the regions. The chief agent of reform
was of course the royal visitation, and what documentary evidence
survives of the visitors' activities shows that they were using
freely the powers granted to them to go beyond the letter of the
Injunctions. One of their principal targets was the devotional world
of the late medieval laity, especially those parts of it associated
with the Virgin. At Lincoln they suppressed the evening service,
common in town churches all over England and often funded by
lay bequests, of the singing of the "Salve Regina". They also
forbade the public recitation of the Little Office of the Virgin, one
of the two traditional constituent elements of the primer, and hence
one of the liturgical services in which literate lay people could
and did actively join. In the parishes they were also suppressing

[24] J. King, *English Reformation Literature*, 1982, p. 151; *Grey Friars Chronicle*, pp. 55–6;
Wriothesley Chronicle, II, pp. 2–3. For the ceremonies at St Paul's on Whitsun see A. Heales,
"Easter Sepulchres", *Archaeologia*, xli, 1869, p. 280. There was evidently a somewhat similar
Pentecost ceremony at Louth in Lincolnshire, where John Leche and Robert Boston were
paid at several times for "latyng doun the holy gost" and "for the holy gost aperyng in the
Kirke roffe" – Louth CWA, pp. 7, 192.
[25] Brigden, *London*, pp. 433–6; King, *English Reformation Literature*, pp. 252–70.
[26] King, op. cit. pp. 95, 102, 258–9.

traditional communal celebrations, banning wakes and the Plough Monday celebrations. The Injunctions they drew up for the deanery of Doncaster forbade the non-liturgical use of holy water.[27]

Cranmer himself carried out a visitation of his own diocese in 1548, and his visitation articles reveal the thoroughness with which a radical interpretation of the 1547 Injunctions was now being pressed on the parishes. Cranmer included detailed queries about the destruction of all images (not merely their removal), and in addition to making sure that they had all been removed from the churches, Cranmer wanted to know if any of the laity "keep in their houses undefaced, any abused or feigned images, any tables, pictures, paintings or other monuments of feigned miracles, pilgrimages, idolatry, or superstition". He wanted to know if abrogated feasts or fasts were being observed, whether there were any lights in the churches other than two on the high altar, and whether the Pope's name and the services of St Thomas had been removed from the books. He asked whether any of the abrogated ceremonies – candles, ashes, palms – had been used that year, and he included among these forbidden ceremonies the Easter sepulchre. This had not been specifically forbidden in any Injunction or other document, but Cranmer seems to have taken the view that the prohibition of the other Holy Week ceremonies, together with the abolition of all lights other than those on the altar, outlawed the sepulchre ceremonies. Gardiner was called to account in May of that year by the Council for carrying out the sepulchre ceremonies at Winchester, and defended himself on the ground that they were legal, a view clearly shared by other conservative bishops. The sepulchre ceremonies were used that year in both the cathedral and parishes of Worcester, for example, though in the cathedral the Easter morning procession from the sepulchre was omitted.[28] But it was not only the lights round the sepulchre of Christ which Cranmer was now intent on extinguishing. Some of the depositions of the 1548 Canterbury visitation make it clear that the authorities were also using the prohibition of lights to prevent candles being lit round the corpses of the dead when they were brought into churches.[29]

Cranmer was also anxious to ensure that the laity on their death-beds should be dissuaded from any traditional obit bequests, "blind devotions", giving only to the poor man's box, and he wanted

[27] VAI, II pp. 166–70, 171–5.
[28] Worcester Record Office, MS 716.093, "Notititia Diocesae" *sub* 1547/8: St Michael in Bedwardine CWA, p. 20.
[29] "Extracts from . . . Documents Illustrating the Progress of the Reformation in Kent", ed. C. E. Woodruff, *Archaeologia Cantiana*, XXXI, 1915, p. 102.

clergy who accepted mass stipends for requiems searched out. He was also anxious to discover any clergy who were encouraging the laity to pray in Latin, to use Catholic primers or other traditional devotions "as in saying over a number of beads or the like". Lay people possessing and using rosaries were to be openly warned by the clergy.[30]

Given the intensity and thoroughness of this sort of scrutiny, the widespread implementation of the reforms of 1547–8 in the parishes comes as no surprise. All over England churchwardens cooperated in the removal and destruction of images and the suppression of traditional services, but this cooperation should not be read as approval. Tudor men and women had stoically endured many religious changes in the reign of Henry. They had seen the monasteries and friaries go, the shrines pillaged, the lights in the parish churches snuffed out, the Pope's name scratched or cut out of the parish liturgical books and their own primers, the abolition of many of the traditional feast days. There had been Protestant preaching, even, in some places, image-breaking and burning. But these early Edwardine changes were recognized as something new, something different. The Marian churchwardens of Stanford in the Vale in Berkshire, stocktaking after six years of destruction, articulated a very generally shared perception when they dated "the tyme of Scysme when this Realm was devyded from the Catholic Churche" not from the breach with Rome in the early 1530s, but from the "second yer of Kyng Edward the syxt", when "all godly ceremonyes & good usys were taken out of the Church with in this Realme."[31]

The changes were by no means uniformly imposed, but all over the country horrified traditionalists watched as the lead given by Cranmer and the royal visitors unleashed a wave of destruction. Robert Parkyn, the parish priest of Adwick le Street near Doncaster, in the comparative refuge of a staunchly traditionalist area, nevertheless recorded that in 1548 all the images were removed from the churches in Lent, and all but the high altar lights quenched. There were no Candlemas ceremonies, no ashes, no Palms, no creeping to the cross, no sepulchre, no paschal candle, no blessing of the font. Traditional fasts were disregarded, and at Rogationtide "no procession was mayde abowtt the fealdes, but cruell tiranntes dyd cast downe all crosses standynge in oppen ways dispittefully." The attack on sacramentals implicit in the Injunctions was also being pursued in the visitation in the north, though it was clearly less successful there than elsewhere, for Parkyn records that

---

[30] VAI, II pp. 176–89.
[31] Stanford CWA, p. 70.

"in many places of this realme (but specially in the sowth parttes, as Suffolke, Norffolke, Kent & Waylles &c) nather breade nor watter was sanctifide or distributte emonge Christian people on Sondays, butt clerely omittide as thinges tendinge to idolatrie." Worst of all was the attack on the Sacrament:

> Yea, & also the pixes hangynge over thallters (wherin was remanynge Christ blesside bodie under forme of breade) was dispittfully cast away as thinges most abominable . . . utterynge such wordes therby as it dyd abhorre trew christian eares for to heare, butt only thatt Christ mercy is so myche, it was marvell that the earth did nott oppen and swalow upp such vilanus persons, as it dyd Dathan and Abiron.[32]

Parkyn has been called "the last medieval Englishman", but if the title is meant to imply that he was unusually conservative, or that his opinions were in any way unrepresentative of other parish clergy, it is misleading. By late April 1548 the Council, alarmed no doubt by the disturbances in Cornwall and elsewhere, thought widespread rebellion a serious possibility. They blamed the unrest to a large extent on the clergy who "of a devilish mind and intent", were inciting and moving the people "as well in confession as otherwise, to disobedience and stubbornness against his majesty's godly proceedings". They therefore forbade any preaching in the parishes without special licence from Cranmer or the Protector. Without such a licence, only the reading of the *Homilies* was permitted. The proclamation was phrased so that it seemed to protect parishes from outside, itinerant, preachers, since any preacher had to show his licence to "the parson and curate, and two honest men of the parish beside". In fact the proclamation silenced the parish clergy themselves, and gave the radical propagandists for the new measures who were actually licensed the monopoly of the pulpits.[33] At the same time, the Council was nervous, for the men most eager and able to justify the changes already made were not always those most anxious to proceed as slowly as the maintenance of order seemed to demand. The licences to preachers contained a strict warning that while they might teach the people to "flee from the old superstitions" they must not "run before they be sent, nor change things without authority".[34] By September the Council issued another proclamation, deploring the fact that some of the licensed preachers had exceeded their commission. They therefore

---

[32] "Robert Parkyn's Narrative" in A. G. Dickens, *Reformation Studies*, 1982, pp. 295–6.
[33] TRP, I no. 303.
[34] R. W. Dixon, *History of the Church of England from the Abolition of the Roman Jurisdiction*, 3rd ed., 1895–1902, II p. 531.

withdrew all licences, and, pending the establishment of "one uniform order throughout [the] realm", forbade all preaching whatsoever, a supremely ironic, or perhaps cynical, action by men committed to the propagation of the preaching of the Word.[35]

The "one uniform order" was, of course, the prayer-book of 1549, authorized by the Act of Uniformity which was passed by both Houses on 21 January 1548/9, received the royal assent on 14 March, and which came into force on Whitsun of that year, though it was already being used in St Paul's and some London parishes from the beginning of Lent 1549.[36]

Hindsight and the far more openly Protestant character of the second prayer-book of 1552 make it difficult for us now to capture any real sense of the radical discontinuity with traditional religion represented by the book of 1549. At an obvious level, of course, it preserved the basic pattern of parochial worship, matins, Mass, and evensong. But it set itself to transform lay experience of the Mass, and in the process eliminated almost everything that had till then been central to lay Eucharistic piety. The parish procession, the elevation at the sacring, the pax, the sharing of holy bread, were all swept away. Nor was it clear what, in the short term, would take their place. Cranmer certainly hoped for the growth of the practice of regular communion by lay people. But he did not attempt to legislate for this, and the book clearly envisaged that in the foreseeable future, most of those present at the parish Mass would be onlookers, not communicants. In a series of instructions at the end of the Communion service, the prayer-book ordered that the old holy loaf rota should now become a rota for households in the parish to pay the communion expenses, and that "some one at the least of that house in every Parishe", or at least a deputy appointed by them, should receive with the priest. Thus, paradoxically, by seeking to ensure that there should be at least one lay communicant, Cranmer enshrined in the rubrics of the book the notion that for most people the parish Mass would continue to be something to see. At the same time, however, he took steps to eliminate the focus which had given meaning and power to that spectacle, by forbidding any elevation or showing of the Host.

[35] TRP, I no. 313.

[36] *Wriothesley Chronicle*, II p. 9. I have used the Everyman Library edition (1910) of *The First and Second Prayer-Books of King Edward the Sixth* in preference to the Parker Society edition, because it reproduces the original spelling: On the prayer-book of 1549 see F. Procter and W. H. Frere, *A New History of the Book of Common Prayer*, 1925, pp. 45–64, and G. J. Cuming. *A New History of the Anglican Liturgy*, 1969; F. E. Brightman, *The English Rite*, 1915; E. C. Ratcliff, *The Book of Common Prayer: its Making and Revisions*, 1949, and "The Liturgical Work of Archbishop Cranmer", *Journal of Ecclesiastical History*, VII, 1956, pp. 189–203.

The prayer-book represented radical discontinuity in other ways too. The traditional cycle of feast and fast days had been nibbled at by successive measures since 1536. Now the calendar of the new book simply bulldozed away most of the main features of the liturgical year, leaving only the great feasts of Christmas, Easter, and Whitsun (shorn of the octaves which extended and elaborated them), and a handful of biblical saints' days – the Apostles, the Evangelists, the Baptist, and Mary Magdalene. All but one of the feasts of the Virgin were abolished, including the great harvest celebration of the Assumption. There was no provision for votive Masses of any sort, or for any of the devotions which had been the mainstay of lay Mass attendance on weekdays, and which might conceivably have been preserved even within the reform. Virtually every town in England had had its Jesus Mass on Fridays, for example, well attended and often a major focus of establishment piety; all this, like the Jesus gilds which had sustained it, was now swept away. That no attempt to perpetuate this aspect of medieval Eucharistic piety would be tolerated was quickly made plain. When the conservative canons of St Paul's attempted in June 1549 to continue the daily Masses of the Apostles and the Virgin in the side chapels by using the proper collects and lections in the book for the feasts of the Virgin and the Apostles, the Privy Council intervened and ordered that henceforth there should be only one communion a day, celebrated at the high altar "without cautel or digression from the common order".[37] At a more obvious level, the switch from Latin to English immediately rendered obsolete the entire musical repertoire of cathedral, chapel, and parish church. Not the least of the shocks brought by the prayer-book at Whitsun 1549 must have been the silencing of all but a handful of choirs and the reduction of the liturgy on one of the greatest festivals of the year to a monotone dialogue between curate and clerk.

Nor was the discontinuity evident merely within the Mass. Despite Cranmer's dislike of the blessing of objects, and the hostile reference to the superstitious abuse of such things in the Injunctions, up to the very end of 1548 the royal visitation had accepted, and even legislated for, the continuing use of sacramentals, in particular holy bread and holy water. Though the parish procession had been forbidden by the Injunctions, the visitors made express provision for the curate to sprinkle holy water before Mass "into three or four places where most audience and assembly of people is", and provided a form of words for the distribution of holy bread. But

---

[37] Foxe, *Acts and Monuments*, V p. 723; though the Council's order did leave a loophole for the provision of an early communion (the old morrow Mass) where "some number of people desire, for their necessary business, to have a communion in the morning".

there was no place for any of the sacramentals in the 1549 book, and once again a central feature of medieval lay engagement with the liturgy was removed at a stroke.

Some parts of the book remained close to their medieval originals. The Office for the visitation of the sick, for example, was a skilful shortening of the Sarum rite. But even here what the Tudor laity would most have noticed was the removal of the symbolic gestures which were often the aspects of the rite which impinged most directly on the lay imagination. A case in point is Cranmer's omission of the moving gesture with which the medieval Office of visitation began, when the priest held up before the eyes of the dying person an image of the Crucified. Similarly, in the rite of anointing, now merely an optional part of the Office, he provided only for a single anointing on the forehead or breast, instead of the medieval practice of anointing eyes, ears, lips, limbs, and heart in turn, an eloquent absolution and surrender of all the sick person's senses and faculties as death approached. This ritual impoverishment, in particular the abandonment of sacramentals, was to feature as prominently in popular rejection of the prayer-book as did the shift to the vernacular.

That rejection came most spectacularly in the West Country, which rose against the new book in June 1549. The western rising was the only sustained armed resistance to the religious changes, but there were smaller disturbances from the West Midlands to Yorkshire. The essentially religious character of the revolts cannot seriously be questioned, and it should be noted that the rebels sought a restoration not only of the old Mass, but of the full ceremonial range of medieval Catholicism. They singled out the sacramentals of holy bread and water, the Lenten ceremonies of ashes and palms, the parish procession on Sundays, but included "all other auncient olde Ceremonyes used heretofore, by our mother the holy Churche". They also demanded the restoration of the cult of the dead. The form of bidding of the bedes commanded for use by the 1547 Injunctions had commemorated the dead only in the most general of terms, in a prayer which made no allusion to Purgatory or cleansing, and in which there was no provision for the actual naming of the dead. Now the rebels demanded that every preacher in his sermon and every priest at his Mass should "praye specially by name for the soules in purgatory, as oure forefathers dyd."[38]

[38] The demands of the rebels are conveniently presented in Anthony Fletcher, *Tudor Rebellions*, 1973, pp. 135–6.

The rebels recognized that the prayer-book was merely one element in a programme which affected their religious life at every level, the dissolution of the elaborate symbolic framework within which the life of their communities had been shaped for generations. There was far more at stake than the merits of English or Latin in liturgy, or even single points of doctrine. It was a perception certainly shared by their opponents. A draft set of visitation articles of this year, probably the work of Cranmer, makes clear the extent to which the Edwardine reform itself was in movement, steadily advancing towards more and more radical forms of Protestantism. So these 1549 Articles specifically repudiated those sections of the 1547 Injunctions which refer to or seem to allow the "popish mass", chantries, candles on the altar "or any such things". They condemned any priests who used any of the ceremonies of the old Mass in celebrating the communion, and forbade the celebration of communion services on behalf of the dead. No bells or crosses were to be borne before corpses, nor were the clergy to precede funeral processions from the deceased's house. Even more significantly, clergy carrying the Blessed Sacrament to the sick, an observance specifically permitted in the prayer-book, were forbidden to honour the Sacrament by having any lights or bells carried before it. References to Purgatory, praying for the dead by reciting their names, invocation of the saints, even the retention of altars, were all forbidden. And in a direct attack on the personal prayer-life of the laity, clergy were ordered to "admonish" any of the laity who prayed upon beads, "and such as will not be admonished, to be put forth from the Holy Communion".[39]

It was not merely the prayer-book which antagonized the laity, but this determination to stamp out immemorial devotional customs, even at the cost of preventing those who continued to use them from "taking their rights" by excluding them from Communion, effectively a redefinition of the community of the parish to include only the reformed. We have a vivid contemporary account of the effect of just such attempted interference in one of the stories told by John Hooker about the Devon revolt. Sometime in Whit week 1549 Walter Ralegh (the father of the famous seaman) was riding to Exeter. Near the village of Clyst St Mary he overtook an old woman on her way to Mass; she was praying upon a pair of rosary beads in her hand. Ralegh, a staunch supporter of the Reformation, challenged the old woman, asking her what she meant by carrying such beads, "sayenge further that there was a punyshemente by the law apoynted agaynste her & all suche as

---

[39] VAI, II pp. 190–6.

woulde not obeye & folowe the same & wch woulde bee putt in
execution vpon theime." The old woman hurried to the church,
where the parishioners, already disgruntled by the imposition of the
1549 prayer-book on the previous Sunday, were gathering for
Mass,

> and beinge impacyente & in an agonye wth the speches before
> paste betwen her & the gentleman begyynethe to upbraye in
> the open Churche verie harde & unsemelie speches concernynge
> religion, saienge that shee was thretned by the gentleman, that
> exvcept shee woulde leave her beades & geve over holie breade &
> water the gentlemen woulde burne theym oute of theire howses
> & spoyle theim.[40]

It is clear from the reference to holy bread and water that the
altercation between the old woman and Ralegh had focused not
on the book, but on the whole question of sacramentals. This,
almost as much as the question of the Mass, was where the reform
challenged lay religion. The enraged parishioners all but lynched
Raleigh, a local mill was burned, and the rebellion escalated.
The incident, not without elements of farce, was to end in black
tragedy. When ultimately Lord Russell was despatched by Somerset
to put down the rebellion, Clyst St Mary was the scene of a
particularly bloody pitched battle, in which the local peasantry were
ruthlessly butchered, along with all the prisoners captured by the
royal forces then and previously. The village was put to the torch.
Archbishop Cranmer's dislike of rosary beads and holy water had
cost the people of Clyst dear.[41]

The disastrous outcome of the open revolt of the West Country
was a firm disincentive to emulation elsewhere, but more oblique
resistance was widespread. The Privy Council considered that the
judges and the local gentry were to blame, and Lord Chancellor
Rich was deputed to harangue the judges on their dereliction of
duty. They were so negligent and slack in implementing the King's
"godly orders", he told them, that far from enforcing them, "you
do look rather, as it were, through your fingers," content that there
should be disobedience to the King's laws and Injunctions. The
result was that in some shires "which be further off, it seemed that
the people have never heard of divers of his majesty's proclamations"
or if they had, the judges winked while the laws were ignored.[42] In
a sermon preached before the court in March 1550 John Ponet
expanded on these themes. All over the land, he declared, the

[40] John Vowell alias Hooker, *The Description of the Citie of Excester*, 1919, part II,
pp. 62–3.
[41] Dixon, *History*, III pp. 73–4.
[42] Foxe, *Acts and Monuments*, V pp. 724–5.

saying was "Believe as your forefathers have done before you," a saying spread abroad "by the judges in their circuits and the justices of the peace that be popishly affected, by bishops and their officers . . . by schoolmasters in their grammar schools, by stewards when they keep their courts, by priests when they sit to hear auricular confession".[43]

In this climate · of discontent and disobedience, all the more alarming because it affected and was promoted by those most vital to the enforcement of order, the judges, the gentry, and the clergy, the arrest of Somerset in mid-October was profoundly unsettling. Since the cause of reform was so closely identified with the Lord Protector, traditionalists all over England believed that soon the Mass would be restored and the Henrician settlement reimposed. The Papists, wrote Hooper, "are hoping and earnestly struggling of their kingdom". It was "noised and bruited abroad that they should have again their old Latin service, their conjured bread and water". The Mass and other Catholic ceremonies were even revived in Oxford. To stop the rot the Council issued on Christmas Day an instruction to the bishops to call in all Catholic service books and any other book, whose retention "should be a let to the using of the said *Book of Common Prayer*". The bishop or his deputy was personally to oversee each of these books "defaced or abolished", so that they were unusable. The same order gave bishops authority to discipline parishioners hindering the celebration of the communion by refusing to take their turn on the rota for paying the expenses of bread and wine. The order was enshrined in an Act "for the defacing of images and the bringing in of books of old Service in the Church" in January 1550, which was even more far-reaching. In addition to calling in all "antiphoners, missals, scrayles, processionals, manuals, legends, pyes, portuyses, primers in latin or English, cowchers, journals, or other books . . . heretofore used for the service of the Church", the Act also ordered the destruction by the end of June of all "images of stone, timber, alabaster or earth, graven carved or painted, which heretofore have been taken out of any church or chapel or yet stand in any church or chapel". The responsibility for this surrender and destruction was laid on the mayors, bailiffs, constables, or churchwardens of every community. For every such book or image they withheld, the local officials were to be fined twenty shillings for a first offence, four pounds for a second, and to be imprisoned at the King's pleasure for a third.[44]

[43] A. Gasquet and Edmund Bishop, *Edward VI and the Book of Common Prayer*, 1891, pp. 257–8.

[44] J. Gairdner, *Lollardy and the Reformation*, 1908–13, III pp. 125–6, 172–4, 181–4; TRP, I no. 353.

The Council was now determined that the time for any compromise with the Catholic past had gone. They were intensely conscious not merely of resistance to the prayer-book, but, more insidiously, of its assimilation to traditional Catholic practice and belief. Gardiner's maddening claim, from his cell in the Tower, that he could find the fundamental teaching of the Mass in the pages of the prayer-book was no isolated piece of sophistry. Many less subtle traditionalists set about making the best of the matter, and in the process seemed set to subvert the aims of the reformers. Bridget, Lady Marney, making her will in September 1549, provided money for doles, for the payment of priests and clerks at her "Dirige", to have twelve old men at her burial and month's mind "and in the service tyme be well and devoutly occupied". A priest was to sing for her soul for two years "yf the kyngs lawes wolle so suffer yt"; if not, the money was to be spent on deeds of charity for the poor folk and on highways. And on the day of her burying she stipulated that "I wolle there be songe soche service as ys sett out or appointed by the King's booke to be used at buryall."[45]

Lady Marney's desire to operate within the bounds of the law is evident, but her unreformed Catholicism is just as clear, and many others sought to press the prayer-book into the same mould. It is perhaps not very surprising that Sir William Bee, a former Carthusian of Mount Grace, having left bequests of a shilling to each of his former brethren, and a mark's worth of white bread for the poor at his burial "to pray for my powr soul", should ask for a "Dirige" and "com'unyon wyth note" to be sung at his funeral in March 1551, as though it were still the Mass.[46] But many of the laity showed the same determination to treat the prayer-book as an English missal. William Kaye of Wakefield in August 1550 asked his wife "to dispose for my saull healthe as she thinkes mete, to have the blessed communion celebrate the day of my buriall withe all other godly prayers conteyned in the common booke of s'vice".[47] Giles Fenis of Arlington in Sussex asked his executors in April 1551 to pay five honest priests "to say service and mynister the holly communyon nowe at this present sett forthe for a uniform to be followed thorow oute all the Reame yf they can be gotten," and left eightpence each to five poor folks who would receive communion at the same time, a clear continuation of Catholic practice.[48] In the same way, the Northamptonshire

---

[45] Will printed in *Transactions of the Essex Archaeological Society*, ns I, 1878, pp. 143–6.
[46] *Wills and Inventories* (Durham), ed. J. Raine I pp. 134–6.
[47] *Test. Leod.*, I p. 256.
[48] *Sussex Wills*, I p. 38; see above, chapter 10, "The Pains of Purgatory", pp. 364–6.

testators who left money in 1550 "to the hyght aulter & now callyd the table of our Lord", or in 1551 for a taper "to be set upon the hey alter & to be tened and lighted ever when the pryst ys at masse" revealed volumes about "reformed" eucharistic practice in Northamptonshire, and about the essentially unreconstructed mentality of the parishioners who stoically accepted the liturgical changes forced upon them by the regime.[49]

This "counterfeiting of the mass" was intolerable to the leaders of reform. It had been condemned in Cranmer's draft visitation articles for 1549, and by the suppression of the "Apostles Communions" in St Paul's. The silencing and arrest of traditionalist bishops like Bonner, Gardiner, and Heath, and their replacement by Ridley, Ponet, and Hooper marked a new and intensified attempt to stamp out all such accommodations with the past. Ridley's Injunctions for the London diocese in 1550 forbade any such counterfeiting in "kissing of the Lord's board, washing his hands or fingers . . . shifting the book from one place to another . . . saying the Agnus before the Communion, showing the Sacrament openly before the distribution, or making any elevation thereof, ringing of the sacring bell, or setting any light upon the Lord's board".[50] Roger Edgeworth recalled in a sermon preached in Mary's reign the shifts to which the determination to avoid any traditional reverence towards the Sacrament drove the reformers. At first, he declared, they had consecrated the Sacrament holding the bread on the paten with their backs to the altar, so that the people might see. But

> because there seemed to muche reverence to be given to the Sacrament by this waie, the people were al driven out of the chauncell except the ministers, that the communion should not be commonlye sene nor worshipped. And anone that way seemed not best and therefore there was veils or curtens drawn . . . that no man should see what the priest did, nor here what he said. Then this way pleased not and the aulters-were pulled downe and the tables set up and all the observaunce saide in Englyshe and that openly that all men mighte here and see . . . and the bread commaunded to be common brede levende with salt . . . And then sone after were all the corporaces taken awaye to extenuate the honoure of the sacrament and laied downe on the prophane boarde clothe.[51]

[49] *Northants Wills*, II pp. 405, 436.
[50] VAI, II p. 242.
[51] R Edgeworth, *Sermons Very fruitfull, godly and learned*, R. Caly, 1557, RSTC 7482, fols 312–13.

Edgeworth no doubt made the most of the flux in which reformed Eucharistic practice found itself in the early 1550s, but there is no questioning the substantial accuracy of his account, at least as far as the capital was concerned. The London chronicles also report the use of the old Lent veil to screen the communion table from would-be worshippers of the sacrament in St Paul's.[52]

But the capital was not the only place in which the consequences of the drive towards radical Protestantism and discontinuity with the past was felt. Hooper's Interrogatories and Injunctions for Gloucester and Worcester, drawn up in 1551, were even more extreme, requiring the ripping out of any steps or partitions where altars had been, the celebration of the communion anywhere except where the Mass had been sung, forbidding the "decking or apparelling" of tables "behind or before" as if they were altars, and any variation of tone or pitch of voice or posture of body, by ministers or people, which might be reminiscent of the Mass. Hooper even insisted that the priest should break the communion wafer into two pieces, not three, since in the Mass the fraction was into three.[53]

All this ran far ahead of the law, but law, like policy, was being made on the run. In May 1550 Ridley ordered the abolition of altars everywhere in his diocese. This was not formally extended to the whole country by the Privy Council till November, but altars were coming down all over the country by then, as the Protestant episcopate and their officials brought pressure to bear.[54] The pressure was applied with extraordinary minuteness, and not just on the question of altars or the celebration of communion. Hooper expected his clergy to police even the prayers and words of encouragement used by midwives at childbirth, lest any saint should be invoked. He set on foot enquiries about any clergy using preambles to parishioners' wills which mentioned the saints. He demanded to know if any reverenced the Sacrament while it was being carried to the sick, or whether anyone showed particular respect or honour to the oils with which the dying asked to be anointed.[55]

It was amid this flood-tide of radicalism that the second Edwardine *Book of Common Prayer* was authorized in April 1552, printed in late September, and brought into use from 1 November.[56] The book of 1552 represented a determined attempt to break

---

[52] *Grey Friars' Chronicle*, p. 67.
[53] VAI, II pp. 241–2, 267–309.
[54] R. Hutton, "Local Impact", 1987, pp. 125–6.
[55] VAI, II pp. 291–308.
[56] Gasquet and Bishop, *Edward VI*, pp. 301–3.

once and for all with the Catholic past, and to leave nothing in the official worship of the Church of England which could provide a toehold for traditional ways of thinking about the sacred. Inconsistencies in fact remained to trouble the Elizabethan church and to provide grist for the mill of puritans calling for further reformation. By the standards that England had known till 1552, however, it was drastic in the extreme. The differences between the two books provide a telling index of the distance which the reform had travelled in just three years from the thought world of medieval Catholicism, and therefore from the instincts of the vast majority of the people.

For all his suspicion of sacramentals in 1549, Cranmer had left in the first prayer-book a number of observances which clearly reflected the theological understanding which made the blessing and the exorcism of things and people meaningful. In the baptismal service, for example, he had retained a striking and full-blooded prayer, adapted from the Sarum rite, in which the priest drove the unclean spirit out of the children about to be baptized, in the name of the Father, Son, and Holy Ghost. As we have already seen, it was the presence of prayers of this sort in the medieval rite which provided the laity with paradigms for countless "magical" charms and invocations.[57] The 1552 book banished this prayer, along with all anointings, in baptism, the visitation of the sick, and ordination. It also dispensed with the chrisom, or white robe given to the newly baptized. Similarly, in confirmation, the 1552 book omitted the ceremonial signing of those confirmed with the sign of the cross on their foreheads. Somewhat inconsistently, this ceremony was retained in baptism, but took place now after the actual baptism, not before, as in ancient tradition. It thereby lost the exorcizing function implicit in its original place in the ceremony.

In the consecration prayer at communion, the prayer of invocation in which the priest called on God to "blesse and sanctifie" the bread and wine with his spirit and word was now dropped, together with the two manual signs of the cross over the elements which endorsed the notion that a powerful act of blessing, affecting the "creatures of bread and wine", was here taking place. Any idea that the communion could be celebrated for a congregation made up predominantly of spectators, as was envisaged, however reluctantly, by the 1549 book, was now abandoned, the rubric stipulating that there was to be no celebration "excepte there be a good noumbre to communicate with the Priest". In a dramatic visual break with

[57] *First and Second Prayer Books*, p. 238; see above, chapter 8, "Charms, Pardons, and Promises" pp. 279–85.

tradition, the prayer-book stipulated that the communion was to be celebrated by a priest wearing neither cope nor vestment, as required in 1549, but a simple surplice, like the parish clerk or the choir. The celebration was to take place not "at God's board", a medieval term frequently used of stone altars, but at a table set in the body of the church, the priest standing on the north side, thereby removing every trace of association with the priest before the altar at Mass. Ordinary wheaten bread was to be used, and any bread or wine left after the celebration was to be taken home for domestic consumption by the curate, thereby abolishing any notion of consecration. This ruling had the added advantage of preventing any worship of the Sacrament as it was taken to the sick, since the Sacrament would no longer be reserved or carried through the streets for any purpose whatever. Instead, the priest was to celebrate the communion afresh in the sick person's house, always provided that there was "a goode nombre to receyve the communion" with them. The book did not flinch from one inevitable consequence of this provision, that lonely people with no close neighbours would be unable to receive communion on their deathbeds. To these, as to any dying person who for one reason or another could not receive their last housel, the curate was to explain that true repentance, firm faith, and hearty thanks for the benefits of Christ would be just as profitable to their soul's health, "althoughe he doe not receyve the Sacrament with his mouth". The one exception allowed for in the prayer-book was in time of plague, "when none of the parysh or neighbours can be gotten to communicate wyth the syck in theyr houses". At such a time the priest alone might communicate with the dying person. Medieval Christians had of course accepted the value of "spiritual communion" for those deprived of the Sacraments, but the gulf between the theology of the book on this issue and the absorbing preoccupation of the majority of the laity of late medieval and early Tudor England with securing "housel and shrift at my last end" is daunting.[58] Later practice was to modify the rigours of this prescription, and in some places the parish clerk attended the priest and received communion with the sick person, but the starkness of the original prescription remains.

If in the rites of the dying the prayer-book of 1552 seems to come from a different world not only from the medieval church, but even from the 1549 book, that gulf is displayed even more starkly in the rites of the dead. Funerals in late medieval England, as we have seen, were intensely concerned with the notion of community, a

---

[58] See above, chapter 9, "Last Things" pp. 319ff.

community in which living and dead were not separated, in which the bonds of affection, duty, and blood continued to bind. The means of this transaction between the living and the dead was charity, maintained and expressed in prayer. The dead, whose names were recited week by week in the bede-roll at the parish Mass, remained part of the communities they had once lived in, and the objects they left for use in the worship of that community preserved their names and evoked the gratitude of the living towards them.[59] The theology behind the 1549 book was well advanced towards reformed teaching, and there was an evident unease about prayers which implied that intercession might effect any change in the state of the dead. Yet the funeral service of 1549 did contain prayers for the dead, and emphasized their community with the living, "they with us and we with them". That sense of the continuing presence of the dead among the living was vividly expressed in the Sarum funeral rite and in the 1549 prayer-book by the fact that at the moment of the committal of the body to the earth the priest turned to the corpse, scattered earth on it and, in Cranmer's translation, said "I commend thy soule to God the father almighty, and thy body to the grounde, earth to earth, asshes to asshes, dust to dust." The dead could still be spoken to directly, even in 1549, because in some sense they still belonged within the human community. But in the world of the 1552 book the dead were no longer with us. They could neither be spoken to nor even about, in any way that affected their well-being. The dead had gone beyond the reach of human contact, even of human prayer. There was nothing which could even be mistaken for a prayer for the dead in the 1552 funeral rite. The service was no longer a rite of intercession on behalf of the dead, but an exhortation to faith on the part of the living. Indeed, it is not too much to say that the oddest feature of the 1552 burial rite is the disappearance of the corpse from it. So, at the moment of committal in 1552, the minister turns not towards the corpse, but away from it, to the living congregation around the grave. "Forasmuche as it hathe pleased almightie God of his great mercy to take unto himselfe the soule of our dere brother here departed: we therefore commit his body to the ground, earth to earth, asshes to asshes, dust to dust." Here the dead person is spoken not to, but about, as one no longer here, but precisely as departed: the boundaries of human community have been redrawn.[60]

The last act of the Edwardine attack on traditional religion was already under way by the time the second prayer-book was

[59] Ibid., pp. 327ff.
[60] *First and Second Prayer Books*, pp. 269–70, 424–7.

imposed by law. The reform had begun in plunder, the stripping and the destruction of the monasteries. Some of the most vigorous opposition to it, such as the Pilgrimage of Grace, had been born out of the fear of plunder. As we have already seen, the Edwardine authorities had demanded in 1547 returns of the valuables of every parish in the land. Further surveys had been carried out in 1549, when once again the reason given was the preservation of the property of the churches from private embezzlement. By 1549 this concern may have been perfectly genuine. Everywhere the treasures of the churches were being rapidly sold off by churchwardens and parishioners, to prevent confiscation. But they were also being stolen in an unprecedented and apparently nationwide outbreak of burglaries in churches in the years after 1547.[61] Yet embezzlement was no monopoly of private men. In 1549 Somerset had ordered the destruction of the Pardon Churchyard at St Paul's, with its famous cloisters painted with the Dance of Death and Lydgate's accompanying verses. The "daunce of Paulls" was one of the most potent symbols of the old theology in London, and its destruction was probably inevitable. But the ideological impact of its destruction was dulled (or, depending on your point of view, sharpened) by the fact that the rubble and wainscoting were carted away to be used in the building of the Protector's own great new house rising in the Strand on the site of the parish church of St Mary le Strand, which he had demolished for the purpose.[62] It was no surprise to anyone, therefore, when the pretence of the protection of the treasures of the churches was abandoned in March 1551, and the Privy Council ordered that "for as much as the King's Majestie had neede presently of a mass of money" all the remaining church plate in England was to be called in and disposed of for his use.[63]

This order was not in fact acted on till the following year, when once more commissioners for every part of the country were appointed to compile new inventories, trace anything which had gone astray since the beginning of the reign, and begin the process of liquidation. They had careful instructions to "use such sober and discrete maner of p[ro]ceding" as to provide "as litle occasion of trouble or disquyet of the multitude as may be".[64] We will look in detail at the effects of this commission in the next chapter: here we need only note that the commissioners were commanded to take charge of all the plate and vestments the churches owned, leav-

    [61] See below, chapter 14, "The Impact of Reform: Parishes", pp. 487–9.
    [62] On the destruction of the Dance of Pauls, see extracts from the notebook of George Vertue in Walpole Society, XVIII, 1929–30, p. 37.
    [63] Inventories of Church Goods for Yorkshire, p. xiv.
    [64] Transactions of the Essex Archaeological Society, IV, 1869, p. 208.

ing only the bare essentials for the worship defined in the new prayer-book – a surplice, a couple of tablecloths, a cup for the communion, and a bell.

It was to emerge from this final Edwardine survey that parishes all over the country had done what they could to prevent the Crown laying hands on their treasures, especially vessels and other objects of precious metal. Some were concealed, many others sold without Crown permission and the proceeds set aside for the use of the parish. Yet in many parishes much remained. The 1549 book permitted the use of copes and vestments, of chalice and paten, candlesticks and chrismatory. Though there had been sales and depredations almost everywhere, and the sumptuous inventories of the pre-Reformation period had in many places dwindled to a handful of vessels and vestments, nevertheless something remained of the material embodiments of the piety of centuries. Now these heirlooms, from the most elaborate monstrance or the most bejewelled vestment down to the humblest kerchief or houseling towel, were to be turned into cash for the benefit of the Crown.

Some of the commissioners baulked at so breathtaking an act of sacrilege. The commissioners for the Weald of Kent had to be pressured by the Council to act, and claimed later to have left as much in the parishes as they could get away with, since "we were very lothe to take any thinge from them." John Huddlestone, whose family was to have a long tradition of recusancy, helped compile the Cambridgeshire inventories for 1549, but refused to assist in the confiscations.[65] But whatever the scruples of individuals, the process of stripping moved swiftly ahead. The commissioners for the Kesteven division of Lincolnshire did not begin their work until 18 June 1553, less than three weeks before Edward's death, yet in the course of one week they disposed of vestments and ornaments, much of them at knock-down prices, to the value of £158 at Stamford, Folkingham, Ancaster, Wellingore, Grantham. Despite the difficulty of handling them, even the bells in the steeples were not safe, and by the end of the process 31,921 pounds of bell-metal was awaiting sale at Grimsby, and Sir William Cecil himself had custody of another 14,555 pounds.[66] The house was swept and garnished. But on 6 July Edward VI died. Queen Jane, the last desperate hope of the reformers, had not long to reign, and by 20 July Mary's succession was assured and proclaimed. It was time to rebuild the altars.

[65] *Arch. Cantiana*, XIV, p. 322; Scarisbrick, *Reformation*, pp. 104–5. Huddlestone signed all the 1549 certificates for Cambridgeshire, but none of the subsequent acts of the Commissioners.

[66] Walker, "Reformation and Reaction", pp. 55–6.

CHAPTER 14

THE IMPACT OF REFORM: PARISHES

The dramatic religious changes between 1547 and 1553 are closely reflected in the records of diocese and parish. Any theory of the weakness of Tudor government in the regions must somehow explain the astonishing degree of conformity achieved in thousands of communities, great and small, throughout the country. From Cumberland to Kent, from Bristol to Bury St Edmunds the images came down in the wake of the royal visitation of 1547/8, the Mass was abolished and the Mass-books and breviaries surrendered in 1549 and 1550. In response to central diktat the altars were drawn down and the walls whited, windows broken or blotted out to conceal "feigned miracles". In 1553 veils and vestments, chalices and chests and hangings, the accumulation of generations of pious donations, were surrendered to the King's commissioners, to be unstitched, broken up, or melted down to meet the spiralling costs of mid-Tudor war-debt and the runaway rapacity of the mid-Tudor Court. By the end of the reign in most churches the altars were gone, the niches empty, indeed many of the niches themselves filled in and plastered over. Whatever the Crown commanded, the people, for the most part, did. When resistance erupted it was often because of specific local provocations, as in the Lizard peninsula in 1548, or because the tensions and changing fortunes of Court life meant that aristocratic and gentry leadership was available to focus and legitimize popular discontent, as was probably the case in the Pilgrimage of Grace, or else because dramatic and unwelcome religious change coincided with social and economic crisis, as in the West Country in 1549.[1]

For historians convinced of the bankruptcy of late medieval Catholicism there is nothing here to surprise, certainly no historical problem. A rotten structure crumbles when kicked, institutions embodying ideas whose time has passed can be dissolved with

---

[1] For a survey of the parochial implementation of the changes see R. Hutton, "The Local Impact of the Tudor Reformations", in C. Haigh (ed.), *The English Reformation Revised*, 1987, pp. 114–38.

impunity. Thus, for A. G. Dickens the fundamental reason for the comparative calm with which the dissolution of the chantries was received was that most people had "ceased to believe in the doctrine of intercessory masses for souls in purgatory", and only a minority "persisted in this belief".[2] The altars could be demolished because the sacrifice offered on them was no longer precious to the people. It has been one of the principal contentions of this book, however, that into the 1530s the vigour, richness, and creativity of late medieval religion was undiminished, and continued to hold the imagination and elicit the loyalty of the majority of the population. By the 1540s, of course, the numbers of committed Protestants were growing, and there were a number of places in which they had come to have a dominant role. Protestantism was a force to be reckoned with in London and in towns like Bristol, Rye, and Colchester, and it was becoming so in some northern towns such as Hessle, Hull, and Halifax. Even in these cases, though, we should beware of overestimating numbers. There can have been few if any communities in which Protestants formed anything like an actual numerical majority. The influence of the reform usually stemmed from the not always very secure social and economic prestige of its more prosperous or articulate adherents. The Kentish town of Cranbrook had produced Protestants from the 1530s onwards, but it was a bastion of traditional religion, whose images were not defaced and whose Rood was being rebuilt in the 1540s. The wills made at Cranbrook to the mid-century are among the most consistently traditionalist in form in the whole of Kent.[3] East Anglian towns are often thought of as "natural" centres of Protestantism, but there were important ones, such as Eye, whose Protestant minorities never got the whip hand, and where Catholicism, or at any rate determined traditionalism, continued to dominate the town's life well into Elizabeth's reign.[4] In such a perspective, the unmistakable evidence of prompt compliance with the Tudor reform does present a problem, and demands not only an explanation but an accurate characterization. In what follows, I want to explore the impact of the Henrician and Edwardine reforms in the parishes, trying to assess the extent to which those reforms can be said to have secured themselves within the localities against a revival of Catholicism in the reign of Mary.

[2] *The English Reformation*, 1989, p. 235.

[3] P. Clark, *English Provincial Society*, 1977, p. 59.

[4] For a maximalist account of the spread of Protestantism up to the accession of Elizabeth see A. G. Dickens, "The Early Expansion of Protestantism in England 1520–1558", *Archiv für Reformationsgeschichte*, XXVIII, 1987, pp. 187–221; for Eye see M. A. Cook, "Eye (Suffolk) in the years of Uncertainty, 1520–1590", Keele PhD thesis 1982.

Injunction twenty-eight of the 1547 set had articulated what was to be one of the central impulses of the royal visitation of that year. Clergy and people were to "take away, utterly extinct and destroy all shrines, covering of shrines, all tables, candlesticks, trindles or rolls of wax, pictures, paintings and all other monuments of feigned miracles, pilgrimages, idolatry, and superstition; so that there remain no memory of the same."[5] Three years later the Council demanded that the old liturgical books should be "defaced and abolished" lest their continued existence prove "a lett to that godly and uniform order, which by a common consent is now set forthe".[6] At the heart of the Edwardine reform was the necessity of destroying, of cutting, hammering, scraping, or melting into a deserved oblivion the monuments of popery, so that the doctrines they embodied might be forgotten. Iconoclasm was the central sacrament of the reform, and, as the programme of the leaders became more radical in the years between 1547 and 1553, they sought with greater urgency the celebration of that sacrament of forgetfulness in every parish in the land. The churchwardens' accounts of the period witness a wholesale removal of the images, vestments, and vessels which had been the wonder of foreign visitors to the country, and in which the collective memory of the parishes was, quite literally, enshrined. Some of this, especially in the capital, was true iconoclasm, expressing deeply held Protestant conviction, destruction as itself a religious act. But it is patent that much of it was nothing of the sort. There was grudging fulfilment of the will of the Crown, and sometimes an attempt to anticipate the actions of the Crown in order to save something from the wreckage.

About the promptness of the removal of the images almost everywhere there can be no doubt, for the wardens' accounts for 1547–8 bristle with references to it: 2s 4d at Ashburton in Devon for taking down "le ymag called le George", and 3s 4d for the removal of "le rode and other images". At Stratton in Cornwall it cost only eight pence "for takyng down of the horse of the Image of seynt George" and another eight pence for the Rood.[7] At Tilney in Norfolk they paid out thirty-five shillings in 1547 "for whytyng of the Churche and stoppyng of the hooles" where the images had stood, while at North Elmham they paid for whitewashing the church in 1548, but recouped by selling the images for 9s 2d. At Ludlow the wardens sold the image of George for eighteen pence, his dragon for sevenpence, with tenpence for "a image of Jhesus".[8]

[5] VAI, II p. 126.
[6] C. Dugmore, The Mass and the English Reformers, 1958, p. 142.
[7] Ashburton CWA, p. 121; Stratton CWA, p. 220.
[8] Tilney CWA, p. 172; North Elmham CWA, p. 43; Ludlow CWA, pp. 35–7.

These activities were duplicated in every region in England, and there is no great mystery about them, since they coincide with the activities of the royal visitors. The deeply traditionalist Suffolk parish of Barking, where the feasts of Becket had long been rumoured as remaining undefaced in the parish Mass-books and breviaries, and whose clergy and wardens resolutely stonewalled reform measures in Henry's reign, was not a community likely to harbour iconoclasts or to welcome the abolition of the cult of images. Yet like conservative parishes up and down the country, at the visitation of 1547 Barking dutifully sold off the six candlesticks and the "egle all of latten" which had adorned the candle-beam.[9] The same process would be repeated at each stage of the reform, as when the regime required removal of altars from 1550 onwards.

Promptness, of course, is a relative term: some parishes delayed implementing commands to remove images or altars as long as it was safe to do so, and sometimes longer. Where parishes dragged their feet the authorities retaliated. In Kent some of the clergy whose parishes delayed the removal of altars in 1550 were excommunicated, even though altars were at that stage still legal.[10] The pace of reform therefore varied somewhat, reflecting perhaps as much the zeal of the commissioners as the inertia of the people. In the Home Counties and East Anglia, the Injunction against abused images was used fairly consistently to remove all imagery. In parts of the Midlands, the west, and the north only Roods and "abused" images seem to have gone to begin with, and the final removal was postponed till 1549. In the end, however, conformity was almost universal.

Such conformity in itself implies nothing about the beliefs of clergy, wardens, or laity in the parishes, and we are certainly not dealing here with mass evidence of spreading Protestant conviction. The Rood and other images came down at Ashburton in 1547, but the figures of Mary and John were new, and had gone up only the previous year. The parishioners of Ludlow in Shropshire complied promptly with orders to remove the Rood and other images in 1547, but in the same year they spent tenpence on making up the canopy to be carried over the Blessed Sacrament on Corpus Christi day, and in the following year celebrated the Easter sepulchre ceremonies connected with the Blessed Sacrament as usual, though elsewhere in England the sepulchre was being treated as illegal.[11] The parishioners of North Elmham sold their Rood-loft images in

[9] The East Anglian, ns I, 1885, p. 68.
[10] "Extracts from Original Documents Illustrating the Progress of the Reformation in Kent", ed. C. E. Woodruff, Archaeologia Cantiana, XXXI, 1915 (hereafter = Kent Reformation) pp. 103–4.
[11] Ludlow CWA, pp. 30–4; for an identical example see Worcester St Michael's CWA, p. 20.

1548 and whitewashed the church, but in the previous two years they had renewed the best canopy for Palm Sunday and Corpus Christi, and made new copes for the boy bishop celebrations.[12] Many West-Country parishes which dutifully removed their images in 1547 and 1548 showed their true convictions in the rising of 1549. At Stratton, which had taken down its images in 1548, the Rood-loft itself was dismantled in 1549, presumably because it was covered in images or had an altar on it. But there were no reformers in Stratton, and evidently nothing had been destroyed, for the parishioners took advantage of the rising to restore the loft. Despite harassment from the Elizabethan authorities, it was not finally removed till the 1570s.[13] There is in fact real danger in reading changes of heart into the evidence of the activities of Edwardine churchwardens. Reglazing in churches in the late 1540s has been taken as "almost certain" evidence of iconoclasm, the triumph of the "campaign against representations of the saints". As it happens, all the town churches of Ipswich were reglazed between 1548 and 1550, and in view of the town's subsequent reputation as a Puritan community, it is tempting to see this reglazing as an indication of the strength of Edwardine Protestantism in the town. Yet it would be quite mistaken to do so. The wardens of several of the churches concerned reported to the Suffolk commissioners for Church goods, who would have been only too pleased to hear of iconoclastic zeal, that the cause of the reglazing was not Protestantism, but a freak storm; the windows had been "decayed and broken with the great tempaste of hayle."[14]

The removal of images and in due course altars was required by authority, and, where necessary, enforced. But the apparently voluntary sale of religious objects was almost as striking a feature of the parish records of Edwardine England as was iconoclasm. Many of the objects sold off were connected with the cult of the saints – silver shoes, crowns, reliquaries, embroidered and jewelled coats – and all these would have had to go as part of the campaign against the cult. But much else was directly associated with the Blessed Sacrament – chalices, pyxes, monstrances – and much of it was the product of the cult of the dead – sumptuously embroidered vestments with the donor's arms or name on them, vessels with commemorative inscriptions, designed to ensure the continuance of prayer for the benefactor. Does their disposal suggest a diminishing of the cults about which they were employed, a lessening of reverence, or a disregard for the spiritual welfare of the dead?

[12] North Elmham CWA, pp. 36, 41.
[13] Stratton CWA, pp. 221, 227, 230.
[14] Hutton, "Local Impact", p. 121; *East Anglian*, ns I pp. 6–8, 42–4.

In some instances it may have been so, but once again the evidence suggests that in most cases the reasons for the sales were practical and the ideological implications slight. Many sales had already taken place in Henry's reign, in part because of widespread fears that he intended to seize parish valuables as he had seized those of the monasteries, but in part also because the outlawing of the cult of the saints had rendered some objects redundant. Some of the Henrician bishops had systematically confiscated and destroyed relics.[15] The empty reliquaries were valuable. In the light of official utterances like the King's letter from Hull of 1541, ordering the removals of "shrines, coverings of shrines" and the like, they were also extremely vulnerable. So in the year after that letter was issued, the wardens of North Elmham sold off to a Norwich silversmith "the Sylver that was upon the Crosse that the relyques wheryn" as well as the silver shoes which were upon "the brown rodes fete".[16] Great St Mary's, Cambridge, had a shrine of St Nicholas, which attracted votive offerings. A meeting on St John's day 1541 of "moste part of the parochianers" agreed to sell at the next Stourbridge fair a silver pair of beads and two coral pairs, which had been given as *ex votos* to the image, the collar of nine gold links enamelled which hung round the saint's neck, and the "lityll Monstre or Relick of St Nicholas oyll". But this was no Protestant repudiation of the cult of the saints, for the rest of the church's images kept their embroidered velvet and satin coats, till the images themselves were abolished in 1550.[17] Less colourfully, at Tilney in 1544 the parishioners sold off the candle-pricket on which votive lights had once burned before the images of the Virgin, since such lights had been illegal since 1538. It is not without interest that they waited six years before doing so.[18]

These were all sales to comply with the requirements of the Henrician Reformation. But there was precedent for the sale or at least the pawning of even the most sacred objects to solve cash-flow problems during extensive building projects, or to meet emergency costs for repairs after accident or disaster. The churchwardens of Louth in Lincolnshire in 1503 had borrowed £6 12s 0d from the Lady Gild and St Peter's gild, pledging "the best chalys belongyng to the hy auter" as security. The Suffolk parish of Cratfield sold a spare chalice, a silver censer and a cross for £21 in 1544, in order to pay for battlements and lead for the church tower. The parishioners of Great Dunmow in Essex met pressing financial needs by selling

[15] See above, chapter 11, "The Attack on Traditional Religion I", pp. 414–5.
[16] North Elmham CWA, p. 15.
[17] Cambridge Great St Mary's CWA, pp. 94–5, 97, 118.
[18] Tilney CWA, p. 164.

off considerable quantities of plate in 1536 and 1537. At the same time, they were not insensible to the symbolic resonance of the sale of holy things, and in 1538 the wives of the parish gathered subscriptions to redeem the best pax, a particularly potent symbol of the parish's identity and unity.[19]

With the accession of Edward the steady trickle of sales already under way in the last years of Henry became a flood. The radical character of the regime was clear from its first months, and the dissolution of the chantries and the series of inventories of parish valuables demanded by the Crown in 1547, 1549, and 1552 persuaded many that confiscations were now imminent. The sales of 1547 and the following years represent not a swing to the reform, but a panic-stricken stampede to prevent theft by the Crown. Wherever one turns in the records one encounters massive sales of plate in 1547 and 1548, as parishes shed particularly valuable second or third chalices, crosses, pyxes, paxes, and monstrances, and set about spending the money on bona fide parish projects which even the Crown could not challenge. Haddenham in the Isle of Ely, a conservative community like most Cambridgeshire villages, sold off a silver-gilt chalice and paten, a processional cross, a pyx and two paxes, raising £42 10s 0d, which was spent on repairs to the church leads, on embanking the town common against floods, on drainage gulleys and dykes, and for "the borde of one pore mayden that was frantyke for the space of 10 wekys".[20] There was no question here of the deliberate shedding of Catholic cultic objects of which the parishioners disapproved, since they retained two chalices and had duplicates of the other items in copper, a metal which would serve just as well as silver in the liturgy but was less likely to stimulate the rapacity of the king's visitors and commissioners. Some parishes, indeed, with a striking lack of foresight, sought to take advantage of the abundance of ornaments and vestments coming on to the market by acquiring coveted cultic objects, just as many had bought up such things after the dissolution of the monasteries. Sometime before 1549 Great Chesterford in Essex sold a double-gilt Cross, two silver cruets, and a pax, and promptly spent part of the proceeds on acquiring a lavish black velvet set of vestments for priest, deacon, and subdeacon with matching copes, for use at requiems, a purchase they must rapidly have regretted.[21]

[19] Louth CWA, p. 33; Cratfield CWA, p. 74; W. Scott, *Antiquities of an Essex Parish*, 1873, pp. 48–9.
[20] *East Anglian*, 3rd series, IX, 1901–2, pp. 96, 105.
[21] *Transactions of the Essex Archaeological Society*, ns X, 1909, p. 95.

Many of these sales of vessels and vestments were pre-emptive, designed to retain for parishes the value of objects certain to be seized by the Crown. They can often be related directly to the stages of official reform. Thus the parishioners of Rayleigh in Essex, despite the absence of its churchwarden, held a meeting after service one Sunday in 1550 and hastily sold off most of their Catholic liturgical books. This action was almost certainly in response to the Act "for the abolishynge and puttinge away of diverse Bookes and Images", which demanded the surrender of all such books to the Crown, and which criticized those who retained them as "pervarse persons" who "ympugned" the King's proceedings.[22] Certainly there was no hint of religious radicalism at Rayleigh. In 1552 the parish still had more than a dozen sets of vestments, its pyx, oil-box, processional crosses, and even two marble super-altars containing relics, the mere possession of which was certainly forbidden.[23]

To judge by its possessions, Rayleigh was a wealthy parish, but even it had sold off £10-worth of plate in 1547. In many parishes such sales were absolutely necessary to meet financial crises precipitated by the government's religious reforms. The Injunctions of 1547 and the subsequent religious changes demanded substantial expenditure from parishes – the construction of parish chests, pulpits, and communion tables, the provision of Bible, *Homilies*, prayer-book, and the paraphrases of Erasmus, the removal of images and the filling and whitewashing of walls. It was standard practice after the removal of the Rood and other images from the lofts to stretch canvas or some other cloth across the front of the loft and the tympanum above it, on which were then painted the royal arms, the Commandments, and other biblical texts. At Smarden in Kent the parish sold a chalice to pay for "a cloth to hang before the rood loft to deface the monuments [and] tabernacles that wer yn the same roode lofte, wrytten with scriptur and the Kynges armes".[24] This could be expensive work: "one Pottie a paynter" was paid £6 by the churchwardens of Houghton in Bedfordshire for "scrypturyng and other payntyng of the churche", and Beckingley in Surrey paid £6 15s 2d for the same work.[25] These financial demands came at precisely the time when the

---

[22] 3 & 4 Edward VI cap. X.

[23] *Transactions of the Essex Archaeological Society*, V, 1873, pp. 117–20.

[24] *Archaeologia Cantiana*, XI, 1877, p. 411 (*Kent Inventories*).

[25] *The Edwardine Inventories for Bedfordshire*, ed. F. C. Eeles, Alcuin Club, VI, 1905 (hereafter = *Bedfordshire Inventories*) p. 28; *Inventories of the Goods and Ornaments in the churches of Surrey in the Reign of King Edward VI*, ed. J. R. Daniel-Tyssen, 1869 (hereafter = *Surrey Inventories*) p. 106.

dissolution of chantries, gilds, and light stocks was depriving parishes of some of their most important traditional sources of funding. The parishioners of Little Ilford in Essex reported to the commissioners on the financial difficulties encountered by Thomas Hutton, their churchwarden from 1547. He had clearly used his ingenuity in keeping costs to the minimum, for the "King's armes with other scriptures" were painted on a ground made up of banner cloths stitched together. Nevertheless there had been unavoidable expenditure, "which charg's the chirche warden and the rest of the parisshe were faine to beare of their own proper cost for they never had no stock to the churche, therefore it hath been verie painefull". Hutton was glad, therefore, to sell some of the church metalwork and albs to "one that came about to enquere to bie latten . . . but what he was he cannot tell".[26]

This was a dilemma experienced in many parishes, as the policies of the regime simultaneously required large-scale expenditure, deprived parishes of the traditional ways of meeting it, but rendered obsolete much valuable ritual paraphernalia which could be sold off to fill the gap. The parishioners of the little church of St Nicholas, Tolleshunt Major, where a grand new tower of brick had been erected in the last years of Henry's reign, were reduced to calling a meeting in 1550 "seyng the church to nede much reparacyon", at which they decided to sell "to such persons as wold bye, all the . . . candylstycks and other old thyngs past use fore the church, as latyn, iron, holy water bockett, prosesshon bell, auter clothes or hangyngs, banners, and suche other".[27] In the same year the parishioners of East Ham, whose financial difficulties were made worse by the theft from the church in 1548 of "the best copes and vestments and all other things worth the conveying away", including the poor man's chest, decided to sell "such things as remained superfluous and unoccupied for the dischargyng of the aforesaid charges and other charges".[28]

With so much desirable material coming on to the market it was a time for entrepreneurs, not only like the scrap-metal man who travelled the Essex parishes and bought the Little Ilford latten and linen, but for "such persons as wold bye" within the parishes themselves. Many local people of means bought up the plate being disposed of at what were often, in a glutted market, knock-down prices. At Great Bromley the principal purchaser when the parish sold off some of its lavish provision of plate in June 1547 was

[26] *Transactions of the Essex Archaeological Society*, ns II, 1884, pp. 239–41.
[27] Ibid., V, 1873, p. 279; N. Pevsner, *The Buildings of England: Essex*, 1954, p. 362.
[28] *Transactions of the Essex Archaeological Society*, ns II, 1884, p. 242.

William Cardinal, lord of the manor and patron of the living. He was also in fact one of the royal commisioners for the inventories of church goods in Essex. The possibilities for corruption in such a situation were obvious, since the sale of all church goods and the subsequent expenditure of the proceeds had to be retrospectively approved by the commissioners. At Brightlingsea, a town parish with rich plate and vestments to protect from confiscation, the wardens "by the assent of the paryshe" seem to have sought to smooth their way with the commissioners by presenting the most influential of them, the Earl of Oxford, with a golden cope.[29]

One of the direct consequences of all this disposal of sacred objects was a dramatic rise in the number of thefts from churches. Sacrilegious theft was not, as some historians have implied, the invention of the Reformation. The accumulation of precious objects which was one of the distinctive features of parochial piety in fourteenth- and fifteenth-century England had been a standing temptation to thieves and was frequently succumbed to in the late Middle Ages.[30] But the legalized looting of the monasteries and chantries by the Crown and its agents in the 1530s and 1540s set an example which others were swift to follow. Moreover, the polemic of the reformers against the very notion of sacred objects, the ritual changes of Edward's reign and the formal desacralizing they involved, removed any religious restraint that thieves might have felt. The presence in every church after 1547 of a poor-box into which contributions were regularly put was an added inducement to thieves. The fact that so much church furniture and equipment was being sold legitimately meant that the sale of stolen goods aroused fewer suspicions than would have been the case at any earlier period. Churchwardens' accounts and the returns to the commissioners for church goods for every county are therefore full of accounts of theft. The commissioners for Hertfordshire compiled a special report on them, and the Essex returns show that some churches were repeatedly robbed. Wennington was robbed three times between 1547 and 1552.[31] At Ashingdon in two incidents thieves stole all the church goods except a chalice, a vestment, an alb, and the chest, even getting away with two bells from the steeple, weighing a hundredweight.[32] At Little Ilford thieves took advantage of the fact that the churchwarden lay dying early in 1551

[29] Ibid., ns I, 1877, pp. 10–16.
[30] On theft of church goods before the reformation see C. Oman, "Security in English Churches A.D. 1000–1548", *Archaeological Journal*, CXXXVI, 1979, pp. 90–8.
[31] *Transactions of the Essex Archaeological Society*, ns II, 1884, p. 184.
[32] Ibid., IV, 1869, p. 215.

to break into the church and steal a cope, four surplices, and all the altar cloths "with all other implements that was in the chirche the which was any thinge handsome to be carried awae". East Ham lost its best vestments and the poor man's box in 1548, and was robbed again in 1552. South Weald lost suits of vestments in velvet, silk, and satin, a copper pyx, a surplice, and even a Bible in two separate robberies.[33]

Not all these thefts were by persons unknown. Prominent local people often took advantage of the disturbance of the period to line their pockets. The outlawing of the use of more than one bell to call to service in the Injunctions was seized on by Sir William Stafford, one of the richest landowners in east Essex, as an opportunity to confiscate bells from the parish churches of which he was patron in the area, at Rochford, Ashingdon, South Shoebury, Hawkwell, and Foulness; he sold the Foulness bells to repair his sea walls on the island.[34] The parishioners of Hawkwell turned in a detailed report to the commissioners, naming the team of carpenters Stafford had employed to strip two bells weighing fifteen hundredweight and all the brass and iron fittings, worth £10, from the steeple, "contrary to the myndys of the seyd paryshioners and withowt ther consents".[35] The commissioners for Hertfordshire reported a series of such incidents, especially the removal of vestments and plate from parish churches by local gentry, like Sir William Cavendish who took a silver chalice from Northaw, John Fitzherbert "nowe of the Kinges Maiesties Court" who took a chalice, a pyx, and a chrismatory from his parish church of Braughing, or Sir Thomas Josylene who took "a Rytch Coppe and a Suytte of vestmentes" from the parish church of Sawbridgeworth.[36] Some of the perpetrators of these removals may even have seen themselves as justified in the interests of reform. Walter Ralegh, whose Protestant zeal had precipitated the rising at Clyst St Mary in 1549, had been imprisoned by the rebels for much of the siege of Exeter in the tower of St Sidwell's church. At the raising of the siege his captors fled the city. Raleigh and two companions helped themselves to the ornaments of the church – a cross of silver, a chalice, a censer and ship, a silver spoon, a collection of velvet vestments, and the best cope of cloth of tissue, worth twenty marks. Despite efforts by the parish, Ralegh seems to have held on to most of these goods. When

[33] Ibid., ns II, 1884, p. 183.
[34] Ibid., IV, 1869, p. 201.
[35] Ibid., IV, 1869, pp. 224–5.
[36] *Inventories of Furniture and Ornaments remaining in all the Parish Churches of Hertfordshire in the last year of the reign of King Edward VI*, ed. J. E. Cussans, 1873 (hereafter = *Hertfordshire Inventories*) pp. 18–19.

asked for the cope he replied that "yf it were not cut already for the sparmer of a bed they should have it."[37]

There is no doubt that incidents of this sort pushed some parishes into selling plate and vestments which they would have preferred to keep. The parishioners of Bramfield in Suffolk, whose magnificent Rood-screen with its fascinating iconography is a testimony to the vitality of traditional piety there in the early sixteenth century, reported that "we had certeyne plate of the church which did lye in custody of the vycar for the shafegarde thereof, and certeine Rasshe persones did attempt & wolde have had yt of the same vycar, wythoute the consent [of the parish] to their owne occupyeinge." The wardens and leading parishioners therefore sold the plate and spent the proceeds on acquiring two coffers for the church and vestry, and on repairs inside and outside the church.[38]

But it is possible that some of these incidents of apparent theft, and many of the seemingly opportunistic purchases by gentry, were in fact more respectable than they appeared. William Gostwick was reported in Edward's reign to have taken and sold a cross of silver-gilt and enamel, a pair of silver cruets, a chalice, and a rich set of vestments from the parish church of Willington in Bedfordshire. The matter was thoroughly investigated in Mary's reign, and it was established that the ornaments had in fact been the property of Gostwick's brother, Sir John Gostwick, lord of the manor, who had been in the habit of lending the ornaments of his private chapel for use in Willington parish church, and in other parishes with which he was connected, on the great festivals.[39] This sort of patronage of parochial liturgy by the gentry was certainly quite common, and it is hardly surprising, once the plunder of local churches by the Crown or by thieves seemed a probability, and churchwardens began to sell the richer items, that the gentry should have reclaimed their property. At East Ham one of the local gentry, Thomas Ecclesfield, had maintained a lamp in the chancel. Since the Injunctions outlawed such lights, he reclaimed the stock as his own property, an action then imitated by the vicar, who had maintained two candles at the high altar.[40]

At Long Melford the Clopton family had a close relationship of religious patronage with the parish, John Clopton having left much of his own chapel furniture to the parish in 1494, including the

<hr />

[37] *The Edwardian Inventories for the City and County of Exeter*, ed. B. Cresswell, Alcuin Club, XX, 1916 (hereafter = *Exeter Inventories*) pp. 77–8.
[38] *East Anglian*, ns I, 1885, pp. 114–15.
[39] *Bedfordshire Inventories*, pp. 25, 30–9.
[40] *Transactions of the Essex Archaeological Society*, ns II, 1884, pp. 244–5.

monstrance used on Corpus Christi and Palm Sunday. The family had a relic of the true cross which was loaned out to the parish wives when they were in childbed, and John Clopton's treasured relic of the pillar on which Christ was scourged was included among the church's possessions in 1529, given by Sir William Clopton, John's son. When the Edwardine spoliation of the church began William Clopton systematically bought up many of the images, and was given a free hand by the wardens to remove material from the Clopton family aisle and chapel, including all the images, "and to do yt at hys plesur". One of these images, of the Virgin and Child in bed being venerated by the Magi, was discovered unbroken under the church floor in the nineteenth century, so it seems likely that Clopton took the images to preserve them.[41] Parishioners in a number of Lincolnshire villages reported in 1566 that during Mary's reign local gentry had loaned vestments, plate, and books to the parishes. In most cases these were returned to their owners at "the defacing of all popery" in 1559. These books and ornaments must in most cases have been rescued or bought from the churches in Edward's reign, and the Marian practice was probably a return to an earlier form of patronage which bound tenants and the lord of the manor with spiritual as well as economic ties.[42] Nor was it only the gentry who rescued ornaments and books in this way. As we shall see, in many parishes in Mary's reign local people brought out and returned sacred objects bought or removed in Edward's reign, and many clergy loaned, sold, or gave back to their parishes books and vestments which they had acquired in this way. Lincolnshire visitation returns for 1565/6 attest this in many cases, and they can be amply paralleled elsewhere. When the commissioners for Berkshire ordered the sale of all the parish goods of Stanford in the Vale in 1553 the vicar, Sir John Fawkener, bought four complete sets of vestments and copes, four assorted chasubles, a spare cope, and an altar frontal, for which he paid £5 16s 8d: he duly sold these back to the parish at cost when Mary came to the throne.[43]

Purchase by individuals was not the only way of rescuing church property from confiscation. Images, books, and relics might be concealed, as Clopton had done at Melford. The churchwardens of St Mary, Stamford, walled their patronal image of the Virgin into its niche, where it was discovered in the nineteenth century.

[41] W. Parker, *History of Long Melford*, 1873, pp. 93–4; G. M. Gibson, *The Theater of Devotion*, 1989, pp. 61–2.

[42] See below, chapter 16, "Mary" pp. 490ff.

[43] L. G. Maine, *A Berkshire Village*, 1866, pp. 97–100.

[44] F. Cheetham, *English Medieval Alabasters*, 1984, pp. 41, 53–4.

Parishioners at Wakefield hid twenty-five alabaster images in the roof of a local chapel. The parishioners of Flawford, near Nottingham, hid three images under the floor of their chancel. The figures were discovered unscathed in the eighteenth century, long after the church had fallen into ruins. And in 1574 the Protestant vicar of Preston reported to his bishop that while digging in his garden he had discovered a great number of alabaster images, which he had destroyed.[44]

Concealment of this sort took those responsible well outside the law, and could only succeed given almost total secrecy or total solidarity within the community. Nevertheless, many parishes did whatever they could short of actual burial to conceal their possessions. The commissioners closely scrutinized the inventories meticulously submitted by the parishes. The vicar of Morebath in Devon, who had concealed the church's vestments, was forced to appear before the commissioners four times before they were satisfied. But they did not go to the parishes to see for themselves that everything was included. It was therefore possible for parishes, provided they submitted a reasonably complete-looking inventory and the wardens could keep their nerve before the commissioners, to conceal a good deal. Many of the Norfolk returns are manifestly "cooked", large and rich parishes returning lists as sparse as impoverished hamlets. Some parishes possessing precious medieval lecterns omitted them from their inventories, and so still have them. At Stanford after the confiscation of 1553 the wardens privately listed "the parcells of goods that was lafte in the Church, and not put in the Kynge's inventory". These included the great standard candlesticks from the sanctuary and the small candlesticks for the altar, the cross, the sacring bell and the handbell rung before corpses, the diadem canopy and veil for the hanging pyx, the lantern to go before the Blessed Sacrament as it was carried to the sick, the Lenten veil, altar-cloths, towels, and frontals, an alb with its stole and fanon, the box in which the Eucharistic torches were kept, and even the mitre for the boy bishop on St Nicholas's feast, in fact much of the necessary and some of the optional equipment for Catholic cult.[45] At Wycombe in Buckinghamshire the wardens, with the connivance of the mayor, concealed three sets of vestments, all the Catholic liturgical books (whose concealment made mayor and wardens liable to heavy fines), two chrismatories, three crosses, an assortment of banners, altar frontals and cloths, the Lent veil, two censers and nine candlesticks. At Mary's accession this church must have been almost fully equipped for the

---

[45] *Norfolk Archaeology*, XXVI, 1935–7, pp. 252–3; Stanford CWA, pp. 99–100.

immediate resumption of Catholic worship with some degree of opulence.[46]

Indeed, one of the striking things revealed by the inventories of 1552 is just how many parishes retained the necessary vessels and vestments for the celebration of the Mass and other Catholic ceremonies up to the very moment of confiscation, despite the steady attrition of embezzlement, burglary, and enforced or voluntary sales. There were parts of the country where the churches do seem to have been stripped by 1552: Cumberland is a case in point. But Cumberland was a notoriously impoverished area, and its churches were probably ill-equipped to start with.[47] In most regions chalices, vestments, chrismatories, holy-water pots, the basic necessities of daily Catholic worship, survived. Much of this of course was in store, or, like the suit of satin vestments embroidered with silver at Hungerford, "altered for the comunyon table".[48] Though both Mass vestments and copes had been permitted for use in the communion service of 1549, the reformers increasingly discouraged the wearing of chasubles, which had unacceptable doctrinal associations, and encouraged "counterfeiting" of the Mass. The rubrics of the 1549 prayer-book prescribed the cope for use when only the first part of the communion service was used, as was stipulated for Sundays when there were no communicants, and there was therefore probably a tendency for this to become the standard Eucharistic garment. There were many places in which the wearing even of copes was frowned on by the authorities, as it would certainly have been in Hooper's dioceses. In any case the abolition of altars and the celebration of the communion service at a long table flanked by wooden benches in the body of the church made any vestment other than the surplice increasingly anomalous. But many churches in Cambridgeshire and in Essex were evidently still using not only copes but even Mass vestments in 1553, for in a number of cases the commissioners, ignoring or unaware of the prohibition of both copes and vestments by the 1552 book, explicitly allowed parishes to retain a chasuble in addition to or even in place of a cope "for the onely mayntenance of deuyne serruyce their".[49] The Surrey commissioners normally qualified the return of copes or vestments by stating that they were

---

[46] Wycombe CWA, pp. 127–35.

[47] H. Whitehead (ed.), "Church Goods in Cumberland in 1552", *Transactions of the Cumberland and Westmorland Antiquarian and Archaeological Society*, VIII, 1886, pp. 186–204.

[48] *Berkshire Inventories*, p. 21.

[49] For example, they left a vestment but no cope at Trumpington, and also at Stuntney – *East Anglian*, ns VI, 1895–6 p. 226, IX, 1901–2, p. 42. The return of copes *and* vestments for the maintenance of worship was commonplace in both Cambridgeshire and Essex.

"to make a communion table cloth". But they were unusually meticulous in enforcing the letter of their commission, and the commissioners from Cambridge and Essex made no such stipulation, sometimes left copes or vestments where there were already coverings for the table, and in several parishes even left oil-boxes. These are certainly an indicator that the commissioners were working to the rubrics of the 1549 prayer-book, not that of 1552, as well as suggesting that parishioners were still requesting anointing, since this too was disallowed by the 1552 book.[50]

It would be preposterous, of course, to imply that the reform made no headway in the parishes, though it is certainly true that the Edwardine regime found it far easier to enforce the removal of images and altars than to make wardens equip their churches for the new worship, by the purchase of Bibles, service-books and the paraphrases of Erasmus.[51] Nevertheless, the sources reveal parishes whose shedding of the materials of Catholic worship does suggest more than mere conformity. At a time when many Essex parishes were retaining and perhaps using their copes and vestments, the fact that Southchurch sold all but an alb, two surplices, and some cloths for the table suggests that there priest and people had embraced reformed ideas about worship. A few miles away at Great Stambridge in 1552 they had kept "an olde cope of sylke" to go with their two surplices, but had sold both their chalices and now used "a Cuppe of wood for the mynistracion". This could just be poverty: the wardens raised £12 18s 8d in total by the sale of their church ornaments, of which the receipts for the chalices accounted for more than half. They claimed to have spent £10 8s 2d on implementing the reform in the parish, and if so, it may be that the sale of the chalices was essential to keep the parish solvent. But £3 8s 2d of that expenditure was on the mending of a highway, and a devout Catholic parish would surely have found other sources of revenue had they wanted to. The conclusion seems inescapable that the wooden cup at Great Stambridge represents Protestant conviction, not economic necessity.[52] It is less clear what is to be made of the state of religion in the hamlet of Lawling, where in 1552 they still had a cope, two vestments, a processional cross, two holy-water pots, the Palm Sunday canopy, their banners, and an abundance of candlesticks. Yet they appear to have been using a glass for the celebration of holy communion, for which the wardens had paid tuppence; the Commissioners confiscated the

[50] *Transactions of the Essex Archaeological Society*, IV p. 228, V p. 241, ns II p. 186.
[51] Hutton, "Local Impact', pp. 124–5.
[52] *Transactions of the Essex Archaeological Society*, V, pp. 125–7.

chalice and left the cope and the glass. The absence of a chalice suggests Protestantism, but the survival in the parish undefaced of so many "monuments of superstition" raises a question mark.[53]

There is a further reason for caution in attributing the use of mean vessels of this sort to Protestant principle. The use of wooden or glass cups at the communion probably did represent a symbolic rejection of the chalice and all its Catholic associations, at least on the part of the priest, but it might also represent the parish's indifference to or contempt for the new service, which was felt not to be the Mass. Hooper complained in 1551 that the people of his diocese "commonly" failed to communicate as the 1549 prayer-book required when their turn on the rota to provide the elements came, instead persuading neighbours who were "disposed" to receive to do so on their behalf. This may have been due to reluctance to communicate outside the traditional Easter period, but it might also indicate repudiation of the rite itself. A report on the lack of progress of the Reformation in the diocese of Chichester, compiled in 1568, claimed that many parishes in Elizabethan Sussex had concealed their old chalices against the return of the Mass, and chose to bear the cost of providing new communion cups rather than profane the chalices by using them for communion. Some parishes pretended that the chalices had been stolen, and "therefore they ministered in glasses and profane Goblets". What was true of early Elizabethan Sussex may have been true also of Edwardine Essex, and in parishes where such rejection of communion was general the decision not to use the traditional vessels might have more than one possible interpretation.[54]

But even in communities with no positive commitment to the reform, the stripping away of the externals of Catholic worship between 1547 and 1553 must often have had a profound if not always conscious effect. Whether done under official pressure or not, the removal of the images of the saints, of the altars, and perhaps most of all the brasses and obit inscriptions calling for prayers for the dead, which were ripped up from gravestones and sold by the hundredweight from 1548 onwards, were ritual acts of deep significance. Like the silencing of the bede-rolls, the removal of the images and petitions of the dead was an act of oblivion, a casting out of the dead from the community of the living into a collective anonymity. They, like the Mass and the saints, were now as they had never been before, part of a superseded past. The imaginative power of the cult of the dead in late medieval England

[53] Ibid., ns I, p. 222.
[54] VAI, II p. 283; P. Hughes, *The Reformation in England*, 1950–4, III p. 129.

had lain in part precisely in its continuity, as generation after generation inscribed its names and imposed its features upon the palimpsest of the parish memory. Through the recitation of the bede-roll and the continued use of the objects which the generosity of "good doers and well willers" had provided, the community was prevented from shrinking to become coterminous with its living members. Once broken, that sense of continuity proved difficult to recapture. The surprising failure of the Marian laity in many regions to re-establish the cult of the dead on anything like its former footing is probably less to do with any scepticism about doctrine than with the loss of this vital dimension of continuity.

For the reformers this act of distancing was in a sense deliberate, a necessary rite of exorcism. In his *Displaying of the popishe Masse* Thomas Becon has a passage in which he attacks the whole notion of commemorating the dead. In the course of it, he parodies the bede-roll:

> And here in your mind and thought . . . ye pray for Philip and Cheny, more than a good meany, for the souls of your great grand Sir and your old Beldam Hurre, for the souls of Father Princhard and of Mother Puddingwright, for the souls of good man Rinsepitcher and good wife Pintpot, for the souls of Sir John Huslegoose and Sir Simon Sweetlips, and for the souls of all your benefactors . . . friends and well-willers.[55]

This is undeniably effective, a rollicking but ultimately chilling reduction of the dead to the status of figures of fun, figures of contempt. From such puppets it was easy, and better, to be free. It is worlds away from More's evocation of the dead, a generation before, as "your late acquaintance, kinred, spouses, companions, play felowes, and frendes". The ripping out of the memorials of the dead, like the three hundredweight "in Brasses" sold to Thomas Sparpoynt at Long Melford for fifty-three shillings in 1548, was the practical enactment of that silencing and distancing. The dead became as shadowy as the blanks in the stripped matrices of their gravestones, where once their images and their inscriptions had named them, and asserted their trust in, and claims on, the living.[56]

The sale of the ornaments accumulated from the bequests of the dead was another act of stripping. Medieval church inventories commonly identified the objects listed there not merely by colour, material, and function, but by the name of their donors. The parish

---

[55] Thomas Becon, *Prayers and Other Pieces*, ed. J. Ayre, Parker Society, 1844, p. 276.
[56] More, *Workes*, p. 288; Parker, *History of Long Melford*, p. 92; D. Dymond and C. Paine, *The Spoil of Melford Church*, 1989, p. 36.

inventory, like the parish bede-roll, was an act of remembrance. The inventories prepared for the commissioners year by year in Edward's reign were altogether different. Though a few wardens included the names of some of the donors, it was of the essence of the Edwardine inventories that they dissociated the goods they listed from their histories. Was the pax of silver sold at St Margaret Patten's in November 1547 to "one unknowen" for 4s 10d the ounce the one given by Agnes Wymeke in memory of her friend Sir Thomas Avelenn priest, on which she had had enamelled the Salutation of Our Lady? Did the job lot of vestments and copes bought by "a maryner" there in 1550 include the white damask cope paid for by Richard and Elisabeth Bowell, which had the life of St Margaret embroidered on the orphreys? These were no longer matters of concern for those charged with taking the reckoning. The strangers paid their tallies, took their merchandise, and carried away the history of the parish, in bundles of velvet and barrow-loads of brass, so much the hundredweight, so much the ounce, so much the yard.[57]

There were more tangible effects on the identity of parishes. In many cases parochial response to Reformation change seems to have been genuinely parochial. The Edwardine inventories reveal parishes all over the country consulting and taking collective decisions about the disposal or the protection of their church goods. But in a situation where so many traditional sanctities were involved, and where so many individuals sought to capitalize on the uncertainties of the time and to line their own pockets, division and resentment were inevitable. In predominantly conservative communities whose natural leaders were reluctant to initiate change the agents of reform, whether motivated by conviction or by opportunism, were bound to encounter hostility. At Long Melford Roger Martin was a member of one of the leading gentry families, deeply involved in parochial life. He was one of those entrusted with church plate after the first inventory was taken in 1547. But he was a passionately convinced Catholic, and as such unacceptable to the Edwardine regime; the commissioners removed the vessels from his custody. Martin was horrified by the spoil of the church, and blamed the Edwardine wardens for their involvement in it. He himself as churchwarden in Mary's reign was to lead the reconstruction of Catholicism in Melford. Intent on recovering as much as possible, he searched and annotated the parish records of the dispersions of Edward's reign, and the bitterness of his

---

[57] *London Churches at the Reformation*, ed. H. B. Walters, 1939, pp. 370–1; London St Margaret Patten CWA, pp. 320–1.

comments throws a vivid light on the divisions brought by the processes of reform and reconstruction. Against lists of linen and other cloths committed to the Edwardine wardens, William Marshall and William Dycke, Martin wrote "The wyche clothes war sold by [them] as many other thynges war for nowght as yt apperyth (although not trulye) in ther accowntes." After an inventory of the parish's magnificent collection of liturgical books, which included the great red Mass-book bound with jewels and relics used as the pax at the parish Mass "the premyssis scattered abrode & delyvered to certen lyght persons wyche payd lytle or nothyng for them, war many of them spoyld and mangelyd," though some remained to be restored to the church in 1553.[58] Marshall and Dycke were evidently all too aware of the hostility their activities were likely to arouse. Unusually among churchwardens' accounts of the period, they preface their accounts for the crucial year 1547–8 by a reference to "the gere takyn down by the Kyngs commandments and vysytors, as in the Kyngs injunccyon doth appere, in the xxviii artykle and other places", a degree of precision suggesting nervous citation of chapter and verse.[59] Something of Martin's bitterness against the work of his Edwardine predecessors is evident in the fulminations of the Marian churchwardens of Stanford in the Vale about what was done in the parish "in the wycked tyme of sysme", though in fact the Edwardine wardens of Stanford seem to have done all they could to stonewall the commissioners and hinder the process of reform.[60] The recriminations of Mary's reign, as searches were launched to identify and exact restitution from those who had profiteered from the Edwardine spoil, reveal how scarred many communities were by the divisions that religious controversy, and the enforcement of religious change, had brought.[61]

Many of these general points about the impact of reform in the parishes can be brought into sharper focus by looking at a single conservative community, the little Exmoor parish of Morebath, whose priest, Sir Christopher Trychay, was vicar from 1520 to 1574. Trychay, a pious, garrulous man with an insatiable enthusiasm for the beautifying of his church, kept the accounts for most of that period, and his record, punctuated with pious invocations – "deus in adiutorium meum intende", "Assiste nobis Sancta Maria", "Sent Anthony ora pro nobis" – offers a unique window into a

---

[58] Dymond and Paine, *The Spoil of Melford Church*, pp. 29–30.
[59] Parker, *History of Long Melford*, pp. 91–2.
[60] Stanford CWA, pp. 72, 118.
[61] For the divisions of a Kentish parish see above, p. 435.

close-knit and largely self-contained community, committed to the old ways but caught up in the revolutionary events of the middle of the century. Morebath was no Eden. The parish had its problems, responsibility for the provision and payment of the clerk proving a recurrent source of strife, and there was serious trouble in 1536 when some of the parishioners refused to pay their share of the clerk's wages. The matter was ultimately resolved by diplomacy on Trychay's part and a firm ruling by a parish meeting. On the whole the incident suggests a community able to deal with its own problems, and with confidence in its priest.[62]

There is certainly no mistaking the Catholic piety of Morebath on the eve of the Reformation. The tiny community had five "stores" – the patronal store of St George, managed by the church-wardens, St Anthony's store, the store of Jesus and St Sidwell, the maiden light and the young men's light. Trychay had introduced to the parish a devotion to the Exeter saint, Sidwell, and his parishioners enthusiastically adopted her cult. But the new image of St Sidwell which was attracting the gifts of parishioners in the 1530s was by no means the sole focus of their piety. From 1531 parishioners were also contributing towards the cost of a new image of the Virgin, they commissioned a new patronal image, and in 1537 they erected and gilded a new Rood, Mary, and John.[63] When, on the night of 20 November 1534 a thief broke into the church and stole the chalice from St Sidwell's altar and the saint's silver shoe, the young men's and the maidens' gilds organized a collection, and raised 32s 8d towards the replacement of the chalice.[64] In 1537 the parish acquired a stained-glass window from the recently dissolved Augustinian priory of Barlinch, just across the moor in Somerset.

The Injunctions of 1538, with their prohibition of lights before the saints, was therefore a blow to Morebath, but the parish took it in its stride. The young men's gild moved the light it had till then maintained before St George onto the candle-beam before the Rood: the maidens' light was now burned before the sepulchre.[65] All expenditure on images, so prominent in the accounts of the 1530s, ceased from 1538. But the vicar was not at a loss for an alternative outlet for the piety of his parishioners. Since 1534 he had been setting aside his tithings from the sheep of Our Lady's store to buy a set of black velvet vestments for use at parish requiem

[62] Morebath CWA, pp. 82–6.
[63] Ibid., pp. 24–5, 32–5, 47, 70.
[64] Ibid., pp. 64–5.
[65] Ibid., p. 105.

Masses. He now encouraged his parishioners to focus their pious giving on this impeccably Catholic, and still perfectly legal, end. The parish also spent twelve shillings on buying a "new bybyll" in 1542. The parish was as yet undisturbed by religious change, and in 1542 Trychay recorded the contributions, in cash and in manual labour, of parishioners to the renovation of the parish house. The vicar was moved by the piety of his parishioners, and in the entry recording each man's contribution noted "ye schall se furder devocion of diversse perssons of the parysse to the churche howse wt out the wyche devocion we had not been abyll to pay and redd men clenely as they ofht to be."[66]

Disaster struck in Edward's reign, though at first all seemed well. The parish duly paid their vicar fourpence to sing King Henry's "Dirige" and Mass. On the Sunday before St Mary Magdalene's day in July 1547 the vicar triumphantly recorded that the long saved-for black vestments had been bought, blessed by the bishop at Exeter, and brought back to Morebath. He made a little speech to the parish on the occasion, which he obviously thought well of, because he entered it into the book, "now lok ye a pon thes vestmentis & the cope and take them at a worthe wt al there fawtis for y have don the best thay y can doo yn gathcryng of the small pennse to gethers y pray God that hyt may be for there sawlis helthe that gave any gefth un to hyt".[67] At the parish audit on 1 November 1547 Trychay duly recorded the expenses incurred in riding to Exeter for the royal visitation, and the making of the poor men's box, and then his world began to fall apart. The accounts for 1547 ended with a detailed memorandum recording the location of the parish vestments, which Trychay had distributed among the farmers of the parish to prevent confiscation by the visitors. John at Court had the precious and long-awaited black set, Nicholas at Hayre the red velvet set and the matching altar cloth of satin, Thomas Rumbelow had the Lent vestments of blue, John Norman of Pole had the best banners of silk rolled up in a board cloth. The best cope was pawned for twenty shillings to William at Coomb, but the transaction was certainly a legal fiction, and he was subsequently reimbursed and the cope recovered.[68]

In 1548 there was, for the first time, only one high warden of the church, and she a woman, Lucy Scely, a widow. She presided over the dismantling of the pieties of Morebath. The Lent veil, the sepulchre hangings, and the frontals from St Sidwell's altar and St

[66] Ibid., p. 128.
[67] Ibid., p. 155.
[68] Ibid., p. 160.

George's altar went for 9s 4d, a banner staff for threepence, the brass candlesticks for four shillings. Morebath celebrated the Lent and Holy Week ceremonies as usual that year: the Lent veil was hung, the paschal candle set up. The annual requiem for benefactors was sung on Palm Sunday as usual. But on St George's day 1549, "by the consent of the hole parysse" the contents of the church house were auctioned off, and some of the church linen distributed to deserving parishioners and the clerk. Two nights later a thief broke into the church and stole the best surplice and the clerk's rochet. In this year too the parish compiled its inventory for the royal commissioners. They put the best cope into the inventory, repaid William Hurley his twenty shillings and set it on record that "so ys cope our owne (under the kyng) as our invitory dothe record".[69] The parish duly bought the prayer-book of 1549 and, in the same year, the Paraphrases, meeting some of the costs by selling off some altar-cloths and the iron bolt on which the patronal image of St George had stood. The parish also contributed, with feelings one can only speculate about, to the expenses of the royal army which put down the 1549 rebellion.[70]

By 1551 the parish funds of Morebath were completely exhausted. The new warden for that year inherited nothing at all from his predecessor. He was obliged to sell the church candlesticks to a brazier in Exeter, and the purchase of a psalter was paid for by a collection of groats from parishioners. Routine expenses for repairs were now major problems: the parish officers used their own money, and borrowed from the more substantial parishioners and from the vicar.

The troubles of the parish were exacerbated by the scepticism of the commissioners (entirely justified) about the parish inventory. Trychay had to make repeated trips to Exeter, and in 1552 they were forced to admit the existence of the concealed vestments. Most were surrendered to the commissioners, but the precious black set was not disclosed. Bitterly, the vicar recorded the pathetic remnants of the possessions of his church at the beginning of 1553, after the wardens had paid out five shillings for the second prayer-book:

> on auter cloth & ii wother auter clothers with ryngis that servyd for curtyngis, a nold auter clothe that came from pole, a diaper towle and a nother poure lytyll towle, a nackyn for the priestis handis, a nolde sylkyn banner, a black hersse clothe of bockeram,

[69] Ibid., pp. 162–3.
[70] Ibid., pp. 163–4.

ii tapers, a lytyll pece of say with a frange, ii sacren bellis, ii lyche bellis, the fotte of the crosse and on length of brasse of the staffe that bare the crosse, the holly water bockytt (de brasse), ii peces of led, a coller of a bel with ii yris a bout . . . the hyer part of the sens and the schyppe, a paynted paper, ii bolts of yre and a hoppe of yre, the wyche hoppe of yre was delyveryd to the clerke to make a new twyste with all for the churche howsse dore.

In addition, the church had debts of twenty-four shillings. Trychay concluded the desolate little list with "God save the kyng", a sentiment which, in the circumstances, can hardly have been entirely wholehearted.[71]

The accession of Mary was pure joy to Trychay. His parishioners rallied to the restoration of Catholicism. A general meeting of the parish settled accounts with all who had loaned the parish money. Many of those concerned, including the vicar, took less than they were owed. Parishioners who had acquired Catholic ornaments during the years of spoil now brought them again, some asking for reimbursement, others giving them as gifts – John Williams of Bery gave back the image of the Blessed Virgin, and the king and the queen from the tableau of St George and the dragon. From "diversse wother perssons" came paintings, books, and parts of the dismantled Rood-loft (Pl. 135). In recording all this Trychay commented, "lyke tru and fayghthefull crystyn pepyll this was restoryd to this churche by the wyche doyngis hyt schowyth that they dyd lyke good catholyke men."[72]

Unsurprisingly, Trychay's view of the Edwardine years was wholly negative. Writing towards the end of Mary's reign a review of the recent history of his parish, he recorded that:

Anno domini 1548 was hye warden of this churche Luce Scely and by her tyme the churche gooddis was sold a way with out commission ut patet postea and no gefth gevyn to the church but all fro the churche and thus hyt continyd fro Lucc ys time un to Richard Cruce and from Cruce un to Richard Hucly and fro Hucly un to Richard Robyns and fro Robyns un to Robyn at More and by all thes mens tyme the wyche was by tyme of Kyng Edward the vi the church ever dekeyd and then deyd the Kyng and Quyne Maris grace dyd succed and how the church was restoryd a gayn by her tyme here after ye schall have knolyge of hyt.[73]

[71] Ibid., pp. 172–3.
[72] Ibid., p. 185.
[73] Ibid., p. 200.

Trychay was a conservative man in a conservative region. The fervour and comparative unanimity with which his parish rallied to the Marian restoration of Catholicism leaves no room for doubt that they shared his loathing of the reform, his joy at its overthrow. But the experience of Morebath, the destruction of treasured objects which had been the focus of communal pride and local identity, the disruption of immemorial custom and the festal calendar, the pressing problems of debt and the narrowing range of options in meeting them, all this was replicated in parishes up and down the land. Even in a parish as solidly traditionalist as Morebath the task of implementing the reforms demanded by government produced division and enmity. Trychay had not a good word for poor Lucy Scely or her successors who had presided over the destruction of his life's work. Elsewhere, in communities where the reforms had their advocates and where the balance of influence between traditionalists and innovators was more evenly distributed, the forces making for division were much more explosive, more disruptive for the community. There were parishes where the reform was embraced with ardour, at least by those with most influence, and where a new solidarity began to emerge on the basis of the new faith.

Even in communities where this was not so, the passage of time and the relentless push of Conciliar policy had its effect. The men and women of Tudor England were, by and large, pragmatists. Grumbling, they sold off as much of their Catholic past as they could not hide or keep, and called in the carpenters to set boards on trestles and fix the forms round the communion tables. Used to obedience, many of them accepted the changes, however un-welcome, as unavoidable. We catch a glimpse of this process of acceptance in the phlegmatic note in their accounts by the church-wardens of North Elmham in 1550, less than a year after the abolition of the Mass, when they sold their antiphoners, grails, missals "and all other kynds of boks of the olde servyce", and, a year later, the sale of the altar, sepulchre, and "serten other old thyngs Afor Acustomed to be occupyed in the chyrche, in the tyme of the servys then". In the same matter-of-fact spirit the wardens of Clapham noted the sale of "dyvers olde stayned clothes for the doynge of ceremonyes lately used in the churche".[74] And the process might be very much more than mere acceptance. Four years of exposure to the matchless and memorable dignity of Cranmer's English services could not be without effect. As we shall see, even

---

[74] North Elmham CWA, pp. 54, 56; *Surrey Inventories*, p. 109.

men of profoundly Catholic convictions found themselves drawing on the rhythms of Bible and prayer-book when they came to express their convictions. Even for the traditionalists nothing would ever be the same again. But when all that is said, the experience of Morebath almost certainly offers us a more accurate insight into what the locust years of Edward had meant to the average Englishman than the embryo godly communities which had begun to emerge in parts of Essex, Suffolk, or Kent, and which historians, dazzled by hindsight, have too easily seen as the inevitable future of Tudor England. In the majority of English villages, as in Morebath, men breathed easier for the accession of a Catholic queen.

CHAPTER 15

THE IMPACT OF REFORM: WILLS

In any assessment of the impact of reform on the laity of Tudor England, the evidence of wills is bound to loom large, and has in fact dominated much of the debate about the limits and expansion of Protestantism. Many historians, from W. K. Jordan to Robert Whiting, have taken the shifting patterns of mortuary provision in wills – bequests for masses, prayers, and charitable gifts to the poor – as indicators of shifting belief. But much of this writing has been dogged not only by misunderstanding and unfounded assumption, but by an insufficient attention to the external pressures which often counted for more than inner conviction in the shaping both of will formulas and specific will provisions. Robert Whiting, for example, commented in a discussion of West-Country wills that it was "*revealing* that in 32 wills made between January 1550 and July 1553, there was not a single attempt to arrange intercessions in any form. Nor was there even one recorded bequest to a religious guild. Gifts to the poor, by contrast, were included in no less than 15 of the 32 wills."[1] Given that all religious gilds had been dissolved in 1547, and their funds diverted either to the Crown or to the poor-boxes, that the *Homilies* of 1547 had denounced "purgatory and masses satisfactory", that the royal Injunctions of the same year denounced trentals, and that successive episcopal visitations all over England in the late 1540s systematically attacked belief in Purgatory, the recitation of the names of the dead in the bede-roll, and the celebration of Masses for the dead, it is hard to see what the absence of obit provisions in wills *reveals*, except that most Tudor testators were possessed of a normal allowance of common sense. Given this avalanche of exhortation and enforcement, and the clear endorsement by the Crown of increasingly radical reforming opinion, it must have been plain to most Tudor property owners that attempts to secure traditional intercessory activities, at least by means of a will, an official document which

---

[1] R. Whiting, "'For the health of my soul': Prayers for the Dead in the Tudor South West", *Southern History*, V, 1983, p. 81.

had to be proved in the ecclesiastical courts, were likely be counter-productive.[2]

As for the growth of provision for the poor in wills, which some historians have taken to be a sign of growing Protestantism or secularism, once again one may be sceptical. Of all the medieval activities held to assist the soul after death the relief of the poor was the only one permitted and indeed actively encouraged by the Protestant authorities after 1547. The royal Injunctions of that year required clergy assisting at deathbeds to dissuade the dying testator from any of the traditional "blind devotions", such as requiem Masses, and instead to give to the poor man's box. The Injunctions justified such charity not in secular terms, but on the traditional and impeccably Catholic grounds that alms to the poor were "given to Christ himself" and would be "mercifully rewarded" with ever-lasting life. It is hardly surprising therefore that funds formerly invested in Masses and "Diriges" should be redirected into poor relief, especially since the Edwardine authorities, in commending such gifts, thereby retained at least one element of continuity with traditional Catholic belief and practice. Many Tudor testators quite explicitly stated that gifts to the poor were an acceptable alternative where the law forbade intercessory provisions such as Masses.

Historians looking for evidence of religious change have tended more particularly to focus on the preambles to Tudor wills, in which the testator committed his soul to God, but often also to the saints, before going on to dispose of his or her property "for the health of my soul". Shifts in the phrasing of such preambles, for example, the omission of any mention of the saints, the expression of reliance solely on the merits of Christ, the repudiation of the value of good works, have all been taken as signs of Protestant conviction on the part of the testator. A note of caution was first sounded by Margaret Spufford, who drew attention to the con-ventional character of many such preambles, and to the role of scribes, like local clerics or scriveners, in their composition or copying. And since her work alerted historians to the problems, even some of the apparently most distinctive expressions of personal Protestant feeling have been shown to be conventional, in the sense of being directly based on model wills provided in precedent books, almanacs, and devotional treatises.[3]

[2] Whiting, "For the health of my soul", pp. 68–78; G. Mayhew, "The Progress of the Reformation in East Sussex 1530–1559: the Evidence from Wills", *Southern History*, V, 1983, pp. 55–6; VAI, II pp. 112, 127, 182, 194, 241, 244, 287, 301–2, 306.

[3] M. Zell, "The Use of Religious Preambles as a Measure of Religious Belief in the Sixteenth Century", *Bulletin of the Institute of Historical Research*, L, 1977, pp. 246–9; J. D. Alsop, "Religious Preambles in Early Modern English Wills as Formulae", *Journal of Ecclesiastical History*, XL, 1989, pp. 19–27; Claire Cross, "Wills as evidence of popular piety

Nevertheless, preambles have been heavily relied on by historians arguing for the rapid progress of Protestantism among the laity of mid-Tudor England. G. J. Mayhew for Sussex, Elaine Sheppard for Norwich, and Peter Clark for Kent have all with varying degrees of sophistication seen in the modification or abandonment of traditional Catholic preamble formulas clear evidence of the spread of Protestant belief, or at least the decay of Catholic allegiance. Professor A. G. Dickens, who pioneered the statistical analysis of will preambles as an indicator of religious change, has recently offered a summary of the current state of research on wills, in which he reaffirms his conviction that the disappearance of any mention of the saints in will preambles provides the historian with a rough but essentially reliable guide of the disappearance of Catholic conviction; the silence of mid-Tudor testators represents for him the "rejection" of the cult of the saints. And in wills stressing salvation through the merits of Christ alone, Dickens and others have discerned a growing and self-conscious Protestant conviction.[4]

If mid-Tudor wills are to provide us with any reliable insight into the reception of reformed beliefs among the people, however, they need to be handled with great care. Above all, we need to be clear about the difference between a Catholic and a Protestant will, a matter much less easy to define than has commonly been supposed. It is of course evident that some will preambles are unequivocally Protestant. Edward Hoppay, a yeoman of Skircoat near Halifax, making his will in May 1548, left no doubt about the matter. Having declared his firm conviction that he was already possessed of salvation by the merits of Christ alone, he went on to insist that

> towchyng the welthe of my saull, the faith that I have takyn and reherced is sufficient, as I beleve, without any other man's work or workes . . . I accepte non in hevyn, neither in erthe, to be my mediatour betwixt God and me, but he onlie . . . and towchyng the distribution of my goodes, my purpose is to bestowe them that they may be accepted as the fructes of faithe, so that I do not suppose that my merite be by bestowyng of them, but my

in the Reformation period: Leeds and Hull 1520–1640", in D. Loades (ed.), *The End of Strife: Death, Reconciliation and Repression in Christian Spirituality*, 1984, pp. 44–57; Margaret Spufford, *Contrasting Communities*, 1974, pp. 319–44, and her "The Scribes of Villagers' Wills in the Sixteenth and Seventeenth Centuries, and their influence", *Local Population Studies*, VII, 1971, pp. 28–43.

[4] A. G. Dickens, *The English Reformation*, 1989, pp. 214–5, and "The Early Expansion of Protestantism in England 1520–1558", *Archiv für Reformationsgeschichte*, LXXVIII, 1987, pp. 213–7; Elaine Sheppard, "The Reformation and the Citizens of Norwich", *Norfolk Archaeology*, XXXVIII, 1981–3, pp. 44–55; Clark, *Provincial Society* pp. 58–9; G. Mayhew, "Progress of the Reformation in East Sussex", pp. 38–67; K. G. Powell, "The Social Background to the Reformation in Gloucestershire", *Bristol and Gloucestershire Archaeological Society Transactions*, XCII, 1973, pp. 117–18.

merite is faithe in Jesus Christe only . . . For a righteouse man lyveth by faithe. And thus I rest in conciencie concernynge my faithe.

Hoppay here explicitly repudiates the help of the prayers and good works of others, and makes it clear that in disposing of alms he does so not to secure "the health of his soul", but as a sign that it is already assured. He is not hopeful, but certain of his own salvation. There can be no question of the Protestant convictions represented by this and similar wills.[5]

But preambles which simply declare trust in the merits or Passion of Christ cannot be assumed to be Protestant or even "reformist". J. D. Alsop, in an article devoted to warning historians of the pitfalls of placing too much reliance on preambles, nevertheless characterizes as a "typically protestant emphasis" the following from 1562: "first I give and bequeth my Soule to almightie God my only sauior, and redemer, by the merites of whose death and passion I am in full hope to be saved."[6] There is nothing necessarily Protestant about this sort of formula; as a matter of fact, this testator went on to ask for prayers for his soul, and many wills containing similar sentiments were made by Catholics in England before, during, and after the Reformation, like Harry Edon of Barningham in Suffolk in 1545. Having first commended his soul to God, "by meritte of whose passion I wholly trust to be saved, and to attayne and come to his glory in heaven", he went on to make provision for "Diriges", Masses, and doles to the poor and to prisoners, even establishing a temporary chantry.[7] This is no rarity, and comparable examples could be produced for any county in England in the period. The late medieval Christian was certainly encouraged to seek the support of the saints at the hour of death as in life. But, in the words of John Bossy, the believer "knew who his saviour was", and was taught to place his trust first and foremost in the Passion of Christ. Though the majority of will preambles are relatively unsophisticated, there were a significant number of pious Catholic wills in the late fifteenth and early sixteenth centuries which articulated these theological convictions, frequently echoing the very wording of the Ars Moriendi, and the pastoral textbooks provided for clergy at the sick-bed. The results, as we have seen, could be very striking. The injunction to "put alle thi trust in his passion and in his deth, and thenke onli theron,

---

[5] It was in fact a formulaic will nonetheless – G. Mayhew has found an almost identical example of the same year in Sussex, and both are closely modelled on the famous will of William Tracy. The same formula was used also by a testator in Lowestoft in September 1558; see East Anglian, ns III, 1889–90, pp. 347–8.

[6] Alsop, "Religious Preambles", p. 23.

[7] Visitation of Suffolke, I pp. 4–5.

and non other thing . . . medil the and wrappe the therinne"[8] is
deliberately recalled in the phrasing of many wills. The distinctive
tone of the will of Sir Roger Townsend of Blythburgh, derived
from just such an internalization of the theology underlying the
late medieval church's deathbed ministrations, will be recalled. As
absolutely as any Protestant, Townsend commits his soul to God,
his maker and redeemer,

> besechyng him for the merytes of his bitter and gloriouse passion
> to have mercy oon me and to take me into his mercy which is
> above all workes, unto whom it is approposed to have mercy . . .
> of the wych numbre of contrite synners I mekely and humbly
> besechith him that I may be oon and one of the predestinate to be
> found.

But he goes on to ask for the help of the prayers of the saints too,
which he sees as being in no way incompatible with the Christocentricity for the opening of the preamble. "And the rather thorow
the meanes of our most blessid lady modre and mayde and of all the
aungells of hevyn and patriarks prophets apostels maters confessours
virgyns and all the hooly company of hevyn and in speciall of
them that I have moost in remembraunce."[9] Certainly such wills
were a minority before the 1530s, but they were impeccably
orthodox. There was no theological reason why orthodox Catholics
should not make increasing use of such formulas when, in the
course of Reformation, it became expedient to do so. This, as we
shall see, was in fact the case. Noting the growth of Norwich wills
making statements of reliance on the merits of Christ from the mid-
1530s, Elaine Sheppard saw them as expressions of "altered times",
and signs of a "change in the air". This is certainly right, but
not, as she concluded, because they provide evidence of growing
Protestant conviction among the will-makers. Moves in the direction
of Protestantism may or may not have occurred, but the wills
tell us more about the external constraints on testators than they
do about shifting private belief. As pressure mounted against
traditional practice in late Henrician and Edwardine England, there
were many reasons why Catholics might use such formulas, for
which there was ample medieval precedent, and there were no
theological objections to their doing so. Wills using such preambles
before the Reformation commonly included bequests for prayers
and alms-deeds which identify them as Catholic, but, given the
growing pressures against the expression of certain Catholic beliefs
in wills in the 1540s and 1550s, we cannot simply assume that the
absence of such bequests in wills with these preambles indicates

[8] See above, chapter 9, "Last Things", pp. 313–27.
[9] C. Richmond, *John Hopton*, 1981, pp. 244–5.

Protestant conviction. And indeed it can be said in general that historians seeking evidence of the advance of Protestant conviction have often read these beliefs into, and not out of, will formulas. Elaine Sheppard considers the will of Thomas Tidman, made in 1557, "ambiguous" because he left his soul "to my savyour Jesus Christ and to his most blessed mother our ladie and to all the hollie angelles and saintes in heaven". She also considers that the wording of this will in 1557 demonstrated the inability of the Marian church to "put the clock right back". There is of course nothing ambiguous here, unless one is under the entirely erroneous impression that pre-Reformation Catholics needed to be told that Christ was in a unique and special sense their divine Saviour, and the saints powerful, kindly, but essentially subordinate human helpers.[10]

The changes in the phrasing and provisions of Tudor wills which have been fairly generally taken by historians to indicate significant shifts in belief are varied, but Peter Clark has characterized Kentish wills in three groups, which broadly reflect the historical consensus. These groups are *traditionalist* wills, in which the soul is commended to God, Mary, and the saints in heaven, *reformist* wills, which omit any mention of the saints, and *Protestant* or *radical* wills, which stress the hope of salvation through Christ alone. A number of historians have tried to refine these categories in order to distinguish wills which display more than one of these supposedly exclusive tendencies, so G. Mayhew discerned six, not three, types of will in Sussex.[11] There are serious difficulties involved in all such attempts at characterization, and I shall not attempt it myself. The difficulties may be illustrated by considering the reformist category of wills, those which omit mention of the saints. A. G. Dickens has laid particular stress on this type, drawing attention to the decline all over England from the early 1540s or even earlier in the number of wills which bequeath the soul to the Virgin and the saints. Accepting that in individual cases the precise form of the preamble may reflect the attitude of a scribe, rather than that of the testator, he nevertheless insists that "anything like a mass-movement to omit mention of the Virgin and the saints must reflect a decline of those cults." There is an obvious sense in which this is true, in so far as the mention of the saints is part of their cult. But if it is meant to suggest that those who omit mention of the saints do so because they no longer value their prayers and help, the matter becomes more doubtful; common prudence might dictate reticence about even deeply held beliefs.

---

[10] E. Sheppard, "The Reformation and the Citizens of Norwich", pp. 52–3.
[11] Mayhew, "Progress of the Reformation in East Sussex", pp. 53–7 and table 1.

To understand this, we need first to reflect on the legal constraints shaping the phrasing and actual provisions of wills in Tudor England. Even before any traditional doctrine was called into question by the Reformation, Tudor testators were accustomed to modifying the religious provisions of their wills to take account of the law. The Crown in the fifteenth and early sixteenth century was consistently opposed to the disappearance of lands into mortmain to support chantries, for economic and not ideological reasons. It became increasingly difficult to obtain licences for chantries, and testators wishing to endow them grew increasingly anxious to secure their wills against legal objection and confiscation. Many pre-Reformation wills display this realism about and deference to the law. Thus James Thompson, a yeoman of Frieston, established in 1528 a group of feoffees for the government of a chantry in his parish church "to be continued from tyme to tyme . . . as long as the kynges lawes will suffer it". In 1527 John Leek, a Boston mercer, left lands to the Corpus Christi gild for a period of ninety-two years or, "yff it may be soffryd by the law", for ever. Thomas Quadryng of Corby left 3s 4d a year towards five tapers before the Rood "during the space that the law of Inglond will admitte".[12]

Mortmain was not the only way in which the law might affect the religious provisions of wills. From 1531 onwards poor-law legislation complicated traditional patterns of charitable giving, and once again one can see Catholic testators taking account of the fact in their wills. The first Act "Concerning punishment of Beggars and Vagabonds"[13] forbade any form of begging without licence, but expressly excepted "common doles used at buryalles or obytes". But the subsequent "Acte for Punyshment of Sturdy Vacabundes and Beggers" of 1536, which required every parish to establish a poor-box, addressed itself specifically to the "inconveniences and infeccions" arising from "commen and open doolis", and forbade the establishment of any such doles or the distribuition of "redye money in almes" other than to the common boxes, diverting existing funds for such purposes to them.[14]

Concern about this prohibition is reflected in a group of wills at Long Melford in the 1530s and 1540s. Roger Martin, a bencher of Lincoln's Inn, in a will full of traditional intercessory and charitable bequests, noted that "because common dooles be prohibit and put awaye be Act of parlyament" he wished there to be no such dole at his obits, but instead a distribution on the day before his

---

[12] Lincoln Wills, II pp. 27–8, 29–30, 75–7, 96; Alan Kreider, English Chantries: the Road to Dissolution, 1979, pp. 71–92.
[13] 22 Hen. VIII cap. 12.
[14] 27 Hen. VIII cap. 25.

anniversary obit of bread and meat to poor householders in Long Melford, and to twenty poor couples at the offertory of the requiem Mass. Sir William Bretyner, a chantry priest who made his will in 1543, provided for a distribution of money to the poor of Melford "and other straunge people being poer comyng and being at my seyd buriall", but they were to be warned "that they shal not resorte nor com unto my seyd thirtie day for any dole, consideringe yt ys prohibitc by the lawe". Any further alms were to be given individually to poor householders at their homes, and this seems to have become standard practice at Melford.[15]

This particular piece of poor-law legislation was enacted after the break with Rome, but it probably had little or nothing to do with Protestant doctrine. The trends towards the rationalization of charity which it encapsulated were already well developed before the Reformation, as we have already seen.[16] What it suggests is that early Tudor testators did not lightly include in their wills provisions which they believed might complicate probate or bring trouble on heirs and executors. With the advent of reform the stakes and the pressures were raised. Famously, the Protestant will of the Gloucester gentleman, William Tracy, proved in 1531 and containing an unequivocal statement of Lutheran belief and a repudiation of the help of the saints and any doctrine of merit, led to his posthumous conviction of heresy, and the exhumation and (illegal) burning of his body. The incident became a *cause célèbre*, and the will itself circulated in manuscript and was published in 1550. Dickens, who accepts that the Tracy incident may indicate ecclesiastical sensitivity to Protestant wills by 1530, dismisses the notion that Catholic formulas might themselves in due course have involved testators in difficulties. He claims that in the last years of Henry there were "no legal or social pressures" to abandon traditional forms, and even the government of Edward VI "does not seem to have seriously threatened to disqualify Catholic wills".[17]

In fact, the matter is not so straightforward. From about 1536 onwards, as we have seen, the tide of official religious action was flowing strongly against devotion to the saints. The lights before their images were extinguished in 1538, their shrines despoiled, and pilgrimages banned. Clergy were encouraged by the Henrician Injunctions of that year to omit the invocations to the saints in the litany, and although the Ten Articles and the *King's Book* permitted invocation of the saints in general, they discouraged resort to

---

[15] Parker, *History of Long Melford*, pp. 223–5.
[16] See above, chapter 10, "The Pains of Purgatory", pp. 362–6.
[17] A. G. Dickens, *The English Reformation*, 1989, p. 215.

particular saints for specific favours, thereby striking a blow at the relationship of patronage and dependence between the saints and their clients which lay at the heart of the late medieval cult. No one in Henry's reign, it is true, *forbade* the bequest of one's soul the saints, but in 1543 the Catholic will of one of the conservative opponents of Cranmer in the chapter at Canterbury came under attack, on the grounds that the will's provision for the recitation of the rosary for the testator's soul contravened the Article on prayer for the departed in the *King's Book*, which forbade the placing of any trust in one particular form of prayer over another.[18] If the expression of one aspect of Catholic belief could call the validity of a will into question, why not others, especially since the cult of the saints was the aspect of traditional Catholicism most directly under official attack in the later years of Henry's reign? In 1544 Cranmer issued his English litany, in which the invocations of the saints, which had till then made up the bulk of the litany, were reduced to three generalized petitions, in which no saint but the Virgin was actually named. This process of attrition was completed on Edward's accession, when all images were removed and defaced, the three remaining collective mentions of the saints were removed from the litany, and the whole cult banished from public worship. By 1551 Hooper was quizzing the clergy of the diocese of Gloucester "whether any of them make or write any man's testament with this style, 'I commend my soul unto God, to our Blessed Lady, and to the saints of heaven,' which is injurious to God, and perilous as well for the salvation of the dead, as dangerous unto the maker."[19]

Against this mounting hostility on the part of the Crown and the Protestant section of the episcopate, the growing tendency to omit the names of Mary and the saints from will preambles becomes more intelligible, but correspondingly less significant in religious terms. Of course it was an achievement of sorts for the reformers to eliminate the names of the saints from the pieties of will-making, if perhaps not altogether at the deathbed; the intimacy between believers and the saints they invoked was nourished by such gestures, and could not indefinitely survive without them. But it cannot be assumed that to omit the names of the saints under official pressure was to reject them, or that this omission can be taken as a sign of growing Protestant conviction. Prudence, not ideology, dictated reticence. In 1543 the first edition of *The Book of Presidents* was published, containing, among other exemplary

18 L&P, XVIII part 2, p. 301.
19 VAI, II p. 306.

documents, a sample will for a London mercer, in which the testator bequethed his soul "unto almightie god, my maker and redemer", and this or similar uncontroversial forms rapidly became popular in wills all over England. But this form was, precisely, uncontroversial: it is seriously misleading to call it reformist, for this is to suggest a dynamic towards Protestantism which in most cases cannot plausibly be demonstrated or assumed. Indeed, in many cases it is manifestly absent, since wills which use this form often include bequests for Masses, prayers, and works of charity which make clear the testator's Catholic convictions.[20]

Nor can it be assumed that even wills lacking such explicitly Catholic bequests are reformist. As the Henrician Reformation proceeded testators came to see the will less and less as a suitable place in which to express religious conviction or to make provision for the health of their souls. Theological polemic, combined with the uncertainties of politics and the rise and fall of Catholic and reformed influences at court, made the religious policy of the regime difficult to fathom and to predict. In many cases, therefore, testators entrusted all such arrangements to the discretion of their executors. This had already been a feature of many pre-Reformation wills. Though most testators before 1530 specified the sorts of religious observances they desired, Clive Burgess found that in Bristol the obit provisions actually carried out in the parish churches far exceeded anything specified in the wills of the deceased, for executors and friends provided far more than was requested by the testator. Clearly, therefore, much of the specifically religious dimension of death even in the fifteenth century fell outside the scope of the will, and many testators in fact left all such arrangements to their executors – "to dispose . . . for the helthe of my soule as I have shewed him in confession"; "my executors . . . to do and to dispose affter theyr discretion"; to dispose "as to her shall seem most expedient".[21] It was a simple and obvious step in trying times to extend this area of discretion. In the 1540s, silence in the will about one's funeral arrangements must have seemed to many an increasingly sensible option, as nervousness grew about what the regime would or would not permit. There are many wills in which this nervousness is evident, as in that of John Hynes of Holy Island, who in 1545 asked for burial and other mortuary arrangements "accordynge to the kynges Maiesties actes statutes and Iniunctions",

---

[20] Alsop, "Will Preambles", *passim*.
[21] C. Burgess, "'By Quick and By Dead': Wills and Pious Provision in Late Medieval Bristol", *English Historical Review*, CII, 1987, pp. 837–58; *Lincoln Wills*, II pp. 3, 9, 12, 14, 15, 16, 50, 64, 65.

or John Hygdon, a Somerset man who in 1552 asked, somewhat optimistically, for a dirge for this soul "if it shall stand with the king's proceedings".[22] Other testators kept their worries to themselves and simply said as little as possible, like Thomas Fairfax, a Yorkshire lawyer who in 1544 asked "to be buried in Christien buriall, to be done by the discression of my executors", a sensible form which became increasingly common and went on in widespread use into Mary's reign and beyond.[23]

We know for certain that some testators of demonstrably Catholic belief said as little or even less. Many London testators in the 1540s made wills which had preambles entrusting their souls to God and to the saints: they can therefore be presumed to have had essentially Catholic beliefs. But many of these wills contain no explicitly Catholic bequests at all – they ask for no Masses or dirges, arrange no doles, mention no month's minds or anniversaries, and many use neutral phrases about their funerals, requesting merely "Christen mannys buryall" or "my bodye . . . brought honestlye to the erthe".[24] On Dickens's principle that the omission of such Catholic formalities implies "rejection", one might deduce that middle-class Londoners in the 1540s were moving away from traditional belief about intercession for the dead. The chance survival of inventories which include funeral expenses for two of these testators, however, throws a very different light on their silence. Katherine Bracye, a haberdasher's widow who made her will in May 1543, bequeathed her soul to Almighty God, to St Mary, and all the holy company of heaven. She left the conventional sum of 3s4d for unpaid tithe, but made no other religious arrangements, simply dividing her property among her seven children. Her will is, to all intents and purposes, a secular document. The funeral expenses preserved in a separate inventory, however, include substantial expenditure on candles, payments to priests and clerks suggesting that at least twenty attended her funeral, and 3s 4d for "mass and dirige at the month mynde". Similarly, in the following year the will of Anys Borde had an identical preamble, and no religious provisions, not even a bequest for unpaid tithe, simply requesting "Crystyn berryall". Once again the inventory reveals that this involved candles, the usual requiem with payments to priests and clerks to be present, and a dole to the "pore peple at the daye [of] her beryall".[25]

---

[22] *Wills and Inventories*, ed. J. Raine, Surtees Society, 1835–60, I. p. 113. Hynes accepted the supremacy, but was otherwise traditionalist in his beliefs; *Somerset Wills*, III pp. 135–6.

[23] *Test. Ebor.* VI p. 188.

[24] *London Consistory Court Wills 1492–1547*, ed. I. Darlington, London Record Society, III, 1967, pp. 74, 75, 77, 79, 94, 110, 123, 132, 143, etc.

[25] Ibid., pp. 101–7, 125–6.

Of course it does not follow that because some testators were silent about their Catholic convictions, all such neutral wills can be counted as Catholic. But it is evident that the silence of a growing number of wills about traditional Catholic religious practices cannot safely be taken as an indicator of reformist shifts in popular belief. Nor is this a matter of a few atypical examples. Even significant regional shifts in types of preamble cannot be taken as a reliable indication of a swing away from traditional beliefs, as can be seen from an examination of the seventy-five wills made between 1540 and 1561 in a single Yorkshire parish, that of Otley, ten miles north-east of Leeds.

Otley, a parish in Wharfedale of a thousand houseling folk in a number of settlements, had none of the radicalism associated with larger urban centres like Halifax. It provides a useful case study nevertheless, both because of the substantial number of wills produced over the key years of reform, and because between 1540 and 1550 the parish had just one curate, Sir Richard Olred, who witnessed and probably drafted the majority of wills, thereby eliminating one variable factor and making less complicated any attempt to interpret shifts in the drafting of parish wills. It is also useful because the Otley wills are to be found in one of the main collections, those from the Leeds district, on which Dickens's pioneering work was done, and so they provide some sort of test of the validity of his overall conclusions. Moreover, in spite of Otley's geographical scatter, or perhaps because of it, individual wills suggest a close-knit community, in which deathbeds and funerals served as a focus of neighbourly concern and community solidarity: many of these Otley wills list by name as many as five or six witnesses, and refer to the presence of "other more". Will-making in such a community can be presumed to reflect common values and assumptions.[26]

Between 1539 and 1543, the years of traditionalist triumph after the passing of the Six Articles, all the wills made in Otley follow a single basic pattern, with only insignificant variations. Testators leave their souls to "Almightie God my maker and redemer, and to our blessed ladie, withalle the holie companie in heaven, to pray for me".[27] All but three of these wills were witnessed by or overseen by the vicar, Richard Olred, who usually signs first, suggesting that he did the drafting. Almost all the testators make explicit provision

[26] A. G. Dickens, *Lollards and Protestants in the Diocese of York*, 1959, pp. 170–2, 214–17. What follows is based on the wills printed in *Testamenta Leodiensia*, ed. G. D. Lumb, Thoresby Society, I and II, 1913–30.

[27] *Test. Leod.*, I p. 67, William Bonde 17 July 1542; see also pp. 12, 15–16, 28–9, 31, 42–3, 65–6, 76, 79, 88–9, 131–4.

for intercessions and acts of charity, though these are varied in character – bequests for candles and torches, dirges and masses, to a gild altar, to highways and to the poor, to light or adorn the pyx, or, less specifically, to be bestowed "where most nede is within the church". Here, evidently, is a serenely Catholic parish, presided over by a Catholic priest.

Change begins quite abruptly after 1543. One of the two wills made in that year, by Richard England of the hamlet of Pool, has no obit provisions whatever and uses a different formula, simply leaving his soul to "Almightie God my maker and redemer". This will too was witnessed and probably drawn up by Olred, and it appears to have been the first of a new type. Of the eighteen wills made in Otley between 1544 and 1549, Olred's last year as curate, twelve were witnessed by Olred, but only two revert to the older form by including Mary and the saints in the bequest of the soul. The rest use "Almighty God my Maker (creator) and redeemer", or simply "Almighty God my redeemer". This shift cannot plausibly be put down to any change in belief. Olred continues to witness and probably draft both types of will, and until 1546 most wills continue to make traditional obit provisions, bequests of rosaries, large- and small-scale expenditure on Masses, alms to the poor, and bequests for highways and the ornaments of the church.[28] From 1547 onwards a new phase begins: most testators omit any explicit obit provisions, and the overwhelming majority of wills contains no provision for Masses, no gifts to the church or highways, no doles to the poor. The one exception, William Waid of Newall, who made his will in October 1549, bequeathed his soul to God without any mention of saints. Nevertheless he left twenty shillings to the poor "to praye for my saull" and five shillings to Olred, presumably for Masses. By contrast George Bramley, who made his will in February 1549, included the saints in his preamble, but left no obit provisions of any sort, merely requesting "christen manes buriall".[29]

We have already seen evidence of the mounting government pressure on the cult of the saints in the early 1540s, which may have led testators to omit the expression of that aspect of their traditional beliefs in their wills, and to adopt the non-provocative form provided in patterns like those in *The Book of Presidents*. In Otley at least that shift was not at first accompanied by any significant lessening of Catholic commitment, as reflected in traditional obit

[28] Ibid., I. pp. 148–9, II p. 78 (including saints); I pp. 109–10, 111, 121, 122, 131–4, 141, 148–9, 161, 170, 188, 204, 209, 232, 233, 237, 250 (omitting the saints).
[29] Ibid., I p. 250, II p. 78.

provision. That break was to come from 1547 onwards, when the accession of a Protestant puppet king and the dissolution of the chantries signalled to anyone with a modicum of common sense the likely destination of money bequeathed for intercession. Crown condemnation of religious institutions as "superstitious" had since the mid-1530s invariably been a prelude to confiscation, and the Chantries Act of 1547 explicitly confiscated not only chantry lands but all funds set aside for obit provision, such as stocks for candles or lamps. Like sensible people, the men and women of Otley decided not to throw their goods away by legally allocating them to what the Crown and the Archbishop of Canterbury were now proclaiming to be "blind superstition".

Richard Olred ceased to be curate of Otley in late 1549 or early 1550. Perhaps he was unwilling to use the prayer-book, for he remained in contact with the parish, witnessing a will there in 1551. With the arrival of the new curate, Richard Somerscale, the homogeneity of Otley will-making seems to break down. Somerscale himself is mentioned in only one will, and witnessed none, and alongside the now standard "Almighty God my creator and redeemer", several new formulas were employed, bequeathing the soul to "Jesus Christe my maker and redemer" and to "the blessed trinitie and the Celestiall company of heaven".[30] As that example suggests, the diversity was by no means necessarily a sign of an advance towards Protestantism, for in the same year a variation of the old formula appears in the will of Lady Isabel Johnson, who left her soul to "Almightie God my creator and redemer, desiryng oure blissed ladie, with all the blessed sanctes in heaven, to praye with me and for me, that my saull and bodie maye come to lif everlastyng throughe the merites of the passion of oure Saviour Jesus Christe".[31]

That will embodies the sort of theological sophistication evident in many of the self-consciously "correct" wills of pious gentry in the late fifteenth and early sixteenth century. No doubt its careful articulation of the primacy of Christ in salvation, and the sub-ordinate role of the saints (who are to pray "with me and for me") reflects a Catholicism rendered more sensitive to the demands of strict orthodoxy by Protestant polemic. As we shall see, Catholic wills of this "correct" sort would become the norm in Marian Otley. Of the six Otley wills made in 1551 three, somewhat surprisingly, are overtly Catholic, two of them identifiable as such

---

[30] Ibid., I pp. 267, 313.
[31] Ibid., I pp. 267–9.

from obviously Catholic preambles, while that of Robert Wilson of Denton, by contrast, used the non-provocative "Almighty God my maker and redeemer" form, but contained a bequest of a shilling to a priest for prayers, and 6s 8d to the poor of Denton "to pray for my saull".[32]

As might be expected in a parish where Protestantism therefore appeared to have silenced traditional pieties but made little positive impression, the accession of Mary marked a decisive change. In the only Otley will of 1553 Nicholas Rodes, making his will on 20 July, the day after Mary's proclamation as Queen but before news of it had reached Wharfedale, used the now standard preamble, omitting the saints. William Pickard, however, making his will in the following February, reverted to the fully Catholic form current in the early 1540s. Thereafter only three of the twenty-eight wills made in Otley before the end of 1560 omit elaborate references to the saints in their preambles. Moreover, one of those three, the will of Alice Stanfield in March 1556, in which she bequeathed her soul simply to "the mercie of my Redemer Ihesus Christe", made such extensive obit provision, for elevation torches, Masses, and "Diriges" both for herself and her husband, and doles to the poor, that there can be no doubt of her Catholic convictions.[33]

Overall, the Marian wills of Otley present a far more striking change in language than anything which had previously taken place. From 1554 the parish had a new priest, Sir Anthony Jackson, whose name occurs sporadically in wills up to 1557. The first two wills he witnessed, that of Agnes Bound in March 1554 and of Richard or Robert Stanfield in July 1555, established a new pattern for the parish. This preamble bequeathed the soul "to the mercye of my Redemer Jesu Chryste, . . . beseching or blessed Lady St Marye and all the sanctes in heaven to praye for me".[34] A very common variation on this form added a reference to predestination, bequeathing the soul "to allmightie God and to the mercye of my Redemer Jesus Chryst, besechyng our blessed laydye and all the celestiall companie of heaven to pray for yt that yt may tayke place emongest the elect people of God".[35]

There is no reason to question the firm Catholic convictions of testators using either version of this new formula. As we have seen from many fifteenth-century examples, there was no contradiction or inconsistency for orthodox Catholics in trusting solely in the

[32] Ibid., I p. 280.
[33] Ibid., II p. 92.
[34] Ibid., II pp. 14–15, 21, 55, 75, 191, 244, 302, 355.
[35] Ibid., II p. 142 (two examples) and see also 25, 58–60 (witnessed by Jackson "my curate"), 97, 111 (witnessed by Jackson), 140, 214, 267.

merits of Christ, and asking the prayers of the living and the dead, including the saints, that the testator might be a partaker of those merits. Nor is the reference to election a sign of reformed convictions, since an emphasis on the doctrine of predestination had been a feature of English theology and piety since at least the fourteenth century.[36] Although the reformers asserted the incompatibility of faith in Christ with a desire for the prayers of one's fellow Christians, Christendom for a thousand years had seen no such contradiction. The comparatively large number of surviving wills from the later 1550s accommodating declarations of trust in the merits of Christ alongside a desire for the help of prayers and good works suggests that the Marian church vigorously set about reclaiming the theological high ground by encouraging preambles which did justice to the unique and sufficient saving power of Christ's Passion and at the same time the value of the prayers of the saints, the celebration of Masses, and the dispensing of charity as means of making that Passion fruitful for the living and the dead. Historians have scratched their heads unnecessarily over wills of this sort, seeing them as muddled, mixed, inconsistent, even as evidence of the failure of the Marian regime to turn back the clock. In fact they represent an important aspect of Marian orthodoxy, the base-line of a Catholicism which was anxious to spell out the teaching which had dominated the Church's deathbed ministry throughout the later Middle Ages, and thereby to neutralize the claims of the reformers to a monopoly of faithfulness to a Christocentric Gospel.

Wills of this sort originated in the fourteenth and fifteenth centuries, but had of course been used by some testators in the 1540s. We have already encountered the Suffolk will of Harry Edon, though that, having been made in the year after the publication of Cranmer's English litany, prudently omitted the saints. Sir Godfrey Foljambe, of Walton in Derbyshire, made a will in January 1541 in which he commended his soul "to Almyghty God, my Savyor and redemer Jeshus Criste, through whose mercy and by the merites of his passion I trust to be a saved soule", and then went on to commend it also "to our blessed Lady Seynt Mary, Seynt John baptist, and all the holy company in hevyn, humbly beseching them to pray unto our sayd Savyor Jeshu Criste to accept the same to his high grace, marcy and endeles joye". He provided for Masses and "Diriges", "with all other suffrages and obsequies to be done and mynistered for my soule and all Christian soules".[37]

---

[36] See above, chapter 7, "Devotions of the Primers", p. 253.
[37] North Country Wills, Surtees Society, 1908–12, I pp. 175–8.

But the incidence of such wills increased dramatically in the Marian period. Otley provided a particularly fine crop, but they were by no means confined to this place, and examples are to be found in all the major collections of the period. They were commonplace in the Leeds region in 1556, 1557, and 1558. Some of these wills contain obit provisions which remove any possible doubt about the genuinely Catholic convictions of the testators, while others have no such provision. A representative example is the will of John Parson of Methley, who left his soul to the holy and glorious Trinity, to the

> blessed and holy St Marye the virgine and mother of God, . . . evermore trustinge and in stedfaste beleve throughe the glorious and paynefull passion of our Lord Jhu Chryst to be one of thos chossen and electe children of God at the laste resurrection and dredfull day of Iudgement, and to company wyth or holy father Abraham, Isaac and Jacobe, and all other the holy company of heaven.

He went on to bestow 13s 4d on bridges, and asked his executors "to dispose for the healthe of my soull as they shall thinke most mete and convenyent".[38] Similar examples could be found in Suffolk and Somerset, in London and Durham. They are sometimes used in the conventional late fifteenth-century way, as self-conscious expressions of passionate Catholic commitment. This appears to have been the purpose of the will of Thomas Trollope, of Kelloe, County Durham, who declared himself to be "a true Christian belevynge all the articles of or catholyke faythe and all other cerymonies wch or mother holy Church doith observe and kepe", before going on to bequeath his soul to Christ "who redemede and bought the same wt his most precyous blode, besechinge the most hollye and pure virgin Mari mother of Jesus Christ and all the saynts of heaven to praye for me". He provided for "solempn masse wth all other obsequys as becometh a man of my behaveyor at the discretion of myne executors", as well as leaving bequests for the re-equipping of the parish church.[39] A will preamble of this sort, combining explicit statements of Catholic orthodoxy with declarations of sole reliance on the Passion of Christ, far from representing the Marian church's failure to turn the clock back, is thus recognizably a triumphant return to and advance upon the programme advocated in the *Ars Moriendi* and pre-Reformation pastoral practice, and in the English deathbed prayers

[38] *Test. Leod.*, II p. 122; for other examples, among many, see pp. 3, 25, 26–8, 34, 42, 45, 83, 143, 165, 196, 273–4.
[39] *Wills and Inventories*, I pp. 174–6.

of the Sarum primers. It would not be too much to claim that such wills constitute a neglected source of evidence of the resilience and creative traditionalism of Marian Catholicism.

But they do more. Retrospectively, they also help to place a question mark against what has been taken to be firm evidence for the spread of Protestantism among the people in Edward's reign. The instant, enthusiastic, and virtually unanimous adoption of Catholic forms by will-makers in Otley at the accession of Mary is of course a strong indication of the persistence of Catholicism there in the 1540s and early 1550s. Yet even in Otley the saints were dropped from wills from 1544, and obit bequests ceased from 1547. The Catholic people of Otley making their declarations of trust in the merits of Christ's Passion in the years after 1554 could presumably have made similar declarations in 1550. But in 1550 they would have been unable to add the prayers to the saints and the requests for Masses and doles which mark the Marian wills out as obviously Catholic. Though their Catholicism would not have been compromised by their reliance on the Passion, it would have been invisible, because of the silence imposed on expressions of other aspects of their inherited beliefs by the dominance of the Protestant minority who controlled the government. Can we therefore be confident that apparently uncomplicatedly Protestant wills in the reign of Edward or the first years of Mary can be trusted as indicators of the acceptance of the Protestant message? A handful of wills from another community, the tiny hamlet of Newton Kyme, two miles from Tadcaster, suggests that perhaps we cannot.

On 22 January 1553 John Empson of Newton Kyme made his will. His formula was of the type generally treated, and counted, by historians as straightforwardly Protestant, since he bequeathed his soul "to almightie God my maker and to his onelie sonne Jhu Christe my lorde and Savior, in whome I putt the holl hope and truste of my salvacion throughe the merites of his blissed passion". There were no obit provisions and no mentions of the saints. The will was witnessed by two of Empson's neighbours, George Cawood and Richard Shipley. As it turned out, George Cawood himself was not long for this world: on 1 September 1554 he in turn made his will. The preamble to his will is identical to Empson's, except that Christ is described as Lord and Redeemer, rather than Lord and Saviour. But Mary had now been on the throne for over a year, and George Cawood included a clause in his will bequeathing twelve pence "for the adorninge of the Churche". There are no other obit provisions, but Cawood's gift of a shilling for the ornamentation of the church to its pre-Reformation glory need not have been made. The reticence established under Henry and Edward died hard, and until 1556 many Marian testators, even in predominantly conservative communities, tended to continue the minimalist practice which had emerged in the last years of Henry, and to confine the provisions of their wills to the secular disposal of property. The conclusion seems inescapable, that George Cawood was well disposed to the restoration of Catholic worship which was by now under way in his parish church.

In May 1556 Richard Shipley, who had witnessed Empson's will with Cawood, witnessed the will of another neighbour, William Barker, this time in company with Christopher Cawood, probably George's son, and one George Wyley. Once again, Barker employed the same preamble as Cawood and Empson, but after the words "merites of his blissed passion", he added that he also left his soul "to his mother and virgine sancte Marie, and to all the holie company of heaven, to pray for me, havynge great nede thereof". That phrase, "having great need thereof", is hardly the sort of addition a scribe would make, for it catches the dying man's voice, and suggests an authentic and heartfelt piety. The Protestant formula which Barker was perhaps given by Shipley is now unmistakably Catholic. Finally, in September 1557 John Empson's widow Anne made her will, and once again Richard Shipley, Christopher Cawood, and George Wyley were called on to act as witnesses. Anne's preamble is uncomplicatedly traditional, committing her soul to Almighty God, to the Blessed Virgin, and to all the company of heaven. The last echoes of the Edwardine regime have died away.[40]

Do these wills show us a Protestant village returning to Catholicism, or a Catholic village whose Catholicism re-emerged with increasing confidence as the Marian regime stabilized? Was John Empson a Protestant, rejecting by his silence the prayers of his neighbours and of the whole communion of saints for the health of his soul? If so, what of his wife, who three years later resigned her soul simply, as generations of her kind had done, into the hands of God, of the Mother of God, and of all the saints? And what of Empson's friends, the tight-knit group of neighbours who stood round each other's deathbeds and witnessed each other's wills? Were George Cawood, copying Empson's preamble but bestowing a shilling about the Catholic ornaments of the church stripped under Edward, and William Barker, adding his urgent plea for the help of the saints, "having great nede therof", thereby parting company with their friend, turning their backs on the Gospel light that had broken on Newton Kyme in the 1540s? It seems more

---

[40] *Test. Leod.*, II pp. 16, 4, 48, 146.

likely that the shifts in the preambles of these wills reflect not a deep-seated change of heart by the testators, but rather shifts in the limits of the possible and the approved. Given the wills made by his wife and friends, it is at least as likely as not that John Empson's will reflects not commitment to Protestantism, but an accommodation to the theologically favoured idiom of a Protestant regime, adopted all the more readily because nothing in it contradicted Catholic belief. This was clearly a close-knit group of neighbours, sharing a community of value. Not the least remarkable feature of these relatively sophisticated shifts in theological nuance is the apparent lack of clerical influence on the wills, for no priest appears as a witness. In the circumstances, radical discontinuity of belief among them seems psychologically improbable. No doubt if Edward VI had lived to manhood, and the silence imposed on the language of Catholic piety had deepened and lengthened, the villagers of Newton Kyme would have absorbed Protestant beliefs and values as the memory of the old religion faded. That, presumably, is what was to take place in Elizabeth's reign. But to put the matter at its lowest, nothing irreversible had happened in Newton Kyme by 1554, and the patterns of Catholic devotion readily, and rapidly, re-established themselves.

CHAPTER 16

MARY

A convincing account of the religious history of Mary's reign has yet to be written. More than any other period of Tudor history, the five years from her accession to her death have been discussed in value-laden terms which reveal the persistence of a Protestant historiography, authoritatively shaped by John Foxe, which still hinders a just assessment of the aims and the achievements of the Marian church. The phrase most commonly used to describe the religious policy of the reign, the "Marian reaction", reveals more about the assumptions of those who use it than about the objectives of the churchmen to whom it is applied. The limitations and presuppositions of this historiographical tradition can be seen in its most distinguished product, A. G. Dickens's account of the English Reformation.[1] Dickens devotes twenty-nine pages to the reign: six of them discuss (and emphasize) adverse public reaction to aspects of Mary's rule, especially her marriage to Philip II. Eight pages are devoted to the Protestant martyrs, six pages to the Protestant minorities who continued to practise their religion during the reign. Only two and a half pages are allocated to a discussion of the positive impact of the Marian church, and the religious attitudes of the broad majority of the nation who accepted and, as I have been arguing, welcomed the return of traditional religion. This brief section is, moreover, entirely confined to the north of England, and therefore makes no use of the most important piece of evidence we have for the objectives, methods, and effectiveness of the Marian church, the returns of Archdeacon Nicholas Harpsfield's visitation of Kent in 1557, surely the most searching visitation carried out in any diocese in the Tudor period.

---

[1] D. Loades, "The Enforcement of Reaction 1553–1558", *Journal of Ecclesiastical History*, XVI, 1965, pp. 54–66; A. G. Dickens, *The English Reformation*, 1989, pp. 287–315, essentially reaffirming the emphases of his *The Marian Reaction in the Diocese of York*, Part I, *The Clergy* and Part II, *The Laity*, Borthwick Institute Publications, nos 11 and 12, 1957. In many ways the most satisfactory account of religion in Mary's reign is A. M. Bartholomew, "Lay Piety in the reign of Mary Tudor", Manchester M. A. Thesis, 1979.

In his discussion of Marian use of the press Dickens does not even mention the most characteristic and impressive product of the Marian church's desire to reeducate the nation in the fundamentals of Catholicism, Bonner's *Profytable and necessary doctryne*, and the thirteen *Homilies* compiled by his chaplains, John Harpsfield and Henry Pendleton, usually bound with it, despite the fact that Cardinal Pole in 1556 required every parish priest in England to acquire and preach from this book.

For Dickens the Marian church was, like its Queen, "the prisoner of a sorrowful past",[2] unable to generate policy or initiate reform, just as she was unable to produce an heir. Miserably failing to rise to the polemical challenge set by the "formidable army of talent" among the Protestant exiles, the regime was trapped in religious and cultural sterility. Instead of creative instruction there were only "the ceaseless processions made by government order round the streets and churches of London". Mary and her clergy failed to discover the Counter-Reformation, and, lacking a "programme of reconversion", had nothing to offer except an unpopular mixture of nostalgia for an irrecoverable past and a version of persecuting Catholicism tainted by association with Spain, certainly nothing which might have evolved into "a broadly acceptable English Catholicism".[3]

There is something intrinsically problematic about the notion of a Marian failure to "discover" the Counter-Reformation, not least because, as yet, there was little that could be called the Counter-Reformation to be discovered. In 1553 the Council of Trent still had much of its most important work to do. Suspended in 1552, it was not to reconvene till both Mary and Pole had been dead for more than three years. When it did so it was to frame what is arguably its most important decree, on the establishment of seminaries, on the model mapped out for Marian England by Pole in 1555.[4] Indeed, the religious priorities in evidence in the attempts to re-establish Catholic belief and practice in Mary's reign closely parallel much that is often thought to be most characteristic of the Counter-Reformation. The leaders of the Marian church did in fact possess a realistic set of objectives, based on a shrewd and fundamentally sound assessment of the impact of reform on the broad mass of the population. Far from pursuing a programme of blind reaction, the Marian authorities consistently sought to promote a

---

[2] Dickens, *English Reformation*, pp. 309–11.
[3] Ibid., p. 315.
[4] W. Schenk, *Reginald Pole, Cardinal of England*, 1950, pp. 143–4; A. D. Wright, *The Counter Reformation*, 1982, p. 154.

version of traditional Catholicism which had absorbed whatever they saw as positive in the Edwardine and Henrician reforms, and which was subtly but distinctively different from the Catholicism of the 1520s. Their programme was not one of reaction but of creative reconstruction, and they did not jettison all that had been done since 1534. The restoration in March 1554 of the ritual calendar as it had been after and not before Henry VIII's prunings is significant, and entirely characteristic.[5] The regime preserved and sought to build on much that had been produced by the reforms of the previous two reigns, and in its teaching did not flinch from adapting and repossessing for Catholic orthodoxy even language reminiscent of Cranmer's communion service.

There is, moreover, considerable evidence that the religious programme of the Marian church was widely accepted, and was establishing itself in the parishes. The Marian visitations have been quarried, even by comparatively sympathetic historians like Philip Hughes, for signs of turmoil and failure. Harpsfield's visitation of Kent in 1557 put the most Protestant county in England under a microscope, and in the process it certainly revealed just how much needed to be done before the restoration of Catholicism was complete. But the returns also reveal the startling extent to which the depredations of the Edwardine regime had already been repaired, and the herculean efforts being made by clergy, wardens, and parishioners to reconstruct the ritual and sacramental framework of traditional religion.[6]

Nor was the effort to reconstruct traditional religion confined to the parish church. Those who have criticized the Marian regime's use of the printing-press have neglected one aspect of the publishing history of the reign which is crucial to any adequate understanding of the religious programme of the Marian church. Thirty-five editions of the Sarum primer survive from Mary's reign, and four of the York primer, compared with a total of seventeen from the reign of Edward. Most of the Marian primers were produced between 1555 and 1558, fifteen editions surviving from 1555 alone. This rate of production swamps that of any earlier period. Quite apart from the demand for Catholic prayer-books to which their sheer number testifies, the Marian primers themselves throw a flood of light on the religious priorities of the reign. Over half of the Marian primers printed in England came from a single

---

[5] TRP, II no. 407 (p. 37).
[6] L. E. Whatmore (ed.), *Archdeacon Harpsfield's Visitation, 1557*, Catholic Record Society, XLV–XLVI, 1950–1. The two volumes are continuously paginated, volume I ending at p. 173. Reference is by page number only.

publisher, John Wayland, or his assigns. The Wayland primers had a distinctive character and content, and carried the regime's stamp of approval. Wayland's first primer in 1555 claimed on its title-page to have been "newly set forth by certayne of the cleargye with the assente of the moste reuerende father in god the Lord Cardinall Pole hys grace: to be only used (al other sette apparte) . . . according to the Quenes hyghnes letters patentes", and his privileged status as Crown patentee was reiterated in successive editions.[7] While they did not in fact command an effective monopoly of the market, his primers clearly represent the religion approved for lay use in Mary's church, and, as we shall see, their character and content disposes decisively of any idea that that religion was merely reactionary or represented an unreflecting return to the pattern which had prevailed before the break with Rome.

Religious Priorities in Marian England

Queen Mary was proclaimed in London on 19 July, and in most of the north by St Mary Magdalene's day, 22 July. It was at once clear that Catholicism would be restored, and some communities proceeded to Counter-Reformation without tarrying for any. At Melton Mowbray the altar stones were put back up immediately, in order to sing Mass and "Dirige" for the King who had put an end to the Mass and prayer for the dead.[8] Robert Parkyn reported that in "many places of the realme" the Catholic gentry commanded the clergy to sing Mass once more "with a decentt ordre as haithe ben uside beffore tyme". But since "ther was no actt, statutte, proclamation or commandementt sett furthe for the sayme", many clergy "durstt not be bolde to celebratte in Latten, thowghe ther hertts was wholly enclynede thatt way".[9] Parkyn was a convinced papalist who had nevertheless conformed under Henry and Edward, and would do so again under Elizabeth. His testimony to both the inclinations of the majority of the clergy and their reluctance to take any initiative without the sanction of "actt, statutte, proclamation or commandementt" demonstrates the extent to which the Tudor state had succeeded in calling its clergy to heel. But all uncertainty evaporated on 18 August, when the Queen issued a proclamation making clear her own desire for the restoration of Catholicism,

---

[7] I have not had access to the first edition, RSTC 16060, and I have used *The primer in Englishe (after the use of Sarum) with many godly and devoute prayers . . . Wherunto is added a plaine and godly treatise concerninge the Masse . . . for the Instruccyon of the unlearned and symple people*, London, John Wayland, 1555; RSTC 16063; Hoskins no. 211 (hereafter = Wayland *Primer*).

[8] J. J. Scarisbrick, *The Reformation and the English People*, 1984, p. 104.

[9] "Robert Parkyn's Narrative" in A. G. Dickens, *Reformation Studies*, 1982, p. 308.

permitting the practice of both religions till such time "as further order by common assent may be taken". She called for national unity, and forbade religious disputation and name-calling or the publication of religious satire or controversy.[10]

This proclamation opened the floodgates of Catholic restoration: less than a week later, on St Bartholomew's day, 24 August, "the olde service in the lattin tongue with the masse was begun and sunge in Paules in the Shrowdes . . . and likewise it was begun in 4 or 5 other parishes within the cittie of London, not be commaundement but of the peoples devotion."[11] By the beginning of September

> ther was veray few parishe churches in York shire but masse was song or saide in Lattin . . . Holly breade and holly watter was gyven, altares was reedifide, pyctures or ymages sett upp, the crosse with the crucifixe theron redye to be borne in procession . . . and yitt all thes cam to passe with owtt compulsion of any actt, statutte, proclamation or law.[12]

It was not of course plain sailing everywhere. London divided on the issue, and elsewhere the presence of strong reformed influences held back the tide of restoration. The Protestant propagandist, John Bland, was challenged by his churchwarden, John Austen, the leading traditionalist in his Kentish parish of Adisham, as early as 3 September. Austen denounced both Bland and his clerk as "heretic knaves" who "have deceived us with this fashion too long". Yet despite the swell of traditionalist feeling in the parish the 1552 communion service went on being used till the end of November, triggering a series of confrontations, priest against churchwardens, in which the communion table was repeatedly dismantled and re-erected. The issue was finally resolved on Holy Innocents Day 1554, the parish's patronal festival, when, because their own priest would not celebrate the old services, they hired a neighbouring traditionalist to come and sing matins, Mass, and evensong for them. The vicar tried to preach against transubstantiation at the Mass, but was pulled down by the parishioners, led by Austen, imprisoned in a side chapel, and subsequently arrested and taken to Dover for trial, and to his eventual terrible death by fire.[13]

The years of schism had left rifts, in many communities, which ran far deeper than any mere intellectual disagreement. The deputation which appeared before Archdeacon Harpsfield in 1557 to

[10] TRP, II no. 390.
[11] *Wriothesley Chronicle*, II p. 101.
[12] "Robert Parkyn's Narrative", p. 309.
[13] Foxe, *Acts and Monuments*, VII pp. 288–9.

represent the Kentish parish of Brookland included John Knell,
almost certainly the son of William Knell, the yeoman of Brookland
who had been executed in 1539 for speaking against the supremacy.
Also in the deputation was William Warcop, one of those who had
informed against him.[14] Religious division was worse in Kent than
in any other part of the country outside London, but Mary and her
bishops were well aware of the tensions and divisions in parishes
everywhere, and were convinced, as Henry had been convinced,
that disputation was no way to resolve them. At the heart of the
Marian regime's "failure" to promote a controversial pamphlet war
was a considered distrust of the social and religious effects of
what Mary's first proclamation called "the playing of interludes
and printing of false fond books, ballads, rhymes and other lewd
treatises" meddling in "question and controversy touching the high
points and mysteries of Christian religion".[15] In the time of schism,
Bonner wrote in the preface to the *Profytable and necessary doctryne*:

> Pernicious, and euylle doctryne was sowen, planted and set forth,
> sometymes by the procedyng preachers sermons, somtymes by
> ther prynted treatyses, sugred all ouer with lose libertye, (a thing
> in dede most delectable and pleasaunt unto the fleshe and unto al
> unruly persons) sometimes by readyng, playing, singing, and
> other like meanes and new devises, by reason wherof great
> insolency, disordre, contention, and moch inconvenience, dayly
> more and more, dyd ensue, to the greate dishonour of God,
> the lamentable hurte, and destruction, of the subjectes, and the
> notable reproach, rebuke and slaunder of the hole realme.[16]

The blustering scurrilities of Bale or Becon did not seem to
the Marian authorities the best model for establishing truth and
stabilizing the religious life of the people, for such "pernicious
and hurtful devices" could only engender "hatred among the
people and discord among the same".[17] Satire and burlesque are
commonly the weapons of those who seek to assail the established
order, wedges hammered into the wall to create or exploit a breach.
This was how the bishops perceived the position of Protestant
controversialists, striving by fair means or foul to shake the religious
convictions of centuries. It was the Protestants who needed to
make an impression, and who sought to deploy the belly-laugh
and the jeer to make their points. The bishops believed that what

[14] *Harpsfield's Visitation*, p. 165.
[15] TRP, II no. 390 (p. 6).
[16] *A Profitable and necessary doctryne, with certayne homelies adioyned thereunto set forth by the reverende father in God, Edmonde byshop of London*, London, 1555; RSTC 3282, preface (unpaginated).
[17] TRP, II no. 407 (p. 36).

they needed to do was not to contribute to, but to quieten the babble of alehouse debate. Their objective was to re-establish the order and beauty of Catholic worship and the regular participation of the people in the sacraments, and to underpin it by a regular and solidly grounded pattern of parochial instruction, which would repair the damage of the schism.

This preference for the beauty of holiness over the cut and thrust of debate was not, in any straightforward way, a rejection of the value of scripture-reading or preaching, though there were those, like Gardiner, who were gloomy about the likely impact of either. As we shall see, the Marian church sought to ensure regular parochial preaching and followed Cranmer's precedent in preparing a set of homilies to be used by "insufficient" preachers. Though the Bibles as well as Erasmus's paraphrases were collected up from the churches during the Marian visitations, Bible-reading or the possession of Bibles was never condemned by the regime. Protestant versions of the Bible were suspect, not English Bibles as such. Pole, as a member of the evangelically minded *Spirituali* of Cardinal Contarini's circle, had a deep sense of the value of scriptural preaching and expounded the Bible daily to his own household. A new English translation of the New Testament was one of the projects agreed and begun at Pole's legatine synod at the end of 1555.[18] But he abhorred religious argument and the spirit of self-sufficiency which he believed indiscriminate Bible-reading by lay people was likely to encourage. Better for the people to absorb the faith through the liturgy, to find in attentive and receptive participation in the ceremonies and sacraments of the Church the grace and instruction on which to found the Christian life. This was the true Catholic way, the spirit of the *parvuli*, the "little ones" of Christ, for whom penitence, not knowledge, was the true and only way to salvation. The object of preaching and teaching was not to impart knowledge, but to cause the people to lament their sins, seek the healing of the sacraments, and amend their lives. As he told the citizens of London, speaking of the Protestant desire to "cleave to Scrypture",

> The whiche only desyre of ytselfe beynge good, yet not takynge the right waye to the accomplishing of the same, maketh many to falle into heresyes, thinkynge no better nor spedyer waye to be, for to come to the knowledge of God and his law, than by readynge of books, whereyn they be sore deceyved. And yet so yt be done yn his place, and wyth right order and circumstance, yt helpethe muche.[19]

---

[18] R. W. Dixon, *History of the Church of England*, IV pp. 456–7.
[19] J. Strype, *Ecclesiastical Memorials*, 1816, III part 2, p. 503.

Pole, a true Augustinian, did not think of the ceremonies of the Church as an end in themselves. The true light and life of the soul "the Spirite of God gyvythe, neyther the ceremonyes whiche the heretykes doe rejecte, nor yet the Scrypture whereunto they doe so cleve". Yet, he insisted,

> the observatyon of ceremonyes, for obedyence sake, wyll gyve more light than all the readynge of Scrypture can doe, yf the reader have never so good a wytt to understand what he readeth, with the contempt of ceremonyes. But the thynge that gyveth us the veraye light, ys none of them both; but they are most apte to receyve light, that are more obedyent to follow ceremonyes, than to reade.

There could hardly be a more decisive rejection not only of Protestantism, but even of any radical Erasmianism which exalted the text over symbolic or ritual gesture. It was not, however, an obscurantist or ritualist position. It had impeccable precedent in sixteenth-century English Catholic teaching, and much the same emphasis expressed in similar terms can be found in John Fisher's Good Friday sermon of the Crucifix. For Pole the restoration of ceremonies, including the "endless processions" which have so exasperated historians, was important because participation in Catholic ceremony was symbolic of acceptance of the grace of God in the Church, and of attentiveness to the truths of God there proclaimed: "of the observation of ceremonyes, begynnethe the verye educatyon of the chylderne of God; as the olde law doyth shewe, that was full of ceremonyes, whiche St Paule callythe *pedagogium in Christum*." This was a message he read not only in scripture and the tradition of the Church, but in the recent history of England. As God made ceremonies the beginning of the good education of his children,

> so the heretykes makythe this the fyrste poynt of theyre schysme and heresyes, to destroye the unyte of the chyrche by contempte or change of ceremonyes; whiche semyth at the begynnynge nothinge. As yt semyd nothinge here amongste you to take awaye holy water, holy breade, candells, ashes, and palme; but what yt came to, you saw, and all felt yt.[20]

In this emphasis on the positive value of ceremony and sacrament, Pole and his colleagues, so often accused of lacking a grip of the realities of mid-Tudor England, were certainly more closely in touch with the feelings of the laity at large than were the reformers. Resentment and rejection of ritual change had lain close to the heart of both the Pilgrimage of Grace and the Western Rebellion, but

[20] Ibid., 502.

it was not only in the dark corners of the land that men and women felt that the repudiation of time-honoured ceremonies was symptomatic of more profound and more drastic discontinuities. Procession, pax, holy bread, and holy water were the formal expressions of the identity of the parish, and the rituals in which pecking-order and precedence were manifested or negotiated. Repudiation of or abstention from such rituals might be a manifestation of the repudiation of neighbourly charity and the unity of the community. Ceremonies which, to the reformers, were unchristian or idolatrous, were somewhere near the centre of things in the religious and communal instincts of the people. The parishioners of Stanford in the Vale dated the "wicked time of schism" not from Henry's reign, but from 1547, when "all godly ceremonyes and good usys were taken out of the Church."[21] Three years before Mary's accession John Ponet complained bitterly of the universal grumbling against the reform, as men said to one another "Believe as your forefathers have done before you... follow ancient customs and usages."[22] In re-establishing the old ceremonial the Marian church was not engaged in irrelevant antiquarianism, but playing one of its strongest cards.

Not that the Marian authorities were unaware of the need to teach the people once more to appreciate and value the ceremonies which had been proscribed by Cranmer and the Council under Edward. Behind the repudiation of ceremonial by the reformers lay a radically different conceptual world, a world in which text was everything, sign nothing. The sacramental universe of late medieval Catholicism was, from such a perspective, totally opaque, a bewildering and meaningless world of dumb objects and vapid gestures, hindering communication. That spirit of determined non-comprehension was very much in evidence in Marian England. It had been the lifeblood of Lollardy, and had been enormously encouraged by the spread of reformed teaching and practice. On Palm Sunday 1556 Laurence Burnaby, a parishioner of Brampton in the diocese of Lincoln, cried out when the vicar smote the door with the foot of the processional Cross and the choir sang "let him enter, the King of Glory", "What a sport have we towards. Will our vicar ronne at the quintine with God Almightie?"[23]

Accordingly, it was realized that any secure restoration of Catholicism must be based on a long-term process of catechesis which would enable lay people to understand and benefit from the

[21] Stanford CWA, p. 70.
[22] See above, chapter 13, "The Attack on Traditional Religion III", pp. XXX.
[23] Strype, *Memorials*, III part 2, p. 392.

ceremonies of the Church. Bonner, who set the pattern here for the rest of the Marian episcopate, required his clergy regularly to "declare, set forth, and instruct the people the true meaning of the ceremonies of the Church". So holy bread was to "put us in remembrance of unity . . . like as the bread is made of many grains, and yet but one loaf, and . . . to put us also in remembrance of the housel . . . which the people in the beginning of Christ's Church did oftener receive than they do use now in these days to do". Similarly, the bearing about of the pax on Sundays was to be explained as a reminder of the peace which Christ left his disciples, "but also of that peace, that Christ by his death purchased for the people". In addition, four times a year the clergy were to preach longer sermons in which they declared to the people

> the signification and true meaning of all other laudable and godly ceremonies used of old time in this Church of England to the best of their power, in such sort, that the people may perceive what is meant and signified by the same, and also know and understand how and in what manner they ought to use and accept them for their own edifying.[24]

The precedent for such explanations was of course Henrician. It had been enjoined in the Ten Articles, and Latimer had adapted medieval materials to provide similar "declarations" for his diocese.[25] As we have already seen, "declaration" of the ceremonies had been a much contested point in the early 1540s, traditionalist clergy frequently refusing to make any such declaration and emphasizing instead the apotropaic character of sacramentals. On the other hand, "declaration" had been one of the devices by which Henrician conservatives like Tunstall and Bonner had staved off the demise of the sacramentals and "laudable ceremonies" whose abolition Cranmer and others sought. The "Rationale of Ceremonial" was the most sustained example of that policy, and some of the model "declarations" Bonner provided for his clergy to use in Mary's reign closely resemble sections of the Rationale. The Marian church's adoption of the policy of declaration therefore demonstrates not only an awareness of a real pastoral need, but a willingness to absorb the lessons of the past, even when it meant canonizing methods developed in schism, and distancing itself, if only by silence, from the apotropaic understanding of the use of sacramentals.

There were in fact many aspects of the Henrician and Edwardine religious changes which the Marian church sought to preserve,

---

[24] VAI, II pp. 361–2.
[25] Ibid., pp. 171–2.

from the provision of registers of births, deaths, and marriages, and a church chest, to an emphasis on basic religious instruction in English. Bonner also ordered his priests to preach quarterly sermons, "to wit on the Sunday or solemn feast", recapitulating the essentials of the faith – the Creed, the Commandments, the avoidance of the seven deadly sins, the obligations of the seven works of mercy, and the seven sacraments. Pole required the clergy to preach every holy day, and before every sermon plainly to recite "and diligently teach" the Lord's Prayer, the Hail Mary, the Creed, and the Ten Commandments in English, "exhorting their parishioners to teach the same likewise to their children at home". Unlearned clergy "being no preachers", were to apply themselves to the study of holy scripture, and to give an annual account of their progress in study to their bishops. In the meantime, they were to be sure to catechize the "youth of the parishioners".[26] Addressing herself to the problem of clergy unable to preach, Mary required each of her bishops to set out "an uniform order . . . by homilies . . . for the good instruction and teaching of the people". This, the expedient devised by Cranmer for a non-preaching clergy, was to elicit from Bonner in 1555 one of the most remarkable books of the reign, a neglected masterpiece of Tudor catechesis, *A Profytable and necessary doctryne, with certayne homelies adioyned . . . for the instruction and enformation of the people.*[27]

The *Profytable doctryne* is a vividly written exposition of the fundamentals of the faith, structured round the Apostles' Creed, the Ten Commandments, the seven deadly sins, the seven sacraments, the Lord's Prayer, and the Hail Mary. It was therefore intended to supply the parish clergy with the material they needed to fulfil the catechetical programme which Bonner had enjoined on them. Remarkably, Bonner took the *King's Book* of 1543, round which the traditionalists had rallied in the last years of Henry's reign, as the framework on which he and his chaplains built the book. By preserving as much as he could of the *King's Book* he ensured a continuity of tone between the doctrine taught under Mary and that "observed and kept in the latter time of King Henry the Eighth", an important factor in the retention of public confidence. This was a crucial perception. Traditionalists in Edward's reign had rallied round the *King's Book*, and however defective it might appear to the eyes of Marian orthodoxy, it could not lightly be set aside. In fact, however, the *Profitable doctryne* is an incomparably better catechetical tool than the rather lack-lustre King's Book. Not only was much in the later book new – the entire section on the seven deadly sins, on

[26] Ibid., p. 402.
[27] TRP, II no. 407 (p. 38).

the Hail Mary, the treatment of the Second Commandment with its apparent prohibition of images, and the article of the Creed which dealt with "The Holy Catholic Church" – but even those sections which retained much of the substance of the *King's Book* were sharpened and turned to account on behalf of the new regime. One of the central concerns of the *Profytable doctryne* was to reaffirm the centrality of the Church in every aspect of the Christian life, and in dozens of additions, large and small, this message was hammered home. So, at the end of the section on the third article of the Creed, "which was conceived by the holy Ghost", Bonner introduces a striking quotation from Augustine, making the point that "Christe is borne of a virgin that we mighte be borne of the wombe of the Churche being a vyrgyn". The discussion on the Church in the ninth article of the Creed now included an extended quotation from Augustine on the unity of the Church, designed to strike an English reader by its applicability to the schism: "Take away, saith he . . . the beame of the sonne from the body of the sonne, the unitie of the lyght, can not suffer no division: break a boughe from the tree, the bough so broken, can floryshe and budde no more: cut of the river from the spring, the ryver so cut of, dryeth up."[28] In the exposition of the way in which the Commandments were to be kept, Bonner introduced a passage from II Maccabees 7 – "We are ready rather to die, then to breake or transgresse the lawes of God which oure fathers kepte" – and added: "But of late dayes, in the tyme of our pestiferous scisme, the new broached brethren, rather woulde tumble to hel headlonge, then they would doo as the catholyke Churche from Chrystes tyme hetherto hath done, concernynge the lawes of God, and the rytes of the sayde catholyke churche."[29]

Nor did Bonner hesitate to wrench the reformers' weapons from their hands and turn them on them. The invocation of the Lollard tradition as offering a witness against Catholic error even before the Reformation was a favourite controversial ploy by reformers. In the newly composed section on images, Bonner cited in support of his position a Lollard version of the Commandments, made "almost eight score yeare agone . . . even in time of heresye", thereby playing Lollards against Protestants. He included in his text an offer to show the original manuscript to "any well dysposyd persons who shall desyre it".[30] The *Profytable Doctryne*, however, is much more than an attempt to score debating points against the

---

[28] The *Profytable and necessary doctryne* is unpaginated.
[29] II Maccabees vii. 37 (Vulgate).
[30] See Margaret Aston, "Lollardy and the Reformation", in *Lollards and Reformers*, 1984, pp. 219–42.

reformers. It is a comprehensive and theologically skilful textbook, far more richly supported with quotations from scripture and the Fathers than the *King's Book*, yet not clogged with technical terms or an excess of learning. Generous quotation from and exegesis of key passages from the New Testament, such as the story of the Annunciation, must have been particularly valuable to parish priests of limited learning. Bonner's book successfully provided both an exposition of the essentials of Christian catechesis and an easily accessible collection of controversial and hortatory material designed to impress on the people the evils of the schism and the privileges of the restoration of Catholic communion.

Alongside the *Profytable doctryne* and designed to supplement it, was published a set of thirteen *Homilies*, largely the work of Bonner's chaplains, John Harpsfield and Henry Pendleton. Most of these were concerned with the great controversial topics raised by the schism and its aftermath – the nature and authority of the Church, the place of the papacy, the presence of Christ in the Sacrament of the altar. But several of the *Homilies* deal with more fundamental issues: the creation and fall, the nature of Christ's redeeming work, and two, on the comparatively uncontroversial topics of the misery of mankind and charity, were slightly revised versions of the *Homilies* of those titles from Cranmer's book. Their adoption into the Marian *Homilies* is remarkable, and another example of the regime's willingness to absorb and use whatever remained of value in the Edwardine reform. The homily "On the miserie of all mankynde", in particular, is striking for its uncompromising Christocentricity, couched in language which, to listeners accustomed to six years of Cranmer's prayer-book, must have been inescapably reminiscent of the theology and even the phrasing of the prayer of consecration:

> He is that hyghe and everlastynge priest, whyche hathe offred him selfe to God, when he instituted the sacrament of the Aultar, and once for all, in a bloody sacrifyce, doone upon the crosse, with which oblation, he hath made perfect for evermore, theim that are sanctifyed. He is the mediatoure, betweene God and man, which payed our raunsome to God, wyth hys owne bloude, and wyth that, hath cleansed us from synne.[31]

That emphasis on Christ and his Passion was a consistent characteristic of the Marian church. It goes a long way towards explaining the phrasing and theological ethos of many Marian wills, which, as we have already seen, have been taken to reflect Protestant leanings,

[31] *Homelies seitte forth by the right reverend Father in God . . .* , RSTC 3285.4, fol. 12.

but which find abundant justification in passages of this sort,
supplied to the Marian clergy for use in catechesis and preaching.

The Profytable doctryne, together with the accompanying Homilies,
is well able to stand comparison not only with the King's Book, but
with Cranmer's Homilies, which it equals in theological grip, and
excels in liveliness and range of illustrative material. Its value was
immediately recognized. Pole planned the production of a similar
work for the whole of the country, but pending its production he
ordered Bonner's book and the Homilies to be bought and preached
from by the parish clergy throughout his metropolitan jurisdiction.
The wardens of Morebath paid 2s 9d for their copy in 1556.[32]
Bonner's book embodied much that was most central to the Marian
regime, in particular its desire to maintain continuity with the
Henrician past, but to reform the Henrician legacy into an orthodox
Catholicism. Pole's legatine synod decided in December 1554 to
produce a formulary of faith for the English church: it is not
without significance that the basis for the new formulary was to be
the King's Book. The sections of the formulary were duly allocated,
and work began. As with the proposed New Testament translation,
nothing came of the scheme, but Bonner's book indicates the sort
of product which would have emerged. Nothing about it suggests
an imaginative or controversial exhaustion. Only the death of
the Queen, and the Elizabethan rehabilitation and enlargement of
Cranmer's collection, drove Bonner's work into an undeserved
oblivion.[33]

The Marian Primers

With the restoration of Catholicism, the reappearance of the traditional Sarum primer was a foregone conclusion. Henry's primer
had run through more than two dozen editions, and had been used
well into Edward's reign. Despite its very real reformed character,
it preserved enough of the characteristics and materials of the traditional primers to be acceptable to conservative lay people, trained
to pray on the old books, once the supply of these old books had
been dried up by royal fiat. Successive editions of Henry's book had
undergone some modification in Edward's reign, but the distinctive
Edwardine primer, issued only in 1553, had effectively jettisoned
every remaining link with the primers current before the break with
Rome. It contained neither the Hours of the Virgin, the "Dirige",
the Commendations, nor the Psalms or prayers of the Passion.

---

[32] Morebath CWA, p. 189.
[33] Dixon, History of the Church of England, IV p. 457.

Instead it consisted essentially of prayer-book matins and evensong, arranged with readings for the days of the week, and a large collection of "Sundry Godly Prayers for Divers Purposes", including prayers for special classes and occupations of men – masters and servants, landlords and tenants, single men, wives, householders, and servants. Heavily didactic and penitential in tone, it is light-years away from the traditional primers, and is an inescapably Protestant book.[34]

There was therefore a yawning gulf in the market which entrepreneurs rushed to fill on the accession of a Catholic Queen. Printers in both London and France quickly produced editions of the traditional Sarum primer in Latin in 1554.[35] Freelance primers of this sort, in both English and Latin, were to continue to appear throughout Mary's reign, most of them printed in Rouen, but some of the best of them by the London-based Catholic printer, Robert Caley, who had worked in exile at Rouen during Edward's reign. Mary's government had no objection to the appearance of such primers, all of which were perfectly orthodox, but the regime was as alert as its predecessors to the importance of the primers for the settlement of religion, and in June 1555 there appeared the first edition of an officially approved primer, in English and Latin, published by John Wayland. Unlike Caley, Wayland was no exile for religion. He had functioned in London throughout the Edwardine period, had been the publisher responsible for Hilsey's *Manual*, and his assigns would later be responsible for the first Elizabethan primer. Presumably he was chosen to print the official Marian primer because of his proven reliability and established connections with government.[36]

Henry's primer had been, effectively, an act of state, as much an official product of reform as the English litany or the revised calendar. The precise status of the first Marian Wayland primer is less straightforward. It was backed up not by a royal proclamation forbidding subjects to use any other, but by letters patent from Philip and Mary, giving Wayland or his assigns exclusive rights to print all primers "which by us our heirs, successors or by our clergy by our assent shall be authorised set forth and devised for to be used of all our loving subjects".[37] Nevertheless, the description on the title-page of the primer as 'An uniforme and Catholyke

---

[34] The 1553 primer is printed in *The Two Liturgies . . . set forth by authority in the Reign of King Edward VI*, ed. J. Ketley, Parker Society, 1844, pp. 357–484; see the discussion in H. C. White, *Tudor Books of Private Devotion*, 1951, pp. 119–21.

[35] Hoskins, nos 203–5; RSTC 16058 and 16059.

[36] H. S. Bennett, *English Books and Readers*, 1970, I pp. 39, 180, 200.

[37] Hoskins, p. 190.

Prymer . . . newly set forth by certayne of the cleargye with the assente of the moste reuerende father in god the Lorde Cardinall Pole hys grace: to be only used (al other sette aparte) of al the kyng and Quenes maiesties louinge subiectes" clearly represented strong official endorsement of the book. Wayland produced at least ten other editions of this primer. All reiterated the royal grant of a monopoly on the printing of primers, but none of the subsequent editions carried the claim to be the one "uniforme and Catholyke Prymer", or the reference to Pole's endorsement. It is clear that, provided the books concerned were clear of heresy, Mary's government did not seek to impose the stranglehold on devotional publishing that Henry's or Edward's Council had done. Nonetheless, there is no doubting the special status of the Wayland primers as an expression of the official religion favoured by the regime, and in fact they dominated the market, no other publisher producing so many editions of a single type.[38]

The Wayland Primers follow the pattern of the reformed or rather modified Sarum primers current in the early 1540s, traditional in content but with the main text in English, and the Latin version confined to smaller print in the margins. They are sparingly and conventionally illustrated with large initials containing scenes from the life of Christ and traditional subjects such as David and Bathsheba at the beginning of the penitential Psalms. The "Dirige" has the image of Death with sceptre and pickaxe. The main contents are entirely traditional – the Little Hours of the Virgin, with the customary suffrages to the saints including Thomas Becket, the penitential Psalms, the litany, the "Dirige", the Psalms of the Passion. Wayland put at the end of the book the "Form of Confession" printed in some traditional primers in the 1530s, and the reappearance of this element of the Tudor primer after almost twenty years' absence was a notable indicator of the Marian church's strong emphasis on the value of the sacrament of penance. The primer also includes traditional devotional material like the "Fifteen Oes", prayers to be used at the elevation, and St Bernard's verses.[39]

Despite the traditional contents, this section of the Wayland primer was strikingly different from the primers of the 1520s and early 1530s, for it lacks any indulgence rubrics and has none of the "goodly painted prefaces" containing miraculous legends or promises so scorned by the reformers. The nearest the primer gets

[38] RSTC nos 16060, 16063, 16064, 16065, 16066, 16077, 16079, 16080, 16082, 16084, 16084.5, 16085, 16086. The firm went on to produce the first Elizabethan primer.
[39] This summary is based on RSTC 16063; Hoskins no. 215.

to any of these is the single sentence "To our blessed Lady against the pestilence" before the hymn "Stella Coeli extirpavit", an invocation to the Virgin against the plague. Moreover, the Wayland primer is almost entirely lacking in the elaborate affective prayers on the Passion of Christ, and the many prayers to the Virgin, the saints, and the Blessed Sacrament which were so dominant a feature of the primers of the 1520s. Marian devotion is strongly present in the hymns and prayers of the Little Hours, of course, but it is not allowed to proliferate through the rest of the book. The elevation prayer provided is a translation of the "Ave Verum Corpus"; once again, the lush elaboration of the Eucharistic devotion of the earlier primers has been cut away. The book, while having all the warmth and tenderness innate in the Little Hours, prayers like the "Fifteen Oes", and scriptural catenas like St Bernard's verses, is much more austerely and theologically "correct" than the pre-Reformation books. This might be readily enough explained by the fact that Wayland's copy text was probably a primer produced for the English market at Rouen in 1536, in which this process of pruning had first been carried out. But the choice of the copy text is itself interesting. The Rouen primer of 1536 was the first straightforward translation of the Sarum primer, without the Protestant agenda evident in later reworkings. The Marian editor selected the most Catholic of the English primers available.[40] The sparer tone and less perfervid atmosphere of Wayland's primer therefore seems deliberate, and this is borne out by the fact that every other primer produced in Mary's reign, whether in English or Latin, shares the same silence about indulgences or miraculous legends. The wonder-world of charm, pardon, and promise in the older primers had gone for ever.

Yet more striking, however, are the non-traditional contents of Wayland's primers, the section of the book which displays most careful editorial treatment by the "cleargy" spoken of on the title-page. After the usual preliminaries of calendar and almanac, the primer has a series of prayers for each morning of the week, quite distinct from the liturgical prayers of the Little Hours. These morning prayers include Erasmus's famous "O Lorde Jesus Christ, which art the bright sonne of the worlde, ever rising, never falling", and at least one, the prayer for Friday morning, was adapted from a traditional Latin prayer, "Piisime deus et clementissime pater".[41] But most of them seem to have been composed specially for the

---

[40] The Rouen primer and its derivatives are discussed in White, *Tudor Books of Private Devotion*, pp. 67–86.
[41] Wayland *Primer*, sig. Bi ff.

book, and they illustrate the extent to which the clerical editors had absorbed the tone and style of mid-Tudor piety familiar from the prayers in Henry's primer. One of the most characteristic of these prayers is the long "general morning prayer" into which is woven the Creed in English and the Lord's Prayer, combining devotion and catechesis. It also displays the striking emphasis on redemption through the Passion of Christ which we have already noted in the *Homilies*:

> Onely this is my comfort oh heavenlie father, that thou dyddest not spare thy onely derely beloved sonne . . . Wherefore through the meryte of hys most bitter death and passion, and thorough his innocent bloud shedyng, I beseche thee oh heavenly father that thou wilt vouchsafe to be gracious and merciful unto me, to forgeve and pardon me all my synnes, to lighten my heart with thy holye spirite, to renue, confyrme, and strengthen me with a right and perfect faythe, and to enflame me in love towardes the and my neighboure, that I may hensforth with a willing and a glad hearte walke as it be commith me, in thy most Godly and blessed commandements, and so glorifie and prayse the ever-lastingly; and also that I may with a free conscience and a quiet heart in all maner of temptatcions, afflictions, or necessities, and even in the very panges of death, crie boldely and faythfully unto thee, and say: I beleve in God the father almighty maker of heaven and earth.[42]

One final feature of the Wayland primers calls for comment. Just before the "Form of confession" with which the book ends, the editors inserted "Fyftie devoute prayers contayning severally what so ever is mete to be prayed for, as by their tytles doth appere". In fact there were more than sixty of these prayers, and like the collection of morning prayers they are printed in English only. They include characteristically Catholic elements – prayers before and after reception of the Sacrament, and prayers for the custody of the five bodily wits. There are also a number of prayers traditionally found in pre-Reformation primers which had been edited out of the books of the 1530s and 1540s, like the prayer of St Bede. But the remarkable feature of these prayers is the fact that nearly two dozen of them come from the collection of "Godly Prayers" in Henry's primer, and some of them are by Protestant authors like Wolfgang Capito and Thomas Becon. Many of the prayers are scriptural paraphrases published by reformers like Taverner in the 1530s. The editor even retained the Protestant rewriting of one

---

[42] Ibid., "a general morning prayer".

of the most beloved Catholic prayers to the Virgin, the "Salve Regina", as a prayer to Christ, "Hail heavenly kynge, father of mercy". These inclusions are deliberate, for the editor has not simply copied *en bloc* from the King's primer to fill his space. About a third of the earlier collection was omitted, some of them very evidently for their reformed tone and content. It was not only Protestant prayers which suffered in this purge. Vives's prayer against the Devil survives, Erasmus's prayer for the Church does not, while a number of those included have been reworked to make them morè securely Catholic, emphasizing ascetic or sacramental elements, for example.[43]

Later editions of this primer add one further element, "a playne and godly treatise concerninge the Masse, and the blessed Sacrament of the aulter, for the instruccyon of the unlerned and symple people".[44] This brief anonymous treatise, which was also published separately, appeared at the end of at least three editions of Wayland's primer. Its title is somewhat misleading, since, although it is clearly written, it makes some demands on its readers, and was apparently aimed at intelligent middle-class lay people, the citizens of London and other towns who formed the buying public for many of these primers.[45] The reformers in the 1530s, like William Marshall and John Hilsey, had included extended sections of polemical material attacking Catholic doctrine in their primers, and to that extent the Wayland ones followed their example. But the Protestant polemic had been incorporated into the text of the primer, mixing devotion with argument. This would have run counter to the whole spirit of the Marian reconstruction, and so the polemical material, more sober and reasoned in tone than Marshall's diatribes, comes in the form of a separate treatise at the end of the book. Nevertheless, its presence there indicates the sensitivity of the Marian authorities to the need to defend and explain the Catholic doctrine of the Real Presence and the Sacrifice, so often attacked in the previous two reigns, to the literate laity.

The Wayland primers are a remarkable and intelligent blend of old and new. In them both traditional and reformed materials have been pressed into service to a Catholicism in which the ancient pieties, to Sacrament and to saint, have their place, but where they are subordinated to a strong emphasis on the centrality of the Passion of Christ. The emergence of a genre of sober and scriptural

---

[43] There is a helpful discussion to which I am indebted in White, *Tudor Books of Private Devotion*, pp. 121–31; collation of contents in Hoskins, pp. 186–90.

[44] It first appear in Hoskins, no. 211, RSTC 16063.

[45] STC nos 16063–5.

prayers adapted to the daily circumstances of life, already evident in
pre-Reformation writers like Whitford, but developed more fully
by Protestant devotional authors like Taverner and Becon, has been
accepted and assimilated. The new prayers in the Wayland primers
show that the clerical editors were capable of producing impressive
examples of their own. Once again, the application of the word
"reactionary" to this religion seems inappropriate, for the Wayland
primers testify to the resilience, adaptability, and realism of the
Marian attempt to restore Catholicism to the people. Professor
Dickens has doubted whether the Marian Church seemed likely to
evolve a distinctive and "broadly acceptable English Catholicism".
On the contrary, that is precisely what is on display in these
officially endorsed books.[46]

The Programme in the Parishes

The Marian authorities, in addition to the perennial task of teaching
the fundamentals of the faith, were alert to the need for a programme of doctrinal instruction designed to combat heresy, to
quicken zeal for the sacraments, and to encourage a loyalty to the
Church and its traditions and rites. They were also concerned to
promote a renewed and reformed Catholic devotion, which took
account of the positive elements in the reformed piety of the 1540s,
shorn of the excesses which had been a target of clerical purists even
before the Reformation. The various episcopal and metropolitan
injunctions concerning catechesis and preaching, Bonner's *Profytable
and necessary doctryne*, and the Wayland primers, all of them
ignored by most of those who have written about the Marian
Church, are the concrete expressions of those objectives. A dimension of the Marian religious programme which has received more
recognition, though usually adversely, is the reconstruction of the
material and ritual structures of Catholicism in the parishes. This
was where royal religious policy impinged most directly on the
people, and it is in the effects of this parochial reconstruction that
we can most clearly discern the responsiveness of the nation to the
restoration of traditional religion.

The programme of practical reconstruction was, once again,
mapped out by Bonner in the articles devised for the visitation of
his diocese begun in the autumn of 1554, and in the Injunctions
subsequently based on them.[47] Bonner's articles were adopted by
other bishops as the basis of their own visitations, and were closely

---

[46] Dickens, *English Reformation*, p. 315.
[47] VAI, II pp. 330–59 (Articles), 360–72 (Injunctions).

imitated in Pole's articles for his metropolitan visitation in 1556.[48]
Bonner's programme was minutely detailed and dauntingly comprehensive. The articles and injunctions are heavily indebted not
only to the legacy of medieval canons and visitation procedures, but
to the royal and episcopal Injunctions produced since the commencement of the schism. The formidable apparatus of religious
enforcement evolved within the reform was now to be turned
against it.

Much in the articles replicates material found in every episcopal
visitation of any period – queries about clerical residence, dress,
diligence, and morals, the last issue being of course heightened
and complicated by the need to separate married clergy from their
"concubines, or women taken for wives". There were questions
about the schoolmasters and midwives, about the practice of
sorcery and the payment of tithes. But the main thrust of the
articles was to tackle the legacy of the schism in all its dimensions.
The best-known aspect of this is of course the search for heresy.
Bonner wanted to know about the doctrine taught by the clergy,
about the circulation of seditious or heretical books, about Protestant conventicles, about priests who administered any rites in
English or held prayer-book services in secret. He wanted to know
the names of any of the laity who, at the sacring time "do hang
down their heads, hide themselves behind pillars, turn away their
faces, or depart out of the church". He asked about those who had
eaten flesh on the traditional fasts or vigils. He asked for the names
and addresses of any printers and booksellers who were circulating
the prayer-book or *Homilies*, or "slanderous books, ballads or
plays, contrary to Christian religion". He also wanted to know
of any lay people who expounded or declared scripture without
episcopal permission, and any who "murmured, grudged or spoke
against" the Mass, the sacraments, or sacramentals such as holy
bread, holy water, palms, ashes, or any "laudable and godly
ceremony", especially prayer for the dead, or who "made noise,
jangled, talked, or played the fool" in church in service time, or
mocked or threatened priests when preaching or celebrating sacraments or sacramentals in the traditional forms. He asked for the
names of any women who declined shrift and housel before a
confinement, or who did not come to be churched afterwards. And
he wanted to know of any lay people who tried to prevent the
priest baptizing their children in the traditional way by immersion
in the font, "being yet strong, and able to abide and suffer it",
seeking instead to have the child "in the clothes, and only to be
sprinkled with a few drops of water".

[48] Dixon, *History of the Church of England*, IV pp 243–4; VAI, II pp. 401–8.

In the detection of heresy, parochial conformity was crucial. Bonner wanted special vigilance to ensure that every parishioner confessed to their own curate in Lent and received the Blessed Sacrament at Easter. He wanted notification of any who refused to take part in parochial rituals like the procession on Sunday, the reception of holy bread or the kissing of the pax. Bonner even demanded to know whether any good singer, who had been a choir-man in Henry's or Edward's reign, now "since the setting forth and renewing of the old service in the Latin tongue, absent and withdraw himself from the choir". One imagines that this particular measure might have been counter-productive, and Henry Clerke, in trouble in the Lincoln diocese during Pole's metropolitan visitation in 1556 for singing the "Sursum Corda" in a pub, was probably one of these reluctant choristers.[49]

The articles and injunctions also addressed themselves to the physical aftermath of the schism. Texts or pictures painted on the walls and which "chiefly and principally do tend to the maintenance of carnall liberty" by attacking fasting, clerical celibacy, the value of good works, or the veneration of the Blessed Sacrament, were to be blotted out. The Edwardine spoliation had stripped the churches of the essential ornaments used for Catholic worship; these were now to be replaced. Every church was to have a high altar of stone, covered with a properly consecrated altar-slab, and not the hastily pulled up grave-slabs which many churchwardens had set there in the first flurry of restoration. The parishioners were to provide forthwith all the books, vestments, and vessels needed for the services. The list is worth setting out at length, for it gives some idea of the sheer scale of the task the parishes now faced.

Every parish had to have the following: a holy-water stoup and sprinkler set by the church door, a legend for the lessons at matins, an antiphoner, a gradual and a psalter for the musical parts of the service, an ordinal or "pie" to guide the priest in the right performance of the services, a missal, a manual containing the occasional Offices like burials and baptisms, a processional, a chalice and paten and a set of cruets, a high Mass set of vestments for priest, deacon, and subdeacon, and a cope "with all the appurtenances", altar frontals and hangings, three linen cloths, two for covering the altar and one for the priest's hands, three surplices and a rochet for the clerk, a processional Crucifix with candles, a cross to be carried before corpses, a censer and an incense boat, a bell to ring at the sacring, a pyx with "an honest and decent cover" to reserve the Sacrament, a great veil to hang across the chancel before the altar in Lent, banners and handbells to carry in Rogation

---

[49] Strype, *Memorials*, III part 2, p. 404.

week, a holy-water vessel to carry about, a great candlestick for the paschal candle, a font with a lockable cover, a chrismatory for the holy oils, and a large Rood and Rood-loft. There was also to be a lamp burning before the Blessed Sacrament.[50]

All these, of course, had been stripped out of the churches, many of them only a year before. The Edwardine commissioners had been instructed to leave in each church a cup, a bell, a covering for the table, and a surplice. Though many churches certainly held on to a good deal more, few, at any rate in Bonner's diocese, can have escaped without the confiscation of vital and expensive equipment; none in the south-east can still have had its images. Agitated deputations of wardens and parishioners lobbied Bonner to tell him that he was demanding the impossible, that all of this could not be provided quickly, but he remained adamant, and the surviving records of his visitation, and the glimpses of it we catch in Foxe, show him forcing the pace with all the vigour of his excitable temperament. He was assisted by one of the ablest figures in the Marian church, his vicar-general Nicholas Harpsfield, who as Archdeacon of Canterbury in succession to Cranmer's brother Edmund was to carry out the exhaustive Canterbury visitation of 1557. London was to be Harpsfield's apprenticeship.[51]

The London churchwardens who protested about Bonner's articles need not be suspected of doing so out of a Protestant desire to obstruct the reconstruction, though some certainly were sympathetic to the reform. Two things emerge with absolute clarity, not only from the evidence of the London visitation, but from churchwardens' accounts and visitation records from all over the country in the years from 1554 onwards. The first is the enormous financial and organizational strain the reconstruction put on parishes; the second is the energy and for the most part the promptness with which parishes set about complying. The work was to go on to the very end of the reign, and there were many parishes in which important items remained unprovided even in 1557 and 1558. But in most of these cases the slow pace of implementation seems to be due to financial or logistical difficulties, not Protestant resistance. The work of destruction could be carried out quickly and cheaply; rebuilding was another matter, not least because the financial returns of dispersal were entirely inadequate

---

[50] VAI, II pp. 365–6.
[51] There is a good discussion of the visitation in G. Alexander, "Bonner and the Marian Persecution" in C. Haigh, *The English Reformation Revised*, 1987, pp. 157–75; see also M. Jagger, "Bonner's Episcopal Visitation of London, 1554", *Bulletin of the Institute of Historical Research*, XLV, 1973, pp. 306–11, and J. Oxley, *The Reformation in Essex to the Death of Mary*, 1965, pp. 179–237.

for the costs of replacement. St John's church in Winchester had sold off a hundredweight and a half of liturgical books as parchment waste in 1550, and had received nine shillings for them. To provide a single set of cheaply printed paper copies of the essential books required for the restored liturgy would have cost several times as much, always assuming that copies could be got, in competition with other churches (Pl. 136).[52] A half-ton altar slab could be levered up and laid in the floor or smashed in hours, a gilded and carved Rood-loft with its images could be reduced to splinters or ashes in an afternoon. To replace such massive or elaborate structures, to commission, carve, set up, and decorate the images demanded resources of manpower, cash, and availability of craftsmen which parishes could not readily command. Yet command them they mostly did, and the implications of that costly compliance have not sufficiently been registered.

Ronald Hutton, after a recent survey of the 134 surviving sets of churchwardens' accounts for Mary's reign, concluded that there was "a considerable homogeneity in the process of Catholic restoration". By the end of 1554 all had rebuilt a high altar, obtained vestments and copes, some or all of the utensils of Catholic worship, and some or all of the books. During the rest of the reign this list was steadily added to, and most churches acquired a Rood with Mary and John, images of one or more saints, a side altar, Rood lights, banners, hangings, and a canopy for processions of the Blessed Sacrament (Pl. 137). Though most of these items were compulsory, "most of the parishes in the sample decorated their churches more than the legal minimum required."[53] The progress of reconstruction at Stanford in Berkshire is fairly representative of this process. In the financial year 1553–4 the wardens recorded the last stage of the Edwardine dissolution, twenty pence for their expenses in carrying their church goods to Edward's commissioners. In the same year the Marian reconstruction begins, with payments for setting up the high altar, for watching the Easter sepulchre, and "in expences goyng abroad to seke . . . the churche stuffe that was lackyng". In 1554 they sold off a "tabull wt a frame the whiche served in the churche for the comunion in the wycked tyme of sysme", and bought and had blessed two chalices, a pyx, and two corporases. Five loads of stone were bought for building the altars, and a painter was paid ten pence "for paynttting a lyttull

[52] Winchester St John's CWA, p. 166. The wardens at Tilney paid 43 shillings to replace their books in 1554 – Tilney CWA, p. 179.

[53] R. Hutton, "Local Impact", in C. Haigh (ed.), *The English Reformation Revised*, 1987, p. 129.

Rode". The wardens claimed six pence in expenses for a journey to Oxford "to seeke bokes", and a carpenter was paid 3s 4d for erecting a lockable shrine or tabernacle on the altar, to keep the Blessed Sacrament in, Pole's legatine synod having decreed that this was the method of reservation to be followed. The financial pressures on them are confirmed by the fact that the pyx they provided was of pewter, as was their chrismatory. In the same year they bought the prayers to be said for the Pope, a whipcord and silk cover for the pyx, and some cords to draw up the trendle of lights before the Rood and the cloth which was drawn up before the Rood during the Palm Sunday liturgy. In 1555 they bought one volume of the breviary, a parchment processional, and "an olde manuell in paper", both of these probably second-hand. They also traded in an old latten basin in part-exchange for a better one to be used for godparents to wash their hands at christenings. In 1556 the wardens travelled to Abingdon to commission a carved Rood, Mary, and John for the Rood-loft. The process of reconstruction was finished off in 1558 when they had a cross-shaped frame made to carry the candles during the singing of Tenebrae.[54]

Stanford was a traditionally minded community. The wardens seem to have dragged their feet about destroying their new Rood on Elizabeth's accession, and had to spend eight pence to certify their eventual compliance to the archdeacon. The parish was in trouble again in 1564 for carrying banners in Rogation week, and in 1566 for tolling the dead-bell all night on All Souls' eve. They had started the reconstruction of the old religion in Mary's reign at once, by re-erecting their altars and resuming observance of traditional ceremonies like the sepulchre, and had thankfully sold off the Edwardine communion table. Yet the process of rebuilding took them four years, and there are signs of forced economy in much that they did. The parishes of Marian England were feeling the pinch, but they were spending substantially to re-equip themselves for Catholic worship.

The Crown and the bishops were well aware of these financial problems. The most obvious way of easing them was to recover as much as possible of the confiscated goods, many of them still in the hands of the commissioners or their delegates. The commissioners for the Weald of Kent were being hounded in 1556 for the return of goods to the churches in their remit, and were anxiously trying to recover them from the Crown officials to whom in turn they had surrendered them.[55] Pole and the other bishops instituted searches

[54] Stanford CWA, pp. 117–20.
[55] *Archaeologia Cantiana*, XIV, 1882, pp. 321–2.

for withholders of church goods who had acquired them illicitly in Edward's reign. Though little plate appears to have been returned, many churches succeeded in securing some at least of their ornaments. Ashburton in Devon recovered its vestments and a cope, though they had to send wardens to London and Exeter to do so. The wardens of Prescot, Lancashire, recorded the outlay of thirty-one shillings in 1554 "in expences in the paroch besynes by the space of xxii days at Candlemas terme, for the obtaynynge of an indenture and oblygation that the churche and chappell goodes shuld be restored to that use wych they wher fyrst gyuen vnto". The fact that there were no large expenditures for replacements over the next two years, only a number of minor repairs, suggests that they succeeded.[56] At Leverton in Lincolnshire the wardens spent two shillings in 1555 "for our horsse and or selfes when we sewed for the vestments" at Lincoln.[57]

Individuals who had acquired church goods were similarly pursued, and they or their executors were often successfully forced to regurgitate their gains or a cash equivalent. The parishioners of Luton pursued the heirs of a former churchwarden, Edward Crawley, for £6 13s 4d worth of goods which he had sold but not accounted for in Edward's reign; the executors gave the church ornaments to the value of the contested sum. The widow of a local gentleman who had acquired two chalices, a coat of crimson velvet "called Jhus cope", an organ, assorted vestments, a bell, and a hundredweight of lead from the parish church of Houghton Conquest was forced or persuaded to carry out repairs and give vestments and ornaments to the value of £32 6s 8d.[58]

By no means all of this was enforced. Many individuals gave or sold back very cheaply the goods they had acquired. We have already seen this process at Morebath, but it occurred in parishes all over England. In some cases the returned goods were probably bought in the first place to preserve them, in others the buyers may have acquired them as a speculation, but either way, in 1554 and 1555 they came back. So at Ludlow Thomas Season was paid an earnest of twelve shillings against a sum of 26s 8d "due to hym for 4 copes bought of hym and restored to the churche".

Many who had acquired church goods in Edward's reign loaned them back to the churches. The parishioners of Cadney in Lincolnshire borrowed a vestment, a cope, an alb, a stole, a chrismatory, and much else from a local gentleman. The curate of

---

[56] Prescott CWA, p. 30.
[57] Leverton CWA, p. 360.
[58] *Bedfordshire Inventories*, pp. 17–28.

Firsby loaned his parish all the liturgical books they needed, which he had probably bought in 1550. Sir James Bancroft loaned a vestment, a Mass-book, and a pax to the parish of Gayton le Marsh. Stephen Bond loaned the parishioners of Greatford a pair of cruets and a pax.[59] Parishes with duplicate items might help out poorer communities. The parishioners of Saleby loaned a handbell to the parishioners of Beesby, though Saleby itself had borrowed a cope, a vestment, and a corporas cloth from assorted parishioners, and a Mass-book and a manual from the vicar.[60] As might be expected, clergy were the commonest source of such loans. Many parishes were spared the expense of re-equipping themselves with vestments or books because their priest was willing to use his own personal property, as often as not acquired during the Edwardine spoliation.

These loans, whether from clergy or parishioners, might in due course become gifts. In 1556 Gilbert Pykeryng of Titchmarsh St Mary left his parish church "the holle sute that I have of purpell velvet with all other things that they have of myn in the churche savyng the vestments with that belonges to the same". In the following year Agnes Andrews left to her parish of Charlton a chalice, a Mass-book, a cope, and "all the vestmentes that I bought of the parishioners of Charleton". And, tragically out of time, the parish priest of Ufford St Andrew in November 1558 left his parish "the table (reredos) that standethe uppon the hygh aulter, a peyr of greate candlesticks, a masse boke, a processioners, and a manuell".[61]

Parishes confronted with having to buy ornaments might do so by levying a cess on the householders, an expedient enforced by the authorities in Pole's diocese where other resources were not forthcoming. But gifts might also be solicited or volunteered. The wives of Morebath collected pennies, tuppences, and the occasional groat to buy Sir Christopher Trychay a new manual to baptize, marry, and bury with. The piety of Morebath or the eloquence of their vicar resulted in a series of such gifts. The young men and maidens raised 13s 10d "voluntaryly" for the ceiling over the high altar, and Trychay recorded individual gifts as well – six shillings from Thomas Borrage to buy the Mass-book, a box to put the Sacrament in from Richard Tywell, price 3s 4d, 6s 8d from Thomas Stephens of Clotworthy for the Crucifix and the painting over the Sacrament, a pair of altar-cloths from John Norman at Court, nine shillings

[59] Edward Peacock (ed.), *English Church Furniture, Ornaments and Decorations, at the Period of the Reformation. As exhibited in a List of the Goods destroyed in certain Lincolnshire Churches AD 1566*, 1866, pp. 83, 90.
[60] Ibid., pp. 43–4.
[61] *Northants Wills*, II pp. 297, 417, 420.

from Joan Morse and her son for the ceiling over St Sidwell's altar.[62]

In his visitation articles for London, Bonner had addressed this issue directly, and had instructed his archdeacons to see that clergy at deathbeds should put the sick person in remembrance "of the great spoil and robbery that of late hath been made of the goods, ornaments and things of the Church", and exhort them to remember not only the poor, but also "according to the old and laudable custom used in times past" to make some gift both to the mother church of the diocese and to the parish.[63] Giving of this sort to churches had of course totally collapsed in Edward's reign, and historians have been disposed to see the absence of any immediate resurgence in gifts to the church in Mary's reign as an indication that parishioners' hearts were not in the restoration. The fact that in 1554 Bonner was actively encouraging gifts seems to sharpen this point, for it is certainly true that in some regions there is little evidence of large-scale giving of this sort till the last years of the reign. In Sussex, for example, a regular pattern of bequests to the church does not seem to have re-established itself till 1557.[64]

This is certainly an issue which needs more regional study. There were counties where the laity does seem to have begun to endow parish churches through their wills more or less immediately. In Northamptonshire there are literally scores of such bequests in the wills of the Marian period, beginning in 1554 and becoming more common as the reign progressed: "unto the reparacon of my parishe churche ij sylke clothes to hange about the sacrament", 3s 4d to buy "a boke called a manuell", "to the settyng upp our ladye aulter 6d", "a table cloth to ly uppon the hye awlter", "my best wether shepe towardes the buying of ij handbelss for the . . . churche", "to the byenge of a cope for the more honourable settynge forth of God's service".[65] These bequests could be matched in many counties. Even in strife-torn Kent bequests to the parish churches for repairs, ornaments, and lights seem to have been beginning again in significant numbers from 1555. It does, however, seem clear that in few places, if any, did such bequests reach the levels achieved in the 1520s and 1530s, and nowhere did they displace the bequests to the poor which had become the dominant form of charitable giving under Edward.

[62] Morebath CWA, pp. 182–3, 200–1.
[63] VAI, II pp 341–2.
[64] G. Mayhew, "Progress of the Reformation in East Sussex", *Southern History*, V, 1983, pp. 53–5.
[65] *Northants Wills*, pp. 278, 296, 300, 301, 310, 317, 357, 410, 415, 428.

It is tempting to see this failure of the older pattern to re-establish itself at pre-Reformation levels as a sign of the erosion of Catholic feeling and the spread of Protestant ideas. All the same, the temptation should be resisted. There were a number of reasons why Catholics should not have reverted to the older pattern. In the first place, the problem of the poor was worrying and more present in the public consciousness of mid–Tudor men and women than in earlier periods. Unease at the growth in the number of the poor was universal, and the draconian legislation of the mid-century and the Elizabethan period is witness to the urgency of lay concern about the problem of poverty. Poor relief was therefore both a meritorious work of mercy and an urgent social necessity. The clergy themselves felt this. Interestingly, between the drafting of his visitation articles, and the subsequent issuing of the Injunctions for London, Bonner changed the directions he gave to clergy about will-making among the laity. Where the articles had highlighted the virtue of giving to the church, the Injunctions stress only the need to remember the poor. The clergy were to "induce them to make their testament . . . and to remember the poor, and especially to solicit for the maintenance of the hospitals of the city of London".[66] Pole himself may well have been responsible for this change. A product of the Catholic reform movement in Italy, he had been deeply impressed by the charitable works of the north Italian *scuoli* or lay confraternities, who supported hospitals, lazar houses, and other good works for the poor. He castigated Londoners bitterly for their indifference to the poor, contrasting the cities of Italy with London, where there were not "x places, neyther of hospytalls, nor monasteryes yn the cyte, nor abowte the cyte; and yet for you they maye dye for hunger". Though he wished to see the restoration of religious houses, the whole rhetorical weight of his treatment of the need to give was on the needs of the poor: "the doctryne of the chyrche ys the doctryne of mercye and almes of God. Whyche mercye is receyved more wyth comforte: but of them that use mercye, and gyve almes to other."[67] Accordingly, Pole's own metropolitan Injunctions required the clergy at deathbeds to exhort the dying "charitably to remember the poor, and other deeds of devotion".[68]

The Marian Church, then, despite the pressing needs of the parish churches, actually continued the Edwardine policy of encouraging testators principally to remember the poor in their wills, and did

[66] VAI, II p. 368.
[67] Strype, *Memorials*, III part 2, p. 484, and cf. pp. 505–7.
[68] VAI, II p. 403.

not press Bonner's original policy of seeking to meet the expenses of reconstruction from bequests. The re-establishment of the pattern of such bequests, therefore, where it occurred, was not the result of pressure from above.

In any case, parishioners stretched to the limits by the immediate demands of restoration in the parish churches, especially where these were being met by compulsory cesses or levies, may well have felt that they had done their bit while living. With the exception of small gifts to lights, the custom of leaving gifts for ornaments in pre-Reformation wills had rarely been designed to provide the routine expenses of the church: these had been met by church ales, by revenue from lands and cattle and buildings, by benevolences from gilds. Gifts in wills were in a sense a manifestation of devotional luxury, the gilt on the gingerbread – a better cope, a richer hanging, a new image. Even had Mary lived, it would have been years before that situation could have been recreated, and the devotional point of the older practice, the performance of a gratuitous, supererogatory, devotional gesture, could be felt again. The will of George Wryghte of Cobham in August 1555 stresses both that devotional drive and its limitations in the prevailing conditions in Marian England, when he directed that his executors should bestow five pounds of wax for a light "When so ever any lighte shall fortune to be erected and sett upp before the Image or picture of Christ or in any other place to thonor and wourschipp of Chryst in memorye of his fyve woundes by whiche he suffired for me and all other beleving in hym".[69]

Two years later James Boswell of Sherburn asked his executrix to give 3s 4d to his parish church "yf yt shall chance that ever saynt Antony light goo vpp and be founde agayne". At Mary's accession, the lights before the images had been out for fifteen years, and few testators were willing to mortgage money on the uncertainties of their reintroduction. As parishioners, they shouldered the financial burdens of restoration with energy, even with enthusiasm; as testators they often left these things alone. There was a sense in which the devotional machinery of popular Catholicism had to be in place and working, up and running, before the old pieties could reassert themselves. And in any case, the destruction and robbery of sacred things had sent a deep shock through the devotional system of Catholic England; it is hardly surprising that confidence was slow to return in many places. Allen Wood, a yeoman from Snodland in Kent, left money for an annual obit, with candles and

[69] L. L. Duncan, "Parish Churches of West Kent", *Transactions of the St Paul's Ecclesiological Society*, III, 1895, p. 247.

doles, but added that "if the same obit by order of law be abrogated hereafter" then the money was to be distributed to the poor. This sense of the provisional character of all such obit arrangements was slow to disappear. In April 1558 Thomas Morritt of Sherburn made his will, bequeathing his soul to Almighty God, "who shed his most pretious Bloyd and was Crucyfyed vpon the Crosse for the redemcion of me and all Synfull Creatours, to the blessed virgyn our lady Sanct Mary his mother and to all the Celestiall company of heaven". He left five shillings to the Blessed Sacrament for tithes forgotten, and for the use of the parish church a rich collection of copes and vestments "vpon this condicion. That yf it shall please the King and the Quenes maiestie and ther successors to call suche thinges into ther highenes possession as of late tyme haythe bene, then the said Copes, Vestements and Tunakles to remane to myne haires for ever". Brian Bradforde of Stanley made a will bequeathing a chalice to Wakefield parish church,

> and also all such coipes vestements and other ornamenttes as I have remaininge in the said churche . . . to the mainteyninge of goodes services ther, so long as the lawes of this realme of England will permite and suffer the same to be used and occupied. Provided alwaies that yf yt shall fortune at any tyme herafter any law, ordinance or statute to be maid here within this Realme of England to the contrarie by reason whereof the said chalice, copes, vestments and the other ornamentes maye not remayne to the vse afforesaid, that then and from thence forth I give and bequeth the same . . . vnto Robert Bradford my sone and his heires.

In the same way Arthur Dyneley of Swillington made a will in May 1558 providing for masses, "Diriges", and a series of doles at month's mind and anniversary, "Provyded alwayes that yf the laws of the realme do not permitte masse and dirige to be done, Then I wyll all the said money to be bestowed and gyuen vnto the poore". Richard Malthous of Roclyff, leaving a set of vestments to the chapel of Sallay in August 1558, added the proviso that "if the uses of vestments do cease in churches or chappells or if the said Chappell of Sallay be pulled downe" the vestments were to be restored to his wife and children. So soon before Mary's death such provisions have a prophetic note, but these men were expressing an unsettled feeling rooted in Edward's reign, not in any foresight about Elizabeth's. The spoliation, even by the spring of 1558, was "of late tyme". More time was needed before Catholic men could feel as confident as their fathers had done that gifts to God's glory in their parish church would actually be used to that end. The lack of such gifts in their old numbers reflects a failure of faith, not in the old ways, but in the constancy of councils and of kings.[70]

The Visitation of Kent, 1557

The visitation of 243 parishes in Kent carried out by Archdeacon Nicholas Harpsfield in August and September 1557 offers us a detailed progress report of the Marian restoration in the county most devastated by the iconoclasm and upheaval of Edward's reign. Kent almost certainly had a greater proportion of committed Protestants than any other part of England outside London, a fact reflected in the numbers burned there.[71] In another sense, too, Kent was a burned-over district, where iconoclasm had been under way since the early years of the schism, and where Cranmer's encouragement and patronage had ensconced a large number of radical clergy in key positions. In Kent, therefore, the Marian regime was to encounter its toughest parochial challenge, and the visitation of Kent shows us the difficulties of the restoration at their most intense. Moreover, the visitation returns allow us to see a moving picture. Harpsfield meticulously recorded every dilapidation, every missing ornament, every breach of Injunction. Having done so, he gave detailed directions about what was to be done to remedy the defect, and the time allowed. Officials were later despatched back to the parishes to check whether the required work had been carried out or the required item supplied, and they occasionally made yet further visits, adding further notes or recording that the parish had finally complied. The returns therefore give us an unrivalled picture of the restoration in progress.[72]

The demands being made on Kentish parishes in 1557 were significantly greater than those on Londoners in 1554. In addition to all the accoutrements required by Bonner, Harpsfield was enforcing the building of at least two altars of stone in every church, a high altar and a side altar, each with its full complement of cloths, frontals, and curtains, a silk set for holidays, a cheaper set for workdays. There were also to be separate copes and Mass vestments for workdays and for holy days. There was to be a Rood

---

[70] *Tudor Parish Documents of the Diocese of York*, ed. J. S. Purvis, 1948, p. 142; *Test. Leod.*, II pp. 121, 171–2, 256–8, 341–4: *Testamenta Cantiana: West Kent*, p. 71.

[71] P. Clark, *English Provincial Society*, 1977, pp. 98–106.

[72] The Injunctions from the visitation have not been found, but the return of the officials to parishes is attested by later annotations on the return where the archdeacon's instructions have not been carried out, usually indicated by the word "non" written above the relevant instruction; where the matter was subsequently set right, the "non" is deleted, indicating a further scrutiny by the officials.

light, which had to be of six or more tapers, depending on the size
of the parish, there were to be a carved patron saint and a carved
Rood with Mary and John, each of the figures at least five feet high.
There was to be a register book and a wardens' account book, kept
in a locked chest, and there was to be a full complement of grave-
digging equipment, mattock, spade, and shovel. The altars themselves were inspected to see that the slabs for the *mensa* were
properly consecrated: where gravestones had been used they were
to be replaced with proper altar-slabs, and the archdeacon and his
men scrutinized the floors of the church to see if any of the pre-
Reformation altar-stones had been set into the ground; those that
had were to be raised and reused or reverently stored. Where altar-
stones had disappeared, the wardens were to institute enquiries,
trace them, and certify their whereabouts to the archdeacon. High
altars which had been made too small for the proportions of the
chancel were to be reconstructed on a larger scale.

There is difficulty about interpreting some items in the returns.
Over forty churches were told to "paint" the Rood, Mary, and
John. This is apt to mislead on several counts. Harpsfield was
certainly not telling these parishes to put up a two-dimensional
painting of the Rood. In the early stages of the restoration many
parishes had stretched canvas over the tympanum above the Rood-
loft, or whitewashed over the King's arms and scriptures already
painted up there, and called in a local painter to fill the space with a
painted Calvary; this arrangement actually survives at Ludham in
Norfolk (Pl. 137). But the bishops insisted that these paintings be
replaced as soon as possible with carvings. Harpsfield rigidly
enforced this ruling, making exceptions in only two cases. At
Queenborough he noted that "they haue no roode Marye nor John
but of paynted clouthe for they say they neuer had other", and at
Boughton Monchelsea there is a note that "the Marie and John and
the patrone of the church be not carved but painted", which suggests that they had a carved Rood imposed against the tympanum,
the secondary figures being then painted in. Harpsfield or his
officials use three terms about the Rood and other images – provide, paint, and set up. In some cases these are clearly different
processes, as at River where the wardens were instructed to set up
the Rood, Mary, John, and the patron saint, "and paint the same".
So it is difficult to be sure whether or not parishes asked to paint
their Rood had an unpainted carving or were being told to get a
carving. Some of the parishes so instructed definitely did possess
the images themselves. At Harrietsham the wardens were instructed
to "painte the roode Marie and John with the patrone of the

churche before Easter"; an official has added in the margin "because they be grene".[73] The churchwardens' accounts of Bethersden, where the archdeacon instructed them to paint the Rood and the patron "decentlie", high-light the difficulties. The parish accounts record the purchase of the Rood, Mary, and John in 1557, along with a pax, a breviary, some candlesticks and a handbell. None of these items was recorded as missing at the visitation, so it seems likely that they were hurriedly purchased before the arrival of the visitors. There is a separate entry for the painting of the Rood after it had been fetched from the workshop at Ashford, and a number of expenses about the trip the wardens were forced to make to show the officials the new holy-water pot, surplice, and processional cross they had been instructed to provide. It looks, therefore, as if the Bethersden requirement to "paint" the Rood meant exactly that. If that is so, many or most of the churches told to "paint" images may already have had them, but were being asked to colour them.[74]

Some of the same difficulties apply to the orders to set up stone altars. Philip Hughes calculated that forty-seven of the parishes "had yet to find" high altars.[75] This is certainly not so: many of the churches told to provide high altars simply had unsatisfactory ones, where the structure was made of wood or was badly built, or where the slab was a gravestone, or too small for the principal altar of the church. Only thirteen churches can be clearly identified as being without a stone high altar, and some of these had reasons the archdeacon was prepared to accept, as at Marden, where there were indeed many heretics but where the chancel was ruinous. The parish was told to erect a permanent altar when the necessary repairs had been completed. There is no suggestion in any of the parishes that there is not at least a wooden altar on which Mass was being said.[76]

Despite these problems of interpretation, the Kent returns make it clear that in virtually every parish by 1557 there was a high altar of stone, with the necessary altar furniture. There was at least one set of vestments, and in over 200 churches more than one. Almost all churches had missals, manuals, processionals, and breviaries, the crucial books for the basic celebration of the liturgy, though a few lacked choir books like the grail and antiphonary. Most churches had a chrismatory for the holy oils, though some of these had clearly been through the wars in Edward's reign, and minor repairs

[73] *Harpsfield's Visitation*, p. 225.
[74] Ibid., pp. 122–3; Bethersden CWA, pp. 107–15.
[75] P. Hughes, *The Reformation in England*, 1950–4, II p. 237.
[76] *Harpsfield's Visitation*, pp. 190–4.

such as the replacement of the pin on which the lid hinged are commonly demanded. Most churches had an Easter sepulchre, though not all had a decent frame to support the lights that burned before it. The commonest defect recorded was the absence of a lock and key for the font cover. Many churches were making do with one processional cross instead of the two required, and some of those, battered survivors from the Edwardine spoliation, had lost the figure of Christ, or needed it fixing back. About half the churches lacked the full complement of towels, altar-cloths or frontals, though most had at least one of everything. There is no discernible pattern in the items missing, and little if anything that can be directly related to rejection of the rituals the objects were designed to serve. Thus forty-four churches lacked a pax, which in some cases might have reflected a dislike of the pax ritual; one of the signs of heresy Bonner required his officials to look for was abstention from the pax. But almost as many churches were short of grave-digging equipment, which can hardly be for ideological reasons, and fifty-nine churches had no register of births, deaths, and marriages.

Perhaps more significant than any of the particular items lacking is the evidence the returns offer of prompt efforts to comply with the archdeacon's requirements on the part of the parishes. Thus, over sixty churches were instructed either to supply, to paint, or to "amend" the statue of their patron saint. Some were using pre-Reformation statues which had been damaged, and at Bonnington the scandalized archdeacon made the parishioners provide silk or linen clothing to cover their patron saint Rumwald, because their statue represented him as a naked boy.[77] It took two visits by officials to clothe St Rumwald, but only a dozen churches of the sixty with defective statues ultimately failed to carry out the improvements required, which does not suggest any widespread aversion to the veneration of images. Similarly, of the forty-four churches lacking a pax, only fourteen failed to provide one in the time allotted: since it was common practice before the Reformation to use a Gospel book as a paxbred, even these fourteen may have had a functioning pax ritual at their Masses.

There were of course, ample signs of heresy, and Harpsfield had clearly earmarked certain parishes for special scrutiny. At Elmstead, Capel le Ferne, Harstone, Hythe, St James's Dover, Littlebourne, and Bekesbourne the wardens were instructed to present any who did not carry and use their beads on Sundays and holidays, or who would not go in procession. At St James's Dover, where the scriptures had not yet been blotted out of the Rood-loft,

⁷⁷ Ibid., p. 264.

the archdeacon noted that "there be not iiijor besides women in the parishe that were bedes."[78] At Chart, Sutton, Ulcomb, and several other parishes lists of singers who would not join the choir were compiled. Harpsfield paid particular attention to the need for preaching in such parishes, and the curates at Pluckley and Bekesbourne, both communities with dissidents in them, were rebuked for not providing sermons. At Sandhurst, Hawkhurst, Benenden, and Cranbrook the archdeacon ordered that the whole parish should be confessed before mid-Lent Sunday, then again in the later part of Lent, and a rota for every household was to be devised to see that all communicated. One member of every household was also to attend the processions on Wednesdays and Fridays. The curates had instructions to bury no one who had declined housel and shrift on their deathbeds, and to give Easter communion to no one who refused to creep to the cross. At Rolvenden, the archdeacon wanted the names of the men who had purchased the Bible and the paraphrases when the parish had sold them off. Heresy was therefore a real problem in some communities, and very much in the archdeacon's mind.

1557 was a year of burnings in Kent, in many of which Harpsfield was involved. But a study of the restoration of traditional religious practice is not the place for a survey of the pursuit of heresy, and I shall not attempt to consider the burnings here. This is neither to minimize their horror nor to suggest that they were without importance in the long-term reaction against the Marian reconstruction. There has indeed been a tendency in some recent writing about the Marian regime to play down their significance, on the grounds that the 300 or so deaths involved were insignificant in a society inured to frequent brutal executions for a whole range of crimes, and in comparison with the more draconian activities of the European Inquisitions. It is certainly true that early Tudor crowds turned out in large numbers to become spectators of the sport of burning Lollards or early Protestants, with little sign of sympathy or misgiving. One needs accordingly to be on guard against importing into the period twentieth-century revulsion at the very idea of torturing sincere and often outstandingly brave men and women to death for their religious convictions. Foxe's accounts of communal solidarity with the victims of the Marian burnings certainly cannot be taken at face value. The animosity of John Bland's parishioners towards their former vicar is eloquent testimony to the bitter legacy of schism. There were many communities with similar scores to be settled, and accusations of heresy might provide the materials of revenge.

[78] Ibid., p. 53.

Yet when all that is said, such attempts to soften the bleakest aspect of Mary's reign can be overdone. There had been burnings before, and in some regions, like the Chilterns or parts of East Anglia, burnings in substantial numbers. But England had never experienced the hounding down of so many religious deviants over so wide an area in so short a period of time. However eagerly the burnings were greeted or initiated in some communities, it is hard to believe that they were not often in the end self-defeating. They must often have aroused sympathy for their victims, though not necessarily support for those victims' opinions.

However that may be, this aspect of the Marian reconstruction made little impact on the Visitation. Diocesan visitation was not the normal method for pursuing heresy, for which there was a separate commission. Presentments in the visitation were almost as much concerned with cunning women and conjurers, butchers who opened their shops during service times, and, perhaps most of all, those who acquired church property in the Edwardine spoliation. Harpsfield was not pressing those presented for suspected heresy too hard; he was primarily concerned to secure conformity. Margaret Geoffrie of Ashford, who had refused to venerate the Sacrament, was required on the following Sunday to "sitte in the myddes of the chancell apon her knees havinge beades in her handes and devoutlie behaving her self and that at the tyme of the elevacion she shall devoutlie and reverentlie woorshipp the Blessed Sacrament and to make certificat thereof".[79] Harpsfield was more flexible on this matter than on some less important issues, and he was clearly exercising some pastoral or prudential discretion, for he did not always insist on the element of public humiliation involved in this sort of gesture of recantation. The wife of Henry Baker of Stockbury was presented because she had stayed away from the ceremonies in her parish church on Holy Cross Day. On examination she admitted to having abstained from communion as well, though she made a satisfactory declaration of her belief in the real and substantial presence in the Sacrament of the altar. She was sentenced to go in procession the following Sunday, perform all the ceremonies reverently, and stand by while the vicar publicly declared her faith, and her negligence in not coming to church. However, "because she did humbly submittte hereself and acknowledged her fault" the archdeacon remitted her sentence, to spare her the public shame, instead warning the churchwardens in due course to provide a certificate of her good behaviour.[80]

Parishes which had had strongly Protestant clergy might of course retain strong Protestant minorities, but the legacy of a Protestant

[79] Ibid., p. 118.
[80] Ibid., p. 244.

ministry might also be debts and resentment which served as a vaccine against the culprit's doctrines. John Austen had challenged John Bland in November 1554 with "Master Parson . . . You know that you took down the tabernacle or ceiling wherin the rood did hang, and such other things: we would know what recompense you will make us. For the queen's proceedings are, as you know, that such must up again."[81] Bland was ashes on the Kent wind by 1557, and the altar and the images stood again in his church, but his parishioners were still being pressed by the archdeacon to "cause the bonde over the rood lofte to be caste in color". At Lydden the parishioners told the archdeacon that their Edwardine vicar had "spoyld the church" and "dyd serve his hennes in the onle holliwater stock". Parishioners sent scurrying round the country-side to recover altar-stones or images disposed of by a Protestant vicar, or whose married priest had turned the parish candle-hearse into a cradle for his children, did not necessarily look back with longing to his ministry. And although heresy was clearly a serious problem in Kent, it is noteworthy that most of those detected in the visitation for suspicious beliefs or practices did in fact accept penance and conform. Fear certainly played its part in this, but so did the removal of the sources of Protestant teaching and the pressure of neighbours and custom. Many of those suspected were probably "waverers and doubters" like the three parishioners of St Botolph's, London, during Bonner's visitation, who declared that "before the Quenes reigne that nowe ys, they were mainteyners and favorers of suche doctryne, as then was putt forth, but not syns."[82] And however unpopular the burnings were, it would be unwise to assume that all who disapproved of them, or showed sympathy with the victims, were Protestants. Neighbourhood was neighbourhood, however frayed by religious difference and the conflicts of the mid-century upheavals. Catholic stomachs too could turn at the smell of scorched flesh, and sympathy for a victim does not necessarily lead one to embrace the doctrine which brought them to the pyre. It is clear that in some communities parochial officials, like the constable or "bosholder", were at best lukewarm in pursuit of suspect neighbours, but though the archdeacon's men were clearly well aware of this, there is no suggestion that they thought the parish officers themselves were suspect.[83]

There was certainly a whole range of pressing problems for the Church in Kent. The break with Rome had meant massive transfers of church property and patronage, most of it into lay hands; as a

[81] Foxe, *Acts and Monuments*, VII p. 289.
[82] Alexander, "Bonner" p. 169, note 51 above.
[83] For example, at Marden; see *Harpsfield's Visitation*, pp. 190–4.

result many chancels were desperately in need of repair, and there was a good deal of litigation about financial responsibility for the upkeep of buildings. The fact that the authorities in 1557 were still in hot pursuit of alienated church goods sold in the early 1540s says volumes about the difficulty of recovery. In most of this heresy was an irrelevance: what was at stake was property, as at Well, a hamlet in the parish of Ickham, where there was a chapel in which the parishioners had been accustomed to have a Mass in Rogationtide. But the farmer of the tithe, a local gentleman called Isaac, had let the chancel fall into ruin, had made hay-lofts in the chapel, a workshop for a weaver, and a kennel for dogs, "and there was such a savour of hogg skynnes that no man coulde abide in the Chappell for stinck thereof".[84] There were also severe problems of manpower. Sequestration of married clergy and the abolition of the chantries meant that many parishes lacked clergy, and in several cases Harpsfield had to make arrangements for parishioners to be allocated to attend services in neighbouring parishes, thereby creating problems for the wardens required to oversee regular participation.

Thus, although heresy did remain a formidable problem in some communities, the overall impression is one of successful if painful recovery, and of parishes doing what they could to meet the stringent requirements of the reconstruction. Bethersden, whose wardens had to troop back to Cranbrook to get a certificate for their new cross, surplice, and holy-water pail, was not a recalcitrant community. Their accounts show steady expenditure from 1554 onwards to acquire all the essentials of Catholic worship. By the late summer of 1557, when they were in trouble with the archdeacon, they had simply not managed to get everything done. Indeed, improvization is more evident than resistance in these returns, like the parish of Longley, where they were using a wooden bucket to keep their holy water in, or Egerton, where they were required to buy a new pax immediately, "bye cause they have none but a nakyd man with the xij sighnes aboute hym", or Charing, where they were using as a pax a small shield with a gentleman's arms on it, a miniature recapitulation of the dynamic of the English Reformation as a whole which the archdeacon was not prepared to tolerate. He demanded to know whose arms they were.[85]

Heresy apart, however, there were some signs in the visitation of real shifts in religious feeling. We should perhaps not attach as much weight as Philip Hughes did to the comparatively large

---

[84] Ibid., pp. 68–9; *Kent Reformation*, p. 107.
[85] *Harpsfield's Visitation*, pp. 171, 173.

number of parishes which had not yet got round to setting up the Sacrament. Of the thirty-six who had not done so before the visitation, all but seven complied in the time allowed, and the logistics of setting up the Sacrament may have had more to do with the delay than theology. But ninety-six parishes had no lamp burning before the Sacrament before the visitation, and the absence of these lights does perhaps suggest an erosion of traditional Eucharistic piety.

Perhaps more significantly, 116 churches, nearly half the parishes visited, had no side altar, and although all but thirty quickly supplied the omission, the initial fact is surely significant. Of course, the basic reason in most cases was certainly financial: most parishes were struggling adequately to provide and adorn the high altar. In a sense, too, side altars were redundant in most churches in 1557. There simply were no longer the clergy to staff them, nor the numbers of Masses being said to make them necessary. But their absence signals the narrower devotional range of Marian Catholicism, a narrowing evident also in the fact that few gilds were re-established in Marian England. Where the parish was preoccupied with raising funds to equip its church for the basic round of services, the devotional elaboration of the gilds was an unaffordable luxury. The layman anxious to show his devotion now would find all the scope he required in the needs of his parish, and the demands of that solidarity were likely to override all others. But the absence of gild and chantry priests, and the altars they had once served, reduced and to some extent refocused the liturgical variety of the parish, as they certainly reduced the layman's control over daily worship. The daily Mass now in most communities was the one parish Mass, and laymen would no longer have the scope to develop or indulge devotional preferences for one Mass over another, one saint over another.

The only image in the nave of most churches now was the Rood, just as the only altar in many churches was the high altar. In Marian parish churches the sharpening of focus on the Crucifix was to a large extent a matter of simple economics. But whatever the reason, the fact was that the only representation of the Virgin in most churches would now be the weeping figure standing under the Rood, where once there might have been multiple images of Mary – the Pietà, the Mother of Mercy, Our Lady in childbed, the Madonna and Child. And the ranks of holy helpers who had once filled every angle of the chancel and presided over the altars were reduced now in most cases to one, or at most a couple. That fact alone would inevitably have an effect in reshaping lay perception of the role of Mary and the saints.

This narrowing of focus was not entirely a factor of the destruction of the old images. There is a deliberation and a consistency evident in the devotional policy being imposed by the archdeacon in the visitation. Where he required the provision of hangings or reredoses for altars, Harpsfield normally specified the imagery which was to adorn them, and it was, invariably, a picture of the Passion of Christ. Similarly, where paxes were lacking the parish was to provide one with a Crucifix embossed on it. These are obvious enough requirements, though pre-Reformation paxes, like pre-Reformation reredoses, often had other designs, such as the Lamb of God. Their imposition is nevertheless noteworthy. They should probably be seen as another dimension of that recasting of Catholicism in response to the reform, with a more marked or at any rate more self-conscious emphasis on the cross and redemption, which we have already identified as a feature of the devotional and doctrinal ethos of the regime. This was an aspect of the Counter-Reformation's deliberate redirection of the exuberant but sometimes unfocused piety of the pre-Reformation laity towards a more evangelical emphasis on Christ and his redemptive suffering, a feature of other parts of sixteenth- and seventeenth-century Catholic Europe as well as of Marian England. The historian of local religion in Philip II's Spain has noted precisely the same tendency by the religious authorities there to steer popular piety towards a more scripturally "correct" devotional emphasis on Christ and his Passion, at the expense of some of the minor saints' cults of regional Spain. In this respect, as in others, Marian Catholicism was at one with the larger Counter-Reformation.

CHAPTER 17

ELIZABETH

The accession of Anne Boleyn's daughter in November 1558 launched the parishes of Tudor England on the third major religious transformation in a dozen years, though the extent and finality of the change was not at first evident to everyone. A proclamation of 27 December 1558 forbade contentious preaching, and for the time being "until consultation may be had by Parliament" required the continuing use of the Sarum rite, modified only by the reading of the Epistle and Gospel and the recitation of the Lord's Prayer and the Creed in English, and the optional use of Cranmer's English litany.[1] As we have already seen, many testators, even in the last years of Mary's reign, had displayed uncertainty about the likely permanence of the Catholic restoration; the succession of a new Queen could only deepen that uncertainty. Two days after Mary's death William Woodman of Eye in Suffolk made a will, leaving twenty ounces of silver to his parish church to be used in the making of a new processional cross "yf the laws of the realme will permit and suffer the same". A month later John Lake of Normanton near Leeds left 3s 4d "to the makinge of one case to the blissed Sacrament yf it may be suffred and yf not my executours to dispose yt to poore folkes". On the other hand, in conservative Battle a testator in December 1558 demonstrated blithe unawareness of impending change, when he left bequests to the restored monasteries of Syon, the Charterhouse, and Greenwich, "desiring every one of the said Howses to make me a brother of their Chapters". The same testator left a Latin and English primer and a pair of new rosary beads to friends, to be prayed for, though shortly the use of both beads and Catholic primers would be declared illegal.[2] But the religious climate of Sussex clearly encouraged optimism. Richard Russell of Lewes, making his will in 1559, asked for Mass and "Dirige" at his burial "according to the laudable custom of this realm".[3]

[1] TRP, II no. 451.

[2] *Proceedings of the Suffolk Institute of Archaeology*, II, 1859, p. 141; *Test. Leod*, II p. 285; *Sussex Wills*, I p. 97.

[3] G. Mayhew, "Progress of the Reformation in East Sussex", *Southern History*, V, 1983, p. 55. Bafflingly, Mayhew considers that this bequest represented "an implicit approbation of the impending protestant reform".

The Act of Uniformity, abolishing the Mass and reintroducing a slightly modified version of the second prayer-book of Edward VI, passed by the nerve-racking margin of three votes in April 1559, and came into use on 24 June. St Paul's Cathedral and a few London parish churches continued to celebrate the Catholic liturgy up till the last legal moment, but a wave of iconoclasm and sacrilegious mockery spread through the City. A Rogationtide procession in the precincts of St Paul's was thrown into disorder by a printer's apprentice who snatched and smashed the processional cross and made off with the figure of Christ, declaring that he was carrying away the Devil's guts. By contrast, at Canterbury the Corpus Christi procession attracted a crowd of 3,000 from the city and the surrounding countryside, including many of the county gentry, in a last public gesture of allegiance to the traditional faith.[4]

Even after the passing of the Act of Uniformity, the introduction of the prayer-book, and the commencement of the draconian royal visitation with its attendant iconoclasm, traditionalists did not abandon hope of the continuance of something of the old order. Sir William Paynter, parish priest of Bardwell in Suffolk, made his will in October 1559, bequeathing his soul into the hands of his Lord God "who hathe redemed yt wt hys moost precious bloode". He asked for burial in the chancel, "honestly as a mynister and a pryste owte to be: yf the lawes of the realme do serve and the procedynggs of the heyghe powers wyll suffer by the ordre of the lawe, to have the observatyons and ryghtes of the catholyke churche".[5] Something of the same desire was probably in the mind of John Hartburne in April 1560, when he made a will requiring his executors to dispose in unspecified ways "for ther profet and my soules health", and asking for burial "with laudabile ceremones as are permitted by the lawe".[6] In a will dated the same year but possibly written earlier, William Mylle, curate of Monkton in Thanet, left vestments and two breviaries "for divine service", and £5 towards the provision of altar-cloths and curtains and the repair of bells. The money was to remain in the hands of his executors for two years after his death, and "if there chance to be any manner of spoyle in the Church within the space of two years", was to be used as they thought best in deeds of charity for the health of his and his parents' souls.[7] Such hedging of bets was not confined to the dying. At the end of their accounts for the year 1559–60, during which they

[4] H. N. Birt, The Elizabethan Religious Settlement, 1907, pp. 504–5.
[5] Bury Wills, pp. 153–4.
[6] Wills and Inventories, pp. 186–7.
[7] Testamenta Cantiana: East, p. 227.

recorded expenses for the removal of the altars and the images on the Rood-screen, the churchwardens of St Petroc's, Exeter, noted that "whearas last year the parson of the parish [the elderly William Herne] gave 6/8 to the church he hath now declared his mind was that it should be distributed to the poor".[8]

The confusion evident in the minds of clergy and laity about the likely direction of the religious policy of the regime is understandable, even as late as 1560, given the ambivalence of the religious measures. The modifications in the Elizabethan prayer-book from that approved in 1552 did seem designed to soften its more starkly Protestant features.[9] The petition in the litany for deliverance from the tyranny of the Bishop of Rome "and all his detestable enormities" was dropped. The new book also omitted the so-called "Black Rubric", which had explained that in kneeling at the communion no adoration of the sacred species was intended or allowed. The words of administration in the 1552 prayer-book, "Take and eat this, in remembrance that Christ died for thee, and feed on him in thy heart by faith, with thanksgiving," clearly implied that Christ was received not in the bread in the mouth, but by faith in the heart. To this formula was now prefixed the form from the 1549 book, "The Body of our Lord Jesus Christ, which was given for thee, preserve thy body and soul unto everlasting life," which, spoken as the bread was delivered to the communicant, was much more patient of a traditional Catholic interpretation of the Real Presence. And whereas the 1552 book had abolished all vestments except the surplice, the Elizabethan book now restored the use of the cope by the priest when holy communion was celebrated, a gesture towards traditional ritual, even though the proper Mass vestment, the chasuble, was not permitted. In 1559 the regime issued an official primer; significantly it was far closer to the Henrician primer than to its more Protestant Edwardine counterpart. It included a "Dirige" service, with a series of prayers for the repose of the souls of the dead. These were definitely not Protestant prayers, and along with the whole of the "Dirige" they disappeared from the Latin primer authorized in 1560. As if by way of compensation, the calendar to the Latin primer restored most of the saints' days observed in Henry's reign, even including the "new feasts" of the Visitation, the Transfiguration, and the Holy Name of Jesus.[10]

---

[8] Exeter St Petroc CWA, p. 458.

[9] F. Proctor and W. H. Frere, *A New History of the Book of Common Prayer*, 1925, pp. 91–115.

[10] The Elizabethan primer is printed in *Private Prayers put forth by Authority during the Reign of Queen Elizabeth*, ed. W. K. Clay, Parker Society, 1851.

In July 1559 Elizabeth issued a set of Injunctions for the "suppression of superstition" and "to plant true religion". Together with an accompanying set of articles of inquiry they formed the basis for a royal visitation of the whole country, which began in London on 19 July, and was extended to the rest of the country in August.[11] Both the articles and the Injunctions were to a large extent modelled on those of Edward's reign, and required the recreation of the essential framework of Edwardine reform – an English liturgy, the provision of Bible and Paraphrases, the abolition of images including those in window and wall, the outlawing of all vestments except the surplice and, at communion, the cope, the suppression of the parish procession and substitution of the English litany, and the abolition of the cult of the saints and of the dead. In particular, clergy were to discourage dying parishioners from making any religious obit provisions other than bequests to the poor and to highways. As in the case of the prayer-book and primer, the Elizabethan visitation articles and Injunctions in some respects took more account of Catholic sensibilities than the Edwardine provisions had done. The Rogationtide procession was to be retained as a religious thanksgiving for the fruits of the earth and a means of preserving boundaries, and a form of prayer for the occasion was to be provided. Congregations were to bow at every mention of the name of Jesus. In removing images, those in windows were to be broken only if the window was to be reglazed. An addition to the Injunctions regulated the orderly removal of altars, forbidding the sort of iconoclastic activity which in fact took place in London, and declaring it to be in any case a matter of indifference whether the communion was administered at altar or table.

The Injunctions of 1559 have therefore been seen by some historians as markedly more conservative than their Edwardine models, and it has even been suggested that their draftsmen envisaged the preservation of non-abused imagery, such as Roods.[12] This would be in line with the conciliatory features we have noted in the prayer-book and primer, but the suggestion does not seem to be borne out by scrutiny of the articles which accompanied and glossed the Injunctions. The Edwardine articles, for example, had called for the destruction of "misused images"; the corresponding Elizabethan article requires the removal and destruction of "all images . . . all tables".[13] However that may be, the actual

[11] TRP II no. 460; VAI III pp. 1–29; C. J. Kitching, *Royal Visitation*, 1975, pp. xvi–xxx; W. Haugaard, *Elizabeth and the English Reformation*, 1968, pp. 135–44.
[12] Haugaard, *Elizabeth*, p. 141.
[13] VAI, II p. 105, III p. 2.

choice of commissioners to carry out the visitation ensured that the Injunctions, far from being a conservative document, would be used to press home a radical Reformation. The active commissioners were overwhelmingly dominated by returned Marian exiles, such as Becon, Horne, Jewel and Sandys, most of whom were subsequently raised to the episcopate, and all of whom were strongly committed to the attack on traditional religion. Despite the conciliatory signals in the prayer-book, primer, and Injunctions, the visitation of 1559 was to establish a pattern of rigorous suppression of the externals of Catholicism which was to preoccupy the episcopate for much of the next twenty years.

Some lessons had been learned from the Marian restoration. It would not now be enough to call for the surrender of Catholic liturgical books or the removal of images. There must be no opportunities for repetition of the scenes at Morebath or Long Melford and the hundreds of other parishes up and down the country where concealed or rescued images, vestments, and books had been restored at Mary's accession, like the reredos for the high altar brought out from the vicarage barn at Cratfield in 1553.[14] Commitment to the new order could only grow if all hope of a restoration of the old was extirpated, and that hope was recognized as inhering in the physical remains of Catholic cult, the "monuments of superstition". The commissioners were therefore to search out "any that keep in their houses undefaced" any such monuments and images "and do adore them, and specially such as have been set up in churches, chapels, or oratories". The progress of the visitation would be marked out by the smoke of bonfires of images and books in market-places and church greens throughout the land. And in what must have appeared an ominous preliminary to a re-run of the Edwardine confiscations, the Injunctions required the churchwardens of every parish to deliver inventories of "vestments, copes, and other ornaments, plate, books, and especially of grails, couchers, legends, processionals, hymnals, manuals, portuesses and suchlike".[15]

Documentation of the 1559 royal visitation is meagre; the Northern Act Book has survived, but is brief in the extreme. Nevertheless, it allows us to see the commissioners enforcing the Injunctions to the letter, and hunting out the images stored undefaced in the vestry at Doncaster, the pilgrimage image of the Virgin at Beynton, the Rood at Rewle, the statues still standing in the church at Rotheburn, and those mysteriously spirited away, no

[14] Cratfield CWA, p. 83.
[15] VAI, III p. 22.

one knew how, at Osmotherley. At Chester those who removed the images were evidently less adept, and the visitors were told that Mistress Dutton had the Rood, two pictures, and a Mass-book from the parish of St Peter, while at St Mary's one Peter Fletcher had "certin ymages whiche he kepithe secreatlye".[16]

Attempts to prevent the destruction of images and ornaments were certainly very widespread. At Morebath, for example, the missal and Mass vestments were entrusted once more to parishioners. We do not know what the commissioners did about the northern cases listed above, but elsewhere there is evidence of their thoroughness and determination. The wardens of Steeple Aston were summoned six times and had to submit three separate bills before the commissioners were satisfied.[17] In both London and Exeter individuals who hid or tried to protect images were forced to destroy them publicly, a pattern which was to be repeated in episcopal proceedings against traditionalists over the next decade. In April 1567 nine parishioners of Aysgarth in Yorkshire, probably successive churchwardens, were required to do public penance barefoot in white sheets at the main Sunday service, and to make a public declaration that they had "conceyled and kepte hyd certane Idoles and Images undefaced and lykewise certain old papisticall bookes in the Latyn tonge . . . to the high offence of Almighty God the breache of the most godly lawes and holsome ordinances of this realme the greate daunger of our owne sowles and the deceaving and snarring of the soules of the simple". They were then to burn the images in the presence of the parish at the church stile, and the performance of their penance was to be certificated to the commissioners.[18]

As that example almost ten years on makes clear, the Protestant authorities found themselves with an uphill task. Although the evidence of surviving churchwardens' accounts makes clear the essential conformity of most parishes, it was a reluctant and partial conformity. The removal of Roods and drawing down of altars which fill the pages of virtually every set of accounts from 1559 to 1561 were not in most cases the result of a landslide of Protestant fervour, but of weary obedience to unpopular measures. Once more the ingrained sense of obligation towards the Crown asserted itself, and the Tudor parishioner's respect for "the lawes of the realme . . . and the procedynggs of the heyghe powers". But like Sir William Paynter, vicar of Bradwell, whose words these are, the majority of parishioners were firmly attached to "the observatyons

[16] Kitching, *Royal Visitation*, pp. 67, 69, 73, 85.
[17] R. Hutton, "Local Impact", in C. Haigh (ed.), *The English Reformation Revised*, 1987, p. 134.
[18] *Tudor Parish Documents of . . . York*, ed. J. S. Purvis, 1948, pp. 145–6.

and ryghtes of the catholyke churche", and many hoped, and most thought possible, a return of the old ways. They had seen all this before – the books and images burned, the altars stripped and demolished, the vestments sold for cushions and bed-hangings. That destruction had had to be reversed, with great difficulty and at enormous cost, and it was the rank and file of the parish who had borne the brunt. Now the newly acquired Roods and patronal statues, the untarnished latten pyxes and paxes and holy-water stoups, the missals and manuals still smelling of printer's ink, which Marian archdeacons had demanded from them, were to be once more pitched into wheelbarrows and trundled to the fire. And all this at the behest of a Queen still unmarried and young enough for childbearing, whose prospects of a Protestant husband, and hence a stable continuation of religious policy, were minimal. Dislike of change, Catholic instincts, hope for a speedy restoration of the old ways, and Tudor thrift, combined to struggle against the instinctive obedience of well-schooled subjects, in a conflict not strong enough for resistance, but which ensured widespread inertia and concealment.

The articles and Injunctions produced for the episcopal visitations of 1560 and 1561 reveal the key areas of official concern about such resistance. Had any parishioner made a will leaving money, plate, or ornaments "for the erection of any obits, dirges, trentals or any such like use"? Did the clergy celebrate communions for the dead "as they were wont to keep their Requiem Mass, or no?" Did any clerks sing psalms "dirge-like at the burial of the dead", or ring long peals at the burial of the dead or at none on feast days for the dead? Were communions being celebrated where there were fewer than three or four communicants? Were all images, altars, holy-water stoups removed, defaced and destroyed, especially representations of the Assumption of the Virgin, of the descent of Christ into the Virgin as a little boy at the Annunciation, "and all other superstitious and dangerous monuments", and any pictures of the Trinity in walls, books, copes, banners, or elsewhere? Were any images or service-books not allowed by law reserved by any man or in any place, and if so, by whom, and where? Were Mass wafers being made, were Mass vestments preserved? Did anyone have in their house abused images from the churches, or devotional objects such as St John's heads or images of St Katherine, St Nicholas, or other saints? Did anyone use rosary beads, or pray with Latin primers or any unauthorized prayer-books?[19]

[19] From Parker's articles for Canterbury, from the anonymous "Interrogatories" of 1560, and from Parkhurst's Norwich Visitation Articles and Interrogatories of 1561 – VAI, III pp. 81–93, 97–107.

These preoccupations recur again and again in episcopal visitations and ecclesiastical court proceedings into the 1570s and beyond.
In the diocese of Lichfield and Coventry in 1565 the bishop, under
pressure from the Court, was driving his clergy to "call upon
the people daily that they cast away their beads with all their
superstitions that they do use", and the clergy to "cast away your
Mass-books, your portesses and all other books of Latin service",
and in any case to extinguish the lights which burned round the
dead at every funeral. He demanded that wardens and sidesmen
fine those using beads a shilling for every offence, and was also
attempting to prevent the laity reciting the "De Profundis" Psalm
for dead neighbours or laying corpses down by wayside Crosses as
they brought them for burial. He was also demanding the surrender
of holy-water stocks, sepulchres, and other ritual paraphernalia
"which be laid up in secret places in your church".[20]

Conditions in Lichfield and Coventry were no doubt worse
(from the reformers' point of view) than in many other places, but
the widespread survival of traditional practices and the equipment
of Catholic worship was by no means confined to the dark corners
of the land. The records of presentments in the Archbishop of
York's Court of Audience, arising out of the visitation of 1567,
throw a brilliantly clear light on this aspect of the state of the
diocese, and demonstrate that it was not only in Staffordshire and
Derbyshire that images and holy-water pots, Rood-lofts, beads,
and Latin primers survived to trouble the Protestant establishment.[21]
John Aylmer, Archdeacon of Lincoln, conducted a routine visitation of the diocese of Lincoln in 1565 which so horrified him that he
lobbied Cecil, Throckmorton, and the Earl of Leicester for the
establishment of a special commission for the county of Lincoln
"for reforming this church and diocese . . . for undoubtedly this
country hath as much need of it as any place in England".[22] The
commission, presided over by the bishop, Nicholas Bullingham,
was duly established, and detailed returns for 180 parishes visited
in March and April 1565/6 survive. The commissioners were
concerned to establish the fate of every image, book, vessel, and
ornament used in Mary's reign for Catholic worship. Each item,
from the Rood and altar-stones down to the cruets and towels had
to be accounted for. If they had been destroyed the commissioners
demanded the date of the destruction, the names of the wardens
who presided, and, if the wardens had since died, the independent

[20] Ibid., III pp. 163–70.
[21] *Tudor Parish Documents*, pp. 15–34.
[22] H. Gee, *The Elizabethan Prayer-book and its Ornaments*, 1902, p. 147.

testimony of eyewitnesses that it had indeed been carried out. Where vestments, vessels, or books had been sold, they demanded the names of the purchasers, and evidence that any imagery on them had been defaced before or immediately after sale. Where this was not forthcoming, the wardens were required to trace and recover the item, and "see it defaced". Large items like sepulchres, loft-timbers, and altar-stones were to be certified as having been broken up or put to irreversibly profane use, such as being turned into benches and bridges or built into walls and chimneys. Where clergy or parishioners had removed books or vestments and had subsequently died, their executors were to be traced and the items accounted for and certified as having been defaced.

The resulting returns therefore provide an extraordinarily detailed picture of the progress of reform in a single county between the visitation of 1559 and that of 1566. Though a dozen or so of the returns are incomplete or too vague to be of much use, the majority give chapter and verse, name and date for every stage of the stripping away of the imagery and equipment of Catholic worship. The picture that emerges from them is unmistakably that of a slow and reluctant conformity imposed from above, with little or no evidence of popular enthusiasm for or commitment to the process of reform.[23]

The general outline of the picture presented by the returns can be crudely established by a simple count. If we take the destruction by the end of the second year of the reign of such major cult items as the altars, the Rood and other images, and the Mass-books, as an indicator of prompt compliance, just forty-five of the 180 parishes qualify as having complied promptly with the main requirements of the Elizabethan settlement. This is, in fact, to stretch the notion of promptness somewhat, since the royal visitation was completed within the first year of the reign, and obedience over the next year hardly constitutes a scramble towards reform. Eighty-two parishes delayed the destruction or sale of important items like the images, books, and vestments for three years or more, many of them only complying after Aylmer's archidiaconal visitation of 1565, and some only within days or even hours of appearing before the commissioners in 1566. Thirty-one parishes spread out the destruction or sale of major items in such a way as to be difficult to

---

[23] The bulk of the returns were edited by Edward Peacock in 1866 as *English Church Furniture, Ornaments and Decorations, at the Period of the Reformation. As exhibited in a List of the Goods destroyed in certain Lincolnshire Churches AD 1566.* Peacock subsequently discovered and edited returns for a further twenty-seven parishes, published posthumously in *Lincolnshire Notes and Queries* XIV, 1917, pp. 78–88, 109–116, 144–51, 166–73 (hereafter = *Monuments of Superstition*).

classify as complying either promptly or slowly, and the remainder
of the returns are too incomplete or too generalized to enable any
classification to be made. Only just over a quarter of the parishes
presenting usable returns, therefore, can be said to have complied
promptly and reasonably comprehensively with the requirements of
the royal Injunctions of 1559. Given the laxity of our definition of
"promptness", even this proportion is certainly an overestimate.
Many parishes, for example, had borrowed all or most of their
books or vestments from clergy, parishioners, or local gentry in
Mary's reign, and hence could comply with the demand to rid
themselves of such things by simply returning them to their owners
in 1559. The fact that in only a handful of cases did they first deface
them, or seek to ensure defacement, suggests no great iconoclastic
enthusiasm.[24]

And even among those complying promptly by destroying
images, books, and ornaments, obedience to "the lawes of the
realme . . . and the procedyngs of the heyghe powers" was often
the operative factor, rather than communal zeal for Protestantism.
The visitation of 1559 is everywhere referred to in the returns
as "the tyme of the defacinge of all papistrie", and it is clear that
much of the destruction was carried out under the eyes of the commissioners or the archdeacons at subsequent episcopal visitations
between 1560 and 1565. Thus the parish of Tallington "burned
spoyled and defaced" its books and images "at the quenes majesties
visitacion".[25] Like many other parishes, Fillingham tried to save
what it could by handing banner cloths, streamers, and copes into
the safe keeping of parishioners, and their liturgical books "weare
taken awaie by whome wee know not", but their Rood and other
images "were broken in peces to be burned afore Mr Archdeacon
Dr Kelke". Since Kelke did not become Archdeacon of Stow till
1563, it is clear that Fillingham harboured no zealots for reform.[26]
At Wilsford the Rood and other images were burned in 1560 "by
the commandment of Mr Bartew", and the liturgical books in
the following year "in the presence of the parishioners and the
parritors", a clear indication of pressure from the bishop.[27] At
Welby they duly destroyed their images during the visitation of
1559, and sent a manual, a processioner, a legendary "and such
like popish peltrie" to Grantham to be burned "according to the
commandment of the Quenes highnes visitors". But for a small

[24] *Monuments of Superstition*, pp. 90–1, 110, 113–14, 157–8.
[25] Ibid., p. 150.
[26] Ibid., pp. 82–3.
[27] Ibid., pp. 163–4.

parish with only one priest these were mostly dispensable liturgical books, and the crucial item, the missal, they kept back, only destroying it after Aylmer's visitation in 1565, along with their pyx, vestments, chrismatory, and handbells. Their original surrender of books, therefore, has all the appearance of a ploy, a strategic retreat to preserve the main position.[28] Similarly the parish of Stallingborough complied with the demands of the commissioners in 1559 by destroying some of their liturgical books, but they retained others which, as they reported on 1 May 1566, they defaced only "on sundaie last". Langtoft adopted the same device, not only with its books, but with its ornaments and vestments, retaining much until 1565 and Aylmer's visitation. At Heydour they recorded that they had duly defaced the Rood and other images in 1559 "but thei were burnt but yesterdaie"; they also still had all their vestments, books, and ornaments.[29]

At Ashby near Horncastle the parish clearly dragged its feet over the "defacing of all papistrie" till at least 1561, when Bullingham became bishop. He visited the parish and was outraged to find it still equipped for Catholic worship, and the wardens recorded, with evident feeling, that "the bowkes that we had my lorde the bysshop was within the chirch and cawsyd his men to Ryve them in peces and did breke the baner staffes and dyd gywe away ower candilstykes of wode."[30] A similar sense of parochial resentment is evident in the return for Market Rasen. This parish had burned its images in 1563, but like most others in the area held on to much of its vestments and equipment until 1565. In that and the year following they sold them off, presumably under pressure from the archdeacon, though without first defacing them, an omission which was to cause some difficulty in 1566. But some items had gone in 1559, as they reported with some bitterness, when "one South the Quenes Majesties Pursevant" took away the liturgical books "who (as he said) had aucthoritie to take the same and what he did with it wee knowe not". Their bitterness was due to the fact that he also took a tin pyx, bound with silver bars, promising "to break it and to redeliver the barres of silver . . . who hath not accordingly restorid the said silver barres and whether the pix be defacid wee are not certaine".[31]

Pressure was not exclusively applied by royal or diocesan officials. Of the eight or nine villages in the Lincoln area whose returns have

[28] Ibid., p. 158.
[29] Ibid., pp. 95–6, 111–12.
[30] Ibid., continuation in *Lincolnshire Notes and Queries*, XIV, 1917, p. 86.
[31] Ibid., pp. 124–5.

survived, all but one held out against reform. At Thurlby the parish kept its images till 1564, and its books and ornaments till the beginning of Lent 1566. At Bassingham the images were retained till Shrove Tuesday 1565/6, and the vestments, books, and pax were distributed for safe keeping to parishioners, till the commission of 1566 forced them to disgorge them. The single exception to this determined conservativism in the area was the village of Auburn, less than a mile from Thurlby and Bassingham, where images, books, and vestments were all duly defaced in 1559. The key to this prompt compliance was not, however, the Protestant convictions of the parish, but the presence there of a returned Marian exile, the younger brother of the lord of the manor, Anthony Meeres; the wardens meticulously recorded after each item "broken and defaced . . . by Mr Mearse".[32]

The questionnaire which formed the basis for the visitation was clearly couched in strongly anti-Catholic terms. It has not survived, but the repetition in many returns of phrases from it indicate its general tone – vestments and vessels characterized as "trifling tromperie for the sinful service of the popish priest, . . . feigned fables and peltering popish books". Many of the returns employ these phrases, but they cannot be taken as any indication of the convictions of the wardens completing the returns, since they were used by parishes who had retained their Catholic ornaments till forced to dispose of them, such as Claxby Pluckacre, where they held on to everything till 1565, or Kelby in Heydour, where the wardens, having revealed that they had sold off their ornaments and burned their books and images "yesterdaie", naïvely assured the Commissioners that "there nowe remaineth no trashe nor tromperie of popish peltrie in our said church of Keilbie."[33]

Only one return, that for Grantham, suggests positive commitment to reformed ideas, and even this may be misleading. This return, prefaced by a flowery introduction to the "Right worshupfull John Aylmer archdeacon of lincoln and professor of the Devyne word of God", records the destruction of the Rood-screen and the sale of its materials in 1559. This was clearly carried out under the eye of the commissioners, for the churchwarden had duly submitted his accounts for the proceeds to "master Bentham master flleetwod and master everyngton then beyng visiters". The return goes on to report the burning of the "papisticall bookes and

[32] Ibid., pp. 34–5, and C. Garrett, *The Marian Exiles*, 2nd ed. 1968, p. 228.
[33] *Monuments of Superstition*, pp. 109–10, and *Lincolnshire Notes and Queries*, XIV, 1917, pp. 111–12; see also Billingborough and Market Deeping, *Monuments of Superstition*, pp. 49, 67–9, and Snelland, *Lincolnshire Notes and Queries*, XIV, 1917, p. 169.

serymonyes" at the Market Cross in the same year, and the sale
of the church plate to provide a silver-gilt pot and ewer "for
the mynistracion of the holye and most sacred supper of oure
lorde Jhesus Crist called the holye comunyon". All this, not least
the terms in which it was reported, suggests some enthusiasm
for the Protestant cause. Yet when asked to report on the state
of religion in his diocese in 1564 Bullingham had been gloomy
about Grantham, where he listed three-quarters of the corporation as either indifferent to or actual hinderers of true religion.
This is borne out by the fact that the town had revived the cult
of St Wulfran, the parish patron, during Mary's reign, and the
Elizabethan wardens had duly sold off a silver and copper shrine for
his relics. The Protestant rhetoric of the return is unlikely therefore
to reflect the attitudes of the parish at large, and it is probably
significant that the warden in charge of the destruction and sales of
1559 was John Taylor, named by Bullingham in 1564 as one of only
three members of the corporation he believed to be "earnest in
religion".[34]

Perhaps an equally detailed survey of conformity to the
Elizabethan settlement in Kent or Essex or Suffolk would yield a
different picture, with less obstruction and more commitment to
the reform in evidence. But the gloomy letters of the bishops to the
Privy Council in 1564, reporting on the lack of enthusiasm for
Protestantism among the majority of office-holders in their regions
make it clear that the situation in Lincolnshire was far from unique,
and some areas were certainly much worse. A report on the diocese
of Chichester compiled in 1568 recorded that many Rood-lofts still
stood, and in many parishes where they had been removed the
wood "lieth still . . . ready to be set up again". In many places the
images were hidden "and other popish ornaments ready to set up
the mass again within twenty-four hours warning". Crosses still
stood on many graves, and when they were removed the people
chalked crosses on the church walls near them. Lay people brought
Latin primers to Protestant services, and women and old people
plied their beads during prayer-book services.[35]

Episcopal visitations frequently singled out funeral ritual as
one of the most recalcitrant areas of continuing Catholic practice,
particularly the use of candles and Crosses about corpses, and the
ringing of peals both before funerals and on All Souls' eve, to
elicit prayers for the dead. The bishops were not the only ones

[34] *Monuments of Superstition*, pp. 87–9; M. Bateson, *A Collection of Original Letters from the Bishops to the Privy Council 1564*, Camden Miscellany, IX (ns LIII) 1895, p. 28.
[35] H. N. Birt, *Elizabethan Religious Settlement*, 1907, pp. 427–30.

concerned at such survivals. The Admonition to Parliament of 1572 complained of the superstitions used

> bothe in Countrye and Citie, for the place of buriall, whiche way they muste lie, how they must be fetched to churche, the minister meeting them at churche stile with surplesse, wyth a companye of greedie clarkes, that a crosse white or blacke, must be set upon the deade corpes, that breade must be given to the poore, and offerynges in buryall time used, and cakes sent abrode to frendes . . . Small commaundement will serve for the accomplishing of such things. But great charge will hardly bring the least good thing to passe, and therefore all is let alone, and the people as blind and ignorant as ever they were. God be mercyfull unto us.[36]

In 1590 the situation in the north-west had hardly improved, ministers complaining that throughout the county of Lancaster and in much of Cheshire whenever there was a death "the neighbours use to visit the Corse, and there everie one to say a Pater Noster, (or De profundis) for the Sole: the Belles (all the while) beinge ronge many a solemne Peale. After which, they are made partakers of the ded manse dowle or Banquet of Charitie."[37]

Funeral practice was, inevitably, one of the areas where feeling remained most conservative. It was by no means the only one. Rogationtide rituals were another, the bishops striving to reduce them to the maintenance of neighbourhood and the policing of boundaries, parishes struggling to retain the traditional supplicatory processions, with banner and surplice. Zealous Protestants might dismiss this "charming the fields", but it proved almost impossible to eliminate. Nearly a century on from the settlement Richard Baxter complained that the

> profane, ungodly, presumptuous multitude are as zealous for crosses and surplices, processions and perambulations, reading of a Gospel at a cross way, the observation of holidays and fasting days, the repeating of the Litany or the like forms in the Common Prayer, the bowing at the name of the word Jesus . . . with a multitude of things which are only the traditions of their fathers.[38]

Those traditions were legion – crossing with the ring in marriage, and moving it from finger to finger as in the pre-Reformation

---

[36] W. H. Frere and C. H. Douglas, *Puritan Manifestoes*, 1954, p. 28.

[37] "A Description of the State, Civil and Ecclesiastical, of the County of Lancaster about the year 1590", ed. F. R. Raines, *Chetham Miscellany*, V, 1875, p. 5.

[38] Vernon Staley, *Hierurgia Anglicana*, III, 1904, p. 8.

service, "Crossinge and knockinges of their breste, and som times
with beads closly handeled" and a whole range of traditional actions
in the communion service: standing while the Gospel was read,
kneeling at the name of Jesus, refusing to receive the bread in their
hands but insisting that the priest place it in their mouths, crossing themselves before receiving, or crossing themselves with the
consecrated bread. John White, Jacobean vicar of Leyland, where
he thought "the whole body of the common people popishly
addicted", found his parishioners using this prayer:

> I blesse me with God and the rood
> With his sweet flesh and precious blood;
> With his crosse and his Creed,
> With his length and his breed,
> From my toe to my crowne,
> And all my body up and downe,
> From my backe to my brest,
> My five wits be my rest:
> God let never all come at ill
> But through Jesus owne will,
> Sweet Iesus Lord, Amen.[39]

Such practices, of course, survived in some regions longer than
others. Bishops and archdeacons in the archdiocese of York and the
dioceses of Chester and Hereford in the 1580s were still enquiring
after the users of beads and primers, and the survival of altars,
images, and the medieval or Marian vestments and books. In
London, Exeter, and Norwich, by contrast, the ritual offences
being enquired after were more likely to be the abandonment of the
fonts by ministers who would not baptize in popish pig-troughs or
who would not wear the surplice.[40]

Given the integration of popular drama into the devotional and
catechetical objectives of the late medieval Church, it was inevitable
that the Elizabethan reform would attack the Corpus Christi cycles
and other religious plays too. This was a formidable and chancy
task, given the amount of civic pride and community effort which
went into the production of these cycles, and there is some evidence
that at first the Protestant authorities walked warily, particularly in
the north and north-west. Once again, however, the grip of the
Tudor regime on the élites who governed the localities was strong
enough to achieve its ends. The vulnerable point of the plays was,
of course, their association with a discredited, or at least forbidden,

---

[39] John White, *The Way to the True Church* in *The Workes of that Learned and reverend Divine, John White*, London 1628, preface (unpaginated).
[40] W. P. M. Kennedy, *Elizabethan Episcopal Administration*, III, 1924, pp. 228, 230, 261 etc.

aspect of the old ritual calendar. The corporation records at York record the decision in May 1561 that "for as moche as the late fest of Corpus Christi is not nowe celebrated and kept Holy day as was accustomed it is therefore agreed that on Corpus Christi even my lord Mayor and aldermen shall in makyng the proclamation accustomed goe about in semely sadd apparrell and not in skartlet", a provision duplicated in other towns.[41] But it was not merely the occasion of the cycles which was objectionable, but their content, with whole plays devoted to the Assumption of the Virgin, or expounding Catholic sacramental teaching. The Mary plays were excised from the York cycle in the early 1560s, and piecemeal bowdlerization was carried out on other cycles too. In 1575 the Chester cycle was performed for the last time "with such corrections and amendments as shalbe thought convenient by the . . . mayor". The nature of these "corrections" can be gathered from the action of the northern ecclesiastical commission with respect to the Wakefield plays in 1576. The commissioners complained that the cycle contained many things "which tende to the derogation of the Majestie and glorie of God, the prophanation of the sacramentes and the mauntynaunce of superstition and idolatrie", and ordered that "no pageant be used or set furthe . . . whiche tende to the maintenaunce of superstition and idolatrie or which be contrarie to the lawes of God and of the realme." The surviving manuscript of the Towneley plays is bowdlerized in accordance with this command, passages on the seven sacraments, especially the real presence in the Eucharist, scratched out and marked "corectyd and not playd".[42] The gilds and corporations responsible for the plays complied with these demands in order to secure the continued performance of the plays, but the noose of official disapproval was tightening throughout the 1560s. In March 1568 Matthew Hutton, Dean of York, wrote to the mayor and corporation about the text of the Creed plays which they had submitted to him for vetting. He reported that though there were many things in it "that I myche like because of thantiquitie", yet there were also many "that I can not allowe because they be Disagreinge from the sinceritie of the gospell". He had evidently been asked to amend anything he found unacceptable, but he declined because the objectionable matter was so integrated with the rest that any such change would alter "the wholle drift of the play". He urged that the plays should be abandoned, "ffor thoghe it was plausible to yeares agoe, and wold now also of the ignorant sort be well liked yet now in this happie

[41] H. C. Gardiner, *Mysteries End*, 1946, p. 72.
[42] Ibid., pp. 78–9.

time of the gospell, I knowe the learned will mislike it and how the state will beare with it I know not."[43] There were no further performances of the Creed play. The Corpus Christi cycle was played again at York in the following year, but that was to be its last performance, though unsuccessful attempts to revive it continued into the late 1570s. In 1572 the Paternoster plays were performed on Corpus Christi Day, an act of defiance which did not go unnoticed. Two aldermen of reformed convictions walked out halfway through the performance in the Common Hall, and were gaoled and disenfranchised by the rest of the corporation for defiance of the ancient customs of the city. Inevitably, they were subsequently reinstated, and the incident seems to have sealed the fate of the plays. On 30 July the Archbishop called in all copies of the plays: they were never performed again, and requests from the corporation for the appointment of a commission to "correcte the same wherein by the law of this Realme they ar to be reformed" were ignored. None of the texts of the Paternoster play has survived.[44]

The same year saw the suppression in York of the St Thomas day "Riding of Yule and his Wife", a festal celebration suspect not for its popery, but for its disorder and half-disguised paganism. The Yule riding involved "disguising", and the figure of Yule carried a leg of lamb and a cake of bread; his wife carried a "rock" or distaff, and nuts were thrown in among the crowd. These were clearly emblems of abundance and fertility, and the presence of the distaff suggests a ritual of disorder, and conflict between the sexes. In 1570 a broadside had been published which tried to launder these observances by attributing religious significance to them all:

The shoulder of the Lambe the man in hande doth beare,
Doth represent the lambe of God which Iews on Crosse did
    reare,
The cake of purest meale, betokeneth very well
The bread of life which came from heaven in earth with us to
    dwell.

This was a nice try, but did not convince. Apart from anything else, it suggests that the author of the broadside had not quite caught the acceptable idiom, and was not as alert as he might have been to the implacable Protestant sensibilities of those with

---

[43] A. F. Johnston, "The Plays of the Religious Guilds of York", *Speculum*, L, 1975, p. 86.
[44] On the suppressions at York see Gardiner, *Mysteries End*, pp. 72ff; Johnston, "Plays of the Religious Guilds", pp. 55–90.

power to stop the plays and games. They would certainly not have relished the Eucharistic overtones of such allegorization, any more than they would have approved of the broadside's interpretation of the nuts as representing "that most noble Nut our Saviours blessed body, springing miraculously from that beautifull branch of Iesse, the pure and immaculate virgin". At any rate, they were not impressed, and in November 1572 the Archbishop wrote to the mayor and aldermen, complaining of the "undecent and uncomely" disguising, which drew "great concurses of people . . . to the prophaning of that day appoynted to holy uses" and withdrawing "multitudes of people frome devyne service and Sermons". They were ordered to suppress the Yule riding.[45]

The same pattern of suppression was repeated elsewhere, though with varying degrees of traditionalist persistence. The Norwich Corpus Christi plays were silenced in 1564, those at Kendal were still being performed in 1586, though the mayor and his colleagues were trying to reduce the frequency of performances, in the face of popular demand that they should be played every year. The Cornish plays may well have continued into the 1590s. In some communities approved Protestant plays on subjects remote from the old and dangerous themes were substituted, like the play of Tobias composed for Lincoln, or Julian the Apostate played at Shrewsbury in 1565. But by the end of the century in most communities the plays were no more than a memory, and, though the young Shakespeare may have witnessed one of the last performances of the Coventry Corpus Christi cycle, which survived into the mid-1570s, only the older members of the audience of *Hamlet* would have known at first hand what "out-Heroding Herod" actually involved. Two centuries of religious drama, and a whole chapter in lay appropriation of traditional religious teaching and devotion, were at an end.[46]

The attempt to obliterate the memory of traditional religion was not confined to the eradication of Catholic ritual and Catholic drama. Both the bishops and their Puritan critics were especially aware of the potent influence of what they called the "monuments of superstition", the physical remnants of Catholic cult which represented both a symbolic focus for Catholic belief, a reminder of the community's Catholic past and its corporate investment in the old religion, and a concrete hope for its ultimate restoration. A document drawn up in defence of Puritan ministers in Kent in the

[45] *Records of Early English Drama: York*, ed. A. F. Johnston and M. Rogerson, 1979, I pp. 359–62, 367.

[46] Gardiner, *Mysteries End*, p. 87.

early 1580s told of the troubles brought on the head of the curate of Ashford because he had destroyed the parish's wooden font cover "coloured, guilded and pictured" with the seven sacraments,

> the B[ishop] giving holy orders and confirming children, the priest saying Masse and Christening with Exorcismes, marryinge, shriving, and annealing, as thei call it, these things being slubbered over with a white wash that in an hour may be undone, standing like a Dianaes shrine for a future hope and daily comforte of old popish beldames and yong perking papists, and a great offence to all that are Christianly minded.[47]

The reversability of whitewashing was an established fact: at Chichester a painting of the Passion of Christ in the Cathedral was whitewashed over in the early 1580s, but "some well wishers of that waie" rubbed at the whitewash so that "it is almost as bright as ever it was."[48] The survival of images certainly did serve to nourish their own distinctive piety. Another of the prayer-charms which horrified John White was the "white Pater Noster", a prayer which depended for its intelligibility on the survival of the familiar image of the Apostle Peter with his keys:

> White Pater Noster, Saint Peter's brother,
> What hast i'th t'one hand? white booke leaves
> What hast i'th other hand? heaven yate keyes.
> Open heaven yate and sticke hell yate:
> And let every chrysome child creepe to its owne mother:
> White Pater Noster, Amen.[49]

The part which the physical remnants of Catholicism might play in the reversal of Reformation was starkly revealed in the northern rising of 1569, when altar-stones and holy-water stoups were unearthed from middens and quarries where they had been concealed, and re-erected in Durham Cathedral and in a number of parish churches in the region. The holy-water stoups were almost as important in this as the Mass-stones, for the crowds that flocked to the Masses being celebrated in November 1569, and to the ritual burnings of Bibles and prayer-books which often went with them, were as interested in securing holy water and other sacramentals such as holy bread as they were in receiving the Pope's absolution or seeing the sacring, just as the women who knelt at the Masses with their long-forbidden beads seem often to have sought Catholic

---

[47] Albert Peel (ed.), *The Seconde Part of a Register*, 1915, I p. 239.
[48] Peel, *Seconde Part of a Register*, II p. 191.
[49] White, *Way to the True Church*, preface to the reader.

churching from the priests celebrating them, or from their newly reconciled parochial clergy. The minute inquisition carried out by the authorities after the quashing of the rebellion into the present whereabouts of the altar-stones and holy-water stoups is a testimony to their awareness of the imaginative potency of such sacred objects, as is, in a different way, the account of Roland Hinxson, churchwarden of Sedgefield, who hid the holy-water stoup in a midden on the collapse of the rebellion, covering it with straw and bidding it farewell with "Dominus Vobiscum".[50]

The Protestant episcopate was therefore keenly aware of the function of the "monuments of superstition" as the "future hope and daily comfort" of those who yearned for the old religion, like Roger Martin at Melford, who noted that the reredos from the Jesus altar "is in my house decayed, and the same I hope my heires will repair, and restore again one day".[51] Accordingly, they set themselves to rid the parishes of them, root and branch. But it is difficult to avoid the impression that in this respect the Elizabethan authorities were finding it harder to secure obedience to the settlement than any previous Tudor regime. Even docile communities which had rapidly implemented the equally drastic measures of Edward's reign now held back. Bishop's Stortford, for example, had rid itself of its Catholic plate, vestments, and images, whitewashed the church, and replaced the altars with a communion table in 1547 and 1548, well in advance of many other communities in the region. The wardens complied with equal promptness with the Marian restoration, and on Elizabeth's accession duly removed the altars again in 1559, sold off the Rood-loft in the following year, and replaced their chalice with a communion cup in 1562. But in 1570 the accounts record the defacing of the windows and the sale to "diverse of the parish" of the Catholic liturgical books, altar-cloths "and suche other stuffe", which had been retained till then in defiance of Injunction and visitation, and noted that this ridding of the Catholic ornaments was "at the comandement of my lord of London".[52]

Bishop's Stortford was one example among many. By the late 1560s it looks as if the diocesan authorities everywhere were seriously worried by the persistence of Catholic sentiment and practice, and were making a determined effort to remove the physical survivals of Catholic cult on which they thought such

[50] J. Raine (ed.), *Depositions and other Ecclesiastical Proceedings from the Courts of Durham*, 1845, pp. 127–205. The Hinxson incident is on p. 193.
[51] Parker, *History of Long Melford*, p. 71.
[52] Bishop's Stortford CWA, pp. 56–7.

sentiment could focus. Churchwardens' accounts from all over the country record the process. In 1568 Great St Mary's parish in Cambridge sold off the Eucharistic canopy, the Lenten veil, the censers, an assortment of vestments, two paxes, a holy-water stoup and sprinkler, a processional cross, and thirteen liturgical books "great and small". And at the same time they picked off and sold to a choir-man the image of the Virgin from a blue velvet altar-cloth, "bi the comaundement of the archdeacon".[53] In the same year the Rood-cloth, banners, stoles, cross, and holy-water stoups remaining in St Edmund's, Salisbury, were sold off, while in the following year at Ashburton the wardens sold the Catholic vestments. At Stratton in Cornwall the chalice, Rood-loft, and books went in 1570 and a communion cup was bought.[54] In 1569 the wardens of Ludlow paid "Higges wief" tuppence to unpick the sign of the cross from an altar-cloth which was still in use for the communion table. In the following year they paid fourpence to a workman to break down the stone pedestals on which the images of St Margaret and the Virgin had once stood (Pl. 140).[55]

Such meticulous removal of the externals of the old religion, "so that there remain no memory of the same in walls, glasses, windows or elsewhere within their churches and houses," was imposed as a matter of policy from above; as we have seen, it was for a time widely if quietly resisted. But it could not be without effect. As the memories of Catholic cultus faded, as even traditionally minded clergy read out week by week the fulminations of the *Homilies* against "papistical superstitions and abuses", and preached their quarterly sermons against the Pope, as the Commissions of the Peace were slowly purged of hinderers of religion, and wardens and sidesmen chosen to police the parishes who were ready to conform to and even to further "this religion", the chances of a reversion to the old ways faded. The process of destruction itself must have had its effect. The parishioners of Hacconby held on to their crosses, censers, pyx, chrismatory, Mass-books, and processioners, and to the great reredos for the high altar "with leaves full of Imageis" until 1562, but thereafter they succumbed to pressure, and all these things were burned or sold. We can only guess at the impact on their sense of the sacred when they saw their priest feed his swine from a trough which had once been the parish holy-water stoup, or heard Thomas Carter jingle about the parish with a bell on his horse's harness which had

[53] Cambridge Great St Mary's CWA, p. 164.
[54] Stratton CWA, p. 229.
[55] Ludlow CWA, pp. 137, 140.

once summoned them to adoration at the sacring.[56] Elsewhere holy-water stoups became the parish wash-troughs, sanctus and sacring bells were hung on sheep and cows, or used to call workmen to their dinner, pyxes were split open and turned into balances to weigh out coin or spice.[57] The insistence of the authorities that all such sacred objects be defaced and "put to profane use" represented a profound recognition of the desacralizing effect of such actions (Pl. 140–1).

And of course in many communities the spread of Protestant feeling was a far more positive thing, as the teaching of convinced Protestant ministers penetrated, and the conformist pieties of the respectable of the parish allowed themselves to be recast into a new mould. The English Bible certainly played a crucial role here. Even in the heat of the northern rebellion there are indications that many of those involved in burning the Protestant books from the churches baulked at burning the Bible, and did what they could to protect it.[58] New pieties were forming, and something of the old sense of the sacred was transferring itself from the sacramentals to the scriptures.

At any rate, by the 1570s there is a perceptible sense of a changing of the guard, even in many traditionalist parishes. At Ashburton, where they had preserved the vestments until 1569, one of the wardens from 1574 onwards annotated the accounts kept by his predecessors. After an ordinance regulating the collection of funds for the light before the Rood, he wrote:

> The men that thys ordinaunses at fyrst dyd make
> Dyd not thynke Godis word plase for to take
> For yff they had lokyed well there unto
> About thys matter had not been somyche adow.
> But nowe the truethe ys cum to the lyghte
> Thys matter ys put clene to hys flyghte
> Myche was spent herein and dyd no man good,
> And for the love there of the pore lackyd fode.[59]

At St Dunstan's in Canterbury, where they kept their vestments till 1563 and were still using a black woollen pall ornamented with a great white cross at funerals in 1566, they made framed benches in the choir for the communicants in 1571, and at the same time paid a mason five shillings "for mending of the Idolaterous steapes of the chancell".[60]

[56] Monuments of Superstition, pp. 93–5.
[57] Ibid., pp. 50, 55, 73, 105, 114, etc.
[58] Raine, Depositions . . . from the Courts of Durham, pp. 185–6, 188.
[59] Ashburton CWA, p. 192.
[60] Canterbury St Dunstan's CWA, pp. 115, 120, 130.

Perhaps the most striking example of this decisive shift of attitude within a conservative community is that which manifested itself in the Northamptonshire village of Scaldwell in 1581. Scaldwell had been an enthusiastically Catholic community under Mary, and its Marian priest, Thomas Fletcher, who died in 1557, had left minute instructions in his will for an almost aggressively Catholic burial, with the best vestments draped over his corpse and the parish chalice held upright on his breast by having his stole and fanon pinned across it, a vivid affirmation of the power of priesthood and the reality of the Sacrament. In 1581 the churchwardens of Scaldwell reported to the Bishop of Peterborough the discovery in the "towne howse" of a cache of "monuments of popery":

> that ys to say the pycture of Chryst callycd the roode, the picture of Saynt Peter, both of wood undefaced, the pycture of the Trinitye and the pycture of Saynt Mudwyn wt hyr cowe standyng by her both of alabaster undefaced, and a table or tabernacle of wood whych in the tyme of popery dyd stande uppon the auter wt a great number of images appertayning to the same.

In the same cache was a wooden coffer containing seven candlesticks of latten, the chrismatory complete with the holy oils, the sacramental canopy, the censers, the sanctus bell and the handbell, the clapper used in place of a bell in Holy Week, the candle-sockets from the sepulchre and Rood-beam, and "a box of wood to fetch candle lyghts to the church in the tyme of popery". Appended to the report was a list of previous wardens with the note that "These men . . . were they that caused the monuments of popery to be easelyd . . . churchwardens when the churche goodes were soude."[61]

And even in communities where no such dramatic repudiation of popery occurred, time did what ideological confrontation could not. At Morebath Sir Christopher Trychay had once more conformed to the new regime. The parish bought the new communion book, the Bible, the *Homilies*, and the paraphrases in 1560, sent the Mass-book off to Thomas Borrage for safe keeping, and the vestments to Edward Rumbelow. The Rood came down in 1562, though we hear nothing of the fate of Sir Christopher's beloved St Sidwell and her altar, re-erected during Mary's reign. The wardens were still describing the communion table as the "auter" in 1568, but a noticeable change came over the parish thereafter. In 1570 the Bishop of Exeter carried out a visitation, very much in the wake of the northern rebellion. Clearly the diocesan officials were not

---

[61] *Northants Wills*, II pp. 403–4; *Northamptonshire Notes and Queries*, I, 1886, pp. 258–9.

satisfied with the communion arrangements at Morebath, and the wardens had to pay William Jurdyn to set a table in a frame, and to spend 2s 7d in providing "ornamentis about the table". In the same year Edward Rumbelow's wife died. He was the custodian of the vestments, and he paid for his wife's grave by giving back to the church "a tunakyll of sylke the wiche ys bestoyd about the tabyll". In the following year the parish received 53s 2d for their chalice and paten, and paid twenty shillings "to the quenes commissioners at Molton" for another, presumably the compulsory exchange of chalice for Protestant communion cup which was taking place all over England from the late 1560s onwards. In 1572 the parish dismantled the Palm Cross in the graveyard, and sold the iron bolts which had held it together; with it they sold the timber which had stood "a bout the syd auter". And in 1573, the last year in which Sir Christopher kept accounts, he recorded the receipt of a communion book and a psalter, the gift of William Hurly and Ellen his wife, worth ten shillings. At the end of the note Sir Christopher added "deo gracias".[62]

These Morebath entries, undramatic as they are, record the passing of a world. In a parish of undoubted traditionalist views, with a priest who had been an ardent exponent of the cult of the saints and of the dead, and who had revived both promptly under Mary, whose loathing of the Edwardine years had been unmistakably set down in the parish records, slowly the Elizabethan order had been accepted. Chalice gave way to communion cup, altar to table, and the vestments, hoarded so long against the day of restoration, were eventually unstitched and resewn to adorn the table of the supper. And as these external changes had been accepted, so attitudes had shifted. By 1573 the old priest, who had urged his flock on to set silver shoes on St Sidwell and lights before the Jesus altar, had come to see in the gift to his church of a handsome communion book and psalter for the new service a cause for prayerful rejoicing. In a thousand parishes in the 1570s and 1580s the same victory of reformed over traditional religion was silently and imperceptibly enacted.

The victory was, of course, neither simple nor complete. The deluge of criticism of the prayer-book by the godly in the 1570s and 1580s was focused as often as not on customs and practices not specified in the book, but which in parochial practice rapidly attached themselves to it, as communities sought in the prayer-book what they had found in missal and manual. Puritans recognized that these things were "rather used of custome and superstition, than by

[62] Morebath CWA, pp. 205–7, 210, 211, 215–16, 226, 234, 239, 246, 250.

the authoritie of the booke".[63] Yet their perception that somehow the prayer-book and the network of Injunction and interpretation which governed its practice gave legitimacy to such superstitious practices was shrewd and accurate. The religious provision in the book for rites of passage such as churching of women, burials, the retention of the sacramental of the sign of the cross in baptism, and the continuity of personnel among the clergy who performed these services, ensured that the supersession of missal by prayer-book would be an ambivalent victory, and the prayer-book itself would be to some extent absorbed into the practice of traditional religion. The elderly ex-friar still serving as a minister at Binfield in Berkshire in 1583, who told his parishioners that "yf ever we had masse agayne he would say it, for he must lyve", was no doubt exceptional.[64] But many clergy in the 1560s and 1570s blessed candles on Candlemas, sprinkled corpses or placed crosses in their hands, wore a surplice to go in procession at Rogation, tolerated funeral, month's minds, and All Souls ringing, and held the communion bread aloft for the veneration of the people. The wardens at Ludlow might unpick the cross stitched into their linen altar-cloth, but the godly struggled in vain to unpick the pattern of traditional belief from the reformed structures of the prayer-book.

For the conformity of the majority did not mean the end of traditional religion. Instead, slowly, falteringly, much reduced in scope, depth, and coherence, it re-formed itself around the rituals and words of the prayer-book. Already in 1566 the parishioners of Braceburgh, reporting to the Lincoln commissioners that they had sold or made away "all the old superstitious ornaments", added "except one cope *which we keape to serve on festivall daies*".[65] There was no such provision in the prayer-book. Copes were prescribed for use at every communion service, though already by 1566 the drift of official practice was in favour of a return to the rubrics of the second Edwardine book, discontinuing the use of copes at all. The parishioners of Muckton appear to have realized this, and when they reported that they too had retained a cope "for the use of servyce", they added "yf yt may be alowed".[66] But at Braceburgh the parish, with no such apology or fears, had already begun to seek new expression for the old rhythm of high day and workday in changed circumstances, to mark the passage of liturgical time within the narrowed bounds of the new order.

[63] Frere and Douglas, *Puritan Manifestoes*, p. 28.
[64] *Victoria County History of Berkshire*, II, 1907, p. 39.
[65] *Lincolnshire Notes and Queries*, XIV, 1917, p. 110.
[66] Ibid., p. 151.

This was not the only such accommodation between old and new. After the northern rising and to offset the Catholic menace, religious celebrations were attached to the anniversary of the Queen's accession day, 17 November. But this was the abrogated feast day of St Hugh of Lincoln, and had customarily been celebrated by bell-ringing in honour of the saint in parishes throughout the Lincoln diocese, from the Humber to the Thames, from Lincoln to Oxford. Ringing for St Hugh, like the All Souls peals, seems in some places to have persisted, despite official disapproval. It merged imperceptibly into the celebration of Gloriana, and the old practice took on a new, and in some ways opposite meaning.[67]

And the prayer-book itself, from a weapon to break down the structures of traditional religion, became in many places their last redoubt. As the godly came to see in the prayer-book, with its saints' days, its kneeling, its litany, its prescribed fasts, its signing with the Cross, little else but the rags of popery, and sought their abandonment, so adherence to the prayer-book became the one way of preserving such observances. Once again, the funeral service was a touchstone. It was in many ways a starkly reformed service, speaking much of predestination, "beseeching thee, that it may please thee to accomplish the number of thy elect". Yet it required the minister to declare of every one he buried that they died "in sure and certain hope" of salvation. Were all the dead elect? The godly answered with an emphatic no, and godly ministers were increasingly unwilling to read over the bodies of drunkards, adulterers, or the merely mediocre words of hope and rejoicing for their deliverance, words that asserted and assumed their salvation. As Richard Baxter put it, "It is a confusion perilous to the living, that we are to assume that all we bury be of one sort, viz., elect and saved: when contrarily, we see multitudes die without any such signs of repentance as rational charity can judge sincere."[68] Yet James Pilkington, Elizabethan Bishop of Durham, commenting on the due rites of the dead, declared that "the comely using of these in God's church is a great comfort to all Christians, and the want of them a token of God's wrath and plague."[69] This was the view of the average English parishioner too, and they would permit no predestinarian scruples on the part of ministers to abbreviate or truncate those rites. Insistence on the due performance of this and the other rites of passage became a frequent bone of contention between traditionally minded parishioners and Protestant clergy.

---

[67] On accession day ringings see D. Cressy, *Bonfires and Bells*, 1989.
[68] R. Baxter, *Reliquiae Baxterianae*, 1696, part II, p. 315.
[69] *The Works of James Pilkington*, ed. J. Scholefield, *Parker Society*, 1842, pp. 317–18.

By the late 1580s loyalty to prayer-book observance was as often as not taken as a mark of traditionalism, not of reformed views. Atheos, the shrewdly characterized Essex countryman in George Gifford's dialogue, *Countrey Divinitie*, is prepared to admit and to defend having prayed to images in Mary's reign. But he has come to detest the Pope and popery, and he is a stout prayer-book man, scornful of Puritan preachers, those "busie controllers", proud of his genial, non-preaching, parish priest, who "doth reade the service as well as any of them all, and I thinke there is as good edifying in those prayers and Homelics, as in any that the Preacher can make: let us learne those first."[70] Writing about 1590, William Perkins thought that most of the common people were papist at heart, given to saying that "it was a good world, when the old religion was, because all things were cheap", that "a man eates his maker in the Sacrament", that they might swear by Our Lady "because she is gone out of the countrey", that they had believed in Christ "ever since they could remember". Yet he also reported the common view that "it is safer to doe in religion as most doe." In that paradox lies the key to understanding the Reformation in the English parishes.[71]

There were of course those for whom the Protestant gospel was a light on the Damascus road, the sense of a burden lifted from their shoulders. Their impact was certainly disproportionate to their absolute numbers, which were probably small in most communities in Elizabeth's early years. Time, the steady pressure of authority lending its weight to the reformed groups within local communities, and thereby tipping the balance of power in favour of the new faith, the impact of education and evangelization – all these would combine to change that. But for most of the first Elizabethan adult generation, Reformation was a stripping away of familiar and beloved observances, the destruction of a vast and resonant world of symbols which, despite the denials of the proponents of the new Gospel, they both understood and controlled. The people of Tudor England were, by and large, no spartans, no saints, but by the same token they were no reformers. They knew themselves to be mercenary, worldly, weak, and they looked to religion, the old or the new, to pardon these vices, not to reform them. When the crisis of Reformation came they mostly behaved as mercenary, worldly, and weak men and women will, grumbling, obstructing, but in the end taking the line of least resistance, like Bishop Stokesley

[70] George Gifford, *Countrey Divinitie*, 1612, pp. 2–3.
[71] William Perkins, *The Foundation of Christian Religion gathered into sixe principles*, 1627, sigs A3–A4.

lamenting his own helplessness in the face of advancing heresy and
wishing that he had had the courage to stand against it with his
brother the Bishop of Rochester.[72]

Their conformity was not always ignoble. Christopher Trychay
on Exmoor conformed and conformed again, but he was no vicar
of Bray. Reading his church book it is hard to see what else such a
man in such a time could have done. For him religion was above all
local and particular, "rooted in one dear perpetual place", his piety
centred on this parish, this church, these people. It was not a matter
of mere fear, though going with his wardens to be quizzed yet
again by the commissioners for church goods in Exeter he would
have seen the rows of rebel heads above the gates, and registered
the fate of those who resisted the Crown. Some priests had led their
people against the new religion, and had been hanged in their
chasubles for their pains, and still the altars had come down, the
royal arms replaced the Rood, the beloved images been axed and
burned. Some priests, probably more than we are likely to be able
to count, refused to serve the new order, and moved away – to
secular life, to a diminished role as a schoolmaster or a chaplain in a
traditionalist and ultimately recusant household, to exile abroad.
But for a man like Trychay there was nowhere to be except with
the people he had baptized, shriven, married, and buried for two
generations. A few years before Trychay had begun to minister at
Morebath the wisest man in England had written:

> What part soever you have taken upon you, playe that aswel as
> you can and make the best of it: and doe not therefore disturbe
> and brynge oute of order the whole matter, bycause that an other,
> whyche is meryer and better commeth to your remembraunce . . .
> you muste not forsake the shippe in a tempeste, because you can
> not rule and kepe downe the wyndes . . . But you must with a
> crafty wile and subtell trayne studye and endevoure youre selfe,
> asmuche as in you lyeth, to handle the matter wyttelye and
> handsomelye for the purpose, and that whyche you can not turne
> to good, so to order it that it be not very badde.[73]

In parishes all over England decent, timid men and women set
themselves to do just that. It was not for them to rule the winds:
the conscience of the prince was in the hands of God, and the
people must make shift to do as best they could under the prince.
While Sir Christopher Trychay was priest of Morebath Protestantism
would be long in making headway, and when it did it would be
tempered, transformed.

[72] S. Brigden, *London and the Reformation*, 1989, p. 227.
[73] Thomas More, *Utopia*, 1910, pp. 41–2.

But the price for such accommodation, of course, was the death of the past it sought to conserve. If Protestantism was transformed, so was traditional religion. The imaginative world of the *Golden Legend* and the *Festial* was gradually obliterated from wall and window and bracket, from primer and block-print and sermon, and was replaced by that of the Old Testament. Cranmer's sombrely magnificent prose, read week by week, entered and possessed their minds, and became the fabric of their prayer, the utterance of their most solemn and their most vulnerable moments. And more astringent and strident words entered their minds and hearts too, the polemic of the *Homilies*, of Jewel's *Apology*, of Foxe's *Acts and Monuments*, and of a thousand "no-popery" sermons, a relentless torrent carrying away the landmarks of a thousand years. By the end of the 1570s, whatever the instincts and nostalgia of their seniors, a generation was growing up which had known nothing else, which believed the Pope to be Antichrist, the Mass a mummery, which did not look back to the Catholic past as their own, but another country, another world.

ABBREVIATIONS

CWA	Churchwardens' accounts
EETS	Early English Text Society
Hor. Ebor.	*Horae Eboracenses: the Prymer or Hours of the Blessed Virgin Mary according to the use of the Illustrious Church of York*, ed. C. Wordsworth, Surtees Society, CXXXII, 1919.
Hoskins	*Horae Beatae Mariae Virginis, or, Sarum and York Primers*, by E. Hoskins, 1901.
L&P	*Letters and Papers, Foreign and Domestic, of the Reign of Henry VIII*, ed. J. S. Brewer, J. Gairdner, and R. H. Brodie, 1862–1910.
LFMB	*The Lay Folk's Mass Book*, ed. T. F. Simmons, 1871.
ODS	*The Oxford Dictionary of Saints*, by D. H. Farmer, 1978.
RSTC	*A Short-Title Catalogue of Books Printed in England, Scotland, and Ireland and of English Books Printed Abroad 1475–1640*, 2nd ed., revised and enlarged, 1976–86.
TRP	*Tudor Royal Proclamations*, ed. P. L. Hughes and J. F. Larkin, 1964.
VAI	*Visitation Articles and Injunctions of the Period of the Reformation*, ed. W. H. Frere and W. M. Kennedy, 1908–10.

BIBLIOGRAPHY

Primary Sources

MANUSCRIPTS

Cambridge

University Library
Add. 2792
Add. 3041
Dd. 5.65.
Dd. 1.15
Dd. 6.1
Dd. 15.19
Ee. 1.14
Ff. 2.31
Ff. 2.38
Ff. 5.45
Ff. 6.8
Ff. 6.55
Gg. 5.24
Gg. 4.16
Hh. 1.11
Ii. 1.36
Ii. 6.2
Ii. 6.8
Ii. 6.43
Kk. 6.10
Kk. 6.20
Kk. 6.47
Ll. 2.2
Mm. 1.36

Corpus Christi College, Parker Library
MS 128

Fitzwilliam Museum.
MS 48
MS 49
MS 50
MS 51
MS 54
MS 55
MS 57

Magdalene College
MS F.4.13
Pepys MS 1584,
Pepys MS 2125.

St John's College
MS E.6
MS E.26
MS E.32
MS L.10
MS S.35
MS 506

Trinity College
MS B.11.20
MS B.11.11
MS B.11.14
MS O.2.53

London

Westminster Abbey
MS 39.

Oxford

Balliol College
MS 354

Bodleian Library
Lyell 30
Tanner 407

Worcester

Record Office, MS 716.093,

PRINTED RECORDS

Parish and gild records: churchwardens' accounts and related documents cited by place-name followed by "CWA" or "Gild" as appropriate

Andover	J. F. Williams (ed.), *The Early Churchwarden's Accounts of Hampshire*, Winchester, 1913.
Ashwell	A. Palmer (ed.), *Tudor Churchwardens' Accounts*, Hertfordshire Record Society, 1985.
Ashburton	A. Hanham (ed.), *Churchwardens' Accounts of Ashburton 1479–1580*, Devon and Cornwall Record Society, ns XV, 1970.
Badsey	E. A. B. Barnard and W. H. Price (eds), *Churchwarden's Accounts of the Parish of Badsey with Addington in Worcestershire 1525–1571*, Hampstead, 1913.
Baldock	A. Palmer (ed.), *Tudor Churchwardens' Accounts*, Hertfordshire Record Society, 1985.
Bardwell	F. E. Warren (ed.), "The Gild of St Peter in Bardwell", *Proceedings of the Suffolk Institute of Archaeology*, XI, 1903, pp. 81–110.
Bath	C. B. Pearson (ed.), *The Churchwardens' Accounts of the Church and Parish of St Michael without the North Gate, Bath, 1349–1575*, in *Proceedings of the Somerset Archaeological and Natural History Society*, XXIV–XXVI 1878–80 (paginated continuously as a supplement to the annual volumes).
Bethersden	F. R. Mercer (ed.), *Churchwardens' Accounts at Betrysden (Bethersden), Kent, 1515–1573*, Kent Records, Ashford, 1928.
Beverley	A. F. Leach (ed.), *Beverley Town Documents*, Selden Society, XIV, 1900.
Bishop's Stortford	J. L. Glasscock (ed.), *The Records of St Michael's Parish Church, Bishop Stortford*, London, 1882.
Bodmin	J. J. Wilkinson (ed.), *Receipts and Expenses in the Building of Bodmin Church, A.D. 1469–1472*, Camden Society, 1874.
Boxford	P. Northeast (ed.), *Boxford Churchwardens' Accounts 1530–1561*, Suffolk Record Society, XXIII, 1982.
Bramley	J. F. Williams (ed.), *The Early Churchwardens' Accounts of Hampshire*, Winchester, 1913.
Bridgewater	T. B. Dilks (ed.), *Bridgewater Borough Archives* III and IV, Somerset Record Society, LVIII, LX, 1945–8.
Bristol	All Saints (a): E. G. C. F. Atchley (ed.), "Some Documents Relating to the Parish of All Saints, Bristol", *Archaeological Journal*, ns VIII, 1901, pp. 147–81.
Bristol	All Saints (b): E. G. C. F. Atchley (ed.), "On the Parish Records of All Saints, Bristol", *Transactions of the Bristol and Gloucestershire Archaeological Society*, XXVII, 1904, pp. 221–74.
Bristol	All Saints (c): E. G. C. F. Atchley (ed.), "Some more Bristol Inventories", *Transactions of the St Paul's Ecclesiological Society*, IX 1922–8, pp. 1–50.
Bristol	St Ewen's: B. R. Masters and E. Ralph, *The Church Book of St Ewen's, Bristol*, Bristol and Gloucestershire Archaeological Society, Records Section, VI, 1967.
Bristol	St Nicholas: E. G. C. F. Atchley (ed.), "On the Medieval Parish Records of the Church of St Nicholas, Bristol", *Transactions of the St Paul's Ecclesiological Society*, VI, 1910, pp. 35–67.
Bristol	St Stephen's: E. G. C. F. Atchley (ed.), "Some Inventories of the Parish Church of St Stephen, Bristol", *Transactions of the St Paul's Ecclesiological Society*, VI, 1910, pp. 161–84.

Cambridge   Trinity: M. Siraut (ed.), "Accounts of St Katherine's Guild at Holy Trinity Church Cambridge 1514–1537", *Proceedings of the Cambridge Antiquarian Society*, LXVII, 1977, pp. 111–21.

Cambridge   St Mary: J. E. Foster (ed.), *Churchwardens' Accounts of St Mary the Great, Cambridge 1504–1635*, Cambridge Antiquarian Society, XXXV, 1905.

Canterbury   St Andrew's: C. Cotton (ed.), "Churchwardens' Accounts of the Parish of St Andrew's, Canterbury 1485–1625", *Archaeologia Cantiana*, XXXII, 1917, pp. 181–246, XXXIII, 1918, pp. 1–62, XXXIV, 1920, pp. 1–46, XXXV, 1921, pp. 41–108.

Canterbury   St Dunstan's: "Churchwardens' Accounts of the Parish of St Dunstan's, Canterbury", *Archeologia Cantiana*, XVI, 1886–7, pp. 289–321, XVII, 1887, pp. 77–152.

Chagford   F. M. Osborne (ed.), *The Churchwardens' Accounts of St Michael's Church, Chagford, 1480–1600*, Chagford, 1979.

Cowfold   W. B. Otter (ed.), "Churchwardens' Accounts of Cowfold, Sussex, 1471–1485", *Sussex Archaeological Collections*, II, 1849, pp. 316–25.

Cratfield   J. J. Raven (ed.), *Cratfield: a Transcript of the Accounts of the Parish A.D. 1490–1642*, London, 1896.

Crondall   J. F. Williams (ed.), *The Early Churchwardens' Accounts of Hampshire*, Winchester, 1913.

Croscombe   E. Hobhouse (ed.), *Churchwardens' Accounts*, Somerset Record Society, IV, 1890.

Dartmouth   H. R. Watkin (ed.), *Dartmouth, vol I: Pre-Reformation*, Devonshire Association Parochial Histories no. 5, 1935.

Dunmow   L. A. Majendie (ed.), "The Dunmow Parish Account", *Transactions of the Essex Archaeological Society*, II, 1863, pp. 229–37.

Great Hallingbury   J. F. Williams (ed.), "Great Hallingbury Churchwardens' Accounts 1526–1634", *Transactions of the Essex Archaeological Society*, XXIII, 1942–5, pp. 98–115.

Grimsby   E. E. Gillett (ed.), "An Early Churchwardens' Account of St Mary's, Grimsby", *Lincolnshire Architectural and Archaeological Society Reports and Papers*, VI, 1955–6, pp. 27–36.

Halesowen   M. O'Brien (ed.), *Halesowen Churchwardens' Accounts 1487–1582*, Worcestershire Historical Society, 1957.

Hawkhurst   W. J. Lightfoot (ed.), "Churchwardens' Accounts of Hawkhurst, Kent", *Archaeologia Cantiana*, V, 1862–3, pp. 55–79.

Knowle   W. B. Bickley (ed.), *The Register of the Guild of Knowle in the County of Warwick*, Walsall, 1894.

Leicester   T. North (ed.), *The Accounts of the Churchwardens of St Martin's, Leicester 1498–1844*, Leicester, 1884.

Leverton   E. Peacock (ed.), "Churchwardens' Accounts of Leverton in the County of Lincoln 1492–1598", *Archaeologia*, XLI, 1867, pp. 333–70.

Lichfield   A. G. Rosser (ed.), "The Guild of St Mary and St John the Baptist, Lichfield: ordinances of the late fourteenth century", *Staffordshire Record Society*, 4th ser, XIII, 1988, pp. 19–26.

Little Waltham   B. S. Smith (ed.), "Little Waltham Church Goods c 1400", *Transactions of the Essex Archaeological Society*, L, 1961–5, pp. 111–43.

London   All Hallows: C. Welch (ed.), *The Churchwardens' Accounts of the Parish of All Hallows, London Wall, in the City of London, 33 Henry VI to 27 Henry VIII (AD 1455-AD 1546)*, London, 1912.

London   St Anne and St Agnes, Aldersgate: W. McMurray (ed.), *The Records of Two City Parishes*, London, 1925.

London St Botolph's: P. Basing (ed.), *Parish Fraternity Register: Fraternity of the Holy Trinity and Ss Fabian and Sebastian in the parish of St Botolph without Aldersgate*, London Record Society, 1982.

London St John Zachary: W. McMurray (ed.), *The Records of Two City Parishes*, London, 1925.

London St Mary at Hill: H. Littlehales (ed.), *The Medieval Records of a London City Church 1420–1559*, EETS, 1904–5.

London Lambeth C. Drew (ed.), *Lambeth Churchwardens' Accounts I*, Surrey Record Society, 1941.

London St Margaret Pattens: W. St John Hope (ed.), "Ancient Inventories of Goods belonging to the Parish Church of St Margaret Pattens in the City of London", *Archaeological Journal*, XLII, 1885, pp. 312–30.

London St Michael's Cornhill: W. H. Overall (ed.), *The Accounts of the Churchwardens of the Parish of St Michael Cornhill 1456–1608*, London, 1883.

London St Peter Cheap: (a) W. Sparrow Simpson (ed.), "Inventory of the Vestments, Plate and Books belonging to the Church of St Peter's, Cheap, 1431", *Journal of the British Archaeological Association*, XXIV, 1868, pp. 150–60.

London St Peter Cheap: (b) W. Sparrow Simpson (ed.), "Accounts of St Peter, Cheap", *Journal of the British Archaeological Association*, XXIV, 1868, pp. 248–68.

Louth R. C. Dudding (ed.), *The First Churchwardens' Book of Louth 1500–1524*, Oxford, 1941.

Ludlow T. Wright (ed.), *Ludlow Churchwardens' Accounts*, Camden Society, 1869.

Luton H. Gough (ed.), *The Register of the Fraternity or Guild of the Holy and Undivided Trinity in the parish church of Luton 1475–1546*, London, 1906.

Marston F. W. Weaver and G Clark (eds), *Churchwardens' Accounts of Marston, Spelsbury and Pyrton*, Oxfordshire Record Society, V, 1925.

Mere T. H. Baker (ed.), "The Churchwardens' Accounts of Mere", *Wiltshire Archaeological and Natural History Magazine*, CVIII, 1907, pp. 23–92.

Milton (Somerset) E. Hobhouse (ed.), *Churchwardens' Accounts*, Somerset Record Society, IV, 1890.

Molland Sir John B. Phear (ed.), "Molland Accounts", *Reports and Transactions of the Devonshire Association*, XXXV, 1903, pp. 198–238.

Morebath J. Erskine Binney (ed.), *The Accounts of the Wardens of the Parish of Morebath, Devon, 1520–1573*, Exeter, 1904.

Norfolk Gilds I "Norfolk Guilds", ed. J. L'Estrange and W. Rye, *Norfolk Archaeology*, VII, 1872, pp. 105–21.

Norfolk Gilds II "Some Norfolk Guild Certificates", ed. W. Rye, *Norfolk Archaeology*, XI, 1892, pp. 105–36.

Northampton J. C. Cox and C. A. Markham (eds), *Records of the Borough of Northampton*, Northampton, 1898.

North Elmham A. G. Legge (ed.), *Ancient Churchwardens' Accounts of the Parish of North Elmham 1539–1577*, Norwich, 1891.

Norwich St Andrew: J. L'Estrange (ed.), "The Church Goods of St Andrew & St Mary Coslany, Norwich", *Norfolk Archaeology*, VII, 1872, pp. 45–78.

Norwich St George: M. Grace (ed.), *Records of the Gild of St George in Norwich 1389–1547*, Norfolk Record Society, 1937.

Norwich St Peter Mancroft: W. H. St John Hope (ed.), "Inventories of the Parish Church of St Peter Mancroft, Norwich", *Norfolk Archaeology*, XIV, 1878–1900, pp. 153–240.

Norwich Churches H. Harrod (ed.), "Goods and Ornaments in Norwich Churches in the Fourteenth century", *Norfolk Archaeology*, II, 1849, pp. 89–129.

Norwich Gilds "The Hitherto unpublished Certificates of Norwich Gilds", ed J. C. Tingey, *Norfolk Archaeology*, XVI, 1905–7, pp. 267–305.

Oxford F. W. Weaver (ed.), *Churchwardens' Accounts of St Michael's Church, Oxford*, Oxford Archaeological Society, 1933.

Peterborough St John the Baptist: W. T. Mellows (ed.), *Peterborough Local Administration*, Northants Record Society, IX, 1939.

Pilton (Somerset) E. Hobhouse (ed.), *Churchwardens' Accounts*, Somerset Record Society, IV, 1890.

Prescot F. Bailey (ed.), *Prescot Churchwardens' Accounts*, Lancashire and Cheshire Record Society, 1953.

Pyrton F. W. Weaver and G. Clark (eds), *Churchwardens' Accounts of Marston, Spelsbury and Pyrton*, Oxfordshire Record Society, V, 1925.

Reading (St Lawrence) Charles Kerry (ed.), *A History of the Municipal Church of St Lawrence, Reading*, Reading and Derby, 1883.

Reading (St Mary's) F. N. A. Garry (ed.), *The Churchwardens' Accounts of St Mary's, Reading, 1550–1662*, Reading, 1893.

Salisbury H. J. F. Swayne (ed.), *Churchwardens' Accounts of Edmund and St Thomas, Sarum, 1443–1702*, Wiltshire Records Society, 1896.

Sheriff Hutton J. Purvis (ed.), "Sheriff Hutton Accounts", *Yorkshire Archaeological Journal*, XXXVI, 1944, pp. 178–89.

Sleaford W. A. Cragg (ed.), "Compotus of the Holy Trinity Guild of Sleaford 1477–1536", *Lincolnshire Notes and Queries*, XXVIII, 1934–5, pp. 91–7.

South Newington E. R. C. Brinkworth (ed.), *South Newington Churchwardens' Accounts 1553–1684*, Banbury Historical Society, 1964.

Spelsbury F. W. Weaver and G. Clark (eds), *Churchwardens' Accounts of Marston, Spelsbury and Pyrton*, Oxfordshire Record Society, V, 1925.

Stanford W. Haines (ed.), "Stanford Churchwardens' Accounts 1552–1602", *The Antiquary*, XVII, 1888, pp. 70–2, 117–20, 168–72, 209–13.

Stoke Charity J. F. Williams (ed.), *The Early Churchwardens' Accounts of Hampshire*, Winchester, 1913.

Stratford-on-Avon J. H. Bloom (ed.), *The Register of the Gild of the Holy Cross, the Blessed Mary, and St John the Baptist, of Stratford on Avon*, 1907.

Strood H. R. Plomer (ed.), *The Churchwardens' Accounts of St Nicholas, Strood*, Kent Archaeological Society, 1927.

Sutterton E. Peacock (ed.), "Churchwardens' Accounts of St Mary's, Sutterton (Lincs) 1483–1536", *Archaeological Journal*, XXXIX, 1882, pp. 53–63.

Tavistock R. N. Worth (ed.), *Calendar of the Tavistock Parish Records*, Tavistock, 1887.

Thame F. G. L. Lee (ed.), *The History, Description and Antiquities of the Prebendal Church of the Blessed Virgin Mary of Thame*, London, 1883.

Tilney A. D. Stallard (ed.), *The Transcript of the Churchwardens' Accounts of the Parish of Tilney All Saints, Norfolk, 1443–1583*, London, 1922.

Tintinhull (Somerset) E. Hobhouse (ed.), *Churchwardens' Accounts*, Somerset Record Society, IV, 1890.

Walberswick R. W. M. Lewis (ed.), *Walberswick Churchwardens' Account 1450–1499*, London, 1947.

Walsall G. P. Mander (ed.), "Churchwardens' Accounts of the Parish of All Saints, Walsall, 1462–1531", *William Salt Archaeological Society*, LII, 1928, pp. 175–267.

Wandsworth   C. Davis (ed.), "Early Churchwardens' Accounts of Wandsworth 1545–1558", *Surrey Archaeological Collections*, XV, 1900–2, pp. 80–127.

Winchester   St John's: J. F. Williams (ed.), *The Early Churchwardens' Accounts of Hampshire*, Winchester, 1913.

Wing   A. Vere Woodman (ed.), "The Accounts of the Churchwardens of Wing", *Records of Buckinghamshire*, XVI, 1960, pp. 307–329.

Worcester   J. Amphlett (ed.), *The Churchwardens' Accounts of St Michael's in Bedwardine Worcester 1539–1603*, Oxford, 1896.

Worfield   "The Churchwardens' Accounts of the Parish of Worfield, Shropshire 1500–1572", *Transactions of the Shropshire Archaeological and Natural History Society*, 3rd series, III, 1903, pp. 99–138, IV, 1904, pp. 85–114, VI, 1906, pp. 1–24, VII, 1907, pp. 219–40, IX 1909, pp. 113–40.

Wycombe   W. H. St John Hope (ed.), "Inventories of the Parish Church of All Saints, Wycombe", *Records of Buckinghamshire*, VIII, 1903, pp. 103–45.

Wymondham I   G. A. Carthew (ed.), "Extracts from Papers in the Church Chest of Wymondham", *Norfolk Archaeology*, IX, 1884, pp. 121–52.

Wymondham II   G. A. Carthew (ed.), "Wymondham Gilds", *Norfolk Archaeology*, IX, 1884, pp. 240–74.

Yatton   E. Hobhouse (ed.), *Churchwardens' Accounts*, Somerset Record Society, IV, 1890.

York   R. H. Shaife (ed.), *The Register of the Guild of Corpus Christi in the City of York*, Surtees Society, LVII, 1871.

PRINTED HORAE, PRIMERS, AND RELATED BOOKS

Horae are listed here chronologically by title, printer, place and publisher, date, RSTC number, and number in E. Hoskins, *Horae Beatae Mariae Virginis, or, Sarum and York Primers*, 1901.

Hore beate Marie v[ir]g[in]is secundum usum Sarum, [Paris] Thomas Kerver for Jean Richard, 1497. RSTC 15885: Hoskins 15.

Hore presentes ad usum Sarum, [Paris] for Simon Vostre, 1507. RSTC 15905: Hoskins 33.

Hore beatissime virginis Marie ad legitimum Sarisburiensis ecclesie ritum diligentissime accuratissimeque impresse / cum multis orationibus pulcherrimis et indulgentiis iam ultima de nouo adiectis, [Paris] for Francis Burckman, 1511. RSTC 15912: Hoskins 39.

Officium beate Marie v[ir]ginis ad usum Sarum, [Paris] for Simon Vostre, 1512. RSTC 15913: Hoskins 40.

Hore beate marie virginis ad usum insignis ac p[rae]clare ecclesie Sarum, [London], Wynkyn de Worde, 1514. RSTC 15919: Hoskins 46.

Hore b[ea]tissime virginis Marie ad legitimum Sarisburiensis ecclesie ritum: cum quindecim orationibus beate Brigitte: ac multis aliis orationibus pulcherrimis et indulgentiis, [Paris], Nicholas Higman, 1519, for François Regnault and Francis Byrckman. RSTC 15924: Hoskins 54.

Hore b[ea]t[issim]e marie virginis ad usum Sarum, [Antwerp], Christopher Endoviensis for Francis Byrckman [London], 1525. RSTC 15939: Hoskins 67.

Hore b[ea]t[issim]e Marie virginis secundum usum insignis ac praeclare ecclesie Sarum [Rouen] for Jacques Cousin, 1525. RSTC 15940: Hoskins 68.

This prymer of Salysbury use is set out a long wout ony serchyng / with many prayers / and goodly pyctures . . . , Paris, F. Regnault, 1531. RSTC 15973: Hoskins 98.

This prymer of Salysbury use is set out a long without ony serchyng / with many prayers / & goodly pyctures in the kalender . . . , Paris, F. Regnault, 1533. RSTC 15981: Hoskins 109.

This prymer in Englysche and in Laten is newly translated after the Laten texte, London, Robert Redman 1537. RSTC 15997: Hoskins 128.

The manual of prayers, or the prymer in Englysh & Laten . . . Set forth by Jhon . . . bysshope of Rochester . . . [London], Wayland, 1539. RSTC 16009.5: Hoskins 142.

The Primer, in Englishe and Latyn, set foorth by the Kynges maiestie and his Clergie to be taught, learned, and read: and none other to be used throughout all his dominions, London, 1545. RSTC 16034–40: Hoskins 174.

The Primer and catechism set fourthe by the Kynges highnes and his Clergie to be taught, learned and read, of all his louyng subjects, all other set aside, corrected according to the Statute mad in the iijrd and iiijth yere, of our soyereigne Lorde the Kynges Maiesties reigne, London, 1551. RSTC 16054: Hoskins 196.

The primer in Englishe [after the use of Sarum] with many godly and devoute prayers . . . Wherunto is added a plaine and godly treatise concerninge the Masse . . . for the instruccyon of the unlearned and symple people, London, John Wayland, 1555. RSTC 16063: Hoskins 211.

This prymer of Salisbury use is se tout a long with hout onyser chyng / with many prayers / et goodly pyctures in the Kalender, Jean le Prest (Rouen) for Robert Valentin, 1555. RSTC 16068: Hoskins 215.

The Primer in Englishe and Latin, after Salisburie use: set out at length with manie Praiers and goodly pictures, London, Robert Caly, 1556. RSTC 16073: Hoskins 220.

The Primer in Englishe and Latine, set out along, after the use of Sarum: with many godlie and deuoute praiers, London, John Kyngston and Henry Sutton, 1557. RSTC 16081: Hoskins 233.

Hore Beate Marie virginis secundum usum insignis ecclesie Sarum, London, assignes of John Wayland, 1558, RSTC 16084: Hoskins 236.

Horae Eboracenses: the Prymer or Hours of the Blessed Virgin Mary according to the use of the Illustrious Church of York, ed. C. Wordsworth, Surtees Society, CXXXII, 1920.

OTHER PRIMARY SOURCES

Books in this section are listed under the headings used in the notes, that is, author, editor, title, or the designations adopted for particular papers or groups of them.

An Alphabet of Tales: an English 15th Century Translation of the Alphabetum Narrationum of Etienne de Besançon, ed. M. M. Banks, EETS, 1904–5.

Anselm, Saint. *S. Anselmi Opera Omnia,* ed. F. S. Schmitt, Edinburgh, 1946–61.

Ars Moriendi, Wynkyn de Worde, 1506, RSTC 788.

The Art or Crafte to Lyve Well, Wynkyn de Worde, 1505, RSTC 792.

The Babees Book, et. F. J. Furnivall, EETS, 1868.

Baker, D. C. (ed.) *The Late Medieval Religious Plays of Bodleian MS Digby 133,* EETS, 1982.

Bale, John. *A Comedy Concerning Thre Lawes,* ed. A. Schroer in *Anglia,* V, 1882, pp. 137–264.

Banting, H. M. (ed.) *Two Anglo-Saxon Pontificals,* Henry Bradshaw Society, 1989.

Bateson, M. (ed.) *A Collection of Original Letters from the Bishops to the Privy Council, 1564*, Camden Miscellany, IX (ns LIII), 1895.

Baxter, R. *Reliquiae Baxterianae*, ed. M. Sylvester, London, 1696.

Bazire, J. and Cross, J. (eds) *Eleven Old English Rogationtide Homilies*, Toronto, 1982.

Beattie, W. (ed.) *Border Ballads*, Harmondsworth, 1965.

Becon, Thomas. *The Early Works of Thomas Becon . . . published in the Reign of Henry VII*, ed. J. Ayre, Parker Society, 1843.

—— *Prayers and Other Pieces by Thomas Becon*, ed. J. Ayre, Parker Society, 1844.

Beds. Inventories. The Edwardine Inventories for Bedfordshire, ed. F. C. Eeles, Alcuin Club, VI, 1905.

Beds. Wills I. *English Wills 1498–1526*, ed. A. F. Cirket, Publications of the Bedfordshire Historical Records Society, XXXVII, 1956.

Beds. Wills II. *Bedfordshire Wills 1480–1519*, ed. R. Bell, Publications of the Bedfordshire Historical Records Society, XLV, 1966.

Beds. Wills III. *Bedfordshire Wills proved in the Prerogative Court of Canterbury 1383–1548*, ed. M. McGregor, Publications of the Bedfordshire Historical Records Society, LVIII, 1979.

Berkshire Inventories. Parish Church Goods in Berkshire, ed. W. Money, Oxford and London, 1879.

Betson, Thomas. *Here begynneth a ryght profytable treatyse . . . the Pater Noster, Ave & Credo in our moder tonge*, 1510, RSTC 1978.

Blume, C. and Bannister, H. M. *Analecta Hymnica Medii Aevi*, Leipzig, 1886–1922, esp. vol. LIV, 1915.

Bokenham, Osbert. *Legendes of Hooly Wummen*, ed. M. S. Serjeantson, EETS, 1938.

Bond, B. (ed.) *Middle English Miracles of the Blessed Virgin Mary*, Huntingdon, 1964.

Bradshaw, Henry. *The Life of St Werburge of Chester*, ed. C. Horstmann, EETS, 1887.

Brome. *A Common-place Book of the Fifteenth Century . . . at Brome Hall, Suffolk*, ed. L. Toulmin-Smith, London, 1886.

Brown, Carleton (ed.) *Religious Lyrics of the XIVth Century*, Oxford, 1924.

—— *Religious Lyrics of the XVth Century*, Oxford, 1939.

—— *Secular Lyrics of the XIVth and XVth Centuries*, Oxford, 1952.

Bucks. Courts. The Courts of the Archdeaconry of Buckingham 1483–1523, ed. E. M. Elvey, Buckinghamshire Record Society, 1975.

Bucks. Inventories. The Edwardine Inventories for Buckinghamshire, ed. F. C. Eeles, Alcuin Club, IX, 1908.

Burton, E. (ed.) *Three Primers put forth in the reign of Henry VIII*, Oxford, 1834.

Bury Wills. Wills and Inventories from the Registers of the Commissary of Bury St Edmunds, ed. S. Tymms, Camden Society, XLIX, 1850.

Calendar of Entries in the Papal Registers relating to Great Britain and Ireland, XIII–XVIII, London, 1955–89.

Cambridgeshire Inventories. "Cambridgeshire Church Goods temp. Edward VI", ed. J. J. Muskett, East Anglian, ns VI, 1895–6, pp. 145–9, 199–203, 225–8, 241–3; IX, 1901–2, PP. 5–9, 23–5, 42–3, 49–50, 73–5, 94–6, 105–8, 117–20, 136–8, 236–8, 248–50, 262–5, 282–3, 301–4, 311–14, 328–30, 348–50, 373–5.

[Capgrave, J.] *Here Begynneth the Kalendre of the new Legende of England*, Richard Pynson, 1516, RSTC 4602.

Chaney, E. F. *Danse Macabre*, Manchester, 1945.

The Chester Mystery Cycle, ed. R. M. Lumiansky and D. Mills, EETS, 1972.

The Clerk's Book of 1549, ed. J. Wickham Legg, Henry Bradshaw Society, XXV, 1903.

Colburn, A. F. (ed.) *Hali Maidhad*, Copenhagen, 1940.

Concilia Magnae Britanniae et Hiberniae, ed. D. Wilkins, London, 1737.

Councils and Synods with other Documents Relating to the English Church, II, AD 1205–1313, ed. F. M. Powicke and C. R. Cheney, Oxford, 1964.

Coverdale, Myles. *Remains*, ed. George Pearson, Parker Society, 1846.

Cranmer, Thomas. *Miscellaneous Writings and Letters*, ed. J. E. Cox, Parker Society, 1846.

Cura Clericalis, Thomas Petyt, 1542, RSTC 6128.

Dante Alighieri. *The Purgatorio of Dante*, London (Temple Classics), 1964.

Davies, J. (ed.) *An Old English Chronicle 1377–1461*, Camden Society, LXIV, 1856.

Davies, R. *Medieval English Lyrics*, London, 1963.

Davis, N. (ed.) *Non-Cycle Plays and Fragments*, EETS, 1970.

—— *Paston Letters and Papers of the Fifteenth Century*, Oxford, 1971–6.

Derbyshire Wills. "Wills at Somerset House relating to Derbyshire", ed. S. O. Addy, *Journal of the Derbyshire Archaeological and Natural History Society*, XLIV, 1923, pp. 42–75.

The Digby Plays with an Incomplete Morality, ed. F. J. Furnivall, EETS, 1896.

Dives and Pauper, ed. P. H. Barnum, EETS, 1976–80.

The Doctrinal of Sapyence [by Guy de Roye], ed. William Caxton, 1489, RSTC 21431.

Dugdale, Sir William. *Monasticon Anglicanum*, ed. J. Caley, Henry Ellis, and Bulkeley Bandinel, London, 1830.

Duncan, L. L. (ed.) "The Parish Churches of West Kent: their Dedications, Altars, Images, and Lights", *Transactions of the St Paul's Ecclesiological Society*, III, 1895, pp. 241–98.

Durham. *The Rites of Durham*, ed. J. T. Fowler, Surtees Society, CVII, 1903.

Durham. *Wills and Inventories [from the Registry at Durham]*, ed. J. Raine and W. Greenwell, Surtees Society, II, XXXVIII, 1835–60.

Dyboski, R. (ed.) *Songs, Carols and other Miscellaneous Poems from the Balliol MS 354, Richard Hill's Commonplace Book*, EETS, 1908.

The Dyetary of Ghostly Helthe, Wynkyn de Worde, 1520, RSTC 6833.

The Fifty Earliest English Wills in the Court of Probate, London, ed. F. J. Furnivall, EETS, 1882.

The Early English Carols, ed. R. L. Greene, 2nd ed., Oxford, 1977

Easting, R. (ed.) *St Patrick's Purgatory*, EETS, 1991.

Edgeworth, R. *Sermons very fruitfull, godly and learned*, Richard Caly, 1557, RSTC 7482

Ellis, H. (ed.) *Original Letters Illustrative of English History*, London, 1824–46.

Essex Inventories. "Inventories of Essex Church Goods", ed. H. W. King, *Transactions of the Essex Archaeological Society*, IV, 1869, pp. 197–234; V, 1873, pp. 116–35, 219–42, 273–80; ns I, 1877, pp. 5–32; ns II, 1884, pp. 165–88, 223–50; ns III, 1889, pp. 36–63; (additions ed. R. C. Fowler and others) ns X, 1909, pp. 228–36; ns XI, 1911, pp. 90–210, 310–20.

Exeter Inventories. The Edwardian Inventories for the City and County of Exeter, ed. B. Cresswell, Alcuin Club, XX, 1916.

Exonoratorium Curatorum, Thomas Godfray, 1534(?), RSTC 10634.

Festial see Mirk, John, *Mirk's Festial* . . .

Fifteen Tokens. Here begynneth a lytel treatyse the whiche speketh of the xv tokens the which shullen be shewed afore the dredfull daye of Judgement, Wynkyn de Worde, 1505, RSTC 791–2, 793.3.

Fisher, John. *English Works*, ed. J. E. B. Mayor, EETS, 1876.

—— *Two Fruytfull Sermons of St John Fisher*, ed. Sr M. D. Sullivan, PhD thesis for Notre Dame University, 1961.

The floure of the commaundements of god, Wynkyn de Worde, 1510, RSTC 23876.

Foxe, John. *The Acts and Monuments of John Foxe*, ed. G. Townsend and S. R. Cattley, London, 1837–41.

Frere, W. H. and Douglas, C. H. (eds) *Puritan Manifestoes*, London, 1954.

Furnivall, F. J. (ed.) *Political, Religious and Love Poems from Lambeth MS 306 and other Sources*, EETS, 1866.

The Gast of Gy: A Middle English Religious Prose Tract, ed. R. H. Bowers, *Beiträge zur Englischen Philologie*, XXXII, 1938.

Gee, H. and Hardy, W. J. *Documents Illustrative of English Church History*, London, 1896.

Gifford, George. *A Briefe discourse of certaine points of the religion, which is among the common sort of Christians which may be termed the Countrey Divinitie*, London, 1612.

Gloucester Chantries. "Chantry Certificates, Gloucestershire", ed. J. MacLean, *Transactions of the Bristol and Gloucestershire Archaeological Society*, VIII, 1883–4, pp. 232–51.

Gloucester Inventories. "Inventories of and receipts for Church Goods, Gloucester and Bristol", ed. Sir John MacLean, *Transactions of the Bristol and Gloucestershire Archaeological Society*, XII, 1887–8, pp. 70–113.

The Golden Legend or Lives of the Saints as Englished by William Caxton, ed. F. S. Ellis, London (Temple Classics), 1900.

The Grey Friars' Chronicle of London, ed. J. G. Nicholls, Camden Society, LIII, 1852.

Grey, D. (ed.) *The Oxford Book of Fifteenth Century Verse and Prose*, Oxford, 1985.

Guylforde, Sir Richard. *The Pylgrymage of Sir Richard Guylforde to the Holy Land, AD 1506*, ed. Sir Henry Ellis, Camden Society, 1851.

Hale, William (ed.) *A Series of Precedents and Proceedings in Criminal Causes, extending from the year 1475 to 1640*, London, 1847.

Happé, Peter (ed.) *English Mystery Plays*, Harmondsworth, 1975.

—— *Four Morality Plays*, Harmondsworth, 1987.

Archdeacon Harpsfield's Visitation 1557, together with Visitations of 1556 and 1558, ed. L. E. Whatmore, Catholic Record Society, XLV–XLVI, 1950–1.

Hertfordshire Inventories. Inventory of Furniture and Ornaments remaining in all the Parish Churches of Hertfordshire in the Last Year of the Reign of King Edward VI, ed. J. E. Cussans, Oxford and London, 1873.

Homelies seitte forth by the right reverend . . . Edmunde byshop of London, RSTC 3285.4.

Horstmann, C. (ed.) *Altenglische Legenden, Neue Folge*, Heilbronn, 1881.

—— *The Minor Poems of the Vernon Manuscript*, EETS, 1892–1901.

—— "Prosalegenden: Die Legenden des MS Douce 114", *Anglia*, VIII, 1885, pp. 102–96.

—— *Sammlung Altenglische Legenden*, Heilbronn, 1878.

—— *The Three Kings of Cologne*, EETS, 1886.

—— *Yorkshire Writers*, London, 1895.

How the plowman lerned his pater noster, Wynkyn de Worde, 1510, RSTC 20034.

A Hundred Merry Tales and other English Jest-books of the Fifteenth and Sixteenth Centuries, ed. P. M. Zall, Lincoln, Nebraska, 1963.

Hymns to the Virgin and Christ, ed. F. J. Furnivall, EETS, XXIV, 1867.

Idley, Peter. *Peter Idley's Instructions to his Son*, ed. C. D'Evelyn, Boston, 1935.

James, M. R. (ed.) *Henry VI: a Reprint of John Blacman's Memoir*, Cambridge, 1929.

—— "Lives of St Walstan", *Norfolk Archaeology*, XIX, 1917, pp. 238–67.

James, M. R. and Jessopp, A. (eds) *The Life and Miracles of St William of Norwich*, Cambridge, 1896.

Jones, E. (ed.) *The New Oxford Book of Sixteenth Century Verse*, Oxford, 1991.

Julian of Norwich. *A Book of Showings to the Anchoress Julian of Norwich*, ed. E. Colledge and J. Walsh, Toronto, 1978.

The Kalender of Shepherdes, ed. H. O. Sommer, London, 1892.

Kempe, Margery. *The Book of Margery Kempe*, ed. S. B. Meech and H. E. Allen, EETS, 1940.

Kennedy, W. P. M. *Elizabethan Episcopal Administration*, Alcuin Club, XXV–XXVII, 1924.

Kent Inventories. "Inventories of Parish Church Goods in Kent A.D. 1552", ed. M. E. C. Walcott and others, *Archaeologia Cantiana*, VIII, 1872, pp. 74–163; IX, 1874, pp. 266–84; X, 1876, pp. 282–97; XI, 1877, pp. 409–16; XIV, 1882, pp. 290–325.

Kent Reformation. "Extracts from original documents illustrating the progress of the Reformation in Kent", ed. C. E. Woodruff, *Archaeologia Cantiana*, XXXI, 1915, pp. 95–105.

The Kentish Visitation of Archbishop William Warham and his Deputies 1511–1512, ed. K. L. Wood Legh, Kent Archaeological Society: Kent Records, XXIV, 1984

Kettley, J. (ed.) *The Two Liturgies . . . Set Forth by Authority in the Reign of Edward VI*, Parker Society, 1844.

The King's Book, ed. T. A. Lacey, London, 1932.

Kitching, C. J. (ed.) *The Royal Visitation of 1559: Act Book for the Northern Province*, Surtees Society, CLXXXVII, 1975.

Lancashire and Cheshire Wills and Inventories, ed. G. J. Piccope, Chetham Society, XXXIII, LI, LIV, 1857–60.

Langland, William. *Piers Plowman: an edition of the C Text*, ed. Derek Pearsall, London, 1978.

—— *The Vision of Piers Plowman*, an edition of the B Text by Carl Schmidt, London (Everyman Library), 1978.

Latimer, Hugh. *Sermons*, ed. G. E. Cowie, Parker Society, 1844.

—— *Sermons and Remains*, ed. G. E. Cowie, Parker Society, 1845.

The Lay Folk's Catechism, ed. T. F. Simmons and H. E. Nolloth, EETS, 1901.

The Lay Folk's Mass Book, ed. T. F. Simmons, EETS, 1879.

Legends of the Holy Rood, ed. R. Morris, EETS, 1871.

Lester, G. A. (ed.) *Three Late Medieval Morality Plays*, London, 1990.

Letters and Papers, Foreign and Domestic, of the Reign of Henry VIII, ed. J. S. Brewer, J. Gairdner, and R. H. Brodie, London, 1862–1910.

The Liber Celestis of St Bridget of Sweden, ed. R. Ellis, EETS, 1987.

The Liber de Diversis Medicinis in the Thornton MS (Lincoln), ed. M. S. Ogden, EETS, 1938.

Lincoln Court. An Episcopal Court Book for the Diocese of Lincoln 1514–20, ed. M. Bowker, Lincoln Record Society, LXI, 1967.

Lincoln Visit. Visitations in the Diocese of Lincoln 1517–1531, ed. A. Hamilton Thompson, Lincoln Record Society, XXXIII, XXXV, XXXVII, 1940–7.

Lincoln Wills, ed. C. W. Foster, Lincoln Record Society, V, X, XXIV, 1914–30.

Liturgies and Occasional Forms of Prayer set forth in the Reign of Queen Elizabeth, ed. W. K. Clay, Parker Society, 1847.

Lloyd, C. *Formularies of Faith put forth by Authority during the Reign of Henry VIII*, Oxford, 1825.

Lloyd, R. (ed.) *An Account of the Altars, Monuments and Tombs existing AD 1428 in St Alban's Abbey*, St Alban's, 1873.

London Churches at the Reformation, ed. H. B. Walters, London, 1939.

London Consistory Court Wills 1492–1547, ed. I. Darlington, London Record Society, III, 1967.

Longland, John. *A Sermond made be fore the kynge hys hyghenes at Rychemunte, uppon good fryday, the yere of our lorde MCCCCCXXXVI by Johan Longland bysshope of Lincoln* [*vere* 1535], RSTC 16795.5.

Love, N. *The Mirror of the Blessed Life of Jesu Christ*, London, 1926.

—— *The Mirrour of the Blessed Lyfe of Jesu*, ed. L. G. Powell, Oxford, 1908.

Ludus Coventriae or the Plaie called Corpus Christi, ed. K. S. Block, EETS, 1922.

Luria, M. S. and Hoffman, R. L. *Middle English Lyrics*, New York, 1974.

Lydgate, John. *The Minor Poems of John Lydgate: Part I*, ed. H. N. MacCraken, EETS, 1911.

Machyn, Henry. *The Diary of Henry Machyn 1550–1563*, ed. J. G. Nicholls, Camden Society, XLII, 1848.

McSparran, F. and Robinson, P. R. (eds) *Cambridge University Library MS Ff 2 38*, London, 1979.

Malden, A. R. (ed.) *The Canonisation of St Osmund*, Wiltshire Record Society, 1901.

Malleus Maleficarum, trans. M. Summers, reprint, London, 1971.

Manipulus Curatorum, Richard Pynson, 1508, RSTC 12474.

Maskell, W. (ed.) *Monumenta Ritualia Ecclesiae Anglicanae*, London, 1846–7.

Meredith, P. (ed.) *The Mary Play from the N. Town Manuscript*, London, 1987.

Middle English Sermons edited from British Museum MS Royal 18 B xxiii, ed. W. O. Ross, EETS, 1940.

The Miracles of Henry VI, ed. R. Knox and S. Leslie, Cambridge, 1923.

Mirk, John. *Instructions for Parish Priests*, ed. E. Peacock and F. J. Furnivall, EETS, 1868, rev. ed. 1902.

—— *Mirk's Festial: a Collection of Homilies by Johannes Mirkus*, ed. T. Erbe, EETS, 1905.

Missale ad Usum Insignis et Praeclare Ecclesiae SARUM, ed. F. H. Dickinson, Burntisland, 1861–83.

Monuments of Superstition. English Church Furniture, Ornaments and Decorations at the Period of the Reformation, ed. E. Peacock, London, 1866. Continued by C. W. Foster in *Lincolnshire Notes and Queries*, XIV, 1917, pp. 78–88, 109–16, 144–51, 166–73.

Moore, A. P. (ed.) "Proceedings of the Ecclesiastical Courts in the Archdeaconry of Leicester, 1516–1535", *Associated Architectural Societies Reports and Papers*, XXVIII, 1905, pp. 117–220, 593–662.

More, Thomas. *The Complete Works of St Thomas More*, VI, *A Dialogue Concerning Heresies*, ed. T. M. C. Lawler and others, New Haven, 1981.

—— *Utopia*, London (Everyman Library), 1910.

—— *The Works of Sir Thomas More*, London, 1557, reprint, London, 1978.

Munby, L. M. (ed.) *Life and Death in Kings Langley: Wills and Inventories 1498–1659*, Kings Langley, 1981.

Mustanova, T. F. (ed.) *The Good Wife Taught her Daughter*, in *Annales Academiae Scientarum Fennicae*, LXI part ii, 1948.

Narratives of the Days of the Reformation, ed. J. G. Nicholls, Camden Society, LXXVII, 1859.

Norfolk Goods. "Norfolk Church Goods", ed. Walter Rye, *Norfolk Archaeology*, VII, 1872, pp. 20–44.

Norfolk Inventories. "Inventories of Norfolk Church Goods 1552", ed. H. B. Walters and others, *Norfolk Archaeology*, XXVI, 1935–7, pp. 245–70; XXVII, 1938–40, pp. 97–144, 263–89; XXVIII, 1942–5, pp. 89–106, 133–80; XXX, 1947–52, pp. 75–87, 160–7, 213–19, 370–8; XXXI, 1955–7, pp. 200–9, 233–98.

Norfolk Wills. "Extracts from Early Norfolk Wills", ed. H. Harrod, *Norfolk Archaeology*, I, 1847, pp. 114–25; IV, 1855, pp. 317–39.

North Country Wills, ed. J. W. Clay, Surtees Society, CXVI, CXXI, 1908–12.

Northants. Chantries. "Chantry Certificates for Northamptonshire", ed. A. Hamilton Thompson, *Associated Architectural and Archaeological Societies Reports*, XXXI, 1911, pp. 87–180.

Northants. Wills I. "The Parish Churches of Northamptonshire, illustrated by wills, *temp.* Henry VIII", ed. C. J. Cox, *Archaeological Journal*, LXIII, 1901, pp. 113–32.

Northants. Wills II. "The Parish Churches and Religious Houses of Northamptonshire: their Dedications, Altars, Images and Lights", *Archaeological Journal*, LXX, 1913, pp. 217–452.

Northants. Visitation. "An Episcopal Visitation in 1570", ed. E. A. Irons, *Northamptonshire Notes and Queries*, ns II, 1907–9, pp. 115–79, 202–8.

Norwich Consistory Court Depositions 1499–1512, 1518–30, ed. E. D. Stone and B. Cozens Hardy, Norfolk Record Society, X, 1938.

Norwich Inventory. Archdeaconry of Norwich: Inventory of Church Goods temp. Edward III, ed. A. Watkin, Norfolk Record Society, XIX (2 parts), 1947.

Ordynarye of crystyanyte or of crysten men, Wynkyn de Worde, 1502, RSTC 5198.

Thordynary of crysten men, Wynkyn de Worde, 1506, RSTC 5199.

Oxford Chantries. The Chantry Certificates for Oxfordshire and the Edwardian Inventories of Church Goods for Oxfordshire, ed. R. Graham, Alcuin Club, XXIII, 1920.

Oxfordshire Wills Proved in the Prerogative Court of Canterbury, 1393–1510, ed. J. R. H. Weaver and A. Beardwood, Oxfordshire Record Society, XL, 1958.

Paston Letters see Davis, N. (ed.) *Paston Letters and Papers . . .*

Peacock, E. (ed.) *English Church Furniture . . .* see *Monuments of Superstition*.

Pecock, R. *The Repressor of Over Much Blaming of the Clergy*, ed. C. Babington, Rolls Series London, 1860.

Peel, A. (ed.) *The Seconde Part of a Register*, Cambridge, 1915.

Perkins, W. *The Foundation of Christian Religion gathered into sixe Principles*, London, 1627.

Pilkington, James. *The Works of James Pilkington*, ed. J. Scholfield, Parker Society, 1842.

The First and Second Prayer Books of King Edward VI, London (Everyman Library), 1910.

Private Prayers put forth by Authority during the Reign of Queen Elizabeth, ed. W. K. Clay, Parker Society, 1851.

A Profytable and necessary doctryne, with certayne homelies adioyned thereunto set forth by the reverende father in God, Edmonde byshop of London, London, 1555, RSTC 3282.

Raine, J. (ed.) *Depositions and other Ecclesiastical Proceedings from the Courts of Durham*, Surtees Society, XXI, 1845.

—— *Fabric Rolls of York Minster*, Surtees Society, XXXV, 1859.

The Rationale of Ceremonial, ed. C. S. Cobb, Alcuin Club, 1910.

"Reculver and Hoath Wills", ed. A. Hussey, *Archaeologia Cantiana*, XXXII, 1917, pp. 77–141.

Records of Early English Drama: York, ed. A. F. Johnston and M. Rogerson, Manchester, 1979.

The Register of Edmund Lacy, ed. G. R. Dunstan, Canterbury and York Society, 1963–72.

The Register of Richard Beauchamp, Bishop of Hereford, ed. A. T. Bannister, Cantilupe Society, Hereford, 1917.

The Register of Richard Mayhew, Bishop of Hereford, ed. A. T. Bannister, Cantilupe Society, Hereford, 1919.

The Register of Thomas Rotherham, Archbishop of York, ed. E. E. Barker, Canterbury and York Society, 1976.

Regularis Concordia, ed. T. Symons, London, 1953.

A Relation, or Rather, a True Account of the Island of England about the Year 1500, ed. A. Trevisano, Camden Society, XXXVII, 1847.

Reliquiae Antiquae, ed. T. Wright and J. D. Halliwell, London, 1845.

"The Revelation of the Hundred Paternosters: a fifteenth-century meditation", ed. F. Wormald, *Laudate*, XV, 1936, pp. 165–82.

Reynes, Robert. *The Commonplace Book of Robert Reynes of Acle*, ed. C. Louis, Garland Medieval Texts I, New York, 1980.

Richmond Wills. Wills and Inventories from the Registry of the Archdeacon of Richmond, ed. J. Raine, Surtees Society, XXVI, 1853.

Rolle, Richard. *English Writings*, ed. H. E. Allen, Oxford, 1931.

—— *Prose and Verse*, ed. S. J. Ogilvie-Thomson, EETS, 1988.

—— see also Woolley, R. M. (ed.) *The Officium and Miracula of Richard Rolle*.

Sarum Breviarium. Breviarium ad Usum Insignis Ecclesiae Sarum, ed. F. Proctor and C. Wordsworth, Cambridge, 1882–6.

Sarum Manuale. Manuale ad Usum Percelebris Ecclesie Sarisburiensis, ed. A. Jefferies Collins, Henry Bradshaw Society, XCI, 1960.

The Sarum Missal in English, ed. F. E. Warren, London, 1911–13.

The Use of Sarum, ed. W. H. Frere, Cambridge, 1895–1901.

Scot, Reginald. *The Discoverie of Witchcraft*, 1584, RSTC 21864.

Sede Vacante Wills, ed. C. Eveleigh, Kentish Archaeological Society Records Branch, III, 1949.

Silverstein, T. (ed.) *Medieval English Lyrics*, London, 1971.

Somerset Medieval Wills, ed. F. W. Weaver, Somerset Record Society, XVI, XIX, XXI, 1901–5.

Speculum Sacerdotale, ed. E. H. Weatherby, EETS, 1935.

Staffordshire Inventories 1552 (North). *The Archdeaconry of Stoke on Trent*, ed. S. W. Hutchinson, London, 1893, pp. 168–90.

Staffordshire Inventories 1552 (South). *The Inventory of Church Goods and Ornaments taken in Staffordshire in 6 E VI (1552)*, ed. F. J. Wrottesly, Collections for a History of Staffordshire, ns VI, 1903, pp. 165–90.

Stella Clericorum, London, 1531, RSTC 23244.

Surrey Inventories. Inventories of the Goods and Ornaments in the Churches of Surrey in the Reign of King Edward VI, ed. J. R. Daniel-Tyssen, London, 1869.

Sussex Wills. Transcripts of Sussex Wills in Four Volumes, ed. R. Garraway Rice and W. H. Godfrey, Sussex Record Society, XCI–XCIV, 1935–41.

Taverner, Richard. *The epistles and gospelles wyth a brief postill upon the same* . . . 1540(?), RSTC 2967–8.

—— *Postils on the Epistles and Gospels*, ed. E. Cardwell, Oxford, 1841.

Testamenta Cantiana: West, ed. L. L. Duncan, London, 1906.

Testamenta Cantiana: East, ed. A. Hussey, London, 1907.

Testamenta Eboracensia: a Selection of Wills from the Registry of York, ed. J. Raine and J. W. Clay, Surtees Society, IV, XXX, XLV, LIII, LXXIX, CVI, 1836–1902.

Testamenta Leodiensia, ed. G. D. Lumb, Thoresby Society, 1913–30.

The thre kyngys of Coleyne, Wynkyn de Worde, 1511, RSTC 5574.

Toulmin-Smith, L. (ed.) *English Gilds*, EETS, 1870.

Tracts on the Mass, ed. J. Wickham Legg, Henry Bradshaw Society, XXVII, 1904.

A Treatise declaryng & shewing . . . *that pyctures & other ymages* . . . *ar in no wise to be suffred in the temples or churches of Cristen men*, 1535, RSTC 24328–9.

Tudor Parish Documents of the Diocese of York, ed. J. S. Purvis, Cambridge, 1948.

Tudor Royal Proclamations, ed. P. L. Hughes and J. F. Larkin, New Haven and London, 1964–9.

Turner, William. *A New Booke of Spiritual Physic for Dyverse deseases*, 1535, RSTC 24361.

Tyndale, W. *Answer to Sir Thomas More's Dialogue*, Parker Society, 1850.

The Book of Vices and Virtues, ed. W. N. Francis, EETS, 1942.

The Vision of the Monk of Eynsham, ed. A. Arber, London, 1901.

The Vision of Tundale, ed. R. Mearns, Heidelberg, 1985.

Visitation Articles and Injunctions of the Period of the Reformation, ed. W. H. Frere and W. M. Kennedy, Alcuin Club, XIV–XVI, 1908–10.

The Visitation of Suffolke, ed. J. Jackson Howard, Lowestoft and London, 1866.

The Wakefield Pageants in the Towneley Cycle, ed. A. C. Cawley, Manchester, 1958.

Wednesday Fast. Here beginneth a lytel treatyse that sheweth how euery man & woman ought to fast and absteyne them from flesshe on the wednesday, Wynkyn de Worde, 1500, RSTC 24224.

Weever, John. *Ancient Funeral Monuments*, London, 1631.

Wells Wills, 1528–1536, ed. F. W. Weaver, London, 1890.

Whalley Act Book. Act Book of the Ecclesiastical Court of Whalley, 1510–1538, ed. A. M. Cooke, Chetham Society, ns XLIV, 1901.

White, John. *The Workes of that Learned and Reverend Divine, John White*, London, 1624.

Whytford, Richard. *A Werke for Householders: A Dayly Exercyse and Experyence of Dethe*, ed. J. Hogg, Salzburg Studies in English Literature, no. 89, 1979.

Woolley, R. M. (ed.) *The Officium and Miracula of Richard Rolle*, London, 1919.

A Worcestershire Miscellany compiled by John Northwood c.1400, ed. N. S. Baugh, Philadelphia, 1956.

Wordsworth, C. (ed.) *Ceremonies and Processions of the Cathedral Church of Salisbury*, Cambridge, 1901.

Wright, T. (ed.) *Three Chapters of Letters relating to the Suppression of the Monasteries*, Camden Society, os XXVI, 1843.

Wriothesley, C. *A Chronicle of England 1485–1559*, ed. W. D. Hamilton, Camden Society, ns XI, XX, 1875–7.

York Breviary. Breviarum ad Usum Insignis Ecclesie Eboracensis, ed. J. Raine, Surtees Society, LXXI, LXXV, 1879–82.

York Chantries. The Certificates of the Commissioners appointed to survey the Chantries, Guilds and Hospitals in the County of York, ed. W. Page, Surtees Society, XCI, XCII, 1892–3.

York Inventories. Inventories of Church Goods for York, Durham and Northumberland, ed. W. Page, Surtees Society, XCVII, 1896.

York Manuale. Manuale et processionale ad Usum Insignis Ecclesiae Eboracensis, ed. W. G. Henderson, Surtees Society, LXIII, 1875.

York Missal. Missale ad Usum Insignis Ecclesie Eboracensis, ed. W. G. Henderson, Surtees Society, LIX, LX, 1872.

The York Plays, ed. R. Beadle, London, 1982.

The York Provinciale, as put forward by Thomas Wolsey in the year 1518, ed. R. M. Woolley, London, 1931.

Secondary Works

Adair, J. *The Pilgrim's Way: Shrines and Saints in Britain and Ireland*, London, 1978.

Alexander, J., and Binski, P. (eds), *Age of Chivalry: Art in Plantagenet England 1200–1400*, London, 1987.

Alsop, J. D. "Religious Preambles in Early Modern English Wills as Formulae", *Journal of Ecclesiastical History*, XL, 1989, pp. 19–27.

Anderson, M. D. *History and Imagery in British Churches*, London, 1971.

—— *The Imagery of British Churches*, London, 1955.

Ariès, P. *The Hour of Our Death*, London, 1981.

Ashley, K. and Sheingorn, P. *Interpreting Cultural Symbols: St Anne in Late Medieval Society*, Athens and London, 1990.

Aston, M. *England's Iconoclasts*, Oxford, 1988.

—— *Lollards and Reformers*, London, 1984.

Atchley, E. G. C. "The Second Gospel at Mass", *Transactions of the St Paul's Ecclesiological Society*

Atkinson, C. *Mystic and Pilgrim: the Book and the World of Margery Kempe*, Ithaca, 1983.

Backhouse, J. *Books of Hours*, British Library, 1985.

Bailey, D. S. *Thomas Becon and the Reformation of the Church in England*, Edinburgh and London, 1952.

Bailey, T. *The Processions of Sarum and the Western Church*, Toronto, 1971.

Ball, R. M. "The Education of the English Parish Clergy in the Later Middle Ages with Particular Reference to the Manuals of Instruction". Cambridge PhD thesis, 1976.

Barfield, S. *Thatcham, Berkshire, and its Manors*, ed. J. Parker, Oxford, 1901.

Barratt, A. "The Prymer and its Influence on the Fifteenth-Century Passion Lyric", *Medium Aevum*, XLIV, 1973, pp. 264–79.

Barron, C. M. "The Parish Fraternities of Medieval London" in C. M. Barron and C. Harper Bill (eds), *The Church in Pre-Reformation Society*, Woodbridge, 1985, pp. 13–37.

Barron, C. M. and Bill, C. Harper (eds) *The Church in Pre-Reformation Society*, Woodbridge, 1985.

Bartholomew, A. "Lay Piety in the Reign of Mary Tudor", Manchester MA thesis, 1979.

Bateman, M. "Cambridge Gild Records", *Publications of the Cambridge Antiquarian Society*, XXXIX, 1903, pp. 14–25.

Beaty, N. L. *The Craft of Dying: a Study of the Literary Tradition of the Ars Moriendi*, New Haven and London, 1970.

Bennett, H. S. *English Books and Readers 1475–1557*, 2nd ed., Cambridge, 1970.

Bennett, J. A. W. *The Poetry of the Passion*, Oxford, 1982.

Bertelli, C. "The 'Image of Pity' in Sancta Croce in Gerusaleme" in D. Freser and others eds, *Essays in the History of Art Presented to Rudolf Wittkower*, London, 1967.

Birchenaugh, E. "The Prymer in English", *The Library*, 4th series, XVIII, 1937–8, pp. 177–94.

Birt, H. N. *The Elizabethan Religious Settlement*, London, 1907.

Bishop, E. "On the Origins of the Prymer" in *Liturgica Historica*, Oxford, 1918, pp. 211–37.

Blake, N. F. *Caxton and His World*, London, 1969.

Blomefield, F. and Parkin, C. *An Essay towards a Topographical History of the County of Norfolk*, London, 1805–10.

Bloomfield, M. W. *The Seven Deadly Sins*, Ann Arbor, Michigan, 1952.

Bober, H. "The Zodiacal Miniature of the Très Riches Heures of the Duke of Berry", *Journal of the Warburg and Courtauld Institutes*, XI, 1948, pp. 1–34.

Bond, F. *Fonts and Font Covers*, London, 1908.

—— *Screens and Galleries in English Churches*, London, 1908.

—— "The Tympanum of the Rood Screen", *Proceedings of the Somerset Archaeological and Natural History Society*, XLIX, 1903, pp. 56–64.

—— *Wood Carvings in English Churches*, London, 1910.

Bond, F. and Camm, B. *Roodscreens and Roodlofts*, London, 1909.

Bossy, J. "Blood and Baptism: Kinship, Community and Christianity in Western Europe from the Fourteenth to the Seventeenth centuries", *Studies in Church History*, XIX, 1973, pp. 129–43.

—— *Christianity and the West 1400–1700*, Oxford, 1985.

—— "The Mass as a Social Institution 1200–1700", *Past and Present*, C, 1983, pp. 29–61.

Bowker, M. *The Henrician Reformation: the Diocese of Lincoln under John Longland*, Cambridge, 1981.

Boyle, L. E. "The Fourth Lateran Council and Manuals of Popular Theology" in T. J. Heffernan, *Popular Literature of Medieval England*, Knoxville, Tennessee, 1985, pp. 30–43.

—— "The Oculus Sacerdotis and Some Other Works of William of Pagula", *Transactions of the Royal Historical Society*, 5th ser. V, 1955, pp. 81–110.

—— *Pastoral Care*, London, 1981.

Bradshaw, B. and Duffy, E. (eds) *Humanism, Reform and the Reformation: the Career of Bishop John Fisher*, Cambridge, 1989.

Bradshaw, H. "On the Earliest Engravings of the Indulgence known as the Image of Pity" in *Collected Papers*, Cambridge, 1889, pp. 84–100.

Brady, M. T. "*The Pore Caitif*: an Introductory Study", *Traditio*, X, 1954, pp. 530–6.

Brand, J. *Popular Antiquities of Great Britain*, ed. H. Carew Hazlitt, London, 1870.

Bray, J. R. "Concepts of Sainthood in Fourteenth-Century England", *Bulletin of the John Rylands Library*, LXVI, 1984, pp. 40–77.

Brigden, S. *London and the Reformation*, Oxford, 1989.

Brightman, F. E. *The English Rite*, London, 1915.

Brown, P. *The Body and Society: Men, Women and Sexual Renunciation in Early Christianity*, London, 1989.

Buhler, C. F. *Early Books and Manuscripts*, New York, 1973.

—— "A Middle-English Prayer-roll", *Modern Language Notes*, LII, 1937, pp. 555–62.

—— "Prayers and Charms in Certain Middle English Scrolls", *Speculum*, XXXIX, 1964, pp. 270–8.

Burgess, C. R. "By Quick and By Dead: Wills and Pious Provision in Late Medieval Bristol", *English Historical Review*, CII, 1987, pp. 837–58.

—— "A Fond Thing Vainly Invented" in S. Wright (ed.), *Parish, Church and People*, Leicester, 1988, pp. 56–85.

—— "For the Increase of Divine Service: Chantries in the Parish in Late Medieval Bristol", *Journal of Ecclesiastical History*, XXXVI, 1985, pp. 48–65.

—— "A Service for the Dead: the Form and Function of the Anniversary in Late Medieval Bristol", *Transactions of the Bristol and Gloucestershire Archaeological Society*, CV, 1987, pp. 183–211.

Burnet, G. *The History of the Reformation of the Church of England*, London, 1850.

Burrow, J. *The Ages of Man*, Oxford, 1986.

Butterworth, C. *The English Primers 1529–1549*, Philadelphia, 1953.

Caiger-Smith, A. *English Medieval Mural Paintings*, Oxford, 1963.

Carey, H.M. "Devout Literate Laypeople and the Pursuit of the Mixed Life in Later Medieval England", *Journal of Religious History*, XIV, 1987, pp. 361–81.

Carpenter, C. "The Religion of the Gentry in Fifteenth-Century England" in D. Williams (ed.), *England in the Fifteenth Century*, Woodbridge, 1987, pp. 53–74.

The Catholic Encyclopedia, ed. C. G. Herbermann and others, New York, 1907–13.

Cattermole, P. and Cotton, S. "Medieval Parish Church Building in Norfolk", *Norfolk Archaeology*, XXXVIII, 1983, pp. 235–73.

Catto, J. "Religion and the English Nobility in the Late Fourteenth Century" in H. Lloyd Jones *et al.* (eds), *History and Imagination*, London, 1981, pp. 43–55.

Cautley, H. Munro., *Suffolk Churches and their Treasures*, 5th ed., Woodbridge, 1982.

Cawley, A. C. "Middle English Metrical Versions of the Decalogue with Reference to the English Corpus Christi Cycles", *Leeds Studies in English*, ns VIII, 1975, pp. 129–45.

Cawley, A. C. *et al.* (eds), *Medieval Drama* (The Revels History of Drama in English I), London and New York, 1983.

Chambers, E. K. *The Medieval Stage*, Oxford, 1903.

Cheetham, F. *English Medieval Alabasters*, Oxford, 1984.

Cheney, C. R. "Rules for the Observance of Feast Days in Medieval England", *Bulletin of the Institute of Historical Research*, XXXIV, 1961, pp. 117–47.

Clapham, A. W. "Three Bede Rolls", *Archaeological Journal*, CXI, 1949, Supplement, pp. 40–54.

Clark, F. *Eucharistic Sacrifice and the Reformation*, 2nd ed., 1981.

Clark, J. M. *The Dance of Death in the Middle Ages and Renaissance*, Glasgow, 1950.

Clark, P. *English Provincial Society from the Reformation to the Revolution*, Hassocks, 1977.

Clay, R. M. *The Hermits and Anchorites of England*, London, 1914.

—— *The Medieval Hospitals of England*, London, 1909.

Cohen, K. *Metamorphosis of a Death Symbol: the Transi Tomb in the late Middle Ages and the Renaissance*, Berkeley, 1973.

Coleman, J. *English Literature in History 1350–1400: Medieval Readers and Writers*, London, 1981.

Comper, F. M. M. *The Life of Richard Rolle*, London, 1933.

Constable, W. G. "Some East Anglian Rood-Screen Paintings", *The Connoisseur*, LXXXIV, 1929, pp. 141–7, 211–20, 290–3, 358–63.

Conway, C. A. "The Vita Christi of Ludolph of Saxony and Late Medieval Devotion", *Analecta Cartusiana*, XXXIV, 1976.

Cook, G. H. *The English Medieval Parish Church*, London, 1970.

Cotton, S. "Medieval Roodscreens in Norfolk – their Construction and Painting Dates", *Norfolk Archaeology*, XL, 1987, pp. 44–54.

Cotton, S. and Tricker, R. *Saint Andrew, Burlingham* (cyclostyled pamphlet) n.p. n.d.

Cowen, P. *A Guide to stained Glass in England*, London, 1985.

Cox, J. C. *Churchwardens' Accounts*, London, 1913.

Cox, J. C. and Harvey, A. *English Church Furniture*, 2nd ed., London, 1908.

Cox, J. C. and Serjeantson, R. M. *A History of the Church of the Holy Sepulchre, Northampton*, Northampton, 1897.

Craig, H. *English Religious Drama of the Middle Ages*, Oxford, 1955.

Cressy, D. *Bonfires and Bells*, London, 1989.

Cross, C. "The Development of Protestantism in Leeds and Hull 1520–1640: the Evidence from Wills", *Northern History*, XVIII, 1982, pp. 230–8.

—— "Northern Women in the Early Modern Period: the Female Testators of Hull and Leeds 1520–1650", *Yorkshire Archaeological Journal*, LIX, 1987, pp. 83–94.

—— "Parochial Structure and the Dissemination of Protestantism in Sixteenth Century England: a Tale of Two Cities" in D. Baker (ed.), *The Church in Town and Countryside, Studies in Church History*, XVI, Oxford, 1977, pp. 269–78.

—— "Wills as Evidence of Popular Piety in the Reformation period: Leeds and Hull 1520–1640" in D. Loades (ed.), *The End of Strife: Death, Reconciliation and Repression in Christian Spirituality*, Edinburgh, 1984, pp. 44–57.

Cumming, G. J. *A History of Anglican Liturgy*, London, 1969.

Cutts, C. "The Croxton Play: an Anti-Lollard Piece", *Modern Language Quarterly*, V, 1944, pp. 45–60.

Cutts, C. L. *Parish Priests and their People in the Middle Ages in England*, London, 1898.

Dal, E. and Skarup, P. *The Ages of Man and the Months of the Year*, Copenhagen, 1980.

Davenport, W. A. *Fifteenth Century English Drama. The Early Moral Plays and their Literary Relations*, Cambridge and Totowa, New Jersey, 1982.

Davidson, C. "The Digby *Mary Magdalene* and the Magdalene Cult of the Middle Ages", *Annuale Medievale*, XIII, 1972, pp. 70–87.

Davies, C. S. L. "Popular Religion and the Pilgrimage of Grace" in A. Fletcher and J. Stephenson (eds), *Order and Disorder in Early Modern England*, Cambridge, 1985, pp. 58–88.

Davis, N. "Some Tasks and Themes of Popular Religion" in C. Trinkaus and H. Oberman (eds), *The Pursuit of Holiness*, Leiden, 1974, pp. 307–36.

Denny, N. (ed.) *Medieval Drama* (Stratford-upon-Avon Studies, XVI) London, 1973.

Dewick, E. S. "On a Manuscript Primer", *Transactions of the St Paul's Ecclesiological Society*, V, 1905, pp. 170–1.

Dickens, A. G. "The Early Expansion of Protestantism in England 1520–1558", *Archiv für Reformationsgeschichte*, XXVIII, 1987, pp. 187–221.

—— *The English Reformation*, 2nd ed., London, 1989.

—— *Lollards and Protestants in the Diocese of York*, Oxford, 1959.

—— *Reformation Studies*, London, 1982.

Dickinson, J. C. *The Shrine of Our Lady of Walsingham*, Cambridge, 1956.

Dixon, R. W. *History of the Church of England from the Abolition of the Roman Jurisdiction*, 3rd ed., Oxford, 1895–1902.

Dodgson, C. "English Devotional Woodcuts", *Walpole Society*, XVII, 1929, pp. 95–108.

Dove, M. *The Perfect Age of Man's Life*, Cambridge, 1986.

Doyle, A. I. "Reflections on some MSS of Nicholas Love's 'Myrrour of the Blessed Lyf of Jesu Christ'", *Leeds Studies in English*, ns XIV, 1983, pp. 82–93.

—— "A Survey of the Origins and Circulation of Theological Writings in English in the 14th, 15th and early 16th centuries", Cambridge PhD thesis, 1953.

Driver, M. W. "Pictures in Print: Late Fifteenth- and Early Sixteenth-Century English Religious Books for Lay readers" in M. Sargent (ed.), *De Cella in Seculum*, Cambridge, 1989, pp. 229–44.

Duff, E. Gordon *Fifteenth Century English Books*, Oxford, 1917.

Duffy, E. "Devotion to the Crucifix and related Images in England on the Eve of the reformation", in R. W. Scribner (ed.), *Bilder und Bildersturm in Spätmittelalter*, Wiesbaden, 1990, pp. 21–36.

—— "Holy Maydens, Holy Wyfes: the Cult of Women Saints in Fifteenth and Sixteenth Century England", *Studies in Church History*, XXIII, 1990, pp. 175–96.

Duggan, L. G. "Fear and Confession on the Eve of the Reformation", *Archiv für Reformationsgeschichte*, LXXV, 1984, pp. 153–75.

Dugmore, C. *The Mass and the English Reformers*, London, 1958.

Dunn, E. C. "Popular Devotion in the Vernacular Drama of Medieval England", *Medievalia et Humanistica*, ns IV, 1973, pp. 55–68.

Earwaker, J. P. and Morris, R. H. *The History of the Church and Parish of St Mary on the Hill, Chester*, London, 1898.

Eden, S. F. "Ancient Painted Glass at Stamford on Avon", *Journal of the British Society of Master Glass Painters*, III, 1930, pp. 156–65.

Eeles, F. C. "On a Fifteenth-Century York Missal Formerly Used at Broughton-in-Amounderness", *Chetham Miscellany*, VI, 1935.

Eisenhofer, L. *The Liturgy of the Roman Rite*, Freiburg and London, 1961.

Eisler, R. "Danse Macabre", *Traditio*, VI, 1948, pp. 182–227.

Elton, G. R. *Policy and Police: the Enforcement of the Reformation in the Age of Thomas Cromwell*, Cambridge, 1972.

—— "Thomas Cromwell's Decline and Fall" in *Studies in Tudor and Stuart Politics and Government* I, Cambridge, 1974, pp. 189–230.

Erler, M. C. "The *Maner to Lyve Well* and the Coming of English in François Regnault's Primers of the 1520s and 1530s", *The Library*, 6th series, VI, 1984, pp. 229–43.

Esdaile, K. A. *English Church Monuments*, Cambridge, 1940.

Evans, J. *Magic Jewels of the Middle Ages*, Oxford, 1922.

Farmer, D. H. *The Oxford Dictionary of Saints*, Oxford, 1978.

Farnham, W. "The Dayes of the Mone", *Studies in Philology*, XX, 1923, pp. 70–82.

Feasey, H. J. *Ancient English Holy Week Ceremonial*, London, 1893.

Febvre, L. and Martin, H.-J. *The Coming of the Book*, trans. D. Gerard, London, 1984.

Fines, J. *A Biographical Register of Early English Protestants*, I, Sutton Courtney, 1982, II, West Sussex Institute of Higher Education, 1986.

Finucane, R. C. *Miracles and Pilgrims: Popular Beliefs in Medieval England*, London, 1977.

Firth, C. B. "Village Gilds of Norfolk in the Fifteenth Century", *Norfolk Archaeology*, XVIII, 1914, pp. 161–208.

Fleming, P. W. "Charity, Faith and the Gentry of Kent 1422–1529" in A. J. Pollard (ed.), *Property and Politics: Essays in late Medieval English History*, Gloucester, 1984, pp. 36–58.

Fletcher, A. *Tudor Rebellions*, London, 1973.

Fletcher, A. J. and Powell, S. "The Origins of a Fifteenth-Century Sermon Collection", *Leeds Studies in English*, ns X, 1978, pp. 74–96.

Fletcher, A. J. "Unnoticed Sermons from John Mirk's *Festial*", *Speculum*, LV, 1980, pp. 514–22.

Foister, S. "Painting and Other Works of Art in 16th Century English Inventories", *Burlington Magazine*, CXXIII, 1981, pp. 273–82.

Footman, J. *The History of the Parish Church of St Michael and All Angels, Chipping Lambourn*, London, 1854.

Fowler, J. T. "The Fifteen Last Days of the World in Medieval Art and Literature", *Yorkshire Archaeological Journal*, XXIII, 1915, pp. 313–37.

—— "On Medieval Representations of the Months and Seasons", *Archaeologia*, XLIV, 1873, pp. 137–224.

Fowler, R. C. "The Religious Gilds of Essex", *Transactions of the Essex Archaeological Society*, ns XII, 1913, pp. 280–90.

Fox, F. F. "Roods and Rood-lofts", *Transactions of the Bristol and Gloucestershire Archaeological Society*, XXIII, 1900, pp. 79–95.

Franz, A. *Die Kirchlichen Benediction im Mittelalter*, Freiburg, 1909.

Friedlander, M. J. *From Van Eyck to Brueghel*, London, 1969.

Friedman, J. B. "The Prioress' Beads 'Of smal coral'", *Medium Aevum*, XXXIX, 1970, pp. 301–5.

Fryer, A. C. "On Fonts with representations of Baptism and the Holy Eucharist", *Archaeological Journal*, LX, 1903, pp. 1–29.

—— "On Fonts with Representations of the Seven Sacraments", *Archaeological Journal*, LIX, 1902, pp. 17–66, LXXXVII, 1930, pp. 24–59, Supplement XC, 1933, pp. 98–105.

Gairdner, J. *Lollardy and the Reformation in England*, London, 1908–13.

Gardiner, H. C. *Mysteries End: an Investigation of the Last Days of the Medieval Religious Stage*, New Haven, 1946.

Garrett, C. H. *The Marian Exiles*, Cambridge, 1938.

Gasquet, A. and Bishop, E. *Edward VI and the Book of Common Prayer*, London, 1891.

Gaydon, A. T. "Ludlow Palmers' Guild", *Victoria County History of Shropshire*, II, 1973, pp. 134–40.

Gee, E. A. "The Painted Glass of All Saints Church, North Street", *Archaeologia*, CII, 1969, pp. 151–202.

Gee, H. *The Elizabethan Prayer-book and its Ornaments*, London, 1902.

Gibson, G. McMurray, "Bury St Edmunds, Lydgate and the N Town Cycle", *Speculum*, LVI, 1981, pp. 59–90.

—— *The Theater of Devotion*, Chicago and London, 1989.

Gillespie, V. "Doctrina et Predicatio: the Design and Function of Some Pastoral Manuals", *Leeds Studies in English*, ns XI, 1980, pp. 36–50.

Gittings, C. *Death, Burial and the Individual in Early Modern England*, London, 1988.

Gjerlow, L. *Adoratio Crucis*, Oslo, 1961.

Glasscoe, M. "Late Medieval Paintings in Ashton Church, Devon", *Journal of the British Archaeological Society*, CXL, 1987, pp. 182–90.

—— "Time of Passion" in M. Sargent (ed.), *De Cella in Seculum*, Cambridge, 1989, pp. 141–60.

Gougaud, L. *Devotions et Pratiques ascétiques du Moyen Age*, Paris, 1925.

—— "La Prière dite de Charlemagne et les pièces apocryphes apparentées", *Revue d'Histoire Ecclésiastique*, XX, 1924, pp. 211–38.

Gratton, J. H. G. and Singer, C. *Anglo-Saxon Magic and Medicine*, London, 1952.

Graves, C. P. "Social Space in the English Medieval Parish Church", *Economy and Society*, XVIII, 1989, pp. 297–322.

Gray, D. "The Five Wounds of Our Lord", *Notes and Queries*, CCVIII, 1963, pp. 50–1, 82–9, 127–34, 163–8.

—— "Notes on some Middle English Charms" in B. Rowland (ed.), *Chaucer and Middle English Studies*, London, 1974, pp. 56–71.

—— *Themes and Imagery in the Medieval English Religious Lyric*, London, 1972.

Green, A. R. "The Romsey Painted Wooden Reredos", *Archaeological Journal*, XC, 1933, pp. 306–14.

Greene, R. L. "The Meaning of the Corpus Christi Carol", *Medium Aevum*, XXIX, 1960, pp. 10–21.

Hadley, G. *A New and Complete History of the Town . . . of Kingston-upon-Hull*, Hull, 1788.

Haigh, C. (ed.) *The English Reformation Revised*, Cambridge, 1987.

—— "Puritan Evangelism in the reign of Elizabeth I", *English Historical Review*, XCII, 1977, pp. 30–58.

—— *Reformation and Resistance in Tudor Lancashire*, Cambridge, 1975.

—— (ed.), *The Reign of Elizabeth I*, London, 1984.

Haines, R. M. *Ecclesia Anglicana: Studies in the English Church of the Later Middle Ages*, Toronto, 1989.

Hall, D. J. *English Medieval Pilgrimage*, London, 1965.

Hanawalt, B. "'Keepers of the Light': Late Medieval English Parish Gilds", *Journal of Medieval and Renaissance Studies*, XIV, 1984, pp. 26–37.

Hanham, H. J. "The Suppression of the Chantries in Ashburton", *Transactions of the Devonshire Association*, XCIV, 1967, pp. 111–37.

Hardison, O. B. *Christian Rite and Christian Drama in the Middle Ages*, Baltimore, 1965.

Harper-Bill, C. "A Late Medieval Visitation – the Diocese of Norwich in 1499", *Proceedings of the Suffolk Institute of Archaeology*, XXXIV, 1977, pp. 35–47.

Harrison, F. L. *Music in Medieval Britain*, London, 1958.

Harthan, J. *Books of Hours and their Owners*, London, 1977.

Harvey, B. "Work and *Festa Ferianda* in Medieval England", *Journal of Ecclesiastical History*, XXIII, 1971, pp. 289–308.

Haugaard, W. *Elizabeth and the English Reformation*, Cambridge, 1968.

Heal, F. "The Parish Clergy and the Reformation in the Diocese of Ely", *Proceedings of the Cambridge Antiquarian Society*, LXVI, 1975–6, pp. 141–63.

Heal, F. and O'Day, R. (eds) *Church and Society in England, Henry VIII to James I*, London, 1977.

Heales, A. "Easter Sepulchres: their Object, Nature and History", *Archaeologia*, XLI, 1869, pp. 263–308.

Heath, P. "Between Reform and Reformation: the English Church in the Fourteenth and Fifteenth Centuries", *Journal of Ecclesiastical History*, XLI, 1990, pp. 647–78.

—— *The English Parish Clergy on the Eve of the Reformation*, London, 1969.

—— "Staffordshire Towns and the Reformation", *North Staffordshire Journal of Field Studies*, XIX, 1979, pp. 2–5.

—— "Urban Piety in the Later Middle Ages: the Evidence of Hull Wills" in R. B. Dobson (ed.), *The Church, Politics and Patronage in the Fifteenth Century*, Gloucester, 1984, pp. 209–34.

Heffernan, T. J. *The Popular Literature of Medieval England*, Knoxville, Tennessee, 1985.

—— *Sacred Biography; Saints and their Biographers in the Middle Ages*, New York and Oxford, 1988.

Herbert, R.-J. "Les Trentains Grégoriens sous forme de cycles liturgiques", *Revue Bénédictine*, LXXXI, 1979, pp. 108–22.

Hicks, M. "Chantries, Obits and Almshouses: the Hungerford Foundations 1325–1478" in C. M. Barron and C. Harper-Bill, *The Church in Pre-Reformation Society*, Woodbridge, 1985, pp. 123–42.

Hillen, H. J. *History of the Borough of King's Lynn*, Norwich, 1907.

Himmelfarb, M. *Tours of Hell: an Apocalyptic Form in Jewish and Christian Literature*, Philadelphia, 1983.

Hirsch, J. C. "A Middle English Version of the Fifteen Oes from Bodleium Add. MS B 66", *Neuephilologische Mitteilungen*, LXXV, 1974, pp. 98–114.

—— "Prayer and Meditation in Late Medieval England: MS Bodley 789", *Medium Aevum*, XLVIII, 1979, pp. 55–66.

Hodgson, P. "*Ignorancia Sacerdotum*: a Fifteenth Century Discourse on the Lambeth Constitutions", *Review of English Studies*, XXIV, 1948, pp. 1–11.

Hodnett, E. *English Woodcuts 1488–1535*, Oxford, 1973.

Hogg, J. "Mount Grace Charterhouse and Late Medieval English Spirituality", *Analecta Cartusiana*, LXXXII part 2, 1983, pp. 1–43.

Hole, C. *Saints in Folklore*, New York, 1963.

Homan, R. L. "Two Exempla: Analogues to the Play of the Sacrament and Dux Moraud", *Comparative Drama*, XVIII, 1984, pp. 241–51.

Homans, C. G. *English Villagers of the Thirteenth Century*, Cambridge, Mass., 1941, reprint, New York, 1960.

Hope, W. St J. and Atchley, E. G. C. *English Liturgical Colours*, London, 1918.

Hoskins, E. *Horae Beatae Mariae Virginis, or, Sarum and York Primers with Kindred Books and Primers of the Reformed Roman Use*, London, 1901.

Houlbrouke, R. *Church Courts and the People During the English Reformation, 1520–1979*, Oxford, 1979.

Howard, F. E. "Screens and Rood-lofts in the Parish Churches of Oxfordshire", *Archaeological Journal*, LXVII, 1910, pp. 151–201.

Howell, A. G. F. *S. Bernardino of Siena*, London, 1913.

Hudson, A. "A New Look at the Lay Folk's Catechism", *Viator*, XVI, 1985, pp. 243–58.

—— "The Sermons of MS Longleat 4", *Medium Aevum*, LIII, 1984, pp. 220–38.

Hughes, A. *Medieval Manuscripts for Mass and Office*, Toronto, 1982.

Hughes, J. *Pastors and Visionaries: Religion and Secular Life in Late Medieval Yorkshire*, Woodbridge, 1988.

Hughes, P. *The Reformation in England*, London, 1950–4.

Hume, A. "English Books printed Abroad 1525–1535: an Annotated Bibliography" in L. A. Schuster *et al. Complete Works of Thomas More*, VIII part 2, New Haven and London, 1973.

Hussey, A. "Archbishop Parker's Visitation 1569", *Home Counties Magazine*, VI, 1904, pp. 109–14.

Hutton, R. "The Local Impact of the Tudor Reformations" in C. Haigh (ed.), *The English Reformation Revised*, Cambridge, 1987, pp. 114–38.

Index of Middle English Prose: ed. A. S. G. Edwards and others, *Handlist I: Huntington Library*, Cambridge, 1984.

Index of Middle English Prose: Handlist II: John Rylands Library, Cambridge, 1985.

Index of Middle English Prose: Handlist III: Digby MSS, Cambridge, 1986.

Index of Middle English Prose: Handlist V: BL Add. MSS 10001–12000, Cambridge, 1988.

Index of Middle English Prose: Handlist VI: Yorkshire Libraries, Cambridge, 1989.

Jagger, M. "Bonner's Episcopal Visitation of London, 1554", *Bulletin of the Institute of Historical Research*, XLV, 1973, pp. 306–11.

James, E. O. *Seasonal Feasts and Festivals*, London, 1961.

James, M. "Ritual, Drama and the Social Body in the Late Medieval Town", *Past and Present*, LXXXVIII, 1983, pp. 3–29.

James, M. R. *A Descriptive Catalogue of the Manuscripts of the College Library of Magdalene College Cambridge*, Cambridge, 1909.

—— *A Descriptive Catalogue of the Manuscripts in the Fitzwilliam Museum*, Cambridge, 1895.

—— *A Descriptive Catalogue of the Manuscripts in the Library of St John's College Cambridge*, Cambridge, 1913.

—— "St Urith of Chittlehampton", *Cambridge Antiquarian Society Proceedings*, X, 1901–2, pp. 230–4.

—— "The Sculptures in the Lady Chapel at Ely", *Archaeological Journal*, XLIX, 1892, pp. 345–62.

—— *Suffolk and Norfolk*, London, 1930.

—— "The Wall-Paintings in Eton College Chapel and the Lady Chapel of Winchester Cathedral" (with E. W. Tristram), *Walpole Society*, XVII, 1929, pp. 1–44.

—— *The Western Manuscripts in the Library of Trinity College Cambridge*, Cambridge, 1900–2.

Jeffrey, D. L. "English Saints' Plays" in N. Denny (ed.), *Medieval Drama*, Stratford-upon-Avon Studies XVI, London, 1973, pp. 68–89.

Jewell, H. M. "'The Bringing Up of Children in Good Learning and Manners': a Survey of Secular Educational Provision in the North of England *c.* 1350–1550", *Northern History*, XVIII, 1982, pp. 1–25.

Johnson, A. M. "The Reformation Clergy of Derbyshire", *Journal of the Derbyshire Archaeological and Natural History Society*, C, 1980–1, pp. 49–63.

Johnston, A. F. "The Guild of Corpus Christi and the Procession of Corpus Christi in York", *Mediaval Studies*, XXXVIII, 1976, pp. 372–403.

—— "The Plays of the Religious Guilds of York: the Creed Play and the Pater Noster Play", *Speculum*, L, 1975, pp. 55–90.

Johnston, S. H. "A Study of the Career and Literary Publications of Richard Pynson", University of Western Ontario PhD thesis, 1977.

Joliffe, P. S. *A Check-list of Middle English Prose Writings of Spiritual Guidance*, Toronto, 1975.

Jones, W. R. "The Heavenly Letter in Medieval England", *Medievalia et Humanistica*, ns VI, 1975, pp. 163–78.

Jordan, W. K. *Philanthropy in England, 1480–1660*, London, 1959.

—— *Social Institutions in Kent 1480–1660*, Archaeologia Cantiana, LXXV, 1961.

Kaplan, S. L. (ed.), *Understanding Popular Culture: Europe from the Middle Ages to the Nineteenth Century*, Berlin and New York, 1984.

Katzenellenbogen, A. *Allegories of the Vices and Virtues in Medieval Art*, London, 1939.

Keen, M. *English Society in the Later Middle Ages 1348–1500*, Harmondsworth, 1990.

Keiser, G. R. "The Progress of Purgatory: Visions of the Afterlife in Middle English Literature", *Analecta Cartusiana*, CXVII, 1987, pp. 72–100.

—— "St Jerome and the Brigittines: Visions of the Afterlife in Fifteenth Century English Literature" in D. Williams (ed.), *England in the Fifteenth Century*, Woodbridge, 1987, pp. 143–52.

Kelke, W. H. "Master John Shorne", *Records of Buckinghamshire*, II, 1869, pp. 60–74.

Ker, N. *Medieval Manuscripts in British Libraries I London*, Oxford, 1969.

Kermode, J. I. "The Merchants of Three Northern English Towns" in C. H. Clough (ed.), *Profession, Vocation and Culture in Later Medieval England*, Liverpool, 1982, pp. 7–50.

Kerry, C. "Hermits, Fords and Bridge-Chapels", *Derbyshire Archaeological Journal*, XIV, 1882, pp. 54–71.

Kettle, A. J. "City and Close: Lichfield in the Century before the Reformation" in C. M. Barron and C. Harper-Bill (eds), *The Church in Pre-Reformation Society*, Woodbridge, 1985, pp. 158–69.

Kiermayr, R. "On the Education of Pre-Reformation Clergy", *Church History*, LIII, 1984, pp. 7–16.

King, J. N. *English Reformation Literature*, Princeton, 1982.

King, P. M. "The English Cadaver Tomb in the late Fifteenth Century: Some Indicators of a Lancastrian Connection" in J. H. M. Taylor (ed.), *Dies Illa*, Liverpool, 1984, pp. 45–57.

Kingsford, H. S. *Illustrations of the Occasional Offices of the Church in the Middle Ages from Contemporary Sources*, Alcuin Club, XXIV, 1921.

Kitching, C. J. "The Chantries of the East Riding", *Yorkshire Archaeological Journal*, XLIV, 1972, pp. 178–85.

—— "Church and Chapelry in Sixteenth Century England", *Studies in Church History*, XVI, 1979, pp. 279–90.

Knowles, J. A. "The East Window of the Holy Trinity Church, Goodramgate, York", *Yorkshire Archaeological Journal*, XXVIII, 1926, pp. 1–24.

—— *Essays in the History of the York School of Glass-Painting*, London, 1936.

Kolve, V. A. *The Play Called Corpus Christi*, London, 1966.

Krapp, G. P. *The Legend of St Patrick's Purgatory, its Later Literary History*, Baltimore, 1900.

Kratzmann, G. and Simpson, J. (eds) *Medieval English Religious and Ethical Literature*, Cambridge, 1986.

Kreider, A. *English Chantries: the Road to Dissolution*, Cambridge, Mass., 1979.

Lancashire, I. *Dramatic Texts and Records of Britain*, Cambridge, 1984.

le Goff, J. "The Learned and Popular Dimensions of Journeys in the Otherworld in the Middle Ages" in S. Kaplan (ed.), *Understanding Popular Culture*, Berlin, 1984, pp. 19–34.

—— *The Medieval Imagination*, Chicago, 1988.

—— *Time, Work and Culture in the Middle Ages*, Chicago and London, 1980.

Lepow, L. *Enacting the Sacrament: Counter-Lollardy in the Towneley Cycle*, London and Toronto, 1990.

—— "Middle English Elevation Prayers and the Corpus Christi Cycle", *English Language Notes*, XVII, 1979, pp. 85–8.

Leroquais, V. *Les livres d'heures manuscrits de la Bibliothèque Nationale*, Paris, 1927.

Levinson, D. J. *The Seasons of a Man's Life*, New York, 1968.

Lillie, W. W. "Screenwork in the County of Suffolk, III, Panels Painted with Saints", *Proceedings of the Suffolk Institute of Archaeology*, XX, 1930, pp. 214–26, 255–64, XXI, 1933, pp. 179–202, XXII, 1936, pp. 120–6.

Loach, J. "The Marian establishment and the Printing Press", *English Historical Review*, CI, 1986, pp. 135–48.

Loades, D. M. "The Enforcement of Reaction 1553–1558", *Journal of Ecclesiastical History*, XVI, 1965, pp. 54–66.

Lozar, P. "The Prologue to the Ordinances of the York Corpus Christi Guild", *Allegorica*, 1, 1976, pp. 94–113.

Lubin, H. *The Worcester Pilgrim*, Worcester Cathedral Publications no.1, 1990.

McCree, Ben. "Religious Gilds and the Regulation of Behaviour" in J. Rosenthal and C. Richmond (eds), *People, Politics and Community in the late Middle Ages*, Gloucester, 1987, pp. 108–18.

McGarry, L. *The Holy Eucharist in Middle English Homiletic and Devotional Verse*, Washington, 1936.

McKenna, J. W. "Piety and Propaganda: the Cult of Henry VI" in B. Rowland (ed.), *Chaucer and Middle English Studies*, London, 1974, pp. 72–88.

—— "Popular Canonization as Political Propaganda: the Cult of Archbishop Scrope", *Speculum*, LXV, 1971, pp. 608–23.

McNeill, J. T. and Gamer, H. *Medieval Handbooks of Penance*, New York, 1938.

Maine, L. G. *A Berkshire Village (Stanford in the Vale), its History and Antiquities*, Oxford and London, 1866.

Mâle, E. *Religious Art in France: the Late Middle Ages*, Princeton, 1986.

Malvern, M. M. "An Earnest 'Monysyon' and 'Thinge Delectabyll' Realized Verbally and Visually", *Viator*, XIII, 1982, pp. 415–43.

Manning, B. L. *The People's Faith in the Time of Wyclif*, Cambridge, 1919.

Marchant, G. (ed.) *La Danse macabre*, Paris, 1925.

Marsh, C. "In the Name of God: Will-Making and Faith in Early Modern England" in G. H. Martin and P. Spufford (eds) *The Records of the Nation*, Woodbridge, 1990, pp. 215–49.

Martin, C. A. "Middle English Manuals of Religious Instruction" in M. Benskin and M. L. Samuels (eds), *So Meny People, Longages and Tonges*, Edinburgh, 1981, pp. 289–98.

Martin, J. W. *Religious Radicals in Tudor England*, London, 1989.

Mayhew, G. "The Progress of the Reformation in East Sussex 1530–59: the Evidence from Wills", *Southern History*, V, 1983, pp. 38–67.

—— *Tudor Rye*, Brighton, 1987.

Meier-Ewart, C. "A Middle English Version of the Fifteen Oes", *Modern Philology*, LXVIII, 1971, pp. 355–61.

Merriman, R. B. *The Life and Letters of Thomas Cromwell*, Oxford, 1902.

Mitchiner, M. *Medieval Pilgrim and Secular Badges*, London, 1986.

de Molen, R. L. "Pueri Christi Imitatio: the Festival of the Boy Bishop in Tudor England", *Moreana*, XL, 1975, pp. 17–29.

Moran, J. A. H. *The Growth of English Schooling: Learning, Literacy and Laicisation in the Pre-Reformation York Diocese*, Princeton, 1985.

Morant, A. W. "Notices of the Church of St Nicholas, Great Yarmouth", *Norfolk Archaeology*, VII, 1872, pp. 215–48.

Morant, A. W. and L'Estrange, J. "Notices of the Church at Randworth [*sic*]", *Norfolk Archaeology*, VII, 1872, pp. 178–211.

Morgan, P. E. "The Effect of the Pilgrim Cult of St Thomas Cantilupe on Hereford Cathedral" in M. Jancey (ed.), *St Thomas Cantilupe*, Hereford, 1982, pp. 145–52.

Morris, C. "A Consistory Court in the Middle Ages", *Journal of Ecclesiastical History*, XIV, 1963, pp. 150–9.

Mortlake, D. P. *The Popular Guide to Suffolk Churches: I. West Suffolk*, Cambridge, 1988.

—— *The Popular Guide to Suffolk Churches: 2. Central Suffolk*, Cambridge, 1990.

Mortlake, D. P. and Roberts, C. V. *The Popular Guide to Norfolk Churches: 1. North-East Norfolk*, Fakenham, 1981.

—— *The Popular Guide to Norfolk Churches: 2. Norwich, Central and South Norfolk*, Cambridge, 1985.

—— *The Popular Guide to Norfolk Churches: 3. West and South-West Norfolk*, Cambridge, 1985.

Needham, P. *The Printer and the Pardoner: an Unrecorded Indulgence Printed by William Caxton*, Washington, 1986.

Nelson, A. H. *The Medieval English Stage; Corpus Christi Pageants and Plays*, Chicago, 1974.

Nelson, P. *Ancient Painted Glass in England*, London, 1913.

—— "The Fifteenth-Century Glass in the Church of St Michael, Ashton under Lyne", *Archaeological Journal*, LXX, 1913, pp. 1–10.

Newman, J. L. and Hudson, J. A. "Sir John Schorne and His Boot", *Country Life*, CXXXI, 1962, pp. 467–8.

Nicholls, A. E. "The Croxton Play of the Sacrament: a Re-Reading", *Comparative Drama*, XXII, 1988–9, pp. 117–37.

—— "The Etiquette of Pre-reformation Confession in East Anglia", *Sixteenth Century Journal*, XVII, 1986, pp. 145–63.

Nichols, J. G. "Walsoken Gilds and Pardons", *Proceedings of the Society of Antiquaries of London*, 2nd series, VI, 1873, pp. 15–19.

Nilsson, M. P. *Primitive Time-Reckoning*, Lund, 1920.

von Nolcken, C. "Some Alphabetical Compendia and How preachers Used Them in Fourteenth Century England", *Viator*, XII, 1981, pp. 271–88.

Norris, M. *Monumental Brasses*, London, 1977.

Norton, C., Park, D. and Binski, P. *Dominican Painting in East Anglia*, Woodbridge, 1987.

Oates, J. C. T. "Richard Pynson and the Holy Blood of Hailes", *The Library*, 5th series, XIII, 1958, pp. 269–77.

O'Connor, M. C. *The Art of Dying Well*, New York, 1942.

Oman, Charles. "Security in English Churches A.D. 1000–1548", *Archaeological Journal*, CXXXVI, 1979, pp. 90–8.

Orme, N. "The Dissolution of the Chantries in Devon", *Transactions of the Devonshire Association*, CXI, 1979, pp. 75–123.

—— *Education and Society in Medieval and Renaissance England*, London, 1989.

—— *English Schools in the Late Middle Ages*, London, 1973.

—— "Two Saint-Bishops of Exeter: James Berkeley and Edmund Lacy", *Analecta Bollandiana*, CIV, 1986, pp. 403–18.

Owen, D. M. "Bacon and Eggs: Bishop Buckingham and Superstition in Lincolnshire", *Studies in Church History*, VIII, 1972, pp. 139–42.

—— *Church and Society in Medieval Lincolnshire*, Lincoln, 1971.

Owst, G. R. *Literature and the Pulpit in Medieval England*, Cambridge, 1933.

—— *Preaching in Medieval England*, Cambridge, 1926.

Oxley, J. E. *The Reformation in Essex to the Death of Mary*, Manchester, 1965.

Page, C. "The Rhymed Office for St Thomas of Lancaster: Poetry, Politics and Liturgy in 14th Century England", *Leeds Studies in English*, ns XIV, 1983, pp. 134–51.

Painter, G. D. *William Caxton*, London, 1976.

Palliser, D. M. *The Reformation in York 1534–1553*, Borthwick Papers, XL, 1971.

—— *Tudor York*, Oxford, 1979.

Palmer, W. M. "Fifteenth Century Visitation Records of the Deanery of Wisbech", *Proceedings of the Cambridge Antiquarian Society*, XXXIX, 1938–9, pp. 69–75.

—— "Village Gilds of Cambridgeshire", *Transactions of the Cambridgeshire and Huntingdonshire Archaeological Society*, I, 1902, pp. 330–402.

Panofsky, E. *Early Netherlandish Painting*, New York, 1971.

—— "Imago Pietatis" in *Festschrift für Max J. Friedlander*, Leipzig, 1927, pp. 261–308.

Pantin, W. A. *The English Church in the Fourteenth Century*, Cambridge, 1955 (reprinted Toronto, 1980).

—— "Instructions for a Devout and Literate Layman" in J. J. G. Alexander and M. T. Gibson (eds) *Medieval Learning and Literature*, Oxford, 1976, pp. 398–422.

Parker, W. *The History of Long Melford*, London, 1873.

Parkes, M. B. "The Literacy of the Laity" in D. Daiches and A. K. Thorlby (eds), *Literature & Western Civilisation: the Medieval World*, London, 1973, pp. 555–77.

Pearsall, D., and Salter, E. *Landscapes and Seasons of the Medieval World*, London, 1973.

Pendrill, C. *Old Parish Life in London*, Oxford, 1937.

Pevsner, N. *The Buildings of England: Cambridgeshire*, Harmondsworth, 1970.

—— *The Buildings of England: Lincolnshire*, Harmondsworth, 1964.

—— *The Buildings of England: North-East Norfolk and Norwich*, Harmondsworth, 1962.

—— *The Buildings of England: North-West and South Norfolk*, Harmondsworth, 1962.

—— *The Buildings of England: Suffolk*, Harmondsworth, 1974.

—— *The Buildings of England: Sussex*, Harmondsworth, 1965.

Pfaff, R. W. "The English Devotion of St Gregory's Trental", *Speculum*, XLIX, 1974, pp. 75–90.

—— *New Liturgical Feasts in Late Medieval England*, Oxford, 1970.

Pfander, H. G. "Some Medieval Manuals of Religious Instruction in England and Observations on Chaucer's Parson's Tale", *Journal of English and Germanic Philology*, XXXV, 1936, pp. 243–58.

Philips, H. *Langland, the Mysteries, and the Medieval English Religious Tradition*, Cambridge, 1990.

Phythian-Adams, C. "Ceremony and the Citizen" in P. Clark (ed.), *The Early Modern Town*, London, 1976, pp. 106–28.

—— *Local History and Folklore: a New Framework*, London, 1975.

Pickering, O. S. "Notes on the Sentence of Cursing in Middle English", *Leeds Studies in English*, ns XII, 1981, pp. 229–44.

Potter, R. *The English Morality Play*, London, 1975.

Powell, K. G. "The Social Background of the Reformation in Gloucestershire", *Transactions of the Bristol and Gloucestershire Archaeological Society*, XCII, 1973, pp. 96–120.

Powell, S. and Fletcher, A. J. "In Die Sepulture Seu Trigentale: The Late Medieval Funeral and Memorial Sermon", *Leeds Studies in English*, ns XII, 1981, pp. 195–228.

Procter, F. and Frere, W. H. *A New History of the Book of Common Prayer*, London, 1925.

Prosser, E. *Drama and Religion in the English Mystery Plays*, Stanford, California, 1961.

Radford, V. M. "The Wax Images Found in Exeter Cathedral", *Antiquaries Journal*, XXIX, 1949, pp. 164–8.

Ratcliff, E. C. *"The Booke of Common Prayer of the Churche of England": its Making and Revisions*, London, 1949.

—— "The Liturgical Work of Archbishop Cranmer", *Journal of Ecclesiastical History*, VII, 1956, pp. 189–203.

Redstone, V. B. "Chapels, Chantries and Gilds in Suffolk", *Proceedings of the Suffolk Institute of Archaeology*, XII, 1904, pp. 21–88.

Reinburg, V. "Popular Prayers in Late Medieval and Reformation France", Princeton PhD thesis, 1985.

Revell, P. *Fifteenth Century English Prayers and Meditations: a Descriptive List of MSS in the British Library*, New York and London, 1975.

Rex, R. "The English campaign against Luther", *Transactions of the Royal Historical Society*, 5th series, XXXIX, 1989, pp. 85–106.

—— "Monumental Brasses and the Reformation", *Proceedings of the Monumental Brass Society*, forthcoming.

—— *The Theology of John Fisher*, Cambridge, 1991.

Rhodes, J. "Private Devotion in England on the Eve of the Reformation", Durham PhD thesis, 1974.

—— "Religious Instruction at Syon in the Early Sixteenth Century", *Journal of Ecclesiastical History*, forthcoming.

Richmond, C. *John Hopton*, Cambridge, 1981.

—— "Religion and the Fifteenth Century English Gentleman" in B. Dobson (ed.), *The Church, Politics and Patronage*, Gloucester, 1984, pp. 193–208.

Ridley, J. *Thomas Cranmer*, Oxford, 1962.

Ridyard, S. *The Royal Saints of Anglo-Saxon England*, Cambridge, 1989.

Rigold, S. E. "The St Nicholas or 'Boy Bishop' Tokens", *Proceedings of the Suffolk Institute of Archaeology*, XXXIV part 2, 1978, pp. 87–101.

Robbins, R. H. "The 'Arma Christi' Rolls", *Modern Language Review*, XXXIV, 1939, pp. 415–21.

—— "English Almanacs of the Fifteenth Century", *Philological Quarterly*, XVIII, 1939, pp. 321–31.

—— "Levacion Prayers in Middle English Verse", *Modern Philology*, XL, 1942, pp. 131–46.

—— "Private Prayers in Middle English Verse", *Studies in Philology*, XXXVI, 1939, pp. 466–75.

—— "Popular Prayers in Middle English Verse", *Modern Philology*, XXXVI, 1939, pp. 337–56.

Robertson, D. W. "The Late Medieval Cult of Jesus and the Mystery Plays", *Proceedings of the Modern Language Association*, LXXX, 1965, pp. 508–14.

Rock, D. *The Church of Our Fathers*, ed. G. W. Hart and W. H. Frere, London, 1903–4.

Rodgers, E. C. *Discussion of Holidays in the Later Middle Ages*, New York, 1940.

Rogers, N. J. "About the 15 'O's, The Brigittines and Syon Abbey", *St Ansgar's Bulletin*, LXXX, 1984, pp. 29–30.

—— "Books of Hours produced in the Low Countries For the English Market in the Fifteenth Century", Cambridge M Litt thesis, 1982.

Rosenthal, J. T. *The Purchase of Paradise*, London, 1972.

—— "The Yorkshire Chantry Certificates of 1546: an analysis", *Northern History*, IX, 1974, pp. 26–34.

Rosenthal, J. and Richmond, C. (eds) *People, Politics and Community in the Later Middle Ages*, Gloucester, 1987.

Rosser, G. "Communities of Parish and Guild in the Late Middle Ages" in S. J. Wright (ed.), *Parish, Church and People*, London, 1988, pp. 29–55.

—— "The Town and Guild of Lichfield in the Late Middle Ages", *Transactions of the South Staffordshire Archaeological and Historical Society*, XXVII, 1987, pp. 39–47.

Rouse, E. C. and Baker, A. "The Wall-Paintings of Longthorpe Tower near Peterborough", *Archaeologia*, XCVI, 1955, pp. 1–58.

Routh, P. E. Sheppard. "Full of Imageis: the Ripon Alabasters", *Yorkshire Archaeological Journal*, LVII, 1985, pp. 93–100.

Rowse, A. L. *Tudor Cornwall*, London, 1941.

Rubin, M. *Corpus Christi*, Cambridge, 1991.

—— "Corpus Christi Fraternities and Late Medieval Piety", *Studies in Church History*, XXIII, 1986, pp. 97–109.

—— "Mastering the Mystery", unpublished paper.

Rushforth, G. McN. "An Account of Some Painted Glass from a House at Leicester", *Archaeological Journal*, LXXV, 1918, pp. 47–68.

—— "The Kirkham Monument in Paignton Church", *Transactions of the Exeter Diocesan Architectural and Archaeological Society*, XV, 1927, pp. 1–37.

—— *Medieval Christian Imagery*, Oxford, 1936.

—— "Seven Sacraments Compositions in English Medieval Art", *Antiquaries Journal*, IX, 1929, pp. 83–100.

—— "The Wheel of the Ten Ages of Life in Leominster Church", *Proceedings of the Society of Antiquaries of London*, 2nd series, XXVI, 1913–14, pp. 47–60.

Russell, G. H. "Vernacular Instruction of the Laity in the Late Middle Ages in England", *Journal of Religious History*, II, 1962, pp. 98–119.

Russell, J. C. "The Canonisation of Opposition to the King in Angevin England" in C. H. Taylor and J. L. La Monte, *Haskins Anniversary Essays in Medieval History*, Boston, 1929, pp. 279–90.

Sacks, D. H. "The Demise of the Martyrs: the Feasts of St Clement and St Katherine in Bristol, 1400–1600", *Social History*, XI, 1986, pp. 141–69.

Saenger, P. "Books of Hours and the Reading Habits of the Late Middle Ages" in R. Chartier (ed.), *The Culture of Print*, Cambridge and Oxford, 1989, 141–73.

St John Hope, W. H. "Notes on the Holy Blood of Hayles", *Archaeological Journal*, LXVIII, 1911, pp. 166–72.

—— "Three Altar Frontals of English Work", *Proceedings of the Society of Antiquaries*, ns XXV, 1912–13, pp. 39–45.

Salter, E. "Ludolfus of Saxony and His English Translators", *Medium Aevum*, XXXIII, 1964, pp. 26–35.

—— "The Manuscripts of Nicholas Love's *Myrrour of the Blessed Life of Jesus Christ* and related texts" in A. S. Edwards G. and Pearsall, D. (eds) *Middle English Prose*, New York and London, 1981, pp. 115–27.

Salter, F. M. *Medieval Drama in Chester*, Toronto, 1955.

Sargent, M. G. (ed.), *De Cella in Seculum: Religion and Secular Life and Devotion in Late Medieval England*, Cambridge, 1989.

—— "The Transmission by the English Carthusians of Some Late Medieval Writings", *Journal of Ecclesiastical History*, XXVII, 1976, pp. 225–40.

Saul, N. "The Religious Sympathies of the Gentry in Gloucestershire 1200–1500", *Transactions of the Bristol and Gloucestershire Archaeological Society*, CXVIII, 1980, pp. 99–112.

Scarisbrick, J. J. *The Reformation and the English People*, Oxford, 1984.

Schenk, W. *Reginald Pole, Cardinal of England*, London, 1950.

Scott, W. T. *Antiquities of an Essex Parish*, London, 1873.

Scribner, R. W. *Popular Culture and Popular Movements in Reformation Germany*, London, 1987.

—— "Popular Piety and Modes of Visual Perception in Late-medieval and Reformation Germany", *Journal of Religious History*, XV, 1989, pp. 448–69.

Sekules, V. "The Tomb of Christ at Lincoln and the Development of the Sacrament Shrine: Easter Sepulchres Reconsidered" in *The British Archaeological Association Conference Transactions*, VIII, 1982, printed in *Medieval Art and Architecture at Lincoln Cathedral*, 1986, pp. 118–31.

Serjeantson, R. M. "The Restoration of the Long-lost Brass of Sir William Catesby", *Associated Architectural Societies Reports and Papers*, XXXI, 1911–2, pp. 519–24.

Sewell, W. H. "The Sexton's Wheel and the Lady Fast", *Norfolk Archaeology*, IX, 1884, pp. 201–14.

Sheingorn, P. "The Sepulchrum Domini, a Study in Art and Liturgy", *Studies in Iconography*, IV, 1978, pp. 37–61.

Sheppard, E. "The Reformation and the Citizens of Norwich", *Norfolk Archaeology*, XXXVIII, 1981–3, pp. 44–55.

Shinners, J. R. "The Veneration of Saints at Norwich Cathedral in the Fourteenth Century", *Norfolk Archaeology*, XL, 1988, pp. 133–44.

Simpson, W. Sparrow. "Master John Schorne", *Records of Buckinghamshire*, III, 1870, pp. 354–69.

—— "Master John Schorne, his Effigy in Painted Glass", *Journal of the British Archaeological Association*, XXV, 1869, pp. 334–44.

—— "On a Magical Roll Preserved in the British Museum", *Journal of the British Archaeological Association*, XLVIII, 1892, pp. 38–54.

—— "On a Seventeenth-Century Roll Containing Prayers and Magical Signs", *Journal of the British Archaeological Association*, XL, 1884, pp. 297–332.

—— "On the Measure of the Wound in the Side of the Redeemer", *Journal of the British Archaeological Association*, XXX, 1874, pp. 357–74.

Smith, L. "The Canonisation of Henry VI", *Dublin Review*, XLXVIII, 1921, pp. 41–53.

Spencer, B. "King Henry of Windsor and the London Pilgrim" in J. Bird, H. Chapman, and J. Clark (eds) *Collectanea Londiniensia*, London and Middlesex Archaeological Society, 1978, pp. 235–64.

—— "Medieval Pilgrim Badges" in J. G. N. Renaud, *Rotterdam Papers*, Rotterdam, 1968, pp. 137–54.

Spencer, H. L. "English Vernacular Sunday Preaching in the Late Fourteenth and Fifteenth Centuries", Oxford D Phil thesis, 1982.

Spufford, M. *Contrasting Communities*, Cambridge, 1974.

—— "The Scribes of Villagers' Wills in the Sixteenth and Seventeenth Century and their Influence", *Local Population Studies*, VII, 1971, pp. 28–43.

Stone, L. *Sculpture in Britain: the Middle Ages*, 2nd ed., Harmondsworth, 1972.

Strype, J. *Annals of the Reformation*, Oxford, 1824.

—— *Ecclesiastical Memorials*, Oxford, 1816.

Sumption, J. *Pilgrimage*, London, 1975.

Sutton, A. and Visser-Fuchs, L. *The Hours of Richard III*, Stroud, 1990.

Swales, T. H. "Opposition to the Suppression of the Norfolk Monasteries . . . the Walsingham Conspiracy", *Norfolk Archaeology*, XXXIII, 1962, pp. 254–65.

Swanson, R. N. *Church and Society in Late Medieval England*, Oxford, 1989.

Tait, M. B. "The Brigittine Monastery of Syon", Oxford M Phil thesis, 1975.

Tanner, N. *The Church in Late Medieval Norwich*, Toronto, 1984.

Taylor, J. H. M. (ed.), *Dies Illa: Death in the Middle Ages*, Liverpool, 1984.

Tenenti, A. *La Vie et la Mort à travers l'art du XVe siècle*, Paris, 1952.

Tentler, T. F. *Sin and Confession on the Eve of the Reformation*, Princeton, 1977.

Thornton, G. A. *A History of Clare, Suffolk*, Cambridge, 1928.

Thrupp, S. *The Merchant Class of Medieval London 1300–1500*, Chicago, 1948.

Thurston, H. "The Medieval Prymer", *The Month*, CXVII, 1911, pp. 150–63.

Trinkaus, C. and Oberman, H. (eds), *The Pursuit of Holiness*, Leiden, 1974.

Tristram, E. W. *English Medieval Wall-Painting*, London, 1944.

Tristram, P. *Figures of Life and Death in Medieval English Literature*, London, 1976.

Turner, V. and E. *Image and Pilgrimage in Christian Culture*, New York, 1978.

Twycross, M. "Books for the Unlearned", *Themes in Drama V: Drama and Religion*, 1983, pp. 65–110.

Unwin, G. *The Gilds and Companies of London*, London [1908], 1938.

Vallance, A. *English Church Screens*, London, 1936.

Villette, J. *L'Ange dans l'Art d'Occident du XIIe au XVIe Siècle*, Paris, 1940.

Walker, J. W. "The Chantry Chapels of Wakefield", *Yorkshire Archaeological Journal*, XXIX, 1927–9, pp. 135–56.

Walker, R. B. "Reformation and Reaction in the County of Lincoln 1547–1558", *Lincolnshire Architectural and Archaeological Society Reports & Papers*, ns IX, 1961, pp. 49–62.

Wall, J. Charles. *An Old English Parish*, London, 1907.

Ward, B. *Miracles and the Medieval Mind*, Aldershot, 1987.

Wedel, T. O. *The Medieval Attitude towards Astrology, particularly in England*, New Haven, 1920.

Westlake, H. F. *The Parish Gilds of Medieval England*, London, 1919.

White, H. C. *The Tudor Books of Private Devotion*, Madison, Wisconsin, 1951.

Whiting, R. "Abominable Idols", *Journal of Ecclesiastical History*, XXXIII, 1982, pp. 30–47.

—— *The Blind Devotion of the People*, Cambridge, 1989.

—— "For the Health of My Soul: Prayers for the Dead in the Tudor South West", *Southern History*, V, 1983, pp. 68–78.

Wickham, G. *The Medieval Theatre*, London, 1974.

Wieck, R. S. *The Book of Hours in Medieval Art and Life*, London, 1988.

Williams, E. C. "The Dance of Death in Painting and Sculpture in the Middle Ages", *Journal of the British Archaeological Association*, 3rd series, I, 1937, pp. 229–57.

Williams, G. "Wales and the Reign of Mary I", *Welsh History Review*, X, 1980–1, pp. 334–58.

Williamson, W. W. "Saints on Norfolk Rood Screens and Pulpits", *Norfolk Archaeology*, XXXI, 1955–7, pp. 299–346.

Wilmart, A. *Auteurs spirituels et textes dévots du moyen âge latin*, Paris, 1932.

—— "Le grand poème Bonaventurien sur les sept paroles du Christ en croix", *Revue Bénédictine*, XLVII, 1935, pp. 235–78.

Winter, C. J. "Discovery of a Mural painting in the Church at Sporle, Norfolk", *Norfolk Archaeology*, VII, 1872, pp. 303–8.

Wolper, T. *Die Englische Heiligenlegende des Mittelalters*, Tübingen, 1964.

Woodforde, C. "A Medieval Campaign Against Blasphemy", *Downside Review*, ns XXXVI, pp. 357–62.

—— *The Norwich School of Glass-Painting in the Fifteenth Century*, London, 1950.

Woodman, A. V. "The Buckinghamshire and Oxfordshire Rising of 1549", *Oxoniensia*, XXII, 1957, pp. 74–84.

Wormald, F. "The Rood of Bromholm", *Journal of the Warburg and Courtauld Institutes*, I, 1937–8, pp. 31–45.

Wordsworth, C. *Notes on Medieval Services*, London, 1895.

—— "On Some Pardons or Indulgences reserved in Yorkshire, 1412–1527", *Yorkshire Archaeological Journal*, XVI, 1900–2, pp. 369–423.

—— "Wiltshire Pardons and Indulgences", *Wiltshire Archaeological and Natural Historical Magazine*, XXXVIII, 1913–14, pp. 15–33.

Wordsworth, C. and Littlehales, H. *The Old service-Books ond the English Church*, London, 1904.

Wright, A. D. *The Counter-Reformation*, London, 1982.

Wright, A. R. *British Calendar Customs*, London, 1936–40.

Wright, R. "Community Theatre in Late Medieval East Anglia", *Theatre Notebook*, XXVIII, 1974, pp. 24–39.

Wright, S. J. (ed.) *Parish, Church and People*, London, 1988.

Wright, T. *St Patrick's Purgatory*, London, 1844.

Wunderli, R. and Brose, G. "The Final Moment Before death in Early Modern England", *Sixteenth Century Journal*, XX, 1989, pp. 259–75.

Young, K. *The Drama of the Medieval Church*, Oxford, 1933.

Zell, M. "The Prebendaries Plot of 1543: a Reconsideration", *Journal of Ecclesiastical History*, XXVII, 1976, pp. 241–53.
—— "The Use of Religious Preambles as a Measure of Religious Belief in the Sixteenth Century", *Bulletin of the Institute of Historical Research*, L, 1977, pp. 246–9.

PHOTOGRAPHIC
ACKNOWLEDGEMENTS

Except where indicated below, the copyright in all the illustrations to this book belongs to the author. Permission to reproduce a number of items in the keeping of the following institutions is gratefully acknowledged: Plate 65, the Society of Antiquaries of London; Plates 16, 77, 85, 88, 91–2, 97, 99, 100, 117–19, the Keeper of Printed Books and the Keeper of Western Manuscripts at the Bodleian Library, University of Oxford; Plates 6, 13, 19, 37, 38, 39, 43, 49, 61, 86, 87, 89, 90, 93–7, 104, 133, the Syndics of the Cambridge University Library; Plates 7, 68, and 114, the Conway Library, the Courtauld Institute of Art, University of London; Plate 75, the Museum of London; Plate 110, the President and the Librarian of Ushaw College, Durham; Plates 66 and 120, the Trustees of the Victoria and Albert Museum, South Kensington; Plate I, the Dean and Chapter of Winchester Cathedral.

INDEX

Biographical information in these entries, apart from the date of death, indicates the role or office of the individual concerned at the time to which the book refers; subsequent offices or distinctions are not noted.